# In the HOT SEAT

# In the HOT SEAT

**Richard Holdsworth**

A catalogue record of this book is available from the British Library.

ISBN 978-0-9558383-4-7 (pbk)
ISBN 978-0-9558383-5-4 (hbk)

To order additional copies of this book please visit:
www.holdsworthwrites.co.uk

Published by: Holdsworth Writes (Publishing)
Greenways, Mustard Lane, Sonning, Berks. RG4 6GH, UK

Tel/Fax: +44 (0)118 9696271
Email: holdsworthwrites@aol.com
Web: www.holdsworthwrites.co.uk

Cover design, layout and typesetting by Image Corporate Ltd.
www.image-corporate.com

Printed and bound in Great Britain by Henry Ling Limited, The Dorset Press, Dorchester DT1 1HD.

*To the Holdsworth family*

*Ron "Nick" Nicola*

*Ken Overend*

*Johnnie Mitchell*

*And all the Australian people*

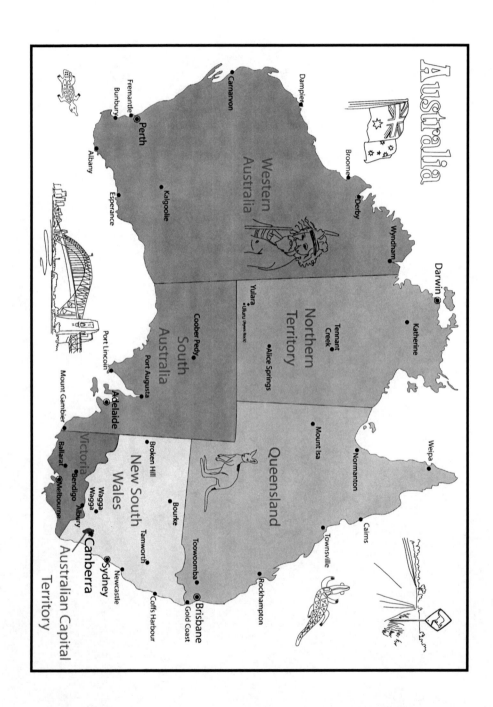

Australia

Western Australia

Northern Territory

South Australia

Queensland

New South Wales

Victoria

Australian Capital Territory

Carnarvon
Dampier
Broome
Derby
Wyndham
Darwin
Katherine
Weipa
Normanton
Cairns
Townsville
Mount Isa
Tennant Creek
Alice Springs
Yulara
• Uluru (Ayers Rock)
Cooper Pedy
Port Augusta
Port Lincoln
Mount Gambier
Adelaide
Perth
Fremantle
Bunbury
Albany
Esperance
Kalgoorlie
Broken Hill
Ballarat
Bendigo
Melbourne
Albury
Wagga Wagga
Tamworth
Bourke
Toowoomba
Rockhampton
Gold Coast
Brisbane
Coffs Harbour
Newcastle
Sydney
Canberra

# Acknowledgements

Prime Minister Paul Keating, Eulogy for The Unknown Australian Soldier, Canberra, 11 November 1993.

The following newspapers and other sources for their coverage of the aftermath of the atomic tests at Maralinga in South Australia: The Green Left Weekly (Australia), The Daily Telegraph (UK), The Age (Australia), the Herald Sun (Australia), together with the BBC news broadcasts.

The front page of The Herald, Melbourne, Saturday, November 23, 1963, courtesy The Herald & Weekly Times Pty Ltd.

The front page of The Adelaide Advertiser, Friday, January 3, 1964, courtesy of The Adelaide Advertiser, Pty Ltd.

The Stock and Station Journal, Adelaide and The Weekly Times, Melbourne, for reports on various farming matters.

Photograph: Warning sign for the Birdsville Track, Queensland, 1964. McKay, Andrew Leslie, 1909-1976. Source: National Library of Australia. www.nla.gov.au/nla.pic-vn4181248.

Drawing: Ned Kelly at bay. Creator: Francis Thomas Dean Carrington. Source: State Library of Victoria. www.slv.vic.gov.au/pic.A/S03/07/80/145.

Ron "Nick" Nicola, for permission to use his story, "I Am the Way" together with the following illustrations:
Chapter 9 – Don't Disturb the Spirits.
Chapter 11 – I Am the Way

The author is also indebted for the research carried out and information provided by Ian Walden, www.ianwarden.com.au

And for the guidance and help given by Kenneth Overend, St Leonards on Sea, East Sussex.

And last, but not least, grateful thanks to my wife Heather Holdsworth for her assistance and research work on her home country, Australia.

# Contents

# Prologue

*"We do not know this Australian's name and we never will. We do not know his rank or his battalion. We do not know where he was born, nor precisely how and when he died. We do not know where in Australia he had made his home or when he left it for the battlefields of Europe. We do not know his age or his circumstances – whether he was from the city or the bush; what occupation he left to become a soldier; what religion, if he had a religion; if he was married or single. We do not know who loved him or whom he loved. If he had children we do not know who they are. His family is lost to us as he was lost to them. We will never know who this Australian was."*

Prime Minister Paul Keating, Eulogy for the Unknown Australian Soldier, Canberra, 11 November 1993,


I stood with my Australian wife, Heather, and her brother Robert and his wife, Margaret, with the hundreds of others on the rolling fields of Flanders on that bitterly cold day exactly 93 years after the battle of Villers-Bretonneux, when so many Australian soldiers fought and died and now lay in their graves at our feet.

And on that day, the Last Post sounded across those fields, and the gentle sobs of those standing with us faded as the sun rose and warmed our faces and brought us back to reality and the year 2009.

And for me, I was drawn to my Australian adventure, years before when I was a lad, leaving the bosom of my family and friends in the little Berkshire village to live the time of my life among the Australian people.

# Chapter 1

# Outward Bound

Ten thousand tons of cargo ship moves slowly ahead, the darkness enveloping her on all sides. The Pilot in charge, Captain at his side. Their faces, intent, outlined in the faint glow of light on the bridge. DEAD SLOW AHEAD. The engine room telegraph clangs its message. "Slowly does it," the Pilot can be heard to say.

The massive gates to King George V dock are behind us. A slow turn to the right then left into the Thames, harnessing the flow of the river, tugs taking the strain. Left is port side, Dad's words come to mind. "A simple little catch-phrase to remember it by, son: There's no red port left."

Now it's right again, starboard, and a biting cold wind whips in from the east, snow flurries stinging our faces. A little knot of hardy souls stand outside their cabins, just a few of the 12 passengers the cargo ship carries, and the deckhands, of course, the men working feverishly to take the ship to sea.

And me, a country boy, just 20 years, never before parted from the love of my family, with Australia and the great adventure stretched out in front of me. I want to watch London depart too. I want to see everything, miss nothing.

Tall cranes to our left, the dock-side cranes that stand like sentries keeping watch over our measured progress. To our right, the sparkling street lights of South London, asleep now.

The Thames widens, we can gather pace… SLOW AHEAD. The engine room telegraph clangs again. Now there's the large black mass of land to our right that is North Kent, the Pilot guiding our way… carefully, not to be rushed, not risking a mishap, there's still Thames traffic even at this hour, past midnight but a new day still to dawn.

Soon the Pilot's job will be done, he'll depart on a tiny motor launch bobbing about in the fast flowing Thames.

"Good luck Captain. Have a safe voyage."

"Goodnight Pilot. See you in a few months no doubt."

"God willing."

The tugs cast off, we are on our own. River traffic become sparse… the lights of London fade behind us. The engine room telegraph clangs yet again. FULL SPEED AHEAD. The engines throb, the whole ship, all ten thousand tons, vibrates as the twin propellers churn the water beneath my feet.

On the deck men are still working busily. Coiling ropes. Lashing tarpaulins. Stashing cargo. And the five huge covered-in crates housing prize cattle, stud horses, securing them on the open deck for the long voyage ahead, two facing inwards, three facing them. Expensive cargo. My cargo, my responsibility. And my passport to the other side of the world.

Now there are instructions shouted. "Clear that deck. Tie that rope. Secure that hatch." The Bosun has been through it all before. "Job done, lads. Time to get some kip. Let's get below."

Darkness is complete. The lights of London just a memory now. The North Sea ahead, then the Channel.

Suddenly a break in the clouds. The moon peeps out.

I say quietly to myself, "Goodbye England… Hello world."

Fifty years on and I still feel I can reach out and touch that moment.

Why on earth wasn't I more anxious for what lay ahead? The days, weeks, months before I'd make a life Down Under – a great one – but I had to get there first.

Survive a stowaway with a knife at my throat, "I'll do for you,

you bastard." And when I did arrive, arrested in the Red Light area of Sydney, lost on the Birdsville Track and bedevilled by Aboriginal spirits in the Outback.

The MV Port Melbourne emerges from the mouth of the Thames and into the North Sea. Another cargo ship passes us, heading for London. "You're going the wrong way, lads… the wrong way."

# Chapter 2

# All at Sea

M.V. "PORT MELBOURNE".

A new day.

Up early, I have work to do, much work to do. But I must see England first, perhaps the last time ever.

Is that it there, in the far distance, through the low, grey clouds hugging the horizon? Is that home? Or what was home until a few hours ago.

I'm taking time off from feeding my bulls, cows and the two horses I've got in my charge. Ship's life is alien to me, of course, and until I get to know my way around, what to do, who to ask, I'll just do what I know best, looking after the animals, mucking them out, giving them fresh straw bedding, attending to them as a good cattleman should. The things that I'd learnt from Ernie Ford, my mentor at the Squire's stud herd over the last two years.

But I must get a last glimpse of England. We're slowly overtaking an old ship, black, grey and rust, smaller than us. A white star on the funnel, laden, deep in the water of the English Channel. Plunging deep into the waves then riding up again shaking the water from its decks.

Do they call them Tramp Steamers? I'll learn I'm sure in the next six weeks at sea, me the one extra crew member to add to the regulation 86; Captain, First Officer, engineers, chippies, electricians, deck hands, everyone to run a ship except look after the cargo of livestock.

Can that be the Sussex coast in the far distance, just behind the Tramp Steamer with the grimy white star, just to the right? The sun lights up the horizon for a moment through a gap in the clouds… then is gone again. Perhaps I've missed my England. Perhaps it slipped by in the last hours of night, while I was asleep in my bunk, dreaming of what lies ahead.

I'm lucky to be here at all. Lads of 20 could still be finishing their National Service, still bashing the parade ground. "Left, right. Left, right. Left… left… left…" But farm trainees get exemption from fighting for their country, the Army, Navy and Air Force. The Government had discovered during the last war that it was necessary to look after those who fed them and anyone learning the art was excused parade ground bashing.

"Thank goodness for that," Mum had said. Having lost a brother, Arthur, fighting in the First World War, Mum was determined her only begotten son wouldn't have anything to do with wars, even if we weren't fighting one at that very minute.

Dad agreed, "You never know, Son. There was the Korean conflict. If you don't look out you'll find yourself in some foreign country fighting an enemy you don't know and can't even recognise."

Left, right…Left, right. Left… left… left… Shoot, shoot, shoot… Yes, shoot or be shot. Don't think about it, I'm saying to myself, scanning the horizon for that last look of home.

"Lost something?" Bosun's standing at my shoulder as I stare out across the white-capped waves, trying to catch a glimpse of a solid outline between cloud and sea. Just a thin sliver would do.

"Lost something?"

"England," I say. "I was hoping to catch a last glimpse."

"You've missed it, son. Passed long ago when you were tucked up asleep." The Bosun could be my strength over the next six weeks. I'll need someone. He seemed a good, sound, solid man from the moment I got on board. And a nice man. "I take it you did sleep well. And the cattle look to be happy too. Not that I know anything about livestock." He's turned, we've both turned, eyeing up the wooden sheds where the animals will spend the whole voyage. "I had the sheds lashed down securely before we sailed. They should be safe. All of you should be," he smiles, half confident, half hopeful.

I better not dwell on the half bit that isn't confident nor the half hopeful bit. Just content myself with the fact that he knows what he is doing while I concentrate on my task.

"Yes," I say. "A great night's sleep but I usually sleep anywhere I lay my head." And I'm telling how I used to doss down amongst the cattle at cattle shows, a camp bed and a sack stuffed with hay as a mattress and one to cover me as a blanket. Ernie had shown me that. And I had not missed a wink. Like I didn't last night.

Bosun smiles again. "Well, I hope you sleep well for the rest of the voyage, even when the going gets rough, this is a cargo ship and not large as cargo ships go, it can be tossed about like a cork on high seas. And no namby-pamby stabilisers either. I've seen grown men, sea-hardened officers too, roll in the scuppers, sea sickness taken over."

It's my turn to smile but I don't know why. I'm not keen on rolling in the scuppers wherever they are, but they don't sound much fun especially if you've been taken over by sea sickness.

"Ever been to sea before, lad?"

I smile. "Just a paddle steamer from Hastings Pier around the Royal Sovereign lightship. A day trip with Dad on holiday, years ago. Two bob return, I think." Then I add, "And a rowing boat on the Thames. One and six for the afternoon. Extra if you lose your oars."

We're both laughing now.

"Well, we'll be in the Bay of Biscay shortly. Let's see how you fare."

Yes, let's see how I fare I think to myself as I return to feeding my charges, five cows, three bulls and two racehorses. Lift the trap door next to their sheds, down a steep ladder into a hold, a dark steel compartment where the animal feed is stored. The hay, straw and the sacks of food stuffs; bran, kibbled oats, maize and high protein cattle nuts. The deck hands must have stashed the lot down here waiting for the cattleman to step forward, me to step forward, take responsibility. Easy for them – the hatch covers would have been off when they loaded the ship in King George V docks. Now I just have this tiny trap door and steep, steel-runged ladder in front of me for the next six weeks.

And there's horse feed down here; this is a relief to find a couple of sacks as I know nothing about feeding racehorses. But there's a little stack in the corner to solve that problem: HIGH PROTEIN HORSE NUTS. THE TRAINER'S CHOICE. If it's good enough for the trainer then it's good enough for me!

It's not quite the bowels of the earth but it feels like the bowels of the ship. Just a single cord and a single bulb casting shadows that move in sympathy with the motion of the ship as it rolls this way and that. And leaving more black bits than rewarding me with bright ones. If I'm truthful this is not where I'm going to be for a minute longer than I have to.

Hump the bales of hay and sacks of feed up the ladder; not easy now, but wait till the going gets rough and sea-hardened men start rolling around in those scuppers. Could be me joining them.

This is no laughing matter. The ladder is steep and the rungs slippery, a bucket of feed in one hand, the other holding on while I get my sea legs. That's what Bosun called it. "Good sea legs, lad. You'll need them when we get into the Bay. Or the South Atlantic."

It was with a wry grin as he admired the cattle, saying how well they seemed to be taking it, oblivious to the ship's movement as it ploughed into a wall of water then coming back up again with the stern, my end of the ship, our end, taking its turn to burrow down into the ocean swell. The cattle were cudding away as if they were back home; a quiet English meadow, a tranquil summer's day. "How'd you get them so contented?"

It's a confidence thing, Ernie used to say, if you are confident and relaxed they are the same. And have respect for you. These are Shorthorns and Herefords, beef breeds, safe in my care even though they weigh a couple of tons and could crush you with ease. But I'm not so sure about milk producers, the Channel Island cattle and their bulls, Guernsey and Jersey, they can be vicious. Ernie said he'd never go in a pen without a large stick at his side and a quick escape route at his back. He was the gentlest man I've ever known with cattle but he still had a warning, "Dangerous they can be, young Richard. If you can't run, don't go in."

I wouldn't. And I'm feeling like that with the two race horses. Wild eyes, flared nostrils, not to my liking at all. I hear them kicking the sides of the sheds with impatience. I'm not confident with them at all and it shows. It'll be my shins they bruise next.

But I've got to make a start somewhere, vicious or not. Can't stand here all day. I've got their feed. It's in the bucket. High Protein Horse Nuts. The Trainer's choice.

"Magisterial Envoy," reads one of the deck-hands. They've come up behind me and have got the horse's name from a card pinned to the door. "Sired by Royal Envoy and out of Sultan's Daughter." And he turns to the lads gathered round, "What the 'ell's all this about then?"

"'is bloody breedin', ain't it?" says one. "'is mum and dad, that's all. Ain't you never 'eard of race 'orse breedin'?"

They're all murmuring now. "Race 'orse breedin'." They agree that's what it means.

"That's right," I say. "Good breeding counts for everything with stud horses. It's the same with my cattle. People will pay good money for top breeding. Like these."

They all stare. I've still got the bucket of nuts in my hand. Half a dozen deck-hands eyeing me up. Some tall, some short, all thick set, tough-looking, tattoos on arms, scars on faces. I'm not sure I'm doing the right thing with what I'm telling them, might be digging a hole for myself. I'm showing affection for a handful of woolly beings on four legs.

They'd already made snide remarks about the friendship I have with them. The only way I know to get the trust of my animals.

"You fancy yer bulls, then, do yer?"

"And cows? Fancy yer cows then?"

They're all laughing. "Snuggle up close to 'em do yer? At night? At night when no-one's lookin'"

"They're paying my fare to Australia." I've got to get that in quickly. "I'd never be able to get to Australia without their help." I nod at the horses. "Not sure about them though. Never looked after race horses in my life."

The deck hands go back to the horses. I put the bucket down. I'm not going in there to be kicked to death with these lads as an audience.

"Magisterial Envoy. What a bloody name... what a mouthful. What's wrong with callin' 'im Dobbin like the milkman's 'orse down our Mum's street?"

They all laugh, even the toughest-looking ones, and their laughter is turned on the one who's speaking. Youngish, short, curly hair, Jimmy from Liverpool they're calling him.

"Can yer imagine Dobbin winning the Derby?" They're pulling his leg.

"Yeah. It's Dobbin by a short bloody 'ead..." Roars of laughter now.

And they're still laughing at Jimmy when they go off to coil ropes or scrub decks or whatever else they do. "Bloody Dobbin." The words come wafting back on the wind carrying sea spray with it. "Dobbin... Bloody Dobbin the milkman's 'orse."

I pick up the bucket, slide the bolts back that secure the door and I'm in. I'd say, "Nice gee-gees, here's your tea." But I'm out again before you can say Jack Robinson. And no kicking!

Phew! Only another six weeks to go.

\* \* \* \* \*

The Bay of Biscay hasn't been that bad.

A couple of the passengers hadn't shown their faces for a day or two and most missed breakfast. They are on the upper decks, out of bounds for us ordinary crew members, but Dougie, the ship's electrician, has been up there to fix faulty switchgear and that's how he knows. And he's telling me in his thick Scottish accent and I'm struggling to make out his words. "Och's and aye's and even a Sassenach or two thrown in.

It's breakfast and half a dozen of us are tucking in, but he's addressing me directly as I'm the newcomer.

"Aye, that's when I bumped into this passenger and wondered why he wasna taking breakfast," Dougie is saying straight into my face. "Sausage, tomatoes, fried eggs, bacon..."

Don't mention breakfast, the passenger told him and dashed to his cabin, slamming the door as he went. "His face was as green as the sea." Dougie has a grin from ear to ear. "I could hear him bringing up last night's dinner even though the door was shut tight behind him."

Mr Mason, the ship's carpenter, had seen them too. "They all looked pretty grim," he's nodding in agreement. "The few that were up and about, anyway. Most weren't."

"Aye, they couldna take it, used to fine living but not the Bay of Biscay." Then Dougie tells me about the top decks being out of bounds. "Don't stray up there, laddie, less ya want a good old telling off." And looks round as if someone might be listening. "Off limits for mere mortals like you and me, us working classes. I'm just telling ya laddie in case ya don't know."

They are supposed to dine with the Captain and First Officer, the 12 passengers, as a perk and a privilege of the trip. "No perks and privileges for them last night. Missed out completely, didn't they?" He's getting a real pleasure from it, the passengers missing out on a plate of fine food. "Best lamb chops cook has turned out in ages. And all the trimmings, mint jelly, the lot... and see what our passengers do with them. Down the pan, I tell yer, down the bloody pan." His voice goes up with his eyebrows as the lamb chops go down. Dougie's enjoying this and I'm enjoying listening.

There's Bosun, Mr Mason the chippie, the two engineers who run the ship's engine room, the radio operator and me at breakfast.

And Dougie, the electrician, of course, enjoying telling his tale.

It's a cosy little dining room, D deck, one down from my own cabin and not much above the level of the sea so the port holes stay locked while the Atlantic breakers swish past. I watch through the thick glass as we roll and pitch under water one moment, out the next. But it feels safe down here; the food is good although not as good as Mum's and I haven't felt sea-sick once. I'm getting those sea legs.

"You're doing fine laddie," Dougie says. "Doing just fine." And it's nice to be told that too.

I'm getting into my routine; up early, checking the cattle and the two horses, giving them their first feed for the day, down for my own breakfast, back up on deck again, the aft deck with the heavy wooden sheds, then mucking them out, keeping them clean and tidy, taking my time grooming the bulls and cows, smart and pristine, that's how I want them and that's how I want them to be when we arrive in Australia.

It's not necessary, not written down as part of my job, like it is keeping them fed and watered and tending to any sickness. I am given a basic vet's kit for that, very basic, you couldn't save a herd of cattle with it. Powders for colic and bloat and a cold poultice for any knocks or bruises. But it's better than nothing and I'm no vet anyway.

I'm going to keep my hand in with the grooming; it might earn me a pat on the back when I get to Australia, even the offer of a job. Mr Evans in Dalgety's London office said I might be lucky. He had known it happen. Dick Evans had taken me on to look after the animals on the voyage. "A shilling a week," he said, with a wry smile. "And all you can eat."

The shilling made me part of the crew, apparently, part of the rules and regulations, he said, and it gave me insurance cover too. "In case of a mishap."

"Mishap," Mum had said, with alarm, stopping half-way through the drying up. "I don't like the sound of that." Mum put the dinner plate down. "A mishap, Son, and you miles from home."

I'd assured Mum they had a very good doctor on board. "To look after the crew and the passengers." I did my most reassuring voice as though I knew what I was talking about. "Very important, passengers, Mum." And that seemed to make her happier. The dinner plate got a jolly good polishing after that.

There were only two more shipments to Australia, according to Dick Evans, two more shipments filling the demand for our stud cattle Down Under. Australian authorities were banning imports for fear of introducing Blue Tongue disease. Not that we have Blue Tongue among our cattle but animals on an open deck could get the disease as the ship passed close to the African coast or stopped at Cape Town, that was the real risk. "It's endemic there, Blue Tongue," Mr Evans had said. "Carried by midges."

So, here I am; curry comb in one hand, stiff brush in the other, just as I have learnt from Ernie Ford. Then standing back and admiring my handiwork… admiring my bulls, admiring my cows, but not showing it when the deck hands come around. They have made those daft comments about cuddling up to them when everyone is tucked up in their bunks and I certainly don't want to be caught talking to them now. And I do that all the time. Getting their confidence as Ernie said. "Make friends of them and they will reward you."

And before I know it we're through the Bay, the ship is slowing and we're sweeping round in a wide arc, clearing the outer jetty, heading into Las Palmas, our first stop, the Canary Islands. "A bunkering facility," Bosun tells me. "The duty on fuel is much less than London. All ships make a bee-line for Las Palmas."

It might be late but the dockside is swarming with traders waiting for the ship to tie up. "Watch out for your wallet," Bosun says. And I'm best advised to keep the door to my cabin locked. "There can be a few unsavoury characters amongst the African stall holders that slip past the Watchman. I don't know how, but they always do."

And Dougie whispers in my ear. "Check your change if you buy anything, laddie. You're as likely to find coins from Morocco and Mombassa in your pocket if you're not wary."

It looks like everything under the sun is being sold on the quayside and now an instant market has popped up on deck. Next to my cattle sheds and where they haven't carried tables on board, they're laying out their merchandise on any empty deck space they can find, squatting down, legs crossed, faces turned up, eyes smiling. A sight to see for a country lad like me. Fabrics, scarves, carpets, rugs… electrical stuff, watches, clocks, radios… jewellery, baubles, bangles, beads. You name it, they've got it. This is a foreign bazaar and just a few hours out of England. Wait till I tell Mum and Dad. And Jill, the girl I left behind.

Wish you were here, Mum and Dad! Wish you were here, Jill!

The bazaar is at my feet. I'm smelling the smells of Africa, herbs and spices, hearing the sounds, the chatter and laughter. And watching the eager faces, the flashing smiles, white teeth, dark eyes, dark skins. Some ebony black, others all shades of brown. Is this what they call a swarthy complexion? Didn't come across the word swarthy at school – but then I didn't come across a foreign bazaar in Lower Fifth with Whacker Worvill my English teacher. Men bartering, heckling, cajoling, persuading. "Zis good for you lady. You buy. Three pounds. She much happy." He's holding up a silk scarf.

The dark eyes, the dreadlocks, the bony, nimble hands, the swarthy complexion. "You feel… you feel quality for you lady. She much happy." How the hell does he know there's Jill back home who'd be bowled over by such a present?

He's on his feet now, his boy is at his side. Same face, same eyes, same skin, same flashing smile. Now he's at my side. "Watch your pockets laddie, watch your pockets," Dougie's words had warned. "The old man distracts while the kid has your change."

It's two against one. It would be so easy to back off. Retreat to my cabin. Lock the door behind me. But if I didn't want adventure, I shouldn't be here in the first place. Shouldn't have fronted up to Dick Evans at the Perth bull sales when I was there with Ernie and asked, "Excuse me, Mr Evans, do you have any vacancies for lads taking cattle to Australia?"

I'm no expert on scarves but the one he's holding looks pretty good to me. Blues, golds and greens, all colours of the rainbow. Haven't seen the likes of this on Right-T-Ho's shelves in the village store. I can see it tied around Jill's face, matching her sparkling eyes. But three pounds? I'll take Dougie's advice. "Offer half what he wants, noo more."

Well, that's set the cat among the pigeons! Dougie's half price has offended the man, abused his integrity. He's looking to the heavens. His eyes roll like he's summoning the Almighty. Hope he's not a Witch Doctor or I'm cursed for life. His little boy tugs my hand. "Mister, you buy. You lady like." Surprise, surprise, he thinks three pounds is a fair price too. A little boy, a perfect copy of Dad, but pint sized. And abused and offended just like pop. His eyes are rolling too.

Crumbs, Mum never had this trouble when buying half a pound of potatoes at the village store.

Dougie had said, "Walk away, laddie. Show no interest. Turn your back."

I'll try that. The hand tugs mine again, he's finished with the rolling eyes. I turn, the man is talking. "Two pounds, my last offer. You buy… you lady like."

We settle on one pound fifteen shillings. I am happy. He is happy. The little boy happy. I have the silk scarf. He has my one pound fifteen. We celebrate, hands meeting hands – in years to come we'll call it High Fives.

"For the girl back home?" Mr Mason, the chippie, has an eye for such things. "The girl who came to see you off?" Jill is pretty, Mr Mason thinks so too. "She'll like the silk scarf, but she'd prefer you to put it around her pretty face!"

I am buying a rug for Mum, just a few feet by a few feet to cover the bare patch in front of our fireplace that just happens to be a few feet by a few feet. This one is hand woven, Bosun assures me. "Some will fall apart before you get them back to your cabin, some won't. This one is quality." But I've never bought anything like this before. "Don't worry, your mum will like that. From her lad, on his great adventure."

I can imagine Mum laying it out in front of the fire then standing back and admiring the effect it's having. The textures, the weave, the colours. When Mrs Wallace from next door pops by she'll say:

"My son bought it for me."

"You miss him, don't you?"

Mum wouldn't show it. A tough spirit, my mum. But years later I heard how the tears ran down Mum's cheeks. But none for Mrs Wallace. "Richard, my son, bought it. In a foreign market. He has good taste."

I go through the same bartering, same words, same debate, and get the same, "You lady like." And I have abused the man on the other side of a pile of carpet that could adorn Buckingham Palace. Five pounds become four, four become three pounds fifteen shillings and three pound fifteen becomes three pound twelve and six. We shake hands on three pound ten. This man's little boy looks up into my face. "You lady like, Mister." I do another High Fives with his dad and have made a chum for life.

I'll post them in Cape Town, I tell Bosun when he asks how I will get them home. "My mum has a sister living in Cape Town. And family and grown up kids. They'll post them for me I'm sure."

But that's a couple of weeks away. The North Atlantic, crossing the equator, then south Atlantic. The bulls and cows and me, we've got all that in front of us. Then there's the horses, still not much fun with them, I can't win them over at all. Become their friend. It's a confidence thing and I have none of that as I open the door to the shed, dash in and out again with the bucket of feed and dodge the flaying feet. Trouble is, mucking out involves a long stay and I get a crack on the shins more than once. And more than just the shins. If it's a kicking you want, step this way.

Give me my cattle any time. I'll reward them. Making something special, a treat, using the bran and molasses I asked for when I signed up. And this is how I'll do it. Take a couple of dozen handfuls of bran, place in the mixing tub; two scoops of sticky molasses dissolved in half a bucket of boiling water, then transfer to the bran. Mix to a crumbly texture. Mrs Beaton would be proud. It smells good enough for anyone to eat.

Bosun is watching, looking over the half door into the cattle pen, leaning on it like a real old countryman, only the piece of straw between the teeth that's missing. "I'm getting to like your cattle. And they don't give me any trouble like some buggers on this ship. And that food you've prepared could put cook to shame."

But it's down there in the bowels. Take your life into your hands with a trip on the steel-runged ladder and the single light to show the way. It'll be better when we start to whittle away at the reserve and flush out the dark corners; but for the moment I'm having to convince myself a few dark corners shouldn't frighten a brave young lad of 20 on his great adventure, nor should the creaking I hear. It's only the cargo bedding in.

Or is it?

I'm sure I'm seeing something, could it be a face in the darkness, white against the blackness, and the shape of a body caught in the light as it swings to and fro. And that's not the ship creaking, it's breathing. Heavy breathing. It sounds tense and agitated. Almost desperate.

"Anyone there?" I try not to let my voice sound hoarse, betray my fear. "Come out so I can see you. Show yourself."

There's that sound again, breathing, a shadow moves and a sack of High Protein Horse Nuts hits the floor, the nuts scattering on the hard steel plate beneath my feet. Then there's the glint of something sharp, a weapon perhaps, something to take the life of a brave young lad of 20.

"Shut ya mouth or I'll do for ya." He has the knife in his hand, one more step and it's at my throat, the cold hard blade, one more move and I'll be slit open wide. Then the words, desperate words. "Just shut ya mouth. I'm hitching a lift back home, to Oz. Ya haven't seen me. Right."

I'm weighing up my options. Get to the steel-runged ladder; not possible. Shout; pointless. Grab the knife; out of the question. I'm not half as brave as I was ten minutes ago and I wasn't very brave then. And I've got to think of Mum and Dad sitting around the fireplace waiting for the news of their son. Then there's the cattle waiting for their bran mash. I can't die in a pool of blood without feeding them first.

"Yes," I find myself saying. "Yes, of course." Then I try, "What a good idea," even though that's daft and anything daft isn't a good idea. But I still don't want that knife slitting my throat, him to do for me. I'll settle for a good kicking from the horses any day of the week.

"You don't have to use the knife. I won't give you trouble." I try not to sound pleading. "I'll help you." My voice is as calm as I can make it. And in the dark he can't see the fear in my eyes nor hear the thumping of my heart.

He is calm now that I've spoken. "That's all right then, mate. Just keep ya mouth shut and you'll be right." The cold steel of the knife is no longer stinging my skin. It's lowered. I see him wipe the blade as though it's blooded. "You'll be okay. Just keep quiet."

And I do. He asks for no more than my silence which is a mercy; no food, no water, nothing but keeping quiet. "I can fend for myself. Don't need an accomplice. I'll keep ya out of all that." He's even going to gather up the High Protein Nuts, Trainer's Choice, and fill the sack. And he has called me mate. Pommie Bastard as well, of course. But mate too. And the knife is put away.

Looking back years later I wonder why the hell I didn't panic, have a fit. Goodness I was only 20 and just freed from Mum's apron strings. Apart from agricultural college and a dozen or so cattle shows I'd never been away from home; and the closest I'd ever come to violence was at the Roxy on a Saturday night with Al Capone and a handful of Hollywood hit men spraying the air with machine gun bullets. I think I even ducked when the cry rang out, "Give it to him Mugsy… Right between the eyes!"

Yes, looking back I wonder why I didn't panic and scarcely lost a minute's sleep. I was all on my own. No-one to turn to. Not even the Bosun now I'd said I wouldn't say anything.

The night watchman had reported a fleeting shadow a couple of nights before. He had given chase, lost it in the corridors, round corners, up stairs. There are enough of all these on the MV Port Melbourne to lose a football team. A young, fit Australian stowaway could outrun any watchman especially if he's as desperate as the man scooping up my high protein nuts at this very minute.

It was all the talk at breakfast. This fleeting figure. Bosun and Mr Mason. Dougie couldn't see it being a passenger unless he was raiding the kitchen, catching up on what he had missed the first two days. "After the lamb bloody chops noo doubt."

Shoulders were shrugged, conversation petered out, nothing

coming to mind and the chat turned to crossing the equator and the antics the deck hands would get up to when we did. The silly rituals handed out to those who had never crossed the line before. Never come face to face with King Neptune. Daubed with paint, the contents of the slop bucket emptied over their heads. And all washed down from the bilge pump. "Och, nay pleasant," said Dougie. "Meeting King bloody Neptune. And if they say they're looking for some nuts to tar, make yourself scarce laddie. They could be yours."

I hoped they would be so preoccupied with other crew members who hadn't crossed the line before that they wouldn't think of me. Wouldn't cotton on to the fact that I had never come face to face with King Neptune. Never had a slop bucket over my head. And if they're looking for nuts to tar, they can have the horses'.

Bosun said it shouldn't include cattlemen, men on a shilling a week, those that weren't full time crewmen. "I'll see if I can keep you out of this," he said.

"Aye, I can remember my first experience." Dougie was still casting his mind back 20 years... or was it 30? It was before the war so it must be 25 at least. "They even got up to those shananicins back then. And don't think they are joking when you see them go for the tar brush." But I'd settle for that and a dousing with the bilge pump against a knife at my throat. "Pommie bastard. Keep quiet or I'll do for ya."

I've already made up my mind. I've told the bloke in the hold I won't break my word, just go about my duties as though nothing has happened. I won't go back on what I'd said.

Of course I'm feeling guilty as my allegiance should be to the Bosun who has been kind to me and to the Port Line for my passage to Australia. But my stowaway has done no harm, other than pinch a few scraps at night. And frighten the living daylights out of a country lad fresh from village life; but what would an adventure across the world be without a knife at your throat every time you go for a bale of hay?

And it will all be over once we leave Cape Town. He said he'll give himself up then.

"They won't turn back just for one stowaway." He laughed. "Or cast me adrift in an open boat, the Poms stopped doing that years ago when they were civilising the world. No, they'll put me ashore the next port of call."

That's Australia, of course, Adelaide.

"Then I couldn't care a toss, mate. I'm home then, thank Christ. You can keep ya fuckin' boat."

I'm still chewing over what's likely to happen when it comes to crossing the Equator. Most especially, what's likely to happen to me. Bosun said he'd keep me out of it if he can – but the deck hands might have other ideas. I'm still thinking about it when Dougie shuffles up at the end of the day, bushy eyebrows, craggy face, filling his pipe from the pouch in his back pocket. I'm going to be treated to more tales from the past as the sun lights up the sky for one last time before dipping over the horizon.

"Don't lose too much sleep over what I said before, laddie. Crossing the Line isn't that bad. But you could always play safe and keep a low profile. Not offer yourself as the sacrificial lamb."

I'm nodding. "I'm hoping that taking a few livestock to Australia doesn't involve all that."

The smoke from his pipe drifts away on a waft of breeze and catches me as it passes. It takes me back home for just that moment and I'm with Mum and Dad in front of the fire, Mum knitting, Dad in his leather chair, puffing on his pipe. Dad always said his St Bruno was the best baccy he'd ever smoked and I'm just about to tell Dougie but he hasn't left King Neptune yet. "Aye, there's worse than being confronted by the king of the sea, laddie. Far worse."

One more puff and I'm learning what it was like to be a merchant seaman in the war. "Bosun served on a merchantman but he'll nae tell you. Just bottle it up, he does, in his cabin and it's nae good for the mind nor soul."

He's fumbling into an inner pocket, a waistcoat pocket, and fishes out a piece of bent metal, about two inches square, jagged edges. "You see this, laddie... you see this here, it's shrapnel. Nearly took my life. Inches away." He fingers it, almost as though he has an affinity for it, shiny from years of fetching it out of the inside pocket and telling his tale. "We were in a convoy, you see, all hell let loose. You were too young to understand, laddie. But I tell you, all hell let loose."

There's another puff of St Bruno and he points the pipe towards the bridge. "Nothing more than a fizz and thud by ma ear, ma right ear, embedded itself into the wheel-house door. I was up there when it nearly took ma ear, and nearly took ma wee Scottish brains…"

He tells me how he dug it out with his pen-knife, a keepsake to remind him, to help his story telling. "I still don't know where it came from. Maybe the cargo ship on our port bow when she blew up. Carrying munitions. One torpedo, that's all it took. The poor bastards didn't stand a chance."

He stops for another puff. I catch more St Bruno.

"Or it could have been from a U-boat gun, they were shelling us too. I tell you, laddie, all hell let loose. It puts crossing the line, confronting King bloody Neptune and the deck hands' antics into perspective."

Dougie is fishing out a crumpled piece of paper from where the keepsake came from. "I keep it safe…Just a few words from a book I read. Great book from a guy on a Corvette escort. No-one sums it up better."

There's a final puff, Dougie clears his throat:

**"What a miserable, rotten hopeless life . . . an Atlantic so rough it seems impossible that we can continue to take this unending pounding and still remain in one piece . . . hanging onto a convoy is a full-time job . . . the crew in almost a stupor from the nightmarishness of it all . . . and still we go on hour after hour."**

"Thirty-thousand of us died, thirty thousand merchant seamen in their watery graves. Bringing home the bacon for Britain at war was nae fun. I tell you laddie, facing King Neptune on the Port Melbourne is nothing to fear, nothing at all."

# Chapter 3

# South Atlantic Blues

The ship's horn is blasting. Once, twice, three times... It can be heard five miles distant but I'm just a few paces away and I jump out of my skin. Either I'll be like Beethoven and prematurely deaf or my life's been shortened by ten years. Perhaps I'll be dead and deaf all at the same time.

The helmsman grins down from the Bridge. "The cattleman's just leapt overboard, Skip."

And the reason – we're crossing the Equator and the deckhands are having a party. For them it's time to celebrate.

Dougie, the electrician, whispers, "Keep your head down, laddie. Lock yourself in your cabin if necessary, make yourself scarce. I've seen this all before."

But I'd like to stay and see what happens. Not every day you cross the Equator, not every day you have your ear drums pierced by a blast from a 10,000 ton cargo ship.

The next threat is being drawn into the deck hands' fun and games. I might hide behind Highland Monarch, the two-ton bull with the sharpest of horns. "Come on lads, come and get me."

Not necessary. They are making all their own fun without drawing me into it. Perhaps Bosun did his bit as he promised. Bosun to the rescue. Good man.

He says they will come up with a crown and beard for King Neptune. And if they're nice to chippie he'll knock them up a trident to carry. Then its slop buckets at the ready. And the tar brush. "They'll go through all that," Bosun says. "If they're going to do it properly. I shouldn't think this crew will let us down."

The passengers, all 12, have gathered on the deck just above me, leaning against the railing looking down on the open decking, the women's pretty dresses blowing in the breeze, the eddies created by the ship as she ploughs across the ocean, the men smearing down their hair. They've come out to watch the ceremony, just like me. It's time to pay respect to King Neptune, King of the Sea. It's what today is all about.

And the lads, the deckhands, those not involved in this King Neptune thing don't want to miss the line-crossing ceremony either. And a glance in the direction of the skirts hoping the wind's going to blow a bit more. Can't blame them, really. Two weeks at sea and four more to go is hard on the hormones. Tan from Newcastle had said already he can't wait to get to Cape Town. He's got a girl there. He's got a girl everywhere, says Jimmy. "Lucky bleeder, for the rest of us it's out on the Town, on the razzle-dazzle. 'ope I get lucky."

The Captain and First Officer have come down from the bridge to watch. Who the hell's steering the ship?

"Don't worry laddie. They've got some sort of auto-pilot contraption," Dougie tells me. "And a man on watch to keep an eye on the auto-pilot contraption... and floating mines."

The bushy eyebrows go up and down. The eyes twinkle. "Just joking, laddie. Just joking."

The deck-hands have a 44-gallon drum prepared specially, filled to the brim. "Och, and I hate to think what they've got in there. And I hate to think what they are going to do with it."

Bosun tells me there's three new recruits signed on for this voyage reporting directly to him. "Three fresh new lads, never been to sea before, never crossed the line. They'll be for it today."

Bosun, Dougie and the rest of the crew have all been through this when they first went to sea. "Every crew member has, laddie. No-one escapes what you are about to see. Even the Captain and First Officer when they were fresh out of college." Those eyebrows again. "There's no escaping it."

"Except the cattleman," I say. "Let's hope he stays out of it."

Here's King Neptune striding out now, taking a few bows and milking the applause from around the aft deck. It's the tall lad, the one who thought Dobbin winning the Derby was daft, he's just wearing shorts and his chest is covered in hair and a bit stuck to his chin, but from where even Bosun is at a loss. But the biggest laugh is for the jerry pot on his head as a crown. "Now where the hell did they dig that up from? It isn't as if a 10,000 ton cargo ship is awash with piss pots. Well, not that sort."

King Neptune is surrounded by a dozen of the lads, most of the deckhands, and they're dressed as maids of the sea with grass skirts made from string and their hair adorned with flowers fashioned from coloured paper. "Give 'em credit," says Bosun. "This crew are doing us proud."

Now they're chanting about King Neptune being King of the Sea, "King of the Sea and all that sail on her..." They sing it out across the decks of the MV Port Melbourne and throw in a few yo ho, ho's to make a great laugh of it, and the passengers are laughing too. And then the lads give King Neptune three hip, hip hoorays. "Hip, hip, hooray, King Neptune, King of the Sea." Even the

Captain's raised a smile even though he must have seen it many times before.

Now here comes Bosun's three new raw recruits led before King Neptune and now we can see where King Neptune's hair has come from – they've lost theirs to the scissors and all that's left is a stubble. Just like Borstal boys. "Och, that'll take ages to grow back. All of six months for me to get ma curly locks back. My old mother hardly recognised her wee laddie the day I got home."

King Neptune is proclaiming them Virgin Sailors, "Never come this way before, never ventured upon my Kingdom," and he's dipping his chamber pot in the drum, scooping the contents and pouring it over their heads, thank God I've not been roped in. Dougie says it looks like it came from the engine room. "I think they've got a mate down there."

Then King Neptune's maids slop them from the leftovers cook dumps overboard every morning.

Shrieks of dismay from the ladies and the men watching; it looks like they wouldn't miss it for the world. And they've got it on camera. Kodak is making a fortune out of this crossing the line.

The three fresh new lads are on their knees, kneeling in front of King Neptune. "To the King, to the King," they chant, "Yer 'ighness, may we be granted the right to cross your line? Some are calling him "Yer 'onour."

And the King replies, "Who comes forth?" And the first is Charlie from Brixton and the next is Jimmy from Liverpool and then Fred from a little place in Yorkshire. There's nothing about my horses, nor the milkman's float and Dobbin's the last thing on their minds now. They're just wishing they could get it over and done with. Charlie, Jimmy and Fred from Yorkshire who always wanted to go to sea but hadn't bargained on yesterday's dinner on his head.

Captain has seen enough and so has the ship's First Officer. Back to the bridge to give the auto-pilot the elbow. And for Bosun it's time to get the lads to clear up and back to work. King Neptune, his maids, the slop bucket and 44 gallon drum. "The fun's over, lads. Back to work." He wants the railings painted and pristine before Cape Town. "No excuses. Get stuck in."

And for me I'm back to enjoying the voyage. I haven't seen the stowaway once although he must be on the ship somewhere. A shadow at night; nothing more than a fleeting figure for the Watchman to chase. During daylight just lying low, keeping out of sight; but he must be watching, listening, and waiting to see if I give the game away, give his game away. "I'll do for ya, Pommie bastard. I'll do for ya if you so much as breathe a word."

I won't. I gave him my promise. But his threat's there while I just spend my time keeping the animals fed and watered, mucked out, and ready for when we arrive in Australia. My future could depend on it, maybe a job in Oz. Mr Evans said there's a good chance and I don't want to miss it.

"They are beautiful, aren't they?" It's a woman's voice, a pleasant voice, and a particularly pleasant one after two weeks at sea treated only to male company. She is standing right beside my cattle pens, smiling blue eyes, flowing hair. Perfect.

But I'm caught off guard. I'm talking to my bulls and my cows, as always, calling them by my pet names, Aggie for Augusta, Bertha for Bapton Bertha and the Shorthorn bull, Highland Monarch, just Monty to me. My mind is elsewhere, I don't hear her come up behind us, didn't hear the tell-tale clickety-clack of the high heels against the background of a working ship.

"Yes," I'm saying, conscious of being caught talking to woolly beings on four legs. "Yes, I think they are great. These are special animals, you know. Full of good breading."

It's daft really, but I'm going a bit red like I used to when I was a kid at school and caught by teacher day-dreaming of escaping the classroom the moment the bell rang. And especially being caught by a woman, this attractive woman. "And they are more than just animals to me, they're friends really, that's why the chat." It's a bit garbled, my explanation. The best I can do in the circumstances. "Not much opportunity of conversation round here."

But I manage a smile to go along with my embarrassment and she is smiling too, confident and reassuring.

"Oh, don't worry. I have a little dog at home, Sheba, I talk to her all the time." Lucky old Sheba, I think. "Like you, I don't have many others to talk to… well, interesting talk."

The big Shorthorn bull nuzzles his wet nose against me. He knows I have sugar lumps in my pocket, nicked from the breakfast table. A treat.

No-one interesting to chat to? What about the husband? I could risk the question. I know there is one; I had seen him taking pictures of crossing the line, silver haired, and the first to succumb to the Bay of Biscay. That's what Dougie said, anyway. Dashing past on his way to ditching the lamb chops and trimmings.

"No-one to talk to?"

"Oh my husband you mean, Eustace, the love of my life." Another smile, this one almost a grimace, she half turns away, I'm not sure if I'm supposed to see or not. "Big in the City and his club. And squash too. So he tells me, anyway. He enjoys his squash."

"I take it you're not talking about the orange variety." I risk the joke to keep the conversation going.

"No, silly. It's a game. Two of them chase a little ball around a room, sometimes four, it doesn't seem to make much difference. The aim is to keep fit, to retain his shape. But ask him to mow the lawn and he gets puffed out."

Her eyebrows are raised now. Smiling blue eyes seem to be telling me something. An encouraging message. The truth maybe?

Perhaps there is an invitation to question more, probe a bit. Eustace, big in the City, big in his club and big with the little ball that you chase round a room. Lots of energy but, it would seem, not for the woman with the smile and fresh new lipstick applied for the trip down the steps to the lower decks and a chat with the lad and his cattle. It would be nice to think that, wouldn't it?

Anyway, my deck is out-of-bounds to privileged fare-paying passengers, all the lower decks are, the working decks. So, what's she doing down here? Bosun will frown. Accidents, he'd say, tripping, twisting an ankle, breaking a leg even. And there's always work going on, ropes coiled, decks scrubbed, fixtures and fittings painted. Bosun doesn't want 12 aimless passengers wandering around when work's going on.

"I can see they think you are a friend." Then she corrects herself with emphasis. "You *are* a friend."

"Thank you," I'm saying and start off on the usual tack about the task of presenting them in prime condition for their new owners in Australia. How I might get a job out of it. I have said all this so many times before, so many on the ship have asked and I don't want to get bogged down once again in describing the daily routine of attending to bulls, cows and race horses on the MV Port Melbourne. How many scoops of bran, how many bales of hay... and how many fork fulls of cow dung thrown over the side each morning. Not with this attractive woman. I'd rather ask about her life, husband, squash, little dog even. Yes, even lucky little Sheba if it scores some Brownie points, keeps her interested, gives me an excuse to keep her chatting, I'll talk about anything you care to name.

"Mrs Wilberforce," she smiles again. "Julia Wilberforce, call me Julia, please." Goodness, that's come out of the blue. Encouragement. I wouldn't have dreamt of that a few minutes ago.

She holds out a hand, a smooth, soft hand and well manicured nails. I hadn't expected that either. "We're on our way to Adelaide to see our daughter get married to Ed in insurance. Big-wig in the Antipodes apparently." The smile returns, "Under-writer, I'm told. Sounds horribly like under-taker to me."

I smile. Mine are rough, working hands... I wipe the palm on my overalls before accepting the offer.

Yes, the message is there. Mr Wilberforce, big in the City, big in his club and big in squash, is only big in her life to pay the bills, give her a large house, little dog, silk scarf and off to Oz to see the under-taker.

We chat about the voyage, the MV Port Melbourne, her husband's choice of a cargo ship rather than a liner. "Likes his seclusion... hates hordes of noisy, ordinary, people. But he soon learnt his lesson when the sea got rough. That laid him low." She chuckles. "He even thought of abandoning ship in Las Palmas and returning home."

I join in that joke. "And what about you? Did you succumb?"

She didn't. "Took to my bed with a good book... nothing else to do. I always said it would be the most boring six weeks of my life. I miss my friends, my own private friends."

31

She's telling me she enjoys a chat with real people. I'm a "real" person. Yes, a real person with bulls, cows, overalls and rough hands.

In the years to come, my next question would go something like this: "To complete a perfect evening, why not come in for a coffee, a tête-à-tête?" But then I'd be the proud owner of a Porsche, a flat on the St Kilda Road backing onto Albert Park Lake and view across what will become the Australian Grand Prix circuit. All glamour and glitz. Now all I've got is a tiny cabin, two bunks, one porthole (steamed up) and a barnacle or two if you look hard enough.

She smiles again. She's even read my mind. "What a pity Eustace is around. I have coffee and mints in the cabin. Very nice mints."

Highland Monarch with the wet nose and sharp horns can't take much more of this. Waiting for his treat, his sugar lumps.

Then it's all over – there is the husband, Eustace, and he's calling from the upper deck. "Julia dear. I'm going down to lunch… coming?"

She trips off. Back up the steps, just a single glance over her shoulder at me and my animals. Highland Monarch stops chewing his cud. "Goodness Monty," I say. "This isn't good for a lad with aspirations."

I fish in my pocket. He gets his sugar lump. Nothing for me though. I've missed out.

There, I go again. Talking to my woolly beings.

Hang on to your hats lads. The South Atlantic is another new experience for a young man who's only had a two-bob trip around the Sovereign lightship and a couple of hours on the Thames in a rowing boat. The sea is not rough, no white caps, but there is a giant swell that comes slanting in from the starboard, and astern, mainly astern, causing the ship to lift and plunge then rise up again like a roller coaster; the last time I enjoyed such a helter-skelter ride was at Henley Regatta fairground, a hot balmy evening with girlfriend Jill.

"Wow. Hold on, Jill."

We hung on.

"Hold onto me," she said. I did! I couldn't stop!

Now the ship buries its bow into this giant swell and the stern lifts and the propellers come thrashing out of the water with the sound of thunder until buried back down again in the next huge surge chasing us across the South Atlantic.

There's five thousand miles of open, unchallenged, sea behind us feeding this surge. All the way from the tip of South America, Tierra del Fuego, Land of Fire.

I'm up on the Bridge, everything laid out before me, the ship's controls, the engine room telegraph, the radar, even Dougie's contraption.

"Self-steering gear," says the Helmsman, scanning the horizon for a floating mine or two. He's invited me up in exchange for deafening me on the day we crossed the line.

"Recovered your hearing lad?"

"What?"

He smiles. "As long as it didn't give you a heart attack. Bosun needs you to get the cattle to Australia."

The radio operator pops his head round the door. "Captain Thompson of the Port Brisbane in contact, Sir. Says he's just left Cape Town. Been keeping our berth warm."

"Ask the old rogue if he left any beer."

They all laugh about Captain Thompson.

The Helmsman says, "Self steering gear. We've come a long way since the days they lashed my predecessor to the wheel when rounding the Horn."

I think I'll get a book out of the library on the early sailing ships taking settlers to Australia. Brunel's great iron-clad ship, the SS Great Britain, made several voyages after her inaugural New York trips and although she was steam-powered with just a few square yards of sail as back-up, the journey time still averaged 70 to 80 days.

Nowadays, of course, any number of airlines will get you Down Under in less than 30 hours. Ironic that while there is First Class, Business Class, the rest travel in what is affectionately referred to as Cattle Class.

My cattle have got accustomed to the swell and the plunging ship. They move in keeping with anything the South Atlantic can throw at them; they are munching away and they look good. I haven't asked the horses but they still manage a kick or two the moment I go near them so there's life there yet.

But it gives the passengers white faces; it's the Bay of Biscay all over again. Unsteady on their feet, clutching the ship's rail as they come up for air. And the hot muggy air does nothing for their well-being. It must be taking its toll on lovely Mrs Wilberforce. No sign of her, no more chats on the aft deck, no more thoughts of mints in the First Class cabin as she slips off her sling-backs then reclines on the deluxe double bed. "Do join me, young Mr Cattleman. Show me what you get up to down on the farm."

I can but dream…

There's a fizzing in the air and the night sky is lit with electrical storms, a firework display of gigantic proportions. Turn the clock back to the Blitz with London on fire. That's how I remember it as a lad standing at my bedroom window, transfixed. "Look Dad. Look."

Dad turned away.

Mum said, "Back to bed, son."

I thought it was fun. But they were thinking of Gran up there in London. We were miles away in the country but it could still be seen. London on fire. But I doubt the passengers are appreciating the sky even if they had seen what I had seen back in 1940. An inferno in the distance. What Dad called a Wagnerian spectacle.

"Gotterdammerung. Twilight of the Gods. Music to fire the imagination, Son. Music you'll understand when you're older."

Dad understood it so much it got him arrested!

Before the war, Mum and Dad had gone to Bayreuth to enjoy this Wagnerian spectacle – long before gallivanting over to the Continent was as easy as popping down to the corner shop. And it had slipped out in casual conversation over a glass of beer at the Red Lion; the locals put two and two together and came up with Funf!

Next evening I looked on in dismay as the village constable, accompanied by a sergeant and a plain clothes man came knocking at our door. "It 'ave come to my attention you been visiting that Nazi Germany, Bank Manager. If you'd like to accompany us down to the Station."

Only doing their duty, Dad said afterwards. Not a Nazi spy, of course. But he does like his Richard Wagner. For the rest of the war he was careful what he said in the Red Lion.

Are your listening, woolly bullies?

We've called into Cape Town. Warm weather, bright sunlight, wide roads. Vast expansive houses, shanty town shacks, Auntie and Table Mountain. A puff of white cloud draped over the top. "The table cloth," Auntie proudly proclaimed as she wrapped Mum's carpet and Jill's scarf, my presents from Las Palmas, and promised to post them next day. By the time I get to Australia they will have arrived home. Maybe I will soon be getting a reply. Maybe Jill will be saying, "Miss you..." I know Mum will be. I had told them to write to me C/o Dalgetys, MV Port Melbourne, Adelaide Docks, South Australia, and Dalgetys promised to forward my letters to wherever I ended up.

Then there's Greg the Stowaway to look forward to.

Some joke. Some bloody joke! But the day can't be far away. "They won't turn back for just one stowaway." It seemed as if he's done it all before. That cocky confidence.

It must be about time for him to show himself, after a day's steaming from Cape Town, perhaps, that's what he promised. But here we are, two days out and I've not seen him since the day he threatened my life, the knife in hand, the light glinting off the blade. It was the best part of four weeks past, but it's still as clear as if it was yesterday.

I go down below to get my cattle feed twice a day. But never without looking over my shoulder and into the dark shadows. "Is that you hiding there, Greg?"

Silence. Silence except for the creaking of the ship.

Another dark corner. "Greg, can you hear me? I've not said anything."

A shilling a week, Dick Evans promised. "And all you can eat." But he didn't say anything about a stowaway jumping out on you for second helpings.

Then suddenly Greg does exist! Large as life. He's true to his word – they won't turn back once we clear Cape Town. That's what he said and he's made sure, doubly sure, by leaving it a couple of days, that bit of extra insurance. Now he's materialised from somewhere, from nowhere. As if by magic, on the aft deck with the deck hands discovering him, not me fortunately and it's the Bosun they're shouting for.

"Get the Bosun Jimmy, quick..." King Neptune takes control. Standing firm. Standing tall. Looking the part. Good job the piss pot's not on his head. "Get Bosun, Jimmy. Quick mate, quick."

Strong, safe, reliable Bosun comes stomping along.

"What's this? A stowaway... on my ship?" My ship. A personal insult, it seems. He prides himself on a tight team. No slackness, no wasters, and no-one he can't account for. But now he's got Greg the stowaway.

The deckhands gather round, watching, they've never come across a Greg before. None of them.

"Christ, where's 'e popped up from?"

"Search me."

"Must 'ave been 'elped by someone... someone on the ship."

"Throw the bastard overboard."

It's not clear if Jimmy is talking about Greg, or his helper.

Greg gives him a long, hard look. Jimmy, who's all for having someone thrown overboard, is getting the look. I remember the words down in the hold that day, "I'll do for you..." Jimmy's a marked man now, good lad Jimmy, shorn of his curly locks after crossing the line. But it's time to back down now. "Well, you know what I mean. Shouldn't be allowed. Stowin' away."

Bosun leads Greg off but not before Greg gives me a sideways glance. No more than a glance. And saying nothing. I hope he's living up to his promise. Keeping me out of this. I have lived up to mine.

It's the Bridge they're heading for. To see the Chief Petty Officer, I guess, he deals with this sort of thing. When I first came on board that's who I was told to see, sign papers, make it official, get my instructions. Then handed over to Bosun and allocated my cabin and bunk. "You're in luck, son, a double cabin all to yourself."

The Captain would have to be told; a stowaway is not an everyday occurrence. Eyebrows raised, questions asked, Bosun under the spotlight. It would be doubted Greg could have survived half-way across the world without help, someone to feed him, water him, to cover for him. Questions will be asked, sure to be.

Then he's gone, leaving the lads excitedly chatting about what has just happened. What they have seen. "'e just walked up to us, cool as a cucumber, I never see where 'e come from. Round the back there, somewhere."

Charlie is pointing to the spare propeller, the huge propeller kept for an emergency, stored on the aft decking, behind my cattle pens. "Over there somewhere," he says.

"Perhaps 'e kipped down under the spare prop." They're all laughing now. "Pity it wasn't connected... would 'ave cut 'is bleedin' 'ead off."

Jimmy turns to me, "Perhaps 'e kipped down with your lot, your bulls and cows."

They're all looking at me now. "That's a thought," says King Neptune. "He'd be tucked up warm and cosy there. Dossed down in the straw. Perhaps you turned a blind eye."

This is getting too close for comfort. "The bulls would trample him," I say. "Trample him to death. He wouldn't stand a chance."

The pressure is off. "Yeah, of course. Them great big 'oofes. I wouldn't want to doss down there."

And Charlie rounds it off. "And a pile of cow shit to lie on."

They're all laughing again.

"Bull shit," says another.

Even more laughter now.

And I'm off the hook.

There's a knocking at my cabin door. "I'm afraid we'll have to put matey in here." It's Bosun. "There's nowhere else," he says. "No other cabin with a spare bunk." He sounds chastened by what he is having to say. Greg is right behind him, in his step, his look unchanged, still surly, bitter. They've issued him with a bunk roll and pillow. Towel. And that's it.

"That's it?" Greg shows mock indignation. "I may not be wanted here, mate, but I got my rights. I'm an Australian citizen. Not a criminal." His lip curls.

"You will take what you're given, and that's it," says Bosun. "And lucky to get that. And I'm not your mate. I'm the Bosun and you take orders from me."

Good old Bosun. This is the tough side not seen before. Yes, good old Bosun, I think to myself, good man. And it doesn't seem as though Greg's said anything. Anything about me coming across him at the point of a knife, weeks ago. "Shut ya mouth and you'll be right. Shut it…"

Yes, it looks like Greg's kept his word. But that's the only concession.

His lip curls again. That face. That look. Maybe he's going to throw a punch, then thinks better of it. Bosun is no pushover, Greg might be a bully but I'd back Bosun in this. Don't be fooled by the kindly nature, affable smile. I'd heard that he'd been known to clap drunken sailors in arms. Greg would be better off looking for a lesser man.

"And don't forget I'm putting you to work after," says Bosun.

If Greg doesn't like the lack of a soft sheet, bar of soap, fancy curtains at the porthole, he certainly doesn't like the idea of work. "Me?" He's stabbing his finger into his own chest to make the point. "Me? I don't 'ave to." It's said in a drawl, like I darn 'ave to. Australian speak. "Me…?" he says. "I darn 'ave to."

"You're on this ship illegally and you'll work when I say." Bosun spells it out. He turns in the cab doorway, "And you'll be charged when we get to Australia. Do you hear? It's an infringement of maritime law."

Now Greg's anger is directed at me. "Bastards, they can't treat me like this." He throws his roll at the bare bunk and follows it up with the towel. "All I'm doing is getting back home. Jumped ship in London a few months back. Then ran out of cash. Bastards, Pommie bastards."

I shrug. There's no point in getting involved. I could be the Lesser Man if he wants to take his anger out on anyone. I get ready to duck. And just because he's kept his side of the bargain – not splitting on me – it doesn't mean he's staying that way.

"I could tell 'em who helped me… I could tell 'em ya knew. Then you wouldn't be Bosun's blue eyed boy." His face is against mine, six inches away, feels closer. I can smell his breath. Christ, what has he been eating these last few weeks? Cook's leftovers? The food dumped overboard each morning?

"And if you're going to Oz, forget it mate. Poms aren't welcome in my country, skinny Poms like you." That lip curls again. "Skinny Pommie bastards…"

He's back to his corner. Fists put to good use. Spreading his bunk roll, tucking in. I'm spared.

Now it's a rant about England. And if I didn't know it already, the Old Country is a lousy country and Oz is great. How it's a man's country where I'll never survive. "No chance, Pom. Take a look at yourself. Your puny white face and your skinny white arms. You won't last a minute. I tell you it's a man's country."

Goodness, if they're all like this in Australia, I'm off back home. Book me the next berth, Captain.

Months later I'll know they're not all Gregs; I'll be one of them. Enjoying Aussie beer, parties on the beach and the great outdoor life, and great Aussie people. "Jeez mate, to think you nearly turned around and went back home."

There's just one relief. He eats with the deck hands and they'll give him stick, can't imagine King Neptune, Big Geordie from Newcastle, and the hardest of them all, Tam from Birkenhead, putting up with him. Not even Charlie, Jimmy and Fred, King Neptune's sacrificial lambs. With their hair shorn down to a stubble it makes them look tougher than they really are. Borstal Boys. They'll give him a hard time I bet.

And there's the relief when he's in the other bunk, gone to kip, as the deckhands call it. "'ope you get some peace and quiet when he puts his 'ead down," says Jimmy. "'e might be a stowaway and a miserable bastard, but 'e won't slit yer throat, 'e don't carry no knife."

Christ, that's a thought. Did Bosun take the knife from him? Did he?

I'm going to be the only man who sleeps his way to Australia with his eyes wide open.

Then there's the other spanner he's put in the works: lovely Mrs Wilberforce and the tête-à-tête when hubbie's not watching. If there was ever any chance of sprucing the place up and inviting Mrs Wilberforce in for the coffee and a mint or two, that's down the drain. It was never more than a fantasy anyway. With Greg around that's sunk without trace.

"Hey Greg, be a good chap and get on the end of the feather duster while I polish the Picasso. I have a guest popping in. And then make yourself scarce for an hour or so. I have mints to nibble."

Can you imagine it? Gorgeous Mrs Wilberforce perched on the spare bunk, long, graceful legs dangling over the edge, slim Mrs Wilberforce, manicured red nails, flowing hair, fresh red lipstick. Yes, that dream's out the window. Or is it the porthole?

Now Bosun's put Greg to work polishing the spare propeller. You can see Bosun's gentle smile as he tells him, "I want to see my face in it." But that's hardly improved Greg's disposition. And he's doing it by hand, spit and polish. "Four hours on, half hour break, then another four. Yes, I want to see my face in it – by Adelaide."

Everything seems to start with an "F" now. "F'kin Bosun, f'kin Captain. And f'kin me!"

The next couple of weeks are going to be f'kin fun!

"For our passengers, I am pleased to tell you we're now entering the Great Australian Bight."

The tannoy booms out. The First Officer is doing his Tour Operator bit. Last week we were shading our eyes against the glare and scanning the Starboard bow for a mother whale and her little one. And the week before we leant over the railing and marvelled as dolphins rode the waves right next to our bow.

Greg's excited about the Great Australian Bight. "You hear that, mate, the Great Australian Bight." He has the emphasis on great. And there's a lot more greats to come. "The Blue Mountains." They're great. "The Murray River." That's great too. Sydney harbour. Surprise, surprise, that's great. But he's reserved the best to last, and I prick up my ears when he comes to the Outback.

"Where a man can get lost and die of thirst in a matter of hours. It's vast, mate, you couldn't even reckon it. It's so great you'd never survive."

I tell him I studied Australia at school in geography under Mr Williams the village headmaster. Round and jolly Mr Williams who inspired me to be here today, telling us about the cities, Sydney, Melbourne, Adelaide, Brisbane, Perth. Darwin in the north and Hobart on the island of Tasmania. And the Outback. And I'd won a book on Australia. Mr Williams had helped me with that too.

"I'm looking forward to seeing it all," I say.

"Now you're talking, mate. But don't think the pavements are paved with gold. You Poms think you can just land in Oz and you're rich."

Just arriving safely in Australia after stumbling across Greg will do me. I'll happily forgo the rich bit.

# Chapter 4

# It's Australia, Mate

"I'm going to win the book, Mum."

"Which book is that, Son?"

"The book on Australia. Teacher told us about it to-day. I'm going to write the best essay and I'm going to do the best drawing and then I'm going to do the best colouring and win."

I was only a ten but remember it as though it was yesterday. The austerity of the post-war years was still upon us but Mr Williams, the village headmaster, somehow persuaded organisations to sponsor awards or secure us invitations to events and places of interest up and down the country. He did it from the heart, for the village children, he was of the "Old School" as Dad put it, and it cost the school nothing.

We spent a day at the Farnborough Air Show and another at Windsor Castle; we travelled to Broadcasting House to see a live BBC radio schools quiz – we even went to an opera, Hansel and Gretel, although I'm not sure we all stayed awake until the end. Canada House sent us prizes for the best story on the beauty of their country; so did the New Zealand Government and when Mr Williams opened a package from the Australian High Commissioner and out popped DISCOVERING AUSTRALIA, the most beautiful book I had ever seen, I said, "I'm going to win that book."

And I did.

\* \* \* \* \*

There's a smudge on the horizon, scarcely discernable at this distance. But a smudge, nonetheless. It is flat and brown. There are no trees, just a few shacks and a couple of poles sticking out of the water with navigation lights to guide the ship.

Have I come all the way for this? It wasn't in my book.

"God's Own Fair Chosen Country," says Greg. He puffs out his chest threatening the fate of the buttons on his shirt front. His face beams – he's a new man! "I've been waiting for this moment for yonks." He's standing at the rail, between Dougie and me. More great breaths fill his lungs like he's come up for air for the last time. "It's God's Own Fair Country," he says again.

"Och," says Dougie, "I find it a wee bit disappointing. The slimy mud flats either side of your river and the muddy brown waters do nae justice to such a fine city as Adelaide. And I've seen crocodiles take men in places more hospitable than this."

Greg's not having this. He knows a good thing when he sees one. "God's Own Fair Country. Every bit of it, Dougie. Crocs and all." But at least he smiles.

The MV Port Melbourne slows. We're turning in a wide loop and heading for the mouth of the river. It's the Torrens my book says.

"That's Adelaide out there, mate, the prettiest city you'll see on a long day's march. And the hills. Have you seen the Adelaide Hills yet, Dougie? On your wanderings, I mean." Greg points in the far distance where we can just make out an undulating range of hills slumbering beneath the heat haze.

"Aye, I've seen your hills, Greg. Very nice too but if you want to see real scenery you'll need to look at the Highlands. And scarcely a stone's throw from the Clyde. Now that's what you call a river. I can see it in ma mind's eye now."

"The Clyde, Dougie? I saw it once and that was enough. And you've got nothing to crow about when sailing up the mouth of the Thames either. It makes our slimy mud flats and muddy brown waters look like the Garden of Eden."

Dougie's still got an imaginary Bonny Scotland in his mind and imaginary bagpipes beneath his arm and gives them a squeeze... his eyes close and words come floating across his lips. It's Scotland the Brave we're getting.

"Land of the shining river, land of my heart for ever...

Hear, hear the pipes are calling... Loudly and proudly callin'...

There where the hills are a-sleeping...Now feel the blood's a-leaping".

Greg's not impressed. "Jeez mate, you'll give this bloke's cattle a nervous bloody breakdown if you go on like that."

Dougie's eyes are open now. "The mountains and the lochs, Greg, you should see the mountains and lochs and then there's the heather. You should see the heather on a good day." He sighs a long sigh and reckons a true Scotsman never travels far from the heather. "I myself have a sprig in ma cabin. I keep it to remind me of the place I love."

"You can stuff your bloody sprig," says Greg, leaning back on the ship's railings as if he owns them. "Now if you are talking about the Gum tree, that's a different matter." Greg's breathing in deep again and zing goes the first shirt button. "I swear I can smell the Gums from here." And he tells us it's a known fact that if Australians are deprived of the smell of the Gum it can be detrimental to their health. "The Eucalyptus Gums. Some scientist wallah did tests. Can't remember his name. But that guy knows a thing or two."

Dougie's not into scientist wallahs. "You can give me chapter and verse another time, Greg. We're about to arrive in that fine city of yours and I've got work to do."

"Don't trip over your sprig," Greg shouts after Dougie. "I'd hate ya to break ya bloody neck."

I stay. Here's a chance to learn a bit about Australia. I'd like to know why the Aussies feel good when they smell the Gum and bad when they don't. Crook is what Greg calls it.

And I stay to get my first glimpse of Adelaide… my first Australian city… I want to see what lies out there for me in the weeks, months, perhaps even years ahead. The deckhands are going about their duties preparing the ship for docking. "Wharfs," says Greg, "Not docks, ya understand. And before you make another blue, the guys are wharfies not dockers."

"What's a blue, Greg?"

"When a bloke calls a wharfie a docker."

"Ok, wharfies," I repeat. "And wharfs. I've got that too."

And he nods with satisfaction and turns and looks down into the dirty brown water as the Pilot's boat struggles against the tide and the Pilot grabs the ladder and hauls himself up on deck.

"You know your way, Mr Bastin." Bosun's words waft across on a hot breeze. "You've done it enough times before."

"It's always a pleasure to come aboard a Port Line ship. Not like some of the old rust buckets we get in here." He has a strong Australian accent, nearly as strong as Greg. Are they all going to talk like that? I wonder

I ask Greg but he just takes it for granted. "No plum in ya mouth here, mate. Best thing is I'll be tucked up in my own warm Aussie bed tonight." Then he seems to think better of it. "If I'm not in some bloody cold prison cell. Bastards."

Bosun says we'll be tying up at berth Number Nine on the South Quay. And tells me the things I've got to do to get the cattle ready for hand over. I'll be losing one of the bulls and two of the cows. Quarantine Island beckons.

I'd been told that by Dick Evans. You just can't dump a load of cattle on Australia and walk away, there's the potential to bring disease to the country, and not just Blue Tongue, there's Foot and Mouth and other diseases that Australia has kept out.

"We'll take them off tomorrow," Bosun's telling me. "There's a big Aussie bloke to handle it… you can't miss him, he stands out a mile. Six foot six and wears a cowboy hat. They call 'em stockman's hats but they still look like they've come out of a Wild West film."

"Blimey."

Bosun smiles. "And he has a lad to help. Batman and Robin, you might say."

"My first Australians. I can't wait."

"Well, you won't bump into these two in your average English high street, that's for sure."

And that doesn't worry me one bit. I haven't come all the way to Australia to see an average English high street.

"They're booked tomorrow, after lunch. Get your animals ready. They'll winch them off and transport them down to the Quarantine Island on a barge. They've done it a hundred times before."

That's a mercy. I've got the animals this far without mishap. That's how we did it in the Port of London and presuming the Australian bloke and his helper know what they are doing it shouldn't be a problem.

We're on the move again. The Pilot's reached the bridge and we are under way. Up river, between the mud flats, and even they're starting to look more hospitable; haven't seen a crocodile in ages. There are still no trees, just low scrub, Saltbush, Greg calls it, and there's a handful of concrete buildings and a small landing stage on the island just round the next bend.

"Quarantine Island," says Bosun. "Where your cattle will be spending the next few weeks, courtesy of Batman and Robin. And before you ask, I'd go down there with them if I were you."

Bosun doesn't have to ask twice.

We're slowing again, the engine room telegraph clangs, DEAD SLOW AHEAD.

There's another cargo ship coming out, heading for the ocean, heading for Greg's Great Australian Bight. It's the sister ship, the MV Port Brisbane, the ship that kept our berth warm in Cape Town. Horns are being sounded, our men rush to the side railing and wave. Their crew waves back. Someone yells, "Are there any white men on board that ship?" And they all laugh. From the Bridge, our Captain gives a sort of half salute, half wave, and the ship's horn's blasted again.

Looks like the Captain of the Port Brisbane gives his half salute too.

"That'll be Thompson," says Dougie. "The old so-and-so, I served under him for years. Enjoys his dram, he does."

"Silly bastards," says the Chippie. "We all know there are no white men on that ship."

Greg says. "I don't know why they're all laughing... they're probably on their way back to Pommieland. Christ I'd be bawling my eyes out."

We're moving slowly and carefully as we do when entering port; for Adelaide read Cape Town and for Cape Town read Las Palmas. It may be the Pilot who is in charge but it is still the Captain's responsibility if there's a mishap.

I watch how it's done; tugs guiding us into Greg's wharves. And the deckhands doing their trick with the rope, the weighted thin one, throwing it like a lasso for the men on shore to grab and pull until they've dragged in the heavy rope to secure the boat. And our deckhands looping our end around the derricks and winding it in, pulling us tight to the wharf. Ten thousand tons of cargo ship and it's manoeuvred as easily as a toy by men who have done it many times before.

And it's Cape Town and Las Palmas all over again once the gangway is down – the ship's a hive of activity. Men from the shipping line, customs officers, insurance agents; just about anyone who has anything to do with our docking is on board. The deckhands remove the covers to the cargo holds, readying the cargo to be winched ashore, and on the wharf the cranes whirr away, trucks and lorries queuing to take it into store and to their new owners. English goods for Aussie customers.

Now the Immigration Officer comes on board along with an Aussie copper. They're not wasting a minute. Greg's escorted away, a police van waiting, no argument, just a nod in my direction. And to the copper I hear him say, "Don't worry, mate. This is home. I won't be doing a bunk."

That's the end of Greg. Survive him and I think I can survive anyone.

* * * * *

This is what I've come for.

I walk down the gangway, past the Watchman on duty, and my feet touch Australian soil for the first time. Down Under. The ground is the same; the air the same (except it is hot and burning) and there's not the slightest hint of a cloud in the clear blue Aussie sky. This is definitely as I remember it in the book I won.

There is a lot of chatter among the dockers, Greg's wharfies. "She's right, mate. Yes, she's right." I catch the words. They're talking about Port Adelaide playing Norwood on Saturday, a needle match. The season has just started. Aussie Rules, the greatest game on earth is what Greg said. "A needle match, mate," the wharfies are saying. "Old rivals."

A mixture of rugby, soccer, hand-ball and all-in wrestling, if you listened to Dougie. "Whatever else you do in Australia laddie, don't get mixed up with that."

Then Bosun says I'm about to get a visitor. A cattleman to see the animals, my stud cattle, the bulls and cows. He runs a stud herd himself, a Shorthorn herd, a hundred miles north of Adelaide, the other side of a place called Angaston, wherever that is. Up country is what I'm told.

I go down to the cattle pens and wait for a big, tall Australian, with one of these stockman's hat. Off it comes and under his arm it goes as he strides towards me. "John Keynes... you must be Richard Holdsworth." This handshake is firm, very firm. While I re-arrange my fingers he wants to talk about my cattle, see how they have fared on the long voyage.

"It's a great opportunity to eye them up," he's saying. Another Aussie accent, not so strong. "And see what the other stud owners have bought." He says he gets on the phone to the local Dalgety's office and knows which ships are coming in and the animals they are bringing. "But there's nothing like seeing them for yourself."

That makes sense, I say. I know Ernie Ford did that. He knew as much about the other herds as they did. Always looking at the animals bought by their owners, assessing them. "Keep an eye open, young Richard. Know what you will be up against."

He's not old, this John Keynes, mid forties I'd say, maybe a bit younger, but seems to know what he is talking about. "I've got a herd of my own… we're building it up… a long way to go yet. Not won any trophies, but hope to one day." He has Shorthorns and Shorthorns that are bred without horns. Polled Shorthorns is what they are called. I heard about Polled Shorthorns back home although we don't have any from what I know and I have only seen them in pictures. They could be the future; the horns are dangerous, not just for us cattlemen but horns can rip another bull or cow in a tight pen.

This John Keynes has enthusiasm and I'm showing him my charges, the Shorthorns and he is casting his eye over them and it looks like he knows what he is talking about.

I tell him where they came from, which herds, which line of breeding. He knows some of if already. The Calrossies and Lord Lovat's Beauforts and he's up with the Glastullich herd of John McGillivray, everyone should be. "I have a Glastullich bull myself although he is old and lame, a bit dodgy in his hind quarters. I picked him up cheaply. He's sired a few calves for me but I'm not sure he will ever work again."

Work meaning breed calves. Dodgy hind legs aren't much use when mounting a cow. Bulls can weigh two tons and more.

I sympathise. A good Glastullich bull is worth having. Worth his weight in gold. But not if he is lame. "Maybe he could be brought back to full health," I ask.

"Maybe. He needs someone who knows how to care for animals."

He's admiring the condition of my bulls and cows. "You wouldn't believe they had been at sea. How long did you say?"

"Six weeks. We left on January 14."

"Six weeks." He's impressed and so he should be. The animals are better than the day they came on board. I have used all my skills, all the skills I learnt. They are in good nick, he's saying. It's nice that he knows and even nicer he acknowledges the fact.

And before I know it he's offering me work, a job, my role would be stud herdsman to look after the animals, to guide the stud forwards, to bring success to the Keyneton herd.

It's quite out of the blue. Just what I have always wanted from the moment I set out. But I didn't expect it would be this easy. He says

I would be paid well, accommodation next to his own house, a Homestead he calls it. "Nothing too luxurious," he's saying.

"I don't need luxury, just a roof over my head." I smile, he smiles, the hat goes back on. "And a bed would help."

This sounds good. A small herd, on the way up, I'm sure I can contribute.

I watch him leave. Giant strides along the deck. He touches his hat as he passes the Watchman and is gone, his feet clattering down the gangway. A Rover, a big old Rover, skirts the wharf, speeds past the cranes and back to Angaston. "Up country somewhere, did you say?" says Dougie. "If Greg were here he'd reckon it's God's Own Country. But I doot it..."

I'd said I'll give him a decision when I get to Sydney. It's the first offer and there might be more, even better. I have yet to see Melbourne and then Sydney, to hand over the cattle at these two ports. We'd shaken hands on it. My fingers crunched again. Perhaps if I'd said "yes" I might have got off more lightly.

I hunt out Bosun. "Guess what...?"

You can't miss the Australian cattleman come to get the cattle, just as Bosun said. Striding along the deck, he's head and shoulders above anyone else, all our heads and shoulders, the officers and deckhands, even Jimmy standing on a bucket polishing the ship's bell looks half his size.

And then there's the hat. Bosun calls it a cowboy hat, they call it a stockman's hat. The lad helping him is striding along, trying to keep up, he's wearing one too. "Batman and Robin. Here they come," Bosun smiles, "Hope you're all ready."

I'm as ready as I'll ever be. This is an important day.

And the barge is alongside too. The big Australian cattleman goes straight to the ship's railing and looks over, shouting instructions so everyone can hear. Everyone for a mile around.

"Did I tell you he's as deaf as a post?" says Bosun.

Now he's shaking me by the hand, and my hand gets another crushing. Twice in two days. What's up with these Aussies – don't they realise a 20 year old Pommie lad is not made of iron? "You the cattleman, Boy? All the way from the Old Country?"

His lad is standing by his side, slightly back, and is smiling. "Old Country," he repeats. "Big Alf's a bit deaf, ya know."

Robin turns out to be Billy and Billy talks with a drawl. From watching too many Hollywood movies, perhaps. He's modelling himself on Billy the Kid. A holster and six-shooter would complete the picture. "Come to take ya cows and bulls," he tells me with this drawl. "To Quarantine Island. Goin' down the river." He makes it sound like goin' deen the river...

And Big Alf says, "Fair dinkum," which must have something to do with getting the cattle down to the Quarantine Island. It wasn't in Whacker Worvill's English dictionary. "That's where we're taking 'em, Boy, the Quarantine Island." And he gives me another fair dinkum, and I get called "Boy" once again which I haven't been called since I was a kid.

They're striding over to the railing again and Big Alf is shouting to the men below and they are shouting back and the crate gets winched up so it's dangling above our heads, spinning round on the end of a steel hawser before being landed with skill in the space between my cattle pens. Big Alf's satisfied with the winchman. "Ya got the job, mate. Now all you gotta do is get 'em landed in the barge without dropping 'em."

The crew have stopped work and are watching and the passengers, those that haven't left, they're watching too. As a spectacle it's almost as good as Crossing the Line.

There's no Mrs Wilberforce and no Eustace; they left ages ago. I caught a glimpse of her on the gangway then tripping off down the wharf her blonde hair blowing in the hot breeze. At least I got a nod from Greg; not one from Mrs Wilberforce.

Big Alf and Billy have top-side all under control; the crane, the winchman, the barge. I have halters on the Shorthorn bull and on the two Hereford cows. "Come on," I say to them quietly, "We're going for a walk. Then you're going to stay in a nice hotel."

\* \* \* \* \*

Big Alf's voice rings out. "Don't bugger about, Billy. Follow me. Get ya head down, Boy. Don't bugger about."

But it isn't Billy that's buggering about. He's leading a Hereford cow and she's not behaving herself, not used to all these antics after six weeks at sea, and solid land beneath her hooves, so she's giving him trouble, tossing her head, yanking at the halter, not wanting to go where Billy wants her to go.

And that's to follow Big Alf. "Come on Billy, ya bugger. Don't hang back."

We're on Quarantine Island; a tug has towed the barge. All of us on board, lock, stock and barrel; two cows, a bull, Big Alf, me and Billy the Kid. Sailing serenely down a muddy river.

A floating menagerie. Fishermen at the side of the river rub their eyes. One drops his catch. "Strewth, what the hell's that? Am I seeing things?"

It's been touch and go. Winching the animals from the deck of the ship, treating them to a boat ride then leading them up a wobbly plank onto the landing stage and solid land. Now Billy is having trouble with the cow and getting a shout from Big Alf for his trouble.

"Come on, Billy. Don't bugger about. We 'aven't got all day. Follow me."

Big Alf has the other Hereford cow and she is doing the same. Tugging on her halter.

"What did I tell ya," says Billy, but Alf doesn't hear or doesn't want to. I have the Shorthorn bull and he is well behaved. He had good sea legs, now I reckon he's got good land legs.

The island is bare except for bushes. I got a glimpse from the ship yesterday and from what I could see it looked barren – and now I know it is. Just these sparse bushes; no more than a foot or so high. Saltbush is what Greg called them. No trees, no grass, nothing green. There is a narrow track and buildings in the distance. Concrete buildings. So much for a nice hotel, I say to Highland Monarch. He'll be roughing it for a while. He and the two cows. No five stars here.

"This way, Billy," the voice booms out again. His skin is parched like leather, his hands and arms, and a voice to match. Billy says deaf people shout because they don't know if they are being heard or not, and Alf doesn't want anyone to miss out.

We've stopped while Billie gets the Hereford cow under control, she has a mind of her own, is tugging at him, but Billy is a strong lad and not likely to let go. The bull I am holding, Monty, is stamping his feet. I soothe him with quiet words. Bulls are not normally upset in my company, Shorthorns anyway. I look down to the parched ground, and see why he is stamping. The ground is moving... or so it seems... thousands of ants, thousands and thousands of them. Huge ants, half inch long, and more, much bigger than ours. Nobody said anything about this. Bloody great ants weren't in the book.

"Only ants," says Billy. "Ain't you never seen a few ants before?"

Not these. Years to come and David Attenborough will give them centre stage on the telly and say what nice little chaps they are... but I'll cringe.

"Wait till you see Bull ants. That's what you call proper ants, Bull ants."

Billy's on the move again.

"Thanks Billy. I can't wait."

"Bull ants bite," says Billy. "And won't let go. Only way to get 'em off is by lighting a match under their backsides. Fair dinkum. I'm not joking."

There's that fair dinkum again. What funny language the Aussies talk. Strewth for strewth, bluey when you call a wharfie a docker and fair dinkum for a whole load of things.

We're coming up to the concrete buildings, the Quarantine Station. There are men in white coats coming out to greet us, nothing more sinister than vets I hope. "In good nick, aren't they?" one says. They are looking them over. Checking them. A clipboard and notes. I'll be surprised if they find anything wrong with my animals.

Big Alf agrees, booming out in his loudest voice, "In top nick." The first man flinches. But Alf's still going. "The boy's done well. Never seen better and I've been doing this since Ned Kelly was a nipper."

"I know," the man says. "I remember you from before. My eardrums haven't recovered." They all laugh. I'm not sure they are joking.

54

The men in white take the animals away. I give a last pat to each in turn. If I wasn't a brave young man half way round the world on my great adventure, I'd say good-bye, talk to them, shed a tear, perhaps. But the men in white are watching, so I won't.

And it's all over. Three of my friends, my companions of the last six weeks have gone. I just wish it was those bloody horses.

"Come on Billy," Big Alf's at it again. "We've got work to do." And to me, "Come on Boy, let's get you back to your boat so you can get moved on."

And on the way back on the barge Big Alf wants to know what I'm doing after Melbourne and then Sydney, dropping off the rest of the cattle and the two horses. "You goin' back to the Old Country? Goin' back home?" I think half the population of Adelaide must know the decision I'm confronted with.

I tell him about the offer I have had from the stud owner up in the country, past Angaston. "I might accept that. I'd like the challenge. It's what I think I can do."

"Well if ya come back through Adelaide we'll pick ya up, won't we Billy? Give ya a home while ya wait. If you don't mind the back porch and a camp bed. The misses cooks a great breakfast. A steak that'll put muscles on ya muscles."

Billy agrees. "Mum's breakfast will set ya up for the day." He seems to know although I don't think he is Big Alf's son and he calls it Mum's tucker. Another new word to learn. For breakfast read tucker.

"If I go," I say. "I haven't made up my mind yet. I've only been in Australia a couple of days and already I have one offer." Dad always said not to take the first that comes along. Hedge your bets. And that's what I'm going to do.

The job is done for Big Alf and Billy, they're going off, they've got a load of sheep to move. "You did a good job, Boy."

"Thanks to your help."

"No sweat," says Big Alf.

"You can't beat Mum's tucker. Fair dinkum," is what Billy says. And I reckon I might take up Big Alf's offer. I'd like a bit of this tucker.

Back on the Port Melbourne the deck hands gather round. "Lost some of yer moo-cows then?" It's the lad who wondered why the cantankerous horse wasn't called Dobbin. "And yer bulls."

"Yes, the Quarantine Station. They have to be there for three months."

"Funny looking blokes who took 'em." This is the tall one who was King Neptune. He has an anchor tattooed on one arm and the word MUM on his knuckles.

I'm agreeing there too. "But they knew what they were doing, Big Alfie and Billy. They looked after them okay."

He's saying I must be sorry to lose them. His mum was gutted when her budgie died, the mum who's on his knuckles, I suppose. "We'd buy her another, I told her. Couldn't get over it, she couldn't. Kept talking to 'im even though we said 'e'd gone to a better place."

They are all concerned about me losing two of my cows and the Shorthorn bull, all gathered round. And King Neptune's mum's budgie… they are sorry about that too. And they all seem to have tales to tell about someone who lost something, even a tortoise that slept night and day. "Never said boo to a goose," says Charlie, "Dad couldn't get over it. Fred, the tortoise. Then one day 'e realised 'e wasn't sleeping, just dead."

Then they have a bright idea. "We're going ashore, all of us. Into Port Adelaide. You wanna come?"

"Yeah," says another, getting excited. "We're going to look round, up the 'igh Street, 'ave a milk shake, then back 'ere, get spruced up and go off to the dance, Port Adelaide Town 'all.

They're all chattering about that. "Saturday night dance."

One called Terry sings, "It's Saturday night and I've just got paid…" and hops about as if he's jiving. They are the words from a rock and roll song. And Charlie says, "No you 'aven't, Terry. You was paid last week like the rest of us."

"Well," he says. "I'm gonna spend it, ain't I. Them Aussie birds are terrific. You comin'? 'elp you forget yer moo-cows?"

And I think I will go to the dance with them. I want to see some terrific Aussie birds, and I've never had a milk shake in my life. Only seen girls drink them through a straw in films. Pretty girls.

And here we are, in a milk parlour, on stools that swivel round, Elvis doing Jailhouse Rock on the juke box, and us having our milk shakes and we are sticking out like sore thumbs. Deck hands with tattoos, some tough-looking with scars, and me in the middle drinking a milk shake, and three of the lads with cropped hair, they make Elvis look like he's just popped out of Sunday School.

I have been to the ANZ bank and got my money – my first Australian money – and the girl just passed it over the counter and smiled and I said "Thanks" and although they have pounds, shillings and pence it looks different from ours, their notes and coins. But everything else is the same as back home in Dad's bank. Except Dad didn't say 'Have a good day.'

Then we've finished our milk shakes and Elvis finished so the lads swagger out and down the High Street looking into the shops and the shops have verandas and corrugated tin roofs and it's a bit like the Wild West but exciting and what with my new money, I think it's great.

And the Saturday dance is great with a five piece band playing the same songs as ours, from our Hit Parade, and the Town Hall is packed to the rafters and we're at the back pushing forwards to see if Terry is right and the girls are as pretty as he says. And they are, the Aussie girls, sitting around the dance floor just like back home, picking and choosing who to dance with and who not and when it's not, the lads having to walk back, red-faced, embarrassed. "Pissin' bloody bird. Didn't want to dance with 'er anyway."

Only here it's a Sheila. "Pissing bloody Sheila."

Another new word to learn.

"I couldn't care a toss," says Jimmy. "Bird, crumpet, tart, Sheila. They all got what it takes, 'ain't they?

"Cor," says Charlie in his London accent and cropped hair. "That one 'ave. Just cop a look at 'er, will yer."

And another says, "I wouldn't climb over 'er to get to you Charlie that's a cert." We're all laughing and the band's into Sweet Little Sixteen and it all makes the village dance back home look a bit tame.

A girl doing a jive twirls round, her skirt swirls up and we see the tops of her stockings and King Neptune says, "I wouldn't mind a twirl with 'er," and the others dare him and he does, and its in the song, Blueberry Hill, and he gets her phone number and might see her next time the ship comes in. "She promised," he says.

And I think I might have a dance too, with the lads egging me on. "Go on, moo cow man. 'ave a dance wiv 'em."

Why not, must start somewhere with these Aussie girls, these Sheilas, and I walk across the dance floor to a girl with dark hair and a polka-dot dress and just catch her saying "yes" and how I must be from England. And in between twirls and the noise of the band we smile and she tells me how she hopes to go there one day, to London. "My Dad came from the Old Country years ago. I'd love to see London."

Then, Elvis and Don't be Cruel comes to an end. It always was too short.

"No phone number, moo-cow, man?"

"No." But it's a start.

Now we're back to the ship, as the lads don't fancy the smoochy number, the last dance; Rock and Roll is what they like. They've been brought up on Rock and Roll.

"Had a good time, lads? says the Watchman back on the ship. And we have.

"Bloody good," says King Neptune who's got the girl's number to prove it. "But I aint lettin' you lot 'ave it. Get yer own numbers."

"Goodnight then."

"Goodnight Watchman."

"Goodnight lads. Sleep tight."

I know I will. There's Australian money in my pocket and no Greg in my cabin.

# Chapter 5

# The Bushman

"What you gonna wear, Boy? What you gonna wear when you get up the Bush?" Big Alf's voice booms out across the store and out onto the busy street.

I hesitate. It hadn't dawned on me I would wear anything other than the clothes I stood up in. My working clothes for an English farm. Casual shirt and trousers and comfy lace-up shoes. Wellington boots, of course, when it got muddy.

Big Alf and Billy are engulfed in laughter at the thought. They fall about and have to steady themselves by holding onto racks of what look like cowboy hats, shirts and trousers.

"Strewth, you gonna wear them?" Billy's pointing at my shoes, my nice lace-ups. "Not them up the Bush surely, mate?"

Big Alfie goes for a couple of strewths too. "What happens when a Goanna lizard pecks your ankles, Boy?" His voice is so loud that people in the street stop and peer in; they too want to know what happens when a Goanna lizard pecks my ankles.

And Billy says, "What about a Black Headed python entwining its way up your trouser leg – what then?"

Big Alf directs my attention to Billy's feet. "Look down there, Boy. That's the kit ya need." I look down and see Billy is wearing sort of semi-high heeled leather boots, elastic sided and they don't stop at his ankles but vanish up his tightly sewn brown trousers. These are cattlemen's Cuban heeled boots that are essential for the Bush – any bit of Bush you care to name.

"Which part you goin' to?" asks Billy, although I had told him 15 minutes ago, when he and Big Alf picked me up at Adelaide Railway Station, in Big Alf's truck with saddles and halters and bits of rope all fighting for space in a cab looking like a rag and bone man's back yard.

"Put ya bags on the flat-bed," Big Alf had said. "Back there. Let the dogs take care of 'em for you."

"Where's that again?" Billy asked as Alf weaved the flat-bed through the early morning traffic on our way out of town.

"The other side of Angaston," I said. "Up country, that's where I'm off to. When Mr Keynes calls for me."

"It's not what you'd call the real Bush," said Billy. "That's a thousand miles on. But it's still good enough for a few nasties to keep you awake at night wondering what'll get ya next."

I hadn't thought of that. Just a few minutes ago I was relaxing in the comfort of the Overlander Express from Melbourne and nasties weren't on the menu.

"Well," said Big Alf," you're in luck, Boy. We're off to Woodville to the best outfitters this side of the Black Stump and we'll get ya kitted out for the Bush before ya can say Ned Kelly's a Sunday School teacher. What would ya say to that?"

I'm very grateful, I had said, as Big Alf parked the truck alongside a store with tin roof, hitching rail and giant cut-out of a man in cowboy clothes and lasso and the words OUTFITTERS TO THE OUTBACK in large letters. The dogs kindly stayed on the flat-bed taking care of my bags while we'd pushed through swing doors like we were entering a Wild West saloon. A vast emporium of all that's great and good for a Hollywood blockbuster. Surely no son of a gun would venture into Dodge City without a visit here first.

"Just take a look round, Boy. This is the kit for you. They got everything a decent Bushman needs." And I'd looked round and I'd seen Billy's Cuban heeled boots and how a Goanna couldn't peck his ankles – and now I'm getting my own pair.

A bloke dressed for the part ambles up. "You blokes right then?" He's the salesman and he's not very impressed with what I'm wearing. "You a tourist or somethin'?"

And the next good laugh is when I mention my Wellington boots. "Mud, Boy. There's no mud in the Bush. It's as dry as an Abo's rucksack."

But there is sun... lots of blazing sun. "Where's ya broad-brimmed stockman's hat to shade that sensitive Pommie skin of yours?

The salesman has the answer. Off the top shelf. It's black and the brim turned up and makes me look like an extra from a John Wayne film and I don't mind one bit.

"Boots next. Get him his boots off the rack Billy."

I slip the Cuban heels on and grow an inch, if not more.

"Strewth," says Billy. "He's half-way there."

"Goannas won't get ya ankles now, Boy."

Next and the salesman is fetching trousers. He calls them strides. Big Alf calls them strides and so does Billy. I put on my new strides.

"Perfect," says Billy. "Just perfect."

I have been to Melbourne on the boat then up to Sydney. I have dropped the rest of the cattle off as my contract said, talked to more stud cattlemen and been offered jobs in the states of Victoria and New South Wales.

I have chewed them over, in the quietness of my cabin, what they would entail, the prospects they would bring, the pay – but none seemed as good as the first, John Keynes and his up-and-coming herd. Up country, South Australia. I've decided. That's my future.

But the best news – I've got rid of those bloody horses. Despite what had gone before – bruised and battered shins, bite marks to my arms and shoulders – and the fact that I had only got close enough to put a brush on them a couple of times, they came up looking ok. I had fed and watered them well and they were in good condition. A life at sea seems to have been a tonic and when the owners had come on board they were impressed enough to give me a tip. A fifty quid tip. Not to be sneezed at – fifty bloody quid!

Best part of ten weeks' wages in one day. They may have been the owners of two of the most vicious horses on Planet Earth but they were generous to a tee, these Aussie horse owners. Or maybe racehorse owners are all rolling in cash.

I have said my sad goodbyes to the Bosun and to Dougie the electrician; Mr Mason the chippie and the others who shared meals with me three times a day, every day for the past six weeks, and the deck hands who at first thought there was something fishy about me having a relationship with woolly beings on four legs.

I have been in jail or, more correctly, a police cell, questioned by two burly plain-clothes detectives, read the riot act and sent packing. "What's a Pommie, wet behind the ears and fresh out of his cot doing down the Red Lights?"

It happened like this. We were in Sydney harbour and the deckhands were laying plans for the Saturday night out as they always did. And the plans included me. "You comin', Rich."

In Adelaide, we did the Saturday night dance; in Melbourne it was St Kilda Junction with its nightlife and in Sydney it had to be Kings Cross and the Red Light district. "See the other side of life," says Jimmy spruced up, excited as a dog with two tails, and egging me on. "Great night out, Rich, Tam from Newcastle says you ain't lived till you've been down The Cross."

"Is this it then, Jimmy? Living it up? The Cross?"

We're sitting on the pavement in a back street, watching the comings and goings, loads of blokes, hands on wallets, fags in mouths; and cars slowly drifting past, sometimes stopping, then moving on, stopping again, and the pavement is the place to be, front row as Jimmy calls it. "To see life as it really is, Rich."

And the girls, sitting in windows, showing what my mum said a nice girl shouldn't show and tarted up like Christmas trees.

Cripes! I've never seen anything this before. Not at the village dance!

"Bloody pros, that's all," says Charlie. "They're all whore-houses. And them's is prostitutes. Ain't yer never seen one before?"

I don't really want to admit I never have. I've stayed in my little Berkshire village all my life. A village hall, a village stores, Mr Right-T-Ho behind the counter, our bus stop and bench seat outside. The closest we got to anything red is the telephone box on the village green. They painted that bright red once.

"Of course," I say, trying to sound slightly irritated that Charlie should even ask. "Lots of them. I've seen lots of them, Charlie."

"I knew you was ok. I knew you was not wet behind the ears like some said you was. Just cus you talk to your moo-cows."

"Not a bit of it, Charlie. Not wet behind the ears. I can't wait to get started."

"Well, 'ang about. We're gonna do some negotiating first. Tossing up which one's best. Don't want to spend our hard earned on the first tart we claps eyes on."

I agree. "That would be daft. Got to negotiate." I was thinking about Dougie's tactics. "Offer half, laddie. If that doesna work, walk away."

"You done that negotiating stuff before, Rich?"

"Well, it got Mum a nice carpet in Las Palmas, Charlie. That was tricky. And the scarf for the girlfriend. Negotiating is my second nature."

Charlie looks at me a bit funny. "What's a bleedin' carpet got to do wiv anythin'?"

But it's too late. No chance to apply my carpet buying skills here in Kings Cross. King Neptune is already in negotiation with a lady who looks as though she might be old enough to be his mum. Her cigarette is making a smoke screen and her exact age is hard to determine. But as Charlie says, "She's big in the melon department."

Whatever King Neptune has said seems to be working.

"The man says yes," the lady from behind the smoke screen is saying. "But one at a time, duckie, I don't want a wrestling match."

"Isn't it past your bedtime, lads?"

A car has pulled up next to King Neptune. The driver is addressing him and King Neptune is telling him we're minding our own business and it's best if he does the same or he might plonk one on him. And before we know it, we're in the back of the car and rushed down to the police station.

Then we are in the cells and as I have never been in police cells before I find they aren't very nice. I'm not sure if you have to spend the rest of your life here just because King Neptune has threatened a policeman. Dad never said what happened when you plonk a policeman in his pep talk before I set out.

Funny beetles crawl about the floor, a dirty looking blanket rests on a concrete slab and this doubles as my bed for the night while naughty words adorn the walls. Goodness is that how you spell it? I could be in here long enough to learn a whole new vocabulary.

There's drunks coming in and swearing. "I'll 'ave you copper. Bugger you... I wanna see my brief."

And coppers aren't much impressed. "Give it a rest, Tommy. We all know ya want a night in the nick and breakfast next morning."

Breakfast? I'm just thinking at least I won't starve in here when the door swings open and we're out and sitting in front of the Sergeant and he's reading this riot act which says we're not to be silly boys, wet behind the collective ears, it's well past our bed-times and we're to get back to our ship and our cosy bunks this very minute.

"If any of my men catch you down the Red Light... it'll be more than the book we throw at ya. Now get out."

And we're shown the door. Out into the warm air and the lights and the night-time activity and the city buzzing.

"Come on," says King Neptune. "What you lot waitin' for? I fancied the old tart with the big tits."

\*   \*   \*   \*   \*

I've accepted John Keynes' offer and I'm going to be a stud cattleman in the footsteps of Ernie Ford. I have travelled back to Adelaide by train, racing through the hot Australian evening and warm Australian night, and because the railway gauge changes at the State border, sprinting down the platform to climb aboard the Melbourne leg.

In years to come, standard gauge track will run right through but tonight it's fun watching the first class passengers in night-gowns and pyjamas dash down the platform; it's all part of life in Australia.

The wharfies on Adelaide Docks had said it, "She's right, mate. She's right." And people are saying it here even when they've been turned out of their comfy beds in the middle of the night.

"She's right, mate." Yes, "She's right."

And it is. I haven't come across a single Aussie with the attitude of Greg the stowaway, nor have I found any of his dire predictions come true, not remotely true. "You over here from the Old Country?" And when I nod and say I am and answer their questions and tell them Berkshire, from a little village 35 miles from London, and they say they have always wanted to go, or have been, it's the Mother Country, the Old Country, dear to their hearts.

And it's the same now that I'm in Adelaide, in the Bushman's outfitters with Big Alf and Billy, and am being fitted up for the job ahead, up country, north of Angaston. Cuban heeled boots to keep out a Goanna, strides tight enough to stop a Black Headed python from entwining its way up my legs and a John Wayne hat that makes me look like I've just ridden in from the Ponderosa.

"He's pretty smart now Billy," Big Alf booms out and Billy nods.

I'm Fair Dinkum and ready for anything the Bush can throw at me.

Or am I?

"Where's your horse, Boy?"

Big Alf runs a business that is legend around South Australia and Adelaide especially. He doesn't have to be in the Yellow Pages – everyone knows Big Alf is the man to turn to if you've got a few livestock to move – even a few thousand. It's all the same to Big

Alf and his helper, Billy, and they've both got horses. Without them they'd be stuffed.

"Yep, stuffed," says Billy with an air of one who knows. "And that's what you'll be up there in the Bush if you haven't got a horse."

"Time to change all that for the Boy," says Big Alf.

And we go out in Big Alf's flatbed truck along a dusty track at the back of Adelaide and find a few paddocks – like our fields but without grass – and there's a couple of dozen horses; big ones and not so big ones, black ones and white ones and black and white ones. "Waiting for the knackers," Billy says. "They'll be dog meat before the day's out."

The truck's bouncing along the dusty track with me and Billy holding on and Big Alf sawing at the wheel doing his best to miss the pot holes and the occasional boulder.

They are scanning the flat, dry, barren land that is these paddocks. Eyes squinting like tiny slits against the glare of the sun and brims of hats pulled down. I'm glad I've got my new John Wayne hat. I pull mine down too. I want to be part of this.

"That's the one, Billy." Big Alf is pointing. "The black one. That's our horse."

"What the hell's he doing in the knackers' yard?"

Big Alf is equally mystified. It seems he owns quite a few horses and they roam about the place, are lent out to people here and there, or put in a paddock where there's a bit more grass. And they also break out and get rounded up for the knackers.

It's my turn to say, "Strewth."

"That's the way of things, Rich," Billy assures me. He seems resigned to it. "Rounded up by some bloke for the knackers. A couple of quid a head he gets."

The truck bounces over a boulder or two and we are airborne for a moment. When we come back down to earth, Big Alf gives the track a few buggers. "Bugger this track Billy, why the hell don't they put the grader in?"

Billy agrees. "The grader will sort it."

When I ask I'm told the grader skins the dusty road surface, fills in the holes and shunts the boulders out of the way.

Billy can't believe we don't have graders in the Old Country. Like horses, you're stuffed without a grader, he says.

We've stopped on the dusty track and Billy has vaulted the fence and talks kindly to Big Alf's horse. He offers him the choice of a sugar lump or the knackers' yard. It's no contest. The bridle goes on.

"I've got ya horse, Alf."

Except it's now my horse. "I'll want him back when you've finished with it, Boy. In the meantime, you'll be stuffed without a horse as Billy says and you can have this one, the Black Horse."

I hadn't thought about having a horse when I set out from the Port of London that freezing night in January with the snow pelting my face and the woolly thermals Mum had packed.

"Strewth," says Billy. "How else did ya think you are going to find ya cattle up there in the Bush?"

I have to admit I have no idea. But I'm very grateful and thank Big Alf and Billy.

Keynes had said that the property was huge – about the size of Berkshire and Wiltshire put together with a bit of Dorset thrown in – and the stud herd would be scattered all round the place. I'd have to go out and find it every now and again. It's obvious – you can't be a stud herdsman without a herd.

"Blokes have died out there in places like that," Billy reassures me. "On walkabout you'd have no chance. Get lost, run out of water. Then that's it." Billy makes as if to slit his throat.

Black Horse eyes me with suspicion. But he seems an altogether nicer horse than the ones on the ship although I've scarcely known him more than a couple of minutes and I'm not a Black Horse expert. I pat him – and he lets me. And I practise some soothing noises. "Good boy, nice horse. How are you today?"

Which is a silly thing to ask, really. He's clearly having a rotten day – a couple of more hours and he'd be in a tin of Doggo Meat.

But we seem to be getting on ok and I'm going to take a leaf out of Billy's book and have a few sugar lumps in my pocket at all times. That seems to be the way to Black Horse's heart. He smiles and I smile; this could be the start of a good relationship.

*   *   *   *   *

Morning. Billy and me are picking up a thousand woolly Merinos from the docks and then dropping them off at Gypps Cross Abattoirs. "No sweat," says Billy. "You've got the Black Horse. Might as well give him a run out."

When I ask what it means by "picking up" I am told they will be on the hoof, all one thousand and it'll be through the town, Port Adelaide, past the Town Hall then police station, dodging the traffic, people, cats and dogs, anything else that comes along or gets in our way. "Droving," says Billy. "Ain't you never done droving before?"

I tell him it's like graders – droving on this scale hasn't got to England yet. Not through the middle of town, anyway.

I've seen pictures, I say. And then there's cowboy films. I've watched Roy Rogers and Trigger in the vast, open spaces of Texas. And the book I won on Australia had pictures of huge flocks of sheep, from horizon to horizon, raising the dust as they swept down hillsides or along dry river beds. But never past the Town Hall in rush hour.

"Nah," says Billy. "Not rush hour. We get it done before the streets get jammed. Anyway we'll have Alf's dogs with us. As long as you're in the saddle by seven you'll be right."

Next I try to explain I have never been on a horse in my life. I have never put a saddle on one, coupled it up to the reins. In fact, I scarcely know which end you couple the reigns to.

"Can't tell a horse's head from his arse?" Billy finds that incredible, and says "Jeez" as though it's the best joke he's cracked in ages.

We're in Big Alf's yard and Big Alf's voice is booming out. "Don't trust the Boy with the bloody nose bag then, Billy. It'll end up on the wrong end."

That's the next funniest thing they have ever heard and Billy still can't believe it. "Never ridden a horse? What the hell do you lot do over there in the Old Country? No droving, no graders and don't ride horses. Funny bloody place."

I'm still explaining some people ride horses, the upper crust and jockeys, but not ordinary people like me. Then it's time to go indoors for breakfast. One of Mum's breakfasts that sets you up for a day's droving and Mum is a little lady with an apron and weary face who looks after Big Alf and Billy and anyone else who pops in, even a Pom who doesn't know a horse's arse from its nose. Mum's sympathetic. "Just because the Queen rides one, doesn't mean to say he's got to."

An enormous plate-full of food lands in front of Big Alf and Big Alf tells me, "You'll soon get the hang of it, Boy."

Bed at Big Alf's is a put-me-up, seen better days, a six legged camp bed with one leg gone lame, on an open veranda with mosquitoes for company, but breakfast soon changes your mind about Australian hospitality. "Get stuck in," says Mum handing me a meal big enough for a bus-full of football supporters. "You poor souls need building up after what you've been through." Rationing hasn't ended all that long ago so I suppose she's right.

There's a steak that overhangs the plate, a couple of rashers of bacon, baked beans, a sausage or two, and tomatoes, all piled high, and after that we're back out in the yard with Big Alf throwing a saddle over the Black Horse, buckling it up, reins next, and then it's me. "Foot in cupped hand, Boy," and Big Alf shoots me up and onto the Black Horse like a jack in the box. "You'll be there all day unless you fall off, so best to stay on."

Black Horse turns and looks at me in the saddle and sets off at a canter even though I haven't asked. What's more important, I don't know how to ask it not to. And to top it all, I've gone and forgotten the sugar lumps.

"Follow me." Billy's on Duke with Big Alf's dogs at his heels and Alf in the truck bringing up the rear with Mum's steak sandwiches to see Billy and me through the day.

Through the day? After Mum's breakfast I wasn't thinking of eating for a month.

There's Big Alf's two pet sheep bouncing about in the back of the truck and we're off to see the boat that serves Kangaroo Island on Mondays, Wednesdays and Fridays and then sails back with the provisions. "Monday," Billy said over breakfast, "that means the sheep. All thousand of 'em. We're picking 'em up then droving them to Gypps Cross."

We're there on the wharf, looking down, and the sheep in the bottom of the boat looking up, but getting them out is no problem because that's what Big Alf's pet sheep have come along for and they're trotting off down the ramp into the boat, mingling with their brethren, turning around then coming up again with their woolly friends following.

Job done. Now it's time for their reward. Billy fetches out a couple of packets of cigarettes and feeds them to the pet sheep and they munch away like there's no tomorrow. "Not filters," Billy tells me. "They stick in their throats."

Me and the Black Horse watch as they gobble them up, a dozen or so each. "Posh Pall Mall or Camel," Big Alf says. "They like them best. But they're not fussy like some smokers."

"Any questions?" Big Alf's voice booms out across the wharf and people stop and look.

There're too many to ask so I don't. I'm on the Black Horse and Billy on Duke and a thousand sheep kicking up the dust at our feet and we're setting out for Gypps Cross which is left out of the dock gates, past the post office and police station, then the cinema where Elvis is on and out onto the back road where we found the Black Horse yesterday. The one for the abattoirs. We're losing a few sheep here and there and stopping the traffic as we go. But Alf's sheepdogs do what sheepdogs do best and that's hustle the stragglers and cut out those who want to dart off into an open shop doorway or even go in to see Elvis.

And everywhere we go, Billy seems to know everyone and everyone knows Billy.

"G'day, Billy. How ya doin'?"

And Billy is doin' fine.

"Give my regards to Big Alf."

Billy will.

"And Mum and her breakfasts."

Billy will do that too.

"I see ya got a new recruit."

"Yep. Fresh off the boat from Pommieland."

"Good luck to ya then."

I'm still on the Black Horse although it gets more uncomfortable by the minute. "Your bum a bit sore?" Billy enquires. "Mine was blue murder for the first few days on a horse."

It is more than sore three hours later when we hand our sheep over to the abattoirs' men in sweat-stained shirts, ten gallon stockman's hats and Cuban heeled boots like mine only theirs are old and weary and mine brand, spanking new. "See you've got a new apprentice then, Billy." Then they are all laughing about the Pom on a horse for the first time in fresh new shirt and strides and shiny new cowboy boots. But I smile and say I'm learning all the time and they say, "Good on ya, mate." And we all seem very happy except my bum isn't.

There are huge holding pens full of sheep at Gypps Cross, a haze of dust, dogs, men, horses, but they all seem to know what they are doing and Billy does too. "I've always wanted to do this," he tells me. But he also likes Elvis Presley and would have bought a guitar, grown his side-burns and sung Hound Dog if Big Alf hadn't come along one day when he skipped school. "Big Alf made me go back to learn what Big Alf never learnt. A real bugger. But Big Alf said it was for the best…learning what he never learnt. Now I can read and write and get the abattoirs' men to sign for the sheep so he doesn't get short changed."

Back home in Big Alf's yard I can scarcely fall off Black Horse and my pants are red with blood.

"I told you," says Billy. "I thought my backside was on fire."

Big Alf tells me the best medicine is to get back on the horse and ride some more.

But Mum takes sympathy. "Poor lad, they don't have horses over there." And gives me a swab soaked in carbolic to kill the infection.

"On fire?" asks Billy.

"And the rest," I say.

I start my new life today. The new challenge. Let's see if I can put into practice all that Ernie Ford taught me. John Keynes is coming down to Port Adelaide to pick me and my bags up and take us to his stud farm, the property, north of Angaston.

"Keep in touch," Big Alf's voice booms out so they can hear ten miles away in Adelaide city.

Mum waves, "He's a nice boy."

Billy says, "I don't know where Mum got that from," and laughs and jumps down from Duke and I think he's going to shake me by the hand or perhaps kiss me but Aussie lads that would be Elvis don't kiss.

Big Alf says he'll send the Black Horse up next week. And the saddle and the bridle and reins. "Seeing as you know which end is which you'll be lost without them." His eyes are moist, mine too. What the hell's going on here? I've only known these people a few weeks and never heard of them before I left England. But now we're one step away from needing our hankies. "The Black Horse, I'll send it up," Big Alf says again. "And the nose bag now ya know the difference between his head and his arse, eh Boy?"

The last thing I hear is their laughter and Big Alf saying, "Saddle up, Billy. We've got work to do."

It's a long drive. Up the North Road, out through Adelaide suburbs, skirting Elizabeth, the satellite town built for Pommie migrants and named after our Queen, through Gawler, Barossa Valley and then into unknown territory. It's dark by now but I am aware the tarmac has petered out; dirt roads have taken over, the sound of stones, gravel, sand thrown up under wheel arches gives that away. Rabbits appear in headlights and dart into the sparse bushes at the side of the track; trees that are called Ghost Gums loom up out of nowhere and piercing eyes peer out as we pass.

"Roos," says John Keynes. "We get a lot round here." And tells me they can inflict a great deal of damage on a car, even kill the driver. "The fully grown roo weighs near half a ton... you know when you've hit one."

Other strange beasts scurry across the track in front of us, or zig-zag, or bound, one, two, three leaps. "Goodness, what the hell's that...?"

The Rover slows, then turns right, the headlights pick out wire fencing and then a wide open gateway, down a bit then up a slight rise and there, perched below a rocky outcrop in the moonlight lies a single-story wooden house, lit up and welcoming and a building to the right and further up, cattle sheds and pens. "Welcome to Keyneton stud," says John Keynes.

Mrs Keynes and five wide-eyed kids stare. Mrs Keynes has the kettle on. "You English like your tea…" The kids are guarded, then not so. "What's school like…? What do you say when you meet the Queen…? What was it like on the boat…?"

I can't wait to see the cattle, the stud cattle I am expected to turn into winners. John Keynes can't wait to show me either. He's keen to confirm he's doing the right thing and his cattle are worthy of my expense. "Let's get up to the cattle sheds right away."

He's reaching for his stockman's hat. The Cuban heeled boots are already on. He's a big man and these are giant strides. He can't wait to get there. Mine are nearly as giant. This is my future. Out into the hot, muggy night. The cicadas singing. The stars twinkling bright above my head. The Southern Cross shines down.

The double door to the cattle sheds swings open. Nothing is different. I have come twelve thousand miles, right across the world, yet the "feel" is the same, the sound of cattle quietly cudding, the smell, the aura of animals at rest, at peace. But there is a difference: you can't see a thing!

"We're too far from civilisation for mains," says John Keynes. "It'll get here one day, maybe ten years, 20, who knows. I'll start the generator." And the generator chugs into life and light floods the pens, the cattle, the walkways, the hay racks, everything I know so well. Yes everything in the pulsating light driven by the generator. There's an open yard with half a dozen cows, 12 or so pens, under cover, for selected bulls, a couple full grown, immense beasts, three or four yearlings and a handful of two year olds. The future, perhaps?

Keynes echoes, "The future?"

Yes, the all-white bull catches my eye. A two year old, I'm told, and then a stablemate, more traditional Shorthorn colours, predominately red with some white. They both look good. The white bull especially… but what's missing? It's his horns… yes this is a Polled Shorthorn, the first I've seen.

"Strange. Strange," I say.

John Keynes looks anxious. "Strange?"

"A perfect Shorthorn… but no horns… how can that be?"

"Bred that way. Polled Shorthorn. You don't approve?"

"Just looks odd without horns," I say. "But a good-looking bull in the making." But I still can't reconcile myself to the missing horns. Somehow they balance a Shorthorn. John Keynes does have a proper Shorthorn, the red and white bull in the adjoining pen.

"What do you think?"

I'm in with him, talking to him, patting, stroking, showing I'm his friend. "Good," I say. "More than that, excellent." But he needs some work I'm thinking, someone to bring him forwards, make him the prime beast he can be. The champion that Keynes wants. "Yes a chance of being a champion. Him and the white bull."

"We've entered both in the Royal Adelaide Show next September, our premier show." He stands back waiting for my opinion. "What do you think?"

I think to myself how there's plenty to work on. The two youngish bulls, the white polled beast and the red horned Shorthorn. "Well, we will have to see. Six months to go, time is on our side."

We agree. There's potential there and time is on our side. Now an evening meal, then bed. I have the shack next door. It was not much more than a store last week. Now it has a couple of squares of carpet on the dusty floor and curtains at the window. Oh, and a bed. That'll do me as I slip off into the world of nod.

Lots to work on, I'm thinking. Lots of potential.

# Chapter 6

## We are the Champions

There's a strange squeaking, grinding sound. I lie in bed trying to work out what it can be. Can it be a gate hinge that needs oiling? There's no wind, so that can't be. An animal in distress? Can't rule that out – Big Alf and Billy had spoken of strange animals doing strange things. "Up country" they said. This is all new to me. Perhaps one eating the other for an early morning snack.

Or can it be someone playing a trick on me? One of the kids putting on a welcoming party, an early morning wake up call, getting hold of an empty tin can and scraping the bottom with a nail on the end of a stick? They didn't look all that innocent.

These same kids convulse with laughter when we meet at breakfast. "It's the magpie," they say.

"Magpie?" Not any magpie that I know.

"The South Australian State Emblem, that's what," the oldest one tells me. A bit of a smart Alec I think we have here, he knows these things, State Emblems. He points out of the window through the shimmering heat haze even at eight in the morning. "Look, there. The black and white bird, our State Emblem, in the Gum tree."

Ok, I own up, I can't recognise a bird that sounds as though it's got its foot caught in a rat trap as their treasured State Emblem. Then lots of laughter again. Mrs Keynes to the rescue. "Back to your breakfasts, children." I am saved further humiliation.

I've been up to the cattle sheds and seen my charges. In the daylight they still look good. I've fed them. Cattle nuts, like we have back home and then filled the byres with hay.

Hay?

Cripes, this stuff is more like barbed wire. What on earth would Ernie say if he saw what I had just forked out for the animals? It's all stalks of dried nettles and thistles; where's our Italian rye grass and the clover? Where's the Trefoil and green, lush Lucerne?

I don't have to think twice, Ernie knew. "That's what you want in your hay, young Richard. If you want to make bulls into champion bulls, that is."

The best I can do is hope the cattle nuts live up to the promise writ large in big bold letters on the side of the sack, HIGH PROTEIN. It'd better be high protein or we're in trouble, I find myself telling the cattle. They seem to be tucking in ok, but there's that look in the white bull's eye, "Have you come all the way out here to give us what we need as champions or not?"

"It's been a bad year for hay making." I hear the stomp of John Keynes' feet come up behind me. The brim of his cattleman's hat is pulled down against the glare of the sun and it's scarcely above the horizon. "Little rain in this part of the world, I'm afraid. And when it does come it's short lived. Just a few millimetres at best. Scarcely enough to lay the dust."

Dust? You can say that again. There's a layer covering my brand, spanking new Cuban heeled boots and all I've done is walk the 100 yards from the tin shack that doubles as my accommodation.

"If I'd known I'd have brought my own." I try a smile but I'm not sure I can afford the luxury of a joke this early on. Good quality hay is the staple diet for all ruminants when there's no lush grass, and there's scarcely a single blade out there in the parched lands of Australia that I can see. Keynes' bit anyway.

"Any chance of buying some in from an area that's had rain?"

Nope!

Well, that settles that! This is a harsh land and if you get a spare bale of hay you hang on to it.

My education is being furthered. "There was a bloke by the name of Goyder – an Englishman like you – came out in the early days of the settlers and became State surveyor and he soon tracked down where there was enough assured rain for arable farming and where there wasn't. We're not in the driest part of the State but the more north you get the lower the rainfall." Keynes draws breath. "Once you get past Barossa Valley, Goyder said it petered out pretty rapidly and he was right."

I avoid the temptation of stating the obvious. The stud's in the wrong place – but we have to live with it. But something has to be done, something if I'm to do my job properly. "What about some decent cereals to compensate? Milled oats and kibbled maize for a start?"

Keynes looks at me as though I've just dropped in from the moon.

I have another go. "You know I'm sure, milled oats and kibbled maize. The maize put through a machine that cracks the maize cornel so the animals get the goodness and it doesn't end up in the field as a pile of cow manure." I pause while he catches up. "And while you're at it, what about bran and molasses?"

My new boss, John Keyes, looks awkward. I'm not getting anywhere. It's time to put all this in perspective, ratchet up the pressure, I've got nothing to lose. "You say the big show, the Royal Adelaide Show, is six months away. We need to make a start right away to get something decent for the show animals... why wait?" I've got his ear. He's still listening. "New feed will build muscle, put meat on the bone while the molasses will give a sheen to the coat; it will give us an edge." Big breath. "Make them champions. That's what you want, isn't it?"

He rubs his chin. "Well, I hear what you say, but laying hands on this feed isn't easy."

"Isn't easy? Surely, you have a wholesaler where you buy in your existing cattle feed?"

Back home it was Percy Stone in Pangbourne. Dad knew him well. He banked at Dad's bank while the Squire bought his cattle feed from Mr Stone's store on the Reading Road. "I'm sure you've got a Percy Stone out there somewhere."

"I'll ask next time I go into the local township."

"Next time," I say. "What's wrong with now? There's no time to lose. I want to make a start."

"Ok, I'll take the truck into town this afternoon and scout around."

That makes me feel happier.

Now onto the next subject to confront our Mr Keynes with. Back home the first thing we did after feeding and mucking out the animals was to walk the fields so you could cast an eye over the breeding herd, cows and heifers, some with young calves. Walking the fields enabled you to make sure they were ok. But the next task was just as important and one Ernie never allowed us to miss and that was exercising the show animals. We had a mock-up show ring for that very purpose.

Building a ring specially out here isn't essential as we can use the small paddock out the back; this isn't a battle I've got to take on. There will be others more important. But exercising our show animals every day is absolutely vital. Ernie Ford would demand it and that's what I'm doing.

"Exercising the show animals is essential. Each and every day." Best way to make my point is give John Keynes the example Ernie always gave. "It exercises them, young Richard, but not only that" – the flat cap pulled down and the dog-end stuck to the lower lip – "it teaches obedience on the end of a halter. Nothing worse than your prize bull taking fright with all the hustle and bustle in the show ring and you chasing after 'im while 'e knocks over tables and chairs and terrifies old ladies." Ernie would roll another and take satisfaction in the example he had just given. "I've seen it 'appen, young Richard. At the Royal Yorkshire show one year I saw it. Tables and chairs, old ladies, the lot."

Keynes smiles. From under the broad-brimmed stockman's hat I watch the smile break into a laugh. A good Aussie laugh. It's one I'll get to know over the next few months. "Fair do's. Sounds ok to me. Your Ernie Ford knows a thing or two."

"Discipline and obedience in the show ring," I am rubbing it in. "And elegance too. Teaching them how to walk, to step out firm and positive at my command and stand four-square when told to come to attention. To hold their heads high, look the part. Catch the judge's eye. Give him a reason to crown them champions."

I might have a convert here in John Keynes. "Fair do's," he says again." But it's a qualified "Fair do's." There's a wry smile to go with it. "It's one thing for your wealthy farmers in the Old Country but this is a commercial operation." He's reminding me of what was said when we met on the ship when he made his offer. "We all have to muck in, multi-task, jack of all trades. Can you drive a tractor? Repair a fence? Mow a crop, plough a fire break?"

A Ferguson tractor is dashing across in front of the cattle pens at this very moment, fence posts bouncing about in a trailer behind, a swirl of dust following at a distance. Keynes points. "There's only Colin the farm hand and me running this place… we need you to chip in from time to time with the everyday jobs." The Ferguson comes to a halt, Colin unloads the posts, a fence goes up as if by magic. "As well as creating a winning herd of Shorthorns, of course."

I'm his expensive recruit from the Old Country. "Winning herd as well, of course," he repeats.

This "chipping in" is no problem for me. I learnt all that at Agricultural College and even at Home Farm under Ernie I had to muck-in at times; we all had to when the busiest months came round. At harvest I was released after playing my part in exercising the show cattle; I took my turn helping gather in the hay, then the grain harvest, teaming up with Billy Milsom operating the Claas combine harvester while I followed with the baler if Bert Fuller, the second tractor driver, was off ploughing, sowing or mowing.

"Good. So we won't fall out then." Keynes seems relieved. The smile looks genuine and I've got a deal I can live with.

"I'll jot down a routine that I'll work to first thing tomorrow morning."

I don't even have to think about it. It's in my head already. Feed the cattle in the byres first thing, the cattle that will be the mainstay of our show team, plus young heifers in the paddocks close to the Homestead. Then I'll grab some breakfast before exercising the show animals, giving them their first lessons in show ring technique, how I want them to perform to win us medals.

And after that I'll be off and away to the outer fields – Keynes calls them paddocks – checking the main breeding herd as I did back home. There's a difference though. Keynes had pointed over the hills and far away, dry, barren hills and the far away is very far away. Out of sight, in fact. Good job Big Alf has sent up Black Horse... now I know what Billy meant and Big Alf shouted. "You'll be stuffed without a horse, Boy."

And what's this John Keynes is saying now? Dingoes, roos, where do they fit in?

"Just make sure a dingo hasn't had the young calves... that the roos haven't flattened the fences."

Time to get Black Horse from the Home Paddock, leap on and show these Aussies what we are made of.

I saddle up just as Big Alf had shown me; halter over head, bit in mouth, reins over horse's neck. "Whoa there, Black Horse. Good boy." I go for a bit of "Whoa there" just to show I know what's I'm talking about. And calling him by his name, he seems to like that too. And a touch of the "Good boy" is nearly as good as a couple of sugar lumps.

I don't think John Keynes and Colin have seen a Pommie lad mount a horse before. And the Pommie lad has only seen him do it a couple of times and earned himself a sore bum for his trouble. But at least my backside has had a few days to heal and there's now a tougher layer of skin between me and the saddle... so here goes.

Hey up! Left foot in the stirrup, right swings up and over and I'm in the hot seat once more. Best of all I haven't fallen off the other side.

My heels, my new Cuban heels – with that layer of dust – dig into Black Horse's flank and with a cry of "Ride 'em cowboy," we're on our way. Colin, open-mouthed, takes time off from driving fence posts into rock-hard ground to watch. I think he's impressed. Out through the gate, left, down the dusty track, and we're heading in the direction of the horizon, Keynes' words ringing in my ears, "Your dinner gets fed to the dogs if you don't get back by eight."

Black Horse has either never seen a horizon or he doesn't recognise one if he has. Much persuasion is needed to keep him in a forward direction, he prefers a U turn and galloping back to the homestead; perhaps he reckons his dinner is at risk too.

But there's an advantage to all this. Clearly he has a built-in compass and knows where his bread is best buttered. And it's not in the direction where I must go, the far-away paddock that Keynes says is where we'll find the herd. At least that is where he indicated with a rather vague sweep of the arm. "Over there somewhere..." He squinted into the blazing sun-light. I squinted too. "Yes, over there somewhere. That's where they were last seen."

I've been equipped with a squishy sort of bag full of water and a sandwich or two from Mrs Keynes. "Don't want you to die out there in your first week."

And if all else fails and we get lost under a scorching sun, I can always let Black Horse have his head and we'll be on our way back home, quick smart, courtesy of the compass. No headlines in tomorrow's dailies. "Pommie Lad Lost in the Barren Outback."

I'm digging my Cuban heels into Black Horse and there's more slaps across the rump. "Come on Black Horse. This is what Big Alf sent you up here for."

We're into what I think they call a canter and a canter bounces my bum up and down on the unyielding saddle and it's very unyielding. Try next gear. Cuban heels dig in flank once more and with more encouraging words we're flying. This must be a gallop. Only top cowboys get up to this speed and I reckon last year's Derby winner would be left at the starting gate.

A flock of South Australia's State Emblems sit in branches and chuckle, rabbits turn and run, flies and mosquitoes pelt my face like grape-shot. Where's my motor-cycle goggles and crash helmet? But at least I know why Hollywood cowboys tie hankies across their faces – nothing to do with keeping their identity from the sheriff but to avoid ingesting a mouthful of nasties.

There's a roo a hundred paces to our left going at full pelt. Byong, byong, byong… How they go! Back at the Homestead that evening and Clever Clogs kids will tell me they have been timed at 40 mph. That means Black Horse and I are doing 50 and close to the speed of light.

The roo has had enough, he's taken fright. And then, out of nowhere we're joined by a flying thing the likes of which neither Black Horse nor I have seen before, amazing he hasn't panicked, thrown me off and galloped back to the Homestead and safety. It's about the size of a Lancaster bomber – and making the same sort of noise – it comes in at an angle, flies parallel, takes a good look, and then buzzes off. Clever Clogs will tell me I have been acquainted with my first Queensland Sugar Wasp and after more laughter I'll be told I should stay well clear of Queensland Sugar Wasps. "They have a nasty sting…" Laugh, laugh… "Yes, very nasty sting. Haven't we told you?"

Now the next problem starts to hit home – it would be so easy to get lost out here. We've been going for the best part of an hour and still no sign of the herd. And one brown patch of dirt looks much the same as another and a pile of rocks is a pile of rocks no matter how you look at it. There is the occasional Gum, but they all look the same and the only visible sign of life is the magpies laughing at my predicament from a tree top. Black Horse has his in-built compass but apart from that, his road sense isn't all that good even if he could answer the question, "Where the hell's the herd and the Far Away Paddock, Black Horse?"

Years ago, in my Boy's Own magazine, the hero would tie the end of his knitted pullover to a twig before entering the labyrinth, but I don't have a woollen pullover and this really isn't a labyrinth but mile upon mile of sameness punctuated with the occasional rocky outcrop, Gum or Saltbush. Then I get the answer – it should have been obvious hours ago – find the boundary fence, follow it on the way out, follow it on the way back and, hey presto, back home before my dinner gets fed to the dogs.

And here it is, looking intact and in good order. No roos have been tampering with this one; bouncing along in giant strides yes, but taking out Keynes' fence, no. Then Black Horse and I come upon a grisly sight – a young calf entwined in the wire, half his poor little body eaten away. The dingoes have got to him before we did. That's what Keynes said, dingoes take to vulnerable calves. I make a mental note that all in-calf cows will be brought into the byres, afforded the protection of a locked gate behind them, straw bedding beneath their feet and herdsman Holdsworth on hand to tend to them.

No point in standing around staring in dismay and feeling sick. The ground is as hard as rock and I don't have a spade to give him a decent burial even if it was as soft as sand.

Over the next barren hillock and the ground seems to vanish before our very eyes. Black Horse and I have stumbled across a wide open ravine and down there is the herd, just what we were searching for, and they are all looking remarkably relaxed given the fact that they are living among roos, dingoes and Queensland Sugar Wasps.

But wait. The cows in this herd are no fools, also down there are a few blades of green grass and something that looks remarkably like it could have been a flowing stream on the day the rains came. A creek, that's what they call it in Oz. Ok, all that is left of this creek is the occasional pool dotted about here and there but at least these pools are giving sustenance to our herd.

"Take a look at that, Black Horse. Have you ever seen such a happy and contented herd in your life?"

Black Horse agrees. There must be a hundred or so cudding away in the shade of a Gum or three, tails flicking at the flies and living the life of Old Riley. Yes, there are a dozen or so calves too, anything from a few weeks to six months I'd guess. Fortunately, none with dingo teeth marks from what I can see from up here.

I dismount and tie Black Horse's reins to a stout branch. "Now, don't go away, I need you to get me home. And keep the compass well oiled."

I'm scrambling down the slope of the rocky ravine, slipping and sliding on pebbles and stones and steadying myself on spindly bushes where I can. This is real Hollywood stuff, all I need is my Smith and Weston and the occasional Red Indian to shoot at. A few pebbles and rocks get dislodged and go bounding down the slope in front of me gathering speed as they go. I'm threatening to join them.

There must be a better way down. A better way that the herd has found. But not for me today. I'm over the difficult bit and about to arrive on terra firma with no broken bones. Black Horse looks over the edge of the ravine. He didn't realise my other skill was abseiling without a rope.

But the grazing herd doesn't seem that impressed and regards me with what I think could best be called disdain, they've not batted an eyelid, contentedly cudding in the shade of the few Gums. A few heads turn in my direction, all passive at my arrival. They really could be at Home Farm, Ernie Ford drawing on his dog-end and calling them "Me Beauties."

Except one. Goodness, out of the herd comes a wild-eyed cow, head down, horns fixed, hooves kicking up the dust; I'm getting out of here. Retreating to the slope, somehow I'm going back up quicker than I came down. Soothing words weren't going to do the trick with this cow – she has a calf to protect and with dingoes on the prowl who can blame her.

I'm back on Black Horse and Black Horse puts the compass into gear. He loves it when his nose is pointing home. No need for Cuban heels in ribs, cries of "Giddy-up." He's off and away. We pass the winner of last year's Derby on the outward journey and he's scarcely out of the blocks.

"How did you get on then?" Keynes is all ears.

I'm trying to dismount as the professionals do rather than fall off. My bones ache from all this bouncing up and down in the saddle. Just don't ask about my bum.

"They're fine," I say. "Down in this wide open ravine, cudding happily. Except a roan cow with young calf... she is a bit too sprightly for me!"

Keynes laughs. "Should have warned you about her. That's Rosemary. Placid as they come until she has a calf to protect.

Should have..."

His voice trails off. I've just told him about the calf entwined in the fence. "What's left of him... or her. Hard to tell. That bit was missing."

The chin is being rubbed ruefully again, the hat pushed back from the forehead. It doesn't take much to convince Keynes that cows about to calve down should be in the safety of the farm buildings. "You have the open yard, straw, security and an eye on their welfare. We'll bring them in."

Keynes agrees. It seems it's the second loss in as many months. "Can't afford that and now you are here we won't."

I sympathise. Several thousand acres to maintain and just him and Colin to do it. Those two can't cover everything. It's time for Keynes and me to round up the cows with calves and cows that are in-calf. Keynes has a sort of cross-country motorbike – I have Black Horse. In his office we scan the records of the herd and come up with a list of the cows likely to calve down in the next few weeks.

The motorbike covers the ground; Black Horse and I get down into the ravine and cull the expectant mothers. I find it surprisingly easy. "Come on boy, that one, the red one." Black Horse turns instinctively and positions himself between the red cow and the rest of the herd. He's done it all before with Big Alf in the saddle. "And that one, Black Horse, cull her out..."

By night-fall we have a dozen pregnant cows culled from the herd and walked back to the safety of the yard along with cows and their young calves. No more dingoes biting their backsides.

"Job done."

"Job well done." Keynes is pleased with our effort, the day's work, and I feel Black Horse and I are making a team. The motorbike is great at covering the ground but you can't beat the good old fashioned team of man on horse to cull animals. Even the Dick Holdsworth and Black Horse team. Ask Roy Rogers and Trigger. They were ace.

"Yes, you did well." Keynes is starting to see a return for the money spent on his extra man, his expensive extra man from England, never mind the knowledge and skills I am bringing to the Keyneton stud.

Now my attention turns to the in-calf cows we've just brought home and my task of watching for signs of an impending addition to the herd. It was Ernie Ford's task back home, mine now.

We scan the list in Keynes' office again. "Matilda could be the first." Keynes is sure she was bulled coming up to nine months before. "She never came back on heat, I kept a close check." His records are good... I trust him. Cows come on heat and can conceive once a month so it's not difficult to work out if you keep your records up to date and your wits about you. "Must be her, this month," he says again.

And so it is.

Matilda is in-calf to Keynes' Glastullich senior stud bull before his hind legs went on him so the resulting calf should be just the sort we want to take the Keyneton stud forward. A heifer calf would be useful... a bull calf could go on and be a future winner two to three years down the line. Whatever, it's a calf that we can't afford to lose. My task to make sure we don't.

And so it is on this evening with Keynes miles away at some graziers' meeting and I'm the man in the hot seat when Matilda shows all the right signs. I'm making my last check for the day, leaning over the railing just like Ernie does, casting an eye over the animals in my charge. Talking to them, of course, just like him. "Me Beauties." The only thing missing is the flat cap and the puff on a dog-end stuck to the lower lip. And the look of a wily old man who's seen it all before. I'm trying to look like a wily young man who's seen some of it before. A pen-full of cows about to calve down, the future for Keyneton stud, my charges. My future.

Ernie would ask, "What do you do first, young Richard?"

And I would reply diligently, "Check the patient and check again."

"And if she looks good, then leave her be. Let nature take it's course."

"And if not?"

"It's best you act then. No time to lose."

It's only on rare occasions you have to intervene, mostly you let nature take its course as Ernie says. Any herdsman will tell you that nine out of ten times cows will calve down by themselves with no outside help. "Leave well alone, young Richard, let nature do the work for you." But there's something not quite right here. It's not what I would call distress. But Matilda is fretting. A dead calf in her? A breach birth? Even twins? Yes, something's up.

"You got to consider everything, young Richard. Don't discount nothing." That's what I must do now.

I've only been a help-mate to Ernie Ford – a sort of mid-wife's right hand man. I've never been the mid-wife on my own. Never been confronted with what I am now.

Deep breath called for here. Hot seat all right.

I gather my kit and clobber and go to work. Bucket of warm water, soap, disinfectant and calving ropes if there are problems. Oh yes, and the towel – I suspect I'll be scrubbing up before the evening's out.

Ernie would say, "Don't be 'asty. There's no point in calving down a cow if she don't be ready." The dog-end would glow in the gloom of the byre. "Look her in the eye... ask her."

I look. I ask. Matilda tells me it's time.

"Take hold of her tail. Yes, her tail, boy." Ernie would look at me intently. "You understand?" I'd nod. "Hold it firm and feel the last joint, the very last joint. If she's ready the joint will be relaxed, so relaxed you can almost bend it double."

And it is! Matilda does not object. Tail in hand, I turn the last joint back on itself, bend it double as he said. "That's the time to go to work." Ernie was always adamant. Fifty years a herdsman told him.

Here, in Oz, in our open yard, the sun setting on another hot sweltering day, I've looked and I've asked. And I've bent the tail as he said. Another deep breath. Time to get down to business.

The cow must go into contraction, of course, push and push again. The water will break and if all goes well there's nothing the herdsman has to do. Soon it will be apparent, a little nose will appear, pair of front feet, and the next push delivers you a bundle of slimy wet skin and bone at your feet. And a bleat. A weak little bleat.

Life! Fresh new life as God intended!

"And if it doesn't, then go to it lad!" Ernie would snuff out the dog-end. "Roll sleeves up to the shoulder, soap the hand and arm, and in you go, find out what's wrong, what's not working. Should be able to feel the nose, the head and pair of tiny hooves either side... just like he's taking a dive... diving out to meet you." I could just see Ernie's grin in the cold, dark calving pen of a midnight hour at Home Farm. "Most likely the feet are hanging back, or neck, and all the pushing from the cow or pulling from you won't solve that." The smile's gone now. "More likely break the calf's neck or rupture the cow."

I'd take a deep breath. "What next, Mr Ford?"

"With your hand in there, get your fingers to find the head, get it up, hold it there, hold it so it doesn't slip back. Get the feet, get them up too, if needs be get the loops of the calving ropes round the fetlocks, then, and only then, give a gentle pull."

The calving ropes are special, made for the job and part of a vet's bag of tricks. But no vet up here, miles from anywhere. I'd got Keynes to buy in a set when I first arrived and, boy, do I need them now.

Back home, as here now, there was tension. Tension you could cut with a knife in the cold, dark cattle pen. Ernie's jacket folded and laid neatly in the straw at the back of the byre, his flat cap still on, his sleeves rolled right up, his face intent. "Yes, gently does it, boy, wait till she pushes... This is life and death. Let nature help you in your work."

Here I am, twelve thousand miles away and the only help I have is the memory of Ernie Ford's words, his advice, and his inspiration.

My hand, my right hand, is deep in the cow now. The pressure is enormous but my fingers find the calf. I've got his head up, somehow I slip the ropes round his fetlocks and I'm encouraging Matilda while gently pulling with the left hand. "Come on, old girl. Come on, we can do it. Push, push."

And suddenly just when I think the battle is lost, when Matilda thinks it is, it isn't; one final push, one last gentle pull, and there's that bundle of slimy skin and bone pops out and flops down at my feet. Quickly, clear the slime from the mouth, the nostrils, get some air into his lungs. And a bleat... yes that bleat... God I've brought a life into this world. I'VE DONE IT! I'm a miracle man!

Some wise old owl once said something about All Work and No Play. Perhaps he had just saved a calf from certain death, spent hours in the saddle searching for the herd and all week wrestling with poor quality hay. He deserved a break too!

"Social life?" says Colin in response to my enquiry. "You mean what does a Pommie lad on the loose do when he's not at work?"

"I don't know about being on the loose, Colin. The boss has lent me a book on Ned Kelly. Apart from reading the life and times of your infamous Bushranger over and over again, there's swatting flies and going to bed early. But you local lads must do something after driving fence posts all day."

"Jeez, we have social events coming out of our ears up here, mate. Dances, barbies, village shows, rodeos, take ya choice. The sheilas will wrench your arm off... a good looking Pommie lad like you." Colin is beaming, sitting astride the Ferguson, another few hundred yards of fence behind him for the day. He turns in the tractor seat and surveys his efforts. "Should keep the bloody dingoes out for an hour or two."

"I reckon," I say, sounding like an Aussie already, "it's what we need, Colin. After what I saw out there in the far away paddock."

Colin nods but he seems more interested in my welfare after dark than dingoes in the daylight. "Not that I need to get out on the night-time prowl myself, you understand. I've got my little wife all lined up." He smiles, satisfied, at having someone ready to cook his dinner and chill his beer after all that fencing. "Cutie," he says. "My little Cutie."

"Cutie's a nice name," I say. "Cute that."

"So let's get you sorted, Rich. Good looking Pommie lad on the loose. The sheilas..." He breaks off, then resumes. "... sheila being a single girl, you understand. Crumpet ya call 'em over there don't ya?"

"Crumpet it is, Colin. Crumpet."

"Well, I've got just the place for you. Just the place. The local hop. They'll wrench ya bloody arm off. I'll get Ray my mate to introduce you. He'll see ya won't miss out."

A girl with reddish, frizzy hair, is taking me by the hand, leading me onto the dance floor. "Ever done the Gay Gordons?"

I'm keen to get to know the local girls as quickly as I can but not this quickly. "No," I say. "Not that I remember."

She's laughing and I'm being propelled around and swapped with others just as enthusiastic about getting me acquainted with this strange dance with the strange name. I get twirled and whirled and spun round in all directions. It's like pass the parcel but at a frenetic pace. And all to music and laughter. And I'm the parcel.

"You're doing ok there, Rich," says Ray, Colin's mate, after I've finished being passed around. "Colin told me you're on the look out for a bit of action. Well, you can't beat this. Every other Friday."

"I can understand it's not every Friday, Ray. It will take two weeks to get over this one."

"Geez Rich, I thought you Poms were goers. I thought you were..." Ray doesn't finish as I am dragged onto the floor for yet another strange dance by another young lass and this one has dark hair and is fitted out with a bright red dress and feet that I can't seem to avoid. She's nimble and I'm a bit of a clod-hopper.

"Sorry," I say.

"Don't worry. You're new here aren't you? From the Old Country?"

"Funny," I say. "The last girl asked that. And the one before. I should put up a sign or hand out leaflets."

We both laugh as I step on her toes once more and make my apologies yet again but there's a certain chemistry here. Ray says afterwards how I'm a lucky so-and-so to have been dancing with her. "She and her sister are the best sheilas around. Everyone wants to date them."

And I'm going to. Well, the one whose feet I have been standing on. I persuade her to skip the Military Two-Step and the Dashing White Sergeant and we go outside for a breath of fresh air and look up at the stars and swipe a mosquito or two and agree to go to the flicks in far away Nuriootpa a week on Saturday. "I can squeeze you in," she says and I'm saying how grateful I am. Being squeezed in. "Between the tennis club, church and domestic science. Night school on Mondays and Wednesdays. Mum insists it'll be a great asset when I line up my intended."

I could suggest we drive down to the nearest big town and the open-air drive-in movies but Rachael, for that is her name, is a nice girl and nice girls don't go to drive-ins on the first date. "You're right there," says Ray. "They think you're going to try it on and you probably would. A Pommie lad from the Old Country looking for a root."

"Root?"

"Root. Shag. A naughty. Whatever the hell you call it over there."

"Well we don't call it a root... that's something on the end of a turnip."

"Ya know what I mean, Rich. They all get up to it at the drive-ins. You're best off at the flicks. She'll like that. All the nice sheilas do."

"The Girl Can't Help It," I say.

"Ya what?"

"The Girl Can't Help It. It's the rock and roll film. Jayne Mansfield, Little Richard, Fats Domino and all the others. She'll enjoy it I'm sure. It's all the rage."

"Well, you're the lucky bugger and no mistake. Just keep ya hands to yourself. I'm told she doesn't put up with any hanky-panky... not first time out, anyway."

Back inside and I'm managing to miss the One Step and a repeat of the Gay Gordons – Dougie the Scotsman and his lot have a lot to answer for if they invented this. And the last dance is a sort of barn dance which involves the whole community. Colin and Cutie. Ray, Ron, Rod. Even the vicar and local copper are out there doing their thing. Arms and legs, hands and feet fly around the place; blokes dressed in chequered shirts and girls in pretty skirts twirling away.

"I'll sit this one out," I say. "I've had enough of standing on your toes for one evening."

My modest joke encourages a smile and a smile that makes me feel as if I'm on the right track with pretty Rachael and her domestic science, Mondays and Wednesdays. Church and tennis. I'd like to steal a kiss, outside under the stars, while everyone is preoccupied with the Barn Dance. But my joke wasn't that good.

We part friends. "I'll see you a week tomorrow, then." There's a sparkle in her eyes and she presses a little piece of paper in my hand. "It's my address. See you at seven o'clock. Tomorrow week. Don't be late."

I think this is a strange way of doing things. Writing out your address in advance and handing it out. A bit like a bus ticket. I wonder if I'm supposed to get it clipped before the night's out.

But if this is the way the sheilas do things, then far be it for me to argue. And she and her sister are the best dates around. Ray said. And I've been squeezed in. "Can't say fairer than that, mate. You're a lucky so-and-so. Go for it."

Back in my tin shack on the farm and I've got hold of a book on ballroom dancing to bring me up to speed, *All You Need to Know on Technique*. I scan the index: Gavotte, Gumboot dance (South Africa) Gigue... Here it is, Gay Gordons. I'll go and practise in the cattle shed with one of my cows. She won't mind if I step on her hooves.

"Fancy the rodeo?" Ray's asking. "There's one this Sunday. Brother Kevin and me are going up. Bronco riding, lassoing, bringing down a steer at full pelt. Dogging, they call it." He's keen to show me a bit of Outback life. "The real thing," he says. "You won't get this at the flicks."

I must look startled. "You only have to watch, mate," he says. "Participating is optional."

"Only if you tell me why I was doing such funny dances the other night. What the hell's wrong with a bit of jiving? Even the quick-step or waltz?

"Ya still on about that dance? I think that sheila has gone to your head, mate."

"Well Rachel is very nice," I say. "But I just wondered about the dances. All the girls I was dancing with are limping now."

"You've got to admit our dances are a sight more friendly, Rich, even if you stood on a few feet. Ya get to know everyone for a hundred miles around before the evening's out. Bugger those dances where you get stuck with the same sheila for ten minutes and all that sloppy music." Ray's standing there in front of me, cowboy hat tilted back, cowboy boots and thumbs stuck in a belt two inches wide. He looks just like the Cisco Kid.

But I suppose there's some sense in what he's saying about their dances as we head off to the rodeo in the ute, Ray, Kevin and me in the front, packed in like sardines. I'd met every girl in the hall and they know me. The Pommie lad here to make John Keynes the champion bull breeder in South Australia.

"I told you they'd wrench your arm off mate, a good looking lad from the Old Country like you."

Ray's ute – I learn it's short for utility, with the front part of a car and the back bit a flat-bed for your tools and stuff – bounces along the dirt road and we're out for a great day. "This'll open your eyes, Rich. I bet you've never seen anything like this back in the Old Country."

Ray's right. I can't believe this. It's a slice of the Wild West. Toughies in full cowboy kit, ten gallon hats, chequered shirts, lariats tied casually round the neck, Cuban heeled boots and chaps flapping in the breeze. Yes, they wear all the gear you see in a Hollywood movie. The only thing missing is a handful of ragged Red Indians sitting around a tepee watching as their land is nicked from them.

The place is packed. It's what the Aussies do for a family day out.

"Stick ya head through here and watch this, Rich."

We've pushed our way through the crowd and arrived at the centre ring and what Ray and brother Kevin stick their heads through is a ten foot high fence strong enough to keep out a Panzer tank. There's a cry of "Ride 'em cowboy!" and a gate in the fence flies open and ejects some unfortunate bloke dressed as Cowboy Joe on a fearsome horse the size of a camel and with the strength of a rhino and Joe is trying to stay on while the horse is trying to get him off. Another problem for Joe – if he hasn't got enough already – he's only allowed to use one hand to hang on (that's the rules) and the beast is bred to throw him off. That's also in the rules.

"The record's less than a minute, Rich. How's that for a day at the races?" Ray wagers 30 seconds and Kevin 20 and Kevin's right. "Beers on you tonight, brother."

Then there's dogging and as Ray had said, dogging is the art of riding alongside a steer at full pelt and throwing yourself at the animal, grabbing his horns and bringing him down to earth in a cloud of dust and broken bones.

The crowd is cheering, the sky is blue and the blood is red. No wonder there are a dozen ambulances in attendance and all leave at the hospital has been cancelled. "Great day out, mate."

Kevin agrees. "I bet you don't have this in the Old Country."

I'd hate to say we're far too sensible but I won't because it has been a great day. And the beers are on Ray.

On the way back, bouncing along the dirt road, Kevin says, "Need to put the grader in." And for the first time in the day I know what they are talking about and I'm on home ground.

"Yes, the grader," I say. "Need to put the grader in. This road's a bastard."


"Ya bulls are looking good, Rich. You reckon we've got a chance?"

It's Colin's lunch break. He's parked the Ferguson in the shade of a Gum and has come over to the pens, leaning on the gate with his broad-brimmed hat keeping the sun from frizzling his face and he's admiring our progress. The bulls are the centre of attention these days. The show's not far off.

"Well, I think we're going in the right direction," I say. "We've done all we can. It's down to the judges now."

"And the work ya do. Don't forget that, mate." Colin had watched the daily routine of walking the bulls and teaching them show ring discipline. "And all that titivating ya give 'em. Jeez, I've never seen anything like it. They get a bath more often than I do." He's got a grin from ear to ear. "Ya treat 'em like bleedin' film stars. Shampooing, drying, brushing."

"You can't win without it, Colin. We'd be lost before we even started. I had a great teacher back home. Let's see how much I've remembered when the big day comes down there in Adelaide."

"Well, the boss reckons we're in with a shout. That's what I heard him say." Colin's overheard the conversation Keynes had with Bill Somerville. They were doing what Colin is doing now. Leaning over the pen, like wise old men, the bulls the centre of attention. "We have a chance," Keynes told Bill. "I reckon the best we've ever had." I heard it too.

Bill Sommerville is the owner of the neighbouring property about 20 miles away as the State Emblem flies. He'd watched our progress ever since I joined John Keynes, he'd taken a special interest. They were now saying how the supreme championship had always gone to a bloke by the name of John Parker. "It'll take a lot to knock him off the top spot," said Keynes.

They were both digesting the fact. This bloke John Parker seemed to be top man with the top bulls. His reputation was spread far and wide which is a long day's ride in Australia.

"Parker has won it so often he's got one hand on the trophy." Keynes was playing down our chances, his neighbour playing them up. "Anyway, John, second place would be better than nothing. Better than you've done before."

I wasn't involved in the chit-chat. Not invited. Anyway, what could I do but my best? Ernie Ford had always consoled himself if he didn't win. "We did our best," he'd say and roll a fresh one and curse if it didn't light up first time or if he spilt the baccy. "Bloody judges... what do they know, boy?"

I look at the white bull and the white bull looks back at me. "He could surprise a few, Colin." And the red bull isn't out of it. "He could be the winner yet."

They are only relative youngsters at two years old, but youngsters often look fresher than bulls that have been around a while. On the other hand older bulls command respect. Or maybe they are over the hill. Maybe we have more than just a reasonable chance as Bill Sommerville said. Could we depose this John Parker and his bull that had won for the past few years?

I'm excited. It's my chance to show what I can do in the show ring. And there could be thousands watching.

We're driving down. An early start but we are still caught in the heat of the day. Keynes is chatty but guarded. "I suppose you've done this many times before? Is it any different over there?"

I have and it isn't! "Except for the rain. We're always looking out for wind and rain even in the English summer. I remember we went to the Royal Lancashire Show at Blackpool and it blew a gale. When they announced the Battle of Britain fly past it wasn't a Spitfire but the flower tent."

Keynes struggles with a smile. He's under pressure. The next couple of days could be make or break.

I think I'll tell him about the time I went to the Perth bull sales with Ernie Ford and the Squire's cattle. "We went up by train. It was in a blizzard. They loaded the cattle in a small wagon and attached it to the back of the night freight to Scotland." I pause so it can sink in. "There was no heating and Ernie and I sat bolt upright... frozen to the wooden bench seat. A 14 hour journey."

I can hear John Keynes draw breath. "Perhaps what we are embarking on isn't so bad after all."

"There was worse to come... we couldn't get out of the wagon when we arrived in Perth, the doors were frozen shut with ice an inch thick. They needed a pickaxe to break in."

Keynes seems pleased it didn't always go smoothly in the Old Country. "This should be a piece of cake then."

Keynes, me and the two bulls in the back of the truck have threaded our way through the outer suburbs of Adelaide, taking care to give the animals a smooth ride.

No point in sudden braking that would risk our valuable cargo. I've put halters on the bulls so they are secured... no roaming around the back. And feed to keep them occupied. Unexpected movements could have them thrown off their feet. All our hard work lost in a moment.

We arrive into a hive of activity; there are at least two dozen trucks unloading, others parking up, some leaving. There are animals everywhere. All hustle and bustle. The Royal Adelaide Show, Woodville show grounds; this could be anywhere in the world. Certainly any show grounds I have been to. Our turn comes to back onto the ramp and lead the bulls off. "Steady, boy, steady."

Two stalls beckon, Keyneton Stud. Shorthorn bull. Keyneton stud. Polled Shorthorn bull. There are other stalls for milk breeds as well as beef and pens for sheep, goats, pigs. A cacophony of noise. Mooing, bleating and squealing. Animals become fractious when they leave the familiarity of their own homes. Opposite is John Parker's reigning champion, a huge bull, and an English lad in a smart white coat tending him. Better put mine on and look the part, mustn't let the side down. Mrs Keynes had washed and ironed it specially.

"Yours look well," I say. "The champion."

"Yours looks good too."

"Depends on what the judge thinks, doesn't it?"

Seems a nice lad, friendly, Tim by name, he's the opposition but there is common goal and a fraternity between herdsmen. No point in taking him outside and offering to give him a walloping. Or him me. We laugh at the thought.

His eyes focus. "Didn't I see you at the English Royal Show one year... your bull won Supreme Champion."

"That was for my boss, Mr Hope, the Squire, and his Basildon herd. It was Pittodrie Kavass, our senior stud bull. Ernie Ford had brought him in. Fancy you remembering."

"I was too busy to chat but I remember you with Mr Ford. Some said the best herdsman around."

"Yes, a great teacher. I'm trying to put into practice everything he taught me. But I doubt we will match you. The reigning Supreme Champion."

"Mr Parker has a pragmatic view. We can't go on winning for ever. The day will come when we are second best. Your two look good..."

"Thanks. But we're not expecting too much. My boss, John Keynes, would be pleased to get anything at all." I think it best to play down our chances, whatever will come out of the ring tomorrow. "Anything, in fact."

"Do you fancy a beer after we've finished here? We could carry on the chat, old times and that."

"Great idea. Do you remember the Royal Lancashire and the flower tent blowing away?"

He laughs. I laugh.

No harm done in drinking with Tim, the opposition. "That's fine. Just give me time to get settled in here, get the bulls tended. Then a drink. But not up too late. It's my first time in charge."

"By the way, do you remember..?"

Five and I'm out of bed. Quick wash, shave, change, grab some breakfast at the B&B Keynes has lined up. The landlady says, "You're keen." And I'm through the show ground gates by six. Ernie would joke, "Up before you went anywhere boy."

The show grounds are already busy. All the herdsmen have only one thing in mind. So don't expect light conversation and meaningless chit-chat. And no smile across the passage-way to Tim, my new found friend, it's judging day, he's the opposition now.

I take the white bull to the washing area and we wait our turn. Wash him down, shampoo, then out with the hair drier, the Curry comb to fluff up his coat, back-comb his tail. A light touch of linseed oil rubbed in to give him that sheen. Then polish his hooves. Stand back and inspect the hard work. "Don't you look good." I think he knows without me telling him. "It's our big day," I say.

"The big day." Keynes is with me now. "Anything I can do?"

"I think I have it under control."

"I was sure you would."

I'm mixing a hot bran mash for the white bull while I prepare his stable-mate. "Sure I can't do something?"

"You can get the boiling water."

Tension building now. The public fills the stands, start to congregate around the judging rings, while some traipse through the cattle sheds. Children are drawn to the show animals. "Look at that one, Mummy. Isn't it big? I'm sure he will win." The little girl is pointing at John Parker's bull.

Tim has him looking good, too bloody good. He's expected to win. I watch out of the corner of my eye. Being older, he doesn't have the coat that my two charges have; but Tim's working his Curry comb and brush to good effect and the big bull, the reigning Champion, looks the part. Looks too good for my two younger, smaller, bulls. Or does he?

Keynes is anxious and it's making the bulls edgy. I wish I could find something else for him to do. "It's time for the judging, just go off and watch with Mrs Keynes and the kids. We'll do what we can."

The stewards call us forward. It's time for the ring. I slip around each bull's neck the loop of ribbon with his allocated number. White bull number 13, unlucky for some. Red bull 33. Polled Shorthorns are in the ring first. I lead out the white bull along with a dozen or so others. White bull strides purposefully. I scarcely have to lead him. All the work we've done back home is paying off; others are skittish, reluctant. Not my bull. Ernie would be proud of me.

The judge, in smart suit, hot under this sun, clip-board under arm, an assistant at his side. He stands stiffly in the centre of the ring. Judge and jury wrapped up in one. He can make our day or ruin it.

We circle him, keeping our distance. I talk to the white bull. "Walk on. Stop. Stand. Head high. Walk on again."

I try to catch the judge's eye, someone said he is over from England. But he's having none of it. Anyway, he's judging the bulls, not my eye. Ernie always said to do your job, lead your charges. "The judge will let 'e know if 'e wants you to come forward."

A nod. The assistant calls out. "Numbers 7, 13, 14, 19 and 21 stand in line please."

So far, so good. We stand in orderly fashion. I'm glad I have my broad brimmed Stockman's hat or I'd get roasted. The sun is strong. The crowd is quiet. Mr English judge walks the line, sizing them up, hand on rump, down to the fetlocks, runs his fingers through the white bull's coat, pressing his fingers into the ribs. Testing the depth of flesh. Next bull, and next... and next...

"The judge's decision. Number 13."

Yes, 13. White bull. Keyneton Gladiator. It is lucky for some. The assistant announces over the tannoy. "Champion Polled Shorthorn." One final pat on the rump from the judge, his eye meets mine now. A ripple of applause. Keynes looks like a cat with a bowl of cream. Mrs Keynes pats him on the back, the kids bounce up and down.

It's not over yet. Now the Shorthorn class. Tim is first in the ring with the reigning champion. Me next, another two dozen other contenders. Same judge, same routine, same tension. We are called forward again, red bull is short-listed just like his stablemate half an hour ago. Tim stands next to me. John Parker's bull is head and shoulders over red bull. None of the others are in it... the judge goes from one to another and back again, knife-edge stuff this. The tannoy crackles to life again. "Number 33. Champion Shorthorn. Keyneton Emperor." More cream for John Keynes, more pats on the back. More jumping up and down for the scallywags. Tim says, "Well done." I sympathise. He has worked hard. Done all he could.

We've got champion of each breed. Now the head-to-head for Supreme Champion. Our white bull against red. Keyeton Stud against Keyneton Stud. Keynes against Keynes. And white bull gets it. "Number 13. Polled Shorthorn, Supreme Champion. Supreme Champion of the Royal Adelaide Show. Keyneton Gladiator."

Life doesn't get much better than this. Keynes shakes me by the hand. John Parker, tall, refined, congratulates Keynes. "We had to lose one day to a better bull and we have."

Tim and I have a drink at the end of the day. The beers are on me.

Back home in the tin shack and a letter is waiting from Mum and Dad. They are coming out to Australia. Can things get any better than this? I doubt it. I really do.

# Chapter 7

# You're a Journo Now!

"A little to the left... Now a bit to the right... That's fine."

I'm lining up fence posts with the boss then driving them into the hard, rocky ground. It's very important because it's a boundary fence and delineates our property from the next.

"We gotta get it right." And I don't argue.

This morning I was picking stones and rocks from the land. That's important too as it's intended for cultivation and rocks bugger up the cultivator. And what did the Good Book say about the corn falling on waste ground but some on good soil? But this is a joke. There ain't any!

Yesterday I re-built a stone wall next to the tractor shed. "I know you're not an up and running bricklayer – but I'd like ya to get it right."

"I'll do my best."

Yes, I want to get it right. I'll be driving off to see Mum and Dad shortly, I want to tell them about successes, not failures. Even building a brick wall.

"Welcome, Mum and Dad..."

Fencing, gathering stones and re-building the wall is fun but it's not looking after stud cattle nor bathing in the glory of the Royal Adelaide Show, and that's because I don't work with stud cattle any more; I'm no longer at the Keyneton stud!

We came back in Keynes' truck. Chattering away merrily with the prize winners riding in the back. Then pinning the winning rosettes in the stalls above the bulls' heads like every successful herdsman does, high up on the walls for the whole world to see. John Keynes had the certificates "Best of Class," "Best of Breed," "Supreme Champion" framed and hung in his office. Colin greeted me warmly, shook me by the hand. "Jeez mate, this really puts us on the map. I bet ya proud."

Keynes had said the next goal would be the Royal Sydney Show, Easter next year, held at the show grounds, just outside the City. He'd entered our two prize winning bulls and we were seeking more trophies. It would be a feather in our cap if the Keyneton stud could repeat the successes of Adelaide.

Keynes said, "Taking the fight to the enemy, that's what I reckon. And after what we've achieved we're gonna scoop a prize or two."

I had smiled. "Of course. Another challenge." I was trawling through my mind as to how Ernie would tackle it. Slimming the bulls down just a bit, that's what I had seen him do, taking them from prime show condition after a big event and then holding them at the lower level. "Just ticking over, young Richard. Ticking over."

The magic words had come from beneath the flat cap, the dog-end stuck to the lower lip. "Watch their condition. Maintenance ration, no more, no less. We don't want them looking like skeletons!" He permitted himself half a laugh. The dog-end went up and down. "Then bring them up again once the next show comes into sight. Onto that high protein diet I told you about." The fag wagged again.

Ernie Ford's words rang in my ears.

And it was time to reach for Freams Elements of Agriculture. Dad bought Freams for me when I went up to agricultural college. A "going away" present, he called it. It was the first thing I packed in my luggage for Australia. The Bible. And with the new challenge ahead, how glad I was. I'd turned to the section on cattle and their feed. I had gone straight to the graphs and charts, grabbed a sheet of paper and sharp new pencil and re-calculated the needs of the animals in this new environment; the starch equivalent, protein equivalent, the trace elements, the roughage. It was all there, Dad was right. A mighty volume.

"Just don't drop it on your toe, Son." Dad had smiled.

I didn't and it paid off. Credits in animal and crop husbandry and I topped my year in agricultural machinery. Plus City and Guilds. Dad smiled again. "That's what dads are for."

Freams was invaluable in calculating the feed levels for my bulls after the Adelaide show ring. It had told me how to calculate their weight. Their needs. What feed I had at my disposal... allowing for the poor quality of the Aussie hay... but utilising the bran, oats, kibbled maize and the rest Keynes had bought in. It didn't tell me anything about temperatures in the 120's though. Ernie hadn't either! Freams isn't a compendium for tropical farming!

Keynes had looked at me intently. "We will be all right in Sydney?"

I smiled again. "No problem. Another challenge."

Then there was the other hurdle. The lovely woolly appearance, used to such effect in grooming the bulls for the show ring in Adelaide – that had gone too. When the temperature tops the 100 degree mark, you don't need a fur coat!

"Not a problem", I said. "This is what I plan to do." And I told him.

But life is full of surprises... and this is what happened next.

I was feeding the bulls their new rations, scoop poised in mid-air over the sack of cattle nuts, bulls snorting and waiting for their tucker when Keynes was at my side.

"Got a moment?" John Keynes looked awkward. Why so flushed?

It wasn't an especially hot day, not more so than usual. "I've got bad news," he said.

"Tell me." I dropped the scoop. I was sure the white bull wondered what had happened to his breakfast. Keynes looked guilty.

"As you know, Colin is to be wed to his childhood sweetheart."

"Cutie," I said.

"Yes, Cutie. But they have nowhere to live."

The white bull, my Best in Class, Best of Breed, Supreme Champion, wanted to know what the hell that had got to do with him, with me for that matter.

"I can't afford to lose Colin, that's why I am offering him your living accommodation, until they find something more suitable, a house or a flat perhaps."

Anyone could see what was coming next. The white bull could see it. The flock of South Australia's State Emblems squawking overhead could. And it was starting to be obvious to me.

"I'm afraid I'm going to have to let you go. I've cancelled our entry at Sydney. I'll concentrate on Adelaide next year. I should be able to handle that myself."

The magpies squawked and raged. It sounded like they were saying, "Told you so."

"Of course I won't prepare the show cattle as well as you did, and I don't have your skills in the ring. But I've learnt a lot. I reckon I'll manage."

We shook hands, I waved goodbye to the kids, Mrs Keynes and Colin. He said, "Sorry ya going, mate."

I gave the bulls one last pat. I was getting good at saying goodbye to animals I'd grown to love.

I had drawn my pay. Still got a good few quid in the bank. I hadn't had much social life. A few girls to go out with. The twice monthly dance. The occasional rodeo with Ray and Kevin. The rest of my spare time was spent accompanying Ned Kelly on his exploits. So the money had just built up; I could always give it back if that would make a difference. But it wouldn't, I knew that. It was John Keynes and the Keyneton stud going forwards – minus me.

At least I had a car to get me home.

Home? Where was home? Big Alf's, of course. "Don't forget, Boy, there's the camp bed waiting when you're this way," the voice had boomed out; it was still ringing in my ears days later. He didn't mention the wonky leg on the camp bed that made sleeping an experience not to be missed. Nor the mosquitoes that shared my veranda and my blood. They'd become quite partial to what flowed through an Englishman's veins.

I had bought a new Volkswagen Beetle at the Royal Adelaide Show. Alabaster Grey, air-cooled engine, great for the hot Aussie conditions. Paid cash, still leaving change to fill the tank a few times over. I had wheels to get me back down to Port Adelaide, Big Alf, Billy and Mum's breakfasts.

I parked the Volksie in Alf's yard. It still looked like a whirlwind had hit it. "Oh it's great to see you, young Rich," said Mum. "You look like ya could do with a good strong cuppa." A huge mug was plonked down in front of me. "How's ya bum... any better?"

Mrs Alf had become my second mum. Second mums could ask questions about bums.

"Right as rain. I rode every day. Alf and Billy were right... couldn't have done the job without Black Horse."

"Too right. Some say the horse has had its day. Not in our world it ain't."

I was on my second mug when Billy rode in on Duke, scattering the chooks and dismounting like they do in films. Big Alf was right behind him in the truck. "Jeez, it's the Old Country back again."

Billy said, "Great to see you mate." He'd been growing his sideburns but still didn't look like Elvis.

Big Alf shook me warmly by the hand. I think it was only the bones in the little finger that were crushed this time. "And to what do we owe this pleasure?" He was still as loud as a fog horn. People in the City of Adelaide could hear. I was sure they were disappointed when they didn't catch my reply.

I shrugged and explained what had happened – somehow feeling guilty about how it all turned out.

"Jeez, don't feel guilty, Boy. He's a silly bugger, make no mistake. Losing ya skills. I watched ya in the ring. He'll never match ya."

Billy couldn't fathom it either. "Too right he won't. What the hell did he do that for?"

I was saying I was very grateful for their reassuring words. And their hospitality. "It's only till I get a job somewhere. Just to tide me over. Mum and Dad are coming out to see me."

"Ya mum and dad?" Mrs Alf was so pleased to hear. "That'll be great. I bet they're looking forward to seeing their boy again."

"They'd be happier if I had a job. I need to get something for a month or so, just to fill in until they arrive. Tide me over."

"Try the employment place up in Currie Street," Billy said. "They'll see you right. That's where I was headed when I bumped into Alf."

"Silly bugger said he was off to be a rock breaker, or summat."

"Rock singer."

"Anyway, summat to do with rocks. I said he could come in with me, I'd got room for a lad who wasn't afraid of hard work."

Mum said, "Billy's a gem."

Billy sat himself down at the breakfast table. A plate of bacon, eggs, chips, tomatoes, beans and steak landed in front of him. English all-day breakfasts were invented right here in down-town Port Adelaide. Billy tucked in. There was a picture of Elvis on the wall, "It's home from home," he said.

"Thanks for that, Billy," I said. "The Employment Exchange. Just something to tide me over." But first my all day breakfast landed in front of me.

"Have to build ya up for what lies ahead, Rich."


"Tide you over?" The man in the Employment Exchange scanned a list on his desk. His finger stopped half-way down. "On the land?" he asked. "And anything?"

"And anywhere," I replied.

He looked up, hopeful. A bare office. A fan in the ceiling stirred the stale air. The pot plant on its last legs. Finding anything positive in here would be a miracle but the man had done it. "Yorke Peninsula, live in, Jack of all trades."

I nodded.

He reached for a card in his index files. "You worked with

cattle?"

"I have some experience."

"And general farm work?"

"Yes, I'm happy with that too. Just a few weeks… to fill in."

He was on the phone to a man on the Yorke Peninsula. A distant voice came down the line. "Drive a tractor?"

The employment man looked in my direction for confirmation. I nodded back. "Fencing?" I nodded again. "Cattle? Yes he has some experience." He hung up. "You're on. Start Monday." He called me a jackeroo. Jack of all trades.

I thought I'd go north on Saturday calling into Keyneton and seeing the sister of the girl who thought I was a bit wet behind the ears. The one who I took to the Odeon to see The Girl Can't Help It. Nothing was said other than, "Thank you for an interesting evening." I don't know whether she didn't get on with Little Richard or Big Richard. Perhaps she wanted a root after all and all I gave her was a peck on the cheek and an ice cream cornet in the interval. And half that had melted in the heat.

But I thought I'd like to redress the balance so had dated her sister. We had hit it off and enjoyed each other's company. Especially in the back of the Volksie.

"Oh, I am so glad we met. I don't know what's wrong with my sister."

"Glad we met too." It was dark but I was sure she was smiling. I was too. Smiles all round.

So that was where I'd go, north to Keyneton, to see the sister that didn't think I was wet behind the ears. Then drive off into the night and kip somewhere in the back of the car and get over to my fill-in job on the Yorke Peninsula ready to start first thing Monday. Then Mum and Dad would be arriving.

But there is only so much smiling you can do in the back of a Volkswagen and I'd have to be a contortionist or a gnome if I wanted to take smiling to the next level. So, it was a big kiss and I was on my way. "Do keep in touch," she said. Another big kiss and the Volksie accelerated away leaving me dreaming of her lovely comfy bed and puffy white pillow. But I was a jackeroo now. They're tough. I was sure they slept in the back of Volkswagens all the time.

Two hours later and I'd found a quiet patch of land beneath the moon, the stars and a friendly Gum and I was trying to get the kip I needed so desperately after all that smiling. But that was easier said than done. A six foot lad and only four feet to stretch out in. Next morning I'd be four feet high and moulded to the shape of a Volkswagen back seat.

Then I discovered it got bloody cold at night. I couldn't believe a country that fried you at 12 o'clock mid-day turned round and froze you exactly 12 hours later. I was mightily glad when the sun made an appearance and the brown flat land emerged from over the front bonnet, the back bonnet and through the side windows. I could see a Caltex petrol station and café just down the road and headed off to thaw out with a hot coffee, bacon and eggs. I parked in the invalids' parking slot. So there were some benefits to being a cripple.

"You all right, mate?" It was Sunday morning and nobody else around so the guy behind the counter had time to chat. I could have clambered onto one of those swivel seats at the bar to continue the conversation but I'd have only fallen off. "Left ya walking stick in ya motor?"

Enough of this cheery banter, Volksie and I had better things to do, miles to cover.

Through typical Australian countryside in this part of South Australia; flat as a tack with dirt roads, straight and wide, and the occasional Gum giving that fleeting moment of shade. Not only the magpies but brightly coloured parrots, parakeets, galahs, flitted from branch to branch marking my progress. Past the next pool of shade... and the next... and the next... And then I found it. My jackeroo's job.

They were at church!

Well, that's what the note on the door of the shed told me. I turned into the yard; wide, dry, simmering in the sun, dead silent. Even the cows and sheep look comatosed hiding in what little shade there was. And where was the farm dog bounding out to greet me? Perhaps he'd gone to church too.

I stepped into the sunlight and tried out my legs again.

Then they arrived, the family. Youngsters, a girl and a boy, five, six year old maybe. Both stared, but I don't suppose they'd seen a jackeroo before. Not one that was bent double, four foot high and the shape of a car back seat. Mr and Mrs, they didn't actually stare but I had the distinct impression my early arrival was not that welcome. It meant looking after me until my official clocking-on time.

"You the jackeroo? We're Mr and Mrs not-expecting-you-until-Monday, Smith."

"Don't worry," I said. "I'm Richard doesn't-want-to-be-paid-until-Monday, Holdsworth."

"That's all right then. Now make yourself comfortable. Here's your room."

The room? The shed, of course. I removed the sign from the door, GONE TO CHURCH, and took up residence. As sheds go, this one was pretty good. You could almost say I'd not seen better. Brick built and there was a bed and a cupboard and a picture of a 1957 Cadillac Fleetwood on one wall and Jesus Christ staring at me from the other. So I had company of the highest order.

"Early start tomorrow, I trust."

"Early it is, Sir."

And it was. I'd never been a jackeroo before. Picking stones from the land, fixing the boundary fence and rebuilding a brick wall. An interesting and varied existence; I could understand the task of clearing boulders from the arable acres but the boundary fence had to be ripped up and re-sited half a yard from where it was because Mr Smith, Boss Man, got it wrong in the first place. I couldn't quite see the point; in a countryside where distances are interminable, what's a couple of feet this way or that? And the brick wall only needed rebuilding because his little lad wanted some entertainment and being God-fearing people you knock down a brick wall if that's what your kid wants.

"Not to worry, here comes the jackeroo, the Jack-of-all trades. I bet he can re-build it."

And I did. A crash course in brick laying was all part of Agricultural College along with ploughing a field, treating foot rot and castrating spring lambs. It might come in handy one day, the lecturer said. How could he possibly have known I'd end up 200 miles from Adelaide in a drought-stricken farm where the owner knocked down walls to keep his son happy?

I worked hard, from sun-up to sun-down. I gave my money's worth and I was rewarded. After the third week we took the day off and drove all the way down to Adelaide to hear Billy Graham, the evangelist. Getting me converted was the aim. I thanked Billy for the thought, but declined the offer of the life-changing experience – walking forwards to be blessed by the charismatic preacher. Dozens did, if not hundreds, so his time was not wasted even if this jackeroo wasn't one.

I'd have liked to shout out, "I've got to get back to building walls, moving fence posts and picking stones if you don't mind. Count me in next time."

A good few hours later and we were back home and still full of fire for Billy.

"Early start tomorrow morning."

"Yes Sir. Very early. I can't wait."

My few weeks are up and I drive out the yard, still wide, still dry, still simmering in the sun. But at least the brick wall is still standing. Mr Boss Man has given me the picture of the 1947 Cadillac Fleetwood as a memento. Jesus Christ stays put. The Cadillac is wrapped in brown paper and I put it on the back seat for safe keeping.

You are a nice man, I think. Even if I can't understand what makes you tick. Other things occupy my mind; I'm off to see my mother and father. Yipee!

"Welcome to Australia, Mum and Dad."

"Welcome to Oz..."

"Welcome..."

I am practising what I am going to say to the parents I haven't seen for a year.

The Volksie hurtles north, around the top of Gulf of St Vincent, then south down the A1 to Elizabeth where Dad is renting a house.

Elizabeth is an all-new satellite town basking on the plains north of Adelaide and under the cloudless Aussie sky.

"And welcome Son." Dad is sweating – it may be the first time but I doubt it will be the last – and Mum busying herself as they settle into their new home. Almost totally new, better than we had in England, by far. Mum will be house proud once the unpacking is done and everything in its place. That includes the table-cloth, the place mats, the napkins. "Now we'll have tea." At least this packing wasn't done in the haste of escaping London and World War Two. The tea pot is at hand right at the top of the tea chest.

Mum had packed everything in such a hurry back in the dark days of 1939 that half the necessities of life weren't found for a week.

"Tell me all about the country you have discovered, Son." Mum and Dad both want to know, and Dad asks about my work. "It sounds very exciting."

I gulp. There is only one way to say this. "I'm afraid the job with the Keyneton stud is finished. I no longer work there. I've been filling in as a jackeroo, a sort of Jack of all trades, up country."

There are no gasps from Mum. Dad doesn't drop his cup. The Holdsworths are not given to panicking. Even showing emotion. True Yorkshire grit.

Mum says, "That's a disappointment, Son."

Dad thinks it opens up lots of opportunities. "In your letters you said there are several stud farms in South Australia. You mentioned one owned by a John Parker... if I remember correctly, your champion beat his best."

I'm explaining that's not practical. "John Parker's stud is hundreds of miles away. Others almost as far. Australia is a big place. They are mostly scattered over the Eastern States."

"Well, we've come out to be near you. Hardly worth it if you are going to be two days' drive away."

Family Conferences were Dad's speciality... and one of Mum's cuppas to go with it. They always worked when I was a kid. We're enjoying one now and Mum and Dad have scarcely been in the country 24 hours. We're not even into our second cup and decisions are already being made.

"I'll go into Town each morning. I can try the Employment Exchange, Billy recommended it – I told you about Billy and Big Alf in my letters – it's where I found the jackeroo's job. But I'll also buy the morning paper, the Adelaide Advertiser and I'll scan the situations vacant."

"Surely there is more than just one morning paper, Son?"

"Just the one, Dad. But it's a broadsheet, quality, there should be jobs in there and some that might suit a lad with a certificate in driving a tractor and milking cows. And bringing out champion bulls."

"In Adelaide?"

We all three look at each other. This is something of a quandary. I have skills suited to the countryside, but to be near my Mum and Dad I have to be in the Metropolis. "Well, I'll go in each day and look."

Next morning the trusty Volksie fires up. We don't turn left towards the Bush but right into the City. We park in Light Square. I buy the Advertiser and my feet walk the streets while my eyes scan the columns.

"We require an invoice clerk," the advert reads. I am not sure what an invoice clerk does so better give that a miss. Insurance assessor; what does he assess? I also turn down the opportunity of being an environmental officer... then assistant anaesthetist. None of this is me at all. I'm just about to give up on city life when...

---

# TRAINEE AGRICULTURAL JOURNALIST

Journalistic experience not necessary –
training will be given. But a sound knowledge
of Agriculture essential.

**Apply: Ron Stewart, Managing Editor,
The Stock & Station Journal,
81A Currie Street, Adelaide.**

---

I look up. It so happens I am in Currie Street. I read the numbers on the office block. I am standing outside 81A. Is this fate?

No time to think, question, no time to wonder whether this should be my future. I am descending the steps, pushing through the glass and chrome door and asking, "Is Mr Stewart in?"

I am addressing a stern lady. She must be 60 if a day. Quite terrifying for a farming lad with straw behind the ear and dung on his boots. "You have an appointment?"

"An appointment? No I don't I'm afraid." I feel a bit silly; I didn't know this world needed appointments. "I have just seen the advert for a trainee agricultural journalist."

"I'll ask if he has time to see you." She turns on her heels. "Wait there."

I wait. Being below ground the office is lit by fluorescent tubes. No natural light. What a contrast to my open fields. And there's so little space; about the size of an overgrown tennis court. It's partitioned off into separate rooms; partitions shoulder height; there are heads bobbing up and down. Mainly female. Blondes, a few brunettes and they are pretty. Men in business suits, collars and ties; smart.

The rattle of typewriters. Phone calls. People in a hurry. This is a busy office. Not that I have been in an office to compare. And I've never been below ground before. Apart from on the Circle Line going to Australia House and getting my passport.

"Mr Stewart will see you now."

I am led in. This is the one part of the office with full height partitions so that if he says "sod off" it won't be heard by the rest. Desk, filing cabinets, drinks cabinet, bottle of Scotch. Coat stand, smart coat, pork-pie hat. Cane. These are the trappings of Managing Editors it seems.

Mr Stewart is businesslike. "Take a seat." I face him across an oak desk stacked with letters, papers and a pile of magazines. A tray that says IN can't take much more. "What can I do for you?"

A dumpy little man but with a sharp eye. Strong Australian accent.

I unfold the Adelaide Advertiser and point to the advert. "I have no experience of journalism but I did well in English at school."

"Which school?"

"Wallingford Grammar, Berkshire, England."

I had been told Aussies don't take much heed of English education, theirs being pretty good, but there is a definite lightening of the mood when I say Wallingford Grammar.

"And agricultural college, also Berkshire. I have a Diploma in Agricultural Management. And City and Guilds in Agricultural Machinery."

Do I detect a half smile?

"And I've just brought out the Supreme Champion at the Royal Adelaide Show. The Polled Shorthorn for John Keynes. And the Reserve Champion. We swept the board."

I have the feeling that if the pork-pie hat and cane could sing and dance they'd do a routine... right now.

But the reply is still curt and straight to the point. "I have other applicants. Leave your details with Miss Tuckworthy and we will be in touch." He waves a hand towards the door.

I am half-way there and he says "When could you start, Holdsworth?"

The Volkswagen Beetle drives with zest back up the North Road to Elizabeth. Dad's delighted, Mum too. But Dad has a suggestion. "The book you created years ago on breeding Beef Shorthorns, your labour of love, it is very impressive."

"I have it with me now. It goes everywhere with me."

I had written it back home in the dark winter nights of Upper Basildon. My homework Mum called it. I researched and recorded everything I could. The famous bulls, the herds, the family trees. And a neat cross-reference at the back. Plus an index, of course, so you could find any bull, any herd, any breeder. All in my best joined up.

"I am sure your Mr Stewart was impressed with what you told him. If he could see your book perhaps it would add to what you have said already, give you a distinct advantage. Why not phone him and ask if you can bring it in?"

Good old Dad! Sound advice! Not that I want to phone, not that I want to trespass on his time once more, that sharp eye, that cane and pork-pie hat. That desk piled high. But I know it is the thing to do.

"Could be your future, Son."

It is. "Welcome to the team, Holdsworth. If your work is as good as that book, then you'll be ok here."

Miss Tuckworthy even gives me a smile.

"I'd like to start tomorrow Sir, if I can."

"What's up with you, Holdsworth? Why Friday?"

"I've never worked in an office before. I'd like to get it under my belt before the weekend. Get the feel of it." I call him Sir as it seems to be going down well.

My wish is granted.

"Start when you like, Holdsworth. As long as it's nine o'clock sharp. Report to Ian Hawker, Assistant Editor."

Ron Stewart is reaching for his hat and coat. "Now you'll have to excuse me, early lunch." He stops as I reach the door. "By the way, Holdsworth. Don't try to teach us. We've been at this a long time."

Before I drive home, I buy a smart jacket, white shirt, tie and trousers. Harris Scarfe, the store that commands Rundle Street, thinks all their birthdays have come at once. Oh yes, and shiny brown shoes. I don't think my Cuban heeled cowboy boots are what's called for here. And it's time to give John Wayne back his hat.

Friday morning and the Volksie stays in the drive. I take the commuter train; I'm a nine to five man now. I have a briefcase and Mum's sandwiches, egg and mayonnaise, neatly wrapped in greaseproof paper. A pencil and Dad's dictionary. I am equipped for my new life.

The glass and chrome door to 81A swings open. It is more imposing than I remember. Trepidation on my part. But a smile from Miss Tuckworthy, perhaps she's not such an Old Dragon after all. "Come this way." I am led into the labyrinth of tiny offices, nooks and crannies, among the bobbing heads behind partitions and into a small, self-contained office. "Meet Richard Holdsworth, the new boy." She is addressing an elegant smallish man of about 40. Impressive, jacket off, tie loosened, sleeves rolled up.

"Take a seat."

He has a worried look as though something is about to go wrong. Perhaps the printing press has broken down. Or his top journalist fallen into a combine harvester. More likely he is contemplating bringing out a paper with a complete novice. Ian Hawker, Deputy Editor, is explaining how the office works, how we get out the paper every seven days. What role I will play. I try to smooth the worried look by sounding up with it all.

"You'll work for me; I'll give you your daily tasks. And Crump, too. Yes, Basil Crump, next door, sub-editor, he puts the paper together." He waves a hand in the direction of the next door office, over the partition. "He's the cornerstone of it all. He's invaluable."

Over the partition where this Basil Crump puts it all together is the main editorial office, the heart-beat of The Adelaide Stock & Station Journal. Compact to say the least, it can't be much more than four paces wide, twice that in length; this could be my home for the next few years. It is feverish activity in a matchbox. A far cry from the wide open spaces of Keyneton Stud or Yorke Peninsula, even the 345 acres of Home Farm, Upper Basildon. There's half a dozen desks, three men typing, one girl, and two empty desks, one being mine, and seat, my hot seat. I put my briefcase down. It looks pretty lonely there.

Basil Crump sits at the head of the room surrounded by papers; this is work in progress, next week's paper. And scissors, pots of gum, typewriter, two phones, or is that a third hidden under a pile of work in progress? He extends a hand. "Welcome, we've not had anyone from the Old Country in our ranks before. Call me Baz."

Giant handlebar moustache, gaunt face, but the eyes are smiling. This is a Flying Officer Kite type – and he is. Ex-RAAF, he flew over the Islands north of Australia keeping the enemy at bay. My fellow journalists include Jason Hopton, also RAAF, tiny tash, rosy cheeks. Such unassuming men who stood tall when their country needed them.

And then there's Ron Tremaine, about my age, sharply dressed, only been with the paper a few months. Finally Dick James not at his desk. "Don't you know the name?" Tremaine tells me he is big in Aussie Rules footie. "He'll be back when the leg is out of plaster.

North Adelaide ruckman." Dougie from the ship did warn me about this game. Now I know why.

Tremaine is the man about town. With two others he runs the Princeton Club, "the place to be seen" he says. He also tells me Patti Morris, Miss South Australia, is the girl on his arm when the day is done. The work day, that is, and Ronnie's world opens up.

I'll be tipping my cap to these men; didn't Ron Stewart say I have nothing to teach them, but everything to learn. And it might be wise to keep in the good books of Ron Tremaine too. But for different reasons. Miss South Australia, eh?

"I'll give you a quick tour," he says. I'm not sure if the smile is a warm greeting or his relief at being able to shed the ignominy of the most recent to join this team of scribes.

"This is the New Boy." I'm being introduced to Kay of Women's Section, brunette, slim and striking. "A knitting competition or two, a theatre review thrown in or book recommendation." Her smile is genuine and welcoming. Tremaine looks bored already. "And general chat... women's things, the little lady behind the man on the land." Lucky man on the land if they are anything like Kay.

Now it's into the main office and Heather Bessen. "Be nice to Heather and you'll get an extra slice of cake when there's a birthday in the offing." Heather is busy with phones, many phones, but I get a smile between, "Good morning. The Adelaide Stock and Station Journal here." Further down in the bowels of the earth is advertising. But Tremaine is fed up with the tour already. He's itching to get back to his desk and enjoy his new role of not being the New Boy.

I'm left in mid air; time to reunite myself with my briefcase, Mum's sandwiches, the pencil and Dad's dictionary. But Basil of the walrus moustache soon has my first task; no respite for the New Boy, time to see if I can string more than two words together. He hands me a sheet of paper with the words PRESS RELEASE across the top. This is from a company that manufactures disinfectants for the cow shed. "I'm counting on you to know all about cow sheds." I'm to turn it into something that will grace his pages. "600 words, top whack."

I turn to leave but more instructions are fired at me. "Take out the Public Relations bull-shit, I want the facts. Something for the readers to get their teeth into."

Yes, Basil was a fighter pilot in the war; seems he's still firing bullets.

My 600 words, minus the bull-shit, something the reader can get his teeth stuck into, has to be typed, of course. While typewriters rattle all around me, my 600 words are typed slowly, painfully, one letter at a time – sometimes two if my finger hits two keys by accident. Could be a crash course in something called QWERTY coming up. "You'll have to be quicker than that, lad."

And typed on slips of paper not much bigger than a man's footprint. Composing the piece is not difficult; typing it takes me past Heather Bessen's morning coffee. I offer my finished effort – my first effort in the world of words – to Basil the ex-fighter pilot. He has a couple of suggestions. A word here and a word there get shot down but the rest land safely. "Good man."

He marks it up for type face and style then sends it to our type setters; hours later it will come back as a galley proof and Basil will snip it up and paste it into his pages. And in a few days it will be on the news-stands for the whole world to enjoy.

## MODERN DISINFECTANTS FOR THE MILKING SHED

Years later, of course, computers will have taken over. The scissors, the pot of paste and the galley proofs will all have gone. Back home and Fleet Street replaced by Wapping… a revolution sweeping the industry.  But for now it's Basil in control and skills I will soon come to admire. And I will hang on his every word.

"Don't pat yourself on the back yet. Wait until you get to cover the intricacies of a wool sale or some Government legislation affecting the pastoral fraternity."

Basil is a pipe man just as Dougie before and Dad before that. It's knocked out while we talk. "So where did you get your farming experience?"

I explain. Agricultural College then on Home Farm for the Squire; Farmer Collins before that, in my school holidays, then bringing the cattle to Australia and finally Keyneton stud.

"I can see Ian Hawker having you down to cover everything on four legs that goes moo or baa, snorts or farts."

"I can milk the House Cow if that helps," I smile, Basil smiles. I think I'll need a touch of humour if I'm not to sink in this new world of mine.

"Well, with the footie star out of action you could relieve the pressure on Jason and Tremaine." The pipe gets filled. "Have to work on that speed though. And the spelling."

Good job Dad's dictionary is sitting on my desk. And a crash course in QWERTY is a definite.

Out of the gloom comes a voice. "Good morning Jason."

"Good morning, Peter."

"How are you today?"

"Fine. And yourself?"

Such pleasantries are my introduction to the Department of Agriculture, Ian Hawker's instructions for the day. "Hopton will take you up there – get you introduced to the men that count." And this introduction is into this gloom. Heavy oak doors, dark parquet floor, wooden panelling; even Old Father Time has nodded off.

"Don't be put off by the sobriety of the place," Jason tells me. "The swan is paddling furiously beneath the surface..." Jason gives a smile. "Good stories come out of the Department. It's a hive of activity. Especially the two guys I'm introducing you to."

Peter Angove is one half, he's the bow-tie man, Press Officer, fat tummy and tiny feet and a replica of my village headmaster who had the knack of getting the best out of us kids, me, Bobby White, Colin the postman's son and Minnow, the little lad.

Then there's the other half of the Press team. Colin is his colleague, tasked with dispensing the information to the four corners of the farming world in the State of South Australia.

I'd been primed as to what to expect a few moments before, striding along King William Street with Jason dodging the early morning shoppers. "Yes, it's a fool who doesn't listen to these guys. I get half my leads from them." Jason taps the side of his nose, the tiny tash twitches. "The boffins, research scientists and men in the field make the stories; these two prepare them for the Press."

Every step brings something new. And I'm recalling Ron Stewart's words, "Remember Holdsworth, don't teach us."

"I re-write what they give me, put my own stamp on it; only a lazy journalist changes the heading and calls it his own."

"I can't imagine anyone doing that."

"You'll be surprised how many do."

I'll do as Jason says. Make my stories my own, even if they are typed one finger at a time – and it takes a week.

"And if you don't and you're caught, Ian Hawker or Ron Stewart will be down on you like a ton of bricks."

"No tons of bricks for me, Jason."

And here's Colin now, the second half of the Press Office, a more youthful man, athletic even. No bow tie here, no fat tummy obscuring the feet he hasn't seen in ages. "England eh? What's the cricket like over there?"

Farming stories can come later. He's a dedicated club man. "You ever turn an arm, swish the old Willow?" He tells me he captains an eleven near Elizabeth, where Mum and Dad are renting their house on the sun-backed Adelaide Plain. "The local league. We're always on the lookout for fresh talent."

"I have been known to bat a bit. Sometimes they trust me to fill the boots of the first or second wicket down."

I don't say my last outing was with the Agricultural College at Maidenhead. The opposing side had a tall, lanky lad of a tractor driver whose fast wayward bowling was to be avoided if you valued your teeth. And pitches pock-marked with rabbit holes and mole hills guaranteed the local dentist never had an idle moment during the cricket season. I gave up filling those first or second men's boots when I saw this lad running in to bowl. Carrying the drinks tray was as close as I wanted to get to danger.

"As you're just up the road in Elizabeth, why not come along for a net one evening?"

"Any tractor drivers in your league?"

"No."

"Good, count me in."

Jason hasn't walked all this way down King William Street for a lesson in cricket. "Did you get the information on Pea Weevil, Peter?"

"I have it on my desk for you, Jason." Then there's Barrel Clover. "I've put aside the latest info on the new strain the boffins have come up with. I think it is something special. It will make a good story."

Colin the cricketer is not to be outdone. He has details for a story that might interest me, yes me. "Mastitis and you being the new Stock and Station Journal animal husbandry man." I hadn't thought of my role in that light but I'm happy to go along with it. Not my favourite subject but I know about Mastitis in milk-producing cows. I was taught at college.

"Yes, it could be of interest. Something to start me off. Thank you Colin. I'll draft something then run it across our Deputy Editor, Ian Hawker."

"And maybe we'll see you in the nets next week. Tuesdays and Thursdays. Just drop by. Match day is Saturday."

Jason and I retreat down King William Street still dodging the early morning shoppers. "Of course you'll need to get yourself acquainted with the conferences, the Department of Agriculture conferences; you'll need to get up to speed on them."

"Conferences?"

"Organised across the State, it's a way of bringing the latest info to farmers out in the sticks. There's usually a speaker or two in the morning, a lunch break and a couple in the afternoon." We cross the road and turn left down Currie Street. "Subjects that the local farmers have requested. And a question and answer session, of course." We stride on past Goldsborough Mort the stock agents. "It's quick-fire stuff at times."

Can I handle this? Mind you I sat through enough lectures at college and didn't falter. Some of the speakers rattled on and I got it all down. "I suppose you need shorthand?"

It's a knowing smile from my new friend. "Well, Hawker and Stewart would like to see us all get shorthand. They both have it as trained journalists, of course. They've offered evening classes...

I haven't taken mine up yet."

"Basil mentioned a course in typing."

"You could. On the other hand I got up to speed pretty quickly and I expect you will too. Baz will throw the work at you... there will be no shortage of time on the keyboard."

"Maybe Hawker will earmark you for the next Department of Agriculture conference. With Dick James away, we could do with some help."

I am earmarked. Cutting my teeth down in Mount Gambier is what Ian Hawker has in mind. He still looks worried and as the printing press hasn't broken down it must be the thought of me – no shorthand and one-finger typing – being relied on to fill a page or two in next week's paper.

"You know the ropes, Holdsworth. Hopton has introduced you to the Department. Conferences for you, starting with Mount Gambier next week." Ian Hawker goes back to the subject matter on his desk... then looks up. "By the way, I like your story on Mastitis. Come up with stories like that and you'll be part of the team."

I'm ambushed on my way out by Ron Stewart, Managing Editor, pork pie hat, cane, and flair, they're all there. "First assignment, Holdsworth? Remember, just get your head down. Don't try to teach us." He points the cane in my direction. "Big things expected of you, Holdsworth. Big things."

So this is Mount Gambier, deep south of South Australia. John Keynes was right – the grass is greener, more rainfall, close your eyes and it could be England's green and pleasant land. And I'm here courtesy of Peter Angrove with the bow-tie and Colin of the cricketing world – and the long drive down.

"How are we doing in the back?"

"Fine, thanks Colin. Fresh notepad and the sharpened pencil. Feels like back at college."

"Today shouldn't be too taxing." Peter Angrove sweeps the Holden into the car park of the local RSL. "Just three speakers. All manageable subjects and just what your editor wants, I'm sure."

These two have it all planned down to the last nut and bolt and I am handed a neatly typed set of notes covering Frank (Sheep Dips) John (Crop Rotation) and Andrew (beef rearing). Yes, it's all here. And it's all happening in the Returned Servicemens' League hall with a stage and testaments around the walls to the brave men and women who gave their lives to fight for freedom and the Old Country in two world wars. It's a respectful place for my first conference. What will they say if I fail?

The Department table is to the left and the Press to the right facing fifty or so farmers keen to learn the latest techniques in modern day farming. And the Press is me and my opposite number from the rival paper, the Chronicle. That's Jim McArdle, a bit up on me in years, a lot older in terms of experience. Jim, reddish hair, thick set and not averse to giving a helping hand.

Rival, Jim is not. "Don't worry, we'll swap notes at the end of the day. I doubt I'll get it all down either."

And before we know it, Frank is into sheep dipping, John into rotating crops and after a liquid lunch Andrew has drawn the short straw and is keeping them awake with his beef rearing.

"The graveyard pitch," Jim calls it. "I've known half the hall snore its way through the first lecture after lunch."

Hang on, what's this? Andrew has a secret weapon. We're just settling back to enjoy a slide show on all that's wonderful in the world of rearing beef when a scantily clad young lady appears on the screen. "Oh sorry," says Andrew with a look of feigned remorse. "Must have put it in by mistake." His audience is wide awake and chortling.

Back behind my typewriter and I endeavour to turn the scribble in my notebook into stories that might see the light of day. My one finger at a time... sometimes two if I'm lucky. The crash course in QWERTY is starting to pay off. A few phone calls to check the points I got on the day and I have the first story to hand over for Ian Hawker to approve. And, surprise, surprise, after a deal of editing, I get a half smile.

Perhaps I'm not that bad after all. In fact, I'm good enough to be pencilled in for the Kangaroo Island conference. "Two weeks' time, Holdsworth. They've got some good stories over there." I'll be flown over.

Meanwhile Baz is working on my first story from Mount Gambier. In 18 pt Times New Roman for my heading:

## CROP ROTATIONS FOR THE MODERN FARM

And my by-line, Arial 12 point:

### By Staff Reporter Richard Holdsworth

It's backs to the wall for the Aussie cricketers! The scribes in the dailies agree, and the sports commentator on ABC breakfast radio isn't arguing. "It's gonna be a long, hard day."

West Indies, the Calypso Kings, are playing Australia and it's the last day of the Adelaide Test and the Aussies are having a rough time of it. They must hang on to save a beating. It's backs to the wall, all right.

And for me, I have another new notepad and the freshly sharpened pencil as I listen to the air hostess announce it's seat belt time, and what to do if we come down in the briny.

I am on the flight to Kangaroo Island and as I have never flown before I am all ears. I'm not sure too many others have either. It's either that or our air hostess is a pretty girl (she is) and the prospect of bobbing about in the sea in a life jacket then blowing on our whistles to attract a passing fishing boat is gripping them.

The guy next to me looks faintly sick. "It's only a short flight," the pretty air hostess is saying. "My name is Amanda and it's Captain Tomlinson at the controls today... he's very experienced."

"That's a bloody relief," says the faintly sick man.

Out of Adelaide Airport, across Investigator Straight to Kangaroo Island. It will be another conference for the new journo from The Stock and Station Journal just as Ian Hawker promised. "Here's your tickets, Holdsworth. Get yourself to the airport by eight. The guys from the Department will be over there waiting for you."

We've taxied out, are sitting at the end of the runway, staring upwards and forwards until the pilot gets the OK, then we're bouncing along, the Pratt and Witneys roaring, and the man next to me gritting his teeth, and with a huff and puff Holdsworth is off the ground for the first time in his life. It's a faithful old Douglas DC3, the same type of aircraft used by the 101st Paratroopers on D-Day on their way to dropping out of the sky on the German forces in Normandy. I watched them go off as a kid. The sky was full of them. Mum and Dad and my sister, Ingie, watched too. "Will they come back Dad? My friends, Harold Heffner, Ben Panzerella and Robert Bowen. Will they come back?"

Today my trip is luxury compared to the men from the 101st; we've got proper passenger seats, the sick bag in the pocket next to me, and the pretty air hostess to tell us all about the whistle and the fishing boat.

The flight's just thirty minutes and we're over Kangaroo Island. Sweeping to the left, then right again, and those wonderful beaches, sand dunes, forests and sparse bush are right below us now, this place has got the lot.

And Amanda is promising us roos, koalas, penguins, wallabies, pelicans, a whole menagerie if we keep a sharp look out.

"Look down there." She's leaning across a seat, over a guy's shoulder and pointing out of a tiny window. "Off the southern tip… a whale passing by on its way to the Antarctic to give birth to its little one." She's probably making it up but it's good dialogue and the guy who she's been draped across isn't complaining.

And before we know it we're bouncing along the runway in a cloud of dust and the guy next to me is putting away his sick bag. "Haven't flown before?" I say. "I'm an old hand."

What we won't see on Kangaroo Island are foxes and rabbits. At the airport building, more like a shack really, I'm being frisked for Declared Weeds. "Don't want any of those buggers over here," says the man in uniform. The great advantage of being an island is if you haven't got them, you can keep it that way.

"Got any spuds?" he's asking now. "And don't say in my packet of crisps."

He's only looking for Potato Blight or some other nasty.

He clears me and I step out into the bright sunlight seeking the men from the Department. Do I hear him calling out, "Parsnips. Anyone got parsnips to declare?"

Back on mainland and the Test Match is coming to a tense conclusion. The Aussies have been holding out all day and the last pair is at the wicket, Slasher McKay and Lindsey Kleine are resisting everything Frank Worrel and his team can throw at them.

I'd spoken to Frankie Worrell the West Indian captain at the Adelaide Oval before the match, at the nets. I'd got in with my Press Pass. A gentleman if ever there was. He beamed at me. "So you think we have a chance?"

I smiled back. "You have a wonderful team that plays with the right spirit of the game."

But as I get back into Adelaide, Ken McKay and Lindsey Kline have held out and the West Indians have been denied victory.

I feel sorry for Frankie Worrell and his Calypso team. These Aussies are not called Diggers for nothing.

# Chapter 8

# I'm Standing Here...

I'm standing here, a sheep-paring knife in my hand, slicing off six inch lengths of German sausage, Mettwurst, while Johnnie Schumacher gets in the beers. It's the end of the sheep sale, the Big Sale, and the men, all two dozen of them, hats turned down against the glare of the sun and shirts stained with sweat are celebrating as only they know how – for this has been the best sale in years.

It's Yelta, up country in Northern Victoria, just over the border from South Australia with New South Wales to the north and Queensland further up. And it's the public bar, the only place to be in town

The Big Sale they called it; pens packed to capacity with no less than 33,000 woolly Merinos, and Johnnie has sold the lot in record time, the best auctioneer in the land. Now we're all taking time out from the day, slaking our thirst and satisfying our hunger – and I'm part of it.

They're an orderly lot, these men, although they've had their fair share of the beer, Carlton lager from Melbourne, and they're giving me my respect, the only Pom among them.

"The beer is warm over there, ain't it, Rich? Where ya come from. The Old Country."

I nod. Let's be honest, our beer is warm. In Dad's pub, the Red Lion, when I was a lad I watched some of the older kids taste the Symonds Best and Old Joe behind the bar laughed and all the others laughed, the constable and the village post-master, when they pulled faces and said how horrid it tasted.

In Australia, when I arrived, it was lager and it was chilled and slaked your thirst. "Yes," I nodded, "Pommie beer is warm, and I never did like it."

And they are laughing too. The sheepmen and the cattlemen in the Yelta bar. "Warm Pommie beer." And I don't need any encouragement to laugh with these men, the source of the background information I will need to write up my story when I get back behind my typewriter and fill the space Baz has put aside:

The aged ewes past their best, or shorn wethers two and four tooth, prime condition, their lives before them, being sold down south where there had been no drought and the grass is lush and green. I had it all down in my notebook. John Parker's year-and-a-half Merino ewes topping the sale at eighty-three shillings and seventy shillings for a pen of 700 sold to a grazier down in Victoria where it was said to have rained sometime in the past six months. Prime wether lambs for up to three quid from north of Wentworth. They'd gone to a sheep man in New South Wales, the Hunter Valley, with feed to spare.

Yes, Johnnie Schumacher had sold the lot, almost single-handed. In one afternoon as he always did. Even though Johnnie had his left ankle in plaster, up to his knee, from slipping and falling from the walk-way at Gyps Cross Abattoirs, Adelaide. The State abattoirs, out there on the road where I had been with Billy and Big Alf when I first got off the boat.

Worse could have happened; the steers in the pen below where he fell could have taken to him, taken his life even. Three and four year old cross-bred steers that had scarcely seen a human being in their lives out there in the Outback – apart from a few wandering Aborigines. But they could easily have finished him off. "Here, Rich, here's the keys. Get more Mettwurst out of the boot of the car. They're a hungry lot. I'll get in another round. More Carlton lager."

I go to the big Chrysler. The automatic that Johnnie can handle with the broken foot. In the yard out the back, in among the trucks and Road Trains that brought the sheep to Yelta. Now they're loading up, next stop their new owners or the abattoirs. There's still the dust, the flies and the heat. But I've got more Mettwurst and Johnnie is getting another round of beers. And I'll be talking to the stockmen, gathering the inside stories, the background to the day.

Staying the pace, hoping to impress Ron Stewart and Ian Hawker, getting the inside story if I can. The Big Sale, they say the best for ages.

*   *   *   *   *

Ian Hawker had been keen I cover it. "You know as much as anyone about livestock and I'm told you get on well with Mr Schumacher. You've been out with him before. Know his ways."

I'm not so sure about Johnnie Schumacher's ways. I only know of his reputation as being as good an auctioneer as you'd find in the State of South Australia. Some say the best.

"I believe he enjoys a drink after his day's work. With the stockmen, with the stock sellers, the stock buyers. Important you mix with them… get to know them. Get the inside story. That's why I've got you down for this job, the best man."

Ron Stewart had said the same. "Into their pockets, Holdsworth."

When our Managing Editor speaks, you listen. Pork pie hat and cane command respect. "I've heard good things about you, Holdsworth. But you've got a way to go yet. Get to know the people you're interviewing. Do you hear me, Holdsworth, into their pockets. That's where you should be."

So, here I am outside 81A and watching Johnnie Schumacher's new car come sweeping down Currie Street. The Chrysler Torqueflite; a bit like an aircraft carrier with a bonnet so big you could land half a dozen sea-going planes right there and still have space for the captain's tea party. A door swings open and I'm into the cavernous interior, sinking into plastic luxury, the best that Detroit money can buy.

"Automatic, Rich. The car, it's automatic, the only thing I can drive with this busted foot."

"Makes sense," I agree as we plough down North Terrace and out onto North Road, the Chrysler wallowing every time Johnnie hits the brake or swerves to miss a pedestrian that hasn't spotted an aircraft carrier coming his way.

"A few more weeks and the plaster comes off then I can kick the cat and the mother-in-law." Young Mr Schumacher smiles; he can't be much more than 30 yet with all that responsibility, the best auctioneer for miles around they say. Perhaps as good as there's been. The smile seems to say so, the cocked hat, the gait, the easy gait even with the busted ankle. "Yes, especially the mother-in-law." His eyes twinkle. "Just joking."

We're clearing the Adelaide suburbs; it's surprising how a couple of tons of steel, chrome and fairy lights eat up the miles.

"V8 under the bonnet, Rich. Top man's limo. You have to be in the company 30 years to get one of these. Or break an ankle. I went for the quick route." There's another chuckle coming from under that hat. He's still wearing it... I've never seen him without it. I wouldn't be surprised if he showered in his stockman's hat.

"I'm impressed, this V8," I say. "I've got a Volksie Beetle. This makes me feel like the President. I'll give a presidential wave next town we hit."

"And I'll get you the out-riders, band playing the Stars and Stripes Forever, a cheer leader and her team of lovelies. Sit on your knee in the back seat."

"Not unless the cheer leader and her lovelies are any good at covering the sale. Getting the details. I'll need as much help as I can get. Full coverage. The boss has strict instructions."

"I want full, in-depth coverage," Ron Stewart had said. "Nothing less, Holdsworth."

I'm not going to admit to being a bit overawed at the prospect of the next couple of days. I'd seen the advertising people and the ad: THE BIG SALE. YELTA. 31,000 HEAD. "I've covered others but nothing like this," I say.

"There's more, Rich. Thirty-one thousand's become thirty-three. But no worries. I'll give you the details over a jar when it's finished,

I'll see you right."

"Thanks Johnnie. The Assistant Editor says this needs to be done in depth. I don't know why but he seems to think I'm the man to do it. Sellers and buyers, prices, the lot. The stories behind each sale, why they are being sold, why the buyers are buying." I stop for breath. "And the Managing Editor, Ron Stewart, says it's about getting into their pockets."

And Johnnie's laughing again. "Bloody pickpockets at the Stock and Station Journal now. Bill Fagin and the Artful Dodger have nothing on you lot."

We're still laughing as we clear Adelaide then Elizabeth comes into sight, neatly laid out, pristine houses, straight roads all basking in the Aussie sun. It must be nudging 90 out there already. I bet it'll be nice when the trees grow a lot more and give some shade.

"How's your mum and dad faring? How are they fitting into life in Elizabeth?"

"Ok. Mum finds it a bit hot and they miss the green fields of England."

"It must be a shock coming straight over from an English winter."

"You can say that again. I left in a snowstorm, arrived to a 100 degrees. And Mum had packed my winter woollies."

The Chrysler Torqueflite ploughs on, the air-con oblivious to the outside temperature. Trees or no trees.

"You know the road?"

"I know the road."

Gawler, then Barossa Valley. We're soon skirting the lush valley with its Lutheran community, the wine growers, the delicatessen owners, everything tells us of the German background; they were early settlers but still talking of the Rhine and Moselle and their German ancestry to this day. I had met a few lads and lasses when I worked for Keynes and they had German forebears although nothing closer than third or fourth generation. But still giving the game away as soon as they opened their mouths. Combing their hairs while we were combing our hair.

The Chrysler sweeps into town. Johnnie Schumacher parks next to a sign announcing HOFFMAN MEATS. "I'm stocking up Mettwurst from old man Hoffman. They tell me it's the finest

German sausage this side of the Black Forrest."

"What's wrong with the tucker where we're staying? I hope I'm not expected to kip under a hedge and scavenge from a dustbin."

There's that sparkle in the eye again. "If the sale goes as well we won't have time for five star cuisine and serviettes tucked into our shirt fronts. It'll be the public bar and celebrating with the buyers and sellers. You'll be glad of your Mettwurst come ten o'clock tonight."

"Qualitaz mit zest," old man Hoffman says. He's reaching for a coil of sausage something akin to a fireman's hose. "Johnnie Schumacher, mein freund. For you der besten."

He smiles in my direction. "I zee you have das new trainee, Johnnie."

"Straight from the Old Country."

"We vill build him up mit za sausage."

I'd like to say something nice but I can't think of it. I could try "I'm a Beethoven fan." But Heil Hitler might go down better.

We retreat to the waiting Chrysler, the outriders and marching girls in the back. It's getting hotter by the hour.

"He seems a good soul."

"You're dead right, a good soul. And with a name like mine, I can't go wrong, can I?"

Johnnie's coil is under his arm. It looks as though it could spring out and get him any minute. "Quick, Rich. Lift the boot lid before it gets me." And we're off with dirt roads taking over from tarmac and into the real Australian red stuff, dust flying and even the air con is struggling to make an impression now. The sun scorches the countryside, catches the chrome on the car and makes the eyes water.

We're chatting about motoring, the Torqueflite against my Volkswagen Beetle, the contrast, how we could get a dozen Beetles in the back along with the cheer leader and her team.

"Jeez, I'm glad I'm not paying the petrol bill for this one," Johnnie says. "What's yours do to the gallon?"

"I can get 40, 50 at a stretch. I can go 200 miles on loose change but as the silly thing doesn't have a petrol gauge, you never know when the loose change is about to run out."

"What the hell do you do when it coughs and comes to a halt?"

"There's a lever down among your feet. Flip the thing over and you are onto reserve tank and away again. Mind you, while I was looking down finding the bloody lever one day, I nearly hit the bloke in front."

"Bang?"

"Well, almost."

We're coming up behind a huge livestock truck, a Road Train, pounding along, little faces of startled animals peering out. One, two, three trailers. Then there's the Mack prime mover somewhere up front in the dust storm it's throwing up.

"On its way to tomorrow's sale, I'd guess. They're coming from all over. It's not called the big sale for nothing."

We're level with the Road Train and its cloud of dust, gravel and stones. They ping against the bonnet and spit at the windscreen as we sweep past. Somehow you can't avoid wincing and putting your hand up to your face.

"You know something," says Johnnie, "I was driving in the Outback last year minding my own business when that happened." We accelerate past the Road Train and its load of little white faces staring out. "But I wasn't so lucky. The windscreen shattered and I couldn't see a thing. Hit a tree and cracked my head open on the dash, blood gushing out of a hole the size of an egg cup... or so it seemed."

"Bloody hell."

Johnnie's description is graphic – too graphic for me. I can see him there, head cut open, blood spurting out. I wouldn't make a St John's Ambulance man; I can't stand the thought of the red stuff, the stuff that flows through your veins and keeps you perky, even though I could be covered in blood and gore calving a cow, had been even as recently as last year at Keynes'.

"Bloody hell."

The heat, the blood, the egg cup. In my mind's eye seeing smiling Johnnie Schumacher's head cut open is more than I can bear.

And the late night last night; when did I get to bed?

"Don't burn the candle at both ends," my doctor had said the other day, looking serious, putting his gadget to my chest and listening while pumping up an oversize elastic band on my arm. "Not at both ends…you young men live life to the full."

Doctor was right. Burning the candle at both ends can make you pass out. Plus Johnnie's graphic description of the day, the heat, his windscreen shattered, his head meeting the dashboard with a crack.

I passed out at school once. Religious education on a hot day. Prayers then hymns, more prayers, more hymns, followed by Reverend Curd rabbiting on. Standing one moment, then I wasn't. I could feel the red stuff that keeps you perky draining from behind my eyes and everything going black – the next I knew and I was on my back and the Reverend throwing holy water at me.

"Good Lord, I thought we'd lost the little boy then." His face was so close to mine I could smell his breath. His whisky breath.

There was a positive side to it. While the rest of the school returned to more hymns, more Reverend rabbiting on in the heat of the day, I sat in the shade of an oak tree enjoying a rapid recovery.

And that's what I'm doing now. Except there is no oak tree and it's Johnnie Schumacher, ace auctioneer, leg in plaster saying, "Christ I thought I'd lost you then."

"Poor constitution," I say. I can just raise a smile. "Plus Rationing. Mum always said it was Hitler's U-boats sinking my orange juice. I thought for years he had it in for me."

There's smiles all round. "I'd better keep away from bashed heads. Anything else?"

"Got any holy water to throw at me?"

"What am I bid...? What am I bid...? Do I see seventy-five? Seventy-five, seventy-five shillings anywhere?"

It is the Yelta sheep sale, the Big Sale, and Johnnie Schumacher has got it under way.

"Look at the quality, gentlemen. Look at the condition, you won't get better from the renowned Avoca Para property of Mr John Parker. Start me somewhere, you won't get better."

Johnnie is in the pen, mixing with them, stick taking the weight off the wonky foot. Hat pitched at an angle, eagle eye catching any flickering sign, any flickering sign of a buyer.

"Seventy then. Seventy shillings. Seventy it is. And they'll make a lot more that that before you're done."

Johnnie Schumacher is warming them up, winning them over. Swivelling round on his good foot, scanning the crowd, searching their faces, 200 or more stockmen, in best stockman's hats, Cuban heels, smart for the day. This is the Big Sale. And dust, yes lots of dust. And flies, millions of them too. Heat and flies. But Johnnie's catching the slightest movement, the wink of an eye, the nod, the touch of the hat, he's the best in the business and not missing a movement here, a movement there. One that means more money for the pen in front of him. More for John Parker.

And he's got seventy. It's a start and that's all he needs. He's off and the bids come tumbling in.

"Seventy-two, seventy-two, seventy-three, four, five. Seventy-five. Don't stop there, gentlemen. The best year-and-a-half ewes you'll see for miles. Seventy-seven, eighty..."

I'm struggling to see the wink of an eye, the nod, anything out of the ordinary that will tell me who's bidding, who I will be chasing up for the inside story.

"Eighty-two and six pence. Eighty-two and six once, eighty-two and six twice... " Johnnie smacks his hands. "Elders Kyneton, Victoria." Alongside Johnnie Schumacher the guys with clipboards scribble the name. Elders, Kyneton, eighty-two and six. 310 prime year-and-a-half year old Merino ewes.

And we're moving on to the next pen while I'm still trying to catch my breath, keep up. Who the hell is buying for Elders in that neck of the woods? I didn't see a thing other than 200 or more stockmen with Sunday best stockman's hats, Cuban heels, dust and yet more dust. And the flies. Did the man in front waft his hand at a fly or did he just pay eighty-two and six for John Parker's year and a half old ewes?

I didn't see any other wink, nod or raised finger that secured the purchase and the story I need to satisfy Ron Stewart, his pork pie hat and cane. "Get in their pockets, Holdsworth. I'm trusting you. This is the big one."

We're on to a thousand head of year old ewes from Ned's Corner Station, Walter Kidman's property, and Johnnie is taking bids at forty-five shillings. "These are great sheep, don't be put off by the condition, we all know there's been no rain in these parts for yonks." Johnnie Schumacher looks round the throng, the throng heaving and shoving to get a glimpse of Mr Kidman's ewes, driven off the land by a lack of feed, shortage of water.

And there are heads nodding in agreement. These are good sheep. "Fifty-five, fifty-seven, sixty." There's a pause. "Come on gentlemen. You're robbers at this price. Ned Kelly has nothing on you lot."

There's smiles and laughter; Johnnie Schumacher is working well. He's got them up to sixty-five shillings. "Sixty-five, sixty-five and sixpence. Once, twice..." His fist smacks into the palm of his hand again. They've gone to New South Wales. But who and where? They might be on the way to the moon for all I know.

Johnnie had said he'd help me when it was over. Get me the details, point out the buyers and the sellers. "No worries, Rich."

The hard-grained, tough, rough men who make a living out of this alien world, the world of saltbush and sand, yet breeding, rearing and selling livestock where anyone else from Planet Earth would struggle. Fancy putting Ernie Ford in this world; he'd do more than chew on his dog-end. He'd swallow it!

But each to his own. Ernie was world champion back home... these men are champions here.

Back to earth, Holdsworth. You're not at Home Farm now. You're a journo in the Outback and entrusted with getting the full facts, the complete story, can't go home without it. Ron Stewart would murder you.

And onto the next pen…
"What am I bid? What am I bid here, gentleman?"

The sale's over. Record time, record prices. Later, in The Stock and Station Journal office I'll be conjuring up something about eager bidding, eager sustained bidding throughout the yarding of 33,000 sheep and the excellent prices paid. And I've got the buyers and the sellers; Johnnie Schumacher has pointed me in the right direction, the guy from Elders, Victoria, and the place in Hunter Valley, New South Wales. It's all down in my notebook, and I've talked to most, got good stories, interesting stories, and captured them on Kodak; Ron Stewart should be happy, will be happy – I hope!

Now we're in the pub, the public bar, and everyone is pleased, celebrating; it's been the best sale at Yelta for years and it's all down in my notebook.

I've got the Mettwurst and the sheep-pairing knife, and the keys to the Chrysler are back in Johnnie Schumacher's pocket. The beers are ordered and the men are lined up in orderly fashion. "Rich, cut the slices, cut a slice each, and the greedy buggers who want more will just have to wait."

And they are all laughing at being called greedy buggers. Stockman's hats pushed back now, faces grimy with dust and sweat, arms tanned by the sun, eyes still half closed against the glare of the day.

Johnnie Schumacher grins; "No pushing and shoving, you lot. And give the lad a chance. He's a Pom and he's new to our ways. He comes from a civilised part of the world."

I'm smiling and pleased at this introduction. And I'm doing as I'm told and cutting off six inch slices of the German sausage and the men are not pushing and shoving because they've been instructed. Taking their turn, not queue-jumping, with the beer in one hand and waiting eagerly for their Mettwurst.

And I'm slicing it up as Johnnie Schumacher says. Buyers and sellers, cattlemen and sheepmen, and there are big names amongst them. Some important men I must get to know if I want to go the extra mile for Ron Stewart.

"Into their pockets, Holdsworth."

There's Jimmy Downie from Alexandria Downs station, the Northern Territory, so far away it's hard to grasp, hard to contemplate if you are from a little village in England where London, 40 miles as the crow flies, is a day's excursion. But that's who I find myself talking to.

Alexandria Downs Station is more than 1500 miles from Adelaide, he's telling me. "Best part of two days on the road, if that's what you call a dust track. Do ya know that, lad? Two days' drive."

"No, I don't," I say. Nor do I know it's 600 miles the other side of Alice Springs and as far as I'm concerned The Alice is the middle of nowhere. Yes, 600 miles the other side of the Middle of Nowhere. More than 14 hours in a four wheel drive. And to get down to Yelta for this sale, to catch up with the market, see what's going on down south, he's been on this road, this dirt road, for two days. "I know, lad. I set out the day before last. Back the day after tomorrow. Five day round trip."

His station, they call them properties, is as big as England and Wales put together, almost four million acres. "That makes ya think, doesn't it? My small patch," he smiles. I smile. "How'd ya reckon that, lad?" asks Mr Downie.

I marvel at the sheer proportions of it all. Johnnie Schumacher had warned me he's one of the biggest station owners around, astute and successful. "How'd ya reckon that back home in the Old Country, lad?" he asks again. "Five day round trip and all for a slice of sausage and cold beer."

"We couldn't," I say above the chatter in the bar, the laughter, the talk about the sale, the success. "We couldn't come to terms with that back home. My Dad walked to the pub, the Red Lion, ten minutes for his pint. I don't think a five day round trip would come into it. Mum might complain."

Now he's telling me something else about the Outback I didn't know. "There're more camels in Oz than any other country of the world. Not many people know that either."

I'm not just surprised, more amazed. "They certainly didn't teach us that at village school. I thought the buggers were all in the

Sahara."

I'm making him laugh and that can't be bad.

Apparently the camels were imported for an expedition in the early days of the settlers. "Yep, for the expedition led by Burke and Wills, an Irishman and a Pom, years back. Ended in disaster. I doubt there's an Aussie who doesn't know it. They teach it in the schools." Jimmy Downie takes a gulp of beer to wash down the dust. "They were crossing the Continent, south to north, then back again. The expedition came to grief, just short of their goal, but they wouldn't have got as far as they did without camels."

It's my turn to take a gulp of Carlton lager. "No, Headmaster Williams didn't mention that. Not once. Taught ten times table and the Great Bard. But he didn't teach camels."

"When the expedition failed the camels were abandoned and started breeding. There were other imports, people saw their value in the Outback. Now we've got thousands of the buggers. Can't keep 'em down. It's like roos… too many bloody roos too."

I'm obviously saying the right things, nodding in the right places, even making him smile. Now I'm getting an invitation to Alexandria Downs Station to see for myself. "Bring your note book, lad, and that camera of yours. And plenty of rolls of film. There's plenty of camels to photograph."

I'm laughing at that and thanking him for the offer to see Alexandria Downs Station, his property, a million miles from nowhere. I wonder if Ian Hawker would countenance such a trip. Or Ron Stewart, the Managing Editor. The two days' drive up, stay, gather the facts, take pics, then two days back. I doubt it.

"What the hell's this, Holdsworth? Bloody camels." He'd lean on his cane, tilt the pork-pie hat. "If I wanted to see camels I'd get down to the bloody zoo."

"Next round coming up," Johnnie says. "It's on Goldsborough's account."

And with my beer comes a message. "In the car coming up you said about your boss, your Editor, wanting stories from the men that count. The big men, the station owners." I nod. "You've been talking to Jimmy Downie and there's John Parker over there. You don't get much bigger than that. Well respected too. Worth fronting up, I'd say."

I know of John Parker, of course. If nothing else, he had the Adelaide champion until I got Keynes' bull to knock him off top spot. I didn't meet him at the Adelaide Show, stud stockmen don't mix with the owners. "Well, he's the guy in the corner," says Johnnie Schumacher. "You just served him a slice of Mettwurst. And his sheep topped the sale."

I've got him in my sights. Worth fronting up, as Johnnie says. And I will, but not opening with the bit about beating his prize bull at Adelaide. Don't think that would go down well, especially as it's said he's a difficult man to get to, has a reputation for keeping himself to himself. Baz told me he's never been interviewed before. "Get to talk to John Parker and that'll earn you a few Brownie points with Hawker and Stewart."

And I'm about to try. "Mr Parker, I'm from the Stock and Station Journal. Have you got time to chat, answer a few questions?"

He looks down on me with presence, authority. Don't be fooled by the sleeves rolled up, sweat-stained stockman's hat, belt holding creased trousers, today he's been working. Out there in the heat and dust. Offering pens of the best sheep.

But with presence. Authority.

It was said he was stopped by a speed cop on his way to Adelaide one day and as his Bentley came to a halt he enquired of the copper, "Do you know who I am?" And the copper didn't; just simply waved him on wishing him a good day. Yes, the man standing in front of me now, the man I am asking if he'll answer a few questions, asking for the interview he's never granted before, carries authority.

But he has time. "You covered the sale today? What did you think? Do you reckon it went well?"

I'm grateful for the positive response. "Well, yes, of course. It was very successful. Buyers from all over the south, Victoria, South Australia, New South Wales. They came from all over."

"The best Yelta sale for two years, at least."

"Yes, so I was told."

And his sheep topped the sale. The pen of 310 one-and-a-half year old Merino ewes, March shorn, knocked down at eighty-three and six to Elder Smith's rep in Victoria. I had found the guy who bought them and had it in my notebook, a Peter Girvan of Taradale, down at Kynton. "Elders were lucky to secure them. The bidding was keen."

He's impressed with my knowledge, my thoroughness in the details I've dug up and got down in writing. "You must come out to the property some time. Tomorrow even, if you are not heading back to your office. It's Avoca Para on the Wentworth Road."

"I'd be very happy with that," I say. "Out on the Wentworth Road. Ten-thirty ok?"

"Ten-thirty it is. My overseer, Jack Gill will be with us. We'll show you round."

Johnnie Schumacher lends me the Chrysler. He has business to do in the Goldsborough's office checking the details of the sale. Making arrangements. "Paperwork," he tells me. "The bane of my life."

"I'll see you back in the office late morning."

"If you survive the interview. I'm told Parker doesn't take prisoners."

What's that expression, a hiding to nothing? But nothing ventured, nothing gained and he was more than civil in the pub last night, enthusiastic even, so here goes. I slip the Chrysler into DRIVE, press the accelerator and we're off and 380 horse power takes over. Cripes this is a doddle... bounding along the dirt track, dust spiralling out behind. No problem finding the Wentworth Road – it wouldn't have arrived this quickly in the Volksie!

It's as dry as the road up from the Barossa Valley that Johnnie and I travelled the day before last. There had been patches of green, emerald green, where the row upon row of citrus fruits were irrigated. But without the water from the Murray there's nothing but dust and scattered Saltbush now. But that doesn't take into account a man such as John Parker.

Turn off the main road, down a graded track, it's now as green as an English meadow on both sides. The Chrysler glides to a halt on a gravel driveway between trimmed hedges and grand house; John Parker greets me, not actually tea on the lawn but we climb the steps into the cool of the house and there it is laid out waiting.

Come out Jeeves!

"Thought we'd have tea in the cool. Too bloody hot on the lawn," he smiles. I agree. And while it is poured I get Avoca Para on a plate… I don't even have to ask the questions. And I reckon the smile is genuine. The guard is down. No need to fear this man, I can hold my own.

I'm handed my cup. "It was the usual arid land before we took over, I'm sure you're up with the conditions in this area. Just ten inches of rain a year if we were lucky. Often we weren't. Sugar?"

I stir.

"That was 15 years ago… dry arid land. We had to do something."

He did, he has. Now it is this lush and green pleasantness my eyes took in the moment I turned off the main road and this resulted in the high productivity that produced the sheep that topped yesterday's sale. Breathtaking. Yes, breathtaking… I was already working out what I'd say, what I'd get down on paper and what Baz would set in type:

---

*In 15 years of ownership of "Avoca Para" station, Wentworth, New South Wales, Mr John Parker has wrought a transformation in the almost waterless and valueless back paddocks to the present prosperity under heavy sheep and cattle stocking, by a bold, imaginative, yet not costly…*

**…use of Darling water**

---

We're onto a second cup and I've still more to learn. I'm scribbling. John Parker took two properties, Avoca and Para, and welded them together to make the 270,000 acre holding he has now.

"Goodness, 270,000 acres. The man I worked for back in

England, George Meredith Hope, the Squire, had just 375 acres. That was recognised as a large property for that part of England."

We smile at the contrast between the two.

"Well, Avoca Para is hardly big for Australia as you must be aware. I saw you talking to Jimmy Downie last night. That's what you call big. A sight bigger than Avoca Para."

We are sitting in the cool of his homestead, the opulent green sward of grass, clover and Lucerne stretching out from the end of the veranda down to the snaking line of Gums marking the banks of the Darling. I can't help but admire everything I see.

"Avoca and Para, two typical light rainfall runs and our only assured water supply coming from the Darling." He indicates towards the line of giant Gums. "The paddocks had to rely upon this meagre rainfall. As I said, just ten inches a year. We were no better than any other property in the area when I arrived, and even that couldn't be relied upon." He takes a breath. "Wouldn't always fill our dams while artesian bores were equally unreliable in their supply."

I nod. If I didn't know about the struggle, about the lack of rain by now I never would. "I'm fascinated to hear how you overcame the problem – I'm sure it would a great story for the paper."

"Well, you would think the River Darling would be the answer. But in this instance the river simply added to our problems."

How the hell can that be? "Surely the Darling is the life-blood. Surely, your stock use it as their source of drinking water."

"You're right, under normal circumstances the river is life-giving. But Richard, the River Darling has an enormous seasonal variation in its flow. One day it is tipping over the banks, a month later a mere trickle. You aren't aware and why should you be?"

I agree, I'm not aware.

"Combine this with steep, slippery banks, and it is a death trap for our cattle and sheep. The only thing to do was take the water to the stock, not the stock to the water. Pumps and a grid of pipes feeding the whole property."

Of course. Simple when you think about it... and the initiative and drive. This could be a good story, a great story, I can see the smile on Baz's face. I already have it mapped out in my head what the typewriter will record next:

> **"In a bold, two-pronged move involving full utilisation of water from the River Darling, Mr John Parker has ensured water and feed for sheep and cattle. Water from the Darling, whose western bank fronts the run, is pumped through more than 60 miles of piping to the back paddocks so that his stock has no more than three miles to walk for water...."**

"Time to see the property."

I can't wait.

John Parker and his overseer, Jack Gill, walk me through the paddocks. Explain it all. They are proud of what they have achieved. I just hope my farming knowledge – Australian farming – does them justice with what I'm going to write.

Jack Gill shakes me by the hand. A tall, willowy man, leathery skin, burnt by the sun and with a handshake like a vice. "Glad ya enjoyed our chat."

John Parker smiles. "Come again. Any time you're up this way." His handshake tells me he means it. I've been the only journo to get to interview him.

"Filled a notebook, Baz. And I got that elusive interview with John Parker."

Baz swivels in his chair. "You got to John Parker? The John Parker?"

"I tackled him in the pub after the sale. He invited me out to the property next day."

Baz's eyebrows show he's impressed. "Better get into Stewart's office. He'll want to know. You'll get medals for this."

"A pay rise will do."

"Don't push your luck, boy."

I hand over a good story. Two good stories in fact. The sale and the interview. "And I hope you can use my pics?"

Baz will give them a fair crack of the whip. "And the shot of the Yelta sale yards. Looks good enough for front cover."

I watch as he works at it, my words, my pics, snipping and

pasting, and making space. Using my pics is a bonus in more ways than one. Pay packet is just 17 pounds a week. It means I have to watch the pennies if I am to get by and still have a life at the end of the day. There's extra for every pic used – seven and sixpence – and a whole guinea, 21 shillings, if you get the front cover.

"I'll see what I can do for you."

My eyes brighten.

"You're a genius, Baz. I'll remember you in my will."

"The pub will do."

"You'll have to wait. I'm off to see Ron Stewart."

# Chapter 9

# Don't Disturb the Spirits

"Prospecting," says the guy from England leaning, relaxed, against the bar as though he's a regular. "For opals mainly. Up the track in Oodnadatta, a place called Skull Creek. You been there?"

"'fraid not."

I am suspicious of skulls, but don't tell him. He's stocky, muscular, looks like he can handle himself if it came to a fight. I could sound a bit namby-pamby if I said I don't like skulls even if only in place names.

He smiles, a good smile. "Daft name, Skull Creek. And it's barren, I've seen nothing like it before and I've been to most places. And it's miles from anywhere. Bloody hundreds of miles."

I'm in a tin shack of a pub just south of Alice Springs. Passing through on my way back to the office after gathering a story on the drought that's gripping the heart of Australia when Nick, for that's his name, fronted up. "Don't hear many Pommie voices up this way. Bit too hot and a bit too bloody harsh. It's not Oxford Street and it's not Piccadilly bloody Circus."

He grins. I grin. He's bang on. Hell, it's 115 degrees in the shade if you believe the thermometer hanging just outside in the shade of the veranda. I saw it as I came in. But how high it was out in the open, where I'd just been, is anybody's guess.

We introduce ourselves. "Ron Nicola. That's where the Nick comes from. And you're Dick Holdsworth, from the Stock and Station Journal. Never bumped into a journalist before."

"It's no big deal," I say. "My background is farming and I scraped through English at school. I can plough a furrow, reap a field and ride a horse – just. And I can't spell."

Nick laughs again. "If I were an Aussie I'd say, 'Good on yer, mate.'"

I think it's better than being thought of as a namby-pamby by the guy who's taking a break from working at BHP, the Broken Hill Propriety. "Having a go at opal mining. On my lonesome. They say it's good for your soul being on your tod once in a while."

I know BHP, is there anyone in Australia who doesn't? It's the biggest mining company in the country, one of the biggest in the world, a huge employer, a huge contributor to the Aussie economy.

He's a foreman plant operator, well paid but reckons it's not something you can do seven days a week, 52 weeks of the year. "And stay sane," he grins again.

Nick says he's done a bit of writing himself. "Nothing special. Just jotted down a few stories I've picked up on my travels. If I was another Will Shakespeare I wouldn't be breaking my back scratching around for opals at Skull Creek I can tell you."

"Well, I expect you have loads of tales to tell. The life and times of Ron Nicola. Skull Creek and all."

We laugh together. "It's nothing special," he says again.

A bloke in a stockman's hat, sweat-stained shirt and Cuban heeled boots, kicks the jukebox into life, feeding it from a handful of shiny zacks and we're treated to the House of the Rising Sun whether we like it or not. "That's the place to be, Tex," he calls out to the man behind the bar. "That's the bloody place." I'd call him a stockman; Nick calls him a Ringer. Whatever, it seems he'd like a slice of that sinful house in New Orleans full of gamblers and women of the night.

I can't think of anything further from this scorched outpost of Australia than the lush Deep South of America with its house of ill repute. But there's another zack and another time around for the Rising Sun. "I'm going back to New Orleans to wear that ball and chain..."

"Wish I bloody was," says the Ringer. "Goin' back there, mate. Better than this forgotten freckin' place you've got here."

Tex nods. "You don't have to stay, Randy, it's a free country. But you'll need another beer before ya get under way. They tell me it's a hell of a way to New Orleans."

"Escaping, that's what I was doing," Nick says. "Up there in Skull Creek. And you never know I might find the big one, the opal, the opal to beat all opals." Nick smiles, a nice smile from a man who doesn't mind the tough life. I reckon Nick could look after himself in a street fight and I certainly wouldn't want to get involved unless he was on my side... or I was on his.

"I suppose I've been called a rough neck from time to time." There's that glint in the eye again. "I was a paratrooper in the British Army, a Red Beret, got out after seven years and thought I'd see a bit of the world and started off with Oz. I'm still here years later."

Here's a toughie if ever there was, prospecting for opals in this desolate environment and a Red Beret before that, the elite. My brain is wondering if there is a story here, if not for the Journal, perhaps for another paper or a fancy magazine. Or for my memoirs, if I ever write them.

"Yep," says Nick. "Too many years leaping out of an aircraft, hitting the ground, learning how to kill, how not to be killed."

All I'd done by that age was go to agricultural college, learn to milk a cow and drive a tractor. Think what I missed!

"ANZAC Day coming up," says Nick. "I could get down to Adelaide, don my kit and march. I might get more recognition than I did back home in the UK. The Aussies respect those who fought for their country. They make a big thing of it. "

ANZAC Day. At least a couple had come and gone while I'd been in Oz. I hadn't even given it a thought. I'd just got my head down and worked on. I was in the Bush. Too busy, I suppose.

But I'd like to hear more from Nick and if I'm going to I need to call up the barman; beat him to reaching for his wallet.

"Same again, mate?"

"Same again."

Then Nick's relating a tale that I had scarcely expected, one that makes the hairs on the back of my neck stand up, about something that chilled his blood, and chills mine too. Days later, looking back on it from the leafy suburbs of Adelaide, I'd scarcely believe what I heard. The tale of the Aboriginal spirits, the Min Min lights, Nick called them.

"Chilled your blood," I say. "What's Min Min lights, anyway, Nick? And what the hell would chill your blood?"

He looks round almost as though he's expecting someone to be looking over his shoulder or listening from the shadows. Someone catching the tale of the Aborigines and these funny lights. "As I've said, I was miles from anywhere… hundreds of miles." Nick's voice is even quieter now, almost a whisper. If the juke box hadn't stopped churning out House of the Rising Sun I doubt I'd have heard a single word. "A barren place, deserted place," Nick whispers. "I wished I'd never stumbled across it. Not on my lonesome, anyway, on my tod. I'm not a big city man but I'd have swapped Oxford Street or Piccadilly Circus for that godforsaken place any day of the week after what happened to me."

Fresh beers are in front of us. I take the first gulp. It's so cold it looks like frost on the glass. "Well, what did happen?"

"It was an area I'd never tried before, reckon no-one had. It was Skull Creek I learnt later." Nick takes his own gulp. He says it was a bit daft. Not only was it off the beaten track and in a place that might not see another white man for ages but he started to realise that it was ancestral land of the Aborigines, sacred land, and this made him feel edgy.

"You see, I'd met this old Aborigine up in the Gulf of Carpentaria, Northern Territory. You know it?" I nod although I only know of it from the map, had never been there.

"Northern Territory, Macarthur River. I was croc shooting when this Witch Doctor stepped out of the bush pointing his spear at me, at my rifle, made me jump. But it seems he was only protecting the women and children of the tribe, not that I knew it at the time." Nick takes a quick look round again. "King Wally. What a name."

I look round too. I'm not so sure I want to be caught talking about this Witch Doctor with the funny name. "Did you say King Wally, Nick?"

"Yep, can you believe it? Witch Doctor to the tribe."

I was trying to visualise Nick's Aborigine, protecting the women and children. The first Aborigine I had ever come across was when I arrived in Australia and I was driving through the Bush and saw one thumbing a lift at the side of the road. Just him, no other, no-one to be seen for miles, just saltbush as far as the eye could see, but the moment I stopped, half a dozen women and children materialised as if out of the ground and climbed into my car.

Nick grins. "That's them. They are masters at appearing from nowhere. It's part of the magic."

I tell Nick how it was only my Volkswagen Beetle, my first car in Oz, a great little family car but not a family of half a dozen. "The poor old Beetle struggled to get going again and when it came to a hill someone had to get out and push."

We're both laughing now. Nick can see my plight. But at least my hitch-hikers weren't like Nick's Aborigine, King Wally, nothing more than a loin cloth and bushy beard to cover his credentials. And a bloody great spear.

"He was about the tallest bloke I've ever seen. Body paint covering the parts his loin cloth didn't. No shoes, no shirt, trousers and no hat, just the spear."

"So, what happened next?

Nick the ex-paratrooper, my new Pommie mate, takes another gulp. "That's the point, we became friends, good friends, and he told me about the Min-Min lights, lights of their ancestors, spirits not to be tampered with. And that's what chilled my blood the other night. Where I was camping up there in Skull Creek. Later I learnt it is where the Abos were supposed to have killed and eaten the early Chinese prospectors looking for gold and opals. That's where the name came from... the skulls. Frightened even a toughie like me."

The jukebox remains silent and Nick's voice is even quieter now, a quiet whisper. "I had my Land Rover for company, of course. And gun, I always carry that. Any good squaddie does. Not that it would have helped for what I was about to see."

"Well, what did you see?"

"The sun's going down and shadows starting to stretch out across the land, the few bushes scattered around, a Ghost Gum here and there and the jagged cluster of rocks I'd picked for company when I'd set up camp. It was then that I noticed it – the shadows on the rocks highlighting protrusions, leaving clefts, markings only man could have made, sinister markings with sinister meanings, I know that. King Wally told me."

A few markings on a rock wouldn't worry me but it's causing Nick to grasp his beer now, his knuckles going white – Nick's Witch Doctor had given him some insight into secrets I knew nothing about. "Yep, that's right, taught me what they meant, how tribal Song Lines criss-crossed the Outback, Tjuringas, thousands of years old, and I was in the very place they met." Nick's looking over his shoulder again.

The Ringer is preoccupied with his beer and Tex is polishing glasses at the further end of the bar. "Mythological spirits could inhabit the area." Nick's voice is still a whisper. "I tell you, Rich, the bloody place was haunted."

We're both looking round now. "Don't laugh... I believe it."

I'm not laughing. When a man who's earned the Red Beret, has leapt out of a plane at 2000 feet with a 90 pound kit on his back, plunged his bayonet into a German soldier – even if it's a stuffed one that hangs limply on a rope like a sack of spuds – then you don't laugh.

"Towards the water hole came flickering lights like fire flies, incandescent, enacting some sort of wavering dance. Min-Min lights, King Wally called them, souls of the dead."

My turn to clutch my beer. My turn to have white knuckles. I'm hoping he's going to tell me it's all a dream. "Perhaps you were mistaken, Nick. A trick of the light as the sun goes down, or something else. There had to be a rational explanation."

"Wish there was, Rich. Wish there was. I thought if I blinked hard enough they might go away."

"And?"

"They didn't. When I finally opened my eyes they were even closer. Much closer. I couldn't believe it. I was rooted to the spot, sweating like hell."

I could see it written on Nick's face, the fear. Can still see it.

"I tell you, Rich, I was terrified and it wasn't down to the hard stuff either. Never touched a drop. Stone cold sober. And bloody terrified."

And this fear is getting to me too. I could have been there. Only the other night I was in the Bush, the blackness, in the staff car, the latest Holden FB, two-tone paintwork, flash wheel trims, chrome bumpers, the lot. None of that would have saved me. I could have taken the wrong turn and stumbled across these Devil-Devil lights of Nick's. I'd done it once already, a wrong turn; it's so easy out there in the dark, on a dusty track, no signs, nothing. Just the blackness. One more wrong turn and I could have been in amongst some of those flickering fearsome lights. And no sharp-shooting gun to defend me either.

"Cripes, mate, a gun wouldn't have been much use. Not against an enemy you couldn't see. Not against what was coming at me through the night."

Nick decided the only thing to do was take the battle to the enemy. The Min-Min lights were almost upon him, dancing, silent, engulfing him. The souls of the dead Abbo warriors. "I turned the radio to full volume, Shake, Rattle and Roll, starting my own dance round the camp fire causing as much rumpus as I could, scarcely daring to look in the direction of King Wally's Devil-Devil lights. And when I did, thank Christ they had gone, vanished, like magic."

I'd have found this hard to believe if I hadn't heard similar stories back in the office from Baz. These funny, frightening Abo lights. "Time for another beer, Nick. Now that it's all over."

But it isn't.

"Worse to come, Rich. I'm dead tired and bloody hungry too. I thought if I stirred the fire and generated a few flames it would keep the ghostly lights at bay."

Nick rubs his chin. "I could also boil the billy and get something in me. They teach you that in the Army." My dad had said that too. From his days in the Air Force I suppose. So it wasn't hard to believe what Nick was telling me. "I made myself a mug-full and was just about to take the first gulp when the night air was pierced by the chilling cry of an animal in distress, as though being tormented, tortured, sacrificed even. Maybe a dingo, I dunno. They say your blood runs cold... well mine did."

The Ringer has returned to the juke box and giving Fats Domino a lease of life on the honky-tonk piano. Blueberry Hill is where the Ringer wants to be now and you can't blame him. I do too.

It's still as black as pitch where Nick is, apart from a few dying embers from his fire, and he's downed his tea. He's just starting to relax and the cry from the dingo is no more, he's got rid of the Min-Min lights, climbed into the Land Rover and locked himself in; time to grab a few well earned moments of sleep. "Then suddenly I'm aware of the fire, embers flaring up, sparks flying into the night sky. This is not possible; it was dead a moment ago, I'd seen to it." Nick looks petrified as he relates his tale.

"And that's not all, Rich, there's something else frightening the daylights out of me…there's a shadowy figure appearing from the incandescent sparks… like a Phoenix rising out of the flames, weaving, dancing, gesticulating, I couldn't bloody believe it. How could it be?"

Rough Neck Nick, paratrooper, man of steel whose side I want to be on if there's a street fight, punches thrown, teeth knocked out, is telling an unbelievable tale.

"Bloody hell Nick, are you serious?"

"Never more serious in my life, mate. I'm not joking. It's the truth, believe me. And I hadn't touched a drop in weeks."

I don't doubt him. Blueberry Hill sounds pretty simple stuff from where I'm standing, and where I'm standing it's as if I'm at Nick's side sharing his fear of the incandescent Devil-Devil figure whispering through the flames, "Be careful Cousin. This is the Home of My Ancestors.  Be careful…"

It's next morning and Nick's just glad to be alive; but that's not all. His belongings are strewn about the place like some poltergeist has been at work. "My gear is scattered everywhere, mate, clothes, boots, billy. Everything."

"Cripes, Nick. What the hell next?"

"I didn't hang about, Rich, I tell you, I grabbed everything I could lay my hands on and threw it in the back of the Land Rover and I was away. Getting to hell out of the place. Fast as I could."

Our glasses are empty again. After a tale like that I should be buying Nick another. And the Ringer. Even Fats Domino if he walked in.

But it's Nick who's calling the barman over to break the spell.

"Funny thing is, as soon I walked in here Tex handed me my binoculars. In the mad rush to get out of the place I must have missed them. As I say, I wasn't hanging about."

"Your binoculars turned up here? In the bar?"

"Tell my Pommie mate, Tex. Tell him you had them, I'm not making it up."

Tex shrugs his shoulders. "An Abo came in, just walked up to the bar and put them down. Said the owner would pick them up

155

later, turned his back and walked right out." Tex shrugs again. "I reckon those buggers know something we don't. And we're suppose to be the sophisticated ones."

The only word to come off my tongue is the good old Aussie one, "Strewth."

"It has taught me a thing or two – prospecting is a mug's game, out there anyway, Skull Creek. And even if I found wealth, what would I do with it? I'd rather have my sanity."

After that I couldn't agree more. "And number two?"

"Respect for the natives, the Aborigines. As Tex says they may not be sophisticated like us, but they have an insight into things we have no idea about. They see things we can't; they feel and hear way beyond our comprehension. And they are in touch with a spirit life we could never grasp."

I had been told how Aborigines had uncanny powers, how they could track people down even where there wasn't a track; on tarmac or across concrete, they could do it, Baz said.

"Black Trackers, Rich, that's what they call 'em. I knew how King Wally could track people, track anything, the ability handed down from his father and his father before him." Nick takes a gulp. "They have an insight… we'll never understand."

I'd love to know about this. A whole new world, the Aborigines and their life, their magical life. "I'd love to find out more, Nick."

"Well, as I said I've done a bit of writing and I did this Abo story that might interest you. It's back where I'm staying – I'll let you have it next time we meet. It's based on real life. And you never know, you might be able to use it one day."

"ANZAC Day," Baz said. "You won't see me behind my desk, Jason neither." Baz was serious. I knew ANZAC Day was regarded as a National holiday throughout Australia, not just a day off, not just barbies in the back yard or down the beach. Nick had said.

"It's a big thing with them," Tremaine told me with a casual air. "All the Old Timers who fought. Opportunity for a piss up." This sounds like one of Ronnie's throw-away lines. Part of his image, I think. "My old man marches… if his legs can take it. Poor bugger, the war didn't do much for him."

"Legs?"

"He was in the islands, fighting the Japs. Up to his knees in swamps with a pack on his back."

I didn't know. Hadn't thought. "He'll tell you one day if you buy him a beer and get him talking." Tremaine had an appreciation for what his father had done, but wasn't going to show it; the islands, the Japs, his father and his legs. "I've heard it all before from Dad," he said.

Baz said to meet in the pub just down the road from the newspaper office. The Grenadier.

"They'll have a good few jars," Tremaine warned. "They all do. And they'll all get pissed. If you don't want the law pulling you over, feeling your collar, then get someone else behind the wheel when you come in."

I heeded the warning. Id let the train take the strain. It was the driver of the 10.15 into Adelaide Station who got me in and I'd walked up from North Terrace to King William Street. Ronnie was right about leaving the car at home and the carriage was packed; so many Aussies wanted to share the day.

Then I'd joined the crowds lining the route, King William Street, ten and twelve deep, watching the march. The band, resplendent, played. The crowd cheered, Aussie flags waved. I caught a glimpse of Baz with the handlebar moustache and Jason with the tiny tash. There they were, striding out. So smart, so focused, such determination written on their faces for the day. Their day.

"Brave bastards," muttered the man to my right. "Brave bastards came through hell." I turned and nodded to him. I shared his thought.

And then they passed, so proud. And I was proud to know them, Baz and Jason, proud to work alongside them. Proud for what they had done for their country, our country, our freedom.

"Brave bastards, all of them," he said again as the last man trailed off down King William Street and out of sight. And the sound of the band trailed off too.

I'm through the door and the pub's heaving. The men are there already, straight off the march, still smart and pristine, their uniforms still blinking in the light of day for the first time in twelve months, spruced up, freshly ironed for the occasion, their wives had seen to that. Digger hats brushed, shirts ironed and jackets festooned with medals.

"Brave bastards," the man at my side had said. "Gallipoli, Flanders Fields, Singapore, El Alamein."

"I'll get them in," I say after I've pushed through. Baz and Jason are already at the bar.

There's a dozen serving, the beer keeps coming, glasses filled as fast as emptied. Beer swills across the counter and spills over the front and down onto the wooden floor. "Cheers," I say, among the noise.

"Cheers."

"Cheers."

"Well, did you enjoy it?" says Baz. "Your first ANZAC Day."

"I did. All those men, all you men… I didn't realise."

"You're not the only one." Jason puts his beer down, wipes his lips with the back of his hand. "The younger generation. It's all past history to them. We're all Old Timers. Yesterday's news."

I nod in agreement. "Back home ours is Remembrance Sunday, a minute's silence, then we get on with our lives as though nothing happened."

There's a pause while it sinks in.

"But I reckon you Aussies respect your war heroes much more than we do. What I saw today in King William Street is proof. The crowds, the sentiment, the appreciation of what you all did."

Did Baz say, "Maybe"?

And Jason, "Perhaps"?

You can scarcely hear in the bar. "There's a room out the back, it's quieter," says Jason. He points. Ruddy cheeks, the tiny tash. "It's quieter there." He has to shout to make himself heard.

Tables, chairs, an aspidistra in the corner, men sitting, leaning over, talking together. Sharing jokes. Yes, it's quieter in here even though it's still packed.

I find myself standing over a table with a group of three soldiers in uniforms of the First World War, chatting about what they went through. Reminiscing, telling their experiences, the details, the days, the nights, their comrades, the dead. Yes, the dead, the men they left behind on the battlefield. Aussie men.

I'm looking down on a man of around sixty, maybe more, it's hard to tell, the hair is all but gone, the face lined. He looks up and asks softly, "Your first ANZAC Day, son?"

"Yes, we have Remembrance Sunday, up in London," I find myself explaining all over again. "I've never been."

He has a pleasant face, pock marked, eyebrows like an overgrown hedge. A little man with sad, blue eyes and just one arm. "Flanders Fields," he tells me. "But not before we had taken the village." Yes, just one arm.

"The village?"

"Villers-Bretonneux." His hand is trembling. His left hand. His only hand. "Villers-Bretonneux," he says again. "Picardy. It comes back to you on ANZAC Day as if it's yesterday. And it was slaughter."

I am not sure if he wants to talk about it. Jason said some bottled it up, their experiences, the trenches in the First World War, Japanese camps in the Second. "Some things you cannot share. Some experiences you keep to yourself. Keep from your loved ones."

The man looks up at me.

"I want to hear," I say.

"You know the song?"

I don't.

And he starts to sing in a low, quiet voice, with a strong Australian accent.

"Roses are shining in Picardy
In the hush of the silver dew,
Roses are shining in Picardy
But there's never a rose like you
And the roses will die with the summer time
And our roads may be far apart
But there's one rose that dies not in Picardy,
'Tis the rose that I keep in my heart.

159

"Villers-Bretonneux," he's saying now. "The orders came down from the top. Drive the Germans out. Drive them out."

He's looking up at me again. His eyes confirm he is there, this minute, now. He can hear the thunder of war, the smell of fear.

"I was part of the 13th Division under Brigadier-General Glasgow and Glasgow was ordered to take the village. In daylight..." He hesitates. "I tell you in bloody daylight and Glasgow told them."

"Told them?"

"The Germans were entrenched, you see. Dug in. And on high ground. Their guns well set and machine gun entrenchments ready. Slaughter it would have been... he told them, slaughter."

I'm feeling pleased for the little man with pock marked face, sad eyes and one arm. Pleased his leader told them what it would be.

"Then Glasgow came up with this plan to surprise them, surprise the Jerries." He takes a sip of his beer. "At night. After darkness fell. No artillery to warn them. That was the trick."

My mind is visualising the darkness, the Germans set, the Aussies outnumbered.

"Yes, outnumbered," he is saying. "Outnumbered ten to one. Not that we knew it at the time, you understand. They didn't tell us at the time."

I think to myself how Churchill said truth was the first casualty in war.

"Then he gave the order, Glasgow did. And we scrambled to get at them. Out of the trenches, out of our fox holes. Over the top we went, every man-jack of us. And the cry went out, 'Get the machine guns. Get the bloody Kraut machine guns – or die.' My mate, Harold on my left, a chap by the name of Nichols from Ballarat on the right, just lads, all of us. Through the swish and patter."

"Patter?"

"The machine guns. A sort of pattering noise and the swish of the bullets and the men dropping like flies, no sound except the thump of them hitting the ground. No time to stop, to look back. No time to help them."

He sighs, draws breath. He is there, now. "We ran hard and fast.

Heads down. Then stood still, motionless, when the Very lights lit up the night sky."

"Standing still?"

"You can't pick up a motionless figure, son. Only a moving one."

I scarcely dare ask. "That where you lost your right arm?"

"Not till it was nearly over. Copped one in the elbow. Smashed the bone. They could have saved my arm but it took time to get the medics in and me away."

I am at a loss as to what to say.

He knows my discomfort. "I hope you never go through it son. Hope you never…"

His voice trails off. The tears in his eyes. Those sad eyes.

"The war to end all wars, they assured us. And we were at it again just a handful of years later. The Jerries and us. What's wrong with them, son? What's wrong with us? So much slaughter. So many of my comrades left back there on the fields of Picardy."

Years later I would stand on those fields and know exactly what he meant. The little man with only one arm.

# Chapter 10

## Lost on the Birdsville Track

"Well, where are you spending your holiday then?" Baz is taking time off from pasting up the news pages, filling his pipe and wondering what a Pommie lad does with his week's break.

"Well, I thought I'd see some of the real Australia, Baz. Go up the Birdsville Track. I've never been there. I need to."

Jason turns on his swivel seat, one eyebrow raised. "Well, no-one can say you're not adventurous."

Tremaine thinks I'm more than adventurous. He thinks I'm mad. "Most people go to the beach for a holiday. This Pom goes Bush. There must be an easier way of doing away with yourself?"

"I'll take it carefully… turn back if the going gets rough."

"At least it's the dry season." Basil sounds positive. It gives me confidence. "Take precautions and you should be ok. There's little risk of flooding at this time of the year."

"Flooding?" I'd never heard anyone mention that. "I thought it was a barren desert."

"Flash floods," says Jason. "In the rainy season there are areas that become awash. Tropical rains in southern Queensland flood the Birdsville Track without warning and recede just as quickly. It's easy to get caught."

"Take your water wings then," says Tremaine.

Baz has been there. He knows. "Ignore that daft bugger. But you need the right kit to get out of a jam if you come unstuck. A lot of people have. Take a spare can of petrol, two if you have the room. And a decent set of tools. It's not a Sunday afternoon jaunt you're going on with the family."

"I've borrowed a spade so I should be able to dig the Volksie out if I get stuck in sand; I'm told it can be a big problem. I've got a towrope, of course, and the local garage leant me a second spare tyre so I should be covered if I get punctures. I'm told there are places where the sand gives way to sharp stones... tyres get cut to shreds." I smile. "As you say Baz, a real Sunday afternoon jaunt."

Both Jason's eyebrows are raised now. "Food and water? Don't forget you need enough to sustain life and limb for a week, preferably more. It's not the leafy lanes of England you know, there's not a service station round every bend."

"I have a pretty fair idea of what I'll have to contend with. I met this guy who was prospecting, the Pommie bloke I told you about, Nick the Red Beret man, he's travelled the Track many times. He warned me what to look out for, what to avoid, how to prepare. And don't forget the trips north gathering stories for the paper. They have given me a feel for what the Outback's like."

Baz seems relaxed about it. "Take a camera and get a few pics, young Richard. Meet a few locals and write up a couple of stories for my pages."

"I'll do my best, Baz. I'll do my best."

"Well, don't do a Burke and Wills on us. They never got back. Never lived to tell the tale."

The Volksie is purring along the A1, going north. Effortlessly, a good 55 to 60 miles an hour. What Burke and Wills would have done for this sort of progress when they set out to cross the

Continent back in the 1860s.

I'd been down to the library and taken out the book Baz recommended on the two ill fated explorers. To see what made them tick. Where they went wrong. What caught them out. It's sitting here on the passenger seat next to me, my companion for the next few days.

No, I don't intend to do a Burke and Wills. Not if I can help it.

Every Aussie kid knows the story, it's taught at school, how their expedition came about, how it came to grief. I'd read the opening pages... flicked through the rest... seen the maps, the pictures. I had a fair idea.

"That'll make you think twice," Baz had said. Two bearded men were staring out at me from the book. Gaunt faces, tight lips.

"And give you nightmares," said Jason.

Tramaine was still thinking I was mad. "Forget the Burke and Wills stuff, mate. Get down the beach, charm the sheilas like every other red blooded male."

At school we'd learnt about the early days of Australia – touched on what the Aussie kids were taught and Mr Rumsey, our geography teacher, told us about the early explorers, and I loved every bit.

"Captain Cook," Mr Rumsey announced and we all sat up and took notice. He was a big, round, jolly man and made discovering anything, anywhere, exciting. He always swept into class wearing his gown and mortar board – he looked great.

"The date is August 22, 1770, children," said Mr Rumsey looking particularly pleased with himself. "That's the day Captain Cook landed on Australian shores. On the Eastern seaboard and he thought it looked so much like South Wales he named it after what he saw... New South Wales."

And with a flourish, Mr Rumsey turned and chalked on the blackboard. *I claim this colony for George III.*

"There children, that's how Australia became part of our empire." He seemed mighty proud of it.

Then we had to write in our exercise books when the first settlers arrived in the new colony and how they established a few scattered farms, raised a handful of cattle and sheep. That was in 1793 with other settlements springing up in the State of Victoria in 1803 and then South Australia,1836. "Have you got all that down, children?"

"Yes sir. Yes sir…"

"Well, what came next boys and girls? What next?"

Mr Rumsey was as excited as if he'd won the football pools and would be getting a cheque from smiling Diana Dors any day. "What next, boys and girls? What next?"

Hands shot up everywhere. "Convicts sir, that's what. Convicts."

"Well done children; pick-pockets, thieves, anyone else?"

"Naughty ladies, Sir. Naughty ladies of the night." Smith Junior knew.

And just when we were about to learn what made these ladies naughty… the bell went.

Baz's book has taken over now.

It tells how the early colonisation was limited to the narrow strip of land within a few hundred miles of the coast. No-one dared venture inland. No-one needed to, this was good, productive country that could sustain the early settlers. Yet man being what man is, there was always the yearning to see what was over the next hill, where the grass was always greener. Even in those early days inter-State rivalry meant a race developed. And when some bright spark reckoned there was an inland sea – bingo, the battle really was on.

Page 33: *'The Royal Society of Victoria was determined not to be left behind in the race. Gold had been discovered in the hills to the north of Melbourne, scarcely a hundred miles away. The wealth it brought opened up the opportunity for funding an expedition to drive through the centre of the new country, reach the northern coast and in doing so discover the Great Inland Sea. And any other prize.'*

I'm drawn to Burke and Wills, one an ex army officer and the other an English surveyor. I read how they won the backing and off they went – to disaster. Turn the clocks back to August 20, 1860, and I found myself in Melbourne's Royal Park with Burke and Wills, their team of men, a couple of dozen camels, a similar number of horses, and a string of wagons. And 12,000 others waving like mad. We need to take a good look, it will be the last time we see them alive.

"Don't do a Burke and Wills on us," Baz had said.

"No, not if I can help it I won't," I replied.

The Volksie buzzes along and I know the way north like the back of my hand. When I cover the Department of Agriculture conferences we use this winding road to get over to the Yorke and Eyre peninsulas. And when I go north for the sheep and cattle sales with Johnnie Schumacher we often go this way.

I am passing through the lush, green, productive lands just north of Adelaide. The modern-day Italian settlers have set up shop, bringing their skills as market gardeners, and the results are here for all to see. And their English is coming along a treat. Here's a sign announcing APPLES FOR SELL. Yes, coming along a treat.

I'll clear all this by nightfall. Getting the city lights out of my eyes, the city sounds out of my ears. Heading for the Bush, I'm planning to reach Port Augusta and get my head down. There are plenty of hotels and I want to look round the old part of the town anyway, do a bit of research, take a few pics for Baz and maybe write something up for when I get back.

Then starting on the difficult bit, off the beaten track, I'll take it easy and get to Lyndhurst next day, on the brink of the Birdsville Track, the goal. Everyone tells me that's where your troubles can start, harsh reality. That's where you can break down and no-one find you for days, maybe weeks. And when they do, you're a bloody skeleton. Baz told me how a family got caught a couple of years back. Eaten by dingoes or those bloody Bull ants. Cripes, eaten alive by ants! Billy said about them when we took the stud cattle to Quarantine Island. "You ain't seen nothing till you've seen Bull ants."

One thing I've got on my side is the Volksie. It's pretty reliable. Didn't Beetles win the Round Australia rallies a couple of years back? Not once but twice, or was it three times? I'd just arrived in the country. Beat all comers and most of it was on Outback dirt roads.

The Volkswagen Beetle is air-cooled, of course, so you can't run out of water like so many vehicles on the Track. I remember an advert from some slick PR guy and it showed the back of the Volksie with a huge jug of water and the words:

**"Water, we don't touch a drop!"**

And air-cooled means there's no radiator to get punctured by stones thrown up by passing vehicles. That happens too.

Dr Ferdinand Porsche knew what he was doing when he designed the Beetle. Engine in the back, over the driving wheels, there's good traction even in sand or snow. Not too much snow on the Birdsville Track but plenty of sand. Short of driving a four-wheel drive, a Jeep or Land Rover, I reckon I'm in the best vehicle man could invent.

Two hundred miles and Volksie and I shoot into Port Pirie and I reach for my Traveller's Guide to South Australia. It's sitting here on the seat keeping Burke and Wills company. Fill up at the BP station, take a break and flick through the pages. Did I know the town is the sixth largest in South Australia and the first outside Adelaide to be granted city status?

Mr Rumsey didn't mention that!

"City status?" The attendant cleaning my windscreen is more interested in the lead-smelting plant trailing a fuzzy drift of smoke over the township and out across the Gulf.

A squeegee in one hand, his other points out into the bay. "Wouldn't bring up my kids here." He's upset with this chimney, coughs and blows his nose. "They say they are going to clean it up. The smelting plant. Can't come soon enough for me."

He's checked the tyres, oil and battery. "Pay in the shop," and I do. Four shillings and ten pence a gallon. Cheap for good, old fashioned service like this. And a lecture on the smelting plant thrown in for free. Then he's onto the next car. "Look at that chimney. Just look at it."

Volksie and I are heading for Port Augusta; that's where I'm putting my head down for the night.

"The crossroads of Australia," my Guide tells me. Kalgoolie is some 1240 miles to the west, Darwin 1550 miles to the north and Adelaide just 200 miles south, the crossroads, it's the meeting point all right. The beer has got to be good, and it is. The mosquitoes good too – to another mosquito. But I've been this way before; Nick Nicola told me, "Get yourself a can of SCRAM, mate. I never go anywhere without my SCRAM. One squirt does the trick."

Next morning I'm up sharp and out early and into the arid world of George W Goyder.

Baz had got me to do a story on Goyder. An interesting guy. How he charted the rainfall in the very earliest days of the settlers and gave it a definition, Goyder's Line, which stands to this day. I remember Keynes telling me about him too. Goyder worked it all out, he said.

"You know he was a Pom, Baz?"

"And a good one."

My research told me he was born in Liverpool, a Scouser, coming to Australia as a 20 year old. That was in 1828. Seems he was a real go-getter. I had bashed my story out, every syllable, every word. My typewriter was on fire. I love researching and writing about people. How he secured a job as a junior surveyor within the South Australian Lands and Survey Department, made his mark and was ultimately appointed as top dog, Surveyor-General. He held that position until his retirement. The years 1861 through to1893. My words had flown off the typewriter. Scouser makes good!

I handed it to Baz:

# GOYDER'S LINE STANDS THE TEST OF TIME

### By Richard Holdsworth

In the early days of settling South Australia, little was known of the rainfall pattern across the State and with no experience to go on, mistakes were made, aspirations dashed, fortunes lost and families destroyed.

There was not only a rush for gold in the early history of South Australia but a rush for land; fresh, virgin farming land. But what form of farming and where?

Just a handful of years' experience is all that the settlers had to go on and no idea whether the rainfall would sustain high yielding arable crops or just simple grazing. Clearly direction was required, and required as a matter of urgency.

The State Government in Adelaide turned to its Surveyor-General, George Goyder and Goyder and his small band of men took to their horses and within two months came up with their recommendations, the Goyder Line. "North of my line," proclaimed Goyder, "and there's only enough rainfall to sustain grazing, south and you can cultivate."

Goyder had never believed in the saying "Rain follows the plough" as many others did. But it didn't help that the next few years were blessed with above average rainfall. Many settlers shunned Goyder and his line, went north and ploughed and sowed to their heart's content. Today the abandoned dwellings and farm buildings are testament to the fact that George Goyder had got it right.

"Looks good to me. If you get your spelling right I'll run it next week."

"Spelling?"

"Two bloody Ls in dwelling. What the hell do they teach you

over there in the Old Country?"

Turn off the A1 onto the B56 towards Hawker, dry, arid country, Goyder country where life can get interesting. Admire the Flinders Ranges. Stop by if you like, set up camp, enjoy the beauty, go for a stroll; that's what the Traveller's Guide tells me. But it also says it is isolated and rugged, a rewarding challenge – but only for the most experienced walker. That's not me, today or any day. Anyway, I've got other challenges ahead.

Hawker is in my sights. High street, a few shops and a welcoming hotel. The guide tells me that in the old days thousands of sheep and cattle passed through on their way south to greener pastures down south – or to market. And to a lesser extent they still come this way today. The little hoof marks in the dust at the side of the road confirm.

Lift the bonnet to the Volksie and top up the petrol. Check the oil and tyres again. Nick Nicola told me that. "Your vehicle is your life-line, mate. Look after it and it will look after you."

Now we're on our way to Parachilna. Flick the pages to the guide book and read how it was an important town in South Australia many moons ago. It also credits the name to the natives, the Aborigines. Apparently it means place of peppermint Gum trees. In years to come I'll learn that peppermint helps a dicky tummy. Clever bloody Aborigines knew already. A herbal remedy. I bet Nick knew all about that.

We've travelled nearly 400 miles since Adelaide and I'm taking a break, in a bar in Lyndhurst and it's bleeding hot even in here. "Does the sun ever go behind a cloud?" I'm asking the man next to me and he picks my Pommie accent. "This place is full of Poms," he tells me. "Can't swing a billy without hitting one. There was a Pom in here the other day, had done a stint up at Broken Hill. Told me how he was taking time off for a bit of prospecting. Opals. I think."

I wonder. It's a small world but could it be? "His name wouldn't be Nick by any chance? His real name is Ron but they call him Nick. Nick Nicola from England."

"That's it, Nick. He was a Pom all right. Had a Land Rover, kitted up, spare wheel, tow rope, spade, the lot. I tell ya, this place is full of 'em these days."

This triggers a dialogue in which I am being told of the good old days before new fangled things like four wheel drives, telephones... even SCRAM. "Ya know something? We didn't have none of them and it didn't do us no harm." My Digger mate, for that is what I reckon he would like to be called, must be 60, or 70 or more. Hard to tell, the brim of the hat is pulled down, the eyes half closed from squinting into the sun and a few days' stubble covers the rest of his face.

"Did ya ever hear the tale of Harry Redford, a drover, son of a convict?"

"Should I?"

"Of course ya should, mate. If you're a journalist as ya say. Harry's exploits were legend, gripped the nation back in the 1870s. Ya should get it all down."

Baz is always looking for a good story to fill his Meerschaum column of truths and half truths that come out of the Bush. I reach for my notebook and start scribbling away, "I'm all ears," I say, and he pushes his empty glass across the counter and it looks like I've taken the bait.

Two slurps and he's into the tale and no stopping him.

"Well, young Pom, as I was telling ya, Harry Redford was a drover of some repute and came the day when he reckoned it was time to use all this skill to earn a quid, a big quid, as against a miserable pittance from them wealthy property owners he was drawing his wage from at the time."

"Where was this then, Digger?"

"Up north, mate. Western Queensland."

My pencil scribbles away. Bowen Downs Station, Western Queensland, close to the Northern Territory boundary.

"Ya got it down, lad?"

I nod. This is going to be good. I know.

"Well, Harry worked out this owner wouldn't miss a thousand head of cattle out of seventy thousand and the seventy thousand scattered across two million acres."

I'm agreeing. Seventy thousand head, two million acres. Black Horse and I wouldn't find them in a week's droving. More than that, we wouldn't even miss them.

"The problem being," says my man, wiping the froth from his lips, "was the fact that they were branded. That buggered him. They'd be recognised the moment he'd offer them at any auction anywhere around abouts Queensland or New South Wales."

"That's some problem." If that's the end of the story, it's not much of a story. Baz would look at me as though I needed my head read. "I hope Harry had a plan B."

"I dunno about any plan B. But Harry certainly wasn't beaten and I'll tell ya how this came about if ya make it worth my while," says my Digger mate, pushing his empty glass across the bar again.

I do as I'm told. And here's plan B even if the Digger doesn't know what a plan B is.

"Well, you can write down in yer book how Harry drove the cattle down south, across country that had scarce seen a white man, let alone a white man and a thousand head of cattle. Yet he did it... and good on him I say."

"Good on him," I agree.

"But wait a minute," says my Digger, gripping my arm. "Just when he was thinking he'd got away with it, and the five grand in his back pocket from the sale of his thousand head of cattle, the Constabulary got to hear and nabbed him and had him back in Queensland and up before the judge and charged with felony."

This is a story with a sad ending, not what Baz wants to hear at all. Our man, Harry Redmond, cautioned, charged and on his way to a long stretch. Then a glint in the eye of my story teller and before I know it I'm scribbling down the next episode in the saga of the drover and his ill gotten gains.

"Judge to Foreman of the Jury, 'What is your verdict, Foreman?'

"And the Foreman replies, 'Not guilty M'lord.'

"And the judge thinking he has misheard, asks again, 'What is your verdict, Foreman?'

"But the Foreman replies again, 'Not guilty.'

"It seems," says my storyteller, "that the jury totally discounted the weighty evidence put before the Court and instead took sympathy on Harry and his Bushcraft skills – plus the audacity of his actions, of course. "You can't beat that," the Digger is saying. "I think it deserves a short, don't you?"

I do. "Cheers to young Mr Redford."

"Cheers to you young sir." He swallows the rum in one go.

I'm off out now, thirst slaked and a story in my notebook for Baz. My friend is still at the bar waiting for the next young Pommie to come by and listen to the tale of the audacious Mr Redford the ace Bushman. I turn and smile from the doorway and my Digger doffs his hat, grimy old stockman's hat, frayed at the edges and corks hanging from the brim. Yes, corks, no Pommie would believe a Digger without corks round his hat, would he?

Marree, I've arrived. I'm giving it the accord it deserves. The Guide tells me it's the junction of the Oodnadatta and Birdsville tracks; it's on the rail link between Adelaide and Alice Springs, a break of gauge since the rail south was re-built in 1957 as Standard Gauge, the track north remaining Narrow Gauge. And it is the rail-head for coals from Leigh Creek shipped to Port Augusta. It is vital for all three reasons. Never mind the fact that cattle and sheep from the Dead Centre and Southern Queensland converge here on their way south.

There's a sign in the High Street that says Birdsville 325 miles

THAT WAY.  And that's where I'm going.

But not before I put on record who I am, where I'm headed, and when I expect to be back. It's a fool who doesn't.

Push through the flyscreen to the door of the local Post Office and greet the man who's seen and heard it all before. "My destination is the Mungerannie Hotel 130 miles up the Track." He reaches for his log, licks the end of his pencil, and starts to write the details that could be the difference between life or death for me out there in the desert.

It's not the full length of the Track that I'm going – that's another 195 miles to Birdsville – but it's enough of a task for me and Volksie and I haven't the time, anyway. Just seven days before my Stock & Station Journal holiday runs out and I'm expected to be back behind my typewriter. But it will give me a good taste of the Track, what it's all about, why it deserves the reputation it has – and it will enable me to announce proudly to Tremaine what I've achieved. "See mate, here I am, large as life. Don't know why you were getting so carried away."

Anyway, if I went north of Mungerannie, I'd have problems I'm not sure Volksie and I could cope with. I'd read about the Gibber Plain with those sun-baked stones, hard as nuts and sharp with it – not healthy for a little car like mine. And once you've passed Clifton Hills homestead there's the Stuart Stony Desert. Another reason I'll give that bit of the Track a big miss.

"No," I say to the man in the Post Office, "I think I'll stick to Mungerannie, take a breather, watch the wildlife enjoy the waters from the bore hole, then head back home. I might down a couple myself, beers that is."

He's taking note of what I'm telling him. "When do ya say you'll be back, lad?"

"A bit under a week, I reckon." He writes that down too. "I've got a Volksie. Registration plate SA 304 251."

"Well, best of luck and make sure you let us know when you pass by here on your way back home. Or else we'll start searching for you and you safely tucked up in your cot down there in Adelaide."

I smile. "And if you don't see me within a month... that's the

175

time to send out the search party."

As I reach the door I hear him call out, "No laughing matter, lad. It's death out there – if ya don't know that ya shouldn't be going." And I'm sure I hear him mutter something about these bloody Poms.

One last check for the Volksie. Plenty of fuel in the tank, plus the reserve. And the couple of jerricans I've scrounged, topped them up too; the trouble with sand is you don't get the mileage you do on bitumen roads, even dirt roads. A good 40 to the gallon comes down to 20 and 20 comes down to ten if the going's bad. I check oil, tyres too.

This is it. Deep breath. Start of the famous, or is it infamous, Birdsville Track.

Funny, it doesn't look much different from the past hundred miles we've been through. Bloody hot, it's like driving through a furnace, can't see a cloud for love nor money, dust billowing out behind the Volksie although we're taking it easy, and the horizon is the same as the horizon we've just breached. There's no snow-capped mountains, no lush green meadows, no cascading waterfalls, nothing to inspire the advertising man and trigger his creative genius as he sits at his typewriter. It's the enormity of the place that tingles the senses, grabs you by the throat, and the thought that you could die here... many have...and they won't be the last. It is so easy. That's what stops you in your tracks.

Stop you in your tracks? Well, I do for a moment, I turn off the air-cooled flat four engine, Ferdinand Porche's masterpiece, and listen. And listen to what? Silence, that's what. Apart from the engine clicking and ticking as it cools down – there's not a sound, no birds, no animals and no human beings. No life at all. I'm out here alone. Completely alone. Cripes, that's eerie.

The Track is wide, seems to be boundaryless, nothing either side to tell me where it starts and where it ends. Just a couple of wheel tracks left by the bloke who was last this way. A day ago? Week? Month even? Half rubbed out by the breeze. Did someone come this way at all?

There's sparse bushes, a few skeletons of trees trying to eke out an existence, a boulder here and there and the all-pervading sand and dust. I know where it gets its name from, the Red Centre. Could equally be the Dead Centre.

And where the wind has come in from the north – or east, or west or south – it's created gracefully sculptured dunes. But treacherous, deep, wide, soul-destroying dunes. Wouldn't want to get stuck in one of these; even with the engine in the back, over the back wheels, giving good traction, it could be a killer. Jason warned, "You really need a four wheel drive for what you're about to tackle."

I'd read of Tom Kruse, the legendary postman of the 1930's and it was said he dumped a reserve of corrugated iron sheets at strategic points along the Track for the times he got bogged down. But I'm no Tom Kruse keeping the Mumgarannie Hotel fed with mail on a weekly basis. And, anyway, I have no idea where the hell he stacked his life-saving sheets of corrugated iron. And even if they've survived to this day. Probably haven't.

If Burke and Wills had passed this way I'd feel sorry for the poor buggers. They were over to the east, of course – it was the same sort of inhospitable terrain in those days I suppose – headed for Swan Hill in northern Victoria, then (after sitting around debating the next move), over the State border into New South Wales and Balranald and Mernindie on the River Darling.

The book says they headed for Cooper's Creek; and it also tells of the incessant disputes. As early as Swan Hill, Burke realised the party was far too heavily laden and with items totally incompatible with their needs. He dumped containers of lime juice, bags of sugar and rice. Some say he had sun shades and inflatable cushions.

Bloody hell!

Plod. Plod. Plod. The camels stepped out slowly, very slowly. And the wagons and horses followed. The progress was painful.

Yes, it wasn't a happy party that passed through Bush country late in 1860.

Volksie and I are a much happier team although wary of the sand where it's blown across the Track and me with nothing more than a shovel to dig us out. We're cheered to see the remains of Lake Harry Homestead, not because it is only remains, but because we know we haven't lost our way and strayed from the Track.

There're no fences, no mile posts, no signs – and as for street lights!

And no floods. Baz had warned how tropical thunderstorms in Queensland's channel country above Innamincka could result in a surge of water filling the dry bed of the Cooper River and, ultimately, spilling out and replenishing Lake Eyre down there in northern South Australia. At those times you have a choice; sit around and wait for the water to subside or head for the Cooper River ferry – but this alternative takes up valuable time, something I can't afford.

Fortunately, Basil was right – no floods at this time of the year. Skip past the Dog Fence too. Yes, this is as it should be, we're not lost – not yet – it's said to be the longest fence in the world keeping dingoes from what is generally regarded as sheep country. North of the fence and the mature cattle are not bothered by the occasional dingo snapping at their heels. A quick hoof in the nuts should see them bury their heads for a day or two.

The sight of Lake Harry Homestead and the Dog Fence brings a bit of confidence. I'm just telling Volksie we can relax; we've covered almost a hundred miles without mishap, when without warning there's a swirling wind, a dust storm, and I'm driving into it, blinded. I've gone for the brakes… I can't see a thing, a bloody thing… and I'm skidding and bouncing and crashing with a thump into some immovable object.

Christ, it happened so quickly. In a split second. One moment sailing along whistling a happy tune, next BANG and I'm in trouble.

I'm leaping out, round the front; we've slid straight into one of those bloody boulders. The front of the Volksie is staved in, bumper a "U" shape, bonnet buckled and spare tyre and wheel trapped in its compartment. Thank goodness for the tyre; it's absorbed some impact, the suspension isn't damaged, the wheels are pointing ahead, not knock-kneed or splayed out. It should still work. It wasn't a heavy shunt, I wasn't going quickly, just feeling my way. Too wary for anything else.

But there's bad news. We're deep into a sand dune. Volksie should get out of this. Rear engine, rear wheel drive, that's what it's all about. If Ferdinand Porsche was here now I'd kiss the bugger. Grab the shovel. Round the back of the car. Dig trenches behind each wheel, make it easy for the engine to pull us free. But this sand is deep, bloody deep. As fast as I dig, more falls in the trench. And there seems no end to it. Within minutes, just a couple of dozen shovel-fulls and the floor of the Volksie is resting on the stuff, beached like a whale with the tide receding. This is desperate; it isn't working and if I can't think of something I'm stuck for good.

At least it's not mid-day and the sun bang overhead. But the temperature must still be topping the130 degree mark and I'm exhausted already, the sweat soaking my shirt, trickling down my brow and stinging my eyes. Desperation is setting in. Starting to panic. There's a cow's skull lying beside the track, bleached white, gaping eye sockets fixing me with an empty stare. Am I going to die like her?

Don't panic, climb back in the car, out of the burning sun and take stock. Have a long gulp of water from the water bag, don't get dehydrated. Keep my wits about me. I have food and water, I can't starve, can't die of thirst. Not just yet anyway. Sit, think, stay calm, what next? Well, I can't expect the rescue services to come past in the next couple of hours. "I'll be back in under a week," I told the smiling man behind the counter in Marree. But I also said to send out the search party in a month. A stupid throwaway line. I might last five days but not ten, let alone a month.

No wonder he muttered, "Bloody Pom."

Maybe someone will come by this way. But when? I had remembered a second spare tyre, fan belt, shovel, tow rope, tools. But I didn't ask how often some guy trots past with the daily newspaper tucked under his arm, cricket scores, cold beer and asking, "In a spot of bother, old chap?"

Yes, relax. Stay calm. I have time to kill. Even have time to finish my Burke and Wills book, see what they did when things went wrong. I might get a few clues.

I must plan. Lay out the limited reserves at my disposal, ration for the worst. Two days, three, longer?  Some of my food will go off. The butter in the sandwiches will melt, become rancid. And the chocolate bar. Keep the lid on the Eski, slam it down the moment I've grabbed something to eat. Not that it's chilled in there, the ice melted long ago, but it's better than the inferno I'm sitting in. Just touching the roof of the Volksie burns your hand. They say you can do a fry-up under the Outback sun and I reckon the roof of my car is just the place for a couple of rashers of bacon and a banger or two.

I have boiled eggs "for an emergency" Baz said. Little did I think I would become one of Baz's emergencies.

That sun-bleached skull is still staring. The dingoes and Bull ants have taken the flesh long ago. It is said that they can turn a body into a skeleton within minutes. Wipe it clean. Bloody hell!

Look away... look away quickly... occupy the mind, set a task, something to do. Make a list of the food. Yes, that's constructive. Make a list.

I've found the couple of packets of digestive biscuits, the sort I have with my cup of tea in our garden back in England, in the spring, between the showers. Goodness, don't start thinking about that, dreaming of the English countryside, the rain, the glorious rain! I'll go balmy!

No, grab a sandwich and munch away. I've got a dozen and I reckon they'll survive a couple of days; I'll scoff half now and the rest tomorrow. Save the biscuits and boiled eggs for day three and four. And I've got a packet of sweets, wine drops, luxury. At this rate I could be living the life of Old Riley at the Ritz. Where on earth is that waiter with my G & T?

Cheer up. Day five, here I come, then rescue! A fleet of four wheel drives arriving on the scene, a flock of light aircraft buzzing overhead.

I'll do as the experts say, break a mirror, build a mound of sand and place the pieces so the light glints and catches their attention. Make an S O S with stones. Anything that can be seen from the air. And jump up and down, of course, scream and shout. IT'S ME. IT'S ME. HERE I AM. DON'T LEAVE ME HERE TO DIE!

The big problem is water. The two plastic jerry cans hold best part of five gallons but it's bloody hot in the back of the car and the water is hot too. Thank goodness the water bag on the front bumper wasn't damaged in the shunt. The water is pretty cool in there. When I first got to Australia and saw a water bag strapped to the front bumper of John Keynes' truck, I said, "Funny, what the hell is it doing out there in the sun?" Keynes showed me how the porous material cooled the water as it evaporated. I have no choice but to fill my water bag from the jerry can and keep it in the shade of the car and hope it does the same.

At least I won't have one problem. Baz said that anyone suffering from dehydration shouldn't gulp fresh cold water despite the uncontrollable urge to do so – Baz said the body rejects cold water and spews it out again. Much better to boil a billy and make tea; I had thrown a few tea bags into the Eski and while I don't have a billy, I have a tin mug – put it on the bonnet, leave it in the sun and it's sure to provide some sort of sustenance. If it's hot enough for a fry-up then it must be hot enough for a cuppa.

Quick, grab the can, pour the water. Christ, in my haste it surges and spills, my vital, life-saving water on the ground, lost in the sand. Take hold of yourself Holdsworth. This is life or death. That drop of water could have been the drop that saves your life on day five. Death just round the corner. The skull is still staring at you.

I don't aim to end up with Burke and Wills. When the chips were down they fell apart instead of keeping their cool. The book says Burke made irrational decisions and didn't convey his thinking to others. He may not have spilt the water, but his actions still cost them dearly.

He established a base camp on the Cooper then sent William Wright, one of his most trusted men, back to Menindie with a handful of others and instructions to bring up a reserve of supplies. Good planning. But with the summer heat in front of him, it was presumed Burke would wait before pushing on – he didn't. Instead he and Wills took King and Gray and set out on the most difficult leg of the journey, that to the Gulf of Carpentaria. But he failed to tell Wright. The fool.

Turn the page and things are getting worse. They are now pitted against dreadful odds. In places it's down to hacking their way through the tropical jungle coming up to the Gulf.

Just short of their goal and with their supplies almost totally exhausted, Burke has no alternative – he gives the order to turn back. By March 4, 1861, and with starvation close, Burke has one of the camels shot – three weeks later a second and then he takes a pistol to his trusted horse, Billie, and they all tuck into poor old Billie too.

This is not bed-time reading. Certainly not when you are stuck on the Birdsville Track. Burke and Wills and their two companions are close to starvation and extreme fatigue has taken over. Scarcely able to put one foot in front of the other they are suffering dreadful pains in the back, weakness of the legs and now dysentery. Then Gray is caught helping himself to the last of the food and Burke has him thrashed in front of the others. Gray dies a couple of days later.

I read on, no way can I put the book down now.

But it only brings further torment. When they finally make it back to the advance camp on Cooper River they find it deserted; the back-up party had waited three months but they, too, were desperately short of provisions and had no alternative but to start the long journey south again; the two parties missed each other by less than a day.

Meanwhile Wright is still in Menindie and he is dallying. If he'd known of Burke's plans to set out to the Gulf without waiting for the cooler weather he might have acted more swiftly. As it was he hung about until late in January. He too was hampered by lack of supplies, straying camels, hostile Aborigines, and no skilled navigator. When he did set out, three of his men died of scurvy and malnutrition. One was Ludwig Becker the German whose sketches of landscapes, natives and wildlife, survived as the one meaningful testament of an otherwise disastrous expedition.

It is the end for Burke; paralysis has taken over, he cannot move. He asks King to place a pistol in his hand and he dies where he lies. King gets help from the local Yantruwanta people, but on returning finds Wills dead too. The Yantruwanta look after King until he is found by a relief party sent from Melbourne. The date, September 15, 1861. So ended the glorious expedition across the continent of Australia, traversing the Outback and passing through terrain similar to the Birdsville region, the very terrain I'm stranded in.

But while I have been daft enough to spill some of my water, I've calmed down now, the tea is brewed and although it doesn't taste like Mum's, it's better than nothing. A couple of lumps of sugar give me energy. Lean back, stretch out, stick my feet out the door on the shady side, close my eyes, save myself for the days ahead. There's nothing else I can do at the moment. I'm going to survive.

I wake with a start, must have dozed off, the sun is setting. Or is it rising? Where the hell am I? Why's a speedometer staring me in the face? And what's a steering wheel doing in my bed?

And there's something itching my right leg, stinging it, I feel down, bloody hell, they're moving. Ants. Ants, millions of them. I'm leaping out of the car screaming, Christ I hate ants. And they're bloody great Bull ants. The Bull ants Billy told me about on Quarantine Island. Wrench my trousers off... swipe them, smash them, get them off me. I'm being eaten alive!

Turn the car upside down for Nick's can of SCRAM... Found it, spray it around... spray everything. Kill the bastards...

I sit down, sit down in the car and cry. Bury my head in my hands and cry. God what the hell's happening to me?

"You all right, mate?"

Who the hell is this? Am I dreaming? Am I hallucinating? A calm voice. A friendly voice.

"You've had a prang. Volksie damaged… but you all right? No bones broken?"

I can't believe it. It's Nick, my Pommie mate. Nick from Broken Hill. "What the hell are you doing here?"

"I'm on my way down the Track. Heading back towards Marree for a bit of a stop-over and I've come across you. I can't believe it. We were only sharing a beer a few weeks back. Small world…"

Nick has his tow rope fixed to the back of the Volksie and his Land Rover yanks it out of the sand as though it is a toy. And it drives. It drives ok despite the whack against the rock.

"Follow me, mate. See you in the bar. I reckon you could do with one. And I've got that story in the Land Rover if you want it. The one I told you about. The native people, the Aborigines."

# Chapter 11

# I Am the Way

Nick's story.

Crouching in the shade of the Acacia tree an old Aboriginal woman draws shapes in the sand, her face wrinkled and wizened with age, deep in concentration... she beckons her granddaughter to come closer. Speaking in short staccato bursts, she places the stones in the sand to indicate the position of watering holes that lie across the Western Desert. Running her first and second fingers in a double dotted line she indicates the distances between the water holes.

Alcheri watches intently as her grandmother runs her fingers through the sand. She is desperate to escape the Government station at Popanji. Over the years many have died in epidemics, some taking to the bottle. Squabbles between rival tribes were commonplace and fights broke out almost every day. She's had enough.

"Grandma – come with us," she pleads.

"No, too old now. Soon to join Sky Hero. He come in dream – fly across in setting sun. Not much time. You still young, go claim your homeland. He will guide you." She erases the scene with the palm of her hand.

Nangarri, the senior man, had been chosen by the Elders to uphold tribal laws. Already experiencing the Dreamtime, he reaches into the dilly bag and grasps the magical quartz, placing it between his teeth. Suddenly, a bolt of lightning turns night into day. Cosmic energy surges into his body and heightens his consciousness, giving powers beyond the boundaries of mortals. Breaking into a chant he quickens his pace, every stride measured and deliberate – following the Dreamtime track of his ancestors – a journey of many days across the Western Desert to the cave of the Rainbow Serpent – a mysterious ancestral spirit from the past – a skilful sorcerer with the power to kill errant tribe members by singing them to their doom. Bone pointing is his speciality. There is no time to lose – the Day of Judgement is fast approaching.

A group of young Aboriginal renegades led by Amadeus the Hawk Man, claim they own the land south of Emu and are entitled to royalties from the mining company that has taken over. The company is not likely to yield without a fight, questioning everything, its spokesman suspicious. He needs proof to identify the renegade Aborigines as the traditional owners, then interpret Tribal Law into the language of the Law of the Crown.

Through careful negotiations he has recruited a one-legged Aboriginal elder known as Stumpy Jack to track down the fabled medicine man Nangarri – the expert on tribal boundaries. If Stumpy Jack could find him, perhaps that would resolve the problem. Eventually he tracks him to Rocky Hill Aboriginal Reserve south of Alice Springs and they set out across the land in the trusty Land Rover.

The vehicle bumps and lurches along the narrow track, bushes brushing the underside of the chassis and leaving a trail of dust that filters up through the foliage behind them. In the distance they see flashes of light dancing through the trees. Suddenly they come upon a shanty of tin roofs under a clump of Ghost Gums. These are half-cylinders of corrugated sheet, open-ended like pig shelters and known as humpies. Little groups of Aborigines sit around in the dust. Dogs scavenge from empty bully beef cans littering the clearing and crows dive-bomb for scraps.

From nowhere steps an imposing figure of a man. He is lean and angular, his skin very black, not the shiny black of the Negroes but a dull black as if the sun has carried away all possibility of reflection. He has a long forked beard and carries a spear. He wears nothing but a loin cloth. On his chest is tattooed a snake with fangs ready to strike. The company man turns to Stumpy Jack.

"Is this Nangarri the medicine man?"

"Yes, he good bloke. Careful what you say."

"Do you know of the Amadeus mob?" he calls from the safety of the Land Rover.

The warrior nods with an air of disapproval.

"Amadeus. He drink. No respect, no Dreaming, no Tjurunga."

"What is Tjurunga?

"Tjurunga sacred emblem, like white man's document – carved on bark of mulga bush – you call title deed. We try Amadeus by tribal court – not by white man. Will call my people together. You know soon what happen."

Cumulus clouds begin to build on the horizon. Mumuna, the voice of thunder, rolls across the plain, spirit winds rage and howl for vengeance. The ancestors show their anger. Someone has challenged the laws of creation. To re-write creation means certain death. A spiritual heritage that has lasted for tens of thousands of years is under threat.

In the east there is the glow of distant fires lighting up the landscape, drawing in tribes from far and wide.

The drone of the didgeridoo resonates through the air, enhancing the drama that is about to take place.

Outside a cave the re-enactment of creation is gathering pace.

The participants themselves have become the early ancestors. Tribesmen in ceremonial dress are amassing and exchanging songs and dances in the Corroboree with rhythmic intensity to the sound of the didgeridoo – proving their ancestral ties in relation to the land.

The Spirit of the Long Grass, Native Black Cat, Possum Dreaming, Hawk Man – establish their tribal grounds using complex word pictures constructed through symbolism, drawing on the imagery and creative power of the Dreaming. Suddenly the sound of a Bullroarer heralds the main participant himself, The Rainbow Serpent.

Blinding sunlight rakes through the Gum trees revealing a tall gaunt figure emerging from the shadows. His stature radiates the power and wisdom of a demi-god. Behind him is a group of Aboriginal women led by Alcheri, who is gently manoeuvring a child in her arms as it tries to suckle. They take their places amongst the magic of music and chant, with the compulsive rhythm of clapping sticks setting the scene. At last, after many years in exile, they have reached their ancestral homeland to claim their inheritance.

Alcheri can still see her grandmother beneath the Acacia tree – she watches as she draws shapes in the sand with her forefinger, erasing scene after scene with her palm as she tells her story. She describes in detail how the white man rounded up her people from their tribal home, forcing those that could be found into cattle trucks then dispersing them throughout Missions in the Outback. Forced re-settlement.

Standing up she continues in anguish. "Whitefella posted Keep Out signs on our land. How we understand what Whitefella write? Many tribal elders hide in bush. Then big bang, BIG BANG! Dust storm fly upward – cover whole Earth. Many disappear. Thunder God took them away."

Alcheri's memories are rekindled as warriors dressed in totemic regalia begin acting out their imitative roles, their painted bodies swaying hypnotically in unison.

The Rainbow Serpent wearing a fantastic head-dress appears in the centre, dancing around the ceremonial fire. He calls on the

Dreamtime spirits to guide him. The stamping of feet reaches a crescendo sending up vaporous dust that adds to the atmosphere of the Corroboree. He circles the tribesmen with his arms menacingly thrust forward, pointing the bone, seeking out the violator of the holy of holies. Finally it rests on Amadeus the Hawk Man.

"You insult our Gods, steal Tjurunga. This land sacred. Belong Maralinga Tribe." The Rainbow Serpent cuts a vein in his arm and lets the blood flow onto the dry earth.

"You dare challenge laws of creation. Royalty money, bad money dreaming." Pushing the bone into the ground now red with his blood, he begins to chant the stanzas of life and death. Suddenly his voice breaks off. An eerie silence descends like a cloud over the ritual. The Rainbow Serpent draws his knife and advances on his prey, now standing transfixed with fear. He slices off a lock of the Hawk Man's hair and ties it to the bone. Crouching, his hand poised like a weapon – he grabs the fire stick and deftly lights the lock of the victim's hair.

Hawk Man stares at the treacherous pointer, lifting his hands to his face as though it will ward off the lethal medium that is pouring into his body. Trembling, he sways backwards and forwards and falls to the ground, writhing in mortal agony, his face horribly distorted, his eyes glossing over, his body twisting.

A primordial cry like an animal in distress pierces the silence. The hair on the pointer flares momentarily – then splutters out.

**In the Eternal Dreamtime an old woman erases the scene with the palm of her hand – and smiles...**

Back in the office Baz agrees there's truth in what Nick says. "The Aboriginies have powers we can't comprehend. A sixth sense if you like, way beyond us ordinary mortals. And he's right about the natives of Australia being treated shamefully over the atomic tests at Maralinga. It is their land, has been for thousands of years. That's the gist of your mate's story."

"Nick told me the authorities tried to move the Tjarutja people before the tests. As you say, their land. But he reckons some skipped off, hid in the bush, not hard for them to do. I think the Brits put up a few signs – KEEP OUT – not that the Aboriginies could read them."

"Could well be. If they had comprehended what was about to happen they wouldn't have stayed. Mind you, who did comprehend what the governments of Britain and Australia were up to?"

"Does the man in the street ever know, Baz?"

Baz swivels round in his seat. It's back to setting next week's pages. One last parting comment, "A bloke in my local said he'd been told servicemen were used as guinea pigs in the trials. They were subjected to the radio active cloud from the detonations."

"For experimental purposes?"

"That's right. To see what the effects were. You can't believe gossip in pubs but in this case his brother was working on the project up there at Maralinga. They were all told to keep it hush-hush."

Heather Bessen is bringing our morning coffee.

"Hope it's not radioactive," says Tremaine.

"What?"

"Forget it."

I stir my coffee, take out Nick's story and read again.

\* \* \* \* \*

Years later, back In England, I get the full story. Well, at least, part of the full story. From BBC radio news bulletins and from UK newspaper articles. And from articles sent to me by friends in Australia who know my interest in the subject. Virtually all of the information had been embargoed by the respective Governments until recently; I can understand why – not much of it makes pleasant reading!

Like so many others, the first I had heard of the proposed atomic tests to be conducted by Britain was in 1957 – a couple of years before I sailed to Australia – when I listened to the proclamation by Harold Macmillan, our Prime Minister. He was pretty up-beat about it:

*"We have made a successful start. When the [nuclear] tests are completed, as they soon will be, we shall be in the same position as the United States or Soviet Russia. We shall have made and tested the massive weapons. It will be possible then to discuss on equal terms."*

In Australia I was not overly conscious of the fact that tests had been carried out and were being continued at that time although Nick had touched on the tests in his wonderful story, "I am the way." "Dust storm fly upward – cover whole Earth. Many disappear. Thunder God took them away." And Baz mentioned them, of course. But it was not until I got back home and started to piece the facts together that I realised what had been happening.

Johnnie Mitch was told of an article in the paper, Green Left Weekly, and he'd popped it in the post straight away saying it might be of interest.

"Something to make you think, mate. It stopped me in my tracks."

 **23 May, 2001. Green Left Weekly.**

**Maralinga: An act of Indefensible Callousness**

*"After years of denial and deceit, the British government has admitted that military personnel were used in radiation experiments during the nuclear weapons tests at Maralinga in South Australia in the 1950's.*

*Confirming statements made repeatedly by veterans over the years, the British ministry of defence acknowledged on May 11 that it used military personnel from Britain, Australia and New Zealand in radiation experiments, but claimed that they were testing clothing not humans. A statement released by the British government that military personnel were "transported or walked in various uniforms to an area of low-level fallout."*

*The admission followed publicity surrounding documents found in the Australian National Archive in February by Sue*

*Rabbitt Roff, a senior research fellow from Scotland's Dundee University.*

*An October 12, 1956, document on "Australian Military Forces – Central Command" letterhead refers to the "Buffalo" series of four atmospheric nuclear tests conducted at Maralinga in September and October, 1956. The document names 70 Australian military personnel and one civilian, plus five New Zealand officers, all listed as exposed to radiation following a September 27 nuclear test.*

*Some men were chosen for "clothing trials" from an "indoctrinee force" of British, Australian and New Zealand military personnel. The men walked, crawled and were driven through a fallout zone three days after a nuclear test at Maralinga.*

*Roff dismisses the British government's claim that it was testing clothing, not humans, and says that thousands of Commonwealth military personnel not directly involved in the nuclear tests at Maralinga were required to be outdoors to observe the detonations."*

Two years later, my ears pricked up when I heard the word Maralinga on the BBC.

**29 April, 2003. BBC radio 4:**

*"For half a century, the Tjarutja Aboriginal people of Maralinga have waited to get their land back. The land is now said by the Australian government to be clean and ready for hand-back - sometime this year. Professor John Keane explores the history of British atomic tests at Maralinga from 1956 to 1963. He finds out how and why the British and Australian governments together confiscated the sacred lands of the Tjarutja people and examines how far Aboriginal people, servicemen and the desert environment were put at risk."*

Then in May, 2003, Johnnie Mitch came on the phone again. He'd put the respected Melbourne newspaper, The Age, in the post and I eagerly awaited what Mike, my postman, would bring.

"It's something else to interest you, mate. It's going back a few years to the build-up to the Maralinga tests. How the site was found and how it was developed."

Yes, it interested me all right.

I phoned John back. "Certainly is an eye-opener, mate. Thanks."

**May 11, 2003. The Melbourne Age:**

**Maralinga's afterlife**

*"Len Beadell stood among the stunted scrub and cast his eyes over the vast limestone and saltbush plain below, stretching northwards to infinity. It was exactly what he and his men had been looking for. They raised their bush hats and gave three triumphant cheers. "We all knew immediately that this was going to be the place," Beadell later wrote. "The saltbush undulations rolled away as far as we could see, even through our binoculars ... We solemnly wrung each other's hands and just gazed about us in all directions for half an hour."*

*Beadell was the leader of a reconnaissance party that had been sent "scrub bashing" in southern Australia 50 years ago, in search of a permanent place to test Britain's atomic weapons. The site he found and recommended was initially code-named X300, but soon became known as Maralinga. The land belonged to the Tjarutja people, though the name did not. Supplied by anthropologists working with Aboriginal people in eastern Australia, it meant "thunder fields."*

*A week later, Bristol freighters began arriving from the UK, bringing in an instant town, designed to house 2000 servicemen and destined to sit in the midst of a fenced-off area the size of England.*

*The main streets of the town sported signs such as London Road, Belfast Street and Durham Crescent. There was a post office, a swimming pool, a chapel, a hospital, even a cinema that screened the latest films from home."*

Then more in my daily post from Australia:

 **January 20, 2010. The Herald Sun, Melbourne.**

**No Compo for Australian nuclear test veterans**

*"THE Government has refused to help Australian veterans who are suing the British Government over radiation exposure during atomic bomb tests in the 1950s and '60s.*

*A group of survivors and their families are joining a class action after 800 British nuclear veterans were granted permission to sue their own Ministry of Defence for compensation.*

*Many of the soldiers, who wore just a hat, shorts and boots, were covered in fallout and were later treated for radiation sickness.*

*They were never warned of the risks involved and many were used as human guinea pigs to test deadly chemicals, including mustard gas.*

*In 1993, the Keating government accepted a $50 million ex-gratia compensation payment from Britain to settle all future Maralinga claims.*

*A condition was that any future compensation won by Aussie veterans would be paid by the Australian Government."*

Next. An article in my Daily Telegraph caught my eye:

 **March 2, 2010. The Telegraph, London.**

### Aborigines to sue British Government over nuclear tests

*"Australian Aborigines and former servicemen are to sue the British Ministry of Defence over diseases and disabilities that they claim were caused by nuclear testing in the Outback more than 50 years ago.*

*A group of 250 people, including 150 former servicemen, say they have suffered cancer, skin disease and deformities because of the fallout from blasts.*

*If they win, the British Government could be faced with a bill for compensation which will run to millions of pounds, according to lawyers for the group, which will be represented by Cherie Booth QC.*

*British lawyers last week travelled to South Australia, where the tests took place, to prepare the case in conjunction with the Aboriginal Legal Rights Movement and document the stories of people living in the area at the time of the testing.*

*Lawyers from London firm Hickman & Rose said the families that had come forward so far were "just the tip of the iceberg" and that they expected many more to follow.*

*Anna Mazzola, a partner at the firm, said that while the British had warned some white farmers that the tests were taking place, the indigenous community was largely ignored.*

*"The British assumed there was no one living there. But [local aborigines] lived off the land, ate the local plants and wildlife and were profoundly affected," she told The Daily Telegraph.*

*"The evidence we have is that little research was carried out into the repercussions of the testing and that's why it's so important that they are held accountable."*

*The group of 100 civilians and more than 150 former servicemen, who claim they were sent to work at the test sites with no protection or warning about the dangers, hopes to launch legal action by May.*

*The claim follows the lead of a class action lodged by former British servicemen also affected by radiation exposure who were granted permission to sue the government last year.*

*Among the Australians seeking compensation are families of the "Woomera babies" – 60 infants who died, some without explanation, during the decade of testing. Woomera lies 600km east of the test site at Maralinga and some believe the town could have been affected by fallout from the nuclear blasts.*

*Other alleged victims of the blasts have told of a "black mist" of fallout descending on their homes after the explosions.*

*In the years that followed the nuclear tests, the lawyers claim that a high number of cases of cancer, skin disease and birth deformities were recorded across several parts of South Australia."*

John asked over the phone one day,"How you getting on, mate?" I replied, "I think you had better watch this space."

Droving 10,000 sheep on a hot day.

John Wayne lent me the hat.

**Black Horse - Now where's the herd?**

**Royal Adelaide Show 1959 - we swept the board.**

Typewriters abound. Jason and I discuss the finer points of Foot Rot.

Margaret and Porsche.

**Waiting for the off. O'Halloran Hill Sprint.**

**Hill climbing at Collingrove - the fun starts here!**

**First day at the Weekly Times, Melbourne.**     **Out in the field - A working Journalist.**

**Ban the Bomb at the Journalists ball. Johnnie Mitch, right with Steve Ackeri and other friends.**

Who's the prettiest of them all - Holdsie, Ackeri and Barnsey off to the (fancy dress) party.

Test Driving a German Claas harvester.

My loved ones in Oz, Dad, Mum and Heather.

Cutting the cake - We're engaged. Mum and Dad Pattison look on.

**Porsche has to go - Puss in Boots to stay.**

**The big day. Me and Johnnie Mitch, my Best Man.**

**Celebrating tying the knot.**

Sail Away. Taking Heather to the Old Country.

We'll be back!

# Chapter 12

# I've got just the job for you

"Take a seat, Holdsworth. I've got just the job for you and it's important. Very important."

"A seat, Sir?"

"Yes, Holdsworth, sit down. This is top stuff."

The Deputy Editor doesn't usually hang about when handing out assignments and you certainly don't get the bum on a seat treatment. But this is serious and time for me to look assured and professional, still a relative newcomer here, but also a capable journo who must do justice to the important – yes, he said it, very important – job. One that merits a seat.

"There's a new irrigation project on the Murray. Up there in the Mallee. It's being opened by the Premier, Premier Playford himself." Ian Hawker looks at me intently. His eyes are level with mine. I try not to blink. "I've arranged for you to go up in Premier Playford's car. Travel with the man himself. Under the same roof you could call it. They don't come much bigger than this, Holdsworth."

I would stand to attention and salute, but Ian's still going. "This calls for the best from you, Holdsworth. The best. Nothing less."

I'm thinking about our Premier, the man who has fought tooth and nail for the State of South Australia, laid his life on the line, making it a sound, sober, law-abiding State every day of his 22 years in office. Aussies would say, "Doesn't seem a day over a hundred."

"Your eyes have glazed over Holdsworth. Hope you're up with this."

"I'm thinking of Premier Playford, Sir."

Ian Hawker's smooth brow turns into a frown; it looks like he's running the rule over me. Although I'm the most recent recruit I've done some reasonable work, even some good work, something that will be known in the years to come as an "exclusive," the interview with John Parker. I was the first – and still the only journalist I know – to get to this man. Yet Ian Hawker gives the impression he's searching for a reason not to give me this task. The top job. The one with Premier Playford that calls for the very best.

"You'll not only cover the event Holdsworth, get all the facts and figures, the speeches, the names, the dignitaries, you will be the representative of The Stock and Station Journal. Do you hear me, the representative?"

"Yes Sir, that's me. I am your man."

Ian Hawker, Deputy Editor, looks slightly less anxious. The frown is fading. Perhaps he's convincing himself that I might just be the perfect solution after all, what with my Grammar School education and youthful English exuberance. I might just woo the austere old sod as he throws the switch on a brand new irrigation project out there on the Murray, then turns to milk the applause from every man, woman and child in his sight. Stray dogs even.

On the other hand I might be the only man he's got. Tremaine is covering a conference on farm management, Jason is Inter-State chasing up some important story and Dick James still not fit enough to go rampaging around the country.

I rise, ready to leave. But there's something more.

"Don't muff it, Holdsworth. Don't muff it."

I can't resist. "No muffits here, Sir."

And then there's even more.

"Holdsworth."

"Yes Sir."

"Glad you got back from the Birdsville in one piece."

I'm to report to the official Government garage, just off Victoria Square and I'm to ask for a man called George Brown, Premier Playford's chauffeur.

It's nine sharp, so's my pencil; sharp that is. No good going out on this assignment and my lead already blunted. And I've got The Stock & Station Journal camera; it's slung over my shoulder, and there's a fresh new notebook in my back pocket.

Goodness, the enormity of what lies ahead starts to hit me. Am I up to it? Ian Hawker asked; not only is Playford the Premier of South Australia with a reputation for not suffering fools lightly, but no journo has been close enough to get a story from him. Now, here's me, thrust in his company and not just a ten minute job either. This is all day. ALL DAY!

Premier Playford, anti-drink, anti-laughter, anti-everything that's enjoyment – or so it seems. This is one assignment I'd happily give to someone else even if it meant I'd miss out on those elusive credits, grabbing The Stock and Station Journal a scoop or two. And for me a Brownie Point to add to the John Parker one.

I've parked the Volksie, sprinted across Victoria Square and here's the Premier's garage, spick and span, and the car, British-made black Daimler Sovereign with flag hanging limply from a little chrome pole on the bonnet. That's spick and span too, gleaming in the heat of the early morning sun. Didn't the guy on ABC radio just tell us that it had already topped the 100 degree mark?

I give a big, broad smile, "Good morning," and extend a hand. Chauffeur Brown is a solid man, seems a capable man, badge on his cap that's freshly polished just like the car, and not a hint of jaunty angle about him anywhere. "I'm Richard Holdsworth from The Stock and Station Journal. I'm to report to Premier Playford's chauffeur? Is that you?"

He ducks the question, but enquires with a half smile, "Warm enough?" And tells me he was in the Old Country a few years back, seeing relatives. "Essex," he says. "Yes, Hornchurch, the mother-in-law you see, her seventieth, born Christmas day. A treat for the wife."

Well, Hornchurch in winter isn't the greatest place on earth, treat or no treat.

But it doesn't seem to have put him off although he says it was a bit parky. "The mercury barely passed zero and here we are knocking on a hundred."

He's a nice man and there's no, "I bet you Poms are glad you're in God's Own Fair Chosen Country." That always tends to kill the amicable chit-chat for a moment or two. Would you believe he's even telling me he enjoyed his time in Hornchurch?

I join in the smiling session. Yes, Chauffeur George Brown is a jolly man. Ex-Royal Navy, it seems. "Ship-shape and Bristol fashion," is the give-away. "Wouldn't want it otherwise." And he shares his memories of Hornchurch even if frost-bite threatened his toes.

"New at the job, lad?"

I nod. I'm getting used to this; explaining about being a trainee journalist, a relative novice, but how I will try not to make a hash of it, be a big disappointment, despite never having met anyone as important as the Premier before.

"Don't worry about Playford. Treat him like anyone else and you'll get on ok." He looks round as if making sure no-one's in ear-shot. "Humour him, that's what I do. And I've got my retirement pension to think about."

He gives a last minute huff to the badge on the Daimler and a quick polish with his hanky. "Speck of dust," he says. "Playford wouldn't like that." Then it's time to make a start. "Here, sit up front with me."

My feet sink into the deep pile carpet and my bum into deep pile leather as the Sovereign purrs into life. "Haven't been late once in 20 years and I'm not about to start now. My pension, you know."

The Premier's house is in the Adelaide Hills. We weave our way through early morning traffic, me looking smug, chauffeur-driven, limousine, Premier's flag fluttering on the front at the heady speed of 25 miles an hour. Poor old Tremaine and his farm management conference; if only he could see me now.

We leave the crowds behind, into the foot hills now, George is making steady progress, all U bends and stiff climbs followed by more U bends and more stiff climbs. The Daimler isn't built for rapid progress under these circumstances nor is George. Back behind us I catch a glimpse of Adelaide basking in the early morning sun. "Be 115 by noon I'll wager." George Brown mops his brow... the cap with polished badge now rests on the back seat. The steering wheel twirls first one way and then the next. The U bends get more U, the climbs more severe. Over the brow of a hill, there's an impressive gateway, the family home, the Playford family home.

Time for me to retrieve George's cap as he sweeps us into a drive bordered by well manicured flower beds and four tyres crunch the gravel as the house looms into view. We agree there aren't too many like this in Hornchurch.

"Out lad. He'll be through the door in a shot and expecting us to be ship-shape and Bristol fashion and us ready to pipe him on board."

Yes, I'm out of the car; Chauffer Brown is out too, cap on now. A little bow is called for as Premier Playford strides forth and into the back seat, sombre black suit and sombre black briefcase to hand. I wonder if his sandwiches are in there, neatly cut and wrapped by Mrs Premier Playford.

George gives a half salute. I think it's time to do as serfs did in bygone days and tip my forelock. I try a friendly, "Good morning, Sir."

"Good morning. Stock and Station Journal isn't it?" His voice is strident, purposeful.

"It is," I confirm.

"Ahh yes. My secretary said."

Greetings over and I return to the front and take my place, Premier Playford in the rear. George slips the Sovereign into first and four tyres retrace their steps and crunch the gravel all over again and we're off on a three hour journey with the opportunity of me making light conversation and gleaning the secrets of Premiership, for those elusive scoops Ian Hawker is so keen to get his hands on.

"Nice day for it, Sir. I can't wait to see the new irrigation system."

"Yes, ahh, yes. Irrigation. Important for the State." The black briefcase rests on his knees. The lid is opened. I catch a glimpse as he scratches around among the contents. The lid is closed. A bit early for the sandwiches I suppose. "Yes irrigation. Important, very important."

Premier Playford seems more interested in the journey, the road ahead and the next corner. I'm not going to get my scoop. Not at this moment, anyway.

We whisk along, George in control, the hot South Australian wind rustling the Gums in a canopy above our heads, Kookaburras screaming to each other, and the Sovereign stirs the dust at the side of the road; second gear, then third, then back to second. "Sharp corner coming up, George." Premier Playford is monitoring our progress, eagle-eyed from the back seat while George is making our progress as unruffled as possible from behind the wheel. "Mind the next bend, George, it can be a little tricky one."

George has that taped too. "I'll mind it, Sir." He has no intention of being caught out by a little tricky one especially with his pension at stake. "I have travelled this route many times before."

I venture another conversation on the irrigation scheme. Important for the State, he said.

"Splendid enterprise. Government and private efforts coming together."

I'd like to keep the chat going if I could. How Premier Playford persuaded companies to come to South Australia, invest in South Australia. Was it not he who was accredited with giving the State its prosperity, a place to live, to set up shop?

But that's all I'm going to get from Playford at the moment. Not what I was looking for one bit, and not what Ian Hawker was looking for at all. "Where's your scoop, Holdsworth? Your scoop?"

Premier Playford is much more interested in the twisting and turning road in front of the fluttering flag, his fluttering flag. "Brake hard for the sharp left ahead. Over the brow of the hill."

Do I detect a sigh coming from George? Did George permit himself the very slightest sound of grief at being told how to do the things he has done impeccably for the past 20 odd years without the slightest mishap, not a single altercation, not even an errant rabbit given a nudge by the shiny chrome bumper.

But there's no stopping our Premier and it's not about investment, irrigation, anything. I wonder why he doesn't open his briefcase again; surely there will be some crucial papers lurking in there next to Mrs Playford's sandwiches. The pictures I'd seen of him in his office showed a desk piled high; if this isn't a bloody good time to knock off some of the outstanding, I'll eat my hat.

But then I'm thrown a lifeline. "Call my office tomorrow. I'll have my secretary prepare something for you." Scoop coming up?

Now it's back to the road ahead.

"I know this well, George... back of my hand. I'll take over the driving if you don't mind... You and the lad take a rest in the back."

George does mind. But there's that pension to think about. No point in telling the Premier how to run things, even the road out to the Murray Mallee.

So, here we are, the most important man in the State of South Australia, the lives of thousands in his hands, all manner of problems to solve, to thrash out, yet he is driving us to the irrigation project 200 miles away in the heat of the day and George and me in the luxury of the back seat like men of prestige. "You can take your cap off now, George. You know I don't stand on ceremony."

George isn't so sure. And from what I hear, I'm not that convinced either. Like a good journalist I did a bit of research on Sir Thomas Playford, asking Baz, "What would you recommend for bedtime reading?

"You can try the Government Press Office, but ten to one that'll be the usual old PR waffle. I'd get myself down to the library if I were you. It won't be long before you trace Playford's dour nature back to his Yorkshire ancestry.

Off I had gone with Baz's words ringing in my ears. "Wowser."

"Wowser," said the man next to me when I settled down with a weighty volume in front of me. "You must be talking about Playford... he's all work and no play, mate. That's what."

"Silence," said a man in grey suit behind a grey desk.

I opened the book and scoured the pages and soon found

plaudits and brick-bats in equal quantities. And what gave him the title of a staunch old sod. "Bloody wowser," said the man next to me again. "Six o'clock swill and on Sundays not a drink for love nor money."

"I won't ask again," said the grey man.

Best read on, said I to myself.

'It was the influence of Playford's mother, Elizabeth, that contributed to his relative Puritanism and social habits. She was a devout Baptist Christian, and it was primarily because of her that he abstained from alcohol, smoking and gambling.

His education was at the Norton Summit school in the Adelaide Hills, one room, one teacher, two assistants and 60 children. Playford, while a quick learner, frequently argued with the teacher and he was the first child to be caned for his troubles. His mother and father farmed locally and young Playford accompanied his father at the East End markets with their produce. Playford junior later called the weekly excursion and associated bartering his "university."

When Father broke a leg, Thomas Playford left school and ran the farm; he was just 13. Even when his father recovered, he stayed on and took control.

A year after World War I broke out, Playford enlisted as a private in the Australian Imperial Force (AIF), and sailed with the 27th Battalion, 2nd Division, for Gallipoli, stopping off in Egypt for training. Australian soldiers frequented Egyptian cities after dark and more often than not fights broke out; Playford and a handful of responsible men frequently dragged Australian soldiers from the drinking houses and brothels of the city of Cairo and the next and the next...

After taking part in the Gallipoli campaign, Playford and his battalion were shipped to Northern France and fought on the Western Front. Playford was shot and wounded and suffered damaged hearing that remained with him for the rest of his life, as did a piece of shrapnel lodged beneath the skin.'

I couldn't help thinking of ANZAC Day. I wondered if the Premier had marched... I didn't catch a glimpse of him. But then I was intent on not missing Baz and Jason. In years to come, I'd be standing on the very soil in Picardie where Playford as a young soldier manned the trenches and fought hand-to-hand with the Germans.

"How are we in the back?" says Premier Playford from the front. The front of the car, that is.

"Yes fine," says George. "Couldn't do better myself."

"Fine, sir," I say.

'After his injury, Playford was offered a desk job in India but preferred to return to his battalion and continued fighting in Belgium and France and he left the AIF as a Lieutenant Officer. Despite his obvious intellectual ability, he shunned the Government offer of free university education for returning soldiers and went back to the family farm. However, in 1932 his life changed when an old wartime friend, Archie Cameron, persuaded him to stand for the newly formed Liberal and Country League party (LCL) and in the election that followed, Playford won and represented the constituency of Murray in the South Australian House of Assembly.

Playford became the 33rd Premier of South Australia in 1938 and at the outbreak of the Second World War showed his mettle as a man with a mission and it was mainly down to him that South Australia became such a vital supplier of munitions for the Allied forces.

Ammunition factories were built in the northern and western suburbs of Adelaide; the small town of Salisbury was turned into the major defence centre while Wyalla shipyard on the Eyre Peninsula launched its first corvettes in 1941 just as Japan entered the war.

All this was done under Playford's watch and against the odds. From intransigent public service workers to Government bureaucracy – there was always something for young Tom to wrestle with. But getting funds from the Federal Government would prove the most difficult....'

"Very quiet in the back," says our driver.

"Cogitating, Sir."

"Yes, cogitating," I agree.

We have the Adelaide Hills behind us and the Daimler is

coasting. In front of us now are the flat, brown square miles that herald the Murray Mallee. The road is as straight as a die. A canon ball couldn't have traced it better.

"Ah, the easy bit," says Playford.

George nods. "It is easy now, Sir."

I think it best to chip in my twopenneth. "You've done a remarkably good job, Sir."

A few goannas scurry across the burning tarmac in front of us, the heat haze shimmering, distorting the road as we approach. From where I am sitting, it looks as though Premier Playford is dipping the Sovereign into liquid pools of haze and cars – the one or two we see – disappear then reappear again from the mirage as if by magic.

But there's no risk of being booked for excess speed. No chance of the wail of a speed cop's siren in our ears and the State Trooper calling up his bosses and saying he has no idea who the young lad and older guy in the back are but they must be important, very important. "They're being chauffeured by the Premier himself, Sarge."

Local dignitaries line up awaiting our arrival. In the scorching sun, best suits, beads of sweat on brows and black shoes polished like new. Did they really expect the Premier in the driving seat? There's no explanation from our leader, no explanation from George the Chauffeur nor young Richard from The Stock and Station Journal.

Best say nothing, I think. Chauffeur Brown hasn't. It goes down as an unexplained mystery.

The Mayor steps forward. "We thought you'd enjoy a small repast before the official duties, Premier. Before you throw the switch, so to speak." Premier Playford is nodding his approval. Light sandwiches, lemonade or clear, cold water. "We are very grateful for you coming… quite the event of the year." I look at George and George looks at me as if to ask, "Where the hell's the beer?"

We're into the RSL hall, packed standing. George tells me it must be the whole community for a radius of a hundred miles. "The population wouldn't miss this for the world."

We stand back while Premier Playford has his plate of sandwiches, white bread neatly trimmed, a cup of tea, best china. Two sugars, offered by a plump, smiling lady, with a freshly ironed pinafore, tied neatly at her side. "Cut fresh this morning they were." She does a half curtsey. "Specially, sir." It seems the Clerk of the Council's wife is a dab hand at sandwiches.

I see Jim McCardle, my opposite number at the rival paper, The Chronicle. Jim thinks I am a lucky bastard. "How'd you wangle that? In Playford's car. Lucky bastard."

I grimace. "Best part of three hours watching my p's and q's, not putting a foot wrong, not blotting my copybook. That makes me a lucky bastard?"

Jim grins, a knowing grin. "But you got the inside story. The irrigation scheme, plus a few scoops into the bargain. You'll be your boss's blue-eyed boy when you get back."

I tell Jim the truth, but not of the invitation to call Playford's office next day. "I got a few words of wisdom from him. But most from research in the library beforehand. It was no fun in the back seat of the car with the Great Man as driver."

"The back seat?" Jim's glass stops half-way to his lips. "Playford the driver?" The glass is put down. He looks startled.

Jim had heard of this sort of thing. Premier Playford wanting to run everything, even down to the driving. "I didn't believe it... now I know it's true." Jim takes up the glass again and gulps his chilled water. "Our hands-on Premier." He nearly chokes on it.

The neatly trimmed sandwiches have been devoured and swilled down; Playford makes a point of thanking the plump lady. It's time for official duties. A short ride to the banks of the Murray and the nerve centre where the irrigation scheme kicks off, paid for by a collective of orchard growers and Government money.

But Premier Playford isn't taking a short ride, he's walking, and so are we. And his jacket stays on – so do ours. Even in the scorching sun. I think there's a touch of Gallipoli and Flanders Fields about this. "A man of steel," the book said. "Always doing the honourable thing." Good job there are no Egyptian bawdy houses in the High Street – he could be dragging a few transgressors back to barracks before the day's out.

George had said the thermometer would top 115 degrees before lunch and he's wrong – it's more like a 150.

"Poms aren't used to this," I say to McCardle. "We melt."

"We all melt mate, not just you lily-white Poms."

We've walked the dusty path to the banks of the mighty Murray. The Mayor, Mrs Mayor, Clerk of the Council and Mrs Clerk of the Council, the lady who's ace with sandwiches. Then the committee and their ladies, the orchard growers, a couple of dozen hangers on and us Press guys. McCardle and me and a trusty soul who immigrated from Llandudno years ago and is the mainstay of the local paper. The sun glints off his glasses, his pencil is at the ready, notebook in hand, trusty Roliflex over his shoulder. Only thing missing is the word PRESS tucked into the brim of his hat. "Up from the City, then, lads?"

We affirm, "Up from the City."

"The town has never seen anything like this," he tells us. There's still a touch of a Welsh twang about him and, come to think about it, the look of Dylan Thomas too. Dai does the news pages, sport, farming (of course) and fills in for the Agony Aunt when she's off sick or goes over to Wagga Wagga to see her sister. "This will fill two or three pages, this will, and best part of the next issue, a real bonus lads."

It is a good story, local growers banding together to grow and market their produce, oranges, pears, peaches, and to dig deep in their pockets for the expensive irrigation plant making it all possible, turning dust into a Garden of Eden. Then the crucial licence to secure a slice of the life-giving Murray water. Playford would be behind them all the way... fighting his corner, fighting their corner, against the State Governments of New South Wales and Victoria who would siphon off the golden liquid before it crossed the border into South Australia.

Yes, this is a good story. McCardle and I are as one on this. And Dai from the local paper. "Boy, can I see the headlines. 'Premier Makes it Happen for Local Producers'."

We'll split up, each tackling a handful of people who can help add some depth to the story, then share the spoils over a jar at the end of the day. "A jar?" I enquire. "Not if I'm going back with

Premier Playford. He'll make me get out and walk."

Jim's playing the good soul now. I can travel back with him, in the pool car, a bog standard Holden. Who wants deep pile carpet and a flag fluttering from the bonnet when you can have a beer to set you on your way? "Tell Playford you've got a lift. Tell him you've got to be back before you melt."

I shirk that one. "I'll tell George, he'll understand."

And George does. "Lucky so and so. I could do with one myself before the sun sinks over the yard-arm."

We toss for the responsibilities. I'd got the few details from Premier Playford on the way up, between the sharp bends and the straight straights; Jim will tackle the Mayor and other Top Brass and the man from the local paper knows the Clerk of the Council. They drink together, it seems. I win the easy bit. I'm to talk to the growers.

Then we'll share the spoils over that beer.

The Mayor's knuckles tap the microphone; in his other hand is a slip of paper to prompt should the sense of occasion get to his memory. And the sun beats down, there's scarcely a square foot of shade to be seen anywhere.

Then a polite round of applause for Premier Playford; no notes for him, it's straight from the hip and he's telling us what a fine fellow he is, what a fine State Government we've got. We are lucky people as the temperature soars and a man next to me says, "I tell ya it was a 115 when I left home an hour ago."

George nods in my direction. "Told you so."

I wonder how many people know what lies behind the man addressing them now. Inspiring the men of the land to grow more, never accept second best, to take inspiration from their leader.

The book said it all:

*'Playford was a tough nut. And he had to be. As Premier he worked with seven different Prime Ministers of Australia during his tenure as State Premier, eight if you count the two terms served by Robert Menzies. And it was Bob Menzies, the best known of them all, who he found hardest to bring to the party. Governor Playford used any ploy, any means, underhand or not to achieve his goal for South Australia and South Australians. Of Playford,*

*Bob Menzies once said, "Tom wouldn't know intellectual honesty if he met it on the end of a pitch fork but he does it all for South Australia, not himself, so I forgive him.'*

Respite for the listening throng as Premier Playford throws the switch and behind us, and to right and left, sprinklers gurgle then hiss into action, the cool, life-giving water, drenching the freshly planted rows of citrus. There's enthusiastic applause now, smiles all round, it's over and we're lucky that only two kids and an old-timer are treated for heat-stroke. It's been a great success.

And I wonder how many in the audience realise that this life-giving water is only there because Premier Playford had fought for it with the same vigour and determination as he showed on the battlefields of Picardie.

I think I'll put that in my story. Ian Hawker wants a scoop... well he's got one. But not what he was expecting. Mind you, I think I'll leave out the bit about Egyptian brothels.

"The Drover's Retreat is down the High Street, boy-o," says Dai. "Past the Texaco garage. Get them in who gets there first." He's even sounding like Dylan Thomas.

Next morning and I'm back in the office. Tremaine asks, "How did you get on, mate? The Pom and the Premier."

"Good."

"Got your story?"

I flick through a dozen or so pages before his eyes. "Baz says it's fine."

Tremaine is onto my pics. Row upon row of citrus trees. Sprinklers whooshing jets of water. Satisfied looks on the faces of eager dignitaries as Premier Playford stands back and watches thousands of gallons of Murray cascade over the sun-burnt land. I had captured it all.

"What's Joe Stalin doing behind the microphone?"

I had also scampered forward to the front row on all fours, past the seated Lord Mayor and Mrs Lord Mayor, Mr Clerk of the Council and Mrs Clerk, plus the other dignitaries, snapped the

Premier from feet up to craggy jaw, steely eyes, grim determination. I rather prided myself I had captured the man and the moment. "I have done the old bugger justice, don't you think?"

"Looks more like a Soviet leader on a bad day."

"Joe Stalin had a tash."

"Joe Stalin without a tash, then."

Ian Hawker is impressed. The story gets the thumbs up. Even dodging the drive back with Premier Playford seems to be overlooked. "I sounded him out on a couple of stories on the way up, Sir. And I'm invited to call his office this morning – there might be a scoop there."

"Good man."

I'm just about to leave.

"Just one thing, Holdsworth. What's Joe Stalin doing in your pics?" Ian Hawker has the hint of a smile on his lips.

"He had a tash, Sir."

"Well, Joe Stalin without a tash."

\* \* \* \* \*

Mum and dad have gone back home. I don't think Mum could take the heat and the town of Elizabeth basks on the flat, open plain to the north of Adelaide – maybe not the best place to set up shop for Pommie migrants. I find it glorious weather but if you've come from England in winter, or even England in summer, some find the Aussie summer a bit hard to take. They decided to leave. Dad fitted everything back in a crate, labelled it all and had a carrier come by and take it to the docks. P&O did the rest.

Well, that's more than a big loss but I have made my life in Oz now. I have a great job, good friends and a future that I could never have aspired to back home. And now that Dad is retired, they can come back to see me from time to time. An extended holiday, perhaps. In the meantime, they have my sister to think about. Ingie (I still call her that from the day I was a kid and couldn't get my tongue round Helen) has a husband and children and needs to see Mum and Dad.

But my parents have gone and I don't have a roof over my head!

Wait a moment. Ronnie is moving out of the parental house in Rostrevor, a pleasant suburb of Adelaide, and has taken a flat much closer to Town in North Adelaide while Patti is dropping by every now and again to demonstrate her prowess in the kitchen. "There's a spare bedroom, mate. If you want."

There's another change. The faithful Beetle has been replaced by a fast and furious Porsche. I spied it in a dealer's yard, gleaming in brilliant white, festooned with flags and bunting and a sign proclaiming CAR OF THE WEEK. Standing out from the crowd. Just a year old, one careful owner, or so the salesman said. Fortunately he didn't try to stretch my imagination by saying it was a dear old soul who only drove it to church each Sunday.

I walked away. Then came back. Then walked away again and came back again – a month later it was still Car of the Week! I can drive a hard bargain here, I told myself. And I had to admit the sleek lines, powerful engine, and promise of thrills to come had me hooked.

"Buy me!" it cried (in German).

"I will, I will!" I replied (in English).

And I did – the faithful Beetle was left at the back of the parking lot and my bank account went into the red like never before and monthly hire purchase payments promised to bleed me dry. How was I ever going to live? Eat again? But she was mine! ALL MINE!

Same fundamentals as the Beetle, same brilliance from the pen of Ferdinand Porsche, but a great deal more pace and charisma. And she's a convertible – let the sunshine in! I drive round to my friends and show off. Steve Ackeri, my Lebanese buddy with the hairdressing place down on the South Road and Dom Zappia, who owns a classy Italian menswear shop in Hindley Street with his brother. And Reno the ace Burrows salesman. They all drool.

"Think of the dolly birds you can pull," says Ackeri.

"You'll be fighting them off," says Zappia.

And Bob Barnes who runs a car accessory store can't believe his eyes. Bob has a blue MG, but no MG is a match for the Porsche, even in Barnsey's hands. He drools too.

Now Tremaine has a parking slot reserved for me and my Porsche outside the Princeton Club. Every Thursday; life is starting to move forward at a pace.

And there could be more to come. Dom Zappia conjures up what it could do on the racetrack. "You could set the world alight with this car." He's eyeing the low-slung suspension, listening to the powerful beat of the air-cooled power plant. "You could blow away a lot of cars that think they are fast."

With his European background, Dom Zappia follows the motor racing scene like I do. He and I know the exploits of drivers who make the most of the Porsche's capabilities. We are as one over the exploits of Stirling Moss in the Porsche Spyders in the Targa Floria and around the twisting Nurburgring in Germany. Not only Moss but a whole host of thrilling drivers, Count von Trips, Edgar Barth, Hans Herrmann; these drivers could put in some great performances against much more powerful cars, Ferraris and Maseratis.

I glean all I can from the pages of the motor racing press; the exploits of the German, Count von Trips, fire my imagination. He had a car similar to the one I've just bought and performed miracles with it – how could I not dream of trying to follow in his footsteps?

'Von Trips started his racing in a Porsche and his successes prompted him to put a call through to the factory and ask about a drive in a factory car. The team manager dismissed the idea but the story didn't end there. Legend had it that the secretary implored her boss. "He sounds so nice and he has won so many races..." Miracles do happen; Graf von Trips got a trial, was successful and was invited to join the official Porsche factory team.

Up until then, the young man from Cologne had not been able to bring himself to tell his parents what occupied his weekends. Now he had to come clean! His name could be in lights, his face on front covers of magazines. He is a dashing figure... Count von Trips.'

Ackeri sits in the driving seat, it's difficult to prize him out. "There's no stopping you now Holdsie." Steve also has an MG. He's also envious.

"This is no Porsche Spyder," I tell him. "And I am not von Trips."

Steve and his family emigrated from Lebanon a few years back; his father is an ace hairdresser and Steve is following in his footsteps, he's the best I've known. He was working for his dad but often late out of bed, slow to get to work. Finally his father got fed up. "Here Steve, I've taken a place for you on the South Road, paid the deposit, don't come back till you're successful."

Now everyone goes there, he calls it a salon, Steve's Salon. In years to come he will be in Brisbane and the most successful entrepreneur in the business with dozens of women's hairdressing salons and enough money to buy as many Porsches as you can park on a football pitch. But for now he's saying, "Hey Holdsie, you gotta go racing in this."

And so I am. The first step is joining the Sporting Car Club, it's the official body of the sport in South Australia. I go to my first meeting, we are sitting in row upon row of hard backed seats and Chairman Charles Berry is addressing us, a splendid fellow who runs a funeral parlour; handy if we kill ourselves! He talks about annual subscriptions, entrance fees, race meetings, regulations. What the hell's wrong with talking about racing a car?

Instead, he wants us to work! "I need volunteers to spend an hour or two on the hill climb, up there in the Barossa Valley. It needs sprucing up."

Hands go up, mine included. And here I am, Sunday afternoon painting fencing, tidying the paddock, trimming the grass; what a great way to get to know everyone, get to know the hill climb, my first track at first hand. But it's still not racing.

I munch my sandwiches in the break, eyeing the track spiralling up the hill in front of me and out of sight; somewhere up there hundreds of feet away is the finishing line – if you make it in one piece! And I thumb through The Bible on the art, The Technique of Motor Racing, it's written by the Italian driver Piero Taruffi, master of the long distance race as well as the short sprint. He won the Mille Miglia, a thousand miles of ordinary Italian roads, through villages, up hills, down long dusty straights, round hairpin corners. A bit over ten hours, all flat out. I flick through the pages, search out the telling words. 'Walk the track where you can. Spot the irregularities in the surface, avoid the loose gravel, get to know the reverse camber.'

Charles Berry peers into the Porsche. He is an impressive man; even with a paint brush in his hand he wears a jacket and bow tie. No, he's not after my sandwiches, he's spied my reading matter. "You've got the book."

"I've got the book."

"Well you know what the man says, walk the track."

I do and I'm hooked. More than that, I apply for a racing driver's licence – provisional for the first half a dozen races – then the full job that signals your intent. And as the Club has just acquired Mallala, a conventional, flat, racing circuit north of Adelaide, I'll have tons of chance to put it to the test.

Mallala is typical of this sort of thing, like Silverstone in England, like Le Mans in France. Not the thrilling "natural" circuits such as Nurburgring in Germany or Spa in Belgium. But it has the distinct advantage that if you come off the track you will be extremely unlucky to find a tree to hit. Run-off areas abound, great for novice drivers like Richard Holdsworth, experimenting in the art of piloting a Porsche round a circuit and running out of road as he discovers the limitations of the car... and himself.

Time to walk the circuit, Piero!

# Chapter 13

# The (Daft) Things We Do When
# We're Young

I am driving into the main street of Victor Harbour. It's full of cars, mainly sports cars, MGs, TRs, Austin Healeys and a few, a very few, Porsches and it's full of people, young people in a high state of revelry. Victor Harbour is a holiday resort and it's New Year's Eve holiday break.

I find a parking slot between an MG and TR4 and a lad I know from the Princeton Club swaggers over and sprawls himself against the side of the Porsche. "Hi Rich, welcome to the party." He's wearing bathers and flip-flops; he also has a chain round his neck and cross and is brandishing a plastic sword. But the thing that really convinces me he is a medieval knight is the frilly girl's knickers over his head, his face peeping out of one of the legs and the row upon row of frills look for all the world like chain mail.

"Great to see you, mate. Come and join in the fun."

He shakes me by the hand and goes off to do battle alongside Richard III at Bosworth or Harold at Hastings – or a parking attendant.

The Princeton Club has moved, lock, stock and barrel to Victor Harbour for the three day break. Tremaine, Ferrier and Bowden are at the local hall setting up for the best nights of the year. And the band, the Penny Rockets, they're setting up too, the best band in the land. The rest of the lads, the likely lads, Ackeri, Dom Zappia, Barnsy and Reno have joined forces with the medieval knight and are busy making mayhem in the High Street.

Yes, these are some of the daft things we do when we're young.

I've driven down from Adelaide in a little over an hour. Sixty odd miles. That's not bad on a winding road, ups and downs, fast corners and slow corners, but mainly slow ones with a couple of hairpins thrown in for the Porsche to enjoy. The record is said to be about an hour; I am no more than a minute or two off the record. But I didn't exceed the speed limit; I've learnt my lesson on this road already.

Driving back home from an invitation MG Car Club race day at O'Halloran Hill a month or so back I'd been caught. It had been a wonderful weekend and a great competition on a challenging track; a standing start and flying finish, two laps, terrific fun. I only just got pipped for the fastest run by an out-and-out racing car and on the way back with lovely Christine at my side had slipped the Porsche through a couple of fastish bends – a bit too fastish for the speed cop on the bike behind me.

Stupid me for not checking the rear view mirror. But I hadn't and he had thrown the book at me.

Anyone who gets pulled over knows the sinking feeling as you realise what you've done. It's too late by the time you've caught a glimpse of him in your mirror, you're sure he's been there for ages. The cop follows for a few moments then roars past and you know your goose is cooked as he signals you to pull over. His helmet, goggles and all-enveloping black leather kit all add to the fear he wants to bring to the party.

He parked the bike (ever so slowly), climbed off (even more slowly) and then walked back to me, his victim, with that "You've had it now, Sir," look on his face. Did I see a hangman's noose sticking out of his back pocket?

Gorgeous Christine, my companion for the weekend, glanced nervously across at me.

"Yes, I'm done for, Christine."

I put my hands up to the speeding but not the chronicle of crimes I was supposed to have committed. Driving dangerously, driving in a manner likely to endanger the lives of other road users, crossing a white line, crossing a double white line, crossing anything… The copper, goggles removed now, menace in his eyes, was ticking off every transgression he could find on the Statute Book. He only stopped when he ran out of fingers.

Don't get me wrong, I have some very good friends in the ranks of the police department. Good, friendly, fun-loving friends you can share a drink with, tell the most disgraceful jokes to, remind them their football team is the worst in the land. And get away with it.

But not the guy standing there scribbling in his notebook, retribution written all over his face. You are right, Ackeri, Porsches do hold an attraction for Dolly Birds. Pity you didn't mention speed cops. The Porsche attracts them like bloody magnets. Always has and always will.

Had I not been "done" within an hour of picking up the car? Taking delivery of my gleaming (nearly new) Porsche from the showrooms down the road from The Stock and Station Journal.

I'd signed on the dotted line and written the cheque; now it was my turn to have fun. Les, the salesman, shook me by the hand, opened the driver's door and beckoned me in behind the wheel to take my place on the hot seat. "It's all yours now, Mr Holdsworth. Enjoy ya new car." Then added, "Take it easy." I bet he went straight back into the office, collected his commission and slipped off down the pub for a jar while I came down to earth with a bang. "Take it easy, Mr Holdsworth. It doesn't half go."

I took it easy all right. Gently merging into the rush-hour traffic, turning right down West Terrace, left up towards North Adelaide. I thought I'd skip the flat for a moment to give it a run on a bit of clear road. Through the gears, into top, relax, no different to the Volksie. Just being careful, considerate. Cripes, I had to; the kit beneath my bum had just cost thousands, I was not about to wreck it.

But careful and considerate in top gear for a Volkswagen is not the same as careful and considerate in top for a Porsche. As Les had said, "It doesn't half go..."

"Step out of the car please, Sir?" The Highway Patrol had screeched to a halt in front of me, blocking my escape, sirens blazing. Blocking my escape? What the hell for? I went white, matching the colour of the car. What had I done?

"Do you have any idea what speed you were doing, Sir?"

That's what I'd done... not looked at the bloody speedo.

"No, officer. I mean, yes. I was just tootling along. It's new to me. I've only just taken delivery."

"Well, I'd give it back if I were you, Sir."

The motorcycle policeman was giving me the same treatment. On my way back from the race meeting at O'Halloran Hill; taking things easy, Christine at my side, doing no more than failing to heed the speedometer and the rear view mirror. And the result, he was standing there accusing me of everything short of the gunpowder plot. Big, burly copper. Any magistrate would surely don the Black Cap. Order up the executioner and have me depart this world all over a bit of a dash in the Porsche. Christine cried for me.

But wait a moment. As luck would have it, Christine happened to be PA to a young solicitor and she persuaded him to take time off from fighting for mass murderers, rapists and gun runners to win my case, shine and move up the ladder. In court the sharply dressed young man soon cottoned on to the fact that the copper had changed the answers to the questions he had fired at me out there at the side of the road; half the pages in his notebook were in a different pen.

"Your pen ran out?" enquired my man, sensing a foot in the door.

The copper could not see the foot. "No," came his reply.

"So how do you account for the answers being in a different ink?

Christine, in the gallery, smiled hopefully. She gave a little thumbs up.

The copper shuffled around awkwardly. He had no reply.

My solicitor moved forward, his neatly tailored suit and assured confidence ready for the telling move. He took the notebook from the copper's hand and passed it with deliberate intent to the magistrate. "Something funny here, M'lord."

"Something funny, indeed. I can't convict on falsified evidence." He took the Black Cap off and stood the hangman down. "Case dismissed."

We gathered on the steps outside the court, the Porsche basking in the sunlight and Christine looking just as mouth-watering. I gave her a big hug. My solicitor emerged, his hand outstretched, the gold cuff-links catching the light. "Glad I could be of some assistance."

The magistrate emerged from the darkness of the court, looked at me, looked at Christine and then at the sleek lines of the Porsche, hood down and ready to fly. "You are a very lucky young man. And very lucky to get away with it…"

I paid the speeding fine and watched my speed and rear view mirror from that moment onwards, and not least on the way down to Victor Harbour for the New Year's Eve break. I wasn't going to spoil a great party.

The band strikes up, the pretty girls are looking their prettiest, the lads jostling for position, a dance or two… or three… These are nights to remember if only for the fact that I am sleeping in the Porsche! Painful? But with reclining cab seats it's not as bad as for the lads in MGs, TRs, Healeys. They have fixed, rigid, straight up-and-down seats. Sleep there, no way! So, best not to go to bed at all for them. For me, forty winks perhaps.

Third night of the Princeton Club New Year's Eve rave and sleep deprivation is kicking in. Bright, personable young men have become walking zombies. The medieval knight has capitulated; lost his zing, couldn't fight off a feather duster. It would have been easier to spend three nights on Mount Everest without oxygen. So, when a lovely girl called Heidi from Latvia says, "You look as though you could do with a good sleep." I couldn't agree more.

"Mount Everest would have been a walk in the park compared with this."

"Sorry?"

"Only a joke. I'm climbing Everest next year, it will be a doddle up against New Year in Victor Harbour."

She laughs, a gay laugh, with sparkle in her eyes. "I have a spare bed in my hotel room. On the sea front. My friend has gone off with a boy somewhere. "

"You're too kind," I say. "I'll gather my crampons, ice pick, oxygen mask and see you outside."

"You don't need those, silly."

"What about the short wave radio? Will I need to call base camp for assistance?"

I think she knows I'm only joking. But her smile comes with a warning. "You'll have to tip-toe into the hotel as they are very strict about visitors after 10.00 o'clock. And we'll have to smuggle you out in the morning."

It's next morning and my new found friend from Latvia looks dismayed. It seems smuggling me out through the front door has become impossible. "The corridor is full of people and a stern-looking lady sits behind the reception desk."

"Not to worry," I say. "Don't forget I've still got my crampons."

I go over the balcony, one foot after another, down the trellis until I finish up among a group of startled guests relaxing on the patio with coffee.

"Just practising for next year. Everest, you know."

I'd pick a rose from the garden and throw it up to her window but I just don't have the energy.

\*　\*　\*　\*　\*

The new year is with us and I'm turning out for Colin's cricket eleven and I have to admit it's good to return to the great game. Colin from the Department of Agriculture, that is. I've been to a few nets and Colin thought I was good enough to face the terrors of Aussie fast bowling.

Strap on my pads, rib protector, insert the box in my pants to save my prize assets. Take guard, then duck and weave, move inside the head-high bouncers, punish the loose ball... and I haven't even got out of the car yet!

Cricket! Ah, the sound of ball on bare flesh. Your knuckles, your head, left elbow, right shin. I can feel the bruises coming on.

"You're first wicket down," says Colin, in his freshly ironed whites. Men from the Department of Agriculture do things properly – even on the cricket pitch. Whites are whiter than white. Bat oiled and in perfect nick. He opens the batting and has won the toss, professionals always do or, as my dear old Village Headmaster used to say, "It's my turn, lads, no matter which way the coin falls."

First wicket down? Yes, all I need to do is listen for the rattle of stumps as the man at the crease misses a straight one, or the cry of glee from first slip as he edges an out-swinger straight into the man's waiting hands. Then I'm in. My turn after all these years.

"You did say they haven't got any tractor drivers, Colin?"

There's not a tractor driver in sight but there's a pretty menacing looking guy running in from the pavilion end and I swear he could plough a mean furrow across my skull were I daft enough to leave my head in the way.

"Wait for the overpitched one," Colin says. "Drive him through the covers and you'll be away."

I wish I was away, I'm thinking, as the bowler who's built like a World War Two bunker, or as the Aussies say, the proverbial brick shit-house, runs in to bowl. He's already accounted for our opening bat, the ambulance men having taken him off for re-assembly and promised to let his next of kin know. And I'm in, taking guard from the umpire, trembling, hardly able to focus, never mind think. "Hold the bat straight, lad. How can I give you middle and leg when it's flapping about like that?"

I take a deep breath, look round, standing there all by myself, a lamb to the slaughter; the nearest human being is the wicket keeper standing back at least 20 paces so he won't get knocked unconscious by the bloke running in like an express train. The proverbial brick shit-house.

I had driven up in the Porsche, hood down, with almost gay abandon. I was lucky enough to be going out with a pretty girl from Sydney and we zipped along enjoying life to the full. Her pretty face, flaxen hair blowing in the wind, long legs stretched out from the tiniest of tartan skirts. Goodness, was that the sort of girl I went out with in those days? Lucky old me!

Christine had gone back to England – on the P&O Line just like

Mum and Dad. Gorgeous Christine gone back to England too. What's wrong with this place? Am I missing something?

Well, I'm not missing Michelle, an absolute charmer from Sydney, and my companion for the day. She's learning to drive and the opportunity of practising on the surrounding grassed area, off the main road, is too good to miss even in a race-bred Porsche.

As the brick shit-house runs into bowl, destruction in mind, Michelle passes by, the Porsche kangaroo hopping its way round the ground as she tries too much accelerator, followed by too much brake. And a dab on the clutch between these two. And the grinding sound of gears thrown in for good measure.

The opposing fieldsmen have seen nothing like this. They have all lost interest in the noble sport of maiming batsmen and are watching. The first ball, fast and furious, rears off a length, catches the shoulder of my bat but instead of being taken by first slip, sails through his hands and over the boundary rope in a flash.

"Four," calls the umpire.

Second ball and by now the bowler also has an eye on Michelle and my Porsche hopping round the outfield. He overpitches. "Hit it, Rich," I hear Colin call from the other end, "Hit it." And I do.

"Four," calls the umpire again.

My fifty comes up quicker than Don Bradman at his best. Unfortunately, Michelle soon tires of grinding gears in the Porsche, lies back and takes a siesta. Clearly it's been a hard day and she's not that interested in following my fate.

The fielders return to fielding and the power-house with the ball returns for a second spell to take his wrath out on our side, me included. His first nearly has my head and the second beats me for pace, my bat nowhere near the projectile as it fizzes through on its way to the wicket keeper. "How's that, ump? Definitely out," he cries knowing full well it's not. Out, that is.

The umpire is not certain. I can hear Colin call out. "Hang about, Rich, he's conferring with the square leg umpire. I'm sure you didn't nick it. I'm sure you're in."

"I'm not in," I say. "I'm definitely out."

Back in the pavilion and the next man in is padding up. "He's not that quick," I say. "I thought it only fair to let him have my wicket after all those fours and sixes we rattled up."

He looks dubious.

"Just wait for the overpitched ones. They're a four all the way."

As we drive back, Michelle says, "I think I've got the hang of the pedal that makes it go quicker. And the one on the left, the one you call the clutch. I've just got to learn how to stop."

\* \* \* \* \*

If I were to drive to the far side of Eyre Peninsula in a day I would be doing a good job. More likely, it'd take a day and a half. It's the best part of 400 miles, that's to say, for us Poms a fair slice of the distance from Lands End to John O'Groats. And I've got to get there at the earliest as I'm down to cover the Open Day at Minnipa Agricultural Centre.

"Four days for two stories, three stories at the most, Holdsworth. I can use your time more profitably," Ian Hawker, Assistant Editor, tells me, his slide-rule in hand. "That's why I've arranged for you to go up with Graham in his Cessna. Next Monday, fly out from a private airfield north of Adelaide."

It's Monday and I'm about to learn something new today. After a hearty breakfast I drive up to the airfield nice and early, and the private airfield north of Adelaide turns out to be two tin shacks and an air sock hanging lazily in the hot morning air. Graham greets me cheerily. "Ever been up in a light aircraft before?"

"Nope."

"Well, you're in for a treat. Let's get fuelled up."

Fuelling up for passengers in a scheduled airliner on a regular service doesn't involve the pilot or passengers. Whether it's First Class, Business Class or even the also-rans herded together like sheep in the back. The pilot orders a thousand gallons of high octane from the ground staff and the passengers fly in comfort totally oblivious of the activity that has gone before – the tankers, fuel pipes, gauges, and half a dozen men who know how to get the vital ingredient into the aircraft fuel tanks.

Fuelling the Cessna is a much more sophisticated business.

Graham is pointing. "If you could stand on that 44 gallon drum I'll hand up the fuel nozzle; stick it in the wing tank... up there above your head... while I go and turn on. Give me a shout when it's full."

I am standing on the drum. I heave the thick, heavy hosepipe and the nozzle over my shoulder, feed it into the fuel tank. "Ready when you are," I call out. I feel the flow of fuel as it surges through the pipe and I hear the splash and gurgle as it fills the tank. "How will I know when it's full?"

"You'll soon know."

I find out in a couple of minutes. "Not to worry," says Graham, optimistically. "You'll dry out quickly. Just don't go near anyone with a match."

This is a crop-dusting aircraft. Not the lap of luxury of an Ansett ANA Boeing with in-flight snacks and a girl with shapely legs mincing her way up the aisle. The crop duster spends its life hedge-hopping at near zero height. And it has other disconcerting features as well.

For example, there's only one seat and that's for the pilot while the rear is occupied by a huge silver metal container housing the crop-dusting chemicals. It starts in the roof of the plane and tapers down to a nozzle below floor level; my seat – if that's what you call a string bag stretched across a metal frame – is immediately to the rear of the giant container. I'm sitting with legs apart, the huge tin container pressed against my wedding tackle. One false move and my appeal to the ladies is gone for good.

"I see you've found your seat then," cries Graham, jumping up and down on the brown grass that doubles as a runway so that on the up bit his eyes are level with the tiny window to my left. "Not maximum comfort, I'm afraid, but I expect you'll get used to it after a bit."

And off we go. "Excuse me Miss, when are you serving the complimentary drinks? And I don't half fancy a packet of your roasted nuts."

I am craning my neck to one side of the huge metal container and can see Graham toying with the controls. The bouncing of the wheels along the grass ceases and we're airborne leaving my stomach and hearty breakfast back there on the airstrip. As we cant over and climb to the right in a tight circle, the roads, houses and trees down below rapidly adopt the dimensions of toy-land. Hey, there's the cricket ground where life and limb was put to the test just last Saturday. It's the size of a postage stamp today.

"We need to gain height to cross the Gulf," Graham calls back over his shoulder. "Regulations you see… single engined aircraft… over water."

This is reassuring. If the engine cuts out I'm sure we'll gently coast down till we reach land then find a convenient air strip with a modern air-conditioned airport terminal, row upon row of potted plants, and a bar where I'll be toasting Graham for his skills. And he'll return the favour, me being a model passenger and not kicking up a fuss one bit.

"I'm afraid that's not likely," says Graham still gaining height. "These things don't glide… more a case of coming down like a brick. But they float for a while."

Ok, I've taken that on board.

"Is there such a thing as a life raft?" I ask more out of curiosity than hope, just in case I've missed the instructions of where to find it, how to get it out of that tiny window and inflated with a bicycle pump while bobbing up and down in my second-best best suit, the one saturated in high-octane fuel. Come to think of it, I haven't seen the bicycle pump either.

"Sorry," says Graham. "Nothing like that either. We're on our own if the engine conks out. A wing and a prayer."

Over the Gulf of St Vincent, skipping across Yorke Peninsula, then Spencer Gulf and finally Eyre Peninsula lies beneath my string bag seat.

And navigational equipment doesn't seem to be on a par with a Boeing 707 either; Graham is peering over the nose of the aircraft seeking a landmark he can latch onto and get his bearings. And that's not easy with a chunk of flat, brown land that stretches from horizon to horizon and not a single distinctive feature worthy of the name.

But, wait a minute, Graham has cottoned onto something. "There's the road I'm looking for." Road? I thought we were going by air.

No it's roads Graham is after. He's dived down to zero height plus two feet to allow for hedges... even if there aren't any. I wonder if he is going to lean out of the window and ask the way. Relax, he has it sorted, he recognises a patch of saltbush and a pile of rocks. Those are his bearings. "Soon be there."

And we are. This man, Graham, has done this sort of thing before. And hedge-hopping for a living gives him a distinct advantage over a Boeing 707 pilot. I bet Qantas wouldn't have achieved this marvel of navigation simply with a South Australian road map. Nor would they have put a 707 down on a few hundred yards of flat brown land between the stones, rocks, and a saltbush or two. And another plus point – Graham's missed the flock of sheep by at least a yard.

Now to work. I know of the Minnipa Agricultural Centre, of course. And I had got hold of the latest booklet from the Dept of Ag. 'The Centre is all about finding the best farming practice, methods, crops, varieties, for low rainfall areas, and if any agricultural land is low rainfall, Eyre Peninsula comes pretty near the top of the list.'

So, it's commendable to say the least. With less than 14 inches of rain to look forward to each year – just about enough to lay the dust a couple of times – farming is as precarious as mountaineering in slippers and a bathrobe. One thing is certain, searching the sky for a rain cloud is the main preoccupation. But Minnipa is here to help the farmer confront the challenge and still win.

What a contrast to back home and agricultural college teachings. And what a contrast to UK farming practice where the farmer nurtures the soil, spreads lashings of fertiliser or manure, cossets the crops and then reaps the rewards. Men work, machines toil, but the (relatively) enormous costs are offset by harvests that burst the grain silos and make the bank manager smile. I know because I was part of making it happen... and Dad knew too as he was the smiling bank manager. "I got me wheat cheque 'ere, Mr 'oldsworth."

Out on Eyre Peninsular it is somewhat different but the men from Minnipa are here to help. And I'm here to write it all down, tell the world and play my part.

In England the traditional crop rotation is the four-year Norfolk rotation, wheat, barley, grass and then fallow. Minnipa has successfully cut the cackle and goes for wheat, fallow, wheat, fallow.

'Preparation of the land prior to sowing is kept to a bare minimum – we cultivate and sow in one operation with direct drilling. The seeder has steel discs that open up the soil and drop the seed into the grove in one operation. And generally straight onto the stubble of the previous year's crop.

We have also experimented by doing away with the rotation altogether – simply following one year's wheat with wheat and then wheat again. There have been trials with legumes, crops that "fix" nitrogen from the air into the soil. But while some have fared well, some haven't. We will report in due course...'

Back home we plough, cultivate, disc-harrow and then spike-harrow before the seed is introduced into a beautifully prepared seedbed. Then we Cambridge roll to compact the soil and tuck the seed in. The worst the UK farmer has to contend with is a waterlogged land; here on the Eyre Peninsula the best the farmer can hope for is a light dusting of rain. Or the worst, the occasional deluge that washes the seed and the soil away. Such is life Down Under.

While Graham goes off to sell himself and his aircraft for a bit of crop-dusting, I get myself heartily involved with the men from Minnipa as they proudly show the visiting throng their latest findings. Farmers are taking notes – learning from the learned men. Me too. I can get at least one good story out of all this, probably two or three. Ian Hawker will be impressed.

'We have tried alternative crops such as chickpeas, but the crop is hard to harvest and there is soil erosion, always a problem with our light, sandy soil.'

I take my hat off to the men who successfully farm the Eyre Peninsula. It will be reflected in the story that will flow from my typewriter when I get back to the office. Ian will be pleased; Baz too.

"You ready?" says Graham. We retrace our steps, or, more

correctly, our flight path. We get back before evening; all this in one day. Air travel is the way for the modern-day journo.

Next morning Ian looks up from his desk. "Go ok yesterday, Holdsworth?"

"Yes, Sir, fine." I wave my notebook in front of his face and pat the trusty Roliflex. "It's in the bag Sir."

"Good man. All in a day's work. And I spoke to Graham last night. Seems we owe you some dry cleaning before Crump strikes a match and you go up in flames."

\* \* \* \* \*

Time to go racing!

The Sporting Car Club is holding a meeting up at Collingrove, the Club hill climb on the edge of the Barossa Valley and I've put my name down. Whoopie! This is for real – against professionals and the demands of real competition. It'll be my first go at hill climbs. I've done a few circuit sprints – O'Halloran Hill being one but this is serious!

Time to put aside the motor racing magazines, the glossy pictures of Moss, Fangio, Ascari and Uncle Tom Cobley and all. It's just Piero Taruffi's marvellous thesis on motor racing technique that stays close at hand while I put theory to test. Collingrove is one of the most challenging hill climbs in Australia.

So, here I am, early morning and on my way. I've collected Margaret, bleary-eyed, just out of bed, and we're zipping along on the pleasant country road out of Adelaide. Margaret, whose dad is a major house builder in the State, has expressed an interest in this motor racing.

"How exciting. I'd love to be part of it." I could see her dark eyes opening wider and wider as we stood outside the Princeton Club late one evening, the Porsche sitting there, saying nothing, but playing its part in the promise of things to come.

"Well, you are welcome to join me but it's an early start. I could do with a bit of moral support." And thinking to myself that if all this works out it might be a short cut into the housing market. "I'll pick you up, first thing."

"Yes, first thing." The smile was effervescent. "Can't wait."

But first thing for yours truly is not first thing for Margaret with the dark eyes and bags of enthusiasm the night before. Apparently, she's only got one leg out of bed when I knock on the door.

"The make-up is going on now," says her father with a smile. Dad's reputed to be behind some of the best homes in and around Adelaide. "Don't worry, I'll get her moving with some well chosen words... or a crowbar."

But he's succeeded. "Good morning," I say, as she appears. I'm hoping there's no lessening of the keenness as she slips into the passenger seat, wrestles the rear-view mirror in her direction and sets about finishing the work the father has so rudely interrupted. Is she supposed to do that, I think to myself, with my rear-view mirror. I mean this is a racing car now, not a boudoir, and she is a VERY lucky girl to accompany the next Stirling Moss.

"What time do you call this?" she says as we zip off up the road and something called eye shadow goes on. "And can't we go a bit slower – my lippie is all over the place."

"It's the early bird that catches the worm," I say, trying to raise a smile, "Or, in my case the spark plug wrench."

It doesn't matter all that much. Margaret is fast asleep well before we've left the suburbs of Adelaide and the paper boys finishing their rounds. Some stand and stare as the Porsche whips past.

We're on the straight road out of Gawler and I've nipped past a few Sunday morning drivers when I find we're coming up behind a Volkswagen Beetle; nothing odd about this except that as soon as the Porsche appears in the driver's rear-view mirror he plants his right foot and takes off. A mere Beetle taking off, accelerating away from my pride and joy, filling the Porsche with reverberations and rattling the fillings in my teeth.

This is no ordinary Beetle! It's Ken Virgin's Beetle, the guy I found myself chatting to at the Club the other evening and learning what he'd done to achieve such startling results – including showing me a clean pair of heels on the Gawler road this very morning.

Clearly, when Hitler told Porsche he wanted a people's car he didn't have Ken Virgin in mind.

"I cut my own gears to suit each individual track," he said, looking up at me. Ken's diminutive to say the least and that alone saves a few pounds in weight for the car to propel off the starting line. "And fitted twin Webbers, of course..." I had better explain they are Italian carburettors normally reserved for the likes of Ferrari and Maserati.

"Bored out too." That means one-and-a-half litres becomes two and two becomes two-and-a-half; 40 horse-power becomes 80 and 80 becomes a 180... or anything you care to name. Ken wouldn't say.

Instead, he tapped the side of his nose knowingly. "Then I had a good old look at the electrics, of course."

"Of course," I replied. "The electrics."

And so as Ken plants his right foot, my teeth rattle and Margaret wakes for a second time that morning. "What's that racket?"

"Ken," I reply with reverence. "Ken Virgin, he's ace with a Volksie."

"Well I wish he wasn't."

We keep pace with the flying Volkswagen, follow it off the Angaston Road, along country lanes and turn in through the gates to the hill climb, taking directions from a steward with a flat cap, clip-board and pen in hand. "Competing?" He studies his list. "Ah yes, Holdsworth. Straight ahead. Follow the road." One day I'll be as well known as Ken Virgin and be ushered through without Mr Flat Cap scanning his list, finding my name and ticking it off. He looks somewhat disdainfully down at me. "New then are we, Old Boy?"

All around is exotic machinery, engines revving, mechanics buried beneath bonnets, legs sticking out from under rear ends, tyres humped here and tyres humped there. Squint your eyes, use a sumpful of imagination, and this could be the paddock at Brands Hatch, Spa, Le Mans.

"Hey, that chap looks just like Jim Clarke! And isn't that Black Jack Brabham over there?"

"Who?" says Margaret. She is very pretty and bright even if household names of the motor racing world are way above her head. But I'm glad I brought her.

The paddock (see how I fall in with the professional terms) is full of guys with Castrol XL flowing through their veins, loads of enthusiasm and some of them – the Ken Virgins of this world – with skills that make you wonder why they don't give up the day job and do this for a living. The legal profession, banking world, or MD of a major motor dealer can't really compete with motor racing. Fortunately the Stirling Moss in them bursts out at weekends and they work their frustrations off behind the wheel of their chosen bit of fun on four wheels.

We've parked in amongst lots of sports and racing cars, Ken's Beetle, a Jaguar saloon, a Rover, the ubiquitous Holden and an Austin A55. An Austin A55? Cripes, can they go round corners without falling over? Or accelerate quickly enough to keep the driver awake? This one can apparently! Cyril Nancarrow is a well known Adelaide solicitor and, boy, does he have fun with his souped up Austin which, like Ken Virgin's Volkswagen, bears little resemblance beneath the bonnet to what the makers originally intended.

Vroom, vroom, vroom… Our Cyril is revving up just three cars from us and Margaret has her hands and well manicured nails over her ears. "Do they really have to do THAT?"

Best to send my girl off to the club house to get our coffees while I do my own bit of Porsche preparation. Only in the case of my Porsche convertible it is simply a case of removing any surplus kit I can find. Spare wheel out of its compartment under the bonnet, jack and tools, wheel trims, of course, unbolt the fold-away hood. And the front and rear bumpers if I can get them off. What else? I walk round the car a couple of times, peer under the bonnet again, search inside the car but all I come up with is a car mat. Good, that must save a couple of ounces and improve performance a whole load!

"Here's yours… milk two sugars."

I'm not certain I should go racing on a mug of coffee. The extra weight would negate the fact that I had just removed the carpet. But to join in the spirit of the occasion, I down mine and smile at Margaret. It's very nice to have such a lovely brunette at my side even if I don't have a mechanic, manager, and physio to get me into the peak of fitness for the task ahead.

Margaret smiles back. I think she is starting to like me and my new found hobby. Or is it the smooth-looking lad next door with a proper racing car that's so low to the ground you'd think it had been run over by a steam roller?

"He's nice, isn't he?"

Margaret has slipped off to chat up Mr Smoothy. How can I compete? He has one of the latest aerodynamic helmets, wrap-around goggles that look as though he's in a goldfish bowl and proper racer's gloves that let you "feel" the car when you're flying through an S bend at 80. Now she's off to buy him coffee and a chocolate bar so he's one up there too. What hope Dick Holdsworth with an old fashioned helmet borrowed from Barnsy and the gardener's gloves Mum left behind when she went back home? And I'm sure my goggles were worn by Monsieur Bleriot as he hopped across the Channel in 1909.

The steward is calling us over; he is reminding us of the rules and regulations that will ensure a happy and accident-free day. "Go on green light, observe the marshals' flags, don't take your hands off the wheel to wave to Mum half way up the hill." Fortunately, he's joking. I think!

And he has the running order for the day. It looks like we've been drawn out of a hat; there are the sports cars, like mine, MGs, Healeys, TR4s, mixed in with the Jag and Rover plus Cyril's Austin, and a sprinkling of proper hill climbers like the smooth lad's flat thing with a wheel sticking out at each corner and a windscreen the size of a fly swat. In there too is Ken's Volksie. The Dark Horse.

Vroom, vroom, vroom. The fillings in my teeth are rattling again.

We are starting to line up, me and Porsche in the queue, in our prescribed running order, behind a dinky little car that seems to be designed for taking granny for a ride on Sunday afternoon. The driver has taken the wheel trims off – the only concession to improving performance other than getting granny to climb out – but then all wheel trims have to be removed in case they fly off to decapitate some innocent bystander in the front row.

"Fingers crossed," says Margaret, but I think she's looking at

Smoothy not me. But she's dastardly good looking which means it could be a duel to the death between Smoothy with all the latest kit and me wearing Mum's gardening gloves, Barnsy's World War One helmet and Louis Bleriot's goggles.

The car in front of the dinky car has got the green light and flies off in a cloud of blue smoke and vanishes over the brow of the first hill and out of my sight for a moment as he flies down into the dip at break-neck speed and then up and out again like he's been fired out of a rocket. I see heads swivel in the crowd to follow him at speed, then I catch another glimpse as he's screaming round the banking, up, up and out of sight over the top.

"Good show," says the steward standing next to me. "Just one more before you, Old Chap." I'm glad he can count. I'd hate to fly up that hill, risking life and limb, only to break the tape at the other end and the steward not being alert enough to set the electrical timer going and capture my effort.

The dinky little car moves onto the starting pad. The sign above reassuringly proclaims START, eager officials chatter around, clip-boards in hands, handlebar moustaches bristling, eagle eyes under flat caps. And a bevy of pretty girls hoping for a date with the fastest driver. I can imagine Margaret saying "My boyfriend." But I'm still not certain if it's me or Mr Smoothy who's preening himself by his racer looking like he's just stepped out of an advert for after-shave.

"First time?" asks my steward. I try to nod but the weight of Barnsy's helmet stops me. So my eyes smile at him through Mr Bleriot's goggles and I mumble something about hoping not to waste his time. "Good lad... take it easy... don't be the first to flip over on the banking."

Dinky car makes a noise like a Formula One Ferrari and takes off in a hail of loosened tarmac and smell of burning rubber. He has something under the bonnet not in the maker's handbook. I bet granny's glad she got out before being catapulted into the back seat along with her knitting by the G forces.

Goodness, it's MY turn now. How the hell can I compete with all that wizardry that has just shot up the hill like a V2 rocket?

I move the Porsche up to the start line. To my right the gaggle of officials stand around a pole with red light and beam that stretches across the track to a receiver on the other side. Smiling faces stare down at me sitting there, heart pounding, and me in my old-fashioned racing kit. And the very real possibility of making a fool of myself.

"When you're ready." The light has gone green which means to say either the dinky car has cut the beam at the other end or has flipped over and is rolling back to earth with granny's knitting in the back.

The art of a racing start is to get the revs up, propel yourself away at maximum speed, yet not so many revs as to spin the wheels and you sit there in a haze of smoke and ignominy. That is less likely in the Porsche with engine and weight over the back wheels; but it remains a very real possibility with the scant racing experience I have.

"When you're ready." My steward seems very anxious to send me to my fate.

First gear, brakes off, revs up, clutch in with a wallop and we fly off like we've been hit in the back by a runaway train. Sharp up, near vertical, into second, over the brow of the rise, wheels off the ground. Down into the trough, bang as we bottom out. Up and up again and I'm on the wall of death. Porsche sticks to it like glue. Fast right, third, brake, back to second, hairpin left, hairpin right, then flash into third and I'm across the line for the flying finish.

Christ it's over in a second. More to the point, under 40 seconds. Under 40 seconds? Goodness, it seemed like an eternity – on the other hand it seemed like no time at all. "First time?" asks my steward when I'm back at ground level again. "Not bad, Old Chap. Not bad at all."

Margaret says, "I thought you were gone for ages."

But then she has been talking to Mr Smoothy with the flat car that ascends the hill so fast it was over in the bat of an eyelid and I wonder why he bothered at all. It must have taken longer to pull on his racing gloves than do the actual racing.

Two more goes before the day is out and I'm starting to get the hang of this hill climbing. My time comes down by half a second and then down again. I could easily get hooked. "Well done, Old

Chap. Hope to see you here again next time."

Driving home, the adrenalin still pumping the heart, the thrills still tingling the senses, I'm thinking I might be invited in for a cup of tea, or something. Just the something would be nice. But all I get is a peck on the cheek. "He gave me his telephone number if you want to talk to him about proper racing."

The lad with the flat car. He'd put it on a trailer and towed it home behind a Bentley. Perhaps he could lend me his all-enveloping helmet and wrap-around goggles next time. I'll offer him Mum's gardening gloves.

No, perhaps I won't. He's given his phone number to my girl. I can't see him parting with much else. And he was fastest for the day, minutes ahead of any other car. Ken Virgin, incidentally, with gears, suspension and engine honed to hill climbing, beat me and my Porsche by a whisker.

The bugger!

# Chapter 14

# Make Way for Melbourne

They say, quit while you're on top.

I have an interview for a position as staff journalist with The Weekly Times, part of The Herald and Weekly Times group in Melbourne. And it is a group too; 97 newspapers, some state-wide and some provincial, some dailies, some weeklies and some monthlies. Plus radio station, 3DB and Channel 7 TV. Of the two dailies, The Sun is the Group's morning paper while the first editions of The Herald hit the news stands some time early afternoon. There are two further editions before they clear the decks and prepare for the night shift and next day's Sun.

But it's the agricultural journal, The Weekly Times that I'm going for. This is the leading farming newspaper for the State of Victoria and, unlike The Stock and Station Journal, has the playing field to itself. There's no rival breathing down its neck.

Joining the largest media group in Australia – some say the largest in the Southern Hemisphere – has its attractions. Big time and big opportunity to develop a career in journalism. Go to the top if that's where I want to be. But I'll enjoy the better pay and a generous pension scheme while I make up my mind. Only if I can impress in the interview, of course. And am offered the job.

I've flown over to Melbourne; early morning flight to Essendon, taxi to Flinders Street. "Which bit do ya want?" says my driver. He's a big Hawthorn fan, the stickers plastered over the taxi tell me. "Which bit mate? There's a hell of a lot of it." And he's right, the grand frontage stretches for miles, this is some building, some media group I'm coming to see.

"Hope your side wins," I say as we pull up outside the grand entrance and I dig into my pockets. "Here, keep the loose change." I'm feeling positive.

"We'll give it a go," he says. "Geelong won't be a walk-over."

Through the doors, vast reception, marble floor, sombre efficiency, smart commissionaire. "Weekly Times Sir? I'll take you up seeing as you're new."

We don't have a lift at 81A Currie Street. And certainly don't have someone to take you by the hand and lead you to where you want to go.

This man has just one arm. Later I learn it is company policy to take on returned servicemen whose disabilities often exclude employment elsewhere. Now that's what I call noble, giving something back to the Diggers who gave so much to us.

The lift jolts to a halt.

"Weekly Times is down on the left, Sir. Third door. Miss Margaret will see you right."

"Hawthorn supporter?"

"Hawthorn, of course."

"Of course."

"My lad's treating me. It's a great day out, Grand Final at the MCG. But only if the Hawks win."

My turn to smile now. "I hope they do."

Miss Margaret does see me right. "Mr Barnes will be with you in a minute. He's expecting you."

This is a big office. A busy office. To the left, through an open doorway, I see an open space, ten desks, maybe 12, typewriters clattering away, The Weekly Times journalists I presume. To the right, the man I've come to see, the Managing Editor, Jim Barnes, emerging from his office, greeting me, smiling and firm handshake to go with it. "Welcome to Melbourne Richard, come in, take a seat. Coffee? Tea?"

Almost an uncle figure. And it's first name terms already. "Good flight? Weather? How's Adelaide looking these days?"

I feel comfortable. Bushy eyebrows, broad man, broad face, lined. He can't be that far off retirement. And the warm smile. I feel I've got my foot half-way through the door already.

Editors never seem to have impressive offices in terms of flamboyance. Not Ron Stewart nor Ian Hawker anyway. They are businesslike and so is this; large desk, scattered files and phone. In fact, three phones. Two black and one red; for emergencies?

Book shelves line one side of the room and behind him windows afford a panoramic view out across parklands and the southern suburbs. The railway, two dozen tracks at least, two dozen busy tracks feeding Flinders Street Station, said to be the busiest in Australia although that is put down to the fact that every train – commuter or freight – has to pass through. There's no bypass to Flinders Street Station.

Over the railway lines is the Yarra River and past that the imposing view of the Melbourne Cricket Ground set in the lush, almost tropical gardens. Hawthorn will be giving it a go there this Saturday, no prisoners taken I suspect.

The small talk is over; the good flight, the weather and Adelaide's disposition and Jim Barnes is explaining and I'm listening. "The Weekly Times is not just for farming people, it's for country people as a whole. We satisfy many interests."

He lists them.

"Animal hygiene, crop protection, horticulture, viticulture, gardening..." He draws breath. "Then there're several pages devoted to readers' health and well-being. We encourage readers to confide in us their problems." Jim has a copy on his desk. The paper rustles as the pages fall open on the section headed, OUR LAWYER GIVES HIS OPINION. "Even legal matters," says Jim.

Whereas The Stock and Station Journal is just that – stock (cattle and sheep) and the stations where they are bred, reared and fattened – The Weekly Times title gives no hint that it is for farming folk; and the actual pages devoted directly to farming take up not much more than half of the whole paper.

"Readers' problems are our problems… it's one of the reasons we are successful."

I'm beginning to wonder why I'm here. I can't help with any of this.

"Women's' pages, knitting, cooking." The list continues.

But hang on, there's help out there. "We have experts, of course, paid to find the solutions to those problems. Our consultant doctor and the solicitor. And others; we don't do it all on our own."

Well, that's a relief. I was about to fall off the edge of the seat.

"We need to bolster our coverage on the agricultural front. Your expertise in farming could be invaluable."

Jim Barnes, Editor, has read my CV. My year at agricultural college, the Benyon estate in Berkshire before that and Farmer Collins before Benyon, in my school holidays. Then George Meredith Hope and the Shorthorn herd after college. Leaving the stud and working my passage with the stud cattle. Yes, I'd detailed everything including my success with John Keynes. And topped off with four years training as a journalist at The Stock & Station Journal. Five years if you count the one we're in.

Jim is smiling again. "I'd like to take you to the top… top floor, I mean. Meet the Managing Editor, Managing Editor of the group. Are you ready for the deep pile carpet?" Jim likes his mild joke.

It would be foolish for me to do anything but agree.

Top floor. Decision-making floor. Serious ambience. Oak panelling, sturdy oak door. Oh yes, once inside there's Jim's deep pile carpet.

The office is as big as a football pitch. Perhaps Hawthorn and Geelong could fight it out here. The Managing Editor rises from the far touchline and we meet in the centre circle, shake hands and more smiles. "Coffee?" I politely decline. "If Jim Barnes says you're the man, then you're the man."

Jim nods.

"Wallingford Grammar, did I hear?"

"You did, Sir."

I'm in. More smiles, hand shakes and we retrace our steps. Jim Barnes tells me there will be a formal offer in the post. "Margaret will take care of that."

Good old Margaret.

The commissionaire is helping visitors as they arrive but he still has time for me. "Will we be seeing you again, Sir?" he asks.

"I think so. I hope so."

He says politely, "I do hope so too, Sir."

"Have a great day on Saturday. Hope the Hawks thrash 'em."

Back home, back in The Stock and Station Journal office, my trusty typewriter on my desk, Baz fretting over the next issue, Jason on another foot-rot story, Tremaine on anything but foot-rot; what to do?

I have been enjoying my time at the Journal. Adelaide is my town, small enough to allow me some sort of presence, big enough to make more friends. And I will miss the ones I've made already if I do go.

Ronnie and I have moved out of the flat; I can't cook, never had to, Ronnie can't and Miss South Australia has dropped the heavyweight cook book on her foot and won't go near it again.

"Why don't you come home?" says Ronnie's mum.

"What about my Pommie mate? Can't leave him. He'll starve." Ronnie doesn't smile while he's introducing me. This is a serious business – starving Poms. "I can't leave my Pommie mate out in the cold."

But Mum smiles. "Sure. You come along Rich. You can't be any worse than Ronnie. And Dad's just finished the extension out the back, you two can share that."

So, we're moving up the road to Rostrevor, and I'm joining the Tremaines – Ronnie senior, Mrs T, lovely Wendy, Ronnie's sister. And not forgetting Chum the dog.

"Just settle in Rich. Part of the family."

That's me. I'm happy to become part of this family. And I'm also learning what it takes to be a swimming champion. It seems Wendy is not only a pretty face but she's a clever girl with it, representing Oz in the Olympics in the recent past. Now she teaches kids the art of the Australian crawl, butterfly and back stroke, gold medal winners to be.

Then Ronnie Senior comes home with a brilliant idea. "Let's make you a swimming pool in the back garden. You can teach the kids there."

And we do. Ronnie senior musters his friends; Greg's on back-digger, Tom on cement mixer and Ronnie Senior and me on shovels. We make a great quartet. Oh yes, Mrs T on refreshments and Carl, the German immigrant from next door is ace at tiling it all out. All we need now is the water! And then a barbie to celebrate. All our friends are invited, Dom Zappia, Barnsy, Ackeri, Reno. The Princeton mob.

How can I leave all these guys, these friends? This family? And my work. Melbourne will have to be pretty good to beat this.

I want one last go at finding if there's a remote chance of becoming another Stirling Moss. The Sporting Car Club has the new race track at Mallala, it was something to do with the Royal Australian Air Force although I can't see how they got off the ground as the straight is as straight as a dog's hind leg. But that's where I find myself driving flat out and it's fantastic, a challenge to the nerves. A challenge to anything you care to name.

It's Sunday, it's free practice and Margaret is on the pit wall, stop watch in one hand, a good book in the other. "Aren't you supposed to go past facing the way you are going? Down the road?"

I was onto the accelerator too quickly when coming out of the corner just before the pits and I spin the Porsche. Then Porsche and I go backwards for a hundred yards or so. "Yes, you are supposed to..." I give up trying to explain Piero Taruffi's art of cornering, the turn in, clipping the apex and then accelerating out down the straight. "Anyway, it's track not road."

There's another ingredient – that sixth sense that separates the brilliant, the geniuses from the just good. Maybe I am the latter – perhaps a day at Mallala is going to tell me once and for all.

There's a whole host of us out on the track – sports cars, saloons and proper racing cars – others in the pits and even more in the paddock setting up their cars. Tweaking the suspension, tuning the engine, adjusting tyre pressures. "Give it a bit more in the front, Tom... take a bit out of the back."

Yes, we're all trying to get the best out of our cars. I'm hoping to offset the tail heaviness of the Porsche – what is called over-steer and its tendency to go backwards off the track – by fitting a plain, ordinary road tyre on the front, and Michelins on the back; it is a well known fact that the Michelins give better grip thus curbing the "tail wagging the dog" effect all us Porsche owners live with. Judging by the spin a moment ago it ain't working.

Years to come and the Porsche engineers will have worked on the car and given it near perfect balance. But for now, Dick Holdsworth, watch your tail!

Off we go again. Past the pits, sharpish left, sweep round to the right, and there in front of me is the dog-leg straight. Miss the jet fighter taking off! Hard down with right foot, thrash through the gears, first, second, third, fourth, top. Rev counter dancing up to the red line each time. Overtake an MG on the inside, good man he's getting out of the way. Then an Austin Healey – hey, that's a lad I know from Adelaide, grim-faced, bare knuckles gripping the wheel, giving it his all. Last time I saw him he was on the dance floor at the Princeton Club doing the Twist with Chubby Checker and a pretty girl from Glenelg.

I bet he'd rather be canoodling with her than doing what he's doing now. If the Porsche is tail heavy, the Healey is front heavy – under-steer – and a bit of a pig on this track. I'll nick past him when he's not looking. I'd wave but he might think it's my fist. I did want to dance with his pretty girl from Glenelg but he wouldn't let me.

Quick look in the rear view mirror, I'm not impeding anyone, set the car up for the dog-leg, flat out and the Porsche is rocked by the slip-stream of a Cooper Climax as it flashes past with the professional at the wheel in his natty overalls, racing shoes, gloves and a cheery wave.

Ok, that's a Formula One car, or was a few years back. But I can't help feeling inadequate at the ease at which he goes past. I should have put up more of a fight... like knocking the bastard off the track!

I have Clem Smith in my sights – the Cooper Climax has done for him too. Yes, even Clem Smith... what a bloke young Mr Smith is. He runs a Holden dealership and races what looks like a primitive Holden FJ, but how it goes! In the pits I peer through the Perspex windows and I know why – there's nothing there! Just a seat for Clem, a steering wheel and three pedals. And a gear lever, of course. The rest has gone! Even the hand-brake! And don't ask where you tap the ash from your fag. The ash tray went along with the floor, ceiling, seats, dash, dinner plates and fondue set! Hell, he's driving an empty can of beans with an engine and wheels!

There's just one thing that has been added – there's a huge chunk of lead bolted over the back axle to hold it on the track. Oh yes, I nearly forgot the Repco engine. "How many horses do you get out of that, Clem?"

Clem is coy. "Nothing much, mate. Nothing much."

But I still can't get past him. Let's head for the pit lane. Signal to the bloke behind me in the red MG, sweep into the pits; let the Porsche brakes cool down, they're red hot after all that work. Margaret rushes at me with a wet sponge.

"What are you doing?"

"Cleaning the windscreen. The man next door does that every time his car comes in. I thought everyone did."

"He's got a racing car. They don't have wipers and screen washers."

"I'm only trying to help…"

"Thank you," I say. I'm grateful, very grateful. "Yes thank you, Margaret." She's doing her best even if she is not up with pit-lane procedure and I love her for it. And that short skirt and lovely legs. "You could get me a cuppa…"

"There's smoke coming out of your car."

"It's just the brakes. They've over-heated." Shall I explain the Porsche has drum brakes… the English cars have just come out with discs. They're better, the latest invention. On second thoughts I won't. "Milk and two sugars. You're a darling."

"As long as you're not on fire."

I throw a kiss from beneath Barnsy's helmet and that Frenchman's goggles. "I'll take you out to dinner tonight."

If I'm honest I'm not going to challenge Stirling Moss. I'm trying my hardest but it isn't working.

The brakes have cooled and Porsche and I are out again mixing it with the good and not so good. We're on the back straight and heading for the hairpin. Brake hard, heel and toe, third, heel and toe again, second, throw her into the apex just as Pierro says... and I'm going backwards again. No, I'm not Stirling. Not even a semblance of him. And I don't think I'll be doing a von Trips and phoning the Porsche factory and asking the Competition Manger for a factory drive. I can't even speak German, for a start!

Clouds of burnt rubber, dirt and dust and another enormous spin. I can hear Margaret's words as she stirs my tea. "Aren't you supposed to....?"


Back home at Rostrevor and it's decision time.

The Stock and Station Journal isn't The Stock and Station Journal as I knew it. Ron Stewart has gone and taken his cane, pork-pie hat and those early lunch excuses to be replaced by a faceless man brought in to impose efficiency. But where's Ron Stewart's contacts that counted, his flair and style with words? Where is his inspiration? Ian Hawker has left for pastures greener too; International Wool Secretariat in London. I'm missing Ian Hawker's leadership too. Another great journalist.

Time to say my goodbyes to Basil and Jason, Kay on Women's Pages, Heather Bessen whose teas and coffees have kept me going – extra slices of cake on birthdays. And the lads and lasses in advertising.

Goodbye 81A Currie Street. You have changed my life, given me an opportunity I would never have enjoyed back home. I owe Ron Stewart. I owe you all, especially Baz's strictures: "Never use two words when one will do. Never use a long word when a short one says the same thing. And if I catch you using 'very' or 'really' more than once in your copy, I'll personally disown you."

I've learnt so much. I think I can call myself a proper journalist now. The certificate says so. And my AJA ticket – Australian Journalists' Association. Can't work without that.

Yes, Melbourne here I come.

But not before a last drive up the Rostrevor Road and a sad

goodbye to the Tremaines. Mrs T who has looked after me like a second Mum, Mr T's good humour and lovely Wendy. I never did master the Aussie crawl and never will now.

Ronnie says, "Goodbye mate. We'll miss you." And he means it. And I mean it too – the Princeton Club gave me a social life and the reserved parking slot made me feel special. I wonder what lucky bugger will fill it?

It's first day in Melbourne. I've served my four weeks' notice at The Stock and Station Journal. Plus a week's break. Now a new hot seat beckons and my heart's fluttering.

I've driven in, down St Kilda Road, right into Flinders Street, past the grand building, into a pretty road through the Botanic Gardens and parked the Porsche. You won't get booked here the sign assures me.

Walk back. Through those imposing doors, heart still fluttering, across the marble floor. Same smart commissionaire in same smart uniform; he seems to know everyone. "Morning Sir... Morning Miss..." and those he knows even better are on Christian name terms. I aim to be one of these one day.

I smile. He smiles. Don't know why, the Hawks were thrashed. We agree not to talk about it.

It's Weekly Times, still third floor, still down on the left and still nice Margaret on reception but this time I'm facing Frank Crawford across a busy Assistant Editor's desk.

"Welcome, Holdsworth."

Hello. What's happened to the Richard?

Frank is a small man, peaky face, serious. He either thinks I'm going to give him trouble or I think he's going to give me trouble. He's Ian Hawker with glasses.

"I run a tight ship here, Holdsworth. Good journalism. Stories from the Top Shelf. Getting beneath the surface."

"In their pockets, Sir?"

"What?"

"That just reminded me of something I was taught by the editor at The Stock and Station Journal. Get into their pockets, he said."

"You're not at The Stock and Station Journal. You're here now."

Frank is not quite on my wavelength, but then I notice an ear-plug and thin cord running down to a tiny radio in the drawer beneath his desktop. When the cricket is on, he's tuned in. Even now, the pundits are assessing the Aussies' chances in the forthcoming Test series. I'd heard it all on the car radio coming in; Frank's listening and from his demeanour he reckons the Aussies will do better than the experts say. Much better.

Where it all happens, getting beneath the surface, creating stories from the Top Shelf, is through the door on the left, the open room I had seen when I came for my interview. It's a longish room, desks ranged down the middle, seven, eight or nine journos facing each other across piles of work. There's a lot of moving around and some are up from their desks going through files, researching for the next story, I expect. What we would have given for this space at The Stock and Station Journal.

I am sitting at the near end, closest to the door, furthest from the window, and next to Stewart Wallace; opposite is David Kidd, along from him is John Wisher, and a couple more. At the far end, in the distance, is that view over Flinders Street, the railway line and out towards the MCG – the gladiatorial stadium for cricketers and footie stars alike.

I expect the Poms will be on the rack as Frank predicts. At least he'll have the latest score without me having to ask. His face will tell all.

Stewart takes me under his wing and that is appropriate as he's the resident expert in all that's good in poultry matters. He's currently answering readers' questions on Bumblefoot, External Parasites and Fowl Pest – and I'm to help.

I'm not so sure this is a good idea. I remember we kept chickens back home during the war – Dad had to if he wanted to supplement our meagre rations, but it doesn't mean I am an authority on poultry ailments. "Thanks Stewart, but I know nothing of Bumblefoot, External Parasites or Fowl Pox."

"Don't worry, when I started I didn't either." Stuart pats a card index sitting on his desk. Now it's sitting on mine.

"Simple," he tells me. "Here, have this letter on Croup from this chap in Warnambool. You'll find the man who knows the answer in the card index."

I phone the man whose name appears on Stewart's card. "My reader's got a problem with Croup. Where do we go from here?"

This man knows. It is a problem of the bird's crop which to the layman roughly equates to his chest. Anyway, it's supposed to be full of small stones to break down the ingested food. If the birds are free range they pick up grit and this grinds down the food. Hey presto – no problem. "Your bloke's chooks are in cages – that's his problem. Feed them a little tray of grit. Ok?" I just have time to get in a "Cheers" before the phone goes dead.

Half a dozen of these and I'm up and running... or is it flying? But is it being a journalist? More like an Agony Aunt for the bird industry. But they are paying my wages and the monthly wages cheque is a lot more than I got in Adelaide so I shouldn't complain. Then there's my pension... I could serve out my time here on problems of the digestive track in hens and retire a rich man. Think of the satisfaction that would bring!

How time flies. A dozen of these, a dozen cheers, and it's morning tea break but there's no Heather Bessen with a smile, hint of the fun she had the night before and a tray of coffees and teas. This is a professional outfit, the big time. It's up to the top floor and the staff canteen. You get your own tray here, mate, coffee or tea and a slice of apple pie. Retreat to one of 40 tables for a good old grilling from your new work mates.

"Adelaide?"

"Which paper did you say?"

"What made you leave... come here?"

I've scraped through with a seven out of ten. Eight if you're being generous. Now it's time to relax, sit back and watch other members of staff go through the tray-in-hand exercise. Typists from the typing pool, clerks from Accounts Department, secretaries working for the top men and pen pushers from the Pen Pushers Department. Then the top notch radio or TV journalists; I'm told some are famous voices and some are famous faces. And some are famous journalists. A hushed whisper called for here. They may be famous but they still get their tray, join the queue, select a slice of apple pie and cuppa before going back to their desks – or microphones or TV cameras – and continue being famous.

"Isn't that..?"

"No he's taller…"

"I'm sure she's…"

"What, with that face..?"

Fed up with spotting celebrities, my colleagues return to targeting me. "When did you come over?"

"Drive over?"

"Where are you staying?"

They are trying to be helpful I'm sure. "Yes, I drove over a couple of days ago. And I'm staying in a pretty basic motel I found at the back of the St Kilda Road. It's cheap but comfortable. Until I find digs or a flat. A flat would be ideal."

That raises eyebrows. This St Kilda Road is a road with prestige; grand houses, apartments and corporate offices abutting onto the glamorous thoroughfare. Outer lanes for vehicles only, the centre for trams and vehicles. The palm trees on the two centre reservations add a touch of glamour, Hollywood style.

"Which part of town are you looking for?"

"In the area I'm in now, I suppose. Seems ok to me and it's close enough to work. Looks like there's a good tram service along St Kilda Road."

"You might try further down, away from the City. It's more cosmopolitan," says Stewart. "And less expensive. If that appeals." Stewart is making suggestions. Helpful suggestions and I'm grateful.

Alternatives are thrown into the ring by David Kid and John Wisher. "North of the river, north of the River Yarra, tends to be less expensive, south more so."

I am told there is another guy from England who joined the Group recently. "From London, I heard," says Stewart. "He's in the Photographic Department, I saw him this morning when I picked up a couple of prints. He may have useful info."

Lunch break and I find my way to the Photographic Department and the Dark Room, one floor down. "Any white men in here?"

An English voice, a very London English voice, calls back.

"Another Pom. Come through, mate. But keep the bloody light out, I'm developing."

It's Johnnie Mitchell who's developing. Ex-London, ex-P&O passenger line photographer, and just joined. "Back-room boy, that's me. On my way to the top."

I can just see his outline in the faint red glow of the solitary bulb. He fishes an over-size print out of the tank and hangs it up to dry. A picture of an over-size Bob Menzies materialises before our eyes. "Where you stayin' then, mate?"

"In the motel just off the St Kilda Road. Only temporary. A bit grotty."

I can just detect a smile in the glow. "And I'm in a less than salubrious lodging house bang in the middle of St Kilda. In amongst the pros and conmen."

I'm not sure if he's joking. "Prostitutes and thieves?"

"It's a touch of the old Soho. Until I get a flat. But the grub is ok. And it's cheap."

"Where did you say?"

"Buy me a beer after work and I'll tell you."

"It's a deal."

"The Phoenix. Lou Richards' place. Next block down from The Herald."

"5.15."

"5.15 it is."

"I'll get 'em in."

The Phoenix is where the journos drink, apparently. As John says you find it just down Flinders Street from the paper. Narrow doorway opens straight into a tiny lobby and steep stairway and when you've negotiated that you're in a small but cosy first floor bar that's packed to the rafters.

Johnnie Mitch has got them in already. "Can't waste valuable drinking time, me old mate. Don't forget the six o'clock swill."

We toast each other. "How Poms will travel."

I look round. Surely some famous voices and some famous faces in here. Not to mention famous journalists. Their political comment influencing half the Nation.

"Isn't that…?

"No, he's taller."

"I'm sure she's…"

"With that face?"

"Anyway, a nice little watering hole you've found, John. And not two hundred yards from our work place. I can see this being popular."

"It'll do until I find a real English pub. One with character. I see the names around Town – good old English names, the Nag's Head, Bell and Bottle, even the Jolly Farmer – but when I get inside there's not a jolly farmer to be seen. No bloody nag's 'eads and the only bottle is a bottle of Fosters."

"Well, I've been in Oz six years and haven't found one. When in Rome and all that, John, we'd better stick to what we've got although I must admit it would be nice to amble into Dad's old pub, the Red Lion. Low beams, well trodden carpet, dart board and shove ha'penny. And Old Joe's irrational humour, a real character. And the locals playing their part. "I see you still got your CLOSED on, Joe."

"Clothes on, clothes on. Course I got me clothes on."

Or the old geezer with his Smiths' crisps spread out on the bar before him searching for the packet of salt. "'ere Joe. No salt."

"What's that? One short?"

John tells me the Phoenix is run by a bloke by the name of Lou Richards and he's also some character. "He is one of their footie legends. Now does a column for The Sun. And a pundit on the box – Channel 7."

"A living legend?"

"In 'is own lunchtime, me old Pommie mate. And 'is beer's good."

"Fancy another then?"

"You've talked me into it."

"And you can tell me about the place in St Kilda among the pros and thieves. Did you say the tucker's ok? And it's cheap?"

"All of that, mate. And a few fleas thrown in."

"Can't wait."

The sign on the wall behind the reception desk says:

**No Guests after 10.00pm**
**No Food in the Rooms**
**No Spitting**

"It doesn't say anything about smiling."

"I saw a bloke smile once... but he was leaving."

Upstairs, first floor, Cell Block C, Sing-Sing. "Did the bloke who built this have shares in concrete?"

"I think it makes it easier to remove the blood stains. A quick scrub down and it's ready for the next bloke."

"Blood stains?"

"Someone was murdered in 'ere last week. Only took an hour to clean the place up and 'ave someone new in 'is room paying rent. It was the second this year apparently."

"Remind me to lock my door."

I've moved in, Porsche parked outside amongst the pros and thieves; I'd have lashed it to a fire-hydrant if I had a chain and padlock. Then a good night's sleep and I wake to find I haven't been murdered once.

And the Porsche is still there although the fire hydrant's been nicked.

John is not wrong. There's a good, honest, Aussie breakfast spread out in front of me, bacon, sausage, eggs, baked beans and steak. No, not the steak. I thought it was hiding under the mountain of beans but I was fooled. That was more beans.

"Morning John. Morning lads."

We have a Kiwi at our table and a cheeky lad from Poland with a name that seems to be made up of Js and Ks and Qs. The nearest approximation to English is Joe and that's what he remains. The Kiwi is from Auckland and is another John. "The best city in the world," he says. "And the best country. Going back as soon as my work contract ends. Can't wait."

Johnnie Mitch's shift ended last night and I'm not on duty until Monday so we are relaxing with a free weekend in front of us.

Some Weekly Times journos will be at agricultural shows up and down the country. My turn will come, Frank warned. He is drawing up a new roster with my name on it. A Saturday morning and afternoon spent gathering stories for the Top Shelf in Bendigo, Ballarat and Yarrawonga. That's the life for RH along with Croup in chicken.

"So let's meet up at the Chevron this evening for a beer."

John the Kiwi knows it well. He's a good lad and has it staked out as his local. "You guys know it I'm sure. It's the posh place on the right, half-way down the posh road." He even has a plan which gets us drinks after six o'clock closing without having to buy a meal or stay the night. He has a disarming grin. "Let's just say I caught the manager giving the secretary horizontal shorthand when it should have been first aid training."

That seems fair enough. Heads nod all round the breakfast table after we've explained to Joe what horizontal shorthand is.

"Meet up and share the info on the parties this evening." London John's optimistic.

"Someone will have an invitation and even if they don't we can gate-crash." Kiwi John has it all worked out. I think he's done it before.

That's the evening sorted. But more than that, Joe, the Polish lad, has heard of an empty flat that is worth chasing up. Everything revolves round St Kilda Road and so does the flat. It's owned by a Collins Street dentist, a Dr Streicher. "And if you get behind in your rent, he pulls your teeth."

We make a note not to get in arrears.

"He welcomes young people… have as many parties as you like he told me." Joe smiles, "He welcomes them."

Getting better and better.

"Only one thing," says Joe. "If we take the flat, can anyone cook?"

Not too many hands are raised.

"Better pack Mum's cook book."

There's hope then – that and the Chinese take-away on St Kilda junction. We shouldn't starve.

"Only trouble is, Mum's book's in Polish!"

Perhaps we will.

Monday morning, back behind my desk and I find I've got a new job. It's the job that falls to all the new boys and involves calling up auctioneers at the centres round the country, getting the prices paid at the previous week's livestock auctions, typing them all up and getting the result down to Bill Kelly and Rupert Trude the Weekly Times type-setters. Tons of detail work. Tons of opportunity of making a hash of it. And tons of telling off as a result. And it all has to be done in double-quick time.

Yes, it's that easy!

Stewart hands me a weird contraption used by switchboard operators from years gone by. "Here, put this on. The trumpet lets you talk to the guy at the other end and the ear-phones leave your hands free to type his reply. It's as easy as falling off a log."

"If it's that easy, Stewart, why don't you fall off the log?"

It seems that everyone has to do it one day and it's my turn this week. And next week, and the next, until another new boy arrives.

I slip the contraption over my head and find myself talking to Newmarket, Bendigo, Dandenong, Ballarat, Wodonga, Geelong, Terang – the list is as long as your arm. Cattle, sheep, pigs, steers, heifers, fatteners, vealers, calves, lambs. This list is as long as your arm too. We're in for fun here.

"Hello. This is The Weekly Times. I'm after last week's auction prices."

"Right mate. Ya ready?"

And he's off, ready or not.

I wouldn't actually say there are smirks on the faces of my colleagues, but there is a distinct air of, "Let's see how good the new bloke is."

In fact, it turns out I'm not that bad. Once I've mastered the very latest technology from years gone by, I'm away. My experience at The Stock and Station Journal gives me a great background to stock prices and the moment I mention Johnnie Schumacher, I'm in.

"Geez, mate. You know Schuie?

I say I do.

"Well, let's get you going with the Newmarket auction prices. You ready?"

"I sure am. Give it to me straight."

And I'm typing like there's no tomorrow. Is that smoke coming from my keys?

"Best heavyweight lambs £4/2/0 to £5/0/0. Extra weighty £5/7/1 to £5/11/1.  First cross Border Leicester/Merino cross ewes 1½ years, August shorn, good frames and condition, unjoined £5/16/0. One year old, September shorn, well bred, medium frames, good condition, £4/15/0."

"You got that?"

"No problem."

"Ok, here's the next lot."

I get that typed up too.

"I tell you what, mate, you're better than the bloke I had last week... And the week before.  Where'd they find you?"

"I'm the new boy. You'll have me until they find a new, new boy. I'm learning all the time."

"Ya doin' just great. Talk to ya next week. And I'll pass on your regards to Johnnie Schumacher when I see him."

Now the man at Bendigo. "Suckers, prime heavy, 82/- to 90/-. Extra to 99/-. Shorn suckers, heavy, 65/- to 74/-. Shorn wethers from... "

Then the others. The last guy, the guy at Terang, wants to buy me a beer next time I'm up his way. "Cheers," I say. "You're on."

Stewart says, "You know him?"

"No, but he seems a decent bloke. I'll pop in next time I'm up in Terang."

Then next part of my training. I'm in the basement with the deafening clatter of the type-setting machines and presses and I'm handing over my copy to Rupert Trude, a stout man with a rosy face and years behind him. And Bill Kelly, who's Ned like every other Kelly I've ever come across in Oz irrespective of what it says on the Birth Certificate.

Rupert and Ned smile. My copy is their responsibility now and I'm on time, ahead of time, in fact. "You got this done quickly." They both turn and look at the huge clock on the wall that rules their day. "We didn't expect this till noon."

"You try extra hard when you're the new boy," I say.

I get a "Well done" for my efforts.

But my luck can't last with Frank around. He'd sent me up country to get a story on a dairy farm. He said it was one of the best dairy farms in the State. My face must have reflected my dismay. This aspect of farming never was my forte and not my first choice even in a list of one. "See the man," said Frank. "Walk the farm, ask the questions and get it all down in black and white. I want the full story."

A Top Shelf job this, but somehow my Top Shelf isn't Frank's.

"Is this the best you can do, Holdsworth?"

I thought I'd covered it. Asked all the questions, written it up. If it had been stud beef cattle, rearing or fattening beef, the Outback, I'd have felt more at home. "I did as you said, Frank. I thought it read well."

Frank wanted more detail. "Milk yields, fluctuations from one season to another. Performance on grass and clover, on legumes, on protein feed."

I'd got the milk yields, that was obvious. And I'd compared this year's against the previous twelve months. But it wasn't enough for Frank. He wanted more. "Get the guy on the phone. Get all the figures. This is Top Shelf stuff this, Holdsworth."

I got the dairyman on the phone. "I need greater detail," I asked, cap in hand.

"How far back do you want to go?"

"Ages."

"What's up with ya bloody Editor? Doesn't he know I've got a farm to run?" I re-wrote and re-wrote again. At last I got half a smile. Grudgingly, but at least it was something.

Maybe it was because the English cricket team had arrived and the lads weren't doing that badly. The radio in Frank's desk was chattering away. Frank's ear-piece twitching. No Poms on the rack at that moment. Except me.

Then a lifeline. There's a demonstration of four-wheel drive vehicles to be covered. Frank surveys the forces at his disposal;

I'm in, the rest wouldn't know what a four wheel drive was if it hit them.

"Get down there Holdsworth and see what you can make of it." And down there is the Mornington Peninsula, bordering the sea and on a patch of sand dunes to test the best. I try them all and come to my conclusions, compare performance and price. And technical spec, of course. Meat and drink to me.

"You can handle it Holdsworth?"

Frank doesn't have to ask me twice. I am on my way. I don't even wait around for the cricket score.

"You want to get behind the wheel?" says the young salesman. He's brimming with confidence. His four-wheelers are the best money can buy. It's what he's telling me while dangling the keys before my eyes. "You know what to do, do you?"

"I'll give 'em a try."

"Don't worry, I'll be alongside you in case you panic."

There are the usual Land Rovers, the conventional ones that just about everyone on the land uses, and the forward-control model favoured by the Military. But the trucks that really catch the eye are the Haflinger from Austria and the Mercedes-Benz Unimog, the daddy of them all.

"You ready?" The lad puts his dark glasses on the top of his head and sits back as though he's being taken on a Sunday afternoon drive. "You'll be ok with me at your side. I drive these things all day."

The little Haflinger climbs the first sand dune like a duck takes to water, then over the top and a chasm opens up in front of us, the earth drops away from the windscreen and we topple there for a moment. Bottom gear, crawler gear, and down we go.

The lad's face has gone white by the time I park up on flat ground. The dark glasses have fallen off and are in the sand dunes somewhere. "I hope you'll take it easy in the Merc." His knuckles clasp the grab handle on dash while the other scratches around for the sick bag.

The Mercedes-Benz Unimog climbs walls, crosses ceilings and comes down the other side. "You a Kamikaze pilot in your previous life?" the lad asks. But the really bad news is it seems I've run over his dark glasses.

Back at base and my story reflects my enthusiasm. I make an impression with Frank. I get my first by-line:

## GO ANYWHERE VEHICLES DO JUST THAT
### By Richard Holdsworth

Yes, it's thumbs up from Frank, although I think that might have something to do with the fact that England is batting and have just lost a wicket. "That's more like it, Holdsworth. Get it down to the type-setters and get it set straight away. We'll give this good coverage." Frank even likes my pics. Goodness, another wicket's gone down – Frank likes them even more.

I almost earn a Top Shelf label for my efforts.

In the canteen, tray in hand, I have an extra slice of cake. And the dolly birds look especially good.

I'll try to get a date some time soon. While things are on the up. I might be in luck. I hope so.

# Chapter 15

# Feet Under the Desk

"Holdsie... Hey Holdsie..."

I know that voice. I know that bloody voice. Can only be one man, Ackeri, the ace hairdresser from Adelaide.

What's going on? What the hell's he doing here? He's supposed to be back there in Adelaide, the short back and sides man. The best short back and sides this side of the Black Stump – any side come to that. And the occasional, "Something extra for the weekend, Sir?" All in Lebanese!

I last saw him outside the barber's shop on the South Road, Steve Ackeri Barber emblazoned over the door, blue MG parked outside and a girl, any girl, at his side. He's never short of them.

"Holdsie, where are you hiding?" The voice reverberates round the concrete bunker, up the concrete stairs and down the concrete corridors and batters my eardrums.

"Here Stevie, first floor. Come on up."

The footsteps get closer and round the corner he comes, unmistakable Steve Ackeri. Christ that bear hug is going to crush me, I can feel it from here. "What the hell are you doing in Melbourne?"

His dark eyes stare up at mine, black wavy hair, hunky guy, great guy, you'd trust your grandma's last fiver with him. "I've come to see you, buddy. Sold up, everything, come to see my Pommie mate in Melbourne. And doing a hair-dressing course. I've changed sex."

"Changed sex?"

"Yeah, women's hair-dressing. I'm gonna be the best in town. The best in the whole of Australia."

Well, that's a relief. And it makes sense. Back in Adelaide I'd told him I was off to Melbourne, new job, new friends, new future.

"What's wrong with Adelaide? What's wrong with your mates here? What have we done?" He was finding my decision hard to take. I wished he'd put the cut-throat razor down.

"Nothing, Stevie. Nothing at all. But I'd told you I've applied for a job in Melbourne. And I got it. Better pay, brighter future. But it's not in Adelaide."

Steve Ackeri couldn't understand. "There's nothing wrong with Adelaide. It's a great place." I didn't want to let him down. We were great mates. "What about the parties we go to? What about the Princeton Club? What about… ?"

I heard what he was saying. Everything he said was true. But I explained once again and he put the razor down. That was my chance. I was getting out.

Johnnie Mitch strides into view. His face white. He looks shaken. "'avent you 'eard? President Kennedy's been shot. 'e's bloody dead, mate. Assassinated."

What on earth is going on? Ackeri has sold up, moved out of Adelaide, left his family, Mum and Dad, and come over to Melbourne. Now President Kennedy is dead. The world's going mad.

"Who's this bloke?" says Ackeri. "Another Pom. What's he saying? What's going on?"

I introduce them. Tall, lanky Johnnie Mitch, from London, with ashen face. Hunky, chunky, Ackeri from Lebanon, not quite so ashen. Hands are clasped. "Hey, if you're my Pommie mate's mate, you're mine."

There's only one thing we can do. Get a drink. Or three. And Ackeri is starving. "I've just driven all the way over. I haven't eaten all day."

The last time I dined out with Ackeri he ordered the menu backwards. Coffee came first and starter last. Something to do with the way they eat in Lebanon it seemed.

"Where's the Lebanese restaurants in this town?"

"I'm not eating backwards with you Ackeri. I don't give a tip to the waiter before I'm shown my table."

Johnnie Mitch watches all this. First Kennedy is assassinated and now his new mate talking about ice cream before soup of the day. "Where did you get this geezer from?"

"Don't worry. He's a genius on the snippers. Australia let him in the moment they saw his CV. They thought he was going to shear sheep."

Johnnie Mitch laughs. Steve is too hungry to laugh. "Where's this food, Holdsie? Where're you taking me?"

"The Chevron. Downstairs. They do bar food. And it's good."

We drive over; Johnnie Mitch would go with Ackeri but he can't. His blue MG is stacked with gear. Turn right across the two-way system on St Kilda Road. Miss the cars coming the other way. Miss the trams coming both ways. Park up. Go downstairs.

Everywhere there is shock, everyone talking. Kennedy dead. "In Dallas in a cavalcade. Two shots." Mitch is an avid BBC World

News listener and knows exactly what's happening. "They've got the guy who fired the shots."

Ackeri can't believe it. "Who would want to kill the President? He was very popular... wasn't he?"

"There are some cranks around," John thinks. "Either one of those or a conspiracy."

The guy behind the bar with the flowery shirt says it has to be the Ruskies. "The Ruskies, dears. It's got to be them."

He arranges three little beer mats on the bar in front of us, meticulously. Then puts our beers down, meticulously. "You boys look peckish, want to have a nibble at my nuts?"

I can't say I am up with politics, certainly not American politics. And nor is Ackeri who is looking round the bar, the downstairs bar, he can't believe it. "Hey, this place is full of poofs!"


Frank has called me into his office. He has a job for me, a job I will enjoy, he says. "Yes, right up your street, Holdsworth."

My piece on four wheel drives has gone down well and he is holding out an invitation to the launch of a new tractor range and it's mine to cover. "A new range of David Brown tractors, they're from your neck of the woods, Holdsworth, and I reckon you should be able to make something of it."

I certainly know the David Brown Group. A major industrial conglomerate in England that also includes Aston Martin cars, one of which appears in the James Bond films. Not my scene, but some get carried away about it. The one used in the films has all those gizmos and gimmicks that appeal to adventurous film buffs.

Frank has the invitation, the details, the Press info, he's pushing it across his desk in my direction, a thick folder. "Your assignment Holdsworth. We'll give you a couple of pages. Plus pics."

I reach out to claim it.

"Oh yes, did I mention the actual James Bond car will be there? The film car. Don't get tangled up with that unless you have to."

I have the folder of facts and figures with a super-smooth James Bond on the cover; he's leaning nonchalantly against the car, a smoking pistol in his hand. I think he's just shot the cat.

Obviously the car's there as a gimmick to draw the Press, radio and TV guys. "They love that sort of thing," says Frank. "Just elbow your way in and get the farming angle, Holdsworth. It's the tractor story I want – that's what you're paid for. And don't get yourself killed."

Frank is his most gritty self today. But then Geoff Boycott is on the rampage; the Aussie bowlers are suffering. The transistor in his desk is running hot. Frank's running hot.

"I know you, Holdsworth. Get you behind the wheel and anything can happen."

I make assurances. I don't think he listens. Boycott has just hit another four.

I get down to the darkroom to search for Brownie, Keith Brown, my photographer for the day. The paper has three staff photographers, but Brownie's much more on my wavelength, my age, my sense of humour. And he likes a jar. I bump into Johnnie Mitch on the way. "Guess where I'm off? The assignment for the day. The James Bond Aston."

"Jammy bastard."

"If you'd listened at school you'd be doing this sort of thing." I duck the roll of film coming my way.

Here's Brownie, he's waiting with camera at the ready. He's heard about the James Bond car too. Masses of film, tripod, spare lens. He's kitted out. I explain all the pool cars have been grabbed by The Herald and Sun lads. And what they haven't taken, the famous voices and faces from radio and TV have. "So, you'll have to rough it in a Porsche, Brownie."

We're heading for Sandown racetrack. It was only a week or two back that Johnnie Mitch and I had been there for a big saloon car race, souped-up saloon cars, plenty of American stuff, V8s and the like, and they had attracted drivers from all over the world. The organisers had even flown in Phil Hill from the States. Phil Hill, Formula One World Champion for Ferrari in 1961 – the year Wolfgang von Trips was killed at Monza – the last Grand Prix of the season. The two had fought it out right until the end, two great drivers, one leading the championship then the other until that fateful race at Monza and Jim Clark's Lotus tangling with the rear of the German's Ferrari and the Ferrari somersaulting into the crowd. When they sorted out the wreckage, von Trips was dead along with 14 spectators.

Johnnie Mitch and I had watched as Phil Hill gave his all in the saloon car race. Now Brownie and I are out at the racetrack. "Good job Phil Hill isn't here," I'm saying. "This Press lot wouldn't know him from Adam and we'd still not get close to the James Bond Aston Martin." Yes, they're out in force, the Press guys, as Frank said, journos, radio and TV. And 3DB radio and Channel 7 TV.

"Great for me," Brownie says. "I can get the pictures Frank wants without those buggers getting in my way." The line-up of new David Brown tractors looks resplendent in shiny red paint, or duco as the Aussies call it. Brownie's snapping away from all angles. He wants me in some of the pics. I can see the headlines, "Our Man Puts The New David Brown Tractors Through Their Paces." I am leaning against the bonnet, lifting the bonnet, pointing out features, the diesel engine, transmission, power steering, hydraulics. Now he wants me in the driving seat. It's a long time since I was driving a tractor; I wonder if I'd remember how, hitching up, turning a furrow, baling the hay. I suppose you never forget these things. Like riding a bike or swimming. And these certainly have a good feel to them. I'm sure sales will be brisk. Hope they will – British is best, and all that.

"You've earned your beer, Brownie. Now let's get and see the Aston. See if we can get near it."

The Aston Martin has gone, they've let some journo out on the track with it and there's a spare car running round, packed with photographers taking pics from the front, the side and the back, the journo in the Aston playing James Bond. There's even a TV camera crew on the back of a flat-bed truck chasing the Aston, capturing moving pics, the James Bond theme.

"Simple minds," I say.

"Makes good viewing though," says Brownie. As a professional he would like to get a bit of the action. Get it on film.

"Come on then. I can't give you James Bond but I can give you

Dick Holdsworth in the Porsche."

We're out on the track and I'm lining up corners, doing a Phil Hill down the back straight, into the fast left hander when the Aston comes straight at us... followed by the Holden with half a dozen photographers hanging out of the windows and the silly buggers are all going the wrong way round the track!

If Brownie wasn't so busy ducking, he'd have a great pic of me (almost) destructing James Bond's indestructible car.

Brownie knows the Sun and Herald guys and gets a ribbing when we get back to the office. "You nearly wrecked our photo shoot, Brownie, you and your farming man with the bit of straw between his teeth. We were getting damned good shots there."

"I'll swap you. I've got some great pics of tractors."

"You know what you can do Brownie..."

We're off to get our flat, or so we hope.

But first dig out our references.

"References?" Johnnie Mitch doesn't have one. He's never been a tenant unless you count the lower decks of the SS Orsova, P&O Line. Me neither. I don't even have the P&O to fall back on. All eyes turn to Joe. "I've got my junior scout certificate from Swiejokrzy-skip. Or is it Swiejokrzy-sky?" He can't even remember his home town. We give that a miss too.

"Not to worry," says Johnnie Mitch optimistically. "We scrub up well. All we need is the deposit. I'll be banker." We rummage in our pockets and soon a pile of cash appears on the breakfast table. "That'll do. Come on you two."

The flat's not that far from our doss house; out the front door, right, past the kebab houses and betting shops then left down St Kilda Road. We walk – almost unheard of but we want a breath of fresh air. "And it will give us the chance to gauge what it's like," says Joe, trotting along enthusiastically between John and me. "See if it comes up to expectations."

"You are joking," says John. "Anything comes up to expectations after back-street St Kilda."

A tram rattles past but it's the only thing to disturb the tranquillity and splendour of the surroundings. It's a million dollars from where we've been with our lives hanging on a thread for the past six weeks.

"Told you so, didn't I?" Johnnie Mitch pats his pocket holding the deposit and our key to a new life. "Now Joe, don't you come out with any of those funny place names and upset the apple cart."

Palm trees, neatly tended flower beds and grand facades replace what we've just left – sleazy back alleys, suspicious characters leaning against lampposts and police patrol cars going about in pairs for company. The smell of freshly mown lawn wafts gently on the breeze. "I'm missing the chippie already," says Joe.

Our mouths are open, our eyes wider still as we enter the leafy front drive. "This is bliss, lads," says John. "We'll have to watch our p's and q's 'ere. No washing on the line on Sundays and as for revving up the Porsche after dark."

Six marble steps – oak door, brass name plate with the name Dr Streicher followed by lots of letters which gives him licence to pull teeth when you don't pay your rent. We knock gingerly. Straighten our ties. Wipe our feet. A small, balding man appears in the doorway. "You like parties, boys?"

We look at each other. "We won't put washing on the line on Sundays," says Joe.

"Revving up after ten is right off the menu," says John.

Dr Streicher fixes us with the sort of stare he reserves for patients who don't pay up. "Didn't you hear me? Do you like parties or not?"

We come clean. We love 'em. Yes, we love 'em. And we're in.

"Good boys. Have as many as you like. And as noisy as you like. And if anyone complains – so much the better. They don't pay enough rent. I want them out."

The flat where we've got to be noisy is at the back in the modern block of 20 or 30, we're second floor, first on the left, hiding behind the grand façade that is 632 St Kilda Road. Our lounge and bedrooms look out over Albert Park. And it's great.

There's a group of lads at the end of the landing watching our arrival and air hostesses on the first floor. They watch too. Joe whistles, they wave.

"Better warn them about the party in case they don't pay enough rent."

"We pay full rent," say the lads.

"Ok, you're in. We're having a party in a week or two. A flat-warming party. You'd better help us make as much noise as possible."

"What about the girls?"

"Oh, we pay lots and lots," says a brunette. Her smile is very welcoming. Later, her undies will swirl around with my underpants in the communal washing machine. Then the tumble drier.

"I've only got a few things to wash… can I come in with yours?"

We'll lean against a table watching them go round and round, me too coy to say anything, her shy smile admitting the same. But our undies will enjoy it.

"And we love a party," the blonde tells us. "Can we bring our friends? They are hostesses too."

We think Ansett ANA will be flying short of a few cabin crew some time soon.

We're off to celebrate, it's Joe's idea. "It's my Polish upbringing," he says. "We celebrate for everything; new house, new flat, new tractor, new donkey – we celebrate."

Down at the Chevron Ackeri joins us. "I'm off to Sydney… time to move on."

"What?"

"I've done the hairdressing course. I did fast track. Finished, passed. I'll give you a perm for free, Holdsie. My introductory offer. Just pay for the highlights."

I don't want a perm, free or not, let alone highlights. Ackeri is off, pastures greener, he aims to set up on his own. "And if it doesn't work out in Sydney, then I'll move to Brisbane." The short back and sides has been ditched in favour of the blue rinse. And something extra for the weekend, Sir? That's gone too; they'll have to trot off down to the chemist's. It's Stefan's Salon now. "I'm going to be the best in Australia. I'm going to be rich and famous."

We'd been to some great shows in Melbourne. Some great parties. New friends, new girls and capped it all with the

Journalists' Ball in fancy dress as a team. We brought the house down. But Ackeri is still leaving.

"You'll miss the flat-warming party."

"I haven't got time for that. I've got things to do. My future."

"Can't you wait a couple of weeks before becoming a millionaire?"

The blue MG vanishes up the Sydney Road. It's loaded with Steve's gear. I don't think he even took it out.

Frank is pleased with the David Brown story and he's pleased with Brownie's pics. First the four-by-fours and now this. I'm on the up. Now he's talking about the impending launch of Ford's new tractor range and how best it can be covered; it'll be down to me. Then the last of the big three, Massey-Ferguson. Ford's is at the Broadmeadows plant on the Sydney Road, it's where they assemble the existing Fordson Major tractor made in Dagenham and the parts shipped out. Massey-Ferguson's launch will be in Sydney. I'm being flown up.

This is rewarding. I've found my niche and I'm making a real contribution to The Weekly Times. And we've moved into the new flat – things certainly are looking up. I don't even have to check to see if the Porsche has disappeared overnight along with the fire hydrant.

Time for coffee and that slice of apple pie in the canteen. The chat is not about tractors nor four-by-fours but the pretty girls who come and go with their trays. Most sit and chat; about girlie things, I suppose. John Wisher and David Kidd reckon it's what they got up to the night before. Stewart chips in his twopenneth. "There's one or two that could do with a good night's sleep." We look more intently at the pretty girls. What DID they get up to?

Other girls dash in, grab a tray, coffee and a slice and dash back to their work. PAs for the Top Brass, perhaps. It's a bit like train spotting without numbers. And very much more rewarding. Even a Great Western King or a Castle locomotive on the Cornish Riviera Express can't compete with a pretty girl in The Herald and Weekly Times' canteen. And some are very pretty – and one especially so.

Wisher, Kidd and Stewart have already dubbed her Puss in Boots on account of the snazzy white boots with fluff at the top. No harm done, light relief and especially after tractors and four-by-fours.

I had seen her in the canteen one lunchtime; our eyes met across the day's special. I wished I'd winked, smiled, dropped my apple pie, any excuse to start a conversation. She turned away and the moment was lost.

Tremaine always said not to miss an opportunity. "She might be the future Mrs Holdsworth." I vowed next time I wouldn't miss my chance. If it came.

Mid-afternoon and I'm in Frank's office and it looks like he's going to give me a hard time. I knew my luck would run out sooner or later. The clock ticks past three and I'm getting my next day's assignment.

"Tea up, Rich," calls Stewart, poking his head round the door.

"Be up in a moment."

"Field trials," says Frank, giving me his serious face. "There's a good story out there at the ICI experimental centre. You'll do it well, Holdsworth. You'll enjoy this. Field trials."

My mind has gone into the world of field trials and it doesn't share Frank's enthusiasm. Comparing one row of plants with another is fine as long as chemicals don't come into it – but when they do I cannot get wildly enthusiastic. 'Row "A" has been treated with so-and-so weed killer, Row "B" is the control and treated with – nothing.' The Public Relations blurb goes into overdrive and I am supposed to swoon. 'Observe the difference... see the dramatic effect... see what our chemicals can do.'

Yes, sometimes it can be dramatic. But equally I am left wondering how much nasty chemical had been sprayed onto the plants to achieve such results.

I am an unabashed organic farming man. I have been from the time I watched my dad build a compost heap at the bottom of our garden and grow healthy crops as a result. Grass mowings, tops from carrots and parsnips, potato peelings – anything Mum didn't use in the kitchen – yes everything that would compost was composted. And autumn was a bonus – leaves were swept up in abundance and piled high. Dad dug it all in and that gave his crops a good start – a natural start, not chemical – and when greenfly struck in spring (as it inevitably did), Dad didn't have chemicals – but he did have a soapy spray. A natural remedy. His greenhouse was stacked with natural remedies instead of cans carrying a Government health warning. Dad had sawdust to sprinkle around his new plants so slugs couldn't get to them and he encouraged a family of hedgehogs – they gobbled up snails as though there was no tomorrow. Natural methods. It costs nothing to be kind to a hedgehog, he said.

But Frank is wound up. He likes his chemicals. He likes his field trials. And he likes the idea of me going out there and covering it all.

"Are you with me, Holdsworth?"

"I am sir."

Writing about natural farming methods, organic farming, and I'm your man. Or, at least, organic methods used in conjunction with carefully managed chemicals if the needs be; I'll write with enthusiasm. And with words our readers will digest, go out and act upon. As a journalist, you feel you've done your job. But not today. Or, more correctly, not tomorrow. Frank is determined – and I am down to get the chemical story first thing next morning.

"Ok, Frank. Give it to me. My turn to do the field trials. I just hope it is something new, something worth reporting. Something I can get my teeth into."

"Err well, it's out at Dandenong, the ICI research centre, as I said."

Frank is procrastinating; the hands of the clock have passed the half past, I'm missing out on my tea and more to the point I've yet to find out what's so special about tomorrow's assignment.

"2,4,5 -T," says Frank. "Doing a great job."

I gulp.

"That's as old as the hills, Frank. We've covered it a dozen times, at least. Can't I have something fresh, new, something to enthuse about?"

"It's your job, Holdsworth. Out there tomorrow, first thing. That's an order."

I see the little wire coming from Frank's left ear and running down into the drawer, his pocket-size radio chirruping away. My face brightens. "What's the score, Frank?"

This is an underhand tactic, a mean question. I know the score perfectly well. Johnnie Mitch belled me a moment ago on the internal. "Boycott and Barber are slaying them... 250 on the board. And still going. Runs coming at a gallop."

"Get out Holdsworth. And if that story isn't on my desk the moment you get back, you're for the high jump."

Next day I am out there, I am walking about in a flat field with row upon row of crops, some doing well, some not doing so well. I am one of a hundred or so people being influenced by what we see and what we're told. The crops that are doing best are the ones that have been sprayed with 2,4,5 -T and as a result the weeds have keeled over and given up the battle for life. These are the crops resplendent with no competition. The rest are being strangled, if not at birth, certainly before they climbed out of the cot.

"There," says the chemical man, with a flourish. He sweeps his arm around in an arc like someone discovering the Promised Land. "See what I mean? See the results. No-one in their right mind would not use our magic wonder weed-killer." He stops short so we can all digest the consequences of what he is saying. "No-one. No-one at all."

You can't dispute what lies before us, the struggling crops being held back by weeds and the brilliant buggers are the ones standing proud and tall. Not an ounce of competition to tarnish their efforts on the way to being the Best Crop in the World.

But I wonder if the results couldn't be just as good under good organic farming methods; a load of cow manure spread on the field beforehand and ploughed in so the crops get off to a good start. And the Norfolk Rotation whereby the land is left fallow one year in four and the weeds are ploughed in and suffocated beneath six inches of soil.

And those chemical weed killers. I couldn't help wondering what else they might inhibit, annihilate, perhaps. "Oh no," says the chemical man. "It doesn't kill anything else; see the crops are totally untouched."

I would be sceptical but I am not paid to be sceptical. Wondering if there was a build up in the soil, especially if you sprayed on this killer year-in, year-out. It is toxic, there must be repercussions.

"How did you get on?" asks Stewart when I'm back in the office.

"I'm a sceptic," I say. "I don't mind chemicals used in moderation. But not saturating the soil."

"Well, you're not paid to be sceptical. Don't go in too heavy or you'll be for the chop. Anyway, Frank's after your blood. I think the Poms are still thrashing our lot down at the MCG. Who's that chap Boycott? He's murdering them."

I slip a sheet of paper in the typewriter. "Wonder Weed-killer Strikes Again." That should make Frank happy.

Years later, of course, 2,4,5 -T has been dropped. Used without restraint and it is not nice, it affects many living creatures not the least because it could be carcinogenic.

Oh dear!

I am in the lift when in steps Puss in Boots. No time to think, no time for the cracking witticism, something that will be remembered till eternity. I'll be getting out at the next floor; ten seconds is all I have. Maybe 15 if I can fumble with the Doors Closed button for a bit longer.

But I have to come out with something. A few arresting words. Something that will make her think, something that will strike a chord. As Tremaine said, miss the chance and you could be missing the future Mrs Holdsworth.

I've got it. "Going up?"

She turns and she smiles. A lovely smile. My heart is doing what it shouldn't be doing. Thump, thump and THUMP. Her blonde hair worn up, rather than cascading down over her shoulders as I have seen before. And high heels today accentuating lovely slender legs. She's slim, trim and that smart business suit. And oh, that smile.

Yes she is going up. "Top floor."

Top Brass, perhaps. A PA to a Top Man? I wonder.

But I can't say that can I? Can't say, "Top Brass." That's daft. But I can try the age-old weather thing. "Nice day, isn't it?"

In fact it is not a particularly nice day. It is overcast, the 3DB forecaster forecasting showers before school's out. I even threw a coat over my shoulder as I left the flat in the morning and hailed the Flinders Street tram.

"Yes, nice. Very nice." And she gives me that smile again.

I am just about to add another weather witticism when the lift jolts to a halt, third floor, my floor, the door whooshes open and I'm gone, wishing I wasn't.

I'm back behind my desk with my heart rate returned to normal while Stewart enquires about the party, the flat-warming party. "Who are you bringing?"

I play my cards close to my chest. "Maybe no-one. I don't know many girls in Melbourne." That is partly true; I haven't been in Melbourne long enough to know many girls. Maybe I won't bring anyone. But I know who I'd like to bring.

Stewart's coming, and girl friend. Plenty of others too. Joe, our flat mate, who's been around a long time, he knows lots of people, lots of girls. The air hostesses have promised. The wolf whistles have worked. The lads at the end flat too, and Johnnie Mitch and I will invite the handful of friends we have made. It is going to be a good party and with music courtesy of the Beatles at full blast, Dr Streicher will be as happy as a sand-boy, a teeth-extracting sand-boy.

Johnnie Mitch has come across a bloke by the name of Ian. "You know, Ian from South Africa." Apparently he has a flat just off Punt Road and we're off round there. "We'll ask Ian."

"Of course."

The girls fall for him, or so it seems. The current one has. She's making us coffee while we explain the party. Ian with the Herrenvolk good looks, square jaw, blonde hair and a career in Hollywood ousting Cary Grant if selling insurance doesn't work out.

"New girl friend, Ian?" Johnnie Mitch enquires.

Ian shrugs. Take 'em or leave 'em, he indicates.

Ian has a theory that if you are on the shelf at 50, not to worry as you book one of the P&O cruises out of Melbourne or Sydney. "The boats are all packed with widows of big property owners, worked themselves to death running a couple of hundred thousand acres and worth a fortune."

"Where does Johnnie Mitch, Joe from Poland and Dick Holdsworth come in?"

"Obvious," says Ian. "They're all looking for some single bloke to lavish all that spare cash on."

It's ok for Ian. Girls find him attractive; some have been known to trip over pavements just trying to get a glimpse... then walk into the next lamppost.

And the other disturbing thing about Ian is he's well read. He has books on his shelves, just as I have records. Books I've never even glanced at, let alone read. For Ludwig van Beethoven, read Brendan Behan. For the Choral Symphony, read Borstal Boy. I pick it up, I am engrossed – can't put it down until Joey comes by.

"What you doin', man?"

"Reading."

"What for?"

"Waiting for you to come by, Joey."

Peels of laughter. Joey lights up a room... any room. He would find a way of making you laugh if you'd just seen Bob Menzies run over by a tram.

"Hi Ian."

"Hi Joey."

Hands are smacked together. High Fives. And a bear hug for them both. They each hail from the same part of the globe – but the other side of the fence. It seems Joey is having a bit of strife getting into Australia. He's in but staying in is the problem; he jumped ship in Port Melbourne and the authorities want him to jump back on again.

Ian is his help-mate and they think Mitch and I could make a difference with our contacts at The Herald and Sun. But the boys from the dailies have already been in contact; photographs have been taken and headlines have been written. 'If this young man is sent back to South Africa, there is no telling what will happen to him…'

Goodness, what did Joey do over there that he got out in such a hurry? But he seems a nice guy, Johnnie Mitch and I will help where we can. "Just let us know and we'll ask around. You coming to the party?"

Ian is. And Joey too. "If I'm invited."

"Of course."

I'm borrowing Brendan Behan. I can't put him down! 'Friday, in the evening, the landlady shouted up the stairs: 'Oh God, oh Jesus, oh Sacred Heart. Boy, there's two gentlemen to see you.'

I knew by the screeches of her that these gentlemen were not calling to inquire after my health, or to know if I'd had a good trip. I grabbed my Pot. Chlor, Sulph, Ac, gelignite, detonators, electrical and ignition, and the rest of my Sinn Fein conjuror's outfit, and carried it to the window. Then the gentlemen arrived…'

It is Saturday morning. There is a knock on the door; I've only just surfaced, Johnnie Mitch is still tucked up, Joe has gone off to work. And it is Joey of the High Fives. "Hi man, hope I'm not disturbing you?"

"Not at all, Joey. What can we do you for?"

He laughs at my joke, which is nice.

"I'm told you know a lot about cars, I wondered if you could help me buy one."

Buy him a car?! No, I've jumped to conclusions, he has the money, all he seeks is a bit of advice, what would suit his needs best, be most reliable, even where to get it.

"Have a seat, Joey. Coffee? Tea? While I put my brain in gear." Joey laughs at that too. And that's also kind of him. But he's anxious to get going. I have the feeling he wants his car before I've finished breakfast.

Johnnie Mitch pops his head round the corner. "Joey me old mate. How's it going?"

"It's going fine, Man. Rich here has just offered to help me get a car. It's wheels I need. I'm fed up with this transport system you've got here."

"You need to get yourself sorted first," I'm telling him. "No point in getting a car and you can't even stay here. Mitch and I have offered to help."

"That's done, Man. It came through this week. I don't need The Sun no more. I've even got my own passport."

We're amazed at how things have developed. How fast. Johnnie Mitch's eye-brows are raised. "Someone pulling strings? Not even Ned Kelly could get a passport that quick."

Coffee downed and we're off to the Golden Mile. A mile of highway, used car lots flanking every side, at every turn; if you stacked each car one upon another it would dwarf Everest. Flags, bunting, promises you can't resist, and eager salesmen waiting for the Joey's of this world.

We go down in the Porsche. Joey likes it. His long brown fingers trace the line of the bonnet, his dark eyes gobble up the folding hood, his sensitive ears say there are warrior drums in the throaty roar. "You can't have it Joey, it's mine." I don't tell him it has speed that could be bad for his health. The last thing Joey drove was an ox and cart.

We've stopped in customer parking at the first used car dealer down the Golden Mile. "We'll start at the top and work down, Joey. You'll have a good idea of what to buy before the end of the day."

Joey is out like a flash. He has seen the first car, an ordinary example of a Ford family saloon. "I like the look of this one."

"Why's that, Joey?"

"It's next to the open gate so I can drive it straight home."

"That's not necessarily the first thing you should consider when buying a used car." I'm about to explain we should look under the bonnet, dip the oil, check the tyres, see if the exhaust is blowing. "We must get a full report from the RACV. No-one buys a second-hand car without a mechanical report."

Johnnie Mitch has found a pleasant little four-door saloon at the back. "This looks more like it... a bargain, Joey. They always park the best at the back and the cars they can't sell at the front... to catch the unwary."

Joey's undeterred – unwary is his second name even with Mitch and me in attendance. What's more the salesman has found him. "Good morning, Sir. I see you are admiring this fine little bobby-dazzler. Two-tone duco. One careful owner. A snip at four hundred."

The one careful owner could have been a tearaway who was only careful about not getting caught. And the two-tone could be rust in all the out of the way places where the likes of Joey never looks.

But Joey is already behind the wheel, making brum-brum noises as though he is on the Starting Grid. "Give me the keys, man."

I have the feeling if the car salesman handed over the keys Joey would be out the parking lot like a flash and half-way home before the salesman could count his commission. Fortunately, he was not born yesterday. "If you'd like to step this way, Sir, we can sort the finances, get the paperwork done, sign the forms."

Joey is in the office, sinking deep in the luxury PVC seating, the salesman pressing his gold-plated pen into Joey's hand while flicking the cigarette ash into the pot plant conveniently situated next to his desk. "Here and here," he is saying. If ever X marked the spot, this was it. Joey is the proud owner of the wheels he craves. I just hope he's not on the road at the same time as I am.

The last thing we hear is the salesman shout to his buddy, "Shuffle them up, Dan. Keep the quality ones at the back for our regular customers."

# Chapter 16

## Ned Kelly. Was He - Wasn't He?

I'm out with big Alf, the senior photographer at the paper and we're whisking along in the Victorian countryside, Seymour, Euroa, Baddaginnie, on our way up north-east. I'm behind the wheel of the pool staff car and grumpy old Alf is at my side.

"Another glorious day, Alf."

Big, beefy, Alf turns to reply but it's not that easy. And he's getting on in years. "What's it like over there, then? The Old Country, I mean."

We're heading out to a dealer who specialises in used farm machinery. Apparently he has a vast range of second-hand equipment and I want to see what he has on offer and what savings can be made. It could make a pretty good piece, interesting and informative, what better for our readers? But we've also taken the opportunity of grabbing a few pics on the way up of a dairy farm just outside Melbourne. They've installed a new herringbone milking system and Frank's keen to get it into the pages.

"Get on the road early, Holdsworth and you'll do it. Take Alf, he's free tomorrow."

"I reckon, Frank. But Alf's hardly Speedy Gonzales. I might have to put a rocket under him if we're to get it all done and tucked up in bed before midnight."

"Stay over if you have to. Just get the stories."

Alf's a pernickety old bugger, even if the results are invariably good. He's been around since the days when Press photographers used flash powder – before the days of flash bulbs. The good old days, Alf would say, when the photographer was king. "Didn't have to rush about the place." He doesn't move much quicker these days – even with the latest kit; camera, light meters and super-fast film.

"The lighting's all wrong..." he'd moan "...and how are ya supposed to get the tripod level on this bloody cowshed floor?" Big, thick-set Alf with his stoop and thinning hair would turn and grumble. "Now the shutter's jammed." And he's a recruit to the photographer's age-old edict – don't go near kids nor animals. Not what you want when you're working for a farming paper.

"They pay your wage, Alf. Anyway, next stop is machinery. Tractors, ploughs and harvesters don't move, blink, swish their tails or fart when you say 'Watch the birdie.'"

"Get us up there then lad, then let's get home."

Baddaginnie, Benalla, Lake Mokoan... It's a clear road and we're on schedule.

He's turning in the seat again. "You haven't answered my question. What's it like over there, then? The Old Country."

The staff car is dipping in and out of pools of shade as we pass clumps of Gums at the side of the road. Rabbits scamper across in front of us and disappear into the bush. "Well, as you ask, Alf, it's ok in the Old Country." I'm going to play safe here. "But I happen to prefer it in Oz with my mate Alf for company."

"I've been told everything's old and falling down."

"Not falling down, Alf. Fallen down. Hitler got most of it. The years have done the rest. So I wouldn't go near it unless you want to be hit by falling masonry."

We're rapidly approaching the outskirts of Glenrowan. "Ned Kelly country," says Alf. "You know the story of Ned Kelly? The real story? Not what they'd like you to believe."

I did know a bit about the Aussie Bushranger. Keynes had leant me a book on the notorious Ned Kelly when I first went up Bush. No mains electricity so I couldn't do much to entertain myself in the evenings other than look out the window, swat flies or read. I could have bought one of those old-fashioned wind-up gramophones with a huge trumpet and a little dog sitting next to it. But no windup, no dog and no Beethoven for the Bush. So, it was Ned Kelly as my companion each evening. "You'll want to mug up on our famous Bushranger," he said it with a smile. "Keep Ned as a reference – you can make up your own mind." And I've still got it. It's the one thing he gave me when I left.

"Yep Alf. I know a bit. I expect everyone does."

I knew the name Ned Kelly even before I set out from England, of course. Along with Don Bradman and Bob Menzies his name cropped up – an unlikely trio. "He was a bit of a lad from all accounts, Alf. A bit of a lad."

"He was persecuted. Picked on unfairly."

"He murdered three policemen, didn't he?"

"He had his reasons. Picked on. And his father before him. Then his wife and brothers. Authority had it in for the Kelly family. The Catholic Irish, down-trodden by authority. They were typical of the early settlers… just trying to eke out a living from the Bush."

"I must admit it would have been tough for the family, especially with a father who'd been transported for thieving."

"Never proved, lad. Never proved that he nicked anything, especially those couple of pigs. But it got him three years' hard labour and a trip to Tasmania."

"He wasn't a Ten Pound Pom then Alf?"

Alf grunts.

"He served his time, moved to Victoria and got a job working for a settler who had a bit of land. Red Kelly showed he was ok. He grafted, married the farmer's daughter and worked his patch of land. I tell you the Kelly's weren't a bad family."

"Didn't Ned save a kid from drowning?"

"You have been reading up on the Kelly family."

"Well, he did didn't he? And the boy's family gave him a sash as a reward. But, Alf, from what I remember he was always in trouble with the law. Sash or no sash."

"I told you. Picked on he was... Like his dad."

We're still debating Ned Kelly as we pull into the yard of the farm machinery dealer, Tom Burfit. Tom's sign says it all, BURFIT FARM MACHINERY Biggest Range in Victoria. His yard is stacked with a huge selection of machines, tractors, cultivators, ploughs, balers, row upon row of them. You name it, Tom seems to have it.

"You the people from the paper?" Big, barrel chested Tom Burfit, the shirtfront stretched to breaking point, sleeves rolled up tightly to his armpits, wide leather belt holding up trousers ten sizes too big. Looks can be deceptive... I'm told he has a good business sense and a good business.

"Yes, Tom. Richard Holdsworth and Alf our ace photographer."

Tom's grip is vice-like. I'm glad to get my hand back in one piece. Alf must see me wince and keeps his distance. He's got an expensive piece of photographic equipment and needs all his fingers to work it.

"We were just talking about your most famous citizen, young Ned Kelly."

"You interested?"

"We can't agree whether he was just a lad on a course of law-breaking or just a lad hard done by."

Tom hitches the over-size trousers. He came from Somerset as a lad with his mother and father; they were farmers back home and there's still a touch of the West Country about him. "Ah, you don't be alone there. If you asked the people round 'ere, 'alf would take one side, 'alf the tuther. But while there be money to be made from the Ned Kelly name, it pays to play it up." Tom has a good, hearty West Country laugh. "I thought of ditching Burfit and making it Ned's Farm Machinery."

Alf doesn't laugh. "As long as the people talk the truth."

"Well, if you be interested, it so 'appens the school is putting on a play about our famous Bushranger. They do it every year. Bit of luck it's on today. You can catch it if you're quick. I'm off down there in the 'our, just put on me best bib and tucker and Sunday best 'at. My Jack plays Ned."

Alf's not too certain. "Kids," he says. "Anyway, we're due back in the office. What would Frank say if we told him we've gone back to school to see Ned Kelly?"

"I'll sort it with Frank. No problem there. I'll get him on the phone. Say we're staying over and doing Tom's story tomorrow and we'll get a couple more stories while we're up here. I know a few contacts up this way and we've already got the dairy story in the bag."

"You'll enjoy the play," says Tom. "I think you'll be surprised. It takes neither one side nor tuther. And my lad does a good Ned. They been rehearsing all week."

"Alf's convinced. Or half so. "If you sort it with the office. I don't want it in the neck when we get back."

The school hall is packed and buzzing. Mums and dads, sisters and brothers and a handfull of ladies fussing round a tea urn. The home-made cakes seem to be doing a roaring trade. There is a gentleman playing the piano at the side of the stage. "Mr Entwhistle, the post master," says Tom.

"Must be dozens in here," says Alf. "Dozens. I hope they get this right."

"They will," says Tom. "My Jack has been learning his lines for ages."

A prim lady appears on the stage calling for quiet. "Miss Philpot," Tom whispers. "Headmistress and not a bad one neither."

The buzz of conversation subsides. "Thank you all for coming, quite a wonderful turn out." Miss Philpot has a firm voice that carries. "Can we all hear at the back?"

We can.

"By popular demand, we're putting on our Ned Kelly play again... that is to say the children are." Miss Philpot beams. "Whether you approve of Mr Kelly or not, we can't ignore him." Feet are shuffled, heads are nodding. "Our notorious Bushranger. The children want to portray his life and let you decide whether he was good or bad." This brings a murmur of approval. "Or a bit of both." More approval.

Miss Philpot consults the slip of paper in her hand. "Act One, the Wombat Ranges. Let me set the scene for you. Ned had been in trouble even as a young man, yet on the occasions that charges were brought many were thrown out of court through lack of sound evidence. This led to resentment among members of the Kelly family as well as his friends who said that Ned was being unfairly targeted by the police. Others said the Kelly's had intimated witnesses. We'll never know."

Miss Philpot draws breath. "On the 15th of April 1878, Constable Fitzpatrick rode out to the Kelly property hoping to find evidence of cattle rustling. There was an argument and Constable Fitzpatrick claimed he was shot in the hand by Ned. Others protested that Ned Kelly was nowhere near the place at the time."

Chatter interrupts Miss Philpot. The Headmistress calls for quiet.

"Mr Kelly doubts he can convince the authorities of his side of the story and with his background fears a long custodial sentence if taken to court and found guilty. He decides to hide out in the Wombat Ranges with Dan, his brother and two friends, Bushmen Joe Byrne and Steve Hart."

Miss Philpot looks round, satisfied. "Our play starts here," she says.

There is mild applause. Mr Entwhistle thumps the keyboard and strident chords fill the hall as if we're back in the days of silent movies.

Unseen hands draw back the curtains to reveal a clearing in the woods. There is a tent, like an Indian tepee, a stack of boxes marked TUCKER and a camp fire. In the background a tape plays the sound of Kookaburras and Parakeets squawking to each other. Two policemen sit around the fire cleaning their guns while two more stand. One is Sergeant Kennedy. He speaks. "I'm gonna get

Ned Kelly. Do you hear? Gonna get him and lock him up for good."

He's only a kid but he doesn't fluff his lines. "Played by John the storekeeper's lad," Tom whispers. "A great little kid."

People around us say, "Hush."

"Some say locking him up is too good for Ned Kelly," says one of the policemen sitting at the fire. "Remember how he shot Constable Fitzpatrick. Could have killed him."

"Fitzpatrick was a liar," pipes up one of the other policemen. "Didn't he get dismissed from the Force? I'm not sure you can rely on his word."

"Well, I'm not going to argue when I meet the Kelly gang. I'll draw my gun first." They're all wearing papier-mache helmets, costumes made by mums and their guns look like they are the product of the woodwork class.

"What's your plan then, sergeant?"

Sergeant Kennedy replies. "Me and PC Scanlon are gonna get out there and track down the gang. I reckon we'll find 'em ok. You two stay here."

Sergeant Kennedy and PC Scanlon leave the stage. There is a little ripple of applause.

The two remaining policemen look around. "What'll we do while they are gone?"

"Let's fire at a few parrots. I could do with some target practice."

"Yeah, right. We'll need to be sharp shooters when the Kelly gang shows up."

They point their guns out over the audience.

"Bang, bang. I got one."

"Bang, bang. I got a couple."

The two policemen are still concentrating on targeting parrots when two Bushrangers creep into the clearing taking them by surprise. "I'm Ned Kelly and this is my brother, Dan. Throw down your guns."

"There," hisses Tom. That's my boy. He's Ned Kelly. Don't 'e act well?"

Constable McIntyre raises his hands. Constable Lonigan goes for his gun. Ned Kelly fires.

"Bang, bang."

Constable Lonigan sinks to his knees then makes a display out of dying throwing his gun in the air as a final gesture. Ladies in the audience giggle. Tom says, "That kid says he's gonna be an actor when he grows up."

"Shush," say people again.

"You've killed Constable Lonighan," says Constable McIntyre. "You're for the rope now."

"He got what he deserves," says Ned. "He shouldn't have gone for his gun."

Dan Kelly says to his brother. "What are we going to do now, Ned?"

Ned says to Constable McIntyre, "When your mates come back you just tell them we're the Kelly gang and they haven't got a chance."

"Yeah, tell them to throw their guns down," says Dan Kelly.

The three children stand around the stage saying nothing. One smiles into the audience. A hand waves back. Constable Lonighan still lies prone. The Kookaburras squawk.

"I'll say that for him," says Alf. "He plays a good dead man."

Onto the stage runs Constable Scanlon and Sergeant Kennedy. "What was all that shooting?"

Constable McIntyre calls out. "These are the Kellys. Surrender or they'll kill you."

Constable Scanlon goes for his gun. "Bang, bang." Ned shoots him dead.

Constable Kennedy runs off into the Bush as Ned Kelly and his brother fire.

"Bang, bang."

"Bang, bang."

Kennedy falls to the ground. We hear him groaning. Ned walks over to him and fires at point blank range."

In the confusion, Constable McIntyre escapes.

"He'll give the game away," shouts Dan.

"We better scarper," says Ned. "Then lie low. They won't find us. We've got friends in these parts. All right minded people are on our side."

The curtains come down. Miss Philpot reappears clutching the piece of paper. "Part One. The disaster of Wombat Ranges," she reads out in a strong voice. "As a result of these killings, the State Government passes the Felons' Apprehension Act and immediately outlaws the gang. It also exonerates anyone who may shoot and kill gang members on sight. Now they will be hunted not only in Victoria but throughout Australia."

A voice from the back calls out, "Quite right too."

Others call, "Keep quiet."

Miss Philpot consults her piece of paper. "Within six months of the Wombat Ranges killings, the gang carries out two audacious bank robberies, the first in Euroa, just along the road from us here and then two months later across the New South Wales border at Jerilderie. At Euroa they take hostages, forcing innocent bystanders into the bank at gunpoint before stealing £2,260. In today's money, ladies and gentlemen, that equates to over £100,000. At Jerilderie, they disguise themselves as policemen and hold the bank manager at gun point. They steal a similar amount of money."

Miss Philpot takes another breath. "The gang is not done. Ned finds out that a friend, Aaron Sherritt, is a police informant and they ride out to his place and murder him too.

There are ohhs and ahhs from the audience.

"I think this is a good time for us to take a break. Mrs Burge and Miss Templeton are ready with the teas and cakes, please form an orderly queue. All proceeds to the school fund. We will re-assemble for the final part of our presentation of Ned Kelly in approximately 15 minutes."

"What do yer think?" asks Tom.

"Good," I agree. "Your kids are doing well."

Alf says, "The tea will come in handy."

Mr Entwhistle signals the end of the 15 minutes with more strident chords on the piano; there's a scramble to return to the seats whereupon Miss Philpot reappears on the stage, clears her throat and announces the scene has changed to the Glenrowan Hotel. "Mr Kelly and his three accomplices have burst into the hotel and are holding 70 people hostage." Miss Philpot looks mildly embarrassed when she announces that the stage isn't large enough to hold 70 hostages. "Anyway, we don't have 70 children." Gentle laughter from the audience. "So we have just seven hostages this afternoon – I hope it won't spoil it for you."

"Mr Kelly and his gang have learnt that a detachment of police led by Superintendent Hare is on its way to Glenrowan by train from Melbourne. This is not good news for the gang. Yet they have one advantage over the police – they have each forged a suit of armour and are wearing tin helmets and heavy breast plates beneath coats sewn from sacking." Miss Philpot looks up from her slip of paper. "I can tell you they create a strange illusion – more like four robots than human beings."

A voice from behind the curtains hisses "Ready."

"Here we are then, the Glenrowan Hotel. Ned Kelly – Act Two."

The hotel is on one side of the darkened stage, but the end wall is left open so we can see inside, see the seven hostages and four gang members while on the opposite side of the stage is a row of bushes.

"What we gonna do now Ned?"

"Yes," says Steve Hart, "a whole bunch of coppers coming up from Melbourne."

"Don't you worry. I've had the track taken up. The train will be de-railed. The coppers that don't die in the crash will be sitting ducks."

The hostages talk agitatedly between themselves. They are distraught. One little girl starts to cry. "That will mean we won't be rescued."

Ned turns to the hostages. "You people brought this on yourselves. If you'd left us alone you wouldn't have been involved in this. My old man was a good bloke, he was treated like a criminal. We were all treated like criminals."

One of the hostages steps forward. "Please, I am Thomas Curnow, the schoolmaster, my wife and child are at home. My child is sick. Please let me go to them. I will not divulge your plans."

Ned looks at his three accomplices. "Don't let the bugger go, Ned," says his brother. "He'll only split on us."

Joe Byrne says the same. "He'll only make trouble for us, Ned."
Ned seems to being weighing it up.

"Please," says the schoolmaster. "I won't say anything."

Ned leads him to the front door and sends him on his way out into the dark. The schoolmaster immediately runs across the stage waving a torch covered with a red scarf. We hear the train come to a halt then the sound of policemen's voices.

The element of surprise that Ned Kelly had hoped for is lost. Policemen appear and crouch down behind the bushes.

"We've still got a chance," Ned tells the rest of the gang. "Fight for your lives."

"Yes, our lives," says Dan.

There's lots of "Bang, bangs" from both sides of the stage.

The hostages cower. Women scream. Men try to shield them from the gunfire.

Ned Kelly emerges from the hotel, lurching from side to side with the weight of his armour, and firing at the police. He makes a fearsome sight and Superintendent Hare runs off in panic. "I'm getting out of here." Other police stand their ground and fire at Ned but the bullets simply bounce off his armour.

"It's Old Nick," shouts one constable.

Another, "It's a black fella wrapped in a blanket."

And a third, "It's the bunyip."

Ned is hit in the hand and drops his gun, then his foot is struck and he falls at the feet of the police. But he is still alive. In the hotel, the other three gang members lie dead. The hostages escape as the police set fire to the hotel signalled by background flashing red lights.

"The lights, Mr Grimshaw. Turn on the lights."

"Oh yes, the lights."

"It really is Ned Kelly," shouts a policeman. "We've got Ned Kelly."

The curtain comes down.

Wild applause.

"My lad done well," Tom tells us. "'e's been doin' that scene for days."

The children are led to the front of the stage by Miss Philpot.

More applause. "Take a bow, children." They do.

   Alf agrees. "He did well. They've all done well. Except that Mr Grimshaw. I'd give him the sack."

   "You can make up your own mind on Ned now," says Tom. "Make up your own mind. I 'ave."

NED KELLY AT BAY.
FROM A SKETCH DRAWN ON THE SPOT BY MR. T. CARRINGTON.

# Chapter 17

# The Party

"We're starving, lads!"

Time for the occupants of Flat 20 to convene a high level meeting. Me, Johnnie Mitch and Joe.

Johnnie Mitch hasn't mastered a three-ring cooker before and the oven is just something the Christmas turkey pops out of miraculously once a year. "I don't need to know, do I? I've enjoyed five star meals from Sun Up to Man Overboard thanks to the Head Chef on the P&O Line."

Me the same; there were no five stars on the cargo ship, the MV Port Melbourne, but the cook turned out good honest meals three times a day, every day for six weeks. Fine sea-faring fare you could say. Before that, of course, there was my mum and Mum never let the Holdsworth family down even in the war with food rationing thrown at her. Then Mrs Keynes and Mrs Tremaine. And how could I forget the all-day breakfasts at Big Alf's?

But Joe is different, he's from Poland. He's continental. Two pairs of eyes turn on Joe. "C'mon mate, time to show us your continental credentials," says Johnnie Mitch. "All you lot have culinary arts coursing through your veins. Knock us up something and be quick about it, we're starving."

We are sitting on the bench seats in our tiny kitchen, facing each other, bare table between us and we're anticipating the top class meal Joe is going to prepare, save our bacon, as it were. But Joe has other ideas. "I can't cook. Mum could and even Dad could. But I can't. I didn't have to."

Dismay turns to despair.

"Yer what?" says John.

I go for a couple of "Yer whats?" too.

But, wait a minute. Didn't Joe from Poland say something about his mum's cook book as we left the doss house back there in St Kilda? John is onto this like a flash. He doesn't let things like that slip through his fingers, especially when there's starvation on the menu. "C'mon Joe, I distinctly remember you tuckin' it under your arm, telling us how it would come in 'andy one day. It's the come in 'andy one day right now."

"That's it," I say. "The going away present from your mum, you said."

Joe seems a bit reluctant. It's hardly the most enthusiastic spirit that rummages around in the box of tricks beneath his bed. After what seems like an eternity, his mum's book arrives on the table and pages are turned, pictures of sumptuous meals stare out at us, banquets even; they're all pleading, "Eat me, eat me." All we have to do is choose something, anything, it all looks wonderful.

"Cripes, Joe," says John. "You're a genius. Get cooking now. I can feel my taste buds being tantalised this very minute." And John points across our kitchen. "There's the cooker, Joe. It's the thing with knobs on. You don't even 'ave to turn it on – that's my contribution."

The fact that Joe's book is in Polish shouldn't make the slightest difference. Joe is Polish isn't he? "Go for it mate," John says. "Put on your chef's hat and pinny…translate and we're off."

But Joe still has that "If there is a hangman's noose hanging outside our balcony I'll put my head in it," sort of look.

"What do you mean, you can't read Polish?" we say as one voice. "You're Polish aren't you?"

"It's been years since I was back home in Poland and I was only a lad. I know a few words but not enough to make sense of all this gobbledy-gook... It's all foreign to me."

John's flabbergasted. "Of course it's foreign, Joe. Your mum is. You can't get more foreign than Polish."

We slump back in our seats, our tiny bench seats. We're phoning Mr Lee's Chinese take-away yet again. "You wanti three Number 11 and three Number 17? And Special Flied Lice? Again... ?"

"Yes, Mr Lee, again. And a pile of Dim-Sims to add to our order. Joe's about to hang himself if we can't put something on the table before him."

Now it's Saturday morning and we're clearing away the dinner plates from last night's Chinese spectacular when Johnnie Mitch has a great idea.

"Listen lads, there's a delicatessen over the road run by some geezer called Serge. That's what I call him, anyway. He's Polish or something, let's take the cook book to him. He'll translate and sell us the necessary."

Brilliant. A decision maker par excellence – no wonder we won the war with people like John on our side. Hitler and co didn't stand a chance.

We're facing Serge, holding Joe's mum's book up to his face across a counter stacked with exotic-looking meats and sausages and lots of other unrecognisable things in packages with foreign names. Serge with the white apron, slicked down hair, fat tummy. "I'm from Hungary. I can't read that stuff."

Our smiles disappear. So near yet so far. Johnnie Mitch turns on Joe. "Why couldn't your mum be Hungarian?"

It looks like we're back to Mr Lee and the Chinese take-away. At least we're in line for a bulk discount.

But John's a Cockney lad and Cockney lads don't let brilliant ideas slip through their fingers that easily. "You don't have to read it Serge me old mate. Just look at the pictures, sell us the ingredients." John has a page open showing what looks like a meat stew… it's bubbling away in a hot pot. John points to a succulent piece of meat. He holds up three fingers.

"You want-a the three pieces of the meats?"

"Three pieces for three very hungry growing lads, Serge."

Serge chops off a huge chunk of meat, cuts it into pieces and wraps it. "That's-a good for you?"

Now it's my turn. I point to the picture of bacon bubbling away in the stew. I hold up the fingers of both hands. "Ten please." Ten rashers will do us. And ten rashers fly off the bacon slicer.

Joe has a go. "Vegetables, Serge? Vegetables?"

Serge goes off and comes back with half a sack. "For you lads. You make-a da stews. " And the garlic. And the ginger. "Make-a da spicy stews for you lads."

We go home. We make-a da stews. A huge saucepan of boiling water. Chop up the potatoes and carrots, the leaks and onions. The strips of bacon, chunks of meat, half a pound of pearl barley and the couple of Knorr cubes Serge threw in for luck. And a handful of herbs. Hey presto. Boil and bubble, toil and trouble. We go down the pub for an hour or so and when we come back our stew's waiting for us. A Polish stew and not a word of Polish do we know.

"Joe, you're a genius! Or, more correctly, your mum's book is." John always knew he could do it. "I had faith in you, mate. Continental blood and all that."

There is so much stew, tons and tons of it. A milestone has been reached. We can go out into the world confident that no one is going to starve at Flat 20.

Serge even has our parcel of food put aside ready each Saturday morning; shortly stew aroma wafts around the flat, out through the open window and is picked up by anyone who happens to be in stew aroma smelling distance. Including the lads along the landing in the end flat. "You jammy bastards having a Polish chef in your midst."

And the girls in the flat below. The air hostesses. "Oh scrummy. Can we come round one evening?"

And then there's Bottle-o.

"Come in mate, sit down. Fancy a plate full? And a helping for your dog?"

"Great lads, you're too generous."

Bottle-o collects, not unsurprisingly, the empty bottles. Cashes them in and lives off the proceeds. And the proceeds are not bad from Flat Number 20. And now he's tucking into a plate of our stew as a bonus.

"You lads are the kindest I've ever come across. Of all my clients up and down St Kilda Road, you're the best."

Bottle-o doesn't seem to have a name. But his dog does. His dog is Muggings and he has fleas so we make him sit outside although as Joe says, his master has fleas and we let him in.

"Where did you say you live?" Johnnie Mitch asks.

"Oh round and about."

"Is that the roundabout where St Kilda Road joins Punt Road?"

"Don't make me laugh. I wouldn't live on a roundabout. No, I live under a tree in the park."

We all think that is fair enough.

"It's a very nice tree," he says, wiping his mouth with the sleeve of his jacket. "Very nice. And very nice stew." But now he has a living to make. "Can't sit 'ere all day. Got to see me clients, collect me bottles."

Joe gives him ours. "And don't forget we're having a party. We'll have lots and lots then."

Bottle-o grins, a toothy grin, except he doesn't have any. Teeth that is. "Come on Muggings… Wealth beyond our wildest dreams. The lads are going to have a party."

We fumigate the place and chase a few fleas with yesterday's Herald rolled up. Why are we so kind to this man? Why are we so generous with our hard-earned stew?

"The Good Lord will remember us one day," Johnnie Mitch tells us. "We won't go unrewarded…"

I'll bear that in mind next time the chips are down.


The Orange Field Days are said to represent the largest agricultural machinery show in the world and Brownie and I are off up there to cover the extravaganza of tractors, combine harvesters, ploughs, crop sprayers, milking machines – everything to make any and every farm work with clockwork precision.

It's a couple of weeks before our party. Just time to get up there, spend a few days getting it covered, back behind the desk, write it all up, and see it into the paper. Then enjoy the run up to the flat warming. Never a dull moment.

The Orange National Field Days have got so big that people fly in from all over Australia. Us included. Our bags are packed, toothbrush, spare shirt, tie, underpants, and we're out at Essendon airport and we're off.

A bit over an hour's flight, mini bus to the vast display, we're in and seeking the Press Office, getting the info, the latest Press info on who's exhibiting, what they are exhibiting and what their machines will do for the farmer.

"There's so much here you could spend all three days and all you'd do is skim the surface," says the Press guy, young man, smart suit, smiling. "Here's the list of the new stuff; maybe you guys might wanna go for that first."

Just a glance tells us he's right. There is a lot of hard work in front of us. We can do with all the help we can get.

"And the winners of the New Implement Competition," the young man is saying, "you'd wanna have a look at them too." He gives us another wad of paperwork. "The winners and runners up, maybe even those that didn't make the medals. Here, have the lot."

We'll soon need a wheelbarrow.

He smiles. We smile. "And the best of luck." He turns to some more Press men coming through the door. "Here's the list of the new stuff guys; maybe you might wanna go for that first."

Brownie has his camera and spare films at the ready. "I brought a hundred rolls. Not sure if that's even enough." Brownie's case looks like it weighs a ton, slung over his shoulder; another wheelbarrow coming up. "Just think how nice the beer will taste at the end of the day, Brownie."

From the new Massey-Ferguson 510 combine harvester down to a simple hand-held tool for implanting hormones into sheep;

from a combined post hole digger and post driver to something that resembles a motor mower that locks onto the tricycle undercarriage of a parked light aircraft and moves it around – they all get awards and all get the Keith Brown and Richard Holdsworth treatment.

We're staying in a hotel, sharing a room, the place is packed, we're lucky to get a bed although we booked weeks before. The bar is packed too. I battle to get to the head of the queue. "Two beers. Sorry mate, make that four. We might get crushed in the stampede for the next round."

The man agrees. "That accent. Do I detect you're over from the Old Country?"

"A few years back. I'm with The Weekly Times in Melbourne now."

"I was in the Old Country last year."

"And?"

"It snowed."

"That sounds about par for the course."

A bloke at my shoulder says, "When you two buggers have finished with the weather outlook for the Old Country, I could do with a beer." He's right. Don't let it ever be said six inches of snow back home stops an Aussie from slaking his thirst out here in New South Wales with the temperature in the hundreds.

Time to find Brownie. He's deep in conversation with a man and that's a bit tricky as the chap is deaf and dumb. It's a fingers and thumbs deep conversation. And lips. He's pointing to his lips and raising his wrist.

"He wants a beer."

"That's bleeding obvious, Brownie."

Then he's got a make-believe knife in one hand and a fork in the other.

"He wants some tucker."

"Even I worked that out."

He cups his first finger and thumb to make an O. Then runs the index finger of his other hand through it, backwards and forwards.

Brownie and I look at each other. "Time to go off and get us a bite to eat, mate and leave that dirty old bugger to his own devices."

As I go off to sleep, dreaming harvesters, tractors, ploughs, fencing machines, trucks, trailers, everything mechanical, I hear Brownie's voice, "I wonder if he's cocked his leg over yet?"

Back in the office I give Frank a run-down of what we've achieved.
 "Good show? Hope you got it covered."
 "Great show. I reckon we got it all. Three notebooks filled. Brownie took best part of a hundred rolls."
 "We'll do this justice. Give it the full treatment."
 "I reckon."
 That's a first ever five page spread for The Weekly Times.

ORANGE NATIONAL FIELD DAYS.... by Richard Holdsworth

**EIGHT GAIN MOST COVETED AWARDS**

Eight machines from an entry list of 23 gained this year's coveted Orange National Field Days New Implements Award.

"Who are you bringing, mate?" Johnnie Mitch and I are enjoying a drink in Lou Richards' pub, the Phoenix, and John wants to know who will be on my arm at the party. "I know Joe's bringing a pretty little thing from where he works. But who's the lucky girl on your arm?"
 "More to the point, Mitch, who are you bringing?"
 "You know me... Keep my options open... I leave it to you guys to bring all the birds... " John downs the last drops. "Then I nick

the best."

"Sounds about right. You old bugger. And now I'm supposed to buy you another beer?" I struggle to the bar and to Lou, Mine Host, as John calls him. I do my best Aussie impersonation, "Fill 'em up, Lou."

Getting a beer is never simple with Lou Richards. "I hear you're after dating one of our best sheilas from the paper. The blonde one."

"Who told you?"

"Forget it. She won't go out with you, mate. A Pom."

"Stranger things have happened, Lou. We're beating your lot at cricket. Maybe your best Aussie bird will go out with a Pom." I check my change after a comment like that. I even check my fingers, and risk a smile. "You never know. She might like someone from the winning side."

"No way, mate. I tell you if she gets hooked up with you I'll buy you the Crown Jewels. If she even goes out with you I'll buy you a beer... you and your Pommie mate over there." There's a glint in his eye.

"You're on, Lou. You're on."

I escape back to John and dump our glasses in the pool of beer in front us. "No wonder they call it the six o'clock swill."

"I see you and Mine Host deep in conversation," says John. "What's Lou the old rascal got to say for himself?"

I tell Mitch. "The trouble is, Mitch, I don't even know where to find her, let alone ask her out. And if I did, ten to one she wouldn't want to... I bet she's got some boyfriend stashed away somewhere. Good looking, athletic or rich. Or all three. Lou's prophecy would come true. And I've got our beers riding on it."

"It'll be easy mate. All you've got to do is find her and use your charms. You could throw in a ride in the Porsche for extra measure. That should turn her head."

"Find her first, John. The paper employs more people than the British Army and I only bumped into her once. In the lift that time I told you about."

"Puss in Boots. Between floors two and three, you said. Not the most romantic place."

"Not Puss in Boots that day, it was high heels and business suit. Very smart. And those legs. And you should see the smile."

"You've got it bad mate."

"Bad if I don't find her. Needle in a haystack stuff John."

"Half are blokes, Rich. That narrows it down a bit."

"I thought you were on my side. I can do without help like that."

"Well I'll keep my mince pies peeled. Then you can make your move. A faint heart and all that me old mate."

Lou calls time. "Let's be having ya... You should know the law by now."

"One last one."

"You're on." Six o'clock swill.

"'ere mate, I've got news for you." John's home from the Night Shift.

"You've won Tatts?"

"No, better than that. I've been told where Puss in Boots is working. In reception, in the Share Department, just temporary. You'd better get your skates on."

I do.

"If anyone asks, Stewart, I'm down in the Dark Room retrieving some pics."

I take the lift. The reception is its usual sombre self. People coming and going. Hushed whispers. If anyone sneezes they'd be asked to explain themselves. But there she is, as Johnny Mitch said, sitting, typing, an area with about half a dozen young ladies, the team behind the public face of the Share Department. But I don't have shares in the company, I don't even know what one would look like, and I certainly can't front up and ask how they are doing. That's down to the manager in charge and he's a po-faced bugger. John says she's just there on secondment from her boss, the Finance Director.

I chicken out. I walk past the share counter and straight into Flinders Street, the sunshine, the breath of fresh air; I'm going to put some wind in my sails, perhaps that'll help me generate the courage I so desperately need. I turn on my heels. Back through the grand doors, I can't stop now, mustn't stop now. "Excuse me." I clear my throat. "Excuse me…"

"Hello," she says. "Can I help?" The look from the manager tells me I shouldn't be doing this. If it's shares I'm asking about it's his job to answer. But she's smiling. "I'll help if I can."

"Yes," I'm saying. "I just wondered if you'd be free to come to our flat-warming party this Saturday. On St Kilda Road. Mostly friends and people from here. From the paper." I resist the temptation to say, "Please."

"It sounds like fun but I'm afraid I'm already doing something on Saturday night. But thanks for asking."

Us Holdsworths don't give up that easily despite Mr Po-face.

"I'd have asked earlier but I'm new to the paper and still finding my feet. It's a labyrinth of a building." I try to sound positive. "Another time perhaps? It is Heather, isn't it?"

The smile says yes, but I've definitely overstayed my welcome. The manager's glaring. If looks could kill and all that.

The lift whisks me back to Third Floor and my desk. "Didn't get your pics then," asks Stewart.

"My what?"

"Pics. You went to the Dark Room."

"Ah yes, the Dark Room."

I try to concentrate; a reader's problem, that'll do it. I take a letter from Stewart's pile.

"Do you mind?"

"Be my guest."

Some chap's budgie keeps falling off his perch. "He was full of life last week…" the letter says. "Can you help? I've had him a long time. He's all I've got."

Time to give up? Don't think so. Budgie needs vitamins, or so Stewart's budgie expert tells me over the phone, and this poor man needs help. And I find it's vitamins that will make him stick to the perch. "Cheers," I say and dash out the reply, feel inspired, and I'm not giving up on Puss in Boots either. And they do say the Lord loves a trier.

Grab the internal phone directory. Flick a few pages. Here it is,

Share Department, Front Desk, extension 210. "Heather, I was talking to you earlier. It's Richard, from the Weekly Times. If you can't make the party on Saturday what about a meal tonight? I'm sure you have a favourite place in good old Melbourne town."

There's a pause – never a good sign.

"Well, the bad news is, I can't do this evening, but if the invitation for Saturday's party still stands, I'd love to come."

I can scarcely believe what I'm hearing. "Of course. Of course. Saturday it is. Seven-thirty. I'll pick you up at yours."

"Shaftesbury Parade, number 72, turn off St Georges Road, mind the trams, fifth on left. Jacaranda tree in the front garden, Dad planted it years ago. You can't miss it."

"Seven-thirty at seventy-two."

We laugh.

Stewart turns in his seat. "What's making you so happy? Can't be the budgie man, surely?"

"Well, I am having some success with a bird, Stewart. All will be revealed Saturday night."

It seems the boyfriend had asked her to the hockey club "do" but he's been laid low by an injury on the playing field and that rules out social activities for a while. And that, in turn, has opened the way for Heather accepting my invitation. Confucius say, one man's gain is another man's loss. Poor hockey club. Poor lad. I hope he doesn't recover too quickly!

But no time to cry now; we're sitting outside Number 632 St Kilda Road admiring the grand frontage.

"Is this you? Very impressive."

"Not me I'm afraid. Us lowly ones are at the back. Ours looks out over Albert Park. Once upon a time a venue for motor racing. I'm told Stirling Moss whisked round this circuit."

She coos at the thought. Stirling Moss. And the palm tress, trimmed grass, Dr Streicher's marble steps. I suspect the cooing is for the grand frontage more than Stirling demonstrating his skill at the wheel of a Maserati 250F.

"We're a bit more basic than that I'm afraid. Forty years pulling teeth bought all this for our full-time dentist, part-time property owner. An agricultural journalist buys part of the rent in a shared two bedroom flat out the back."

We laugh about the disparity. Johnnie Mitch was right, Heather is PA for the Finance Director. She confirms her status at the paper and it is some role. "They thought it needed more experience, but I seem to be holding it down. It's pressureful at times."

Pressureful? She lights up a cigarette. Surely it can't be that bad. But I can't frown, not this early on in a relationship – if there is to be one – and there is an ash-tray in the car… somewhere.

"We're early for the party. Let's pop round to see a friend, Ian from South Africa. He's on the invitation list."

We'd filled the bath with ice and stacked it with bottles. We saw to that earlier, Joe, John and me; it's a sure-fire way to guarantee a good party in Oz. We've swept the floor, dusted the pot plant and put the stew in the fridge. "Yes, we've got time to see Ian. He's a sociable soul… there's always a coffee on."

Ian obliges. Ian the good looker with the theory that if you get to 50 and desperate you go on a cruise and bag yourself a wealthy widow. Why wait till 50 and desperate, why not go now? But not the subject to be aired in front of Ian's new girlfriend, nor mine. It's good to introduce Heather. "Heather Pattison… Ian… " And, "Heather Pattison, meet Ian's girlfriend, Rebecca…"

Joey is there too. The wheels are outside, parked half on the pavement, half on the road and half in the hedge.

"Joey, meet Heather. She's also at the newspaper."

Joey's eyes light up. "So where's this scallywag been hiding you? He never mentioned such a pretty girl. Keeping you to himself?"

Heather has a smile for Joey too. Joey who has a physique that looks for all the world as if he could scale Table Mountain with one foot tied behind his back. "We only met the other day, Joey, at work."

"I've had some contact with your paper. The guys in The Sun have been very good to me. I've got my passport thanks to them."

Heather smiles. Those sparkling eyes. Joey smiles. Those sparkling teeth.

I'm more interested in Joey behind the wheel. Every time I hear a crash, I think of him. "How's the driving going Joey?"

"I'm not going to let it beat me, Man."

"Have you run over the bloke who walks in front with the red flag?"

Joey folds up with laughter. "I got him first day."

Joey's going to drive round to the party if he can get his car out of the hedge. "On second thoughts, Man, I'll come with you if you can squeeze me in."

"Be my guest, Joey. Leave your car here – parking is never easy on St Kilda Road." I am thinking of the Porsche. It hates being hit by medium-sized Ford saloons trying to make a parking space where there isn't one. "You can come with us if you can clamber in the back."

Heather volunteers. "I'll get in the back, Joey." And she does with dexterity and elegance. Either that or Porsches are her second home. Joey is grateful. "I don't think they design these things for six foot six, spear-throwing South Africans."

Joey's sensitive ears pick up the party even before I've had time to park. And he's out of the car and running. "Man, the place is jumpin'. Is dat the Beatles?"

"It sure is."

"I wanna hold your hand…"

I'm holding Heather's. I'm not going to let go. Not if I can help it.

"Yeah, yeah, yeah…"


Next morning. Next morning. It's so bad they named it twice.

Why on earth did it come round so quickly? And who forgot to draw the curtains – make a note not to invite them next time. Shafts of Aussie sunlight are fine but not the morning after the night before.

Now Bottle-o's dog is barking at our front door somewhere. What do I mean, our front door somewhere? We've only got one to bark at. Muggins either wants second helpings or he's after his master's bottles.

"Come on in Bottle-o. Don't trip over the mess. Hate you to suffer a work-related injury."

"Boys, your place looks like a bomb's hit it."

We have to agree. Joe and me. John is still in bed. Yes, Johnnie Mitch found somewhere to lay his weary bones. Not that he didn't have to fight for it tooth and nail. Joe too.

I pitched someone out of mine in the wee hours after I had taken my new-found girlfriend home. All the way to Thornbury. Through town, out on St Georges Road, turn right at Shaftesbury Parade, no trams to miss at this time. Fifth on left. There was the Jacaranda tree Dad planted all those years ago. It looked great in the moonlight... so did my new girl-friend; we kissed on the doorstep.

"Thank you so much. It has been a lovely evening." Heather smiled up at me. "You certainly know how to put on a good party."

"You made it," I said. Puss in Boots had been a hit. Not just a pretty face, she could hold a conversation, compete with the best. And between that, boy could she dance, my legs were still catching up.

Our lips touched again.

A bottle of Champagne had gone pop somewhere inside my head. I was seeing stars, nightingales were singing, the milkman and his horse wending their weary way down St Georges Road looked like Cinderella and her coach. I might have been walking on air but they weren't going to get a kiss. I don't kiss horses. Nor milkmen, come to that.

Puss in Boots, Puss in Boots! I'll kiss you again and again.

Is this it? Is this the girl I have searched for every year for the past ten years? Even if she smokes, if that's the only down-side, I can live with that for the moment. I don't want my kids to grow up with a puffing mum. But don't count your chickens and all that. Things may change. She may give me the boot... Bob and his hockey club are the competition. Hockey sticks at dawn. The party had gone well. Hadn't dropped any clangers. John, Joe, Joey, Ian, and his new girl friend, and all the chums, they had enjoyed themselves, enjoyed meeting Puss in Boots. And she enjoyed meeting them.

Joey stayed to the bitter end. He had trouble with our settee; you can't believe you can go to a party and have trouble with a settee, but Joey did. "I was only minding my own business, Man, sitting on it when it broke."

"How can you break a settee by sitting on it?"

"Porky Pam sat on me sitting on it."

Two dedicated policemen had called in at midnight. "We've had reports of a disturbance."

They were offered a beer or two, or four… six… "Thank you sir, we're on duty. Now about this disturbance."

Everyone was enjoying themselves. John, Paul, George and Ringo going at it, the volume turned down just a notch to show we were responsible citizens.

The officer's radio, the one attached to his lapel, made a crackling noise. He turned his head and shouted, "Yes Sarge. Yes, at Flat 20. We're here now."

He looked to the heavens.

"Yes disturbance. It's all under control, Sir. Officer Green and I are part of the disturbance."

Officer Green nodded in an official way.

The radio went silent and he didn't even have to say "Over and out." I thought they always had to do that.

"Now what were you saying about a couple of beers, Sir?"

And now it's morning, those shafts of sunlight are streaming through the gap where the curtains should be and Bottle-o's dog is barking. It's a bad start to what should be a good day.

We've said our thanks to Constables Swindlehurst and Green. Thrown out the stragglers. Cleared up. Had a bowl of stew. Thank goodness for the meat stew. It has medicinal properties which is a mercy as we're aiming to get fit for a trip to Station Pier where the P&O Arcadia has tied up. Johnnie Mitch's last ship. He wants to catch up with old friends. Have an English beer, or two.

"What, after last night?"

I'm picking up Puss in Boots, yes Heather wants to come. And Heather's friend, Carol, and Joey too. Ian and girlfriend. The more the merrier.

We wander around the great ship taking in the luxury. The sweeping staircases, spacious dining rooms, enormous ball rooms, bars, swimming pools; everything that a modern ocean-going liner has to offer.

We're all getting high on this fantastic world; Ian and girl friend announce they are getting engaged.

"Engaged?" What happened to age 50 and marrying a rich farmer's widow?

Puss in Boots is star-struck with the Arcadia. "Think, just five weeks and it will be in London."

"Southampton," says John. "Two hour train ride through beautiful English countryside to London. The perfect introduction."

"Can't wait," says Heather. "It's been our dream, hasn't it, Carol?"

It has been their dream since they were kids at school. England. The Queen, Buckingham Palace, the Houses of Parliament. The Tower of London.

Yes, it's not Bob and his bloody hockey club I'll have to arm-wrestle. It's Birdcage Walk.

"Are you on this planet, Holdsworth?" Frank's piercing eyes fix me from over his glasses. It's down to earth day, Monday morning.

"I'm on this planet, Sir."

"I'm told you are going out with our Finance Director's Personal Assistant. A pretty girl and bright with it. She's not going to your head I hope?"

I assure Frank that Heather Pattison is not going to my head. "Feet on the ground, Sir. I'm ready for anything."

"Good. I've got something special for you. A worthwhile story. Critical in fact."

I'm still being fixed by those beady eyes from above the rim of his glasses.

"As you know the country is preparing itself for the bush fire season. Everything is tinder-dry. The worst risk for years – I want to see what's being done out there in the countryside, what recommendations the authorities are making. As a responsible paper we need to get involved. Tell our readers."

"It's right up my street, Sir. A worthwhile story as you say."

"Make sure your feet are on the ground, Holdsworth. No star-gazing. This is a serious business."

He doesn't have to tell me. This could be good. I had first-hand experience of bush fires when I was in South Australia and of what the Department of Agriculture and the Country Fire Service were doing. They were all fired up about bush fires. It was my modest joke... but they didn't see it like that. And you can't blame them.

I'd driven through the countryside after a fire had passed. Twenty-four hours later and the smell of the burning, the smoke, the stifling smoke, Gums still crackling, popping, still festering with fire. It had passed at such a terrifying pace; back home in England we couldn't fathom it. People seeing it from afar couldn't understand why people died, why they didn't get out and run, out-drive the fire.

It moves too quickly, that's why. When I first arrived at Keynes' he told me of the day a fire passed his place, just to the east. A dreadful day he called it, a complete fire ban was operating in the State; there was searing heat and wind the speed of a train. He knew the people involved, the properties; Bill Somerville had phoned in a panic shouting down the line that the fire had just gone through his property, it was coming Keynes' way and it covered the 20 miles in just 20 minutes. He just had time to get himself together when it swept through. A mile a minute, sixty miles an hour. Keynes' eyebrows were raised telling the tale. Mine too!

He was a man prepared and he was making sure I was if it happened again, if it occurred while I was there.

Wise man, in England I'd seen nothing like it, of course. Couldn't even visualise it. We have ice, cars skidding, people killed. And floods, people drowned, properties swept away. In Oz it's Bushfires.

"If it's going to be a bad day," Keynes said, "they'll warn us over the radio. The day the fire came through was classified as Extreme Risk... but there's worse, one up from there, Catastrophic, then down through Extreme to Low Risk."

Keynes said if the radio warned of either of the top two it was time to get out. "Don't bugger about waiting until the fire is on top of you. Unless you are geared to handle it and plan to stay, then get in the car and go."

I wondered what was coming next from John Keynes. I'd come to look after his stud cattle, not race ahead of a fire or stay and risk being roasted alive.

"I'd get the kids and the wife out, get them in the car, and get them out of it. But I'll stay to defend the property." He drew breath. "It's your choice; you can join them and get away. But I'd stay and it's your decision if you want to wade in and help. The property is well prepared to withstand a fire."

He had shown me. The elementary things, buckets of water, hose, hand pumps. The rainwater down-pipes on the house needed to be blocked; then the whole roof doused so that the gutters filled with water. It would be my job to remove everything close to the house that would burn. "Furniture, blinds, door mats, anything you can lay hands on that will catch alight. Remember the heat is intense, the fire does not have to make contact to combust."

I was not sure if John Keynes was out to terrify me or not. "And, remember, burning embers can travel ahead of the main fire. A mile is not uncommon, more has been known."

Keynes' property was well prepared as he said and a well organised property stood a good chance. Fire breaks had been ploughed around key paddocks, just a few yards wide and then a second, 50 paces in from the first. And on cool, calm days the grass burnt off between the two. The dam was topped up and all trees, bushes and undergrowth close to the house and buildings had been cleared long ago. Yes, Keynes explained it all. It seemed his property stood a good chance.

And he was keen I stayed. It was just him against the elements.

And I'd volunteered.

"Yes Frank, I can do this story. I have personal experience."

"Go for it Holdsworth. I want to see your copy on my desk as soon as you're done."

Those eyes pinned me again. "Feet on the ground, Holdsworth."

"Sir."

\* \* \* \* \*

More than 40 years on from the time I researched and wrote my story on Bushfires for The Weekly Times, I found myself in Melbourne watching the events of early February 2009. On the television, in the papers and in the clouds of black and grey smoke obliterating the horizon – I had landed in Melbourne just days before the worst bush fires in the history of the State of Victoria were to break out.

It was a period of extreme Bushfire weather conditions; there had been drought for a long time and then the temperatures began to rise through the 90's to over a hundred and more. Then the winds came. That's all you need. Perhaps a bolt of lightning setting fire to the tinder-dry foliage or the winds bringing down a power line. More than 200 people died and 400 were injured.

Later and Heather and I were back home in cold, damp, dreary, England, watching the aftermath on our television screen. Then the dreadful statistics; as many as 400 individual fires were recorded on the worst day, 7 February 2009.

"It's Black Saturday," said Johnnie Mitch when I phoned.

"Are you ok?" I asked.

"Yep. It was the north-east of Melbourne, away from the suburbs. More than 2000 homes gone, 78 individual townships…"

John drew breath. Even over the phone, a distance of 12,000 miles away, I could see the picture John was painting. "More than 7000 are homeless… they've put out appeals for temporary accommodation, tents, caravans, anything."

I sat down, the phone still pressed to my ear. We had been there just a few days ago and my own experience in South Australia brought it all home to me. I knew what they were battling. I had driven through countryside that had been swept with fire just a few hours before. And I had helped Keynes prepare for the day one might come our way.

"You still there, mate?"

"Yes John, still here."

"They're appointing a Royal Commission into it all. Trying to make recommendations so it never happens again. I'll send you a copy when it's out."

"Yes please, John. I'd like to see it…"

*Professor David de Kretser AC, the Hon. Bernard Teague AO, Ms Susan Pascoe AM, and Mr Ronald McLeod AO 31/07/2010*

## Commission draws to a close

The Commissioners presented their final report to the Governor of Victoria, Professor David de Kretser AC on the morning of 31 July 2010. The report was then presented to the Premier and tabled in Parliament, making it available to the public. You can view the report here. Alternatively, you can order copies from the Victorian Government via Victoria Online or by phoning 1800 463 684. This means that the 2009 Victorian Bushfires Royal Commission has now concluded its task, and ceased to operate. Thank you to all of those who contributed to the work of the Commission.

# Chapter 18

## Headlines – Porsche Gets the Boot

"I'm in unchartered waters here, lads. Totally new ground."

I'm seeking understanding from my two flat mates, that's all I'm after. Not much to ask. A sympathetic ear. Four sympathetic ears in fact.

Heather Pattison arriving on the scene has blown me off course. Up till now the important things in life could be counted on the fingers of one hand. "Isn't that right, lads?" Nods all round. "Whimsically speaking, of course."

"Work at Number One, play Number Two, then the Porsche at Three. Mum, Dad and my sister, Ingie. My family... that's four isn't it?" There are more nods. "And then you two flat mates. That makes five."

"Six if you count us as two," says Johnnie Mitch.

"Eight," says Joe. "If you count your mum, dad and sister individually."

"Can we stick to the point," I say. "This is serious. I'm telling you with Puss in Boots on the scene, it's unchartered waters. I've been blown off course."

"Yes, serious," says Joe.

And serious because I'm the one who has mastered the three-ring cooker and I'm the one who's worked out the recipe for the hearty stew that goes on the three rings. Ok, they know Serge in the deli; but I am the man who has taken up the mantle of turning a raw bundle of veggies and lumps of choice meat into the most succulent plateful for dinner. Herbs, ginger root and bay leaf to add that extra dimension. For tea, or lunch... or even breakfast.

"If Heather Pattison becomes Number One in my life, who knows what might happen to me and the magic tucker, lads?"

John looks at Joe. Joe looks at John. These are grim expressions.

But life is never that straightforward, especially where women are concerned. "Is it, lads?"

They are nodding again.

"For a start, I haven't won her over yet. Then there's the small matter of the boyfriend, Bob of hockey fame. Once the splints come off he'll want to assert his rightful place and not just on the field of play."

"Ah, the boy friend," says Joe.

"And there are other contenders, or so rumour has it. Did I hear that there's some golf player lurking in the shadows fresh off the Eighteenth? A professional with a Jag and one of those bags full of sticks. Part of the mystical world of the golfer that seems to carry weight with the ladies. Woods, irons and putters...all part of the allure."

"It's a mystical world, all right," says John. "Not up my street at all. But it gets 'em in."

Joe shakes his head. "Grac w golfa."

"What?"

"Grac w golfa. To play golf."

"I thought you didn't speak Polish."

"That and futbol I remember," says Joe. "I was taught at school."

"Can we just get back to my predicament, please? What I'm saying is the world of the pro-golfer is one that I can't compete with. Those putters and parties, those holes-in-one and hotels in Florida..."

"Put like that and who can," says John.

"Let's be honest," says Joe. "You don't stand a chance."

This golfing pro, shall we call him Hal because that is, apparently, his name, has the Jag, but that is no competition. I explain to the lads that when I worked for the Squire he would say how butchers and betting men bought Jags, men of class bought Mercs. "Anyway, I've seen off more Jags on the race track than you can point a stick at. They are no competition."

"That puts you one-up, mate," John says.

"Apparently she's been out with him on more than one occasion, Jaguar or no Jaguar. I'm told he picked her up from the office for lunch. And he's shown her the bright lights of Melbourne too. I'd like to extinguish Hal's bloody lights. And I don't mind how."

"Answers on a self-addressed envelope," says John.

"Judge's decision is final," says Joe.

Now, there's another obstacle.

Frank has me down for a stint up country and one that could really de-rail my efforts to stay in contention. "Your machinery pages read well, Holdsworth. We'd like more. More write-ups, more in-depth articles." Frank reminds me the Christmas break is just around the corner. "You need to have a few stories up your sleeve, have a reserve to fall back on. Remember, everything shuts down over the holiday break."

I do know. Australia's summer holidays come over Christmas and New Year. Most go up country or down the beach. They make a big thing of it. "I've got loads of good stories up my sleeve, Frank. Tons to fall back on. And Press releases from all the major manufacturers. And if they lack detail, I'll get on the phone to my contacts. No problem filling pages now or ever."

It doesn't make the slightest difference. I've got to go. Me, up country while Hal the pro and his putter are given a free rein to woo the girl of my dreams. And there's Bob the steady boyfriend to consider, he could still be a stumbling block to my aspirations. And now there's something else to worry about – Heather hankers after doing the overseas trip, the trip of a lifetime. She talked about it on the Arcadia. Where would that leave me?

The last thing I need is to be sent up country on an extended trip when I have so much going on in my head. There's a little birdie tapping away, "I think you want to marry this girl…" And I reply, "I think I do."

I try one more time. "What about my Christmas shopping, Frank? Even a lad like me needs to buy something for his loved ones. I don't want to rush it and I've no chance if I'm a hundred miles the other side of the Black Stump."

"If you're referring to the PA to the Finance Director, she'll still be here when you get back. And there's plenty of time before the Christmas tills stop ringing… if that's what your intention is."

I retreat, defeated. Up country, miles from anywhere, leaving the competition a free hand. Bob the hockey and Hal the golf able to steal kisses beneath a fresh sprig of Mistletoe while I'm left with the left-overs. Mistletoe isn't Mistletoe if it's all limp and lifeless. Fancy asking, "Will you be mine…" and all I get in reply is, "Darling, your berries have dropped off."

"Don't go on so," says Stewart clutching a bird problem in his hand. "She's barely 20 and needs a bit of freedom. She'll see the light in good time."

"Thanks for nothing, Stewart. That's the sort of reassuring news I could do without. Now go back to your own bird problems."

And Ian, South African, with the whirlwind romance under his belt is no help either. He's going for a divorce!

"A divorce? Hell, you've been married ten weeks!"

"Yep, couldn't stand it. Marriage is no fun at all. Take a tip from one who knows." It's true; ten weeks' married bliss has taken its toll. His blonde wavy hair has lost its wave… the ice blue eyes have lost their ice. "Marriage is not all it's cracked up to be, Rich. I speak from experience."

"Ten weeks is hardly experience," I point out. But it's water off the proverbial duck's back to Ian. "Don't go near it," he tells me.

Joey with the Ford family saloon relates what happened. "All that lovey-dovey stuff went down the pan, Man. Minutes after the minister did the 'Will you?' stuff." Joey thinks this joke is the funniest he's heard in ages.

"That's all very well, Ian," I say. "But you don't have Heather Pattison in your sights. I have a little birdie tapping away in my head and he's giving me a message. And its not his nest he's talking about.

"Funny time to send us off. Coming up to Christmas," Brownie says. "What have you done to offend Frank now?"

"Frank says we need more stories… a back-up, he says. No rest till we've got them in the bag. I've lined up the big Case American tractors then onto Claas German harvesters. That should keep the bugger happy. Two of the best. And stop off at a couple of other places while we're going that way. Hope you've got plenty of film."

We're half-way up country and I'm looking over my shoulder and wondering what's going on back home in Melbourne.

"You sure your heart's in this, mate?" says Brownie as we leave the Dandenongs way behind. "Something seems to be bothering you."

"No, Brownie. I'm right here with you. Can't wait to get stuck in. We're a team, remember. My eloquent words… your eloquent pics."

Brownie's behind the wheel today and the Victorian countryside flies past. "These new Holdens don't half go."

"The question is, Brownie, do they stop?"

I make sure my belt is on as the next corner comes rushing at us. My head doesn't want to meet the new Holden windscreen going the other way at 60 miles an hour.

"The big Yankie tractor," I say. "J I Case. They'll pull the skin off Frank's proverbial Christmas custard."

I'd seen Dan McRae at the Orange Fields Days. He was representing the mighty big American tractors and after Frank's latest exhortations I called him and lined up a road test – only in the case of a tractor, more a field test. "Hey Dan, can you get your biggest hooked up to a couple of ploughs, a cultivator or disc harrow. For pics and a story. We'll give it the full treatment. Stick anything behind your best machine. Uncle Tom Cobley and all if you like."

"That's a funny Pommie expression ya got there, mate. But I'll get them hooked up anyway. Your Uncle Tom what's-it Cobley. That'll give ya something to fill ya pages."

"Thanks Dan."

"The big mean machines, Brownie. I'm sure Dan will be showing us what J I Case can do with an acre or two of hard Australian soil behind its drawbar."

"Will it satisfy Frank do you reckon?"

"I bloody hope so. I told Frank I had some serious thinking to do when it came to the Finance Director's PA – and this is his response. I'm sure he's taking it out on me because of the cricket. I blame Geoff Boycott myself."

Out there with Dan and his Yankie tractors and the dust is flying. You can see these machines were bred on the vast open spaces of the States and over the border in the rolling plains of Manitoba. "What do you reckon then, Rich?" Dan pulls up next to Brownie and me. The cloud of dust settles gently over us. "That impress you guys?"

"It sure does, Dan. Sure does."

Back in the car we're putting miles on the clock for our next assignment – the German Claas combine harvesters.

"You can lower the Stars and Stripes now, Brownie. And start humming the German National anthem. We're off to see the best combine harvesters in the business."

"Don't you mean headers?"

"You call them headers. Back home we call them combine harvesters. And before that we had binders."

"Don't remember them at all." Brownie's trying to swat a fly that's found its way into the Holden. The Holden veers from one side of the road to the other and back again.

"Don't worry mate. I've still got my seat belt on."

Brownie gives up the fight with the fly and the Holden returns to my side of the road.

"Well, when I started farming I can remember these binders. I worked my school holidays at Farmer Collins' and the binder cut the corn, put it into sheaves and the farm hands went around the field making little stacks of six, or eight. The old hands called them stooks. You heard of stooks, Brownie?"

"Nope. But they sound hard work."

"I was told to leave the ends of the stooks open so the air got through. 'Keep 'em open, Boy. Let nature do its work.'"

"Nature's a wonderful thing," says Brownie. "I've taken half a dozen swipes at that fly and still I can't get the bugger. He must have built-in radar."

I take up today's Sun and kill him stone dead with one swipe. "Now where was I?"

"You were telling me why you call headers combine harvesters."

"Well, you can learn something here my old son as I came top in harvesting machinery at college and I put it to good use when I joined the Squire as he'd just bought a German Claas harvester. The best, Brownie. The best."

"And...?"

"And what sets it apart is the heart of the machine and the heart is the cylinder that spins at over a thousand revs a minute beating the grain from the corn. The farm hands call it a drum, a threshing drum. 'God speed the drum, Boy,' as it hummed into life. 'God speed the drum.'"

"I bet your college lecturer was pleased to have you in his ranks."

"Young Mr Thorogood was a bloody good lecturer. He had a mock up of the machine and he explained it all. 'Gather round lads,' he'd say. 'Anyone who thinks size doesn't count needs to think again.' His enthusiasm was infectious and we were all listening, and when size comes into it everyone listens. 'Puny little drum works well, a bloody big one works better.' And he got us to write it all down. Size matters if you want your sacks filled fast."

Brownie is overtaking a truck hogging the middle of the road. I take a breather and let him get on with it.

"The same follows for the combine harvester, Brownie. When the combine replaced the binder and stationary thresher. The Claas we're on our way to see has the biggest drum, biggest by far. And it works just as Mr Thorogood said."

Brownie is impressed. "You can come back to my place any day and swat flies. We've got hundreds of the buggers."

We've returned home and my imposed exile doesn't seem to have done too much harm. I've been on the phone to Miss Pattison and have been invited out to Thornbury and an official meeting with

Mum and Dad. I met Mum Pattison when I first picked Heather up for the party date; none of this hooting the horn and gesticulating, "Get in babe" from the comfort of the driver's seat.

Nope, this girl is special. I'd done it properly. And I listened to what my Mum and Dad taught me. "You'll not win a girl's heart that way, son." I'd parked up, tripped lightly along the path, skipped past the Jacaranda tree, politely knocked on the front door and I'm in.

And the next day when we went down to see the Arcadia.

And next, "We're off to see friends..."

And I'm here again.

"Heather's expecting you." That's Mum Pattison, a lovely mum figure; her cookies are as good as anything I've ever tasted. And Robbie, Heather's brother, old enough to have passed his eleven plus if he'd have been back home in the Old Country.

"You a St Kilda fan?" I think it best to say "Could be." I don't want a confrontation at this early stage.

I know my way down the hallway and here's the girl of my dreams. Am I permitted a little kiss on the cheek?

And I am as I catch the chat behind me. "Walks funny, doesn't he?"

But I've got a nice smile. I hear that too as I stroke the cat and that scores a couple of Brownie points.

"Where's Dad Pattison?"

"Down his club. He'll be back shortly."

"Oh, and sister Gaye?"

"Keith and Gaye might pop in later."

"That will be nice. I'm glad they came to the last party. They make a super couple. Young newly weds."

Johnnie Mitch said, "Don't get too carried away, mate. Could be they only came to cast an eye over you. Make sure little sister isn't going out with a total waster."

"I've yet to pass the real acid test, Mitch. That'll be Dad Pattison. Stroking the cat is one thing. Praising the cookies is another point scorer. The real test is the eagle eye of Heather's father. I'm meeting him later. I'd better not mention the cricket."

"And the funny walk, mate."

"All this scrutiny, Mitch."

"It's what you've let yourself in for. And at the end of it there'll be trials and tribulations if Ian's experience is anything to go by. Are you sure you know what you're doing?"

"Yep. I've thought it through and the little birdie tells me I've found the girl of my dreams. He says I should be doing something about it. And I reckon I will."

Dad Pattison is home from his club. I stop stroking the cat, straighten my tie, avoid the funny walk (what funny walk?) and extend a hand. "Heather might have mentioned me?"

This is a stout man and that's not only in physique, but stout in spirit, and those big, bushy eyebrows remind me of Bob Menzies, Aussie Prime Minister and leader of men. I'm not sure if Bob Menzies was suspicious of Poms but Dad Pattison certainly is.

"She has a regular boyfriend you know. Bob is part of the family." He lets that sink in. "And he's a sportsman."

"And a St Kilda fan," Robbie adds to Bob's credentials.

I smile down at young Rob. Or up, he's a big lad for his years. "Don't forget I am too," I say. "And the flat overlooks the ground. Can't get closer than that." I smile; this must be a points scorer if ever there was. I can even hear the cries of pain as boot hits shin each Saturday afternoon. But think it best not to claim points for that.

"Sportsman?" I rack my brains... what can I reply that will impress? Ping-pong champion at Upper Basildon Youth Club – no, don't think that will cut much ice. "Have I told you about my time at the wicket?" I throw that into the equation as nonchalantly as I can. "Scored a 50 off some ferocious bowling not long ago."

It goes down well. "A 50 eh? Fancy a beer?"

Yes, Heather's Dad, the Bob Menzies look-alike, is offering me one of his cherished ales out of his reserve in the fridge. "Carlton Bitter?"

"Of course."

You wouldn't ask for anything but Melbourne beer when in Melbourne. Aussies are not only devoted to their local footie team (quite rightly) but also their local beer. If I'd replied, "Have you got an Adelaide West End or a Sydney Three X's," I'd have been shown the door. This simple fact rules in all but exceptional circumstances. I remember being in an Adelaide club once and amazed to hear Adelaide men ask for the Melbourne Carlton beer. When challenged, the reply was firm but logical, "It's on the bottom shelf… when the sheila bends down she shows her arse…"

Dad Pattison knocks the top off two Carton bottles. "Cheers."

I don't think I'll tell him the tale of girls' arses in Adelaide at this moment. "Yes, cheers."

I relax a bit. But not too much. Just because my flat overlooks the hallowed ground of St. Kilda, because I've scored a 50 against Aussie bowlers and know a bottle of Carlton from a West End, doesn't mean you can marry a man's daughter.

And Dad Pattison seems to have a problem with one of his own even wanting to go out with a lad from England when there are so many good, decent, upstanding, Aussies around.

And then there's young Robbie to impress. He's standing in front of me this very moment with bat and ball in his hand… and a challenge.

"Fancy a game?"

"Bowlers have been known to wilt when I stride to the wicket." Did I say that? How can I be so foolhardy? And now young Robbie Pattison wants to put this to the test. "We have a pitch in the back yard. I'll give you a few looseners."

Heather is joining us. "I want to watch my man perform."

Oh, I say to myself. I'm "Her Man" am I? That's one up for me.

"And see fair play," Heather adds. "I don't want to see anyone come to harm."

Does she think I'm going take this back-yard friendly so seriously that young Rob gets a cracked rib or two? Or is she thinking the boot is on the other foot? Does my Heather know something I don't?

Well, a few looseners from a lad of 12 can't do any harm. And this pitch is scarcely a dozen strides long, between the gold-fish pond and back fence. Robbie's all ready. "I'll be Australia and you can be England." He tosses a coin in the air and when it hits the ground says he'll bowl.

"I didn't hear me call," I say.

"You don't have to. I've always wanted to bowl at an English batsman. I'd rather have Geoff Boycott but you'll have to do."

Heather is sitting on the patio, her knees under her chin. Even in jeans and casual top this girl looks ravishing. And that smile. "Fun isn't it?"

Young Robbie trots off to the gold-fish pond, turns and runs in like a man possessed, or lad, it's hard to tell when someone's running full pelt at you with fire in their eyes. I don't see the ball, only hear it crash into the fence behind me.

"A loosener?" I enquire.

"It was. Wait until I get up to speed."

Heather is nonplussed. "Careful Rob. Richard's taking me out tonight. I want him in one piece."

Young Rob doesn't hear or if he does, chooses to ignore his sister's words.

He sprints in and bowls at the speed akin to Ray Lindwall on the day he destroyed the English team in a matter of a few overs, along with his mate Keith Miller. The ball traverses the dozen paces like lightning and arrives at my end well before I can move my bat. And well before I can move my legs. "Don't worry," I say, "I don't think anything's broken."

"Poor darling," I hear Heather's soothing voice. "Are you all right?"

In the field of play they'd be calling for the stretcher. In the Pattison back-yard I'm batting on...It's worth a fractured kneecap just to be called darling.

At this moment I can see my reputation in the Pattison household diminishing at a rapid rate. I could easily lose a gallon of blood, break a leg, suffer a fracture of the skull, death even. Perhaps I am going to die... perhaps Junior Ray Lindwall has a bouncer in his armoury that will knock my brains out.

Heather is standing up now, she looks nervous. She sounds nervous. "It's only a game, Rob. A game. Nothing to prove."

But the words are lost on brother Rob as he turns for his run in, feet pounding the ground by the goldfish pond and the goldfish taking cover. "Robbie, Robbie," cries Heather as I stand frozen to the spot awaiting my execution – I'll never hear those words from the Man of the Cloth now, "Will you, Richard Michael Holdsworth, take this woman, Heather Jean Pattison?' And then the bit about, "For better or for worse."

The next ball is just as quick as the last – but this time I am quicker. I swipe it with a mighty blow and it sails over young Robbie's head and strikes the garage door with a satisfying thud. "Six," I call. "It hit the garage on the full."

The next bounces once before vanishing into Dad Pattison's rockery patch. "Four."

When it is all over and the garage door dented a dozen or so times and the rockery a tangle of destroyed plants, I call a halt. "Enough of a lesson for one day. Time to take your sister out to a show."

Robbie grins. "You win." Yes, he is a nice lad after all and normality returns to the Pattison household.

Heather says nothing. She doesn't have to. I've got two of the last tickets for the Beatles' concert. John, Paul, Ringo and George. Yeah, yeah, yeah. They are everywhere. Television, radio and they've made the Hit Parade their own. Beatle mania. And I've just shown my mettle among these wonderful Aussie people. I feel good.

Even the little birdie is telling me how well I'm doing. The golfer is not part of the future, he chirrups. Even Bob is a Melbourne lad and isn't going to budge. Heather has her eyes set on far-away, very far away. Maybe I should be thinking the unthinkable… far, far away for me too. Perhaps it could be a double berth on the high seas.

We had stopped and casually glanced in jeweller's windows, hand in hand, when out for the day. We looked at her favourite style of diamond ring. And looked again. My eyes popped out of my head. "I could do a lot of travelling for that money," she said. "Even two people could."

Was that a hint, or was it not? She's certainly right about the cost. It could buy the shop – and if it's travelling you're talking about, it could even buy the ship!

And for that sort of money I could fulfil my own dream and enter the Porsche in the Bathurst 500; buy a truck-full of racing tyres and a professional pit crew to rush at the car every few laps with tools in hand just like Le Mans. Polish my windscreen, pat me on the back and give me a humbug to suck as I fly off again into the night.

I scan my bank account. Where on earth has the money gone? My Weekly Times' salary is good and I've paid off the Porsche long ago. I know I don't scrimp on the housekeeping; only the best meat cuts from Serge; we don't hold back when it comes to entertaining friends and I've had professionals come in and clean the carpets after each party. But it doesn't explain why my cupboard is bare, the bottom line registering nil and even nil is in red. Where on earth has the money gone?

But the ring problem won't go away; it has to be confronted some time soon if I am to make this happen. And what better time or place than over a serious drink. I call Johnnie Mitch on the Darkroom extension and suggest a jar or two at the Pheonix. "I'll get 'em in, mate."

By ten past five John is questioning, "How much?" And when I tell him he replies, "You could enter the Porsche in the…"

"I know, I know," I say. "I've been through all that. But I've had to ditch all such aspirations. Even the Porsche might have to go."

"The Porsche go? I don't believe it. A few months back and you'd have got out of bed on a damp night to give it a cuddle. You have got it bad, mate, haven't you?"

Lou Richards, ex-footie star and columnist for The Sun, TV pundit, and Mine Host, leans on the bar next to me. "She won't marry you, Rich. What would the world be coming to? A Pom."

He's already lost the wager over whether Heather would go out with me or not. He issues instructions to his bar tender. "Here, pour these two Poms a beer." His sorrow is palpable. "But she definitely won't marry you."

I would say something about him sticking to being a once-upon-a-time footie star, columnist for The Sun and Mine Host at The Phoenix, but I don't as I remember he ruined many an opponent's dreams with a boot in the right place. And as he is my side of the bar and I'm a bit vulnerable in the Right Place, I decide to keep quiet.

Anyway, Lou's a great soul and has just bought Mitch and me our beers I won't push my luck.

Back at the flat I cast my eyes over my bank statement again. I still can't believe where the money has gone; ok I have flown to Adelaide a couple of times and had a whale of a time; Porsche had a new tonneau cover after some bright sparks used it as a trampoline and, finally, there was the funny noise in the engine room that meant an expensive investigation.

"I'll be fine once next month's pay cheque lands on my desk," I tell John. "Trouble is I can't wait.

"How much did you say?" John enquires.

"A set of racing tyres?"

"Not them. The bloody ring."

"Couple of hundred and a bit more."

"It so happens I have that kind of money in my account. How about if I lend it to you till the wages department comes good?"

I can't believe this. My old flat mate from London, fellow Pom, stayed put while WWII raged all around, watched as V1s and V2s came crashing down, is now offering to be my banker.

"Do you mean it? Do you really mean it?"

"Just until your pay cheque hits your desk. We'll shake on it, gentleman's hand-shake. But no kissing..."

No kissing! Bugger! As John fishes in his pocket and comes out with his cheque book I breathe a sigh of relief. It's signed and sealed. I'm off to Mr Expensive Jewellers in Collins Street to come out moments later with a little box containing the prized ring – the sparkliest of sparklers. "Don't you get the whole shop for this?"

But I've got to chose the right moment, the occasion, it's just about the most important question you'll ever ask. "Will you? Will you?" And pray the reply is, "Yes, yes, YES."

The office party on Christmas Eve sets the scene for celebration. And Heather's family are gathering at home in Thornbury for the annual pre-Christmas get-together. If I have got a "Yes, yes, yes," what better time and place? "Surprise, surprise. I've just whisked your daughter off her feet."

I've got the ring. All I've got to do is show restraint at The Weekly Times' break-up party. Side-step Lou Richards' comments in The Phoenix. And book our favourite restaurant.

"A bottle of champers?"

"Better had," I say.

"Well it is Christmas Eve."

Goodness, how this little box becomes a big box when it's in your inside top pocket. I spend the meal slumped forwards over my several courses so the bulge won't show. I could pop the question here, in the midst of the revelry, waiters waiting, drinkers drinking, eaters eating.

But no, this has got to be done in the comfort of my own Porsche. Outside number 72, Shaftesbury Parade.

"Will you…? Will you…?"

I produce the little box, flip the lid, the diamond nearly dazzles us, and Heather, my intended, the woman I want to spend the rest of my life with throws her arms round me, and I get a great big kiss.

I think that is a YES!

"Will you, will you," becomes, I WILL. I WILL."

The loveliest girl in the whole of Christendom has said YES!

"Yes, I will. Of course."


The SS Fairstar slips gently from its berth at Station Pier accompanied by the usual razzmatazz; horns sounding, bands playing, streamers streaming; Johnnie Mitch is capturing it all on camera. Heather clutches our streamers, Mum and Dad on the other end, our last tenuous life-line with Australia for the next year while we explore the Old Country, Europe, the world.

The thin paper threads snap, we are on our way, on our own. The propellers churn the water beneath our feet. The bow turns towards the open sea, the horizon beckons. Hey, there's a smart cargo ship on its way in and it's my old ship, the MV Port Melbourne. "You're going the wrong way."

The deck-hands are preparing the ship for docking. Do I recognise faces among the men whose lives I shared for six weeks? Is that Charlie and Big Tam? Is that Mr Mason the chippie and is that Dougie, Dougie the electrician. You're goin' the wrong way, laddie."

Are we going the wrong way?

Maybe. But I've got my Aussie bride and I've had eight fantastic years. And we'll be back. Be back one day…

# Aussie Update

# All You Need To Plan Your Trip

Australia today is a country of 22 million people drawn from many parts of the world, but since WWII, mainly from Europe, Italy and Greece, and to a lesser degree the other Balkan States. Of recent, Australia has welcomed many people from Vietnam and the Far East. After WWII the Australian population was bolstered by an influx of British – the Ten Pound Pom – their passages subsidised by the Australian government.

Australia was first colonised in 1770; therefore not many Aussies can claim to go back further than five generations drawn from the Old Country – some (a minority) coming out in shackles.

If this is a rich diversity – take a look at the Australian countryside! Very few countries can claim to entice the enthusiastic traveller with such an enormous variety, from the sophisticated cities, through lush English-type farming lands to the dry, barren Outback and the stunning mountains and deserts of the far north of Western Australia. Then there is the north of Queensland, equally deserted and scarcely explored, but in this case the attraction to the adventurer is the tropical wet lands and rain forests.

Yes, Australia has it all!

# ADELAIDE and South Australia

I have to admit to a great affection for the city of Adelaide. As I have said earlier, it is my kind of city; large enough to allow you to continually expand your circle of friends and discover something new, yet not so big as to make you feel a tiny cog in a very large wheel. Well, that is how I felt at the time.

Of course, Adelaide – like much else in Australia – has changed significantly from when I lived and worked in South Australia; gone are the six o'clock swill, the inability to get a drink with a meal on a Sunday and a Premier who cosseted the place and its inhabitants like a mother hen. Adelaide is very much a city of the twenty-first century, with a population of more than 1.28 million, the fifth largest in Australia, and a wealth of festivals and other social events to keep the most fastidious happy.

In short, you will not be disappointed if it is on your itinerary alongside the bigger cities that catch the eye, Melbourne and Sydney.

In the Adelaide Festival of Arts it has one of the world's greatest celebrations of the arts; it is internationally renowned and attracts leading performers from around the globe as well as, of course, from within Australia. This is at one end of the spectrum; perhaps Adelaide's Schützenfest is at the other. Translated it literally means shooting festival – and there are some shooting competitions – but today it is a highly popular festival held in January each year with the attendance being over 20,000. Festivities involve German food, beverages, dances and music. More information: www.schutzenfest.co.au

In fact, there is a whole host of food/wine festivals in and around Adelaide. Tasting Australia is just one of several food and wine related events held in Adelaide each year. The first Tasting Australia was launched in 1997 by Ian Parmenter and David Evans, for which they received the Jaguar Award for Excellence from the Gourmet Traveller. It attracts more than 200 national and international journalists, and several thousands of visitors. You can learn more about this and other food/wine festivals on: www. southaustralia.com/winefoodevents.aspx

This is just a tiny snap-shot of Adelaide. Within a train ride is Glenelg, Brighton, and the attractions of wonderful sandy beaches. Further down the coast is Moana beach stretching almost as far as the eye can see and unique in that you can drive a car onto the hard, compacted sand. And the Aussies do! Set up a barbie, crack a few beers, spread out and enjoy yourself! The Aussies do that too!

## City Climate

Of all the major Australian cities, Adelaide is the driest with a semi-arid climate. Rainfall is light and infrequent throughout summer. The winter is like a spring day in England!

# Barossa Valley

Less than a couple of hours' drive from Adelaide is the Barossa Valley, a world-renowned area for wine production and, as such, a popular tourist destination. The Barossa Valley Way is the main road through the valley, connecting the main towns of Nuriootpa, Tanunda, Rowland Flat and Lyndoch.

The success of the wine industry in the Barossa Valley is celebrated every two years with the week-long Barossa Valley Vintage Festival that draws visitors from all over the world and has entertainment for all tastes including a huge street parade, concerts and gourmet dining.

The Valley was the destination for many Germany immigrants two and three generations ago and clearly it is their influence and skills in wine making that has helped put the name Barossa Valley on the world map.

The specialities are the red wines, in particular Shiraz. Normally large proportions of Barossa Shiraz are used in Penfolds Grange (possibly Australia's most famous wine). Other main grape varieties grown in the region include Riesling, Semillon, Grenache and Cabernet Sauvignon. There are also some fortified wines traditionally produced in the region. The Barossa Valley should be high on your priority list.

**Useful contacts:**
General information on Barossa Valley from the Visitor
Information Centre. 66-68 Murray Street, Tanunda, SA 5352
Phone 1300 852 982 (within Australia) or +61 8 8563 0600
(International)
Email: visitorcentre@barossa.sa.gov.au

# Kangaroo Island

My visits to Kangaroo Island were all work-related and I saw none
of the tourist attractions now being promoted by the Visitor Centre.
Perhaps they hadn't been exploited in my day but they are
certainly worth exploring now for Kangaroo Island is a pristine
wilderness - a place that has offered protection to substantial
populations of native Australian animals, a place of beauty and a
place of escape. If you traverse its 155km length (just over 100
miles) you'll find soaring cliffs, dense forests, towering sand
dunes, wetlands and massive arcs of bone-white beach.

You'll want to see the rock formations in the 33,000-hectare
Flinders Chase National Park. There's also the 1909 Cape du
Couedic lighthouse and wildlife aplenty, including kangaroos,
koalas, echidnas (spiny anteaters) and the endangered Cape
Barren geese.

**More information:**
Kangaroo Island Gateway Visitor Information Centre
Howard Drive, Penneshaw, SA 5222.
Phone: +61 8 8553 1185
email: tourismKI@tourism.sa.com

# Birdsville track

The Birdsville Track is not the traditional "must see" venue for the
tourist with a camera slung round his (or her) neck and not
intending to get dust on a new pair of brogues. But for me,
Birdsville Track is as much a "must" as the Australian cities. The
Track connects Marree in central north of South Australia and

Birdsville in the south-west corner of Queensland. Therefore it gives you a very good insight into the Heart of Australia.

It was pioneered in 1880 as a stock route for droving cattle down from Queensland to the railhead at Marree and thence to markets in Adelaide. The cattlemen needed five to six weeks to cover the 524 km (302 miles) arduous journey.

Going in the opposite direction, Afghan traders led their camels north delivering goods to the scattered homesteads on the way to Birdsville. The camels were replaced by vehicles in the 1930s and these replaced by Road Trains 30 years later. The track became notorious for the challenge it posed and many people lost their lives in this remote and extremely hot area of South Australia.

Today the Birdsville Track is a good dirt road when dry. But it still goes through arid, remote areas and vast empty spaces. It can be exhausting and it is better to take two or three days and explore each area. Less than halfway between Marree and Birdsville there is the Mungerannie Roadhouse - the only supply point along the track. A visit at the bar for a cold drink is a must! And it is something of an oasis in the desert with a bore hole, and the Mungerannie Wetlands is a magnet for those who enjoy bird watching.

Just over the Queensland border is the town of Birdsville. Once you see the pub – you know you have travelled the full length of the Track! A cold beer awaits you! Well done!

The Track is safer than when I tackled it – but it still needs care and comprehensive planning. Take adequate provisions. YOU HAVE BEEN WARNED

**More information:**
www.simpsondesert.fl.net.au

# MELBOURNE and Victoria

Melbourne is the wining and dining capital of Australia and it is reputed to have one restaurant for every 30 people who live there.

That means, even with a population of four million, you can still find a restaurant for a last minute booking! And it is as varied as you want - the Europeans brought their cuisine in the 1950's, followed by the Far East in recent decades.

It is also an international cultural centre with events and festivals for drama, music, art, literature, film and television. It was voted a UNESCO City of Literature – not once but three times – and shared top position in a survey by The Economist of the 'World's Most Liveable Cities' – a survey based to a large degree on Melbourne's broad cultural offerings.

The Australian Ballet is based in Melbourne, as is the home of the Melbourne Symphony Orchestra. There are more than 100 galleries, most notably Australia's oldest and largest art gallery, the National Gallery of Victoria.

I lived in amongst all this for two years and thoroughly enjoyed every minute. Mind you, it is a great deal more sophisticated now – think of the fun I would have if I was still a St Kilda Road resident!

Take, for example, dining on one of the city's fleet of historical trams known as the Colonial Tramcar Restaurant. The company operating these glossy, burgundy restaurants say they represent the first travelling tramcar restaurants in the world and ensure a delightfully innovative approach to dining. And just because it's meals on wheels, there's no reason why it won't be anything other than a memorable experience. Surprise your partner – tell her (or him!) to dress up – you are off on a tram ride.

**More information:**
Phone: + 61 3 9696 4000.
Email: reservations@tramrestaurant.com.au

## Moomba Festival

The Moomba Festival is a huge outdoor Melbourne festival held on the Labour Day long weekend (4 days from Friday to the second Monday in March). It started in 1954 as a focus of city celebrations and activities.

The word Moomba is said to have come from an Aboriginal

word meaning Let's get together and have fun.

After the parade, celebrations continue throughout the day along the Yarra River. There's a host of activities for both young and old at this festive carnival time when Melbourne lets its hair down.

## These Sporting Aussies...

Melbourne is home to three major annual international sporting events. The Australian Open – one of the four Grand Slam tournaments on the tennis circuit; the Melbourne Cup – for horse racing enthusiasts, and the Australian Grand Prix (Formula One).

And the city is home to the National Sports Museum, located at the Melbourne Cricket Ground. As well as being the largest cricket ground in the world, the MCG is the spiritual home of Australian Rules football - the spectacular sport which has a fanatical following. Given the opportunity to go to the AFL Grand Final in September, grab it with both hands.

But for me, a cricket fan, the greatest day out is the first day of the Melbourne Test at the MCG on Boxing Day. There are usually at least 90,000 people in this fantastic venue – 89,998 are Aussies and just me and my mate Johnnie Mitch being Poms! A bit intimidating but join in the fun and everyone will make you welcome. Very welcome.

And it doesn't stop there. Early in the motor racing calendar the whole Formula One circus moves to Melbourne. And on the very site that our flat overlooked at Albert Park – the greatest drivers and cars in the world do battle.

## Shrine of Remembrance

Visit the Shrine of Remembrance, Victoria's memorial to the men and women who have served Australia in armed conflicts and peacekeeping operations throughout the nation's history.

The shrine was designed by returned veterans Hudson & Wardrop. Inspired by one of the seven wonders of the ancient world – the tomb of King Mausolus at Halicarnassus – their design was chosen from 83 competition entries.

Anzac Day. Every year, the Dawn Service commences on the Shrine Forecourt at 6am and the Anzac Day March along St Kilda Road starts at 9.00am and assembles at the Shrine by 1.00pm for the Commemorative Service. Be proud to be there.

**More Information:**
www.visitmelbourne.com
www.melbourneaustralia.org

## City Climate

Melbourne has a moderate climate but is well known for its changeable weather conditions, having a reputation of four seasons in one day. However during much of the year – and spring especially – Melbourne enjoys extended periods of mild weather and clear skies and is very appealing to UK visitors. In contrast, the summers can be punctuated by days of extreme heat and in winter there are times when you will definitely need your overcoat.

After the glitter and glitz of the city, the shopping sprees and the days of world class sport, it is time to see what the Victorian countryside has to offer. Here are just three ideas…

## Bendigo Tour with Echuca and Murray River Cruise

The Murray River is not known as Australia's "Old Man River" for nothing. In the early days it was the paddle steamer highway for wool bales and wheat sacks; today you can re-live the era of sweat and tears as you ride the riverboat down the Murray to the town of Echuca, once Australia's busiest inland port.

The tour that caught my eye included a paddle-steamer cruise, the port of Echuca and the nearby town of Bendigo. And a true Bendigo highlight is to relive the miner's experience by travelling underground in a miner's cage; you can do that at the Central Deborah deep-shaft mine.

**Useful contacts:**
Email: enquiries@travelaust.com.au
Phone: 02 9580 6466 (Within Australia) Phone: +61 2 9580 6466 (International)
www.bendigotourism.com

## Go Gold Prospecting

The discovery of gold in the 1850s is the most significant event in the evolution of the State of Victoria. Fuelled by extravagant stories of wealth gained in the 1849 Californian gold rush, gold fever hit Victoria following the early discoveries in and around Clunes, Warrandyte and Ballarat.

However hopefuls coming to the Victorian goldfields were required to pay high fees for mining licences but were denied the vote and couldn't buy land. By 1854 it came to a head. When the appeal to the government for justice was refused, diggers declared that they would stop buying gold licences and, beneath the diggers' flag – the Southern Cross – they made a stand.

Before dawn on 3 December 1854, government troops stormed the diggers' flimsy stockade at Eureka Lead, Ballarat. In a fiery battle that lasted only 20 minutes more than 30 men died. The diggers' leaders were charged with high treason but were acquitted. Within a year they had won the vote and the hated gold licence was abolished.

Visit Ballarat and discover more about the Eureka Stockade.

## Get the feel for Ned Kelly!

Glenrowan is a small town in the Wangaratta area of Victoria, 184 km (115 miles) north-east of Melbourne on the Hume Highway. In the township, tourists can explore the Kelly siege sites where Bushranger Ned Kelly made his last stand and was eventually captured by the police contingent after a siege and shootout.

Also visit Old Melbourne gaol in Russell Street, Melbourne,

where you walk the road to the gallows. It is Victoria's oldest prison and where 135 people including Ned Kelly were hanged. Learn about the lives and crimes of the men, women and children who were banged up here. You'll be pretty relieved when they open the gate and let you out at the end of your visit.

**More information:**
www.glenrowantouristcentre.com.au
www.nedkellysworld.com.au

## Philip Island

Philip Island – some 80 km (50 miles) from Melbourne – is a popular destination for tourists and Aussies alike; with events as diverse as the Art and Soul Summer Festival and the Fantastic Noodles State Junior Surfing Titles and the Phillip Island Jazz Festival to Pyramid Rock Festival.

As they say, there's something for everyone! So what have I left out? Goodness, the World Superbike Championship and the Australian Motorcycle Grand Prix. This is a truly international event not to be missed by bike fans the world over.

## Australian Ski Resorts

Ski resorts attract thousands of visitors each year and are located in the states of Victoria, New South Wales and Tasmania. Some of the most popular resorts are in the Snowy Mountains in NSW – Thredbo, Charlotte Pass, Perisher Blue and Selwyn Snowfields. And at Hotham, Falls Creek, Mount Buller, Mount Buffalo and Mount Baw Baw in Victoria. Tasmania's resorts are Mount Mawson and Ben Lomond.

**More information:**
www.ski.com.au
www.skicentral.com/australia.html
www.totaltravel.yahoo.com/promotions/ski

# SYDNEY and New South Wales

Think of Australia and you think of Sydney. One of the great cities of this world, Sydney can hold its head high with the best. It is modern, sophisticated and the place to head for if you are taking a trip to Australia if only for the magnificent harbour and the unique opera house. The harbour has a thousand-and-one inlets and coves with splendid homes and places for eating with a vista that is hard to beat. Sydney harbour alone is worth visiting – Captain Cook did!

Sydney has been voted "World's Best City" by readers of US travel magazines Travel & Leisure and Conde Nast Traveler. And the features that swayed judges are not hard to find. It is the epitome of a multicultural city with restaurant and cafe scene enhanced by outstanding local fresh produce and world-class wines. Sydney is home to some of Australia's leading arts organisations such as Opera Australia, Sydney Symphony, Sydney Dance Company and Sydney Theatre Company.

On the other side of the coin, I'm pleased to see that Kings Cross still exists! And how! Kings Cross buzzes with nightclubs, live music and the fleshier side of life. After dark, a never-ending procession of revellers hit Darlinghurst Road, while others head to more upmarket scenes in Potts Point and Woolloomooloo.

And the place with more noughts in its name than a Bank of England overdraft is the "in" place resulting from the redevelopment of the waterfront – particularly on the Finger Wharf – and counting amongst its residents the actor Russell Crowe.

There are five major national parks around Sydney with 8,000 square kilometres of open space... enjoy the great outdoors as the Sydney-siders do. And then there's Bondi beach; even if you are not a surf freak, you'll have to get down there and watch. At least you'll have a tale to tell the next time you are leaning against the bar at your local back home.

## City Climate

Sydney has a temperate climate with warm summers and cool winters and rainfall spread throughout the year. The warmest month is January and the coolest is July. Winter temperatures rarely drop below 5C (41F).

## The Blue Mountains and beyond

The coastal region running from Queensland to Victoria is the home to many beaches, coastal lakes and National Parks. The Great Dividing range hosts the Blue Mountains, the Snowy Mountains, the wineries of the Hunter Valley and the New England Tablelands.

**The Blue Mountains National Park** is part of the Greater Blue Mountains World Heritage Area and protects an unusually diverse range of vegetation communities. There are rare and ancient plants and isolated animal populations tucked away in its deep gorges.

**The Hunter Valley** is another major tourist destination and has a large number of vineyards, restaurants, golf courses and country guesthouses. For horse racing enthusiasts, the Upper Hunter area around Scone is one of the largest horse breeding areas in the world.

**The Snowy Mountains** – as the name might suggest, offers skiing in the winter but also excellent bushwalking in the summer with a wide array of wild flowers to enjoy.

**Byron Bay** – in the far north-east of NSW – is renowned for its great surf breaks, some of the best in the world. Cape Byron is the most easterly point in mainland Australia and the first place to witness the sun rising. It is located near some of the best examples of sub-tropical rainforest on the east coast. This is the St Ives of Australia - with resident artists, festivals and many other events throughout the year. It has a thriving health and wellbeing industry with many day spas and healing/alternative health practitioners. It also has a claim to fame for fabulous cuisine in the award-winning cafes and restaurants as well as a popular wedding destination. Byron Bay is surrounded by picturesque countryside filled with small farms growing local crops which are sold direct at the many farmers' markets.

**More information:**
www.australia.com/nsw
www.visitnsw.com
www.visitbyronbay.com

# BRISBANE and Queensland

I have to admit to never having been to Brisbane so I am relying on friends' experiences and my own research to back up their views. But everyone says what a great place Brisbane is – and my friends are not the only people who wax lyrical; Brisbane is the third most popular destination in Oz for international tourists after Sydney and Melbourne.

What do they head for? It seems it is the South Bank Parklands, Roma Street Parkland and City Botanic Gardens, Brisbane Forest Park and Portside Wharf. Want to see Koalas? Well the Lone Park Sanctuary was the world's first koala sanctuary when opened in 1927.

I am told Brisbane has a growing live music scene, both popular and classical. The Queensland Performing Arts Centre located at South Bank consists of the Lyric Theatre, a concert hall, Cremorne Theatre and the Playhouse Theatre. The Queensland Ballet, Opera Queensland, Queensland Theatre Company and other art groups stage performances in the different venues. Classical music is not forgotten – it is also the venue for the Queensland Symphony Orchestra's regular concerts while Brisbane is said to house the largest community choral scene in Australia. Something to sing about!

## City Climate

Brisbane has a humid subtropical climate with hot, humid summers and dry, mild winters. From November through March, thunderstorms are not uncommon with the more severe accompanied by hail stones, torrential rain and destructive winds. Brisbane also lies in the Tropical Cyclone risk area. Maybe bring your umberella!

## The Gold Coast and The Barrier Reef

Queensland is known as the Holiday State and includes such attractions as Surfers Paradise, Noosa, Cairns, Port Douglas, as well as the many islands within the Great Barrier Reef.

The Great Barrier Reef is actually made up of around 2600 different reefs. It is 2000km (1250 miles) long, starting just south of the Tropic of Capricorn. The reef is called the 'Barrier' Reef because it is an outer reef, situated along the Australian continental shelf with the channel between the coastline and the reef reaching a depth of up to 60m.

Make sure you take a tour in either a glass bottom boat or semi-submersible boat to see for yourself the glory of the coral spectacle. Of course, the luckiest tourist is the one who can snorkel or dive – he/she gets a fantastic view on what's below the waves.

## Rainforests - Atherton Tableland – Cape York Peninsula

Explore the northern Rainforests of Daintree and Cape Tribulation National Parks, driving north from Cairns and Port Douglas.

The Great Dividing Range aligns the coast with mountainous views, while inland, beautiful scenery can be found in the Atherton Tableland along with agricultural land – the most productive being the Darling Downs. Further north the wilderness grows deeper. It incorporates a barren outback of desert, empty roads, and small towns. The whole area comes into bloom after the rains.

The Cape York Peninsula is also affected by rain, many of its dry riverbeds flood and after heavy rain the roads can be impassable, so check road conditions before starting your journey. It has two seasons, the Dry Season and the Wet Season. The Dry Season is between May and November. The Wet Season is between November and April. Although thunderstorms and monsoons are common during the wet season, the period between December and April is also known as the "Green" Season. You will need to get permits to camp in certain areas around the Cape York Peninsula as they are Aborigine reserves.

**More information:**
www.qld.gov.au
www.australianexplorer.com
www.capeyorkinfo.org
www.bom.gove.au (Bureau of Meteorology)

## DARWIN and Northern Territory

Darwin is Australia's only tropical capital city and lies on a magnificent harbour. It is a very modern city, having been almost completely rebuilt after Cyclone Tracy all but wiped it from the map on Christmas Eve in 1974.

It is the hub of the Northern Territory's fishing charter industry and enthusiasts come from all over the world to catch barramundi – some over a meter in length.

Some visitors to Australia start their holidays in Darwin. The international airport is on many major routes so it is easy to access, as is the rest of the Northern Territory which is at your fingertips with air services and charters to even the most remote areas. Darwin is also the gateway to Kakadu National Park, Nitmiluk National Park (Katherine Gorge) and Arnhem Land.

**City Climate**
Darwin's warm tropical climate and moderating sea breezes mean that an outdoor lifestyle can be enjoyed all year round. But watch out for thunder storms, there are on average 90 days of tropical storms a year!

## Arnhem Land – Aboriginal Homeland

Arnhem Land to the east of Darwin is what is called the "Top End" of Northern Territory. It is the Aboriginal homeland where the

Dreamtime lives in song and dance. Arnhem Land is sacred to the Aborigines and there are areas where you will need permission to enter.

You can visit the north western and north eastern corners of Cobourg Peninsula and Gove, and Oenpelli near Kakadu's East Alligator River. The area also has some magnificent rock art, which is a big attraction, along with its natural beauty. Mining is a large part of the Eastern Arnhem Land and you can visit the bauxite mine at Nhulunbuy with a free tour each Friday.

**More information:**
www.australianexplorer.com/arnhem_land.htm
www.goaustralia.about.com
www.Ealta.org

## Alice Springs

Alice Springs (or The Alice) received its name in 1933, although it was developed in 1871 as a telegraph repeater station between Adelaide and Darwin. The town's expansion was slow and the old road to Adelaide wasn't replaced until 1987. Although the town is fairly modern and a moderate size, it is set amongst the harsh outback, although ideally situated next to some of Australia's great wonders.

From the top of Anzac Hill there are great views overlooking Alice Springs and the Eastern MacDonnell Ranges and Western MacDonnell Ranges. To Aboriginal people the hill is Untyeyetweleye and the home to the Corkwood Dreaming Story.

Within the town there is the opportunity to visit the Radio Communication Centre of the Royal Flying Doctor Service and gain an insight into the history and day to day operations of this wonderful service.

The RFDS began as the dream of the Rev. John Flynn, a minister with the Presbyterian Church. He witnessed the daily struggle of pioneers living in remote areas where just two doctors provided the only medical care for an area of almost 2 million square kilometers. Call the doctor in an emergency and in those days he'd roll up two days later on a horse! Flynn's vision was to provide a mantle of safety for these people and on 15 May 1928, his dream became a reality with the opening of the Australian Inland Mission Aerial Medical Service (later renamed the Royal Flying Doctor Service) in Cloncurry, Queensland.

Today, they own a fleet of more than 50 fully instrumented aircraft with the very latest in navigation technology and operate out of 21 bases across Australia and annually fly the equivalent of 25 round trips to the moon. The doctors and flight nurses are responsible for the care of nearly 270,000 patients! They've come a long way from that first flight in 1928 which saw the Flying Doctor airborne for the first time.

## Uluru / Ayres Rock and Kata Tjuta

Uluru, or Ayres Rock, is one of Australia's most recognisable natural icons. The world-renowned sandstone formation stands 348 m (1,142 ft) high with most of its bulk below the ground. It measures 9.4 km (5.8 miles) in circumference.

It lies 335 km (208 miles) south-west of the nearest large town, Alice Springs; Kata Tjuta and Uluru are the two major features of the Uluru-Kata Tjuta National Park. Uluru is sacred to the Pitjantjatjara and Yankunytjatjara Aboriginal people of the area. It has many springs, waterholes, rock caves and ancient paintings.

Uluru is notable for appearing to change colour as the light strikes it at different times of the day and year, with sunset a particularly remarkable sight when it briefly glows red. Although rainfall is uncommon in this semi-arid area, during wet periods the rock acquires a silvery-grey colour with streaks of black algae forming on the areas that serve as channels for water flow.

There is Kata Tjuta, also called Mount Olga or The Olgas, a rock formation about 25 km (16 mi) west of Uluru. Special viewing areas with road access and parking have been constructed to give tourists the best views of both sites at dawn and dusk.

**Useful contacts:**
www.nttravel.com.au/darwin.html
www.environment.gov.au/parks/uluru
www.outback-australia-travel-secrets.com/ayres-rock-australia.
html
www.nt.gov.au

# CANBERRA and ACT - Australian Capital Territory

Learn about Australia's culture, history and way of life in the nation's capital. Explore political past and modern democracy at Old Parliament House and Parliament House. Find out more about Aussie sporting heroes at the National Institute of Sport and Science and see lightning being made at Questacon – the National Science & Technology Centre. This planned city – one of the few in the world – is famous for its lake, parklands and native bushland surround. I am told that beneath the foliage Canberra offers stylish restaurants, hip bars, boutique shopping and a non-stop calendar of festivals and events.

## City Climate

Canberra has a relatively dry Continental climate with warm to hot summers and cool to cold winters with fog on occasions and frosts too. The area rarely gets snowfall through the winter but the surrounding mountains are often snow-capped.

# PERTH and Western Australia

I've not been to Perth nor anywhere in Western Australia – more fool me! And I aim to rectify the fact next time I'm Down Under. As the Aussies say, "You've missed out, mate". And I have! Just take a look at what is promised on the official website:
   *"Get active and enjoy the sunshine, natural parklands and beach lifestyle of Perth, one of the country's most beautiful cities and the*

*capital of Western Australia. The weather is fantastic, the beaches are clean and uncrowded, and the city, situated on the banks of the Swan River, is in a postcard-perfect setting. Explore the bushland, landscaped gardens, lakes and lookouts of huge Kings Park overlooking the city. Take a kayak to Rottnest Island's secluded beaches and bays. Feast on seafood and soak up the carnival atmosphere in historic Fremantle. Swim, surf, fish, windsurf and sail at Cottesloe or Scarborough beach, then skip between the boardwalks, beaches and marinas of the Sunset Coast."*

But that's only the half the story. Like so much of Australia, Western Australia is vast and offers huge diversity for the traveller.

## City Climate

Perth has a Mediterranean climate and receives moderate though highly seasonal rainfall. Summers are generally hot and dry lasting from December to late March with February generally being the hottest month of the year. Winters are relatively cool and wet with rainfall between May and September. The rainfall pattern has changed in Perth and south-west Western Australia since the mid-1970s. There has been a significant reduction in winter rainfall and a greater number of extreme rainfall events in the summer months.

## Western Australia's South West

Australia's south-west was chosen by Lonely Planet as one of the world's Top 10 Regions for 2010. Discover towering forests to whale watching, fine food and wine to world-class surfing. Australia's south-west offers some of the most varied travel experiences in Western Australia.

Margaret River and its surrounds are a popular destination for world-class wineries, top surfing and fun family holidays. Locals head here in winter too, responding to the lure of cosy log-fires, brisk walks along the beach, horse riding through the bush, and mountains of delicious local produce.

## Kimberleys from Broome to Kununurra

The Kimberley region in Western Australia's north extends from Broome in the west to Kununurra and Lake Argyle in the east. It covers around 421,000 sq km and is bordered by the Indian Ocean in the west, the Timor Sea in the north, the Great Sandy Desert in the south and Northern Territory in the east. It is vast, rugged and largely unexplored – you'll not want to tackle it alone but there are numerous accompanied tours using four-wheel-drive vehicles and guides with vast experience.

Broome is situated on a peninsula with the tidal mangrove waters of Roebuck Bay one side and the Indian Ocean and the spectacular Cable Beach on the other. Cable Beach is home to one of Australia's most famous nudist beaches. But if you aren't interested in nude bodies, perhaps you'd prefer to see dinosaur footprints! At Gantheaume Point and 30 meters out to sea are massive footprints from the Cretaceous Age 130 million years ago. Take a look and marvel – they are exposed at low tide.

The town has an interesting history based around the exploits of the men and women who developed the pearling industry, starting with the harvesting of oysters for mother of pearl in the 1880s to the current major cultured pearl farming enterprises. The riches from the pearl beds did not come cheap, and the town's cemetery is the resting place for 919 Japanese divers who lost their lives working in the industry in earlier days.

The West Australian mining boom of the 1960s, as well as the growth of the tourism industry, helped Broome develop and diversify so that Broome is one of the fastest growing towns in Australia.

Lord Alistair McAlpine, a member of the British aristocracy, is largely responsible for the Broome of today. Lord Mac fell in love with Australia, and invested very heavily in Broome during the 1980s. He developed a great deal of the town, building Cable Beach Club in the fashion of the historic Broome buildings of yesteryear, thus ensuring the continuation of the influence of the many cultures of Broome.

**Roebuck Bay:** Between March and October you can catch the romantic magic of "Staircase to the Moon" - a silvery illusion created when a receding tide and the reflection of a rising moon combine to create a stunning natural phenomenon.

Broome has a tropical climate with two seasons. The dry season is from May through November with nearly every day clear and temperature is a balmy 30C. The wet season extends from December through March with maximum temperatures around 35C and high humidity. Tropical cyclones and thunderstorms play a large part in the erratic nature of the rainfall and heavy rains can close many of the roads.

**More information:**
http://www.westernaustralia.com
www.kimberleyaustralia.com

## THE OUTBACK

For me, the Outback is the real Australia. Cities are cities the world over and even given the fact that the Australian conurbations are fresh, modern and fantastic, there is just so much shopping you can embark on, so many restaurants you can sample and so many museums you can wander around . The Outback is DIFFERENT! The distances, the vastness, the jaw-dropping scenery and the friendliness of the people – when you find them!

The simplest way of exploring the Outback is in a comfy seat in a luxury coach. Try Greyhound. Take, for example, the Ayres Rock Tour. You can spend time marvelling at Uluru (Ayres Rock), take a guided walk to the sandstone domes of the Lost City and the Valley of the Winds at Kata Tjuta. Greyhound says you'll enjoy Bush tucker and the option of a camel ride. My Pommie mate, Nick Nicola would enjoy listening and learning about the spiritual tales of Dreamtime – in fact he'd probably be telling them!
More about the Outback later.

# HOBART, LAUNCESTON and Tasmania

**Hobart** is Australia's smallest and most historic capital and is in close proximity to beautiful natural surrounds. The city was settled in 1804 by Lieutenant Governor Collins and grew rapidly as the clearing house for British and Irish convicts. Its place on the Derwent River became the perfect protected deepwater harbour, and now every December and January it welcomes weary but exultant contenders from the Rolex Sydney to Hobart Yacht Race.

Like so many Australian cities, Hobart and Launceston are "big" in fine food and wine. In Hobart, head down to Salamanca Place to find 19th-century waterfront warehouses dating back to the 1830s whaling days. Today, they house cafes, restaurants, galleries and art studios; it's the ideal place to wander or enjoy alfresco dining.

**Launceston** is Tasmania's second largest city and has redefined itself as a cultural hub with vibrant cafes, museums and open parkland. It is a small compact city and as such is easy to explore. Walk the elegant streetscapes and through century-old parks, situated beside revitalised areas such as Launceston Seaport and its waterfront eateries. Take the boardwalk link to the Seaport to Inveresk and visit one of Australia's best regional galleries, the Queen Victoria Museum.

The cooler climate that Tasmania enjoys encourages wine growing and Tamar Valley should be on every visitor's list; so too the Cataract Gorge - a striking urban reserve.

## City Climate

Hobart has a mild temperate climate and during the summer it has the most hours of sunlight of any city in Australia with up to 15.2 hrs on the Summer solstice. In winter Hobart rarely receives snow but the adjacent Mount Wellington is often seen with a snowcap.

Launceston has a cool, temperate climate with four distinct seasons. Being located in the Tamar Valley it is surrounded by many large hills and mountains. This means weather patterns can change considerably in a short period of time.  Winter is also the

354

season with the least amount of wind and winters are renowned for foggy mornings.

## More information:
www.tas.gov.au
Phone:  03 6230 8235 (Within Australia)  +61 3 6230 8235 (International) ·
Email reception@tourismtasmania.com.au

---

**For UK residents, Australia House could be your first point of contact before planning your trip to Australia.**

www.uk.embassy.gov.au
Australia House
The Strand
London. WC2B 4LA

---

# GETTING ABOUT

It goes without saying that Australia is a huge country, comparable to the United States of America. Therefore, distances are great and travel must be planned well in advance if you aren't to miss half the country even in a stay longer than four to six weeks. In fact, to do justice to the many fine cities and the countryside within driving distance of those cities could easily take up all of that time and you have still not seen a fraction of the uniqueness that Australia has to offer – the Great Interior.

If you are a tourist from the Northern Hemisphere your natural inclination will be to hire a car or, perhaps, be that bit more adventurous and take advantage of the freedom that a camper van has to offer. Hotels are not dotted about the Outback as they are in Europe, but there is space aplenty to pull up, make a meal and take to your bed; as long as you follow the advice given by authorities and your hire company, this is the way to get the feel of the real Australia. See below for more details.

There is a road around the periphery of Australia – well, as close to the edge as the terrain allows. But unless you are in the country for months, you are not going to do this. But a car combined with the plane or train (or both) is a great idea. For example, take the Great Ocean Road out of Melbourne to Adelaide and you will capture two fine cities while also taking in some outstanding scenery on the way. You might then take The Ghan train north from Adelaide to Alice Springs (or go right through to Darwin). Or train-it all the way to Perth and fly back to Sydney.

I have mentioned Greyhound coaches. Greyhound does not simply go from point A to point B (it does that as well) but it offers a whole host of adventure holidays all over Australia. Accommodation, tour guide, itinerary... AND that comfy seat in air conditioned luxury! In short, the coach operator could be a vital cog in your plans to see as much of Australia as possible in a relatively short stay Down Under. Greyhound Australia travels to over 1100 destinations in Australia daily, has over 100 years' experience, carries 1.3 million passengers and covers over 20 million miles a year.

**Want to learn more? Go to:**
www.greyhound.com.au
Phone: 1300 473 946 (Within Australia)
Postal address:
PO Box 1475
Eagle Farm QLD 4009

---

## CAMPERVAN HIRE:

The next step up is hiring a campervan. The advantages are obvious – set your own agenda, stay a while or move on. And I should know as I was a manufacturer in the UK for nearly 30 years.

There is nothing like finding a campsite in the middle of nowhere, raising the roof, preparing your own tucker and then lowering the bed and nodding off to sleep with the Great Unknown out there. A little bit timid about that? Well, find a campsite where there are a few other friendly souls, a nearby pub and beer and laughter aplenty.

There are dozens of hire companies in Oz, but I suggest you make contact with the largest, Britz Campervan Hire with 11 locations dotted around Australia including Adelaide, Alice Springs, Brisbane, Darwin, Hobart, Melbourne, Perth and Sydney.

**More information:**
www.britz.com.au
Phone: 020 7569 3075 – UK Office

---

## SELF DRIVE CAR HIRE:

If the thought of camping in the Great Outdoors (especially when your only companion is a kangaroo) then you might consider self-drive car hire. Numerous International car hire companies operate in Australia and all have offices at the major airports. To name just three – Avis, Europcar and Hertz.

## TOUR PACKAGES

There are, of course, a number of agents both in the UK and in Australia who offer assistance in not only seeing Australia (and New Zealand, of course) but will also help you with travel, accommodation and a variety of packages to save you doing the "leg" work. I don't doubt they are all good but Freedom Australia is one recommended by friends:
www.freedomaustralia.co.uk
Phone: 01992 514913  - UK Office

One of the services the company offers is the self-drive tour with an itinerary and pre-booked accommodation so that much of the hassle is taken out of the planning and the travel itself. You can combine tours or add extra days in your favourite places. One particular package that may appeal is what they call the Pioneer Trail – Sydney to Adelaide.

Their information says: "Discover the real Australia as you follow the footsteps of the early settlers on an Outback adventure through New South Wales to South Australia."

Days one and two. Head west from Sydney for your first night in the spectacular Blue Mountains. Visit the Three Sisters and walk or take the cable car into the forest clad valleys of this World Heritage area. Spend your first night at the Comfort Inn Grosvenor MacQuarie. The mountains give way to large cattle and sheep stations as you journey on to the old pioneer town of Dubbo. Here you spend your second night at the Comfort Inn Blue Lagoon.

And so it goes on – days three to five - Cobar to Broken Hill, taking in the mining town of Cobar then across the Darling River and staying at Broken Hill where you are able to tour the old mines.

Days six to seven, cross the South Australian border to the Murray River town of Renmark then south to the fertile irrigated country and its citrus orchards, followed by Barossa Valley, then onto Adelaide.

The company offers similar self-drive tours around Alice Springs including Ayres Rock, Kings Canyon, the deepest canyon in the Centre. Again accommodation is booked in advance and there is an itinerary with two or four-wheel-drive vehicle provided. They call this tour the Red Centre Adventure.

**Another recommendation and another company, this time an Australian one – Australis Inbound Tours & Travel.**

This company says: *"Explore Australia's wonders with this extensive selection of adventure tours, camping safaris, accommodated tours, outback 4WD Safaris, day tours, cruises, rail journeys, and air safaries."*

In South Australia alone, Australis offers 14 days in and around Adelaide; Barossa Valley two trips; Kangaroo Island, seven; Cooper Pedy (opal mining) two days and Eyre Peninsula, six days.

**More information:**
www.travelaust.com.au

---

# Bring out the adventurer in you!

If you really want to get a taste of what it was like to be a pioneer or become a stockman for a day or two, here's a couple of ideas for the adventurous traveller Down Under.

Why not help in droving a herd of cattle in the Outback? It is a real adventure, and for me beats lying by a pool all day. And the clever South Australian Government will help get you climb in the saddle. Called The Great Australian Outback Cattle Drive, you'll be among drovers herding cattle along the legendary Oodnadatta Track.

This is what the preamble says:

*"The beginning of a historic journey, a unique journey – your journey. Get ready to sit back and be part of a historic adventure, moving a real herd through real Outback wilderness.*

*On your first afternoon, you'll be a part of the handover and counting of the cattle, the official start of the cattle drive. The next morning it's down to business. The scenery is spectacular with sandy dunes and wide flat corridors covered with native plants such as hopbush and horse mulga. You will follow the remains of the original Ghan railway track as well as what is left of the Overland Telegraph Line critical in the settling of Australia's interior. Hear stories of the settlers, their successes and failures, along with historical accounts by descendents of original inhabitants, the indigenous people.*

*Your village of superior tented accommodation is Anna Creek, 26 kilometres from William Creek."*

**More information:**
South Australian Visitor and Travel Centre
Ground Floor, 18 King William Street
Adelaide, South Australia 5000
Phone: 1300 655 401 (Within Australia) or +61 8 8303 2220 (International)
Email: informationandbookings@southaustralia.com

---

**If you are still with me...** *the National Geographic Adventure Magazine rated walking with camels across the Simpson Desert as* **"... one of the 25 Greatest Adventures In the World".**

The Outback Camel Company says: *"We have been exploring the vast deserts of inland Australia since 1976 after successfully completing Australia's first commercial camel expedition - across* the Simpson Desert. Using our string of pack-camels to carry all the supplies and equipment, we honour the tradition of the pioneering 'Afghan' cameleers who played such a crucial role in the exploration, development and sustenance of inland Australia.

Our camels represent the last living link to the golden days of exploration by camel in Australia, as we are the only camel tour operator in the country that actively and continually explores all of the continents' great deserts without restricting ourselves to one area, and we present a range of treks & expeditions travelling through some of Central Australia's most remote areas.

All our desert journeys are walking treks – they are not camel riding safaris. Duties include shepherding the camels in the mornings & evenings whilst they feed and, under the supervision of the cameleers, helping to saddle the camels and load the equipment. Your Outback Camel Company cameleers cook all the meals on the campfire but help from aspiring chefs is always welcome!"

## More information:

PO Box 132
Fortitude Valley. Qld. 4006
Phone: 1 300 669 780 (Within Australia)  + 61 7 3850 7600
(International)
E-mail: peter@backtrack.com.au

# AIR TRAVEL

I found nine domestic airlines listed for Australia.

Aeropelican
Newcastle,
New.South.Wales.
Australia  +61 (02) 49 289 600

Air North
Darwin,
NorthernTerritory.
Australia +61 (08) 89204000

JetStar Airways
Melbourne,
Victoria.
Australia +61 (03) 9092 6401

National Jet
Adelaide,
South.Australia.
Australia  +61 (08) 8154 7000

Rex Regional Express
Sydney,
New.South.Wales.
Australia  +61 (02) 9023 3555

Qantas Airways
Sydney,
New.South.Wales.
Australia  +61 (02) 9691 3636

SkyWest Airlines
Perth,
Western.Australia.
Australia  +61 (08) 9478 9999

Tiger Airways
Australia     Melbourne,
Victoria.
Australia  +61 (03) 9335 3033

Virgin Blue
Brisbane,
Queensland.
Australia  +61 (07) 3295 3000

# TRY A TRAIN

You could do a lot worse than considering the train for at least part of your travel throughout Australia; I am not talking about commuter trains, although of course the suburbs of most Oz cities are served by efficient trains and some are also served by trams. No, I am talking about inter-state trains that add a real dimension to your enjoyment of this vast country especially if comfort and not speed of travel is high on your priority list.

Take, for example, The Ghan which connects the south of the Continent with the north and taking in Alice Springs plus two of the unique areas of Australia, the Red Centre and the tropical Top End of the Northern Territory. Tickets on The Ghan allow you to stop off, tour around, stay a night or two (in Alice Springs) then resume your journey.

And the train journey? Choose between standards of service, the Gold Kangaroo with day and night sleeper accommodation utilising ensuite single or twin berths and the Standard Kangaroo which offers a sleeper cabin as an option. The Gold service includes dining at no extra cost – Standard travelling passengers have access to the excellent restaurant but pay for their meals.

Whistle Stop Tours in the northern town of Katherine offer you the opportunity to experience the inspiring wonders of Nitmiluk (Katherine Gorge) before your rail journey concludes in tropical Darwin, the relaxed capital city of Australia's Northern Territory.

Departing twice-weekly from Adelaide (Sun & Wed) and twice-weekly from Darwin (Wed & Sat), The Ghan travels through the heart of Australia. The total distance you have covered is 2,876 kilometres or 1846 miles.

**Be even more adventurous** – why not take The Indian Pacific train which connects Australia from side to side, east to west, Pacific to Indian oceans?

This is one of the word's longest – and greatest – rail journeys. The Indian Pacific doesn't go for speed – it cannot possibly compete with air travel nor does it give the flexibility of a car. But think what you miss if you fly, and what effort you expend if you drive.

Like The Ghan, there are two standards for travellers; Red Service provides "Daynighter" seats that recline. Purchase drinks, snacks and light meals from the Diner/Buffet car. Showers and toilets are at the end of each carriage. Gold Service offers a choice of Twin and Single Sleeper cabins and guests have access to a dedicated lounge car with comfortable chairs and complimentary tea and coffee. Full breakfasts, two-course lunches and three course dinners are all included and served in the finely-appointed restaurant car. Twin cabins feature a comfortable lounge that converts to an upper and lower berth with ensuite facilities. Single cabins have a wash basin with showers and toilets at the end of the carriage.

At various places along the route, you'll be offered the chance to purchase sightseeing tours to make the most of your epic journey. You can discover the silver mining legacy of Broken Hill, take in a tour of Adelaide, stretch your legs at the remote outpost of Cook on the Nullarbor Plain, or view the amazing "Superpit" in Western Australia's mining capital of Kalgoorlie.

Departing twice-weekly westbound from Sydney (Sat & Wed) or Adelaide (Thu & Sun), and twice-weekly eastbound from Perth (Wed & Sun), this epic train takes a leisurely three nights to cross an entire continent.

## Other notable Australian trains:

- Travelling along Queensland's stunning coast, the Sunlander makes the 1660 km (1031 mile) journey from Brisbane to Cairns in 32 hours, three times a week.
- The Overland journeys between Adelaide and Melbourne during daylight hours, operating both ways three times aweek.
- The Southern Spirit is the latest addition and offers a sensational new way to see the golden triangle of Australia's south east : Adelaide / Melbourne / Brisbane

- Introduced in 1982, the XPT is short for 'Express Passenger Train' and travels the route between the big east coast cities of Melbourne, Sydney and Brisbane.

**More information:**
www.railaustralia.com.au

---

**Please note:** In this last chapter of my book I have not tried to provide a definitive coverage of the vast country nor have I looked into each and every way of exploring every single part, where you stay, what you do. Your own research will find things I haven't... subjects I have not detailed or, perhaps, even mentioned. I have merely tried to provide a "taster" for the places in Australia I got to know and love... plus other areas known to my friends.

The information is as accurate as I can make it at the time of printing (November 2010) but you would be highly recommended to check - I am not infallible!

It is over to you now! If you have a computer then research is so much easier in all manner of ways. If not, get in touch with Australia House. I'm sure they will help... and, of course, your local travel agent.

One final point – don't forget New Zealand! While in the Southern Hemisphere, why not nip over to see the twin islands that make up New Zealand? More like England in climate and – in parts – in the countryside and the towns. And there is some fantastic scenery too and being a much smaller country than its bigger neighbour, you really can cover a lot of ground in a relatively short time. Yes, you owe it to NZ – and to yourself!

May I wish you well when visiting Australia – for me, it never fails to excite on every return visit.

Best of luck!

Richard Holdsworth

# About the Author

**Richard Holdsworth has enjoyed several Lives!**

Hardly an exemplary scholar, Richard scraped through his 11 plus but came top at milking cows and driving tractors for the Squire in Bumblethorpe – the village at the centre of **Six Spoons of Sugar**. At 20, with Agricultural College behind him, Richard worked his passage on a cargo ship taking stud cattle to Australia. In the Outback he worked on Keynton Station, brought out the Supreme Champion bull at the Royal Adelaide show, became a journalist with The Stock and Station Journal, and later joined the Melbourne Herald and Weekly Times where he met Heather, his Australian wife to be.

**What happened next?**
Back in Britain they built their own Volkswagen campervan, explored every nook and cranny around Europe, borrowed £150 from the Midland Bank, and set up a fledgling business building campervans that eventually took top honours and sold worldwide. After selling the business in 1995, Richard went on to design and consult for major UK motorhome manufacturers and he established a leading German manufacturer on the UK market. In between times he preserved one of the last locomotives built in the GWR Swindon works – Western Ranger D1013.

## World War II and Six Spoons of Sugar

Richard wanted to tell the story of the war through the eyes of a little boy snatched from the leafy suburbs of South London to a country village in the depths of Berkshire. Named after his Father's hero, German composer Richard Wagner, he was always going to be treated with suspicion by the village kids and there were more bad days than good. But by the time the 101st Airborne "Screaming Eagles" arrived in the village, life was on the up and Richard made many friends. Now some 60 years on, he has tracked down some of the survivors – the men he once looked up to and asked, "Got any gum, chum?" Harold Heffner from Ohio tells it like this, "I remember your Pa…and I remember you kids… You all made us very welcome."

**Six Spoons of Sugar** was launched in the UK in September 2008, in Melbourne, Australia in January 2009 and at the 101st Airborne Reunion in Indianapolis, USA, in August 2010.

## Australia and In the HOT SEAT

In search of a future as a young man of 20 after the grim aftermath of WWII, Richard grasped the opportunity to take stud cattle to Australia and found himself in the hot seat on the high seas. Things could only get better and they did. His hard work and training brought success for the bulls in his charge – winning Supreme Champion at the Royal Adelaide Show. This lead indirectly to another hot seat – rising to the challenge of agricultural journalist first in Adelaide and then Melbourne. The land of sun, sea and surf – he rose to the occasion while enjoying all the fun that takes a young man's fancy. Richard enjoyed being in the hot seat….

**The Future**
The third phase in Richard's life takes place back in the UK and 1969 finds him embarking on a business venture – manufacturing motor caravans. Working alongside his wife, Heather, he gets to the elite top three in the UK and sells to Germany, Japan and Scandinavia too. It occupied close-on thirty years of highs, highs and the occasional lows.

Does it make a story? Well, it's a great way to re-live the past, says Richard.

So, watch this space!

**Verpackungsaufschriften als Text -** ⌐sche Analyse

Inaugural-Dissertation
zur Erlangung des Doktorgrades
der Philosophischen Fakultät
der Universität Düsseldorf

vorgelegt von
Sonja Steves
aus Leverkusen
1999

**Statt eines Vorwortes – ein Dankwort:**

An dieser Stelle ist es Zeit, „Danke" zu sagen - an alle, die mich bis hierhin begleitet haben.

Mein ganz besonderer Dank gilt meinen Eltern, die es mir immer ermöglicht haben, meinen Weg zu gehen. Danke auch an Jenk ...
Ein ganz dickes Dankeschön an Tina und Dominique für das „lecker Essen" und die vielen aufbauenden Worte.
Vielen Dank an Tine, Doris und Steffi fürs Korrekturlesen und all die wertvollen Kommentare.
Mein herzlicher Dank an Nitsche und Phil für die unglaublich tolle technische Betreuung – ohne Euch könnte heute niemand dieses Buch in den Händen halten.
Mein Dank gilt ebenso Kerstin, der besten Grafikerin weltweit, die dem Buch dieses geniale Cover verpaßt hat.
Danke Normi dafür, daß Du immer an mich geglaubt hast.
Danken möchte ich auch Gatsby für den Ausgleich, den er mir immer wieder verschafft hat.
Natürlich möchte ich mich an dieser Stelle auch bei Herrn Prof. Dr. Rudi Keller bedanken, der mich mit so viel Geduld und Mühe betreut hat.
Die Liste ließe sich unendlich fortsetzen. Um den Rahmen der vorliegenden Arbeit nicht schon hier zu sprengen, einfach ein pauschales Danke an alle, die sonst noch irgendwie beteiligt waren.

Sonja Steves

## Drei Knusperdosen drei Schicksale

Meine Lieblingslektüre sind Lebensmittelverpackungen.
Andere mögen es für richtig halten, sich die Zeit an der
Bushaltestelle mit Reiterromanen und Schilderungen
brenzliger Situationen zu vertreiben. Ich jedoch habe
immer einige Nudeltüten und Frühstückszerealien dabei,
um sie in öffentlichen Verkehrsmitteln zu studieren.
Auch nachts pflege ich Konservenbüchsen u.ä. mit ins
Bett zu nehmen, damit ich vor dem Einschlafen noch etwas schmökern kann. Was stehen da für schöne Dinge
drauf! »Füllhöhe technisch bedingt.« Genau wie bei mir.
»Abtropfgewicht 225g.«Wie hoch wohl mein Abtropfgewicht ist? Ich hoffe aber, der liebe Gott verfällt
nicht so bald auf die Laune, mich abtropfen zu wollen,
denn ich möchte ja noch viele Nahrungsmittelschachteln
lesen."

Max Goldt (1994), S. 69, s. auch letzte Seite

INHALTSVERZEICHNIS

# 1. Einführung in die Thematik

## 1.1 Einleitung

Wir leben in einer Zeit, in der in einem europäischen Land wie Deutschland ein sehr hoher Lebensstandard genossen wird. Die Wirtschaft lebt vom Konsum. Die Bürger konsumieren Waren aus den verschiedensten Bereichen – angefangen bei den Nahrungsmitteln, über Kosmetik und Haushaltswaren, von Kleidung und Schmuck zu Heimwerker-, Hobby- und Sportbedarf bis hin zu hochtechnisierten Geräten wie Hifi-Anlagen, Computer u.v.m. Selbst die Waren zum alltäglichen Leben dienen nicht mehr nur der reinen Lebenserhaltung. Mit ihnen wird schon beim Einkauf in den heute üblichen riesigen Warenhäusern eine Erlebnisqualität mitgeliefert. In Kombination mit der Werbung wird versucht, den Kunden zu Hause vor, bei und nach dem Gebrauch ein einzigartiges Produkterlebnis zu vermitteln.

Das Angebot der sogenannten Standardkonsumartikel des täglichen Lebens ist von den Grunderhaltungsmitteln zu einer ausgesprochen reichhaltigen Palette der verschiedensten Produkte aus allen Lebensbereichen expandiert.

Die Konsumenten haben die Kaufkraft, aber auch die Qual der Wahl. Sie bestimmen durch ihren Kauf den Marktwert eines Produktes.

Den Anbietern obliegt die schwierige Aufgabe, ihr Produkt über die Werbung und die Verpackung dergestalt mit positiven Eigenschaften auszustatten, daß die Kunden einerseits schnell und dennoch ausführlich über das Produkt informiert werden, und daß gleichzeitig die kaufstimulierenden Attribute dem Vergleich mit Konkurrenzprodukten standhalten bzw. besser erscheinen als diese.

Es gilt, die Aufmerksamkeit und das Interesse auf das Produkt zu lenken, um im Anschluß das zu erreichen, was zählt: daß die Kunden das Produkt tatsächlich kaufen.

Die große und immer wiederkehrende Frage, die sich dabei stellt, ist: Wie erreicht man es, ein Produkt aus dem breiten Angebot zu exponieren und erfolgreich zu verkaufen?

In einem ersten Teil wird nach der Vorstellung des Problemhorizontes und der Festlegung der Arbeitsfragen, der Stand der Forschung präsentiert.

Im Anschluß wird die Produktverpackung als Untersuchungsgegenstand eingeführt. Dabei werden verschiedene Perspektiven der Verpackungen erarbeitet – von der Einführung des Begriffes „Produktverpackung" über die allgemeinen Funktionen bis hin zu der Beziehung Verpackung und Verbraucher.

Darauf folgt ein zeichentheoretischer Abschnitt. Es wird ein kleiner Überblick über gängige Zeichenmodelle geboten. Aus diesen Modellen wird ein geeigneter Ansatz zur Analyse von Produktverpackungen ausgewählt und diskutiert.

Unter Berücksichtigung allgemeiner Analysekriterien wird aus dem theoretischen Teil ein Analysemodell entwickelt, das ein einem zweiten Teil einen praktischen Anwendungseinsatz findet. Exemplarisch wird an ausgewählten Beispielen die Praktikabilität des Modells vorgeführt.

Die Produktverpackungen sollen sowohl aus der Sicht der Anbieter im Hinblick auf ihren Marktwert als auch aus der Perspektive der Konsumenten bezüglich ihrer Eignung kritisch betrachtet werden.

Die gesamte theoretische Auseinandersetzung soll durch zahlreiche Beispiele einen ständigen Realitätsbezug waren. Dabei sollen positive Verpackungslösungen als Empfehlung vorgestellt werden. Weniger ideale Beispiele sollen durch einen Optimierungshinweis ergänzt werden.

In einem Schlußkapitel sollen neben einem Resümee und einem Fazit noch die Aspekte Erwähnung finden, die über eine rein wissen-schaftliche Auseinandersetzung mit dem Thema hinaus allgemein gesellschaftliche Gesichtspunkte berücksichtigen.

Es werden für die Darstellung die allgemein gültigen Abkürzungsregeln Einsatz finden. Abkürzungen, die darüber hinaus verwendet werden, werden an Ort und Stelle erläutert.

Der Vereinfachung halber wird im Text normalerweise die übliche männliche Allgemeinform verwendet. Dabei ist die weibliche Form jedoch immer mitgedacht.

## 1.2 Der Problemhorizont

Der Problemhorizont ergibt sich aus den für die Anbieter zur Verfügung stehenden Mitteln, mit denen sie verkaufsfördernd agieren können.

Die Werbung ist das geläufigste Instrument, das genutzt wird, um Waren vor einem möglichst breiten Publikum anzupreisen. Sie umfaßt die gesamte Spannbreite der verkaufsfördernden Maßnahmen.

Besonders viel Aufwand wird im Bereich der Fernseh-, Funk- und Printmedienwerbung betrieben. Diese Medien erreichen ein großes und vielschichtiges Publikum und sind deshalb zur Verbreitung von Werbebotschaften sehr beliebt.

Werbemaßnahmen werden aber auch vor Ort am sogenannten „point of sale" durchgeführt. Neben ausgefallenen Maßnahmen wie Probierständen, Promotern mit Werbegeschenken, auffälligen Hinweistafeln sowie extravaganten Warenständern etc., ist die Produktverpackung in den Läden das Medium, das zum Zwecke der Vermarktung eingesetzt wird.

Ein Merkmal haben alle Maßnahmen gemeinsam, die der Werbung und damit der Verkaufsförderung dienen sollen - es wird versucht, mit den Verbrauchern zu kommunizieren. Kommuniziert wird über die Sprache, jedoch in Deutschland nicht nur über die allgemein gängige deutsche Sprache. In der Werbung werden gerne klangvolle klangvolle Wörter aus anderen Sprachen verwendet (z.B. der katalanische Name „Freixenet"), sowie neue Wortkombinationen (z.B. Skin Illuminating Complex).

Die Sprache wird in den verschiedenen Werbemedien mündlich (Fernseh-, Rundfunk- und Direktwerbung[1]) und schriftlich (Verpakkungen, Zeitungen/Prospekte, Plakate, etc.) eingesetzt.

Da Werbung gerne auch mittels Sprache betrieben wird, bietet sich in diesem Bereich ein spannendes Forschungsfeld für Linguisten.
Damit einher geht jedoch die Schwierigkeit, aus den oft sehr abgehobenen und praxisfernen Theorien einen Ansatz auszuwählen, mit dem sich ein Analyseinstrumentarium und damit ein Anwendungsbezug herstellen läßt.

Sämtliche Werbemedien zum Gegenstand der Untersuchung der vorliegenden Arbeit zu machen, ist eine Utopie, denn entweder würde der Rahmen dieser Arbeit gesprengt oder es müßte auf einer sehr allgemeinen Ebene gearbeitet werden.
Ich habe mich daher entschlossen, die sprachliche Gestaltung der Produktverpackungen von Standardkonsumartikeln zum Untersuchungsgegenstand der vorliegenden Arbeit zu machen. Dieses Kommunikationsmedium ist noch so gut wie gar nicht erforscht. Dabei bieten Produktverpackungen von Standardkonsumartikeln eine Fülle von sprachlichem Material, mit dem wir uns alle tagtäglich bewußt oder unbewußt auseinandersetzen (müssen). Ein Ziel ist es dabei, zu zeigen, daß Verpackungsaufschriften als Sonderform von Text betrachtet werden können. Produktverpackungen sind oft aufwendig genutzte, jedoch von werbesprachlichen und linguistischen

---

1       Der Begriff „Direktwerbung" wird verwendet, wenn die Verbraucher persönlich von einem Vertreter vor dem Laden oder zu Hause angesprochen und über das Produkt im Sinne des Anbieters informiert werden (ein sehr bekanntes Beispiel hierfür sind die „Vorwerk"-Staubsaugervertreter als Direktwerber). Man spricht ebenfalls von „Direktwerbung", wenn Referenten eines Anbieters potentielle Vertreiber besuchen und ihr Produkt anpreisen (insbesondere bei Medikamenten eine gängige Praxis).

Untersuchungen konsequent nicht beachtete Kommunikationsmedien, so daß sie sich hervorragend eignen, die Möglichkeiten eines Anwendungseinsatzes linguistischer Theorien zu überprüfen.

Nach der Fixierung des konkreten Untersuchungsgegenstandes will auch das theoretische Modell sorgfältig ausgewählt sein, das auf seinen Anwendungseinsatz hin überprüft werden soll.
Ich habe mich dazu entschieden, den Untersuchungsgegenstand der sprachlichen Gestaltung von Standardkonsumartikeln aus semiotisch-semantischer Perspektive zu bearbeiten, auch wenn dieser Weg auf den ersten Blick eine ausgefallene Perspektive der Betrachtung verspricht.
Die meisten Untersuchungen, die sich mit Sprache und Werbung beschäftigen, nähern sich diesem Thema über die technischen Besonderheiten wie dem gezielten Einsatz rhetorischer Stilfiguren.
Es bietet sich jedoch an, eine semantisch-semiotische Perspektive einzunehmen, da viele Produktverpackungen reichhaltig mit sprachlichen und anderen Zeichen ausgestattet sind. Ich möchte mich mit dieser Arbeit auf das Abenteuer einlassen, meinen Untersuchungsgegenstand auf diesem augenscheinlich ungewöhnlichen Weg zu erforschen.

Innerhalb der beiden Disziplinen Semiotik und Semantik gibt es ein reichhaltiges Angebot verschiedener Zeichen- und Bedeutungstheorien.
Bei der Auswahl stellt es sich als Schwierigkeit heraus, einen Ansatz isoliert zu betrachten. Viele Modelle haben nur einen kleinen Aspekt ihrer Disziplin zum Thema und bauen aufeinander auf.
Da in der vorliegenden Arbeit ein praktisches Kommunikationsmedium (Verpackungen von Standardkonsumartikeln) Gegenstand semiotisch-semantischer Untersuchungen werden soll, bietet sich ein

13

zeichentheoretisches Modell an, in dem auch der Kommunikationsaspekt berücksichtigt wird.

Aus diesem Grund habe ich die von Keller vorgestellte Gebrauchstheorie ausgewählt. Mit dieser Theorie soll das linguistische Fundament der vorliegenden Arbeit gestaltet werden. Darüber hinaus wird überprüft, ob es möglich ist, aus dieser Theorie einen Anwendungseinsatz abzuleiten.

Keller diskutiert die Basiselemente der Peirceschen Zeichentheorie und entwickelt darüber hinaus einen gebrauchstheoretischen Ansatz, der auch zur praktischen Anwendung geeignet ist.

Nach Keller schließen sich Gebrauchstheorien und andere Theorien nicht unbedingt aus.[2] Diesen Hinweis möchte ich als Anregung verstehen und überprüfen, inwieweit die Gebrauchstheorie von Keller Parallelen zu Erläuterungsansätzen aus anderen Disziplinen erkennen läßt.

---

[2] Keller (1995), S. 102

14

## 1.3 Die Arbeitsfrage und das Ziel der Arbeit

Die **Leitfragen**, die jedem Arbeitsschritt zugrunde gelegt werden, lauten:

- *Lassen sich Aufschriften auf Produktverpackungen von Standardkonsumartikeln des täglichen Lebens als Textsorte klassifizieren?*
- *Ist es möglich, eine Zeichentheorie, die auf einer Gebrauchstheorie basiert, am Beispiel der Zeichen auf Produktverpackungen in der Praxis anzuwenden und nachzuvollziehen?*
- *Läßt sich auf der theoretischen Basis linguistischer Grundlagen ein Analysemodell entwickeln, mittels dessen sich die textuellen Qualitäten von Verpackungsaufschriften sowie die Qualitäten der Verpackungen als Zeichen und der Zeichen auf Verpackungen ermitteln, bewerten und vergleichen lassen?*

**Ziel** der Arbeit ist es, nachzuweisen, daß es durchaus möglich und gewinnbringend ist, linguistische Modelle aus der Disziplin der Zeichentheorie auf einen Untersuchungsgegenstand des Alltags anzuwenden.

Es soll gezeigt werden, daß neben Erläuterungsansätzen aus den stärker empirisch orientierten Wissenschaften wie Psychologie, Soziologie, Kommunikationswissenschaften und dem Marketing

15

(Marktforschung) auch die Linguistik eine erkenntnisreiche Perspektive für den Einsatz im Alltag liefern kann.

Damit verbunden ist der Wunsch, über eine leicht verständliche und gut nachvollziehbare Darstellung all denjenigen Mut zu machen, die sich bislang abgeschreckt von abstrakten und komplexen Theorievorstellungen, noch nicht getraut haben, aus der Perspektive einer linguistischen Theorie, Dinge des Alltags zu betrachten.

**Angestrebt** wird als Fazit der theoretischen Überlegungen die Entwicklung eines Kriterienkataloges, der eine Bewertung von Verpackungen von Standardkonsumartikeln ermöglicht. Idealerweise bietet ein derartiger Kriterienkatalog ein Beurteilungsraster, mittels dessen Verpackungen bewertet und miteinander verglichen werden können. Die Beurteilung und der Vergleich anhand eines Analyseschemas soll nicht nur den gezielten Einsatz von Kritik provozieren, sondern optimalerweise auch eine standardisierte Richtlinie bieten, um Verpackungen zu optimieren.

## 1.4 Der Stand der Forschung

Der Aspekt der sprachlichen Gestaltung der Produktverpackungen von Standardkonsumartikeln des täglichen Lebens ist bisher in der Forschung der verschiedenen Wissenschaften nur auf wenig Interesse gestoßen.

Dies läßt sich mit der Tatsache begründen, daß die Verpackung eines Produktes Teil einer absatzwirtschaftlichen Strategie ist, die zum Verkauf der Ware beitragen soll.

Die Verpackungen werden in der Regel von Ingenieuren und Designern gestaltet. Erstere sind für eine technisch optimal umsetzbare und wenig (kosten)aufwendige Verpackungslösung zuständig, letztere für eine optisch ansprechende Umsetzung. Dementsprechend stammt auch die zur Verfügung stehende Literatur mit dem Thema „Verpackungen" hauptsächlich aus den Kreisen der Techniker, Designer oder Betriebswirtschaftswissenschaftler.[3]

---

[3]    In diesem Zusammenhang sind folgende Werke zu nennen:
a) Literatur zum Thema Verpackungen aus dem Bereich Graphik-Design:
- Braem (1985)
- Buck; Vogt (o.J.)
- Crowel; Weidemann (1968)
- noAH (1992)
- Petersen (o.J.)
- Leitherer, Wichmann (1987)
- Schilder-Bär, Bignens (1994)

b) technisch orientierte Literatur zum Thema Verpackungen:
- Fürst (1973)
- Wachtel (1965)
- Behaegel (1991)

c) betriebswirtschaftlich orientierte Literatur zum Thema Verpackungen:
- Bräuer (1958)
- Männicke (1957)
- Swankin (1967)
- Sander (1972)
- Debrunner (1977)
- Hacker (1987)

17

Tendenziell in die Richtung der Fragestellung, die der vorliegenden Arbeit zugrundeliegt, geht die Abhandlung von Monika Medeyros mit dem Titel "Anmutungshafte Verpackungsgestaltung als Mittel der Produktpolitik".[4] Medeyros legt den Schwerpunkt auf die Marktkommunikation und stellt die Funktion von Verpackungen als Kommunikationsinstrument in den Mittelpunkt. Jedoch bearbeitet Medeyros ihr Thema aus einer psychologischen Perspektive. Hervorgehoben werden psycho-physische Aspekte der Wahrnehmungstheorie. Ihr Ziel ist es, über psychologische Experimente eine Gestaltungs- und Wirkungsanalyse anmutungshafter Verpackungsaspekte durchführen zu können, um prägnante Verpackungscharaktere (sogenannte „Verpackungs-looks") systematisieren zu können.

Der Abschnitt über die "Zeichen als Mittel anmutungshafter Verpackungsgestaltung" ist bei Medeyros sehr knapp gehalten. Durch den Hinweis auf eine Beziehung zwischen Zeichen und Bezeichnetem läßt sich zwar eine Referenz auf de Saussures Theorie zur Struktur des sprachlichen Zeichens herauslesen, jedoch wird dieser Aspekt nicht näher expliziert.

Diskussionswürdig ist meiner Ansicht nach der von Koppelmann übernommene Absatz zur Wortbedeutung in diesem Abschnitt.[5] Demnach ist die *Wortbedeutung* gleich dem *Wortinhalt* und wird geprägt vom "Bedeutungskern als dem Hauptinhalt des Wortes, vom mitschwingenden Gefühlston und von der assoziativ verursachten Umgebungsatmosphäre des Wortes. Gerade die miteinander verwo-

---

[4] Medeyros (1990)

[5] Medeyros (1990), S. 218 übernimmt in diesem Abschnitt eine Erläuterung der Wortbedeutung von Koppelmann (1981) zur Grundlage ihrer weiteren Ausführungen.

18

benen Gefühlstöne und Nebenvorstellungen des Wortes müssen be-
achtet werden."[6]

Auf der Grundlage linguistischer Semantiktheorien läßt sich hier
einlenken. Es wird versucht, die Definition des Begriffes „Bedeutung" im Hinblick auf den emotionalen Aspekt zu präsentieren, um
diesen Akzent der zentralen Fragestellung zu berücksichtigen, der
Medeyros` Arbeit zugrundeliegt.

Die Tatsache, daß bei der Erläuterung eines Begriffes wie „Wortbedeutung" in fachfremden Disziplinen nicht auf  linguistische
Theorien zurückgegriffen wird, und die dadurch entstehenden Defi-
nitionsprobleme sowie die Einseitigkeit der Perspektive, begründen
die Notwendigkeit, sich dem Thema aus linguistischer Sicht anzunehmen. Das aufgeführte Beispiel zeigt, daß semantische Themen
durchaus in anderen Disziplinen und auch für das praktische Arbeiten
von Interesse sind. Es besteht augenscheinlich Nachholbedarf, linguistische Ansätze in der praktischen Anwendung als allgemein nutzbar
zugänglich zu machen. Die vorliegende Arbeit soll dazu beitragen,
diesen Nachholbedarf auszuräumen.

Medeyros beläßt es bei dieser Äußerung zum Thema Zeichen.


Ebenfalls zu betrachten ist eine Arbeit von Horst G. Kaltenbach mit
dem Titel: "Die Rolle von Produkt und Verpackung in der
Marktkommunikation"[7] aus dem Bereich Marketing. Kaltenbach legt
seiner Darstellung das allgemeine Prozeßmodell der Kommunikation
zugrunde, auf dem er seine beschreibende Funktionserläuterung der
Kommunikation zwischen Anbieter und Verbraucher über das Produkt und die Verpackung aufbaut. Meiner Ansicht nach ist es ein
Mangel dieser Abhandlung, daß Kaltenbach nicht erläutert, aus wel-

---

[6]
      Medeyros (1990), S. 216-240
[7]
      Kaltenbach (1975)

chen Grund er sich für das allgemeine Prozeßmodell der Kommunikation entscheidet. Nach diesem Modell werden Aussagen und Nachrichten von einem Kommunikator verschlüsselt, über ein Medium an einen Rezipienten gesendet, der die Nachricht wieder entschlüsselt.[8] Problematisch erweist sich an diesem Modell, daß die Kommunikation lediglich oberflächlich betrachtet wird. Die Rolle der Zeichen auf Verpackungen wird dabei als Träger einer Aussage definiert, die eine codierte Nachricht transportieren. Damit wird eine viel diskutierte linguistische Position aufgegriffen, die in der Anwendung zu Problemen führen kann, da empirisch  nicht belegt werden kann, daß Zeichen tatsächlich verschlüsselte Nachrichten transportieren, die vom Empfänger der Nachricht entschlüsselt werden müssen.

Kaltenbach macht nicht darauf aufmerksam, daß er mit diesem Modell ein generelles Transportproblem von Kommunikationsinhalten anspricht, denn er verfolgt in seiner Darstellung zunächst die Produktausstattung, deren funktionalen Einsatz in der Marktkommunikation, um dann mögliche Wirkungsvariablen zu systematisieren und schließlich Maßnahmen zur Realisierung der Kommunikation von Produkt und Konsument vorzuschlagen, z.B. in Form von speziellen Aspekten der Produktausstattung.

Der Einsatz von Zeichen auf Verpackungen wird dabei nicht weiter berücksichtigt.

Insgesamt zeigt auch diese Arbeit die Notwendigkeit, gängige Theorien zur Erläuterung der Funktion von Zeichen mit ihren Vor- und Nachteilen gegeneinander abzugrenzen und einen Ansatz auszuwählen, der zur Erläuterung des Phänomens geeignet ist, daß Zeichen auf Produktverpackungen Kommunikation mit Konsumenten ermöglichen, und daß durch Zeichen auf Produktverpackungen Kommunikation mit den Konsumenten erreicht werden kann.

---

[8] vgl. Kaltenbach (1975), S. 21

Winfried Nöth hat es sich mit seinem Arbeitsheft "Semiotik. Eine Einführung mit Beispielen für Reklameanalysen"[9] zum Ziel gemacht, eine umfassende Einführung in die verschiedenen Richtungen der Semiotik zu geben. Er bezieht allerdings nicht eindeutig Position, d. h. er versucht nicht, einen konkreten Anwendungsbezug zwischen Semiotik und Reklame herzustellen. Statt dessen erläutert er linguistische Theorien mit Beispielen aus der Reklame dort, wo es sich anbietet, ohne jedoch die Anwendung zu problematisieren.

Nöths Beispiele zum ikonischen, indexalischen (wie er es nennt) und symbolischen Zeichengebrauch in der Reklame sind nicht mehr auf dem aktuellsten Stand. Daher werden in den Kapiteln zur Erläuterung der Grundverfahren der Interpretation nach einer gebrauchsorientierten Zeichentheorie nur dann Bezüge zu dieser Arbeit hergestellt, wenn sich ein geeigneter Zusammenhang ergibt.

Das Wort "Reklame" im Titel Nöths Arbeitsheftes wirkt ungewöhnlich und wird heute zuweilen als altmodisch oder gar abwertend interpretiert. Das Wort "Werbung" scheint geläufiger. Nöth erläutert in seinem Werk nicht, aus welchem Grund er sich für den gewählten Terminus entschieden hat.

Mir jedoch gibt die Verwendung des Wortes "Reklame" Anlaß, eine Unterscheidung der Terminologien "Reklame", "Werbung" und "Public Relations"(PR) für diese Arbeit festzulegen. Der Unterschied dieser drei Begriffe läßt sich mit folgender Situation gut beschreiben: Wenn ein junger Mann ein Mädchen kennenlernt und ihr sagt, was für ein toller Kerl er ist, so ist das Reklame. Wenn er ihr sagt, wie reizend sie aussieht, so ist das Werbung. Wenn sich aber das Mäd-

---

[9]    Nöth (1975)

21

chen für ihn entscheidet, weil sie von anderen gehört hat, was für ein toller Kerl er ist, dann ist das PR.

Demnach zielt Reklame auf Selbstdarstellung, was oft etwas plump oder aufdringlich erscheint. Werbung intendiert ein Mehrwertgefühl der Rezipienten und PR drängt auf eine größtmögliche Verbreitung einer positiven Einstellung zum PR-Objekt.

Idealerweise werden bei der öffentlichkeitswirksamen Vermarktung eines Produktes alle drei Aspekte der zielgerichteten Kommunikation und über ein Produkt eingesetzt. In diesem Fall wird das Wort Werbung gerne auch als Oberbegriff für alle Maßnahmen der werblichen Kommunikation eingesetzt.

Koppelmann versucht in seinen "Grundlagen der Verpackungsgestaltung"[10] die Zeichen auf Produktverpackungen mittels eines linguistischen Ansatzes zu erläutern. In Anlehnung an de Saussure beschreibt Koppelmann, daß sich die Trennung von Wortform und Wortinhalt als zweckmäßig erwiesen hat. Darüber hinaus unterscheidet er zwischen Bedeutung und Benennung. Er führt diesen Ansatz jedoch nicht weiter aus, sondern beläßt es bei der Übernahme der Terminologie, um diese auf die Verpackungzeichen zu übertragen und zu unterscheiden zwischen dem, worüber man informieren will, und dem, wie man das Mitzuteilende zu gestalten denkt.[11]
Die Äußerung Koppelmanns zeigt ebenfalls, wie notwendig es ist, zeichentheoretische Ansätze in dem Problemfeld der Produktverpackungen nutzbar zu machen. Seiner Ansicht nach „hat sich eine Trennung von Benennung und Bedeutung, von Wortform und Wor-

---

[10] Koppelmann (1971)

[11] vgl. Koppelmann (1971), S. 115

22

tinhalt [...], von Sinn und Sinnträger als zweckmäßig erwiesen"[12].
Diese Aussage sollte meiner Auffassung nach etwas ausführlicher
diskutiert werden.

Ich werde mich im folgenden bemühen, die Diskussion um den Einsatz der von Koppelmann verwendeten Terminologien nachzuholen
und zu ergänzen.

Desweiteren umfaßt für Koppelmann der Begriff „Zeicheninhalt" den
gesamten Informationsgehalt der verschiedenen Verpackungszei-
chen.[13] Diese Übertragung ist meiner Ansicht nach vereinfacht.
Selbst im Sinne de Saussures läßt sich der "Zeicheninhalt" (signifié)
nicht einfach als Zeichenbedeutung und schon gar nicht als Sammel-
begriff für mehrere verschiedene Zeicheninhalte bzw. -
informationsgehalte verstehen. Dieser Punkt wird im Zusammenhang
mit den Überlegungen zu den Anwendungsmöglichkeiten einer geeigneten Zeichentheorie weiter erörtert.

Koppelmann unterscheidet zwei Sorten von Zeichen, die zur Gruppe
der warendarstellenden Zeicheninhalte gehören und Informationen
verschiedener Art über die Ware verbreiten sollen: die namenmäßi-
gen und die beschreibenden Zeicheninhalte.[14]
Diese Einschätzung ist semiotisch differenzierter zu betrachten, denn
die Klassifizierung "beschreiben" und "benennen" ist nur ein Teil der
vielen Zeichentheorien, wie z.B. der Gebrauchstheorie. Um die Phänomene der wirkungsintendierten Einsatzmöglichkeit von
sprachlichen Zeichen auf Produktverpackungen adäquat erläutern zu
können, ist eine umfassendere Betrachtung der Klassifikationsvaria-
tionen von sprachlichen Zeichen auf Produktverpackungen zu

---

[12]
    Koppelmann (1971), S. 115
[13]
    vgl. Koppelmann (1971), S. 115
[14]
    vgl. Koppelmann (1971), S. 115

empfehlen. Auch hier zeigt sich meiner Ansicht nach erneut der Bedarf, das Thema der Zeichen auf Produktverpackungen aus der Perspektive der Linguistik zu bearbeiten und eine vertretbare Systematisierung der Zeichen auf Verpackungen vorzunehmen. Die Linguistik bietet die Möglichkeit, sprachliche Wirkungseffekte sehr viel differenzierter zu analysieren und darauf aufbauend mit Hilfe systematischer Erläuterungsmodelle aktiv zu gestalten. Dementsprechend werde ich die Diskussion über die hier vorgelegten Terminologien in den Abschnitt meiner Arbeit verlegen, in dem eine Auseinandersetzung mit Kategorien bzw. Typen von Zeichen stattfindet.

Diskussionswürdig ist meiner Ansicht nach ebenfalls Koppelmanns Benennung von informationserleichternden Zeichen auf Verpackungen als sogenannte „Supplementzeichen". Ihm erscheint es aufgrund ihres Informationsgehaltes möglich, "die informationserleichternden Supplementzeichen in ‚bedeutungslose' und ‚bedeutungshaltige' Zeichen zu gliedern. Beide Arten treten zu den schon vorhandenen Zeichen hinzu, allein haben sie keinen Sinn."[15] Zur ersten Gruppe gehören seiner Auffassung nach Striche, Linienzüge, Balken, Farbpunkte etc., soweit sie keine Vertretungsfunktion aufweisen. Diese seien nur durch ihren hinweisenden Charakter gekennzeichnet und sollen die willkürliche Aufmerksamkeit richten, die unwillkürliche fesseln. Bedeutungshaltige Supplementzeichen beschreibt er als solche, die neben der Hinweisfunktion auch in gewissem Maße Vertretungsfunktion ausüben. Allerdings seien diese Zeichen nur dann verständlich, wenn man die eigentliche Information kennt (wie z.B. bei Ausrufungs- und Fragezeichen, Farbbalken etc.).[16]

---

[15] Koppelmann (1971), S. 111f

[16] vgl. Koppelmann (1971), S. 112

Koppelmann enthält den Lesern bei diesen Ausführungen seine Definition bzw. seine individuelle Gebrauchsregel des in der Semantik viel diskutierten Begriffes „Bedeutung" vor. Meiner Ansicht nach gilt es, die Verwendung des Begriffes „Bedeutung" zu klären, bevor man Zeichen als "bedeutungslos" und "bedeutungshaltig" klassifiziert. Geht man z.b. davon aus, daß die Bedeutung eines Wortes sich nach der Wittgensteinschen Auffassung über seine Gebrauchsregel in der Sprache manifestieren läßt (vgl. Kap. 6.3), und daß der Sinn die Intention des Zeichenverwenders erkennen läßt, dann erweist sich Koppelmanns Einteilung insofern als problematisch, als jedes verwendete Zeichen intendiert und nicht "einfach nur so" verwendet wird. Dementsprechend ließe sich das, was Koppelmann als „Zeichenbedeutung" bezeichnet, als Sinn des Zeichens auffassen und somit seine Einteilung als "sinnlos" und "sinnhaltig", bzw. "intendiert" und "nicht intendiert" verstehen. Damit wäre seine Einteilung in vielen Fällen unangemessen, denn die meisten Zeichen auf Verpackungen sind mit einer Intention dort aufgedruckt worden, auch wenn es sich nur um einen Strich oder Punkt handelt, der eine Markierung für die Verpackungsmaschinen kennzeichnen soll. Es wäre ein viel zu großer technischer Aufwand nicht intendierte Zeichen auf Verpackungen aufzudrucken. Die allermeisten Zeichen sind mit einer Intention auf die Verpackungen aufgedruckt und dementsprechend *sinnvoll*, was der Kategorie "bedeutungshaltig" von Koppelmann zu entsprechen scheint.

Ich möchte die Diskussion an dieser Stelle abbrechen und der Auseinandersetzung um eine für den praktischen Einsatz in dem Bereich der Produktverpackungen geeignete Theorie nicht vorgreifen.

Dieser Überblick über die Rezeptionsgeschichte des Themas zeigt, daß bislang nur in ganz wenigen Werken Produktverpackungen als

25

Untersuchungsgegenstand betrachtet wurden. Noch weniger haben sich die Autoren mit den Zeichen auf Produktverpackungen auseinandergesetzt.

Die Vorstellung weiterer Werke, die "Produktverpackungen" thematisieren, erfolgt erst dann, wenn sich ein direkter Nutzen in der hier erfolgenden Erörterung ergeben sollte.

Ich erachte es im Anschluß an dieses Kapitel für sinnvoll, den Untersuchungsgegenstand einzuführen.

## 1.5 Der Untersuchungsgegenstand: Produktverpackungen von Standardkonsumartikeln des täglichen Lebens

### 1.5.1 Die Erläuterung des Begriffes "Verpackung"

Das französische "emballager - einwickeln, verpacken"[17] erinnert noch an die alte Gebrauchsform des "Ballen"- und "Bündel"-Bindens zur Zeit des flandrischen Wollhandels. Die Wollballen gelten als Urform der Warenverpackung.[18]

Im Englischen wird "pack" mittlerweile nicht nur verwendet, um auf eine Warenverpackung zu referieren. "Pack" wird darüber hinaus zur Bezeichnung einer britischen Maßeinheit gebraucht. Dabei entspricht 1 Pack = 108, 862 kg. Zudem ist das "Pack" von "Pac" eine alte deutsche Zähleinheit für Papier: 1 Pack = 150 Ries = 150.000 Bogen.[19]

Heutzutage wird im Bereich des Marketing Wert auf einer Unterscheidung zwischen "Verpackung" und "Packung" gelegt. Das Wort Verpackung findet Verwendung, wenn die Produkthülle benannt werden soll. Der Begriff Packung hingegen kommt zum Einsatz, wenn man sich über eine bestimmte abgepackte Menge (Produkt und Hülle) äußern möchte, z.B. eine „Packung Zigaretten".[20]
An diese Terminologie möchte auch ich mich im folgenden halten.

---

[17] Langenscheidts Taschenwörterbuch Französisch-Deutsch (1982), Stichwort "emballager"

[18] vgl. Kluge (1989), S. 522

[19] vgl. "Brockhaus Die Enzyklopädie" (1998), Bd. 18, Stichwort "Pack"

[20] vgl. Sander (1972), S. 522 und Medeyros (1990), S. 6

## 1.5.2 Allgemeine Funktionen von Verpackungen

Nach Koppelmann sind folgende Funktionen unabdingbar, um eine Verpackung als solche zu identifizieren:

1. Schutzfunktion
2. Transport- und Lagerfunktion
3. Werbe- und Identifizierungsfunktion
4. Gebrauchsfunktion[21]

Dieser Katalog umfaßt lediglich die allgemeinen Grundfunktionen von Verpackungen.[22] Um die typischen Produktverpackungen zu charakterisieren, die in der heute üblichen Form der Supermarkt-Discounter zu finden sind, läßt sich diese Liste ergänzen.
So ist es z.B. eine typische Funktion von Verpackungen, Waren zu portionieren und diese Portionen wiederum zusammenzufassen.
Desweiteren ist es eine sehr ernstzunehmende Funktion von Verpak-kungen, nicht nur das Produkt vor der Umwelt zu schützen, sondern auch die Umwelt vor dem Produkt.
Die Werbefunktion und die Identifizierungsfunktion lassen sich um die Informationsfunktion ergänzen. Neben der Identifizierung und diversen Werbemaßnahmen muß auch gewährleistet sein, daß die Konsumenten mittels der Verpackung die notwendigen Informatio-nen über das Produkt und den Umgang mit selbigem erhalten.

---

[21]     vgl. Koppelmann (1971), S. 12

[22]     Die Grundfunktionen werden je nach individuellem Schwerpunkt des Autors anders gewichtet. Ich verzichte darauf, die einzelnen Kategorisie-rungen zu diskutieren und belasse es dabei, die allgemein üblichen Funktionen von Verpackungen hier zusammenzustellen, um dem Leser ei-nen Einstieg in das Thema der Produktverpackungen zu erleichtern.

Sander betrachtet die Verpackung als Informationsmedium und schlüsselt die Informationen in einem umfangreichen Katalog auf, von dem hier ein Überblick genügen soll:

- Eigeninformationen
  (Präsenz-, Verpackungsherkunfts- und Verpackungsqualitätsinformationen)
- Inhalts-, (Packgut-)informationen
  (Art-, Herkunfts-, Qualitäts- und Quantitätsinformationen)
- Packstoffinformationen
- Formen- und Größeninformationen
- Informationsleistungen von Verpackungsfarben
- Informationsleistungen von graphischen Zeichen
  (Schriftzeichen, Bildzeichen, Supplementzeichen)[23]

Laut Koppelmann lassen sich sämtliche Funktionen von Verpackungen zwei Kategorien zuordnen, den originären und den attributiven Verpackungszwecken. Originär muß die Verpackung den Ansprüchen des Schutzes, des Transportes und der Lagerung gerecht werden. Zu den attributiven Zwecken zählen Verkauf und Verwendung.[24]

Ich möchte darauf verzichten, auf die technisch-ökologisch-ökonomischen Funktionen einzugehen und es den Experten auf diesem Gebiet überlassen, dieses Thema zu erörtern.

---

[23] vgl. Sander (1972)

[24] vgl. Koppelmann (1971), Kap.3, S. 37-41

## a)     Die Werbefunktion

Die meisten Konsumgutverpackungen werden heute als Werbeträger funktionalisiert, da sie das Produkt zwingend begleiten.[25]
Es bietet sich aus diesem Grund an, die Verpackung auch dahingehend zu nutzen, das verpackte Produkt zu bewerben. Werbung läßt sich dann verstehen, als Einsatz von Maßnahmen, die auf Verhaltenssteuerung abzielen. Im Falle der Produktverpackungen werden die verschiedensten Zeichen in der Gestaltung derart arrangiert, das Produkt optimal hervorzuheben und die Konsumenten dahingehend zu beeinflussen, das Produkt zu kaufen.[26]

Die Werbung, die über Produktverpackungen veröffentlicht wird, gehört zur sogenannten "Display-Werbung". Ein "Display" ist die Warenauslage. Diese besteht in der Regel aus den Verpackungen und den Regalen sowie Ständern am Verkaufsort. Verpackungen werben als Display, indem sie zu einem Blickfang werden und mit werbenden Informationen ausgestattet sind.

---

[25]     Die Verpackung begleitet ein Produkt mindestens bis an die Kasse. Zuweilen werden danach lästige Umverpackungen oder sperrige Kartons in mittlerweile häufig bereitgestellten     Entsorgungsbehältnissen zurückgelassen. Im Maximalfall steht die Verpackung auch nach demvollständigen Verbrauch des Produktes noch im Haushalt zur Verfügung, entweder als Nachfüllpack oder zweckentfremdet als Aufbewahrungsort für andere Produkte.

[26]     Demnach werden Produktverpackungen mit Werbung vom Typ „Rekbme" ausgestattet.

30

## b)    Die Identifikationsfunktion

Neben der Werbefunktion ist es noch wichtiger, mit einer Verpakkung die Identifikationsfunktion zu erfüllen. Nach Debrunner ist ein
sofortiges Erkennen von Produkt und Marke von großer Bedeutung,
da die spontane Identifikation bei dem schnellen Einkaufen in unserer Zeit oft über die Auswahl aus dem Angebot entscheidet.[27]

Bei der Identifikation des Produktes sollte für den Kunden garantiert
sein, daß er erkennen kann:

- um was für ein Produkt es sich handelt
- wie das Produkt heißt
- evtl. von welchem Hersteller es gefertigt wurde.

Ein gewichtiger Vorteil einer eindeutigen Identifizierbarkeit des Produktes ist die damit einhergehende Abgrenzung von den
Konkurrenzprodukten. Desweiteren sollte die Identifikationsfunktion
einer Verpackung auch eine Unterscheidung zwischen verschiedenen
Produkten aus einem Hause gewährleisten.

Ist die Identifikation und damit das Wiedererkennen anhand be-
stimmter charakteristischer Merkmale gewährleistet, können
Veränderungen im Design werbestrategisch vorgenommen werden.
Die Kunden identifizieren das Produkt anhand der charakteristischen
Merkmale dennoch. Darüber hinaus lassen sich mit einem im Trend
liegenden Verpackungskonzept neue Kunden locken.

---

[27]      vgl. Debrunner (1977), S. 67ff

31

## c)    Die Imagefunktion

Im Zeitalter des Individualismus sind Käuferschaften grundsätzlich nicht mehr homogen. Die Kunden unterscheiden sich nicht nur hinsichtlich demographischer Merkmale wie Alter, Geschlecht, Nationalität, sozialer Herkunft, Einkommen, Religion, Bildungsniveau u.v.m. Geleitet vom unterschiedlichen Bedarf und Geschmack differieren auch die Vorstellungen von Angebotsleistungen. Die Konsumenten bewerten die Offerten und wählen die Alternative aus, die subjektiv den größten Nutzen erwarten läßt. Nach Anghern definiert sich der Wert eines Angebotes in der Beziehung zwischen dem Gut und dem wertenden Menschen.[28]

Da es nicht möglich ist, für jeden potentiellen Kunden ein individuelles Angebot auf den Markt zu bringen, muß ein Arrangement zwischen individueller Bedürfnisbefriedigung und der Kosten/Nutzen-Kalkulation der Anbieter hergestellt werden. Dementsprechend werden bestimmte Selektionskriterien ausgewählt, nach denen man Zielpersonen in Gruppen kategorisiert. So läßt sich z.B. die Zielgruppe der Erwachsenen von der Zielgruppe „Kinder" differenzieren sowie sich die Zielgruppe „Frauen" und „Männer" auseinanderdividieren lassen u.v.a. Diese sind maßgebend für die Produktdifferenzierung.

Die Imagefunktion einer Verpackung besteht darin, "das Produkt präzise gemäß der Zielgruppe zu profilieren. Die Verpackung soll zeigen, an wen das Angebot besonders gerichtet ist, und die Gestaltung hat so zu erfolgen, daß die Zielgruppe positiv angemutet wird. Nur diejenige Packung wird vom Verbraucher verstanden und akzep-

---

[28]    vgl. Anghern (1968), S. 122

32

tiert, welche in ihm die erwünschte Stimmung auslöst und seinen Erwartungen entspricht."[29]

Die Imagefunktion soll die Käufer im gefühlsmäßigen Bereich bei der Kaufentscheidung unterstützen. Verbraucher wählen bevorzugt Produkte, die sie gestalterisch besonders ansprechen und ihnen zusätzlich ideelle Werte wie Luxus, Jungsein etc. verschaffen und das eigene Lebensgefühl aufwerten.[30] Darüber hinaus soll diese Funktion zur Pflege des persönlichen Images und damit zu sozialer Anerkennung im jeweiligen Umfeld des Konsumenten beitragen. Das persönliche Image markiert die Zugehörigkeit zu einer bestimmten Gruppe. Man versucht, mit dem Verkauf von Image auch einen sozialen Status zu verkaufen.

Darüber hinaus bemühen sich die Hersteller, den Kunden ein Persönlichkeitsprofil des Unternehmens über die Imagefunktion zu vermitteln, die sogenannte „corporate identity". Es sollen den Verbrauchern gewisse Wertvorstellungen suggeriert werden, die ihren Bedürfniszustand im Moment der Kaufentscheidung ansprechen.

**d)    Die Informationsfunktion**

Die Selbstbedienung hat sich heutzutage als Verkaufsform für Konsumgüter durchgesetzt. Diese Entwicklung läuft konträr zu der Feststellung, daß eine große Differenzierung und Komplexität der Produkte diese erklärungsbedürftiger macht.

---

[29]   Somogyi (1972), S. 73

[30]   vgl. Debrunner (1977), S. 73

33

Für die Hersteller ist die Verpackung ein ideales Medium, dem Kunden die notwendigen Informationen und Erläuterungen zukommen zu lassen. Bis zu einem gewissen Grad können die Verpackungen Verkäuferfunktion übernehmen. Allerdings ist die Aufnahmebereitschaft der meisten Kunden begrenzt. Die Informationen sollten daher kurz und knapp, dennoch leicht verständlich und gut nachvollziehbar und möglichst ohne Brille lesbar sein.

Auf Produktverpackungen befinden sich die unterschiedlichsten Informationen. Angefangen von den gesetzlich vorgschriebenen Informationen wie Mengen-, Preis-, Inhaltsstoff-, Haltbarkeitsangaben etc. über Gebrauchs-, Verbrauchs- und Entsorgungsinformationen bis hin zu ganz speziellen Produktinformationen, Informationen zu Gewinnspielen und/oder Kampagnen, Informationen über das Unternehmen, ist alles auf Verpackungen zu finden - manchmal sogar Informationen zu Produkten aus einem ganz anderen Unternehmenszweig.[31]

Die Informationen auf Produktverpackungen werden von den Kunden zu unterschiedlichen Zeiten rezipiert. Am Verkaufsort sind vorwiegend die Informationen zum Packungsinhalt interessant sowie alle Informationen, die das Produkt mit anderen Angeboten vergleichbar machen.

Zu Hause sind insbesondere die Ge- und Verbrauchs- sowie die Entsorgungsinformationen von Interesse. Die Konsumenten versuchen, die Informationen möglichst rational aufzunehmen. Daher ist es für die Anbieter schwierig, Informationen, die nicht direkt mit dem Produkt oder dem Gebrauch in Verbindung stehen, auf der Verpackung dergestalt unterzubringen, daß sie auch gelesen werden.

---

[31] Es wird z.B. auf einer Nestlé Cornflakes-Verpackung Werbung für ein Handy gemacht.

Wie die Zusammenstellung der Funktionszuweisungen verschiedener Autoren erkennen läßt, werden Verpackungen gerne als Kommunikationsmedium instrumentalisiert.

### 1.5.3   Die Verpackung als "silent salesman"

Im Zeitalter der Selbstbedienungsläden kommt der Verpackung eines Produktes neben ihren technischen Funktionen immer stärker auch die Funktion ihres eigenen Verkäufers zu. Eine Verpackung fungiert, wie Hardt-Mautner es treffend formuliert, als "silent salesman".[32]

Was früher die Aufgabe der Verkäufer war - die losen Waren zu portionieren, abzupacken, die Kunden zu beraten, Informationen zum Ge- und Verbrauch weiterzuleiten und vor allem die Kunden zum Kauf zu animieren - müssen heutzutage die Produktverpackungen leisten.[33] Diese kleine Aufzählung zeigt, daß die technischen Funktionen von Verpackungen wie Schutz, Portionierung, Lagerung und Transport selbstverständlich und damit nebensächlich geworden sind. Viel wichtiger ist die Kommunikationsfunktion geworden. Jede Verpackung muß beraten, Informationen zum Ge- und Verbrauch über das Produkt weiterleiten - und jede Verpackung muß dies besser tun, als die Verpackung eines alternativen Produktes.

---

[32]   vgl. Hardt-Mautner (1992) - auch Dichter (1981) attestiert: "Eine Verpackung ist so etwas wie ein Verkäufer".

[33]   Heutzutage hat das Verkaufspersonal in den Supermarktdiscountern hauptsächlich die Aufgaben, die Regale aufzufüllen und zu kassieren. Qualifizierte Informationen zu den einzelnen Produkten sind nicht in dem günstigeren Preis solcher Läden inbegriffen.

35

Darüber hinaus müssen Verpackungen heutzutage dazu beitragen, den Kunden das Gefühl zu geben, weit mehr zu kaufen als das verpackte Produkt. Die Verpackung muß Kunden ein erstrebenswertes Lebensgefühl und damit ein einzigartiges <u>Produkterlebnis</u> anbieten, um konkurrenzfähig zu bleiben.

Meiner Ansicht nach vermitteln viele Verpackungen heute nicht den Eindruck eines <u>stillen</u> <u>Verkäufers,</u> sondern eines Verkäufers, der mit anderen Mitteln als der Stimme danach schreit, daß nach der Packung gegriffen und diese in den Einkaufswagen befördert wird.

Verpackungen und die Verkäufer in den sogenannten "Tante-Emma-Läden" unterscheiden sich im Hinblick auf ihre Kommunikationsfähigkeit jedoch dahingehend, daß die Kunden früher auf das Verkaufsgespräch angewiesen waren, um an ihre Waren zu kommen, die hinter der Ladentheke unerreichbar für die Kunden aufbewahrt wurden. Dementsprechend war es den Kunden aber auch nicht möglich, das Verkaufsgespräch zu umgehen.

Die Produktverpackungen in den modernen Ladenregalen hingegen müssen von sich aus die Aufmerksamkeit und das Interesse inmitten der Konkurrenz auf sich ziehen. Der Kunde ist nicht auf die Beratung durch die Verpackung angewiesen. Liefert eine Verpackung nicht die gewünschten Informationen, greift man einfach zu einer anderen.

Da mit diesem Konkurrenzdruck alle Verpackungenhersteller zu kämpfen haben, werden der Druck und die Bemühungen der Anbieter um eine attraktive Gestaltung ständig gesteigert.

Es bietet auch Vorteile, daß die Verpackungen Verkäuferfunktion übernommen haben: So bietet sich für jeden Anbieter die Möglichkeit, ohne den wenig beeinflußbaren Faktor der individuellen Kanalisation durch Verkaufspersonal direkt auf die Kunden wirken und damit selbständig Einfluß nehmen zu können. Die Anbieter können sicher sein, daß die gewünschten Produktinformationen bzw. die

Kommunika-tionsinhalte, die die Hersteller kommunizieren möchten, den Kunden auch zur Verfügung stehen, und zwar exakt den Vorstellungen der Anbieter entsprechend.

Das einzig große Problem dabei ist, daß die Informationen zwar optimal bereitgestellt sein können, wenn aber die Verpackung nicht die Grundvoraussetzung erfüllt, daß sie betrachtet wird, erreichen die Kommunikationsinhalte niemals ihre Adressaten.

Die Aussagen auf den Verpackungen werden in Kombination mit der Produktwerbung in bestimmten Zeitabschnitten durch folgende Marketing-Ziele bestimmt:

- Marktschaffung
- Marktausweitung und
- Markterhaltung.[34]

Bei der Marktschaffung geht es zunächst darum, ein Produkt einzuführen und es dem Verbraucher vertraut zu machen. Dies geschieht in Kombination mit einer individuell für das Produkt maßgeschneiderten Produktwerbung in den Massenmedien. Nur so ist es möglich, einer großen Menge von Verbrauchern das Produkt vorzustellen. Es ist wichtig, daß der Kunde die Verpackung des Produktes in der Werbung sieht, um sie später im Laden wiedererkennen und dem beworbenen Produkt zuordnen zu können.

Hat sich das Produkt eine etablierte Marktposition erkämpft, wird es notwendig, diese auch zu erhalten, denn die Konkurrenz schläft nicht. Darüber hinaus ist es das Ziel der meisten Unternehmen, sich in weiteren Märkten mit neuen Produkten auf der Basis bereits bewährter Werte ein zusätzliches Standbein zu sichern. Oft wird versucht, ein Element eines bereits etablierten Verpackungsdesigns dahingehend zu nutzen, neue Produkte durch eine optische Verbindung mit den bereits bekannten Werten leichter in den Markt integrieren zu können.

Die Glaubwürdigkeit der Aussagen auf Verpackungen ist insbesondere bei neuen Produkten ein wichtiger Aspekt für die Kaufentscheidung der Kunden. Wird das Produkt von den Verbrauchern akzeptiert und gekauft, tritt nach einiger Zeit der sogenannte "sleeper effect" ein.[35] Demnach haben die Kunden dann genügend eigene Erfahrungen mit dem Produkt gemacht, um selbiges beurteilen zu können Sie nehmen dementsprechend die Glaubwürdigkeit der Aussagen auf der Verpackung weniger wichtig.

In Amerika hat man eine Gesetzesvorlage gegen irreführende Verpackungen und Beschriftungen verfaßt, deren Aussagen in der Grundintention auch in der deutschen Rechtssprechung verankert sind. Nach dem "Fair Packaging and Labeling Act" ist mit ordentlichen Rechtsverfahren gegen folgende Geschäftspraktiken vorzugehen:

- undeutliche Mengenangaben
- irreführende Bebilderung
- Werbung mit Rabattversprechen, wenn keine Sicherheit besteht, daß der Inhalt auch wirklich den Käufer erreicht
- Bruchteile von Gewichten
- unvollständig abgefüllte Schachteln (Mogelpackungen)
- unbrauchbare Portionsangaben
- mangelhafte Angaben der Zusammensetzung, falls diese wichtig sind[36]

---

[34] vgl. Kaltenbach (1975), S. 32-40

[35] Kaltenbach (1975), S. 86

[36] Swankin (1967), S. 89ff

Die meisten dieser Punkte unterliegen jedoch der individuellen Aus-
legung. Dementsprechend häufig kommt es dann auch zu einem
Rechtsstreit. So haben z.b. Mitglieder der Umweltschutzorganisation
Greenpeace die Forderung an die Firma Maggi gerichtet, daß genma-
nipulierte Produkte auf der Verpackung als solche gekennzeichnet
werden sollten.[37]

Die meisten Produkte werden in einer Produktverpackung präsentiert.
Es gibt aber durchaus auch Artikel, die ohne Verpackung angeboten
werden. Man versucht, den fehlenden Platz für eine Beschriftung
dadurch zu kompensieren, daß man diese Produkte wie Obst, Brot
und Fleisch mit Aufklebern oder kleinen Anhängern bestückt. Dadurch kann das Produkt wenigstens mit einem Produktnamen als
Wiedererkennungsmerkmal ausgestattet werden und eventuell auch
mit Werbeinformationen zwecks Produkterläuterung etc.
In seltenen Fällen wird nur eine bloße Verpackung dargeboten. Dies
geschieht in der Regel ausschließlich zu Werbezwecken. So wird z.B.
zuweilen eine überdimensional große Verpackung eines Produktes
als Blickfang in einer Schaufensterauslage ausgestellt oder ein Hoch-
haus als Riesenaspirinschachtel verhüllt (s. Abbildung 1)[38].

Insbesondere bei Nahrungsmitteln wird die Darbietung von Produkt
und Verpackung bevorzugt (s. Abbildung 2).
Zu diesem Zweck müssen die Verpackungen entweder mit einem
Sichtfenster ausgestattet werden, so daß der Blick auf das zu kaufen-

---

[37]
    o.A. Greenpeace-Zeitung 4/98
    Hinweis: In Amerika ist die Kennzeichnung genmanipulierter Produkte
    sogar verboten.
[38]
    PR-Gag der Bayer AG Leverkusen anläßlich des 100. Geburtstags des
    Schmerzmittels "Aspirin".

de Produkt in der Verpackung freigegeben wird,[39] oder das Produkt wird im originalen oder im zubereiteten Zustand auf einem meist fotorealistischen Bild auf der Verpackung präsentiert[40].

Gerne werden auch gänzlich durchsichtige Verpackungsmaterialien verwendet, die mit Aufklebern ausgestattet werden, wie man das z.B. von Nudeln, Brot, Käse und Wurst und diversen Getränken in Glasflaschen kennt.

### 1.5.4  Verpackungen und Verbraucher

Eine wichtige Größe bei der Erfolgsrechnung der Anbieter ist die Einstellung der Konsumenten. Einstellungen sind gedankliche Konstrukte, die sich über folgende Merkmale einkreisen lassen:

- Einstellungen sind hypothetische Konstrukte, die oft nicht direkt beobachtbar sind.
- Sie können sich auf Gegenstände beziehen.
- Sie werden teilweise im Verlauf der individuellen Entwicklung erlernt oder herausgebildet.
- Sie können als System interdependenter Einheiten verstanden werden.[41]

---

[39]  Beispiele für diese Form der Darbietung sind Nudelverpackungen, diverse Pralinenkästen, Kartoffelchipstüten etc.

[40]  Besonders beliebt ist diese Präsentationsform auf Konservendosen.

[41]  Vgl. Kaltenbach (1975), S. 80; Roth (1967) und Hermanns (1972). In der Auflistung der Merkmale von Einstellungen wurde zusätzlich die Möglichkeit berücksichtigt, daß Einstellungen auch auf individuellen Empfindungen und Erfahrungen basieren können.

Ein erster Kommunikationserfolg im Sinne des Marketings ist er-reicht, wenn ein Konsument eine Einstellung zu einem Produkt gewinnt. Eine Einstellung allein reicht aber nicht aus. Es muß eine Einstellungswirkung erzielt werden. Folgende Einstellungen können zu einem Produkt gewonnen werden:

1.) <u>Null-Wirkung</u>
Es wird weder eine Einstellung zu dem Objekt gewonnen, noch eine bestehende tangiert.

2.) <u>Bekräftigung einer Einstellung</u>
Das Produkt ist z.B. gut für persönliche Zwecke geeignet.

3.) <u>Schwächung der vorhandenen Einstellung</u>
Das Produkt eignet sich für persönliche Zwecke nicht optimal.

4.) <u>Umkehrung der vorhandenen Einstellung</u>
Es handelt sich um einen Fehlkauf oder Glücksgriff.

5.) <u>Es wird eine Einstellung zu einem Objekt gewonnen</u>
Es entsteht zum ersten Mal die Situation, daß ein Produkt für einen bestimmten Zweck gebraucht wird, oder man glaubt, es zu brauchen.[42]

---

[42]    vgl. Kaltenbach (1975), S. 80

Über die Produktverpackung läßt sich schon im Laden Einfluß auf die Einstellung der Kunden nehmen. Im Idealfall wird ein Verhalten ausgelöst - das Kaufverhalten. Das Kaufverhalten läßt sich in drei Gruppen einteilen, die unseren Einkauf bestimmen:

- impulsives Kaufverhalten
- habituelles Kaufverhalten
- rationales Kaufverhalten[43]

Das impulsive Kaufverhalten läßt sich noch einmal in vier Kategorien untergliedern:[44]

1.) reines Impulsverhalten
Es handelt sich dabei um einen reizgesteuerten Kauf, der das "normale" Kaufverhalten durchbricht.

2.) Erinnerungskauf
Der Konsument nimmt Reize (Produkte) wahr, die ihn daran erinnern, daß er ein Produkt benötigt - z.B. weil seine Vorräte aufgebraucht sind, oder Reize, die ihn daran erinnern, daß er bereits früher mit dem Produkt gute Erfahrungen gemacht hat. Aufgrund dieses Anstoßes wird das Produkt gekauft.

3.) suggestiver Impulskauf
Ein Produkt, das der Konsument zum ersten Mal sieht, spricht seine Bedürfnisse stark an. Es wird unmittelbar und

---

[43] vgl. Kroeber-Riel (1992), S. 384

[44] vgl. Kroeber-Riel (1992), S. 385. Kroeber-Riel übernimmt die in der Konsumentenforschung gängige Einteilung des impulsiven Kaufverhaltens nach Stern (1962), jedoch in einer aktualisierten und zusammengefaßten Version.

ohne längeres Nachdenken zur Befriedigung dieser Bedürfnisse gekauft.

4.) geplanter Impulskauf

Der Käufer hat vor, ein bestimmtes Produkt zu kaufen. Er betritt den Laden in der Erwartung, daß er ad hoc aufgrund von Sonderangeboten, Verkaufsförderungsmaßnahmen u.s.w. noch weitere Produkte kaufen wird. Er ist auf einen Sonderkauf eingestellt.

Es ist strikt zu unterscheiden zwischen impulsivem und ungeplantem Kaufverhalten. Während beim impulsiven Kaufverhalten ein Produkt aufgrund eines von ihm ausgehenden Reizes (meist über die Verpackung) gekauft wird, wandern ungeplante Produkte in den Einkaufswagen, weil man z.B. im Laden nach Anregungen für ein Abendessen gesucht hat.

Echtes impulsives Kaufverhalten charakterisiert ca. 10-20% unserer Einkäufe. 40-50% unserer Käufe sind nicht geplant. Man spricht bei Impuls- oder Spontankäufen von einem sogenannten „Soforteffekt".[45]

**Habituelles** Kaufverhalten resultiert meistens aus großer Vertrautheit und Zufriedenheit mit einem Produkt. In einem solchen Fall sind es weniger die spontan aufgenommenen Reize, die im Laden den Kauf auslösen, sondern vielmehr der Wiedererkennungseffekt eines gesuchten Produktes bzw. seiner Verpackung.

Bei **Gewohnheitskaufverhalten** spricht man von einem **Langzeiteffekt**.[46]

---

[45] vgl. Kroeber-Riel, S. 389
[46] vgl. Kroeber-Riel, S. 394

**Rationales** Kaufverhalten basiert auf dem Vergleich mehrerer Alternativen. Es werden subjektiv sachlich die Vor- und Nachteile der in Frage kommenden Alternativen gegeneinander abgewogen. Gleichzeitig ist das Preis-Leistungsverhältnis ein gewichtiges Entscheidungskriterium. Soll nach rationalen Kriterien eine Kaufentscheidung getroffen werden, kommen die auf der Verpackung aufgedruckten Informationen besonders im Vergleich voll zum Tragen. Bei längerfristig geplanten Kaufentscheidungen werden oft institutionalisierte Orientierungshilfen wie Verbraucherzentralen und Testhefte zu Rate gezogen.

Ist der Reiz eines Produktes entsprechend groß, kann von einem ursprünglich rationalen Kaufplan auf einen Spontankauf umgeschwenkt werden.

Einstellungswirkungen bewirken oft Verhaltenseffekte für den Einkauf:

- Null-Wirkung - keinerlei Verhaltenseffekt
- Verhaltensänderung ohne Rollenwechsel - z.B. größere oder kleinere Einkaufsmenge als früher
- Rollenwechsel oder Umkehrung von Verhalten - z.B. ein Käufer von Niedrigpreisprodukten wird zu einem Käufer von Höchstpreisprodukten, oder aus einem Käufer wird ein Nichtkäufer
- neue Rolle - z.B. erstmaliger Kauf oder erstmalige Verwendung eines Produktes mit spezifischer Nutzenstiftung[47]

Es hat sich herausgestellt, daß nicht nur Produktwerbung, Verpackung und das Produkt selbst auf die Konsumenten beeinflussend wirken. Ein Einflußfaktor in der Kommunikation der Verbraucher

---

[47]   vgl. Kaltenbach (1975), S. 83

untereinander sind die sogenannten „Meinungsführer". Meinungsführer oder -bildner verarbeiten überdurchschnittlich viele Informationen und tragen durch kritische Weitergabe zur Meinungsbildung in der jeweiligen Gruppe bei und kanalisieren das Interesse weiterer Personen. Meinungsbildung nach diesem Prinzip bezeichnet man als "two step flow of communication".[48] Meinungsführer können nachhaltig Einfluß auf das Kaufverhalten nehmen.

Beim Kaufverhalten der Verbraucher unterscheidet man zwischen programmiertem und nicht programmiertem Kaufverhalten. Beim nicht programmierten Kaufverhalten suchen die Verbraucher nach Orientierungs- und Entscheidungshilfen auf den Verpackungen, die ihnen die Kaufentscheidung im Sinne eines optimalen Preis-Leistung-Nutzen-Verhältnisses erleichtern sollen. Auch Verkäufer und Bekannte können hier beeinflußend bzw. meinungsbildend und damit kaufentscheidend wirken.

Markentreue Verbraucher kaufen programmiert, das heißt, sie ersparen sich die Qual der Wahl einer neuen Kaufentscheidung und greifen immer wieder auf ein bewährtes Produkt zurück.[49] Diese reflexartig ablaufende Kaufentscheidung spart zudem Zeit.[50] Läuft die Kaufentscheidung eines Produktes erst einmal programmiert ab, ist es äußerst schwierig, das Interesse auf alternative Produkte umzulenken, denn deren Reize werden nicht einmal wahrgenommen.

Ziel der Anbieter ist es, über die Verpackung zu einem nicht programmierten Kauf zu stimulieren. Im Idealfall überzeugt das Produkt dermaßen, daß es immer wieder gekauft und aus dem nicht programmierten ein programmiertes Kaufverhalten wird.

---

[48] vgl. Katz und Lazarsfeld (1964), S. 31
[49] vgl. Katona (1962), S. 196ff
[50] vgl. Knappe (1981), S. 200

45

Man versucht in der Regel, mit den Texten auf Verpackungen von Standardkonsumartikeln zum Kauf zu motivieren, indem man die menschlichen Grundbedürfnisse reizt.
Diese sind nach Maslow:

**Selbstverwirklichung**
**Anerkennung**
**(Selbstachtung/Prestige)**
**Soziale Bedürfnisse**
**(geliebt werden/Fürsorge)**
**Sicherheitsbedürfnisse**
**physiologische Bedürfnisse**
**(Hunger/Durst)**[51]

Dabei ist zu unterscheiden, zwischen dem, was zum Überleben gebraucht wird (needs), und dem, was man sich wünscht (wants).
Es ist insofern sinnvoll, die Grundbedürfnisse über die Verpackung anzusprechen, als diese triebgesteuertes Verhalten und damit ein Kaufverhalten auslösen können. Ein großer Teil der Waren wandert in den Einkaufskorb, weil im Laden über die Verpackung ein Grundbedürfnis motiviert und damit ein Triebverhalten ausgelöst wird (z.B. "Lust auf etwas Süßes")[52]. So kann durchaus auch programmiertes Kaufverhalten überlagert werden, oder es wird zusätzlich ein alternatives Produkt aus dem gleichen Bereich gekauft, das die Befriedigung eines Triebes verspricht.
Zu diesem Zweck werden Worte eingesetzt, deren Gebrauch mit emotionalen Wertigkeiten besetzt sind. Die Strategie dabei ist fol-

---

[51]  vgl. Maslows (1977), vgl. auch Corell (1992), S. 27ff und zur schematischen Darstellung

[52]  Auf den „Balisto" und „Bounty" Großpackungen wird mit der „Lust auf etwas Süßes" insofern gearbeitet, als der Begriff „Lust" als Schlüsselreiz eingesetzt wird, um auf eine Erweiterung des Inhaltes hinzuweisen – „Lust 1 mehr aufzureißen" oder „Lust 1 mehr zu genießen?".

46

gende: "Man muß nicht einfach Strümpfe verkaufen, sondern schöne Füße!"[53] Dementsprechend werden nicht einfach Haarpflegeprodukte verkauft, sondern "schönes Haar" (Nivea) scheint im Preis inbegriffen zu sein. Ziel ist der Effekt, die Kunden intim anzusprechen. Die emotionalen Reize werden in der Regel unbewußt aufgenommen ("Das Geheimnis, jünger auszusehen" - Oil of Olaz).

Ist es einmal gelungen, mit dem Kauf eines Produktes ein Grundbedürfnis zu befriedigen, kann aus dem ersten impulsiven Kaufverhalten durchaus ein habituelles werden.
Man klassifiziert passend zum jeweiligen Kaufverhalten folgende Produktgruppen:[54]

**Convenience goods:**
Es handelt sich hierbei um Produktalternativen, die jeweils zu den individuellen Bedürfnissen der Kunden passen. Es entsteht kein kognitiver Spannungszustand - die sogenannte *Dissonanz*[55], denn die Kaufentscheidung ist eindeutig. Convenience goods sind typische "Impulskauf-Artikel". Die Rezeption der Verpackungsaufschriften geschieht spontan am Verkaufsort mit einer dem Produkt gegenüber positiv geneigten Einstellung. Daher sind die Chancen besonders groß, daß verschiedene Aussagen verkaufsauslösend wirken.

**Shopping goods:**
Produkte dieser Gruppe verursachen während des Kaufprozesses in der vorhergehenden Entscheidungsphase große Unsicherheit. Die Produktunterschiede sind sehr vielfältig. Dementsprechend differieren die Produktaussagen sehr stark. Der Kunde hat große

---

[53]      Packard (1958), S. 45

[54]      vgl. Kaltenbach (1975), S. 93f

[55]      Zu den Theorien der kognitiven Dissonanz vgl. Manz (1993), S. 157ff

Schwierigkeiten bei der Entscheidungsfindung. Ihm bleibt nichts anderes übrig, als durch Informationsaktivitäten und rational abwägende Rezeption die Dissonanz zu reduzieren und ein akzeptables Produkt aus dem meist vielfältigen Sortiment auszuwählen.

**Speciality goods:**
Die Auswahl ist bei Produkten dieser Gruppe sehr begrenzt. Es bestehen deutlich ausgeprägte physische und funktionale Unterschiede. Manchmal ist das Angebot derart eingeschränkt, daß der Nachfrager gezwungen ist, ein Produkt zu kaufen, das von vornherein seine Nutzenerwartungen nur unvollkommen befriedigt.

Zusammenfassung
Dieser erste Teil diente der Einführung in die Thematik. Es konnten folgende Punkte als Aufgabenstellung und Zielsetzung dieser Arbeit festgemacht werden:

- Verpackungen als Textsorte
- eine gebrauchsorientierte Theorie der sprachlichen Zeichen in der praktischen Anwendung
- linguistische Grundlagen als Basis für ein Analysemodell von Verpackungsaufschriften.

Neben dem Arbeitsziel und den Leitfragen konnte erarbeitet werden, daß der bisherige Stand der Forschung in der Auseinandersetzung mit der textuellen Gestaltung von Standardkonsumartikeln nur unbefriedigend ist. Es läßt sich Nachholbedarf auf diesem Gebiet feststellen.

Zur Einstimmung in die Materie wurden die verschiedenen Eigenschaften und Funktionen von Verpackungen vorgestellt. Darüber hinaus wurden die unterschiedlichen Kaufverhalten der Konsumenten demonstriert.

Bevor es daran geht, ein praktisches Analysemodell für die Untersuchung von Verpackungsaufschriften zu entwickeln, sollen im nächsten Teil die theoretischen Grundlagen aus linguistischer Sicht diskutiert werden.

## 2. Zeichentheoretische Grundlagen

## 2.1 Die Gebrauchstheorie sprachlicher Zeichen

### 2.1.1 Zeichen und Zeichenhaftes

Die folgenden Ausführungen basieren auf einer Arbeit mit dem Titel "Zeichentheorie" von Keller.[56]

Schon der Versuch, den Begriff „Zeichen" zu erläutern, gestaltet sich als ausgesprochen kompliziert. Zeichen haben die Eigenschaft, sinnlich wahrnehmbar zu sein. Allerdings ist dieses Merkmal auch das einzige, das den verschiedenen Definitionsversuchen gemeinsam ist.

Wir kennen die verschiedensten Zeichen aus dem täglichen Leben. Tagtäglich orientieren wir uns an den sogenannten *Verkehrszeichen*. Autos haben *Kennzeichen*, wir schauen uns *Zeichentrickfilme* an, wir geben unseren Mitmenschen *Zeichen*, wir legen in unser Buch *Lesezeichen*, unsere Schrift besteht aus *Schriftzeichen*, wir kommunizieren *sprachliche Zeichen* und erwarten, daß die Waren im Selbstbedienungsladen *ausgezeichnet* sind.

Diese und viele andere Zeichen bestimmen unser Leben – oft, ohne daß wir diese Tatsache bewußt wahrnehmen. So ist z.B. auch das Fahren eines Autos bzw. die Wahl einer bestimmten Automarke zeichenhaft, wie auch der Verzicht auf ein Auto. Ebenso ist die gewählte Kleidung oft ein Zeichen dafür, was man vorhat (Besuch der Oper oder eines des Banketts oder Gartenarbeit, Sport treiben, Beerdigung, Hochzeit, Karneval u.v.m.). Kleidung ist häufig ein Zeichen für das Wetter.

---

[56]　Keller (1995)

49

Das Besondere an Zeichen ist, daß es nicht ausreicht, sie wahrzunehmen - sie müssen auch als Zeichen interpretiert werden. Die Interpretation der Zeichen um uns herum bestimmt im wesentlichen unser Verhalten im Alltag.

Die Interpretation der sprachlichen Zeichen unserer Gesprächspartner bestimmt unsere Kommunikation im Dialog.

In unserer Gesellschaft wird ständig alles mögliche interpretiert. Es ist unmöglich, sich dem zu entziehen - "Man kann nicht nicht kommunizieren."[57] Selbst der Versuch, sich nicht zeichenhaft zu verhalten, wird interpretiert.

Normalerweise ist uns daran gelegen, die Zeichen, die unseren Mitmenschen Anlaß zu Interpretationen geben, nachhaltig nach unserem Geschmack zu beeinflussen. Nach Maslow ist eines unserer Grundbedürfnisse das Streben nach sozialer Anerkennung.[58] Soziale Anerkennung wird uns nur dann zuteil, wenn unsere soziale Umwelt Zeichen an uns interpretiert und positiv bewertet. Zu diesen Zeichen gehören unser Aussehen, unser Besitz, unser Verhalten, unsere Kommunikation etc. Wir haben die Möglichkeit, auf viele Dinge Einfluß zu nehmen, die an uns bewertet werden, z.B. indem wir uns ganz bewußt verhalten, reflektiert Dinge sagen oder nicht sagen. Dabei überlegen wir uns vorher, wie unsere Äußerung oder unser Verhalten von unseren Mitmenschen aufgenommen, interpretiert und bewertet werden könnte. Wir bemühen uns dann, unser (kommunikatives) Verhalten so zu gestalten, wie wir glauben, daß es von unseren Mitmenschen positiv bewertet wird.

---

[57] Watzlawick, Beavin und Jackson (1967/1974), S. 53 und Watzlawick (1974), S. 96

[58] s. Bedürfnispyramide, S. 25

Ebenso versuchen wir, unser Aussehen, unseren Besitz und unseren alltäglichen Konsum derart zu gestalten, daß Außenstehende einen möglichst positiven Eindruck von uns gewinnen.

In unserer Gesellschaft ist folglich ein Mittel, unser Image zu gestalten, unser *Konsum* bzw. unser *Nichtkonsum*.

Diese Absicht greifen auch die Anbieter von Standardkonsumartikeln auf. Es wird den Kunden mittlerweile häufig über die Aussagen auf den Verpackungen explizit ein ideeller Mehrwert mit dem Kauf des Produktes versprochen. Dieser ideelle Mehrwert soll zu sozialer Anerkennung beitragen. Man sollte im Sinne Packards nicht versuchen, einfach Strümpfe zu verkaufen, sondern "schöne Füße".[59]

Allerdings leben wir heute in einer Zeit des immer größer werdenden Individualismus. Nicht jeder bewegt sich im gleichen sozialen Umfeld. Dementsprechend sind auch die Werte verschieden, die positiv betrachtet werden. Aus diesem Grund ist es schwierig, die Werbung, die Verpackung eines Produktes und das Produkt selbst so zu gestalten, daß sie für eine möglichst große Zielgruppe ein Zeichen für ein angestrebtes Image verkörpern.

---

[59] Packard (1958), S. 45

## 2.2.2 Erste Ansätze zu einer Theorie der sprachlichen Zeichen

Sprachliche Zeichen sind in der Linguistik ein zentrales Thema. Man hat ihnen als Grundelemente verschiedener Zeichentheorien einen eigenen Bereich gewidmet - die Semiotik.

Platon und Aristoteles entwickelten als erste jeweils die Grundlagen eines eigenen Zeichenmodelles. Jedoch vertraten die beiden großen Denker zwei verschiedene Zeichenauffassungen. Platon vertritt eine instrumentalistische Zeichentheorie. Demgegenüber stehen die Grundzüge einer repräsentationistischen Zeichentheorie des Aristoteles.[60]

Platons Theorie basiert auf der Annahme, daß die Benennung der Dinge von den Menschen - genauer von einem sogenannten „nomothetes" („Wortbildner") vorgenommen wird und damit auf Vertrag und Übereinkunft basiert (384d)[61]. Daraus ergibt sich die Frage, ob es sinnvoll ist, bei der Benennung eines Dinges zwischen richtiger und falscher Benennung zu unterscheiden. Keller weist bei seiner Auseinandersetzung mit diesem Aspekt auf das Problem hin, daß eine Sprache nicht einfach als ein Benennungssystem von sprachunabhängig gegebenen Dingen angesehen werden kann: "Viele Kategorien werden durch die jeweilige Sprache erst geschaffen und nicht einfach benannt; außerdem ist das Benennen nicht die einzige Handlung, die wir mit Wörtern ausführen."[62]

---

[60] Die nun folgende kurze Präsentation der beiden Zeichenmodelle wurde verfaßt in Anlehnung an: Keller (1995)

[61] Zitiert wird Platon (Kratylos) nach der üblichen Stephanus-Numerierung. Die Zitate stammen aus der Übersetzung von Schleiermacher (1957).

[62] Keller (1995), S. 25f

In Platons Dialog "Kratylos" wird die These aufgeworfen, Wörter verhielten sich zu ihren Referenzobjekten wie Eigennamen zu ihren Trägern. Dabei ist die Kategorie der "Eigennamen einer der seltenen Fälle, wo der Mensch willentlich und bewußte Akte der Referenzfixierung vornehmen kann, z.b. durch die Taufe"[63], ebenso durch die Ausstattung eines Produktes mit einem Produkt- bzw. Markennamen. Nach Keller sind Eigennamen aber eine Ausnahme, die in diesem besonderen Kontext nicht die Regel bestätigen. Man darf sich durch das Beispiel der Eigennamen nicht dazu verleiten lassen, daraus zu generalisieren, daß die Benennung der Beliebigkeit einzelner Individuen unterliegt.

Die Beliebigkeit bzw. Arbitrarität wird zum zentralen Aspekt der Saussureschen Zeichentheorie rund 2000 Jahre später.

In der Diskussion zwischen Kratylos, Sokrates und Hermogenes ergibt sich die Feststellung, daß es eine den Dingen gemäße Richtigkeit der Bezeichnungen gibt. So wie man Handlungen richtig oder falsch ausführen kann, ist das Reden eine Handlung und das Benennen Teil des Redens - dementsprechend kann man Objekte nicht einfach nach eigenem Gutdünken benennen (387d und 391b), wie es einem gerade in den Sinn kommt.

In dem Dialog „Kratylos" wird der Charakter des Werkzeuges eines Wortes als eines seiner spezifischen Eigenschaften in den Vordergrund gestellt (388c). In diesem Zusammenhang werden die wesentlichen Funktionen von Sprache - die Kommunikation, Klassifikation und Repräsentation - ersichtlich.[64]

---

[63]    Keller (1995), S. 26

[64]    vgl. Keller (1995), S. 29

Keller macht in seinen Ausführungen auf zwei Fehlschlüsse aufmerksam, die sich für Sokrates Argumentation als verhängnisvoll erweisen: den instrumentalistischen und den rationalistischen Fehlschluß.

Nach dem instrumentalistischen Fehlschluß sind alle Werkzeuge, auch Wörter, aufgrund ihrer spezifischen Beschaffenheit für ihren Zweck geeignet. Dementsprechend sei ihre Beschaffenheit von dem Zweck diktiert, den sie zu erfüllen haben. Keller erläutert, daß der Schluß formal gültig ist. Der Fehlschluß kann durch zwei Optionen auf die Prämissen verhindert werden. Entweder rechnet man Wörter nicht zu der Gruppe der Werkzeuge oder man geht nicht davon aus, daß alle Werkzeuge eine von ihrem spezifischen Zweck diktierte Beschaffenheit haben.

Bei der ersten Option nimmt man an, daß Worte nur im metaphorischen Sinne Werkzeuge sind, wobei die Metapher sich nicht auf eine zweckbestimmte Beschaffenheit bezieht.

Keller bevorzugt die Option, daß es Werkzeuge gibt, die ihren Zweck erfüllen können, allein durch die Konventionalität ihres Gebrauches.

Als rationalistischer Fehlschluß wird die Annahme vorgestellt, daß alle zweckmäßigen Einrichtungen, die nicht von Natur aus da sind, Ergebnisse kluger Planung und weiser Durchführung von ebenso klugen Menschen sind.

Keller entwickelt hieraus eine Erklärung zur Entstehung von Wörtern:

"In Wahrheit sind die Wörter (mit wenigen Ausnahmen) nicht Schöpfungen begnadeter Künstler, sondern unbeabsichtigte Nebeneffekte des alltäglichen Kommunizierens ganz normaler Menschen. Sie sind Ergebnisse von Prozessen kultureller Evolution".[65]

---

[65]    Keller (1995), S. 32

54

Auf Produktverpackungen sind beide Sorten von Worten zu finden: Worte als Schöpfungen mehr oder weniger begnadeter Künstler (Verpackungstexter im weitesten Sinne) und Worte des alltäglichen Kommunizierens ganz normaler Menschen.

Wie noch beispielhaft gezeigt wird, werfen beide Sorten für die Gestalter von Verpackungstexten Probleme auf.

Die Worte des alltäglichen Kommunizierens werden dann verwendet, wenn das Verständnis des Textes durch die Kunden garantiert sein muß. Das heißt, es ist empfehlenswert, insbesondere bei Texten mit komplizierten Inhalten wie Gebrauchs-, Bedienungs-, Zubereitungsanleitungen, Produktinformationen etc. Worte zu wählen, die ein möglichst einfaches und schnelles Verstehen durch die Zielgruppe garantieren. Dabei stellt sich die Frage, welche Worte ein Verständnis durch die Zielgruppe garantieren und ob es überhaupt Worte gibt, die ein Verständnis garantieren. Um die Wahrscheinlichkeit so groß wie möglich zu gestalten, daß die Worte auf den Produktverpackungen verstanden werden, ist eine Analyse der Zielgruppe inklusive deren Sprachgewohnheiten notwendig. So wählt man z.B. bei Produkten für Jugendliche augenblicklich gerne Anglizismen, da die Sprache der Jugendlichen von diesen geprägt ist (Tuffi Shakes, Kellogg's Flakes, Kinder-Country). Gleichzeitig bedeutet der Gebrauch von Anglizismen für viele Jugendliche eine Imagepflege, die soziale Anerkennung verspricht.

Für Personen, die sich einer gebildeten Schicht zugehörig fühlen, was ihr Kaufverhalten dahingehend charakterisiert, daß sie gerne Geld für teure Luxusartikel ausgeben, werden insbesondere Kosmetikartikel bevorzugt mit französisch oder englisch klingendem Vokabular ausgestattet. Auch in diesem Fall verheißen elegant französische und englisch klingende Worte wie "Skin Illuminating Complex"

(Eliszabeth Arden) oder "Lift Activ Yeux" Exklusivität und damit Imagepflege.

Es liegt der Verdacht nahe, daß insbesondere die Fremdworte in ihrem deutschsprachigen Verwenderkreis nicht unbedingt verstanden werden, sondern daß allein der Gebrauch ihrem Benutzer eine soziale Wertsteigerung zuteil werden läßt.

Dementsprechend schwierig gestaltet es sich, herauszufinden, welche Worte dank ihres konventionellen Gebrauches ihren Zweck zu erfüllen im Stande sind. Der Zweck ist in diesem Falle, die Kunden zum Kauf zu bewegen.

Bei Produktverpackungen, die eine möglichst breite Zielgruppe ansprechen sollen, wie z.B. diverse Nahrungsmittelverpackungen, wird meist versucht, die Wortwahl am allgemein gängigen konventionellen hochdeutschen Sprachgebrauch zu orientieren. Aber auch in diesem Fall gibt es keine verläßlichen Meßwerte, die ein optimales Verständnis garantieren, bis auf eine größtmögliche frequente Verwendung. Letztendlich hängt die Wahl der konventionellen Worte häufig von der subjektiven Einschätzung des Personenkreises ab, der die textuelle Verpackungsgestaltung verantwortet.


Würden Verpackungen sprachlich ausschließlich mit konventionellen Worten der Zielgruppe gestaltet, wäre es stilistisch schwierig, individuelle Akzente zu setzen und das Produkt differenziert vorzustellen.

Zu diesem Zweck werden Worte eingesetzt, die von Keller als Ergebnisse der Schöpfungen (mehr oder weniger) begnadeter Künstler vorgestellt werden. Ziel ist es, mit Hilfe von Wortneuschöpfungen oder neuen Wortkombinationen den Verpakungs-text sprachlich von anderen ab- und hervorzuheben sowie das Interesse der Konsumenten zu wecken.

Aber auch bei den Wortneuschöpfungen ergibt sich die Schwierigkeit, daß sie im Idealfall selbsterklärend sein müssen. Auf Produktverpackungen steht wenig Platz für Erläuterungen zur Verfügung. Darüber hinaus interessieren sich die Verbraucher in der Regel nicht für Produkte, deren Verpackungsaufdrucke sie nicht auf Anhieb verstehen. In seltenen Fällen reizt die äußere Aufmachung der Verpackung dermaßen, daß sich Kunden dafür interessieren, ohne daß direkt ersichtlich ist, welches Produkt sich in der Verpackung verbirgt.

Eine hilfreiche Möglichkeit, eine völlig neue Wortschöpfung z.B. als Namen für ein Produkt einzuführen, ist die Werbung. Nur so kann man den Kunden erläutern, daß sich z.B. hinter "Rask" eine "Zahnbürste für Ihren Hund" (Pedigree) in Form eines Kauknochens verbirgt oder hinter "Rei in der Tube" ein Waschmittel.

Wortneuschöpfungen und neue Wortkombination auf Produktverpackungen müssen entweder aus einem allgemeinen Sprachverständnis heraus erschließbar sein, wie das Wort "knisprig" auf Vienetta-Eiscremeverpackungen von "knusprig" und knisternden "Crisps" abgeleitet werden kann, oder sie müssen auf der Verpackung erläutert werden, wie "Anti-Aging-System" auf der Rückseite der Coral-Verpackung.

Wortneuschöpfungen und neue Wortkombinationen auf Produktverpackungen sollten nicht einfach nach dem persönlichen Gusto eines kreativen Schöpfers eingesetzt werden. Sie bilden den ganz seltenen Fall, daß sie ihrem Zweck entsprechend entwickelt werden - aufzufallen, abzuheben und dennoch verständlich zu sein.

Bevor es daran geht, Wortneuschöpfungen und andere Wortklassen auf Produktverpackungen zu untersuchen, gilt es erst einmal die zeichentheoretischen Grundlagen festzuhalten.

Aus dem Dialog Kratylos lassen sich vier Gedanken zusammenfassen, die auch heute noch Gültigkeit haben:

1.) die relative Arbitrarität der Zeichen,
2.) der Handlungscharakter des Redens,
3.) der Werkzeugcharakter der Sprache,
4.) die Funktionsbestimmung der Sprache: Kommunikation, Klassifikation und Repräsentation.[66]

Es empfiehlt sich, drei Betrachtungsebenen klar auseinanderhalten, wenn man über Zeichen, deren Beziehung zur kognitiven Welt und zur Welt der Dinge reden bzw. schreiben will, wie dies in der vorliegenden Arbeit geschehen soll:

1.) die linguistische Ebene der Zeichen (Wörter, Sätze)
2.) die epistemologische Ebene der kognitiven Korrelate (Begriffe, Propositionen) und
3.) die ontologische Ebene der Dinge, Wahrheitswerte und Sachverhalte.[67]

Ich möchte diese Unterscheidung für die vorliegende Arbeit übernehmen. Dementsprechend läßt sich über eine Verpackung, "Verpackung" und *Verpackung* diskutieren.

Bei einer Verpackung wird Bezug genommen auf die tatsächliche Hülle des Produktes. Die Schreibweise "Verpackung" erfolgt, wenn es um den Begriff der Verpackung geht, und wenn das Zeichen *Verpackung* eingesetzt wird, ist das deutsche Substantiv betroffen.[68]

---

66
vgl. Keller (1995), S. 35
67
Keller (1995), S. 36
68
Diese Kennzeichnung der Betrachtungsebenen gilt selbstverständlich auch für alle anderen Worte.

Mit dieser Festlegung ist ein Reglement für die Verwendung relativ beliebiger typographischer Zeichen festgelegt worden (normale Schrift - Bezug auf das reale Objekt, Anführungsstriche - Referenz auf den Begriff und kursive Schrift - betrifft das Substantiv). Die Festlegung dieser Regeln soll für den Leser eine Orientierungshilfe bieten, damit er die beabsichtigte Referenz leichter nachvollziehen kann.

Der Zeichenauffassung von Platon läßt sich das Zeichenmodell von Aristoteles gegenüberstellen.

Das Zeichenmodell Aristoteles' konstituiert sich aus drei zentralen Elementen und zwei Relationen:[69]

Laut ➔      Vorstellung       ➔   Ding
symbolisiert                        bildet ab
(konventionell)                     (natürlich)

Die Fortschritte der aristotelischen Theorie gegenüber Platons Modell lassen sich an folgenden Punkten festmachen:

1.)     Die Wahrheit und Falschheit wird nicht mehr Wörtern zuge-
        schrieben, sondern nur der Rede.
2.)     Die Bedeutung von Wörtern und Namen wird nicht als zu-
        sammengesetzt
        aus der Bedeutung von Wortteilen oder Lauten angesehen.

---

[69]
    vgl. Aristoteles (1920), S. 1; s. zur schematischen Darstellung auch
    Keller (1995), S. 38

59

3.) Die Bedeutung von Eigennamen wird nicht etymologisierend gedeutet.

4.) Symbolcharakter wird nur konventionell symbolisierenden Lauten zuge-sprochen. Damit wird eine erste Unterscheidung von Symbolen und Symptomen getroffen.

Keller weist auf drei Fehleinschätzungen für eine gebrauchsorientierte Zeichenauffassung aus heutiger Sicht hin:[70]

1.) Die Welt der Dinge sowie die der Vorstellungen wird objektivistisch konzipiert. Die Sprache ist für Aristoteles ein konventionelles Nomenklatursystem kognitiver Abbildungen vorgegebener Dinge.

2.) Konvention wird mit Übereinkunft gleichgesetzt.

3.) Die Relation des Symbolisierens bleibt unexpliziert.

Keller schlägt vor, das System unserer Begriffe nicht wie Aristoteles als Spiegel unserer Welt zu sehen, sondern als Spiegel unserer Auseinandersetzung mit der Welt.

Darüber hinaus wird eine Unterscheidung der Begriffe "Konvention" und "Übereinkunft" empfohlen.

„Konventionen" sind Verhaltensregelmäßigkeiten von Individuen, die durch die wechselseitigen Erwartungen des sozialen Umfeldes meist unbewußt erzeugt werden. „Übereinkünfte" sind hingegen explizite Absprachen. Dementsprechend sind sprachliche Zeichen in der Regel keine Erzeugnisse expliziter Übereinkünfte, sondern sie entstehen durch Konventionen.

---

[70] Keller (1995), S. 39

In den Texten auf Produktverpackungen sind ebenfalls hauptsächlich sprachliche Zeichen zu finden, die auf Konventionen beruhen. Jedoch sind die Texter von Verpackungsaufschriften immer wieder bemüht, sprachliche Zeichen einzusetzen, die durch explizite Absprachen kennengelernt und gelernt werden.

Die gängigen sprachlichen Zeichen, d.h. die, die durch Konventionen in den alltäglichen Sprachgebrauch übernommen werden, befinden sich auf Produktverpackungen von Standardkonsumartikeln, weil sie die Grundausstattung für ein Kommunikationsinstrument mit einer sehr hohen Verstehenswahrscheinlichkeit bieten - der deutschen Sprache.

Es ist jedoch Ziel der Anbieter, Akzente zu setzen, wo es nur geht. Dementsprechend bietet es sich an, auch die Sprache auf den Produktverpackungen dahingehend zu nutzen, das Produkt hervorzuheben. Zu diesem Zweck werden gerne gestalterisch beeinflußbare Elemente innovativ konzipiert. Wenn z.B. plötzlich das altbekannte Spülmittel „Palmolive" mit dem Zusatzlabel „ultra" angeboten wird, zeigt sich die Produktverpackung neu. Im Idealfall hebt sie sich ab und sticht ins Auge. Um dieses Ziel zu erreichen, werden z.B. Wortneuschöpfungen eingesetzt. Die Übereinkunft dieser Wortneuschöpfungen besteht darin, daß den Konsumenten in der Regel über die Werbung mitgeteilt wird, nach welcher Anwendungsregel das Wort eingesetzt wurde. Durch häufige Wiederholungen und ergänzende Erläuterungen auf der Verpackung lernt der Verbraucher den Gebrauch des Wortes - z.B. eines Produktnamens - kennen. Nach entsprechend häufigen Wiederholungen wird die Gebrauchsregel verinnerlicht und in das eigene Repertoire übernommen. Dann reicht lediglich das Wort als wahrnehmbarer Reiz, um als Reaktion das Abrufen der dazugehörigen Gebrauchsregel zu provozieren.

Ist z.B. der Markenname "Zewa" häufig genug in Verbindung mit dem Werbeslogan "wisch und weg" rezipiert worden, so daß der Begriff nach dem Schema der klassischen Konditionierung in Verbindung mit der dazugehörigen Gebrauchsregel verinnerlicht wurde, löst der Name "Zewa" die Anwendung der Gebrauchsregel aus - etwa "Zewa wisch und weg ist der Name für eine Küchenrolle".

Ebenso werden die Gebrauchsregeln für Begriffe gelernt, die durch Konventionen entstehen. Das Reizvolle bei der Gestaltung von Verpackungstexten ist die Chance, in erster Instanz Einfluß auf diese Konventionen zu nehmen, indem man Worte für den Verpackungstext neu konzipiert, die zunächst als Erzeugnisse einer individuellen Übereinkunft vorgestellt und eingeführt werden, um dann, wie alle anderen Worte, konventionell weiterverbreitet und verwendet zu werden.

Festzuhalten bleibt, daß Aristoteles mit seiner repräsentationistischen Zeichenkonzeption Wörter dahingehend charakterisiert, daß es ihre Aufgabe ist, Dinge zu bezeichnen, indem sie Vorstellungen symbolisieren, die Abbilder der Dinge sind.
Für Platon heißt kommunizieren, dem Adressaten Mittel an die Hand zu geben, die es ermöglichen, die Gedanken des Sprechers zu erschließen. Platons zentrale Frage ist dabei, wie es Wörter schaffen, etwas über Gedanken zu verraten. Ihm gelingt es nicht, die Frage angemessen zu beantworten.
Aristoteles dagegen stellt diese Frage erst gar nicht.

Die Frage ist für die Gestaltung und Interpretation von Verpackungstexten insofern relevant, als es nur möglich ist, Sprache auf diesem Medium gezielt einzusetzen, wenn man weiß, wie die Wirkungsmechanismen funktionieren. Aus diesem Grund gilt es, eine Antwort auf die Frage zu finden, die es erlaubt, eine Strategie zu entwickeln, die

Wirkungen von Sprache durch ihren gezielten Einsatz zu beeinflussen.

Zu Zeiten Aristoteles' und Platons gab es noch keine strenge Unterscheidung zwischen den Disziplinen Philosophie und Linguistik. Es ist nach wie vor Ziel der Philosophen, möglichst global zu denken und sich weniger in detaillierten Einzelanalysen zu verzetteln. Eine solch spezielle Einzelanalyse betrifft z.B. die Frage, wie der Mensch kommuniziert. Dieses Problem gehört zu den Arbeitsaufgaben der Linguistik. Darüber hinaus setzen sich auch immer wieder Philosophen mit derartigen Fragen auseinander. Dementsprechend sind viele sprachwissenschaftliche und zeichentheoretische Theorien vom philosophischen Denkkonzept beeinflußt. Für die Sprachwissenschaftler ergibt sich dadurch immer wieder Diskussionsbedarf.

Ähnlich, wie sich die Theorien Platons und Aristoteles' gegenüberstehen, bilden auch die zeichentheoretischen Konzeptionen Freges und Wittgensteins als moderne Vertreter ein Kontrastprogramm. Frege gilt als prototypischer Vertreter einer repräsentationistischen Zeichentheorie und Wittgenstein als Repräsentant einer instrumentalistischen Zeichenauffassung.

## 2.3 Modernere Modelle sprachlicher Zeichentheorien

Ein in der Linguistik viel diskutiertes Thema ist der Begriff „Bedeutung" Diese Diskussion wird derart wichtig erachtet, daß sich ein eigenes Forschungsgebiet, die Semantik, entwickeln konnte.

Am Beispiel der Namen demonstriert Keller die Schwierigkeit, die Bedeutung eines Namens in seinem tatsächlichen Referenzobjekt zu betrachten. Es gibt eine ganze Reihe von Namen, die kein tatsächliches Referenzobjekt haben, z.B. weil der Namensträger bereits verstorben oder eine Fantasiefigur ist. Dennoch sind diese Namen nicht bedeutungslos.

Es existieren noch immer Namen von Produkten, die eine Bedeutung haben, obwohl es das dazugehörige Produkt nicht mehr gibt; z.B. wissen Konsumenten der älteren Generation noch immer Namen wie "Banner"[71] dem Produkt Seife zuzuordnen.[72]

---

[71] Der Slogan zu der Seife lautete: „Banner bannt Körpergeruch".

[72] Insbesondere in der Automobilindustrie lassen sich eine Reihe von Namen finden, die einem Modell zugeordnet waren, das schon lange nicht mehr gebaut wird. Namen wie "DKW" und "Borgward" sind dennoch insbesondere für die Menschen, die diese Autos "live" erlebt haben, mit einer Gebrauchsregel verbunden und haben damit noch immer eine Bedeutung. Dabei stellt sich die Frage, warum Autonamen so gut behalten werden – so gut, daß "Mercedes" wieder einen "Maybach" auf den Markt bringen will, "Bugatti" von "VW" wieder gebaut wird und von "VW" sogar geplant wird, wieder einen "Horch" zu produzieren.Ein Auto war und ist ein Gebrauchsgegenstand, in dessen Abhängigkeit sich ihre Nutzer immer wieder gerne begeben. Darüber hinaus ist es Prestigeobjekt und Statussymbol. Ein Autokauf ist normalerweise eine gut überlegte und lang geplante Entscheidung. Eine ganze Reihe von Autobesitzern personifizieren ihr Auto und empfinden eine Art persönliche Beziehung zu ihrem Gefährt. Aus diesem Grund werden die Gebrauchsregeln des jeweiligen Fahrzeugnamens besonders gut verinnerlicht und behalten. Dementsprechend weiß jemand einen Autonamen noch über Jahre und Jahrzehnte adäquat zu verwenden, nachdem das letzte Modell gebaut wurde.

Frege ist es als Mathematiker ein Bedürfnis, Begriffe derart scharf zu begrenzen, daß man zweifelsfrei entscheiden kann, ob ein Gegenstand unter den Begriff fällt oder nicht.[73] Der Begriff „Primzahl" läßt sich als Begriff mit scharfen Rändern definieren, weil im Gegensatz zu allen anderen Zahlen bei der Eigenschaft der Teilbarkeit ausschließlich das Merkmal „teilbar durch 1 und sich selber" aufweist. Diese Bedingung ist ausreichend, um zu entscheiden, ob eine Zahl eine Primzahl ist oder nicht. Viele Begriffe, die wir alltäglich verwenden, lassen eine derart strenge Zuordnung nicht zu. Es handelt sich dann um Begriffe mit unscharfen Rändern. So handelt es sich in den meisten Fällen, in denen wir von „Wasser" reden nicht um das, was der strengen Definition von $H_2O$ entspricht, sondern um ein wasserähnliches flüssiges Gemisch mit verschieden Zusätzen. Weder Regenwasser ist reines Wasser noch unser Tafelwasser, geschweige denn unsere Haar-, Rasier-, oder Duftwässer.

Keller erläutert, daß die Unschärfe unserer Alltagsbegriffe durchaus kein Manko der natürlichen Sprachen ist. Eine Sprache, die nur aus Begriffen mit scharfen Rändern besteht, kann keine natürliche Alltagssprache sein, denn eine Präzisierungsverpflichtung steht einer Grundeigenschaft der Menschen entgegen - der Bequemlichkeit. Begriffe mit scharfen Rändern erfordern eine genaue Prüfung ihres Einsatzes im Gegensatz zu Begriffen mit unscharfen Rändern.

In der Werbung wird immer wieder versucht, Begriffe mit scharfen Rändern vorzustellen, nämlich dann, wenn es darum geht, einen Produktnamen bzw. eine Produktbezeichnung zu präsentieren, mit denen der Kunde im Laden auf den Verpackungen konfrontiert wird. In der Regel werden die scharfen Ränder den Verbrauchern über die ganz

---

[73]     vgl. Frege (1971), S. 90

65

speziellen produktspezifischen Eigenschaften und Leistungsmerk-
male suggeriert. Auch wenn es eine große Menge alternativer
Produkte gibt, sind alle Anbieter bemüht, ihr jeweiliges Angebot als
einzigartig herauszuheben. Bei einem Begriff mit scharfen Rändern
kann ganz klar entschieden werden, ob ein Gegenstand unter den
Begriff fällt oder nicht. Ziel der Anbieter ist es, die Ränder der Produktbezeichnung so scharf zu gestalten, daß ganz klar nur ihr
jeweiliges Produkt die Kriterien erfüllt, die der Begriff fordert. Um
zu vermeiden, daß auch andere Produkte die Kriterien erfüllen, ist es
notwendig, möglichst neue und bislang unbekannte Leistungsmerk-
male und Eigenschaften zur Charakterisierung des Angebotes zu
nennen. Die Kunden sollen lernen, anhand der Bezeichnung eines
Produktes zu erkennen, daß es strenge Kriterien erfüllt, um diese
Bezeichnung tragen zu dürfen. Zusätzlich sollen die Kunden glauben,
daß nur diese spezielle Kombination von Leistungsmerkmalen den
individuellen Bedürfnissen gerecht wird. Aus diesem Grund müssen
die Verbraucher z.B. lernen:

"Nur wo Nutella draufsteht, ist auch Nutella drin!"[74]

Allerdings interpretieren viele Anbieter die Begriffe selber großzügig
bzw. mit unscharfen Rändern, die sie als Bezeichnungen für die verschiedensten Produkte wählen, und die sie als Bezeichnungen mit
scharfen Rändern vorstellen.
Wenn man sich z.B. einmal anschaut, was alles als "Fruchtsaft" titu-
liert wird, stellt man fest, daß die Auffassungen differieren, was
darunter zu verstehen ist. Als Begriff mit scharfen Rändern ist

---

[74]    Werbeslogan für Nutella - ein Nuß-Nougat-Brotaufstrich. Problematisch
        für die Anbieter ist, daß der Produktname zum Gattungsnamen fürNuß-
        Nougatcremes geworden ist, was es un-bedingt zu verhindern gilt, wenn
        man will, daß die Kunden ein bestimmtes Produkt kaufen.

Fruchtsaft der Saft echter Früchte, wie es in der Werbung gerne gezeigt wird (beckers bester, Valensina). Schaut man auf den Produktverpackungen in dem Verzeichnis der Zutaten diverser "Fruchtsäfte" nach, zeigt sich, daß von Seiten der Anbieter der Begriff vielfältig ausgelegt wird, für alle möglichen Säfte, die irgendwie nach Frucht zu schmecken scheinen. So findet man unter den Zutaten Hinweise auf Wasser, Zucker, Farbstoffe u.ä., die auf eine künstliche Flüssigkeit schließen lassen. Streng genommen handelt es sich in dem Moment nicht mehr um Fruchtsaft, in dem der Flüssigkeit ein weiterer Inhaltsstoff beigemengt wird - sondern um ein Fruchtmixgetränk.

Anbieter von Marken wie „Valensina", „beckers bester" und „rio d'oro" versuchen, ihre Produkte abzuheben, indem sie den Begriff "Fruchtsaft" präzisieren und mit scharfen Grenzen definieren. Die Präzisierung erfolgt allerdings nach ihrem individuellen Gusto. Die drei Produkte werden in den Medien und auf den Verpackungen damit beworben und charakterisiert, daß der Saft nur von ausgewählten und "sonnenverwöhnten" Orangen (Valensina, rio d'oro) stammt. Damit wird ein Akzent gesetzt, der ein optimiertes Preis-Leistungsverhältnis vorstellen soll.

In besonders strittigen Fällen hilft der Gesetzgeber beim Abstecken der Ränder einer Bezeichnung nach.

Wie großzügig man bei der Interpretation von Produktbezeichnungen verfahren kann, zeigt Loewy mit einem Beispiel. Allgemein sind "Drops" als ungefüllte kleine runde und leicht säuerliche Fruchtbonbons aus England bekannt. Dementsprechend verunsichert ist man als Kunde, wenn auf einer repräsentativen Packung "Drops" nach dem Nahrungsmittelgesetz pflichtgemäß zu lesen steht:

"Hergestellt aus Natriumglutomat, dehydriertem Albumin, Glyzerin, Kohlenwasserstoffderivaten, Glukose, Holzkohle, Lezitin, benzoesaurem Natron, Zitronen- und Kleesäure unter Verwendung künstlicher Aromen und garantiert unschädlicher Farbstoffe."[75]

Hinter dieser Produktbeschreibung hätte sich ebensogut ein hochchemischer Reiniger verbergen können. Für Konkurrenzanbieter wäre es hier leicht, eine Alternative zu präsentieren, indem die Ränder des Begriffes "drops" als Bonbon aus Frucht verschärft werden. Ein Bonbon aus reiner Frucht bietet nicht nur ein abgehobenes Leistungsmerkmal, sondern auch ein Argument für einen höheren Preis.

Keller kritisiert an Freges repräsentationistischer Theorie, daß sie keine Antwort auf die Fragen gibt, was man kennt, wenn man eine Sprache hinreichend kennt, und worin das sprachliche Wissen besteht, über das man verfügt, wenn man den Inhalt eines Zeichens kennt. Er erläutert, daß rein repräsentationistische Theorien nicht vorgeben und auch nicht vorgeben sollten, zu beschreiben, wie wir Sätze verstehen. Ein derartiger Erklärungsversuch würde voraussetzen, daß erläutert wird, wie Repräsentation zustande kommt. Einen Logiker wie Frege interessiert jedoch der inhaltliche Teil, der das ausmacht, was er den Sinn nennt.[76]

Einen weiteren zeichentheoretischen Ansatz bieten Theorien, die auf der Vorstellung eines sogenannten "Common Sense" aller Menschen basieren. Als Vertreter einer solchen Theorie ist Peirce zu nennen. Er erläutert den Common Sense als Orientierungsleistung, die wir alle

---

[75] Loewy (1953), S. 269

[76] vgl. Frege (1969) S. 105 und 128ff, vgl. auch Keller (1995), S. 5

als Ausgangspunkt gemeinsam haben. Nach ihm gilt für uns Menschen:

"Indem wir uns für Ziele entscheiden, legen wir fest, nicht nur wer wir sein werden, sondern wie unsere Welt beschaffen sein wird."[77]

Nach dem Common Sense haben die Menschen viele Vorstellungen gemein. Die Anhänger der sogenannten Vorstellungstheorien vertreten die Auffassung, daß die Bedeutung der sprachlichen Zeichen die Vorstellung ist, die mit ihnen verbunden ist. Sprachliche Zeichen dienen dem Transport von Vorstellungen, die von einem Sprecher dekodiert und von einem Hörer enkodiert werden. Die Verständigung funktioniert, weil alle Sprecher einer Sprache über einen Common Sense an Vorstellungen verfügen.

Keller macht auf eine Reihe von Problemen bei der Anwendung dieser sogenannten Vorstellungstheorien aufmerksam.[78]

Demnach läßt sich diese Theorie am ehesten an Wörtern *wie Haus, Auto, schwimmen, backen* etc. nachvollziehen. Diese Begriffe beziehen sich auf konkrete und sichtbare Gegenstände und Handlungen, die in der Regel alle Sprecher einer Sprache wahrnehmen können. Die mit den Wörtern verbundenen Vorstellungen lassen sich auch einigermaßen zuverlässig testen, indem man z.B. Versuchspersonen die Begriffe nennt und dazu die Bilder malen oder darauf zeigen läßt. Ganz unzuverlässig testen läßt sich jedoch, welche Vorstellungen Personen mit Worten wie *abstrakt, Gedanke, unendlich* u.s.w. verbinden. Auch wenn man Testpersonen Definitionen oder Erläuterungen zu den einzelnen Begriffen finden läßt, kann man nicht

---

[77]   Peirce (1993), S. 7

[78]   vgl. Keller (1995), S. 58

69

davon ausgehen, daß die Ergebnisse ein zuverlässiges Bild ergeben, ob und wenn ja, inwieweit die Vorstellungen deckungsgleich sind.

Bei der Annahme, daß die Bedeutung eines Ausdrucks die damit verbundene Vorstellung ist, kommt man darüber hinaus in Erklärungsnotstand, wenn man sich fragt, mit welcher Bedeutung sprich Vorstellung der Begriff "Vorstellung" verbunden ist.

Geht man davon aus, daß Vorstellungen eine Art geistiger Bilder sind, so können diese selber nur verstanden werden, wenn sie interpretiert werden.

Ein weiteres Problem dieser Theorie ergibt sich aus der dazugehörigen Didaktik. Vorstellungen lassen sich insbesondere dann schwer vermitteln, wenn Worte dazu verwendet werden, sich auf einer abstrakten Ebene auszudrücken. Darüber hinaus ist eine Kontrolle von Vorstellungen genauso schwierig wie ihr Vergleich. Wenn Kommunikation aus einem reinen Austausch von Vorstellungen bestünde, so müßte man diese auch mittels anderer Medien als der Sprache austauschen können.

"Eine Vorstellung haben" setzt ein Verstandenhaben voraus.[79] Man kann eine Vorstellung erst dann haben, wenn man einen Ausdruck richtig verstanden hat. Es ist unmöglich, eine Vorstellung von einem Begriff zu haben, bevor man ihn verstanden hat. Daraus ergibt sich, daß Vorstellungen eher Begleiterscheinungen des Kommunizierens, nicht aber sein substantieller Bestandteil sind.

Dementsprechend hat jemand einen auch nicht mißverstanden, wenn er sich bei dem Wort *Urlaub* Sonne, Meer und Strand vorstellt, während man selbst vom Klettern in den Bergen träumt. Dieser Mensch hat lediglich eine falsche Hypothese von dem, was für den anderen Urlaub ist.

---

[79] vgl. Keller (1995), S. 59ff

Es wäre keinesfalls widersprüchlich, wenn dieser Mensch behauptet, mich zwar vollständig verstanden zu haben, sich aber keinesfalls einen solchen Urlaub vorstellen kann. Eine Äußerung richtig verstanden zu haben ist unabhängig davon, eine Vorstellung zu haben, die in der Intention des Sprechers liegt.

Ein sprachlicher Ausdruck kann über seine Bedeutung eine Vorstellung erwecken. Jedoch ist die Vorstellung nicht die Bedeutung selbst. Eine Beschreibung eines Produktes wie „Scheibletten" kann mir eine Vorstellung vermitteln. Dazu muß ich aber erst die Beschreibung verstanden haben. Das wiederum setzt voraus, daß ich die Bedeutung der Worte bzw. ihre Gebrauchsregeln in der Sprache kenne.

Die Vorstellungstheorie läßt sich nur dann auf die sprachlichen Zeichen auf Produktverpackungen anwenden, wenn man es lediglich bei einer Untersuchung der Produktbezeichnungen beläßt. Mit etwas Glück ließe sich vielleicht auch noch die ein oder andere Ge- oder Verbrauchsanweisung mit Hilfe dieser Theorie erläutern.

Nach der Vorstellungstheorie würden die Produktbezeichnungen die Vorstellungen des Produktes transportieren, das sich in der Verpackung befindet. Als vorstellungsunterstützende Maßnahmen ließen sich dann die Abbildungen des Produktes im originalen oder im verwendeten Zustand auf der Verpackung interpretieren.

Problematisch wird es, mit dieser Theorie die Worte auf Produktverpackungen zu erklären, die sich nicht auf einen Gegenstand beziehen. So sind z.B. Geruchs- und Geschmacksrichtungen sinnlich wahrnehmbar, sie unterliegen aber dennoch dem individuellen Geschmack. Was für den einen scharf ist, ist für einen anderen fad und was für den einen frisch wie Zitrone riecht, riecht für den nächsten möglicherweise unangenehm aufdringlich. Vorstellungen von etwas können individuell verschieden sein.

Geschmackshinweise wie "Pfefferminze" und "Hagebutte" auf Tee-verpackungen lassen sich vorstellungstheoretisch dahingehend erläutern, daß diese Begriffe zum Transport der Vorstellungen eines Tees vom Anbieter eingesetzt werden, der nach Pfefferminze oder nach Hagebutte schmeckt. Nun müßte der Verbraucher nach der Common-Sense-Theorie die Botschaft entschlüsseln und seine Vor-stellung von Pfefferminz- und Hagebuttentee abfragen. Es stellt sich die Frage, wie diese Botschaft vorstellungstheoretisch zu interpretie-ren ist, wenn jemand noch nie Pfefferminz- oder Hagebuttentee probiert hat und dementsprechend keine Vorstellung dazu abrufen kann, obwohl er in der Lage ist, die Teesortenbezeichnung adäquat zu verwenden.

Noch weniger lassen sich Geschmackshinweise wie "Märchenzau-ber" oder "Tropenfeuer" mit dieser Theorie erläutern oder Geruchshinweise wie "Poison" oder "Aprilfrische". Erstens stellt sich bei diesen Ausdrücken jeweils die Frage, wie es möglich ist, damit einen Geschmack oder einen Geruch zu bezeichnen, denn es handelt sich um keinen konkreten, für jeden sinnlich wahrnehmbaren Geruch oder Geschmack, sondern um Bezeichnungen, die einen Geruch cha-rakterisieren und die Interpretation durch die Verbraucher kanalisieren sollen. Bei derartigen Bezeichnungen können die Kun-den, die den Tee bereits einmal probiert haben, eine Vorstellung des Geschmacks abfragen, die auf der Erfahrung des Probierens beruht. Diejenigen, die einen solchen Tee noch nicht probiert haben, können keine erfahrungsbedingte Vorstellung abrufen. Ihnen bleibt nichts anderes übrig, als sich im Geiste ein Bild davon zu machen, wie ein solcher Tee nach dieser Beschreibung wohl schmecken könnte – sie müßten sich quasi eine Vorstellung von der Vorstellung machen. Das Problem ist, daß ich mir nur eine Vorstellung von einem Produkt wie „Pfefferminztee" machen kann, wenn ich die Bedeutung von Pfef-ferminztee kenne.

Es zeigt sich, daß man mit einem vorstellungstheoretischen Erläuterungsansatz die vorgestellten Beispiele nicht optimal erklären kann. Der Ansatz reicht nicht aus, um konkret die Frage zu beantworten, welche Mechanismen durch Sprache auf Verpackungen ausgelöst werden, damit ein Produkt tatsächlich gekauft wird, und wie dieses Verhalten nachhaltig beeinflußt werden kann.

Es empfiehlt sich deshalb, eine andere Theorie als Erläuterungsmodell heranzuziehen.

Keller erläutert, daß das Haben oder Nicht-Haben von Vorstellungen völlig irrelevant ist "für die Frage, was der Sprecher meint mit dem, was er sagt und was der Hörer versteht."[80]

Seiner Auffassung nach sind Vorstellungen keine Bestandteile des Kommunizierens.

Er definiert dazu passend „Bedeutung" nicht als das, was kommuniziert ist, sondern als das, was Kommunizieren ermöglicht.

"Der Begriff der Bedeutung soll den Aspekt der Interpretierbarkeit des Zeichens erklären."[81]

Wenn wir uns des Kommunikationsinstrumentes Sprache bedienen und etwas meinen, liegt die Absicht unserer Äußerung darin, unsere Adressaten zu einer bestimmten Interpretation zu bewegen. Ziel ist es, über die Bedeutung herauszufinden, wie es möglich ist, daß der Adressat erkennt, was der Sprecher meint, bzw. wie der Sprecher es schafft, dem Adressaten zu erkennen zu geben, was er meint.

Die gebrauchstheoretischen Erläuterungen Wittgensteins zum Begriff der Bedeutung bieten eine geeignete Grundlage für eine gebrauchso-

---

[80]    Keller (1995), S. 60
[81]    Keller (1995), S. 61

73

rientierte Theorie. Wittgenstein formuliert eine neue Perspektive der Bedeutung eines Wortes mit der Aussage:

"Die Bedeutung eines Wortes ist sein Gebrauch in der Sprache".[82]

Wenn die Bedeutung eines Wortes als sein Gebrauch in der Sprache definiert wird, so muß man unterscheiden zwischen dem jeweiligen situationsabhängigen individuellen Gebrauch mit einer augenblicklichen Intention und einem allgemeinen Gebrauch in verschiedenen möglichen Situationen mit verschiedenen möglichen Intentionen.

Keller erläutert, daß man einen Sprecher verstanden haben muß, um die Bedeutung seiner Wörter zu kennen. Daraus folgt, daß die Bedeutung nichts sein kann, was einem beim Verstehen hilft. Folglich ist die Bedeutung die Basis des Verstehens und nicht dessen Ergebnis. Daraus ergibt sich für Keller, "daß mit dem Ausdruck *Gebrauch* nicht einzelne Gebrauchsinstanzen gemeint sein können, sondern nur die Gebrauchsweise in der Sprache, die Regel des Gebrauchs."[83]

Keller faßt die Grundaussagen der Wittgensteinschen Definition von „Bedeutung" wie folgt zusammen:

"Die Bedeutung eines Wortes einer Sprache L besteht in seiner Gebrauchsweise innerhalb von L. Das gilt für alle Wörter einer Sprache. Wenn du weißt, wie ein Wort verwendet wird, wenn du die Regel seines Gebrauches in der Sprache L kennst, weißt du alles, was es zu wissen gibt. Wenn du jemandem die Bedeutung eines Wortes bei-

---

[82]    Wittgenstein (1994), § 43

[83]    Keller (1995), S. 65

74

bringen willst, so bringe ihm bei, wie dieses Wort in der Sprache verwendet wird."[84]

Nach genau diesem Prinzip funktioniert die Werbung, wenn es darum geht, den Kunden die Gebrauchsregel einer Wortneuschöpfung oder eine neue Regel eines bereits bekannten Wortes beizubringen, die dazu dient, ein Produkt zu bezeichnen oder zu charakterisieren. Es wird erläutert, nach welcher Regel das Wort verwendet wird - für ein Produkt mit den Eigenschaften x, y, z und nur für dieses Produkt. So lernen die Verbraucher beispielsweise über die Werbung, daß der Name „elmex" auf einer Zahnpastatube nur dann auf selbiger steht, wenn sich in der Tube eine medizinische Zahncreme befindet, die sensible Zähne und freiliegende Zahnhälse vor Zahnhalskaries schützt.

Ein bereits bekanntes Wort, das mit einer neuen Gebrauchsregel als Produktbezeichnung vorgestellt wird, ist der Name "Bounty". "Bounty" ist bereits bekannt als Name für einen Schokoriegel mit Kokosraspelfüllung. Jetzt wird dem Verbraucher in der Werbung vermittelt, daß der Name "Bounty" auch mit einer neuen Gebrauchsregel verwendet wird, nämlich dann, wenn sich in der dazugehörigen Verpackung "DIE TOLLE SUPER-SAUGWEG WISCHKRAFT-ROLLE" befindet. Damit die Kunden diese Gebrauchsregel nicht bis zu ihrem nächsten Einkauf vergessen, ist der Werbeslogan zur Erinnerung noch einmal neben dem Namen auf der Verpackung aufgedruckt.

Produkteigenschaften wie z.B. "knisprig" (Vienetta) oder "Anti-Aging-System" (Coral) werden dem Kunden ebenfalls über die Erläuterung in der Werbung und auch auf der Verpackung beigebracht und visuell veranschaulicht. In der Vienetta-Eis-Werbung wird den

---

[84] Keller (1995), S. 65

Kunden das Geräusch und das Wohlbehagen vorgeführt, das knispriges Eis bei einem romantischen Zwei-Personendinner auslöst.

Das "Anti-Aging-System" des Waschmittels „Coral" wird den Kunden als besonderes farberhaltendes Waschsystem vorgeführt. Die Kunden lernen über die Werbung und den Verpackungsaufdruck, daß das "Anti-Aging-System" besonders gut Verfärbungen und Ausbleichen der Wäsche verhindert. Damit wird den Verbrauchern die konkrete Verwendungsregel des Wortes in der Sprache beigebracht. Darüber hinaus soll den Kunden zusätzlich eine zweite Regel beigebracht werden: Ein Waschmittel ist dann mit "Anti-Aging-System" ausgestattet, wenn es besonders gut zum häufigen Waschen bunter Sachen geeignet ist. Wenn man häufig bunte Kleidungsstücke wäscht, sollte man Waschmittel mit "Anti-Aging-System" verwenden. Es gibt nur ein Waschmittel, daß die Bedingungen der Gebrauchsregel für das "Anti-Aging-System" erfüllt - das Waschmittel Coral, aus diesem Grund sollte Coral gekauft werden.

Es gibt Worte, die mehrere Bedeutungen haben, d.h. es existieren mehrere Regeln ihres Gebrauchs in der Sprache. Ein Beispiel für ein solches Wort ist "scheinen". Eine Gebrauchsregel für dieses Wort ist, daß es verwendet wird, um eine „Aktivität" der Sonne zu charakterisieren. Eine weitere Gebrauchsregel für dieses Wort ist, es zu verwenden, um auszudrücken, daß etwas einen Eindruck erweckt.

Die Tatsache, daß für ein Wort mehrere Gebrauchsregeln in einer Sprache existieren, soll nicht zu dem Trugschluß führen, daß ein Wort je nach Situation, Kontext und der Intention des Sprechers verschiedene Bedeutungen hat. Wenn man davon ausgeht, daß Bedeutungen dazu dienen, als Sprecher etwas meinen zu können, so wäre das Verständnis untereinander unmöglich, wenn die Bedeutung mit dem gleichgesetzt wird, was verschiedene Sprecher von Äußerung zu Äußerung meinen. Damit ein Adressat herausfinden kann, was mit einer Äußerung in einer bestimmten Situation beabsichtigt wurde, muß es ein übergeordnetes Konzept geben, das situations-und kontextunabhängig ist. Dieses Konzept kann durchaus mehrere Gebrauchseinsätze in unterschiedlichen Verwendungssituationen vorsehen. Sender und Adressaten ist das Konzept bekannt. Der Sender verwendet normalerweise seine Ausdrücke nach den konzeptionalisierten Gebrauchsregeln. Dementsprechend kann der Adressat mit dem Wissen um diese Konzepte die Äußerungen quasi rückinterpretieren.

Die Bedeutung einer Schachfigur zu kennen, heißt zu wissen, wie man sie ziehen darf und wie nicht. Jedoch ist es etwas anderes, die Bedeutung bzw. die Möglichkeiten zu kennen, eine Figur zu ziehen, als den Sinn eines bestimmten Zuges von einem Spielpartner zu verstehen. Zusammenfassend bleibt festzuhalten:

"Die Bedeutung ist eine Technik, und genau deshalb können wir sie lehren und lernen und modifizieren."[85]

Darüber hinaus bleibt zu bemerken, daß sich in diesem Zusammenhang kein neues Repräsentationsverhältnis einschleicht. Die Bedeutung eines Wortes wird nicht durch den Gebrauch repräsentiert, sondern die Bedeutung eines Wortes ist sein regelhafter Gebrauch in der Sprache.

Die beiden Grundprobleme der repräsentationistischen und der instrumentalistischen Zeichentheorie lassen sich wie folgt auseinanderdividieren:

---

[85] Keller (1995), S. 66f

- Das Grundproblem einer repräsentationistisch begründeten Zeichenauffassung ist ein Transportproblem:
Wie schaffen die Zeichen es, Ideen von A nach B zu transportieren?

- Dagegen ist das Grundproblem einer instrumentalistisch begründeten Zeichenauffassung ein Beeinflussungsproblem:
Wie bekomme ich meine Adressaten dazu, zu erkennen, was ich denke, was ich von dir möchte, was du tun oder glauben sollst?
Die Zeichen werden als Mittel der Beeinflussung konzipiert.
Sie haben deshalb den Charakter spezieller Werkzeuge. [86]

Die zweite Zeichenauffassung hat genau das Problem zur Grundlage, daß auch viele Texter für Werbung und damit auch für Verpackungsaufdrucke beschäftigt: Wie kann ich meine Adressaten dahingehend beeinflussen, das zu tun, was ich möchte - mein Produkt zu kaufen? Allerdings ist die Problemstellung für die Texter insofern verkompliziert, als die Adressaten nicht unbedingt den Eindruck gewinnen sollen, daß das einzige übergeordnete Ziel der Äußerungen auf Verpackungen ist, daß sie die Verpackung in den Einkaufswagen legen und kaufen.

Die Problemstellung läßt sich demnach aus instrumentalistischer Perspektive auf die Verpackungen angewendet wie folgt formulieren:

Wie beeinflusse ich als Texter die Verbraucher dahingehend, zu erkennen, was ich möchte, was sie glauben sollen, und wie schaffe ich es, daß die Verbraucher das Produkt kaufen und dabei das Gefühl haben, das Produkt aus eigenem Antrieb zu kaufen und nicht nur, weil ich das will?

---

[86]    vgl. Keller (1995), S. 73f

78

Das Phänomen der Begriffe mit scharfen und mit unscharfen Rändern sowie deren Einsatz als Verpackungsaufschriften wurde bereits erläutert. Es ist eine weitere Klasse von Begriffen zu ergänzen, mit der sich ebenfalls Wirkungen im Konsumgütermarketing erzielen lassen - die Begriffe mit Prototypenstruktur.

Prototypenstrukturen sind bereits aus der Biologie bekannt. Man hat eine Versuchsreihe mit jungen Möwen durchgeführt, um zu überprüfen, ob es einen Prototyp der Möwen gibt, auf das die Jungvögel reagieren. Den Jungmöwen wurden Schnabel-attrappen in verschiedenen Formen und Farben vorgehalten. Dabei wurde ihre Re-aktion getestet. Es stellte sich schnell heraus, daß die jungen Vögel nur auf Schnabelattrappen reagierten, die eine dem Original ähnliche Form hatten, ähnlich groß waren, eine ähnlich gelbe Farbe und vor allem einen roten Punkt an der Seite hatten. Die Vögel reagierten nicht, wenn die Attrappe originalgetreu nachgebildet war, aber der rote Punkt fehlte. Die Reaktion der Vögel äußerte sich durch ein Klopfen gegen den Schnabel, als Zeichen, Futter aufnehmen zu wollen.

Aus diesem Versuch ging hervor, daß die Schnabelform und -farbe zwar ein wichtiges Erkennungsmerkmal bei Möwen ist, daß das Prototyp eines Möwenschnabels aber nur durch das Merkmal „roter Punkt an der Seite" vollständig ist und beim Möwennachwuchs eine entsprechende Reaktion hervorruft.[87]

Auch in der Linguistik wurden Experimente zur Erforschung von Prototypen durchgeführt. Eleonor Rosch hat eine Reihe bekannter Studien zur Erforschung der Prototypikalität von Begriffen vorgestellt. Mit diesen Versuchen konnte gezeigt werden, daß verschiedene

---

[87] Eine anschauliche Darstellung der Reizewirkung von Möwenschnabelattrappen befindet sich in: Vogel/Angermann (1984b), S. 405

Versuchspersonen einheitlich diverse Elemente einer Kategorie als unterschiedlich typische Beispiele für eine Kategorie beurteilten. So wurden z.B. Rotkehlchen und Spatzen als typischere Vertreter der Kategorie "Vogel" bewertet als Hühner und Gänse. Jedoch wurden Hühner und Gänse wiederum als typischere Vertreter dieser Kategorie gewertet als Strauße und Pinguine. Die Beurteilung als bevorzugt typischer Vertreter der Kategorie wurde mit der Länge der Reaktionszeit bemessen. Je schneller ein Proband einen Begriff einer Kategorie zuordnen konnte, desto prototypischer erschien dieser ihm für die Kategorie.[88]

Selbst Prototypentheoretiker sind sich uneinig, welche Aussagen aufgrund dieser Ergebnisse in bezug auf die Prototypikalität von Begriffen getroffen werden können.

Keller schließt sich hier der Auffassung von Lakoff an, daß die Leute ein bestimmtes kognitives Modell z.B. des Begriffs "Vogel" haben und daraus die unterschiedlichen Bewertungen dessen resultieren, was ein typischer und was ein untypischerer Vogel ist. Dementsprechend beurteilen wir einen Gegenstand, der unser Stereotyp erfüllt, als prototypisch.[89]

Bei der Auseinandersetzung mit der Prototypikalität von Begriffen ergibt sich erneut die Gefahr, in eine repräsentationistische Perspektive zu verfallen. Es gilt immer zu bedenken, daß es zwar durchaus möglich ist, ein kognitives Modell zu einem Begriff im Kopf zu haben, aber daß man dieses kognitive Modell im Rahmen der instrumentalistischen Zeichentheorie unabhängig von der Bedeutung des Begriffes auffaßt.

---

[88] Rosch (1975)

[89] vgl. Lakoff (1987), S. 39ff und Keller (1995), S. 91f

Für Produktverpackungen sind Zeichen mit Prototypenstruktur insofern interessant, als jede Verpackung dem Kunden zwar etwas Neues
und von den anderen Verpackungen Verschiedenes zu bieten haben
sollte, gleichzeitig aber auch etwas Vertrautes, das ein Wiedererkennen ermöglicht. Die meisten Produktverpackungen sind prototypisch
konzipiert.

Die äußere Gestalt der Produktverpackungen ist das erste Zeichen,
das im Laden auf die Wahrnehmungsorgane der Verbraucher einwir-
ken kann. Wenn man einmal die Regalreihen entlangläuft, fällt auf,
daß z.B. Geschirrspülmittel von den verschiedensten Anbietern in
ganz ähnlichen Plastikflaschen verkauft wird. Auch die Waschmittelkartons ähneln sich fast alle, ebenso die Verpackung der meisten
anderen Reiniger. Zwar wird heutzutage zusätzlich zwischen Kom-
paktwaschmitteln, Reinigungskonzentraten, Vollwaschmitteln und
Vollreinigern unterschieden, aber in den jeweiligen Kategorien sind
die Verpackungen von der Form her fast identisch. Ebenso wird Kaffee in der Regel in rechteckigen 500g-Blöcken angeboten, Zahncreme
in Tuben oder Dosierspendern, Cremes im Töpfchen, Müsli und
Cornflakes im 375g-Karton, Schokolade als Tafel, Marmelade im
Glas u.v.m.

Die Verpackung wird meistens den Alternativprodukten ähnlich gestaltet, weil die Verbraucher ein prototypisches Konzept von einer
Verpackung für ein bestimmtes Produkt im Kopf haben und im Laden den Blick sekundenschnell über die Regale schweifen lassen. Die
Verpackung, die dabei dem Stereotyp entspricht, wird als Zeichen für
eine bestimmtes Produkt wahrgenommen und mit Interesse fokussiert. In der Regel stehen die konkurrierenden Produkte der
verschiedenen Anbieter nach Warengruppen sortiert nebeneinander
im Ladenregal. Aus diesem Grund wird der Blick der Kunden meist
durch eine ganze Regalreihe oder - spalte stereotyp aussehender Verpackungen fixiert. Dann erst kommen die Unterschiede zum Tragen.

So werden die verschiedenen Geschirrspülmittel bevorzugt in einer jeweils anderen Farbe präsentiert, und bei Waschmitteln sowie bei den anderen Produkten variiert die Verpackungsgestaltung deutlich.

Wenn eine gänzlich neue Verpackungsform für ein Produkt eingeführt werden soll, ist es ratsam, den Kunden diese neue Form über eine entsprechend konzipierte Werbung vorzustellen und zu erläutern. Im Idealfall gelingt es, den Verbrauchern über die Werbung zu vermitteln, daß eine bestimmte neue Verpackungsform ein Zeichen für ein bestimmtes Produkt ist. Ein Beispiel für die Einführung einer neuen prototypischen Verpackung sind die Kartons für Kompaktwaschmittel. Man war jahrzehntelang die riesigen 10kg-Kartons oder Trommeln gewohnt. Darüber hinaus wurde Waschmittel häufig nach dem Motto "viel wirkt viel" verwendet. Den Konsumenten mußte nun erklärt werden, daß es durchaus möglich ist, mit weniger Menge mehr Waschkraft zu erreichen. Dazu wurden noch eine Reihe anderer Vorteile des kleineren Waschmittelkartons vorgestellt, z.B. der leichtere Transport, die Platzersparnis und eine größere Umweltverträglichkeit. Hat eine Firma erst einmal den Anfang gemacht und mühsam über viel (kosten)intensive Werbung eine neue Verpackung etabliert, ist es ein leichtes für die anderen Anbieter, nachzuziehen und die neue Verpackungsform ebenfalls als Zeichen für die eigene Produktalternative aus derselben Warengruppe anzubieten.

Besonders Me-too-Anbieter profitieren von prototypischen Verpackungen als Zeichen für ein sogenanntes „No-Name"-Produkt[90]. Ein schönes Beispiel hierzu sind die sogenannten "Billigmarken", die für Aldi u.ä. Superketten hergestellt werden. So wird z.B. Frischkäse wie "Bressot" und "Le Tatare" in kleinen runden Töpfchen mit Plastik-

---

[90] Vor allem bei Hygienepapieren, bei Tiefkühlkost und ist vielen Verbrauchern die Marke egal. Mehr auf die Marke geachtet wird bei Süßwaren und Alkohol. (vgl. Ahlert, B.(Hg): „Der Griff zu ‚No Name'", Wirtschaftsteil der Eckernförder Zeitung, 07.10 1999)

deckel verkauft. Im Aldi-Geschäft stehen fast die gleichen Töpfchen, ebenfalls mit Frischkäse als Inhalt. Der einzige Unterschied ist lediglich der Produktname, z.B. "Miree" und der niedrigere Preis. Die Kunden kaufen wegen des optischen Stereotyps der Verpackung ein Produkt, das sie aufgrund der mit dem Markenprodukt identischen Verpackung weitere markenidentische Merkmale in bezug auf eine positive Qualität des Inhaltes assoziieren läßt.

Darüber hinaus liegt es im Interesse der Anbieter von Standardkonsumartikeln, Produktbezeichnungen zu etablieren, die von den Verbrauchern prototypischer bewertet werden als andere. Dies läßt sich größtenteils durch hochfrequente Werbung erreichen. Da mittlerweile Waschmittel, Schokolade und alle möglichen anderen Standardkonsumartikel genauso zum täglichen Leben dazugehören wie Vögel, Pflanzen etc., lernen Kinder auch von ihren Eltern, was typische Vertreter für Waschmittel, Geschirrspülmittel, Schokolade etc. sind. Die Kinder lernen dabei diejenigen Produkte als typische Vertreter kennen, die die Eltern vorzugsweise benutzen. Darüber hinaus ist es möglich, das Kaufverhalten der Durchschnittsverbraucher über die Werbung zumindest dahingehend zu beeinflussen, daß sie ein neues Produkt kennenlernen, in ihren Wissensbestand integrieren und vielleicht sogar einmal ausprobieren. Das heißt, es ist durchaus möglich, daß ein Verbraucher ein Produkt nicht selber verwendet, es aber dennoch als typischen Vertreter einer Gattung benennen kann.

So sind z.B. Begriffe wie "Pril" und "Palmolive" typische Vertreter für Geschirrspülmittel, "Tempo" für Taschentücher, "Persil" für Waschmittel, "Milka" für Schokolade, "Tesa" für einen durchsichtigen Klebestreifen u.v.m.

Jedoch liegt in der Prototypikalität von Begriffen, die ein Produkt bezeichnen, auch eine Gefahr. Ist ein Begriff erst einmal zu *dem* prototypischen Vertreter einer Warengattung geworden, wird dieser Begriff oft dergestalt in die Alltagssprache übernommen und konventionalisiert, daß er als Produktname die ursprünglich allgemeinsprachliche Bezeichnung des Gegenstandes ersetzt. Dann wird z.B. um ein "Tempo" gebeten, wenn man ein Papiertaschentuch haben möchte, um "Uhu", wenn man Flüssigkleber braucht u.s.w. Die für das Marketing negativen Aspekte dieses Phänomens werden in dem Kapitel über die Symbole und das symbolische Interpretationsverfahren erläutert.

Wie bereits erwähnt, dient die Sprache unter anderem der Klassifikation. In diesem Zusammenhang ist auf zwei Phänomene aufmerksam zu machen, die auch auf Verpackungen Verwendung finden, um eine Einordnung in das Warensortiment zu ermöglichen bzw. um die Struktur eines Produktes erkennen zu lassen.

Es handelt sich bei diesen beiden Phänomenen um Taxonomien und Meronomien.[91] Taxonomien strukturieren Klassen in Teilklassen, und Meronomien strukturieren Gegenstände in Teile. So ist z.B. die Produktbezeichnung "Orangennektar" ein Teil folgender Taxonomie:

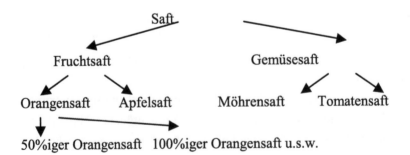

---

[91]     vgl. Cruse (1991), S136ff, s. auch Keller (1995), S. 95f

84

Meronomien strukturieren z.B. Produkte in ihre Teile. Ein anschauliches Beispiel bieten hierfür sämtliche technische Geräte, die in den dazugehörigen Bedienungsanleitungen zerlegt vorgestellt und erläutert werden. Eine Meronomie umfaßt bei den Standardkonsumartikeln z.b. aber auch die einzelnen Bestandteile einer Backmischung.

Die Festlegung einer Taxonomie durch die Anbieter kann durchaus nützlich sein, wenn ein Produkt auf dem Markt positioniert werden soll. Man kann mit Hilfe einer Taxonomie seinen genauen Standpunkt bestimmen. Dabei finden sich mit etwas Glück Lücken, die noch nicht durch ein anderes Produkt abgedeckt werden - sogenannte Marktlücken, die es einem Anbieter zumindest eine Zeit lang erlauben, konkurrenzlos eine Marktführungsposition innezuhaben.

Die Ausarbeitung der Meronomie eines Produktes ist besonders dann hilfreich, wenn es gilt, ein Produkt umfassend mit seinen einzelnen Bestandteilen zu erläutern. Mit Hilfe einer Meronomie lassen sich nicht nur die einzelnen Komponenten eines Produktes erfassen, sondern auch ihre Beziehung zueinander. Allerdings finden Meronomien vorwiegend in Bedienungsanleitungen technischer Geräte ihren Einsatz, z.B. in Erläuterungen von Fotoapparaten, Videorekordern u.v.m.

Der Einsatz verschiedener sprachlicher Effekte ist nur dann erfolgreich, wenn es gelingt, mit den Konsumenten zu kommunizieren. Kommunikation läßt sich nach dem Griceschen Grundmodell[92] als Methode der Beeinflussung von Menschen charakterisieren, "und zwar dadurch, daß man dem anderen mittels Zeichen (im weitesten Sinne) zu erkennen gibt, wozu man ihn bringen möchte, in der Hoff-

---

[92] Grice (1975), S. 245ff

nung, daß diese Erkenntnis für den anderen ein Grund sein möge, sich in der gewünschten Weise beeinflussen zu lassen."[93]

In dem vorliegenden Anwendungsbeispiel ergibt sich allerdings ein Spezialfall der Kommunikation. Man möchte zwar mittels Zeichen den Konsumenten etwas zu erkennen geben und hofft, daß diese Erkenntnis ein Grund ist, daß sie sich in der gewünschten Weise beeinflussen lassen, jedoch sollen die Kunden nicht unbedingt das übergeordnete Ziel erkennen, daß hinter allen Bemühungen lediglich die Absicht steckt, sie zum Kauf des Produktes zu bewegen. Die Kunden möchten und sollen faktisch überzeugt werden.

Zeichen sind generell "Hinweise mehr oder weniger deutlicher Natur, die den anderen zu Schlüssen einladen und ihm Schlüsse ermöglichen sollen".[94] Mit eben diesem Ziel werden auch die Zeichen auf Produktverpackungen eingesetzt. Die Handlungsfolge für den Adressaten ist dabei zunächst das Wahrnehmen der Zeichen, dann der Prozeß des Schließens der Zeichen - das sogenannte Interpretieren, dann das Verstehen und bei den Produktverpackungen schließlich das Überzeugtwerden und letztlich das Kaufen.

Es bietet sich an, an dieser Stelle einen kleinen Exkurs in die Welt der Werbefachleute zu unternehmen, um zu vergleichen, wie die Funktion von Zeichen aus der Sicht der Praktiker charakterisiert wird.

---

[93]  Keller (1995), S. 105
[94]  Keller (1995), S. 106

Die Werbetexter halten sich an eine schlichte Formel, nach der die Konsumenten durch die Zeichen in vier Phasen aktiviert werden sollen:

| A | $\rightarrow$ | to capture attention |
|---|---|---|
| I | $\rightarrow$ | to maintain interest |
| D | $\rightarrow$ | to create desire |
| A | $\rightarrow$ | to get action[95] |

Mit dieser Formel wird psychologisch stärker der Aspekt der Beeinflussung als der reinen Kommunikation akzentuiert.

**Die erste Phase** - das Aufmerksam machen - wird in dem zeichentheoretischen Ansatz nicht explizit genannt, weil es sich dabei um die Grundvoraussetzung der alltäglichen Kommunikation handelt. Diese Phase kann aber ohne Probleme dem Ansatz hinzugefügt werden, wenn der Anwendungseinsatz es erforderlich macht.

**Die zweite Phase**, "to maintain interest", entspricht ebenfalls dem, was nach Grice zu den Voraussetzungen gehört, damit Kommunikation überhaupt stattfinden kann. Nur wenn Interesse für den Kommunikationsbeitrag vorhanden ist, kann davon ausgegangen werden, daß die Kunden bereit sind, den Beitrag wahrzunehmen und zu interpretieren.

Der Vorteil von Kommunikationsbemühungen auf einer Verpackung im Laden ist, daß eine Person diese nach eigenem Gutdünken ignorieren kann, ohne eine soziale Regel zu verletzen, unhöflich zu sein und eventuelle Konsequenzen fürchten zu müssen. Dagegen ist es in der Alltagskommunikation aus Gründen der Etikette selbstverständ-

---

[95] Jacobi (1963), aber auch Nöth (1975), S. 51 und Högn und Pomplitz (1990), S. 41

87

lich, daß man den Kommunikationsbemühungen der Mitmenschen zumindest Gehör schenkt, ob der Beitrag interessant zu werden verspricht oder nicht.

Schafft es die Verpackung, mit der Beschriftung auf den ersten Blick interessant zu wirken, ist ein Erfolg erreicht, denn wenn der Kunde sich für ein Produkt interessiert, setzt er sich meistens etwas intensiver damit auseinander.

**Die dritte Phase**, "to create desire", beschreibt einen ersten Erfolg, nachdem die Kommunikation über die Verpackung stattgefunden hat. Es wurde z.B. erreicht, daß ein Kunde beim Anblick von Milka-Schokolade mit dem Hinweis auf die Geschmacksrichtung "Noisette" und dem dazu passenden Bild ein Verlangen verspürt, diese Schokolade zu naschen. Bei Genußartikeln wie Süßwaren und Nahrungsmitteln gelingt es leichter, ein Bedürfnis zu wecken, z.B. über ein ansprechendes Bild des Produktes, einer Zutat oder des Produktes im zubereiteten Zustand auf der Verpackung in Kombination mit den schriftlichen Produkthinweisen, z.B. "köstlich" (becker's bester).

Schwieriger gestaltet es sich bei weniger genußintensiven Gütern wie Reinigern und Waschmitteln, einen Wunsch zu wecken. Um so intensiver sind die Bemühungen auf diesem Gebiet. Gerade bei Reinigern ist es Usus, die Konsumenten einerseits über besonders starke Leistungen zu beeindrucken (z.B. Keimfreiheit, porentiefe Reinheit, riesige Wäschemengen schaffend etc.). Um derartige Produkte ähnlich attraktiv wie Genußmittel zu gestalten, werden gerne die Sinne angesprochen. Dazu werden sie z.B. mit intensiven Gerüchen von Zitrone über Pfirsich bis Tannenbaum oder Meeresbrise ausgestattet. Welche Wirkungen durch den Einsatz sprachlicher Zeichen konkret erzielt werden können, soll in einem späteren Abschnitt erläutert werden.

**Die vierte und letzte Phase** beschreibt das übergeordnete Ziel sämtlicher Kommunikationsbemühungen, "to get action", was nichts anderes meint, als daß das Produkt gekauft werden soll. Die Kaufhandlung wird ausgelöst, wenn das Verlangen in Phase drei groß genug ist. Um die Kaufhandlung auszulösen, muß nicht nur der Kommunikationsbeitrag erfolgreich gewesen sein, indem er verstanden wurde - er muß darüber hinaus so überzeugend und so ansprechend gewesen sein, daß aus dem Wunsch ein Verlangen wird, das Produkt zu konsumieren.

In der Regel ist der Kauf eines Produktes ein Beleg dafür, daß die Kommunikation mit dem Konsumenten gelungen ist. Dabei muß die Kommunikation nicht unbedingt dergestalt erfolgreich gewesen sein, daß der Kunde mit dem Produkt im Vergleich vor allen anderen Alternativen besonders überzeugt ist. Manchmal bietet eine Produktalternative lediglich das geringste Übel oder es ist das einzige Angebot. Aber auch im letzten Fall ist es wenigstens geglückt, kommunikativ kenntlich zu machen, daß es sich um das Produkt für den gewünschten Zweck handelt.

Im schlimmsten Fall gelingt es einem Produkt nicht, zu kommunizieren, oder es kommuniziert mißverständlich, weil es für etwas ganz anderes gehalten wird, als es eigentlich ist.

Im Anschluß an die Auseinandersetzung mit der kommunikativen Wirkung von Produktverpackungen stellt sich die Frage, wie sich unverpackte Produkte überhaupt verkaufen lassen. Diese Frage ist relativ leicht zu beantworten, schaut man sich einmal die Struktur der heute gängigen Lebensmittelläden an. Die einzigen Produkte, die den Verbrauchern zuweilen noch unverpackt angeboten werden, sind Obst und Gemüse, Brot, Fleisch, Fisch, Wurst und Käse u.ä. Fleisch, Fisch, Wurst und Käse werden im unverpackten Zustand aus hygienischen Gründen hinter entsprechenden Ladentheken durch

Verkaufspersonal angeboten. In diesem Fall übernehmen die Verkäufer wieder aktiv ihre Rolle und ergänzen oft die Funktion des meist einfarbigen Einpackmaterials um die Merkmale Beratung, Werbung und Information. Jedoch unterliegen diese Aspekte der individuellen Einschätzung des Verkäufers und können von den Anbietern nicht ohne zusätzlichen Aufwand beeinflußt werden. Brot wird ebenfalls an einer im Supermarkt integrierten Bäckereitheke angeboten. Obst und Gemüse werden in Behältern oder Kisten zum selbständigen Abfüllen und manchmal auch Abwiegen durch die Kunden bereitgestellt. Hierbei ergibt sich allerdings das Phänomen, daß die Kunden normalerweise keine Produktalternativen zur Auswahl haben. Sie können lediglich wählen zwischen Kiwis und Nicht-Kiwis, zwischen Bananen und Nicht-Bananen aber nicht zwischen Chiquita- und Dole-Bananen. Fleischtomaten, Strauchtomaten, Kartoffeln und die verschiedenen Apfelsorten scheinen auf den ersten Blick Produktalternativen zu sein, die zueinander in Konkurrenz stehen. Bei genauerer Betrachtung der dazugehörigen Schilder stellt man jedoch fest, daß die Sorten so unterschiedlich im Geschmack (süß, sauer, fruchtig etc.), in der Konsistenz (fest, mehlig) und in ihrem bevorzugten Verwendungsbereich (zum Backen, für Kompott, festkochend u.s.w.) sind, daß sie wie unterschiedliche Produkte gehandelt werden können.

Dennoch stellt man bei genauer Betrachtung fest, daß es sich auch die Anbieter unverpackter Produkte nicht nehmen lassen, kleine Etiketten oder Schildchen mit einem Namen wie "Chiquita" oder "Dole", „Braeburn" etc. auf Früchte und Gemüse zu kleben.

Zuweilen werden neben losen Früchten und losem Gemüse auch abgepackte Tabletts mit Folie darüber oder Netze angeboten. Mit dieser Art der Verpackung versucht man, das Obst und Gemüse besonders frisch und steril wirken zu lassen, die Kunden glauben zu machen, ein gutes Angebot erwischt zu haben, wenn sie eine bestimmte Anzahl zu einem etwas günstigeren Preis kaufen können als die lose Alternative, auch wenn ursprünglich gar nicht geplant war, so viel zu kaufen; und die Fläche der Verpackung wird wieder gerne für Labels, Etiketten u.ä. genutzt.

Die Unverpacktheit der dazu in Konkurrenz stehenden Produkte ist ein eigenes Zeichen. Die Kunden sollen das Fehlen einer Verpackung dahingehend interpretieren, daß sie selbst dazu angehalten sind, genau die gewünschte Menge zusammenzustellen und vor allem die Produkte auswählen zu dürfen, so daß der Kauf schlechter Ware ausgeschlossen scheint.

Darüber hinaus ist mit dem Zeichen der Unverpacktheit beabsichtigt, die Kunden zu der Interpretation zu bewegen, daß diese Produkte ganz frisch und ohne viele Zwischeninstanzen vom Erzeuger kommen.

Gerade in der heutigen Zeit, wo die radioaktive Bestrahlung von Obst und Gemüse und lange Aufenthalte in Kühlhäusern immer wieder Schlagzeilen machen, bietet Obst und Gemüse, das in Kisten verkauft wird, wie es beim Bauern geerntet wird, für viele eine dankenswerte Alternative, für die man auch bereit ist, etwas mehr Geld auszugeben.[96] Es scheint zunächst befremdlich, daß loses Obst und Gemüse teurer angeboten wird, da augenscheinlich doch viel weniger Aufwand damit betrieben wurde.

Den Kunden soll ein neues Einkaufserlebnis vermittelt werden, und das läßt man sich bezahlen. Man darf selbst aussuchen, angucken, anfassen und in den Mengen abpacken, die man meint zu brauchen.

---

[96]
    Inwieweit unverpackte Früchte und Gemüse nicht bestrahlt und lange unreif gekühlt wurden, bleibt dahingestellt - durch den Verkauf in Kisten wie beim Bauern werden diese Frischwaren auch als Waren "vom Bauern" interpretiert.

Man sollte meinen, daß nun viel weniger gekauft wird, da man nicht mehr gezwungen ist, eine bestimmte Menge zu nehmen. Tatsächlich verhält es sich jedoch so, daß ein Ausgleich dadurch geschaffen wird, daß lose Äpfel nicht nur teurer, sondern oft auch größer als abgepackte sind.

Festzuhalten bleibt zur AIDA-Formel, daß zwar die Ziele genannt werden, die mit Werbung in den verschiedenen Medien erreicht werden sollen, aber man wird als Anwender völlig darüber im Unklaren gelassen, wie kommunikative Zeichen in der gewünschten Form wirken und wie man diese Wirkung nachhaltig beeinflussen kann.

Aus diesem Grund erachte ich es für sinnvoll, die AIDA-Formel mit den formulierten Zielen der werblichen Kommunikation über Produktverpackungen zu beachten. Zur konkreten Erläuterung des Phänomens der Kommunikation durch sprachliche Zeichen und der Möglichkeiten der Beeinflussung durch selbige, werde ich vorzugsweise die Zeichentheorie zu Rate zu ziehen.

## 2.4 Zeichentypen

Keller erläutert, daß beim Phänomen der Kommunikation durch
Sprache, die Fähigkeit zu interpretieren primär ist. In der Regel wird
die Interpretationsfähigkeit des Adressaten zugunsten des Kommuni-
zierenden ausgenutzt. "Interpretieren heißt (u.a.), auf der Basis von
systematischen oder als systematisch unterstellten Zusammenhängen
Schlüsse ziehen".[97]

Allerdings ist im Bereich der Konsumgüterwerbung zu beachten, daß
der Einsatz der Interpretationsfähigkeit für ein bestimmtes Produkt
ganz besonders der individuellen Bereitschaft der Einkäufer unterliegt. Das heißt, die Anbieter als Kommunizierende müssen ihre
Kommunikation auf die Bedürfnisse ihrer Adressaten abstimmen und
sie dürfen deren Gunst keinesfalls überstrapazieren. Die Kunden als
Adressaten haben heute den Vorteil, daß sie ihre Fähigkeit zu interpretieren bei den Produktverpackungen nur so lange und intensiv
einsetzen brauchen, wie es ihnen beliebt.

Interpretiert werden systematische oder als systematisch unterstellte
Zusammenhänge. Diese Zusammenhänge machen ein Zeichen inter-
pretierbar und lassen sich dementsprechend als die Bedeutung der
Zeichen charakterisieren.

---

[97] Keller (1995), S. 112

93

Keller erläutert, daß es genau drei Arten von systematischen Zusammenhängen gibt, die für Interpretationen nutzbar gemacht werden können. Das sind:

- **kausale Zusammenhänge**
- **Ähnlichkeiten**
- **regelbasierte Zusammenhänge.**

Entsprechend lassen sich folgende Interpretationsverfahren unterscheiden:

- **das symptomische**
- **das ikonische und**
- **das symbolische Verfahren der Interpretation.**

Nach der Terminologie von Peirce lassen sich dazu passend drei Typen von Zeichen unterscheiden:

- **Symptome bzw. Indizes**
- **Ikone und**
- **Symbole**[98]

Peirce Zeichentheorie wird vielfach als Grundstein der Pragmatik charakterisiert. Zu den hervorzuhebenden Besonderheiten seiner Zeichenauffassung zählt die Annahme von Referenzbeziehungen zu einem Zweiten - einem Objekt und einem Dritten - seinem Interpretanten. Er geht davon aus, daß die Kommunikation mittels Zeichen auch unbewußt funktioniert.[99]

---

[98]     vgl. Keller (1995), S. 113

[99]     vgl. Peirce (1993), S. 64

An dieser Stelle ist die Frage berechtigt, aus welchem Grund nicht die Zeichentheorie Peirces zur Überprüfung eines Anwendungseinsatzes herangezogen wird, wo offensichtlich alle notwendigen Referenzen zur Erläuterung von Zeichen auf Produktverpackungen vorhanden sind. Doch diese Frage läßt sich schnell beantworten. Peirce Zeichentheorie ist ein repräsentationistischer Ansatz. Auch er geht davon aus, daß ein Zeichen auf einer Vorstellung aufgebaut und diese dann zu einem Adressaten transportiert wird. Es ist bereits ausführlich erläutert worden, warum diese Position hier nicht weiter verfolgt wird. Die Ausarbeitung seiner Theorie der Zeichen wird mit zunehmendem Alter sehr komplex und umfangreich. Die Theorie ist auf einer abstrakten Ebene anzusiedeln.[100] Aus diesem Grund bevorzuge ich für die vorliegende Arbeit einen stärker plakativen Ansatz. Für einen Anwendungseinsatz einer linguistischen Theorie in der alltäglichen Werbepraxis präferiere ich ein meiner Ansicht nach ausgesprochen anwenderfreundliches Modell, daß hier abgerundet vorgestellt und angewendet wird.

Aus diesem Grund soll für die vorliegende Arbeit der Hinweis genügen, daß die zur weiteren Bearbeitung ausgewählte Klassifikation der Zeichen auf Peirce zurückgeht, hier aber die gebrauchsorientierte Ausarbeitung Kellers auf ihre Anwendbarkeit im Konsumgütermarketing überprüft werden soll.

## 2.5  Die drei Grundverfahren der Interpretation

### 2.5.1  Das symptomische Verfahren

Das symptomische Interpretationsverfahren greift in Situationen, in denen kausale Zusammenhänge kommuniziert werden. Dieses Ver-

---

[100]    vgl. zur Biographie Peirces auch Arroyabe (1982), S. 7ff

95

fahren bezieht sich auf die Interpretation von Symptomen oder Indizes.

Ein Beispiel bieten die Windpocken, die als Symptom die Krankheit nach außen sichtbar machen. Das Auftreten von Symptomen kann in der Regel nicht beeinflußt werden. Sie entstehen nicht intentional und sind daher auch nur in gewissem Sinne Zeichen.[101] Symptome sind Anzeichen für etwas, können aber durchaus auch ein Teil des Ganzen sein, so wie die Windpocken ein Symptom für die Krankheit sind, aber auch ein Teil von ihr.

In der Kommunikation gibt es nur sehr wenige sprachliche Äußerungen, die sich als Symptom bezeichnen lassen. Ein Beispiel sind die Freudschen Fehlleistungen. Dabei rutscht dem Sprecher ein nicht in den Zusammenhang gehörendes Wort mit einer völlig anderen Bedeutung heraus, das im Klang aber häufig dem verwechselten Wort sehr ähnlich ist. Es wird diesen Versprechern nachgesagt, daß sie die unterbewußte Meinung des Sprechers verraten. Man spricht bei diesen Versprechern auch von „Symptomhandlungen"[102]. Demnach sind auch diese sprachlichen Zeichen keinesfalls intentional - zumal sie desöfteren Unannehmlichkeiten nach sich ziehen. Darüber hinaus können Dialekte oder Akzente als Symptom der Herkunft einer Person interpretiert werden. Zuweilen wird die Sprache einer Person als Symptom ihrer Herkunft interpretiert.
Es gibt auch auf den Produktverpackungen Symptome, die einer kausalen Interpretation bedürfen.

So ist beispielsweise ein symptomisches Zeichen in Zusammenhang mit Produktverpackungen deren Aufbewahrungsort. Wird die Ware

---

[101]    vgl. Keller (1990), S. 118

[102]    Freud (1982), S. 487

96

im Kühlregal eines Geschäftes gelagert, kann man das als Symptom dafür werten, daß es sich um schnell verderbliche Ware handelt. Diese Art der Aufbewahrung ist bei verderblicher Ware normalerweise nicht von den Herstellern beeinflußt, denn Transport und Lagerung im gekühlten Medium sind wesentlich teurer. Es ist ebenfalls ein Symptom, wenn uns Waren, die wir eigentlich im Kühlregal vermutet hätten, plötzlich in einem normalen Regal begegnen. Beispiele für solche Waren sind H-Milch-Produkte (die haltbar gemacht wurden), verschiedene Käse- und Wurstsorten.

Hier greift ein weiterer Punkt der von Keller vorgestellten Kriterien zur Unterscheidung der Symptome von anderen Zeichen:

"Es ist prinzipiell offen, wofür ein Symptom Symptom ist. Denn ein Symptom kann als Symptom all dessen interpretiert werden, was aus ihm kausal erschließbar ist."[103]

Aus der Tatsache, daß bestimmte Waren, die man im Kühlregal vermutet hätte, nicht dort aufbewahrt werden, ist kausal erschließbar, daß es sich dabei um Waren handelt, die weniger schnell verderblich sind. Allerdings interpretieren manche Verbraucher einen derartigen Aufbewahrungsort negativ, weil sie frische Produkte als nicht lange haltbar kennengelernt haben, und unterstellen, daß diesen Lebensmitteln Konservierungsstoffe beigemengt wurden, die nicht gesundheitsfördernd sind. Der Kauf oder Nichtkauf des Produktes hängt in einem solchen Fall davon ab, wie und wann das Produkt vom Verbraucher konsumiert werden soll, welche Produktalternativen es gibt und wie überzeugend die Verpackung präsentiert wird.

---

[103] Keller (1995), S. 123

Viele Kunden interpretieren nach wie vor den Preis eines Produktes als Symptom für seine Qualität. Diese Kunden gehen davon aus, daß der Preis zugleich Auskunft über das dazugehörige Leistungs-Verhältnis der Produkte gibt. Gleichzeitig gehen diese Kunden davon aus, daß der Preis den Rohstoff- und Produktionskosten angeglichen wird. Demnach interpretieren sie bei einem hohen Preis einen großen Herstelleraufwand und qualitativ hochwertige und teure Rohstoffe. Folglich werden weniger teure Produkte oft als sogenannte "Billigware" abgetan.

Diese Einstellung wird häufig auch auf die verschiedenen Geschäftstypen übertragen. Einer kleinen teuren Boutique oder einem exklusiven Feinkostgeschäft wird hochwertigere Ware zugesprochen als Supermarktdiscountern wie Aldi.

Symptomisch interpretierbare Merkmale von Verpackungen selber sind z.B. Flaschen mit Kindersicherungsverschluß. Der Verschluß läßt sich dergestalt deuten, daß es sich um ein giftiges oder zumindest unverträgliches Produkt handelt. Verschiedene Medizinflaschen sowie diverse giftige Reinigungsmittel, Pestizide etc. sind mit einem Kindersicherungsverschluß ausgestattet. Sogar Flaschen selber können symptomisch interpretiert werden – als Symptom für Flüssigkeit. Entsprechend lassen sich Tuben als Symptom für Zähflüssiges interpretieren.

## 2.5.2 Das ikonische Interpretationsverfahren

Das ikonische Verfahren eignet sich für Zeichen, die Ähnlichkeiten mit dem Gegenstand ihrer Abbildung aufweisen. Man nennt diese Zeichen daher Ikone.

Laut Keller sind Ikone „echte Zeichen". Sie sind, im Gegensatz zu Symptomen, Kommunikationsmittel. Kommunikationsmittel sind Mittel, die von einem Zeichenbenutzer dazu verwendet werden, um einen Adressaten [...] zu beeinflussen; d.h. dadurch zu beeinflussen, daß man dem Adressaten mittels Zeichen (im weitesten Sinne ) zu erkennen gibt, wozu man ihn bringen möchte, in der Hoffnung , daß diese Erkenntnis für den anderen ein Grund sein möge, sich in der gewünschten Weise beeinflussen zu lassen."[104]

Ein typisches Beispiel für Ikone sind die stilisierten Männer und Frauen auf Toilettentüren, Wegweisern zu Umkleidekabinen etc.

Dabei darf der Begriff "Ähnlichkeit" nicht streng wörtlich genommen werden. Stilisierte Männer und Frauen auf Schildern sind den real existenten Frauen und Männern vollkommen unähnlich. Auf diese Form der Ähnlichkeit kommt es nicht an. Was zählt ist, daß das ikonische Zeichen die Fähigkeit besitzt, bei seinem Rezipienten die vom Sprecher beabsichtigte Assoziation zu erzeugen.

Die Interpretationsmethode basiert auf einem assoziativen Schluß - das ikonische Zeichen "erinnert" seine Adressaten an etwas, was ihm sehr ähnlich erscheint. Das Ikon muß einen Assoziationsimpuls geben.[105]

---

[104]      vgl. Keller (1995), S. 123

[105]      vgl. Keller (1995), S. 125

Bei der Kommunikation lassen sich lautliche, gestische und graphische Ähnlichkeiten unterscheiden. In der Auseinandersetzung mit Verpackungsaufschriften begegnen einem primär graphische Ähnlichkeiten und sekundär zuweilen auch lautliche (z.B. das Knacken beim Öffnen eines Verschlusses).

Fast auf jeder Verpackung gibt es ikonische Zeichen. Es ist besonders bei Verpackungen ohne Sichtfenster sehr beliebt, eine Graphik, die den Inhalt oder einen Inhaltsstoff abbildet, auf die Frontseite aufzudrucken.
Als Beispiel bietet sich die Tetra-Pak-Verpackung des Apfelsaft "vitafit" an. Unter der Produktbezeichnung "Apfelsaft" ist ein reifer rotgelber Apfel mit einem Blatt am Stiel und Wassertropfen vor einem grünen Hintergrund abgebildet. (Bild siehe S. 167)

Es handelt sich dabei um das Ikon eines realen Apfels. Den Kunden gelingt es aufgrund der Abbildtreue des fotorealistischen Bildes eines Apfels, assoziativ darauf zu schließen, daß dieses Zeichen von den Anbietern mit einem bestimmten Zweck eingesetzt wurde. Die Betrachter sollen es zum Anlaß der Interpretation nehmen, daß sich echte Äpfel in der Verpackung befinden. In diesem Stadium des Schlußprozesses, der in Bruchteilen von Sekunden durchgeführt wird, muß zum vollständigen Verständnis der Absicht, mit der dieses Zeichen eingesetzt wurde, die Relation zu seinem Kontext - die Verpackung - mitberücksichtigt werden. Dieses Ikon befindet sich weder auf einem Obstnetz, auf einer Obstschale noch auf einer Tiefkühlverpackung o.ä. Das Ikon befindet sich auf einem Tetra-Pak unter der Überschrift „Apfelsaft". Die Tetra-Pak-Verpackung eines Produktes ist schon alleine ein Symptom dafür, daß es sich um ein Produkt von flüssiger oder zähflüssiger Konsistenz handelt. Das Ikon wird ergänzt durch das Schriftzeichen "Apfelsaft", das wie alle Schriftzeichen über die Gebrauchsregeln gelernt und angewendet wird und daher ein Symbol ist. Damit sind genügend Merkmale gegeben, um relativ sicherzustellen, daß die Konsumenten zu dem interpretativen Schluß gelangen, daß das Ikon eines Apfels eine optische Information bezüglich der Inhaltsstoffe des Produktes bieten soll.

Ikone stehen auf Verpackungen selten alleine. Es bietet sich an, Abbildungen mit Textelementen zu kombinieren, um die gewünschte Wirkung zu steuern, zu verstärken und um Informationen zu erweitern, die über die Abbildungen nicht mitgeteilt werden können.

Auf Verpackungen wird gerne mit mimischen Ikonen zur Aufhebung der Anonymität und zur Überzeugung der Kunden gearbeitet. Besonders beliebt ist die Darstellung eines Gesichtes auf der Verpackung. Die bekanntesten Gesichter auf Verpackungen sind u.a.:

- das Gesicht des Jungen auf jeder Kinderschokoladenschachtel
- das Gesicht des kleinen Jungen auf der klassischen Brandt-Zwiebacktüte und
- das Gesicht des Mr. Proper auf jeder Mr.-Proper-Reinigungsflasche.

Diese Ikone (s. Abbildung 3) repräsentieren zwei ikonentypische Ausprägungsformen. Alle drei Gesichter sind in Form eines graphischen Ikons auf die Verpackung aufgedruckt. Sie unterscheiden sich lediglich in ihrer Ausprägungsform und in der Gestaltung.
Darüber hinaus ist der Schrifttyp auf der „Brandt"-Zwiebacktüte ein Ikon für Tradition.

Alle drei Gesichter haben einen strahlend fröhlichen Ausdruck und wirken sehr sympathisch. Sie sollen die Anonymität der Ware und der Läden aufheben und die Zufriedenheit der Verwender demonstrieren.

Das Jungengesicht soll einerseits die Zielgruppe der Kinder und Jugendlichen als primäre Konsumenten direkt ansprechen. Gleichzeitig soll aber auch bei den Eltern die Assoziation ausgelöst werden, daß die gesunden und glücklichen Kinder durch die Schokolade zu ihrem strahlenden Lächeln verführt werden.

Der Junge vermittelt durch das Ikon der frischen Gesichtsfarbe den Eindruck, kerngesund zu sein. Es wird versucht, Kinderschokolade über den Hinweis, daß darin sehr viel Milch und wenig Kakao enthalten ist, als sinnvolle Ernährungsergänzung zu verkaufen.

Das Lächeln des Jungen übernimmt die Funktion, den Blick freizugeben auf die makellosen schneeweißen Zähne des Jungen, die als Zeichen unterschwellig argumentativ gegen die Sorge eingesetzt sind, Schokolade verursache Karies.

Dieses Gesicht ist seit über zwanzig Jahren unverändert auf den Schokoladentafeln zu finden.[106]

Mr. Proper steht nicht für die zufriedene Kundenschar - er personifiziert die Wirkung des Produktes schon seit vielen Jahren. Das Wort "proper" steht für die Eigenschaften "sauber" und "nett".[107] Der Mr. (oder wie es in der Rundfunk- und Fernsehwerbung klingt: Meister) Proper demonstriert durch sein muskulöses Äußeres Stärke - er ist die Verkörperung der Reinigungskraft. Sein strahlendes Lachen soll den Kunden ebenfalls als Zeichen die emotionale Wirkung der Anwendung des Produktes demonstrieren. Mit Mr.-Proper soll das Putzen

---

[106] Es wurde einmal versucht, das Verpackungsoutfit der Kinderschokolade völlig neu zu ge-stalten. Diese Unternehmung wurde von Mißerfolg gekrönt. Die Veränderung stieß auf absolute Ablehnung. Seitdem wurde kein Versuch mehr unternommen, die Verpackung zu verändern.

[107] Duden Bd. 1 (1980), Stichwort "proper", S. 550

spielend leicht sein und keine Anstrengung kosten. Zum Mr. Proper Frontseitenetikett ist zu bemerken, daß die gesamte Beschriftung englisch klingen soll, bis auf den Hinweis "BAD", der den Kunden mittels eines bekannten Wortes zwischen den englisch klingenden Worten, das Gefühl von Vertrautheit und Wiedererkennung vermitteln kann.

Wie gezeigt, ist es im Sinne des ikonischen Verfahrens möglich, mit graphischen, mimischen und gestischen Ikonen im Bereich der Verpackungsgestaltung zu arbeiten. Ziel des Einsatzes von Ikonen ist es, den Kunden über Assoziationen positive Werte des jeweiligen Produktes zu vermitteln.

Viele Ikone werden hochfrequent eingesetzt. Der Übergang zur Symbolwerdung ist dann fließend.


### 2.5.3   Das symbolische Interpretationsverfahren

Bei Symbolen wird den Rezipienten die Interpretation durch die Regelhaftigkeit des Gebrauches ermöglicht. Grundsätzlich ist die Beziehung zwischen dem Symbol und dem, was es assoziieren soll, arbiträr und basiert nicht wie bei den Ikonen auf Ähnlichkeiten. Keller erläutert:

"Zu wissen, was ein Symbol bedeutet, heißt wissen, zur Realisierung welcher Intention es unter welchen Bedingungen verwendbar ist [...]. Das Ziel des Interpreten ist es, die Intention des Sprechers herauszu-

103

finden; das Mittel ist der Schluß auf der Basis der Kenntnis der Gebrauchsregeln der verwendeten Zeichen."[108]

Dabei ist das, was der Sprecher meint und was es für den Interpreten herauszufinden gilt, der Sinn.

Vorauszuschicken ist, daß im sprachwissenschaftlichen Sinne sämtliche Wörter Symbole für das sind, was sie bezeichnen. Der Zusammenhang ist arbiträr und das Interpretationsverfahren basiert auf der Regelhaftigkeit des Gebrauches.
Bei graphischen und mimischen Symbolen interpretiert man zwar nach dem gleichen Verfahren, jedoch ergibt sich der symbolhafte Charakter der Dinge nicht selbstverständlich wie beim Gebrauch sprachlicher Zeichen. Der Symbolcharakter in außersprachlichen Bereichen ergibt sich ebenfalls durch frequenten Einsatz, bis eine Regel der Interpretation entsteht - allerdings handelt es sich dann um eine kleine Besonderheit.
Typische Symbole aus dem täglichen Leben sind Verkehrszeichen wie Stop- und Vorfahrtsschilder, Ampeln etc.

Auf Verpackungen wird ebenfalls oftmals mit Symbolen gearbeitet. Eines der häufigsten auf deutschen Warenverpackungen vorkommende Symbol ist der sogenannte "grüne Punkt". Die Menschen haben über eine umfangreiche Kampagne in den Medien, Informationsschriften der Städte etc. gelernt, daß dieses Zeichen alles das kennzeichnet, was nicht im normalen Hausmüll entsorgt werden soll, sondern im "gelben Sack" oder im Altpapier. Zusätzlich soll der „grüne Punkt" als Zeichen für Wiederverwertbarkeit Umweltfreundlichkeit suggerieren.

---

[108] Keller (1995), S. 129f

104

Der grüne Punkt hat keinerlei Ähnlichkeit mit einer Verpackung, einem Produkt oder dem, was mit der leeren Verpackung passiert. Trotzdem weiß fast jeder in Deutschland, was mit den gekennzeichneten leeren Verpackungen zu passieren hat.

Der regelbasierte Schluß beim Anblick des grünen Punktes wurde dergestalt verinnerlicht, daß das Symbol auch dann noch erkannt und der Regel entsprechend umgesetzt wird, wenn es auf diversen Einwegverpackungen nicht in seiner original grünen Farbe erscheint, wie z.B. auf verschiedenen Coca-Cola-Produkten in rot-weiß.

Die meisten Firmenlogos sind ebenfalls mit Symbolen kombiniert. Die Regelhaftigkeit des Auftretens läßt sie zum Erkennungszeichen für Produkte aus dem jeweiligen Hause werden, wie z.B. der Stern aus dem Hause „Daimler Benz".

Nicht immer ist es im Bereich des Konsumgütermarketing erwünscht, wenn ein Begriff symbolisch interpretiert wird. Oft stehen die Anbieter dann vor der Schwierigkeit sich etwas Neues einfallen lassen zu müssen, um ihr Produkt stärker von den anderen Alternativen zu differenzieren. So geschehen z.B. bei den „Haarpflege-Spülungen". Dieser Begriff ist mittlerweile als Produktbezeichnung derartig ausgereizt, daß zu einer neuen Produktbezeichnung gegriffen wird, wie „Balsam-Spülung" (Poly Kur) oder „Vitamin-Balsam" (L'Oréal). Der Begriff „Balsam" ist mittlerweile auch bei den Geschirrspülmitteln beliebt (Pril Balsam).

Nach dem gleichen Prinzip bieten Fertignahrunghersteller nicht mehr einfach nur „Nudelgerichte" an, sondern gleich einen „Nudelspass" (Maggi). Dieser Begriff soll vor allem das „Produkterlebnis" zum Ausdruck bringen. Der Begriff „Spaß" impliziert in diesem Zusammenhang ein Vergnügen in einem bislang ungewohnten Kontext und lenkt damit von den unbequemen Eigenschaften der Nahrungszubereitung ab.

## 2.6 Zeichen und ihre Metamorphosen

Wenn man davon ausgeht, daß sprachliche Zeichen über die Interpretation ihres Einsatzes in der Kommunikation bestimmt werden, so ist es möglich, daß Zeichen nicht Zeit ihrer Existenz einer Kategorie zugehörig bleiben müssen. Wenn z.B. ein Symptom nachgeahmt wird mit der Intention, einem Adressaten etwas zu verstehen zu geben, ist das abgebildete Symptom aufgrund seiner Ähnlichkeit ein Ikon.

Wenn bei hochfrequent eingesetzten Symptomen aufgrund der Regelhaftigkeit ihres Einsatzes das regelbasierte Schlußverfahren eingesetzt wird, dann sind diese Zeichen zu Symbolen geworden. Das gleiche Phänomen läßt sich auch bei hochfrequent verwendeten Ikonen beobachten, die dann ebenfalls zu der Klasse der Symbole gehören.

Keller faßt das Phänomen in einen prägnanten Satz:

"Auf lange Sicht wird alles zu Symbolen".[109]

Der Übergang vom Ikon zum Symbol ist häufig fließend. Als Beispiel bietet sich die Symbolifizierung verschiedener Firmenlogos an. Das Kaisers-Kaffeekännchen, die After-Eight-Uhr, die Tchibo-Bohne, das Knorr-Fähnchen, der Maggi-Tropfen, die Iglo-Gabel

---

[109] Keller (1995), S. 186

106

u.v.m. - alle diese Firmenzeichen sollten aufgrund einer Ähnlichkeit einen Assoziationsimpuls geben.

Die Kunden wurden so häufig mit diesen Ikonen in der Werbung, den Ladenregalen und zu Hause konfrontiert, daß bald kein assoziativer Schluß zur Interpretation des Zeichens mehr notwendig war. Ein regelbasierter Schluß hatte das assoziative Verfahren abgelöst.

Die regelbasierten Schlüsse zur Interpretation von Symbolen bieten folgende Vorteile:

- Ihre Abbildtreue verliert an Relevanz
- Die Situationsgebundenheit des Gebrauches wird gelockert.[110]

Der erste Punkt wurde bereits mit der Variation des grünen Punktes auf Coca-Cola-Einwegflaschen erläutert. Ziel der Hersteller ist es, daß die Verpackung insgesamt zum Symbol für das dazugehörige Produkt und idealerweise auch Symbol für die dem Produkt zugeschriebenen positiven Eigenschaften wird. Dann hängt ein Wiedererkennen nicht mehr von einzelnen schriftlichen oder graphischen Symbolen wie dem Firmenlogo ab.

So wird beispielsweise „Milkaschokolade" schon durch den Schriftzug und die lila Farbe der Verpackung erkannt, ohne daß man den Schriftzug erkennen kann. Suchard hat es bei „Milka" geschafft, daß das Lila alleine zum Symbol für „Milka"-Produkte in der „Milka"-Qualität geworden ist.

Über die lila Verpackung wird auch die Einführung weiterer „Milka"-Produkte erleichtert. Die „Milka-lila-Pause" wird ebenso wiedererkannt und zugeordnet, wie die „Milka-lila-Herzen" etc., was

---

[110]    vgl. Keller (1995), S. 169

eine Evidenz dafür ist, daß die Situationsgebundenheit der Symbole gelockert wird.

Die Anbieter von Me-Too-Produkten versuchen, den Vorteil zu nutzen, daß bei Symbolen die Abbildtreue an Relevanz verliert. Sie vertrauen häufig darauf, daß der Aufwand der Originalanbieter gewirkt hat und die Verpackungen der Originalprodukte Symbolcharakter bekommen haben. Anbieter von Me-Too-Produkten versuchen über eine möglichst große optische Ähnlichkeit in den Absatzmarkt des Originalproduktes einzusteigen.

Me-Too-Produkte sind Ikone der Originale mit sehr starker Abbildtreue. Die Kunden sollen über die Ähnlichkeit die Qualität und den Nutzen des originalen Markenartikels assoziieren und durch den niedrigeren Preis zum Kauf verlockt werden. So ist z.B. die Flasche des von Lidl-Märkten angebotenen Shampoos "Cien" den Flaschen des Shampoos "Timotei" verdächtig ähnlich. Ebenso weist die Verpackung der Damenbinde "Siempre" aus selbigem Hause Abbildtreue zu den Verpackungen von "always ultra" auf. Darüber hinaus lassen sich beide Namen mit "immer" in das Deutsche übersetzen.[111]

Ideal ist es, wenn die Ähnlichkeit so groß ist, daß es gar nicht zu der inneren Diskussion kommt, ob der originale oder der nachgeahmte Artikel den Vorzug erhält. Allerdings handelt es sich bei derart nachgestellten Logos zum Teil um illegale Kopien des Originals.[112]

---

[111] Viele No-Name-Produkte kommen aus demselben Hause des Markenproduktes, dem sie ähnlich sehen.

[112] Hinweis: Besonders in Singapur, Hong Kong und Bangkok boomt der Markt imitier-ter Produkte immer noch. Allerdings handelt es sich um Betrug, wenn die Kunden hereingelegt werden, was jedoch nur ganz selten der Fall ist. Vielen Kunden ist es äußerst angenehm, für wenig Geld ein imitiertes Original erstehen zu können und ihrerseits beispielsweise eine kopierte Rolex oder ein kopiertes Lacoste-Shirt als Symbol für einen gehobenen Lebensstatus wirken lassen zu können.

Ein weiteres Beispiel für die weniger deutliche Situationsgebundenheit von Symbolen ist die Erweiterung der Produktpalette der Firma Tesa. Das legendäre „Tesa" ist mittlerweile als Bezeichnung für durchsichtigen Klebefilm in den allgemeinen Wortschatz übergegangen. Das Logo mit dem Schriftzug "Tesa" auf rotem Hintergrund mit einer blauen Ecke ist zum Symbol für den Markenartikel geworden.

Das ursprüngliche Ikon eines abgezogenen Klebestreifens ist durch die hohe Frequenz in der Werbung und im Handel zum Symbol geworden. Über das „Tesa"-Symbol und das „Tesa"-Outfit konnten weitere Klebebänder erfolgreich auf dem Markt etabliert werden. Von Vorteil ist es, das gesamte „Tesa"-Sortiment in einem exponierten Ständer anzubieten, damit der Kunde sich beim Kauf des altbewährten „Tesafilms" bereits mit den weiteren „Tesa"-Podukten vertraut macht und sich bei Bedarf daran erinnert, daß es u.a. noch „Tesa"-Gewebeband in verschiedenen Farben gibt, „Tesa"-Isolierband, „Tesa"-Haushaltsband, „Tesa"-Krepp, „Tesa"-Packband, „Tesa"-Teppichbodenverlegeband und „Tesa" doppelseitiges Klebeband. Der Markt wurde über das bewährte Symbol darüber hinaus um andere Bereiche erweitert. So gibt es mittlerweile auch „Tesa"-Klettband, „Tesa"-Flüssigkleber, „Tesa"-Fliegengitter u.ä.
Pack-, Teppichboden- und Kreppband sowie Flüssigkleber wurden schon längst von anderen Firmen angeboten. Die Tesa-Produkte sind quasi Me-too-Produkte. Jedoch hat es die Firma Tesa geschafft, über ihr Firmensymbol auch diese Produkte zu Markenartikeln zu machen und über diesen Aspekt den Kunden das Gefühl von Qualität zu vermitteln. Beim Pack- und Teppichbodenband ist Tesa der bekannteste Markenanbieter - im Bereich der Flüssigkleber jedoch nicht. Dort haben sich bereits „UHU"- und „Patex"-Klebstoffe derart bewährt,

daß der Produktname Institution bzw. Symbol für Weich- und Hart-
kleber geworden ist.

Hat es eine Firma einmal geschafft, ihr Logo als Symbol zu etablieren, heißt die Maxime zunächst: "Bloß nichts verändern".[113] Es sollte
nach Möglichkeit vermieden werden, den Kunden das zu nehmen,
was sie mit soviel Werbeaufwand gelernt haben: die Wiedererkennungsmerkmale.[114]
Deshalb bereitet die Firma Tuffi ihre Kunden schon weit vor Erscheinen des neuen Outfits vor: „Freuen Sie sich auf unser neues
Design" steht auf der Verpackung zu lesen. Tuffi hat sich eine gute
Strategie einfallen lassen, die Kunden auf das neue Design vorzube-
reiten. Drei Seiten der Verpackung sind wie gewohnt gestaltet. Der
Slogan steht jedoch auf einer Seite, die bereits im neuen Design präsentiert wird. So gewöhnt man die Kunden langsam an das neue
Design, ohne zunächst auf die Wiedererkennungsmerkmale verzichten zu müssen.

Die Maxime „nichts ändern" ist dann wieder aufzuheben, wenn das
Produkt einer Firma dergestalt etabliert ist, daß es droht, ein Symbol
für den Prototypen des Produktes zu werden (vgl. Kap. 6.3). Dies ist

---

[113]    Statement von K. Steindel, Art Direktor der Köster und Vorhauer GmbH in
         Düsseldorf

[114]    Die Hersteller des Geschirrspülmittels "Pril" gaben den Sonderstatus ihres
         Produktes auf, als sie dessen Verpackung mit den Prilblümchenaufklebern
         für nicht mehr zeitge-mäß befanden. Dabei waren die zum Symbol gewor-
         denen Prilblümchenaufkleber auf der blauen Flasche liebgewonnenes
         Erkennungszeichen. Mit der Einführung einer durchsichtigen Flasche mit
         einem neu designten Etikett wurde Pril der Sonderstatus genommen und
         zwischen die ähnlich aussehenden Konkurrenzprodukte wie Palmolive etc.
         ein-gereiht. Gerade die Prilblümchen hatten sich derart etabliert, daß man
         Jahre später im Zeitalter der Technomode bei bestimmten Blümchenmu-
         stern auf Kleidungsstücken von Prilblümchen spricht.

110

z.B. neben dem „Tesa"-Klebeband bei den "Tempotaschentüchern" erfolgt. Ein "Tempo" ist mittlerweile zum umgangsprachlichen Ausdruck für ein Papiertaschentuch geworden. Das Wort "Tempo" wird regelbasiert interpretiert und symbolisiert den Prototypen eines zusammengefalteten, an den Rändern geprägten Papiertaschentuches einer bestimmten Größe aus einer wiederverschließbaren 10er Plastikpackung. Das Problem ist, daß mittlerweile jemand, der um ein "Tempo" bittet, keinen gesteigerten Wert darauf legt, ein Papiertaschentuch der Firma "Tempo" zu bekommen, sondern ein Papiertaschentuch, das den prototypischen Eigenschaften eines solchen entspricht. Diese Eigenschaften weisen z.B. auch weitestgehend die Papiertaschentücher "Softies", "Ja", "Cien" und als Ökovariation "Mach mit" auf.

Mittlerweile versucht die Firma Tempo, mit verschiedenen Maßnahmen wieder ihren alten Marktführerstatus zurückzuerobern. Zu diesen Maßnahmen gehört zunächst die Strategie, die herkömmlichen Tempo-Taschentücher über besonders herausragende Eigenschaften aufzuwerten und der Konkurrenz überzuordnen. So werden beispielsweise die besondere Dicke sowie die ganz besondere Weichheit und Nasenfreundlichkeit der Taschentücher als zu bevorzugende Eigenschaften vorgestellt.

Eine weitere Maßnahme ist die Einführung verschiedener Produktvarianten wie z.B. Tempo mit Eukamentol oder Minzgeruch, die bei einer Erkältung die Nase frei machen sollen.

Darüber hinaus wird die Produktpalette ergänzt um die Tempo-Minipaketchen für besonders kleine Handtaschen.

Auf die Dauer wird die Firma Tempo weitere Maßnahmen zur Aktualisierung ihrer Produkte durchführen müssen, denn die Konkurrenz schläft nicht.

Es gibt in jeder Sprache die Möglichkeit, mit einer Stilfigur das regelbasierte und das ikonische Schlußverfahren miteinander zu kombinieren.

## 2.7 Metaphern

Das Wort "Metapher" stammt vom griechischen "metaphérein" - an einen anderen Ort tragen. Es handelt sich dabei um eine Stilfigur, die schon in der griechischen Rhetorik bekannt war.

Metaphern können allerdings weit mehr leisten, als nur ein Stilmittel zu sein. In neueren Ansätzen hat man sich davon gelöst, Metaphern als rein stilistisches Phänomen zu betrachten. Der Faktor des Gebrauchs wird dann mit in die Analyse einbezogen.

Keller fügt seinen Erläuterungen der Grundverfahren der Interpretation einen anschaulichen Ansatz zum metaphorischen Verwendungsaspekt hinzu. Er demonstriert seinen Ansatz an einem umfangreichen Beispiel:

- Jemand erzählt einen platten Witz.
- Der Rezipient reagiert mit der Antwort: "Au, das tut weh!"

Folgende Erläuterungsschritte sind nach Keller hier notwendig:

- oft wird auf einen plötzlich auftauchenden, unerwarteten körperlichen Schmerz reflexartig mit einem Aufschrei wie "Au" reagiert.
- → "Au" kann als Symptom für Schmerz interpretiert werden.

- Es gibt Situationen, in denen ein "Au" simuliert wird, um einen Mitmenschen zu dem assoziativen Schluß anzuregen: "Au - Du tust mir weh!"

  → "Au" ist in solchen Fällen als Ikon des Symptoms für körperlichen Schmerz zu beschreiben.

- Hinreichend frequenter Gebrauch der simulierten Version führt dazu, daß eine

  Gebrauchsregel entsteht. Dadurch wird "Au" zum Symbol für spontanen körperlichen Schmerz.[115]

Ein Witz produziert allerdings keine spontanen körperlichen Schmerzen. Dennoch wird die Reaktion solange als rationale Handlung interpretiert, bis ausreichende Evidenzen vom Gegenteil überzeugen.[116] Da eine kausale Interpretation der Aussage nicht zu einem brauchbaren Ergebnis führt, ist auf ein assoziatives Schlußverfahren zurückzugreifen. Eine Interpretation nach dem regelbasierten Verfahren reicht nicht aus. Wenn auf das Ergebnis das ikonische Verfahren angewendet wird, entsteht eine Metapher.

Der Satz "Au, das tut weh!" wurde als Reaktion auf den Witz nicht dazu geäußert, körperliche Schmerzen zum Ausdruck zu bringen. Vielmehr sollte der simulierte Hinweis auf körperliche Schmerzen die assoziative Erkenntnis veranlassen, daß die Äußerung aufgrund "seelischer Schmerzen" als Reaktion auf den Witz kommuniziert wurde. Die Metapher ist die Ortsveränderung des Wortes "Au", das

---

[115]
    vgl. zum gebrauchstheoretischen Ansatz von Metaphern: Keller (1995), S. 174ff

[116]
    Frank (1980), S. 43 Sie bezeichnet diesen Tatbestand als eine „Default-Annahme" („so lange nichts dagegen spricht" Annahme).

auf einen Ort übertragen wurde, an den es ursprünglich nicht gehör-
te. [117]

Die genaue Beschreibung der Verwendung von "Au" im obigen Beispiel lautet: "Es liegt die metaphorische Verwendung des zum
Symbol gewordenen Ikons eines Symp-toms von Schmerz vor". [118]

Zu der metaphorischen Verwendung des zum Symbol gewordenen
Ikons eines Symp-toms für Schmerz kommt noch ein ironischer Verwendungsaspekt hinzu.

Eine Metapher entsteht demnach, wenn der Interpret auf die Interpretation mittels regelbasiertem Verfahren das ikonische Verfahren
anwendet.

Metaphern sind für Verpackungsaufschriften ein beliebtes Mittel, den
Text positiv aufzubereiten. Ein schönes Beispiel dazu befindet sich
auf der Rückseite der „Kellogg's-Cornflakes"-Verpackung, auf der
mit vielen anschaulichen Bildern ein Text gestaltet wurde, dessen
Überschrift "Das Sonnenscheinfrühstück" lautet.

Ganz wörtlich genommen würde "Sonnenscheinfrühstück" nach einer
regelbasierten Interpretation aussagen, daß hierbei Sonnenschein
gefrühstückt wird, so wie bei einem Müslifrühstück Müsli und bei
einem Sektfrühstück Sekt gefrühstückt wird. Der nachfolgende Text
lehrt den Konsumenten, daß neben der regelbasierten Interpretation
das ikonische Verfahren angewendet werden muß. Denn nach Ansicht der Anbieter gehört zu einem Frühstück weit mehr als die
ausreichende Menge an Frühstücksmitteln. Ein Frühstück soll den
Tag mit guter Stimmung beginnen lassen. Aus diesem Grund verkaufen        verschiedene    Anbieter    nicht    einfach    nur    eine

---

[117]    vgl. Kurz (1982), S. 9

[118]    Keller (1995), S. 175

Frühstückszerealie[119], sondern wie im Falle Kellogg's den Sonnenschein als sonnige Atmosphäre gleich mit dazu.

Die Sonne ist ein alter Topos und steht unter anderem sogar als Symbol einer Gottheit für Fruchtbarkeit und Wärme. In unserer heutigen modernen Welt symbolisiert die Sonne für Frühling und Sommerzeit und damit einhergehend für gute Stimmung. Die Sonne ist somit uralter Topos, der sehr häufig metaphorisch bzw. mittlerweile symbolisch verwendet wird.

Immer dann, wenn der Begriff „Sonne" nicht zur Beschreibung als Zentralkörper unseres Planetensystems und als unseren nächsten Stern beschrieben wird[120], ist es mittlerweile ebenso regelbasiert, die Jahreszeiten zu assoziieren, die von der Sonne bestimmt sind, sowie die von selbiger aktivierten Prozesse wie Leben, Wachstum, Blüte, Wärme und damit für die Menschen auch gute Laune und fröhliche Stimmung.

Ganz im Sinne Packards wird hier versucht, weit mehr als nur ein Frühstücksprodukt zu verkaufen. Es soll ein ganzes Frühstückszeremoniell inklusive guter Laune verkauft werden.

Metaphern bieten die Möglichkeit, auf elegante Weise Produktleistungen vorteilhaft auszudrücken. So ist beispielsweise der Ausdruckskomplex zu "Geschmack" in vielen Fällen metaphorisch zu interpretieren. Ausdrücke wie "geschmacklich voll", "geschmackvoll", "voll im Geschmack" beinhalten mehr als eine Beschreibung des Geschmacks. Mit dem Adjektiv "voll" läßt sich keine konkrete

---

[119]  Der Begriff "Frühstückszerealie" ist ein Fremdwort, das auf den ersten Blick aussieht wie ein Fachwort. Die Getreideflocken lassen sich unter der Bezeichnung „Frühstückse-realien" leichter in Kombination mit wissenschaftlichen Erläuterungen als gesunden und damit notwendigen Ernährungsbeitrag verkaufen.

[120]  vgl. Brockhaus (1982), S. 81 - Stichwort "Sonne"

Geschmacksangabe machen. Ein Ausdruck wie "geschmacklich voll" läßt sich übertragen interpretieren als „den ganzen Mund, evtl. sogar Körper, voll Geschmack".

Ein Wort wie "geschmackvoll" ist sogar im allgemeinen Sprachgebrauch doppeldeutig. Einmal läßt es sich interpretieren als Synonym zu "geschmacklich voll", gleichzeitig aber auch im Sinne von "von gutem Geschmack bei der Auswahl zeugend".

Auch der Ausdruck "voll im Geschmack" läßt sich aus zwei Perspektiven interpretieren. Einmal wiederum als Synonym zu "geschmacklich voll". Darüber hinaus ist ebenfalls eine Interpretation bezogen auf eine positive Wirkung im sozialen Umfeld möglich, im Sinne von 'voll im Trend'.

Metaphern können als Reiz für bildhafte Assoziationen wirken. Wie bereits erwähnt, tragen Worte, die bildhafte Assoziationen hervorrufen, dazu bei, daß die Worte schneller und leichter erfaßt und nachweislich länger behalten werden.

Voraussetzung ist dafür allerdings, daß der Rezipient die Metapher als solche erkennt. Dazu ist es notwendig, daß ihm die Bedeutung bzw. der regelhafte Gebrauch des metaphorisch verwendeten Begriffes bekannt ist. Nur dann können weitere Interpretationsprozesse durchgeführt werden. Dabei ist jedoch ebenfalls wichtig, daß der Bereich, in den die Bedeutung übertragen werden soll, dem Rezipienten geläufig ist, um metaphorisch wirken zu können.

Hayakawa bemerkt zu diesem Problem ganz treffend:
„The question is not whether metaphors are used, but whether the metaphors represent useful similarities."[121]

---

[121]  Hayakawa (1972), S. 108

Demnach sind Metaphern in Verpackungstexten nur dann sinnvoll, wenn

a)   die Metapher aus einem geläufigen Gebiet stammt,
b)   die Metapher als solche erkannt werden kann und
c)   die Metapher das Verständnis auf keinen Fall erschwert.

Metaphern stellen einen Anspruch an das Abstraktionsvermögen der Rezipienten. Dabei sollte ein gewisses Maß nicht überschritten werden. Schließlich handelt es sich um Verkaufstexte, die schnell verstehbar und gut merkbar sein sollen.

Nach diesen einschränkenden Minimalbedingungen ist nun auch ein positiver Grund zu nennen, warum Metaphern eingesetzt werden sollen:

Das Besondere einer Metapher ist, daß sie dem Betrachter eines Produktes eine neue zusätzliche Perspektive der Betrachtung verschaffen können. Wirkungsintendiert eingesetzt bieten sie daher ein ideales sprachliches Element, mit dem sich Einfluß auf die Perspektive nehmen läßt.

Metaphern, die über gegenständliche Begriffe gebildet werden, sind generell einfacher verständlich. In der Regel liegen die Gebrauchsregeln bei gegenständlichen Begriffen klar auf der Hand. Wenn das Wort *Sonne* in einer neuen Begriffskombination metaphorische Verwendung findet, werden zunächst die allgemein gängigen Gebrauchsregeln zu diesem Begriff abgerufen. Der Begriff "Sonne" wird sehr häufig im nicht wörtlichen Sinne verwendet.

Durch eine hohe Gebrauchsfrequenz wird zwangsläufig jeder metaphorisch verwendete Begriff zu einem Symbol.[122] Der ursprünglich metaphorische Gebrauch fordert von den Rezipienten assoziative Rückschlüsse. Ein regelbasierter Gebrauch erlaubt den Rezipienten regelbasierte Schlußverfahren, ein Verfahren, das für den Verwender wesentlich weniger aufwendig ist. Bei der Verwendung des Begriffs "Sonnenscheinfrühstück" wurde darauf gesetzt, daß für die Wortteile eine regelbasiertes Schlußverfahren angewendet wird, das als allgemein bekannt vorausgesetzt wird. Die Verwendung der beiden Wortteile in einer neuen Kombination macht die Metapher aus. Bei ausreichend frequentem Gebrauch wird auch hierbei das assoziative Schlußverfahren einem regelbasierten weichen.

Idealerweise wird der Begriff „Sonnenscheinfrühstück" immer in Kombination mit dem Kellogg's Produkt abgerufen, so daß der Begriff „Sonnenscheinfrühstück" zu einem Symbol für ein atmosphärisches Traumfrühstück mit Cornflakes wird.

In einem weiteren Schritt gilt es, auch den Umkehrschluß zu sichern - daß die Cornflakes zum Symbol für ein Sonnenscheinfrühstück werden. Der positiv wertende Aspekt der Interpretation soll Teil der Gebrauchsregel und damit der Bedeutung werden.

Es gilt bei der Verwendung jeder Metapher zu überprüfen, ob sie von den Konsumenten mühelos verstanden werden können. Abstrakte Metaphern stehen häufig in Zusammenhang mit einem suggerierten individuellen Produkterlebnis (z.B. „Happy End", Toilettenpapier). Bei Metaphern mit einem sehr hohen Abstraktionsniveau sollte darauf geachtet werden, daß sie mit den entsprechenden begleitenden Maßnahmen (TV-Spots, Werbeplakate etc.) eingeführt werden, da sie sonst ein Verständnisrisiko bergen können.

---

[122] vgl. Keller (1995), S. 183

Ein schönes Beispiel ist die „Marlboro"-Werbung mit Cowboys, Freiheit und Abenteuer. Die Metaphern Männlichkeit, Freiheit und Abenteuer in der Werbung für Zigaretten liegen auf einem sehr hohen Abstraktionsniveau. Aus dem Grund wird versucht, den Kunden diese Perspektive über die Darbietung von Werbefilmen, Plakaten und Events nahezubringen. Im Fall „Marlboro" ist dies sehr gut gelungen. Die überaus aufwendig gestalteten Werbemaßnahmen stehen immer unter dem Produktlogo "Marlboro". Darüber hinaus werden mittlerweile zusätzlich eine ganze Reihe von Artikeln aus dem „Marlboro" Outdoor-Euquipment sowie „Marlboro"-Touren angeboten. Auf diese Weise haben die Konsumenten gelernt, bei bestimmten Bildern die Zigarettenmarke Marlboro zu assoziieren. Neben schönen Bildern z.B. aus den Rocky Mountains in den USA wird in den Filmen unterstützt durch eine sehr intensive musikalische Untermalung, durch die kräftige und rauhe Stimme des Kommentators und durch eine sehr warme farbliche Gestaltung der Bilder versucht, die Zuschauer das "Marlboro-Feeling" erfahren zu lassen. Das Publikum soll die Bilder nicht nur sehen und im Sinne des klassischen Konditionierens als Schlüsserreiz für die Assoziation von Marlboro-Zigaretten erlernen, sondern auch das Lebensgefühl von Freiheit und Abenteuer erfahren. Das Lebensgefühl soll wiederum als Lebensqualität erfaßt werden, die ein Stück weit durch den Konsum der Zigaretten erfahren werden kann. Um sicherzugehen, daß diese Intention auch beim Publikum ankommt, wird ein Slogan eingesetzt, wie: "Feel the flavour".

Darüber hinaus werden die Zigaretten über die Attribute „Natur", „Natürlichkeit erleben" und „der Mensch in der Natur" insofern vorteilhaft präsentiert, als man vergißt, daß diese ein Suchtmittel sind und krebserregend sein können.

Obwohl diese Metaphern auf einem sehr hohen Abstraktionsniveau liegen, haben die Verbraucher keinerlei Verständnisprobleme, denn ihnen wird durch die Werbung die Aufgabe abgenommen, den Zusammenhang zum Produkt herzustellen. Der Zusammenhang wird in den Filmen und auf den Plakaten gerne durch rauchende Cowboys sowie durch die Einblendung des Logos hergestellt. In Amerika ist Zigarettenwerbung verboten. Die Firma Philip Morris ist mittlerweile nicht mehr unbedingt auf Zigarettenwerbung angewiesen, denn die Zuordnung des Logos „Marlboro" zu einer Zigarettenschachtel ist allgemein bekannt. Die „Marlboro"-Anbieter werben weiter. Jedoch werden statt Zigaretten in den Werbemaßnahmen Outdoor-Artikel u.ä. in Verbindung mit dem „Marlboro"-Logo beworben. Damit zielt die Werbemaßname indirekt auf die Zigarette.

Die Kunden haben bereits über die Werbung gelernt, das „Marlboro"-Logo und Outdoor Artikel mit „Marlboro"-Logo als Zeichen für „Marlboro"-Zigaretten zu interpretieren. Damit sind diese Artikel zum Symbol für die Zigaretten geworden. Ihre Interpretation läuft regelbasiert und automatisch ab.

## 2.8 Anspielungen

Das Charakteristikum von Anspielungen liegt genau wie bei Metaphern in der Tatsache, "daß sie sich immer auf etwas textuell schon Vorhandenes beziehen".[123] Wills grenzt Wortspiele und Anspielungen pragmatisch dergestalt voneinander ab, daß er nach Saussure erstere als langue-fundiert und letztere als parole-fundiert vorstellt. Demnach basieren Wortspiele auf kodifizierten Wörterbucheintra-

---

[123] Wills (1989), S. 3

gungen oder grammatischen Regeln, Anspielungen dagegen auf Texteinheiten unterschiedlicher Provenienz.

"Anspielungen sind ihrem Wesen nach 'relationale' Ereignisse, d.h., sie stehen in einem jeweils von Fall zu Fall zu bestimmenden Abhängigkeitsverhältnis zu einer wie auch immer gearteten historisch lokalisierbaren Formulierung"- dem Bezugselement.[124]

"Diese Bezugselemente werden gleichsam in neue Formulierungssituationen eingespielt. Sie besitzen im individuellen oder kollektiven Bewußtsein einer Sprachgemeinschaft einen mehr oder minder profilierten Stellen- und Erinnerungswert."[125]

Wills bezeichnet die Verwendung von Anspielungen in einem Text als eine Art Kollagetechnik. Es wird kein Stoff verwendet, der erst geformt werden muß, sondern es wird auf Material zurückgegriffen, das semantisch und formal bereits festgelegt ist. Die Strategie einer Anspielung ist, daß das Bezugselement in seiner spezifischen Besonderheit in der neuen Kontextsituation erhalten bleibt.

Als Beispiel eignet sich hierfür der rückseitige Verpackungstext auf "rio d'oro"-Apfelsaft-Tetra Paks. Die Überschrift lautet: "Die schönsten Äpfel sind viereckig". (Bild s. S. 183) Dieser Slogan spielt deutlich auf den für „Milka-lila Pausen" veröffentlichten Werbespruch an: "Die schönsten Pausen sind lila". Der Vorteil dieser Anspielung auf dem Tetra Pak liegt in der Tatsache, daß den Konsumenten der Spruch bereits bekannt ist und nur durch die Verknüpfung mit neuen Elementen eine witzige Nuance kreiert wird, die das Interesse der Kunden wecken soll. Hier wird versucht, über den Werbespruch eine Beziehung zwischen Produkt und Verpackung herzustellen. Gleichzeitig sollen die Verbraucher über die erläute-

---

[124]    vgl. Wills (1989), S. 3

[125]    vgl. Wills (1989), S. 3

rungsbedürftige Überschrift dazu angeregt werden, den Text genauer durchzulesen.

Das Fazit des Textes mündet wiederum in einer Anspielung: "[...] Und natürlich bruchsicher - damit Sie auch morgen noch kraftvoll zugreifen können". Dieses Text-element spielt auf den „Blend-A-Med"-Werbeslogan: "Damit Sie auch morgen noch kraftvoll zubeißen können" an. In der „Blend-A-Med"-Werbung wird dabei herzhaft in einen Apfel gebissen. Der Apfel verkörpert hier das gemeinsame Attribut, mit dem der Wiedererkennungseffekt erleichtert wird. Hier läßt sich eine neue Verknüpfung eines bereits bekannten Slogans eine ironische Komponente im Text interpretieren, denn es wird mit einem No-Name-Produkt auf einen Markenartikel referiert. Das leicht entfremdete Textelement soll als Schlüsselreiz wirken und die schon gelernten Assoziationen zu Blend-A-Med wie Qualität und Gesundheit auf den Saft übertragen lassen.

Es läßt sich bei diesem Text über die Satzkonstruktionen diskutieren, denn teilweise sind die Sätze lediglich als elliptische Aufzählungen konzipiert, was stilistisch sehr stark verkürzend wirkt. Es wäre sinnvoll gewesen, die Aufzählungen, die nicht in einem Satz vorgestellt werden sollen, in einer übersichtlichen Spiegelstrichtabelle vorzustellen o.ä. Dann wären die einzelnen Leistungen wie "vitaminschonend, recyclebar, prima zu stapeln und natürlich bruchsicher" deutlich herausgestellt und würden nicht in grammatisch inkorrekten Sätzen im Text untergehen.
Dennoch ist es hier gelungen, einen witzig-frechen Verpackungstext über eine Verpackung zu entwickeln, der zum Lesen einlädt.

## 2.9 Der Verhaltensaspekt von Zeichen

Um die Erläuterung der Begegnung von Konsumenten mit Produktverpackungen und Zeichen auf Produktverpackungen zu komplettieren, ist die Auseinandersetzung um einen letzten Aspekt zu ergänzen: um den Verhaltensaspekt, der durch wirkungsintendiert eingesetzte Zeichen zu erzielen beabsichtigt ist.

Kellers gebrauchsorientierte Theorie der Zeichen ist ein linguistischer Ansatz, der nicht von vornherein auf eine Anwendung im Konsumgütermarketing angelegt ist. Er legt den Schwerpunkt auf die Auseinandersetzung mit den Zeichen an sich, und daher bleibt er bei den durch Zeichen ausgelösten Verhaltensmodalitäten allgemein.

Der Schwerpunkt der vorliegenden Arbeit liegt in der Auseinandersetzung mit den Zeichen auf Produktverpackungen. Deshalb wird der Verhaltensaspekt hier auch nur der Vollständigkeit halber kurz vorgestellt.

Verhaltensorientierte Ansätze gehören schwerpunktmäßig in die Disziplin der Psychologie. Psychologen setzen sich allerdings selten mit dem Wesen der sprachlichen Zeichen auseinander. Einer der wenigen ist Charles William Morris. Allerdings bevorzugt er in seiner zeichentheoretischen Diskussion einen repräsentationistischen Ansatz, auf den hier nicht näher eingegangen werden soll, da ich mich für ein gebrauchsorientiertes Zeichenmodell als Grundlage dieser Arbeit entschieden habe. Er selber relativiert seine Zeichenauffassung mit den Worten: "Wir können es an diesem Punkt ruhig den Wissenschaftlern überlassen, in ihrem Bereich weitere Verfeinerungen vorzunehmen".[126]

---

[126]     Morris (1981), S. 81

Von Nutzen für die vorliegende Arbeit sind Morris` Erläuterungen zum sogenannten "Zeichenverhalten".

Da das übergeordnete Ziel aller Bemühungen, Zeichen auf Verpakkungen wirkungsvoll einzusetzen, das Auslösen eines Verhaltens - des Kaufverhaltens - ist, halte ich es für sinnvoll, hier eine kurze Zusammenstellung der wichtigsten Aspekte zu diesem Thema zu geben.

Morris erläutert den Begriff "Zeichenverhalten" als zielgerichtetes Verhalten, bei dem Zeichen die Kontrolle ausüben.[127]

Er differenziert zwischen dem *Reizobjekt*, das auf einen rezeptorischen Nerv eines lebendigen Organismus einwirkt, und der *Reaktion*, als Aktion eines Muskels oder einer Drüse eines Organismus.[128]

Dabei können als Reizobjekte jegliche Formen von Zeichen gelten, die ein Reaktion auslösen sollen.

Verpackungen werden mit sprachlichen Zeichen und durch ihre Form als Einzelreize zu einem Reizobjekt konzipiert, das als Reaktion im Idealfall den Kauf auslöst.

Dabei spielen auch die Farben der Verpackung eine große Rolle. Es wäre z.B. nicht möglich Orangensaft in grünen Tetra-Paks anzubieten, da der Einsatz der Farbe Grün bei einem Tetra Pak als Symbol für Apfelsaft gelernt wurde.[129]

Dieses Beispiel zeigt den engen Zusammenhang der beiden Betrachtungsperspektiven eines Zeichens – das Zeichen als

---

[127]  vgl. Morris (1981), S. 80

[128]  vgl. Morris (1981), S. 80

[129]  vgl. Frieling (1980), S. 18ff zu den Empfindungs- und Gefühlsqualitäten von Farben.

Wahrnehmungsreiz und bei erfolgreicher Wahrnehmung als Interpretationsreiz.

An dieser Stelle sei der Kreis zu den in Kapitel 5.4 „Verpackungen und Verbraucher" vorgestellten Einstellungswirkungen und Arten von Kaufverhalten geschlossen.


## 2.10 Zielgruppenadäquanz der sprachlichen Zeichen auf Produktverpackungen

Im Alltag werden verschiedenen Gruppen von den Sprachwissenschaftlern und Verhaltensforschern sprachliche Besonderheiten zugesprochen.
Gängig ist insbesondere die Unterscheidung der Alltagssprache in verschiedenen sozialen Schichten, in den unterschiedlichen Generationen bzw. Altersklassen und insbesondere die Unterscheidung geschlechterspezifischer Sprache.
Auch auf Produktverpackungen lassen sich Tendenzen beobachten, zu versuchen, Zielgruppenadäquanz durch einen vermeindlich angemessenen Sprachgebrauch herzustellen.

Ein schönes Beispiel bieten insbesondere diverse Kosmetikartikelverpackungen, auf denen man versucht, über geschlechterspezifischen Sprachgebrauch eine Spezialsierung des Produktes für Männer oder Frauen zu präsentieren. Den Kunden soll auf diesem Weg im Zeitalter der Forcierung gleichberechtigter Anerkennung der Geschlechter und der besonderen Berücksichtigung des weiblichen Geschlechts, ein persönliches und den spezifischen Körpereigenschaften angepaßtes Produkterlebnis geboten werden.

125

So wird das Deo „City" für Männer in verschiedenen Produkterlebnisqualitäten mit folgenden Reizwörtern charakterisiert: *Fire, Fashion, Exiting.* Der Einsatz englischer Worte soll zusätzlich einen emotionalen Reiz bewirken.

Auf dem „adidas Shower Gel" versucht man mit idealen männlichen Attributen zu werben und bietet die Typen „dynamic", „classic" und „sport" an. Gerne wird ein –Produkt in diesem Bereich in verschiedenen Typen angeboten. Den Kunden soll die Möglichkeit gegeben werden, die verschiedenen Wesensmerkmale auf die eigene Person zu projizieren, den passenden Typ auszuwählen und das Gefühl zu haben, mit dem Produkt individuell beraten zu sein.

Den von Kraft und Sportlichkeit geprägten Produkttypen speziell für Männer stehen völlig andere Charaktere bei den Produkten für Frauen gegenüber. Diese unterscheiden sich äußerlich in der Regel schon durch eine sanfte Farbgebung im Gegensatz zu den eher dunkel und kräftig gehaltenen Farben der Verpackungen für die Männer.

Das Dané Deo als „Parfum Deodorant" angeboten und damit mit einem differenzierenden zusätzlichen Wert ausgestattet. Die verschiedenen Typen „Reflexion", „Fantacy", „Creation", „Romantique", „Etoile" und „Elegance" unterstreichen durch ihre französisch wirkende Schreibweise den Parfümcharakter und damit den Mehrwert. Den Konsumentinnen werden mittels dieser Produkttypenbezeichnungen sinnliche Attribute im Sinne der klassischen Rollenklisches der Frau angeboten.

Auf den „Fa" Deodorants wird sprachlich nicht auf weibliche Wesenmerkmale gesetzt. Mit den Typenbezeich-nungen „spirit of freshness –spring flowers" oder „spirit of freshness – exotic garden" u.ä. wird stärker auf den individuellen Erlebnischarakter des Produktes gezielt. Dabei wird jedoch mit Begriffen gearbeitet, die entsprechend den allgemeinen Rollenvorstellungen besonders auf Frauen eine emotionale Reizwirkung haben.

Viele Kosmetikfirmen versuchen ihre Produkte über eine akzentuiert emotionale Sprache an die Frau bzw. an den Mann zu bringen.[130] Gerade Produkte, die auf Attribute wie Schönheit, Jugendlichkeit etc. gerichtet sind, sind nüchtern betrachtet reine Luxusartikel. Um dennoch einen breiten Absatzmarkt zu etablieren wird versucht, den Wunsch zu wecken, den allgemeinen Schönheitsidealen zu entsprechen und gleichzeitig eine Notwendigkeit dieser Produkte glaubhaft zu machen.

Bei der Studie emotionaler Aspekten von Verpackungstexten auf Kosmetikartikeln eignet sich die Methode des semantischen Differentials von Osgood, um herauszufinden, welche Gefühle und Assoziationen die emotionsgeladenen Adjektive eines Textes hervorrufen. Bei dieser Methode werden Versuchspersonen zu einem Adjektiv Eigenschaftslisten vorgelegt, anhand derer diese angeben sollen, welche Emotionen das Adjektiv in ihnen weckt.[131] Man kann auch versuchen, über Befragungen von Testpersonen herauszufinden, in welcher Form diese emotional angesprochen werden. Beide Methoden sind gängige Praktiken in Marktforschungsinstituten. Mit dieser Methode wird einerseits abgefragt, in wie weit die Testperson die Regel des Gebrauches eines Wortes beherrscht. Dies ist besonders bei neuen oder weniger gängigen Worten wichtig, um Verständnisprobleme zu vermeiden. Darüber hinaus versucht man,

---

130    Es ist allgemein bekannt, daß Frauen eine deutlich emotional ausgerichtete Sprache mit vielen Diminutiva und Euphemismen nachgewiesen werden kann. Das männliche Pendant dazu ist eine sachliche und nüchterne Sprache. Trömmel-Plötz (1982), S. 46

131    vgl. Osgood, Suci und Tannenbaum (1967): Die Arbeit mit dem Titel: "The measurement of meaning" ist dem semantischen Differential gewidmet.

die individuelle Erlebniskomponente eines Adjektives für den jeweiligen Konsumenten in der Testphase herauszufinden. Ziel ist es, ein möglichst viele Personen ansprechendes Produkterlebnis mittels Worten (hier Adjektiven) mit Schlüsselreizfunktion zu vermitteln.

Über die Kombination von Wort und Farbe wird versucht, eine spezifische Zielgruppenadäquanz des Produktes vorzustellen, um den Konsumenten neben der jeweiligen Nutzenausrichtung noch einen Erlebnis- und damit einen auf dem Markt differenzierenden Mehrwert des Produktes anbieten zu können.

## 2.11 Resümee und Zusammenstellung der Aspekte für ein Analysemodell zur Untersuchung der Qualität von Produktverpackungen

Schon bei der Vorstellung des gebrauchsorientierten Ansatzes der Zeichen von Keller konnten einige Anwendungsbezüge exemplarisch demonstriert werden. Jetzt gilt es, die Aspekte zusammenzustellen, die sich zur Analyse von Zeichen auf Produktverpackungen generell heranziehen lassen.

Einer dieser Aspekte wird gebildet durch die Kategorisierung verschiedener Begriffstypen:

- die Begriffe mit scharfen Rändern und
- die Begriffe mit unscharfen Rändern.

Per Definition läßt sich eindeutig entscheiden, ob ein Begriff scharfe oder unscharfe Ränder hat. Auf Produktpackungen wird allerdings gerne versucht, Begriffe je nach beabsichtigter Wirkung gezielt als der einen oder anderen Kategorie zugehörig zu präsentieren.

Eine weitere Kategorie bilden die Begriffe mit Prototypenstruktur. Wie schon gezeigt, befinden sich auf Produktverpackungen immer wieder Begriffe, an denen sich eine Prototypenstruktur festmachen läßt. Einerseits ist dies von Seiten der Anbieter aufgrund der steigenden Bekannt- und Beliebtheit zunächst erwünscht. Andererseits kann Prototypikalität durchaus auch negative Auswirkungen auf den Absatz verursachen. Aus diesem Grund sind dem Faktor Prototypikalität und den dazugehörigen Marketingmaßnahmen insbesondere bei der Untersuchung der Verpackungsform Beachtung zu schenken.

Taxonomien werden relevant, wenn es darum geht, ein Produkt zu klassifizieren und in das gesamte Angebot einzuordnen. Taxonomien werden gerne werbend eingesetzt, wenn die Produktvielfalt des Angebotes demonstriert werden soll (z.B. auf „Tuffi"-Milchtüten).

Meronomien werden eingesetzt, wenn ein Produkt in seine Teile strukturiert wird, wie das z.B. in einer Gebrauchsanweisung praktiziert wird.

Im Mittelpunkt des Interesses werden die verschiedenen Zeichen auf den Produktverpackungen stehen. Diese werden als Index, Ikon oder Symbol zu klassifizieren sein.

Darüber hinaus ist der Zeichencharakter der Verpackungen selbst zu analysieren.

Das Augenmerk wird deshalb auf den Zeichencharakter der Verpackung an sich und auf die damit verbundenen Wirkungen auf die Betrachter zu richten sein.

Ferner werden die drei Grundverfahren der Interpretation sowie das metaphorische Interpretationsverfahren im Zusammenhang mit dem jeweiligen Zeichen zu berücksichtigen sein.

Nicht zu vergessen sind die Referenzbeziehungen der einzelnen Zeichen untereinander sowie die Gesamtkomposition der Zeichen auf der Verpackung.

Die sprachlichen Zeichen werden auf die Intention ihres Einsatzes hin untersucht, sowie auf die Möglichkeit, mit ihnen Wirkungseffekte zu erzielen.

Dazu wird auch eine Analyse der sprachlichen Stilelemente gehören. Wenn Besonderheiten bezüglich des Zeichenverhaltens zu vermuten sind, wird auch dieser Aspekt Beachtung finden.

Mit diesen sprachwissenschaftlichen Erkenntnissen an der Hand gilt es nun, ein Analysemodell zu konzipieren, mit dessen Hilfe sich Produktverpackungen analysieren, vergleichen und bewerten lassen.

## 2.12 Text und Verpackungsaufschriften als Textsorte

In der Linguistik finden Texte in einer eigenen Disziplin besondere Berücksichtigung: in der Textlinguistik.

Allgemein wird der Begriff „Text" dann verwendet, wenn man auf die größte sprachliche Einheit referieren möchte. Dabei stehen die Sätze grammatikalisch und inhaltlich in einem Zusammenhang.

Auch auf vielen Produktverpackungen lassen sich Texte ausmachen. Darüber hinaus befinden sich auf vielen Verpackungen Fragmente, die als Teile eines Textes klassifiziert werden können.

Es stellt sich die Frage, ob es sinnvoll ist, Verpackungsaufschriften als Textsorte aufzufassen.

Wawrzyniak definiert Texte im Hinblick auf ihren kommunikativen Aspekt:

"Kommunikation erfolgt durch Texte, die zwischen den Kommunikationspartnern (Sprecher und Versteher, Schreiber und Leser) ausgetauscht werden. Unter Texten verstehen wir hier sowohl schriftliche als auch mündliche Äußerungen, die unterschiedlicher Länge sein können: von einem Ein-Wort-Text bis hin zum Gesamttext eines mehrbändigen Romans."[132]

Für die Auseinandersetzung mit Verpackungstexten ist der Hinweis auf mögliche "Ein-Wort-Texte" wichtig, da sich insbesondere auf Frontseiten von Verpackungen einzelne Worte wie "neu, professionell, classic" etc. befinden oder stichwortartige Sätze, die demnach ebenfalls textuell zu klassifizieren sind.

Zur Benennung verschiedener Textarten legt Hausenblas eine Klassifizierung vor:

- "linguale Texte (immer mit paralingualen Elementen)
- außerlinguale Texte
- gemischte Texte (entweder mit der Dominanz von lingualen oder außerlingualen Elementen)"[133]

Im Zusammenhang mit Verpackungstexten ist besonders die letzte Textart zu betrachten, da es sich dabei häufig um Kombinationen von Geschriebenem und Bildmaterial handelt. Nach Hausenblas läßt sich auch in solchen Fällen von einem Text sprechen.

Viele Konsumenten hegen großes Mißtrauen gegenüber den Darstellungen von Funktions-, Leistungs- und Werbeinformationen auf Verpackungen. Die Bewertung eines Werbetextes im weitesten Sinne durch Kunden wird sehr kritisch vorgenommen.

---

[132] Wawrzyniak (1980), S. 7

[133] Hausenblas (1977), S. 148

"Ein nicht individuell bezogener Text, den wir kostenlos bekommen können, macht uns mißtrauisch ("Ist bestimmt Reklame!"), wir erwarten immer, daß sich ein Emittent einen Vorteil vom Text verspricht.

Dieser Tauschwert [...] hat wichtige Konsequenzen [...]. Oft nämlich überwiegt der Tauschwert eines Textes seinen Gebrauchswert."[134]

Der Tauschwert bzw. der Preis werden vielfach als Zeichen für Qualität interpretiert. Er kann sogar zum Kriterium der Beurteilung der Glaubwürdigkeit eines Verpackungstextes werden. Das heißt, daß die Texte auf teuren Markenverpackungen zuweilen sogar eher eine Chance haben, akzeptiert zu werden und damit Einfluß nehmen können, als Texte auf sogenannten Billigverpackungen.

Männicke charakterisiert 1957 geeignete Texte für Produktverpackungen wie folgt:

"In möglichst kurzer, präziser Form soll der Text auf der Packung dem Käufer das Wesentliche über die Ware bekanntgeben. Je nach dem potentiellen Kundenkreis ist ein origineller und einprägsamer, werbewirksamer Text zu verwenden, dessen beste Form in einem zugkräftigen Slogan gefunden wird. Treffen die Worte in so eindrucksvoller Weise wie zum Beispiel der Slogan eines Zellglasherstellers: "Cellophan zeigt, was es schützt und schützt, was es zeigt" die charakteristischen Eigenschaften einer Ware, so kann von einer echten Wirkung des Textes gesprochen werden. [...] Der Umfang des Textes richtet sich nach dem zu verpackenden Produkt und nach dem Kundenkreis der Ware. Je kürzer der Text, um so einprägsamer ist er für die Verbraucher, daher sollte immer wieder

---

[134] Meyer (1983), S. 29

132

geprüft werden, ob der Text noch weiter gekürzt werden kann, ohne dadurch unverständlich oder sogar wirkungslos zu werden."[135]

Die Auseinandersetzung mit Texten auf Verpackungen fand marginal schon in den 50er Jahren statt. Kropff empfiehlt eine ganze Reihe von Merkmalen in den Text einzuarbeiten:
"Name des Produktes in der Form der Wortmarke,
Name und Anschrift des Herstellers der Ware,
Angaben über die verwendeten Rohstoffe,
Eigenschaften und Wirkungen der Ware,
Angaben über das Mischungsverhältnis der einzelnen Produkte,
Qualitätsangaben,
Gebrauchsanweisungen,
Gewichts- und Preisangaben, durch den Gesetzgeber vorgeschriebene Inhaltsangaben."[136]

In weiten Teilen ist der Inhalt dieser Ausführungen mittlerweile veraltet. Viele der von Kropff empfohlenen Angaben wie Inhaltsstoffe, Preis, Gewicht, etc. sind heute Pflicht, um den Kunden eine bessere Möglichkeit des Vergleichs zu bieten.
Das Kriterium der Einprägsamkeit durch Kürze ist zwar durchaus relevant, dennoch versuchen viele Hersteller den auf der Verpackung zur Verfügung stehenden Platz optimal für die textuelle Gestaltung auszunutzen. Es wird versucht, den Kunden über längere oft kurzgeschichtenartige Texte (z.B. Tchibo Feine Milde), so viel wie möglich über die Produktleistungen und Werbeinformationen mitzuteilen.

---

[135] Männicke (1957), S. 75f
[136] Kropff (1953), S. 100ff

Aufgrund der wenigen Hinweise, die in der Literatur zu finden sind, ist anzunehmen, daß man sich zur damaligen Zeit nicht besonders mit den Strategien der Textkonzeption und Textdarstellung auseinandergesetzt hat.

Lediglich Bräuer macht sich in einer Arbeit selbigen Jahrgangs Gedanken über Wirkungsmechanismen von Verpackungstexten: "Aussagen über das Material, über die Art der Ausführung der Ware und deren äußere Erscheinung, über ihren Grundnutzen sowie über den Preis wenden sich primär an das Rationalpotential im Menschen. Gewicht, Herkunft und Eignung der verwendeten Materialien, ihre Härte, Festigkeit und Elastizität sollen Fachmann und Laien eine Vorstellung von der Beschaffenheit des verpackten Gutes vermitteln. Handelt es sich bei dem Fabrikat um eine Sonderleistung, so wird dies durch Kennzeichnung der Urheberschaft, Patent- und Lizensnummer - auch etwa einer detaillierten Erläuterung über neue Verfahrensweisen und Verbesserungen - nicht nur eine rechtliche Vorschrift erfüllt, sondern darüber hinaus durch den bestätigenden Hinweis auf die Sonderleistung eine zusätzliche Werbeleistung erzielt. Das Prinzip des Markenartikels - direkte Fühlungnahme mit dem Verbraucher - erfährt seine entscheidende Realisierung durch die Werbung im allgemeinen und durch ihren informativen Dienst im besonderen."[137]

Bräuer geht zwar auf Inhaltlichkeiten ein, bleibt jedoch sehr allgemein und verzichtet gänzlich auf Beispiele. Ein Hinweis auf die Strategien der Texte auf Verpackungen ist in der Literatur nicht zu finden.

---

[137] Bräuer (1957), S. 93

Eine Analyse der Strategien zumindest an ausgewählten Beispielen ist jedoch notwendig, um einen Zusammenhang zu den Wirkungsmechanismen herstellen zu können, die Verpackungstexte auslösen sollen.

Mit der Interaktion von Text und Bild als einer Strategie und der Wirkung von Werbesprache hat sich Conen in einer Arbeit auseinandergesetzt. Das erklärte Ziel dieser Arbeit war es, "zu zeigen, daß 'grelle' Werbetexte beim Rezipienten Abneigung, zurückhaltend formulierte Texte hingegen Sympathie erzeugen".[138]
Er führte dazu ein Experimente durch, in dem Versuchspersonen „grelle" und „zurückhaltende" Texte vorgelegt wurden, die die Probanten „erleben" sollten, um von dem Erlebnis Mitteilung zu machen. Das Experiment zeigte jedoch, daß die Hypothese nicht aufrecht erhalten werden kann.[139] Conen gelangt zu der Empfehlung, es dringend zu vermeiden, Unähnlichkeiten zwischen Bild und Text innerhalb des Verpackungsaufdruckes zu akzeptieren, da dies zu einem Sympathieverlust von Seiten der Kunden führt.[140]

Einen konkreten Hinweis geben Högn und Pomplitz, der hier als Merksatz festgehalten werden soll:

"Je spezifischer das Produkt, um so spezifischer muß die textliche Ansprache sein".[141]

---

[138]  Conen (1985), S. 8
[139]  Conen (1985), S. 110
[140]  Conen (1985), S. 8
[141]  Högn und Pomplitz (1990), S. 28

135

Die Texte auf Verpackungen sollen die Vorzüge des Produktes überzeugend darstellen und den Kontakt zu den Verbrauchern knüpfen.

Idealerweise bildet ein Verpackungstext die Klammer um alle für die Verbraucher wichtigen Informationen. Diese sollten leicht verständlich dargestellt werden. Dabei kann der Text sprachlich nach Belieben des Anbieters gestaltet werden, z.B. stilistisch sehr seriös wirkend, witzig oder wissenschaftlich etc.

In einigen Fällen trifft der Text regelrecht auf Rezipientenerwartungen, z.B. dann, wenn die Kunden nicht in der Lage sind, das Produkt ohne Anleitung adäquat zu ge- oder verbrauchen. Dann hat der Verpackungstext gute Chancen, gelesen zu werden.
Daher ist es empfehlenswert, die Makrostruktur dergestalt übergreifend anzulegen, daß der Focus gezielt über zusätzliche Informationen gelenkt wird.
Ein gutes Beispiel bietet hierzu die Fischstäbchenverpackung von „Iglo". Der Blick der Kunden wird auf der Suche nach der Zubereitungsanleitung über zusätzliche Produktinformationen gelenkt (Hinweis auf die Verwendung hochwertigen Alaska Seelachses, Kundenhotline), die das Produkt stärker von anderen differenzieren und dem Kunden besondere Qualität demonstrieren.

Mit dem Abschluß dieses Kapitels bleibt festzuhalten, daß im vorangegangenen theoretischen Teil eine ganze Reihe verschiedener Ansatzpunkte, die als Grundlage dienlich sein können, vorgestellt wurden.

Im folgenden wird es Aufgabe sein, auf dieser Basis ein Modell zu entwickeln, daß sich für einen praktischen Einsatz zur Analyse von Produktverpackungen eignet.

## III. Ein Modell zur Analyse für Produktverpackungen von Standardkonsumartikeln

Ein großes Angebot, wie bei den Produkten und den Produktverpak-kungen, verleitet immer zum Vergleich und der daraus resultierende Wettbewerb zum Ranking.

Die Anbieter streben danach, daß ihre Produkte bevorzugt gekauft werden und dementsprechend auch im Wettbewerb Spitzenpositionen einnehmen. Sie setzen zu diesem Zwecke Werbemittel wie z.B. Pro-duktverpackungen ein. Rankings sind für Produktanbieter insofern von Interesse, als sie kompromißlos die Marktposition erkennen las-sen. Über einen längeren Zeitraum betrachtet, kann man die Stabilität des Angebotes im Vergleich überprüfen. Es gibt durchaus Produkte, die mit viel Werbung auf den Markt gebracht werden und sich an-fangs großer Nachfrage erfreuen. Allerdings kann es passieren, daß, nachdem die erste Neugier der Verbraucher befriedigt ist und das Produkt die Erwartungen nicht erfüllte, die Nachfragekurve steil nach unten fällt.

Ebenso kann ein etabliertes Produkt, dem von Seiten der Verbraucher eine konstant positive Einstellung nachzuweisen ist, über die Jahre im Ranking nach unten sinken, z.B. weil es nach Ablauf des Patentes wesentlich mehr Konkurrenzprodukte gibt oder weil ein Produkt bzw. dessen Outfit nicht mehr aktualisiert wurde.

Regelmäßige Rankings lassen positive Entwicklungen feststellen und negative Tendenzen im Ansatz erkennen, so daß rechtzeitig Gegen-maßnahmen eingeleitet werden können.

Für unentschlossene Verbraucher bieten Rankings von Produkten und Produktverpackungen eine Orientierungs- und Entscheidungshil-fe. Ihnen werden anhand objektiver Kriterien umfassend die Eigenschaften des Produktes oder der Verpackung inklusive deren

Vor- und Nachteile im Vergleich präsentiert. Vielen Verbrauchern kommt eine übergeordnete Bewertungsinstanz in dem Bestreben entgegen, ein möglichst optimales Produkt für das eingesetzte Geld zu erstehen. Dabei stellt sich bei noch nicht ausprobierten Produkten immer wieder die Frage, ob das Produkt hält, was die Verpackung verspricht.

Entschlossene Verbraucher sind in der Regel nur sehr schwer zu beeinflussen. So können z.B. Konsumenten, die Gewohnheitskäufer sind und schon viele gute Erfahrungen mit einem Produkt und seiner Verpackung gemacht haben, nur schwer mit wertenden Informationen einer übergeordneten Instanz erreicht werden, weil ihre Wahrnehmung diesen gegenüber blockiert ist. Sie werden erst dann beginnen, sich über Alternativen zu informieren, wenn sie mit ihrer Wahl nicht mehr zufrieden sind.

Rankings lassen sich nur auf der Grundlage vergleichender Fakten bilden. Man kann z.B. ein Ranking zum Beliebtheitsgrad verschiedener Produkte aufstellen, ausgehend von den Verkaufszahlen. An einem solchen Ranking lassen sich zwar Verkaufszahlen ablesen, aber keine Aussagen z.B. über den Faktor "Qualität".

Ich erachte es für sinnvoll, den Vergleich erst in einem zweiten Analyseschritt anzustreben. In einem ersten Schritt sollten mit Hilfe eines geeigneten Analysemodells die zu betrachtenden Objekte ausführlich auf ihre Eigenschaften hin untersucht werden. Bei mehreren Untersuchungsobjekten ergibt sich der Vergleich leicht aus der Gegenüberstellung der einzelnen Analyseergebnisse.

Die Schwierigkeit, ein universal anwendbares Analysemodell für Produktverpackungen von Standardkonsumartikeln zu erstellen, liegt darin, daß viele sinnvoll erscheinende Untersuchungskriterien durch die subjektive Bewertung desjenigen beeinflußt werden können, der die Untersuchung durchführt. Viele Kriterien, die den Stil und die Gestaltung betreffen, lassen sich nicht objektiv und neutral feststellen, da sie eine Frage des persönlichen Geschmackes sind. Insbesondere die sprachliche Gestaltung von Produktverpackungen läßt sich nicht repräsentativ einfach mit *gut* oder *schlecht* bewerten. Bei diesem Aspekt kann eine Bewertung nur als individuell gekennzeichnete Ergänzung des Betrachters der wertfreien Analyse der eingesetzten sprachlichen Mittel angeschlossen werden.

Es ist vor jeder Anwendung festzulegen, was man erreichen möchte. Möchte man z.B. eine Analyse für sich selber als Tester erstellen, so liegt die Subjektivität durchaus im Interesse des Betrachters.
Ist man an einer allgemeinen Einschätzung einer oder mehrerer Verpackungen interessiert, so sollten möglichst viele verschiedene Betrachter eine Analyse nach dem gleichen Schema vornehmen. Nur dann erhält man einen repräsentativen Überblick über die allgemeine Einschätzung der Verpackung.

Ich werde im folgenden ein Analysemodell für Verpackungen von Standardkonsumartikel entwickeln. Der Schwerpunkt soll auf der sprachwissenschaftlichen Untersuchung liegen. Dabei sollen die aus der gebrauchsorientierten Zeichentheorie Kellers herausgearbeiteten anwendungsadäquaten Aspekte besondere Berücksichtigung finden. Technische, psychologische, soziologische, designerische und sonstige Aspekte werden der Vollständigkeit halber in den Grundzügen ebenfalls aufgegriffen.

**Ziel** dieses Arbeitsschrittes ist es, ein universell einsetzbares Analysemodell zu entwickeln, in dem folgende übergeordnete Untersuchungskriterien Berücksichtigung finden:

- die technischen Aspekte der Verpackung
- die Zeichen auf der Verpackung
- das Verpackungsdesign
- die Produktadäquanz der Verpackung
- die Zielgruppenadäquanz der Verpackung

## 3.1 Die technischen Aspekte der Verpackung

Bevor die Untersuchung der Kommunikationsfunktion der Verpackung erfolgt, ist zu überprüfen, ob allgemeine Grundfunktionen der Verpackung erfüllt sind. Dabei sind meiner Ansicht nach folgende Punkte zu berücksichtigen:

**a) Schützt die Verpackung das Produkt und die Umwelt ausreichend?**

Verpackungen sind nur dann sinnvoll, wenn sie ausreichend stabil sind. Verbraucher vermeiden es, beschädigte Verpackungen zu kaufen. Insbesondere bei luftdicht verpackten Lebensmitteln wirken und sind beschädigte Verpackungen unhygienisch. Darüber hinaus verderben viele Produkte bei einer Kontamination mit der Luft sehr schnell.

Die Verpackung sollte auch einen ausreichenden Schutz der Ware beim Transport garantieren.

Allzu dünne Folien reißen gerne, und dünne Plastikbecher halten nur wenig Druck aus. Für die Käufer ist es höchst ärgerlich, wenn z.B. ein Joghurtbecher in der Einkaufstasche platzt und neben dem Verlust der Ware auch noch Verunreinigungen der anderen Waren und des Transportmittels (Tasche) zu beklagen sind.

Auch wenn dünnes Glas im Kostenfaktor für die Anbieter günstig erscheint, ist es wegen der hohen Bruchgefahr als Verpackungsmaterial nicht zu empfehlen. Da in Gläsern in der Regel flüssige Waren verpackt werden, ist damit zu rechnen, daß ein kaputtes Glas nicht nur einen Haufen unangenehmer Scherben verursacht, sondern auch eine Menge Unflat.

Deckel bieten ebenfalls eine große Fehlerquelle. Undichte Deckel lassen Produkte entweichen, verunreinigen die Verpackung und lassen Luft an das Produkt bzw. Kohlensäure entweichen. Bei Getränkeflaschen hat man deshalb mittlerweile Sicherungsringe und Klebeetiketten für die Verschlüsse entwickelt, die vor dem ersten Gebrauch Ungeöffnetheit garantieren.


Es ist nicht nur darauf zu achten, daß das Produkt vor der Umwelt und die Umwelt vor dem Produkt geschützt wird - die Verpackung muß die Ware in der Verpackung dergestalt schützen, daß z.B. die Plätzchen zum Tee nicht völlig zerbröckelt und damit nicht mehr servierfähig zu Hause ankommen. Zu diesem Zweck werden viele Keksschachteln mit einem Plastikschiebefach ausgestattet, das die Plätzchen vor Quetschungen schützt. Ähnlich verfährt man auch mit abgepacktem Obst und Gemüse, bei dem man die Folie mit einem Papptablett stabilisiert, was zusätzlich optische Vorteile bewirkt. Der Nachteil solcher Stabilisierungsmaßnahmen ist, daß sie zusätzliches

Verpackungsmaterial erforderlich machen, was die Kosten erhöht und die Entsorgung erschwert.[142]

Grundsätzlich sollten die Waren so verpackt sein, daß zu erkennen ist, ob die Verpackung original verschlossen ist oder bereits geöffnet wurde. Unversiegelte Kartons verleiten nebenbei Langfinger dazu, Waren zu entwenden, zu ergänzen oder gar auszutauschen. Darüber hinaus ist es oft nicht möglich, eine Verpackung mit ihrem Inhalt umzutauschen, die nicht mehr original verschlossen ist.

**b)     Läßt sich das Produkt in der Verpackung angenehm transportieren?**

Bei dieser Fragestellung interessiert hauptsächlich, ob es den Kunden gelingen kann, das Produkt in der Verpackung ohne besondere Vorkommnisse nach Hause zu transportieren. Der Transport vom Hersteller in den Laden ist dabei das geringere Problem, da in der Regel geeignete Transportgeräte zur Verfügung stehen.

Besondere Transportschwierigkeiten bereiten Waren, deren Verpakkungen die Schutzfunktion nicht ausreichend erfüllen, Kühlwaren und sperrige bzw. schwere Güter.

Bei Kühlwaren muß garantiert sein, daß die Verpackung die Kälte und damit das Tiefgefrorensein der Ware so lange konserviert, wie der Kunde für den Transport vom Laden nach Hause benötigt, d.h. wenigstens eine halbe Stunde. Da tiefgekühlte Produkte kein zweites

---

[142] In bezug auf die Schutzfunktion von Verpackungen sind Glühbirnenkartons ein beeindruckendes Beispiel. Diese leicht zerbrechliche Ware, die zudem äußerst unangenehme Scherben verursacht, wird im Gegensatz zu vielen anderen weniger gefährlichen Produkten wie z.B. Keksen nur durch einen dünnen Karton geschützt.

Mal mehr eingefroren werden sollen, bieten einige Firmen ergänzend Kühltüten an. Auf diese Weise bleibt nicht nur die Ware länger gefroren - es bietet sich auch ein weiteres absatzträchtiges Objekt.

Eine transportgerechte Verpackung für sperrige bzw. schwere Güter stellt ein generelles Problem dar, da die Verpackung die Eigenschaften des Produktes nicht beeinflussen kann.

In solchen Fällen sind innovative Tricks und Kniffe gefragt. So werden z.B. 10kg-Waschmitteltrommeln mit Tragehenkeln ausgestattet. Sehr transportfreundlich ist auch die Konstruktion, die z.B. von „Warsteiner" oder „Frühkölsch" angeboten wird: Bierkästen zum Halbieren. Diese erleichtern das Tragen wesentlich und sind bedeutend weniger schädlich für den Rücken des Trägers, ebenso wie die Umstellung von Glas- auf Petflaschen verschiedener Wasser- und Limonadenhersteller.

Die Transportabilität eines Produktes kann durchaus ein Kriterium der Kaufentscheidung sein. Wenn man die Ware nämlich nicht nach Hause transportieren kann, verzichtet man eher darauf, sich eine Transportlösung zu überlegen, insbesondere wenn geeignetere Alternativen zur Verfügung stehen.

c)      **Ist es möglich, das Produkt in der Verpackung adäquat zu lagern?**

Diese Frage ist besonders bei Produkten relevant, die nicht nach dem erstmaligen Gebrauch verbraucht sind. Dann spielt z.B. die Wiederverschließbarkeit der Verpackung eine große Rolle.

Die Anbieter von „Golden Toast" und „Brand Zwieback" haben eine pfiffige Idee zur Wiederverschließbarkeit ihrer Verpackungen umgesetzt. Beide Verpackungen sind zugeschweißt. Das heißt, man beschädigt beim ersten Öffnen auf jeden Fall die Verpackung und steht dann vor dem Dilemma, das Produkt entweder umfüllen zu müssen oder beim behelfsmäßigen Zusammendrücken der Öffnung in Kauf nehmen zu müssen, daß zumindest beim Toastbrot die erste Scheibe schnell trocken wird. Diesem Mißstand wurde Abhilfe geschaffen, indem man der Verpackung jeweils einen speziellen Wiederverschlußklebestreifen zugefügt hat. Wenn man darauf achtet, die Verpackung vorsichtig aufzureißen, kann diese leicht wiederverschlossen und bis zum Verbrauch des Produktes verwendet werden. Der Vorteil solcher Wiederverschließstreifen ist, daß über eine Beschriftung desselben ein zusätzlicher Werbeeffekt erzielt werden kann. Wesentlich einfacher ist die Handhabung jedoch bei Toasttüten, die mit einem kleinen Klämmerchen verschlossen sind und mit selbiger wiederverschlossen werden können.

Für die Frage nach einer entsprechenden Lagerung bleibt festzuhalten, daß die Verpackung eine Lagerung des Produktes bis zum absoluten Verbrauch möglich machen sollte und daher leicht wiederzuverschließen sein sollte.

Viele Anbieter offerieren ihre Produkte zu Aktionen in Schmuckdosen („Frolic" in der Schmuckdose, „Persil" in der Schmuckdose etc.) oder anderen Aufbewahrungsobjekten („Klinex" in der Frischebox), oder es werden zusätzliche Aufbewahrungsmittel auf den Markt gebracht (z.B. die Dose zum Knäckebrot – „Wasa").

**d)   Portioniert die Verpackung das Produkt sinnvoll?**

In der Werbung werden ein ganze Reihe von Verpackungen angepriesen, die Produkte ganz unterschiedlich portionieren, z.B.:

- Familienpackung („Landliebe Landmilch" 1,5l)
- Familienvorratspackung (Sunil)
- Vorratspackung
- Singleback (Brot)
- Triopack („Rauch" Eistee)
- Kombipack
- Riesenpack
- XXL („Ritter Sport")
- Doppelpack („El'Vital" Haarpflege)
- 10er-Pack („Cien"-Toilettenpapier)
- 6Pack (Bier)
- 5er-Pack („Knorr"-Salatsauce)
- 4er-Sets (Joghurts wie „Nestlé LC1", „Danone für Kinder", „Fruchtz-
  werge" etc.)
- Super Sparpackung (blend-a-dent)
- Frischebox („Dickmann minis")

Bei der Betrachtung der verschiedenen Portionierungseinheiten fällt
auf, daß gerne zur einfach portionierten Produktverpackung zusätzlich Verpackungen mit größeren Produktmengen angeboten werden.
Die Verpackungen mit größeren Portionen werden zusätzlich beworben. Die Kunden sollen den Eindruck gewinnen, daß sie im
Verhältnis Geld sparen, wenn sie gleich eine größere Produktmenge
auf einmal kaufen. Die Anbieter hoffen darauf, daß nach dem Kauf

145

einer größeren Produktmenge auch mehr des Produktes verkonsumiert wird, insbesondere bei Süß- und Knabberwaren.

Viele Kunden sind zufrieden, wenn sie den Eindruck haben, Geld gespart zu haben, auch wenn dies objektiv betrachtet gar nicht der Fall ist.

Oft werden Verpackungen von vornherein mit größeren Portionsmengen angeboten. Das kann z.B. bei Brot sehr ärgerlich sein, wenn z.B. ein Single weiß, daß lediglich große Portionen angeboten werden, er aber im Verbrauch keinesfalls so schnell sein wird, daß das Produkt vor dem Verderb komplett verbraucht sein wird. In seltenen Fällen wird ergänzend eine Verpackung konzipiert, die auf die Belange von Singlehaushalten abgestimmt ist. Als eigenes Angebot auf dem Markt wird auch diese Verpackung besonders beworben (z.B. „Unox ein Teller" Gerichte, „Singleback" bei Brot oder „Iglo Geflügeldippers"-1 Portion).

In einigen Fällen werden entgegen der Strategie, möglichst viel von einem Produkt zu verkaufen, auch Minimengen angeboten - bei Süßigkeiten, die als Snacks unterwegs verzehrt werden sollen und mit Vorliebe in Ständern vor der Kasse angeboten werden.

So gibt es z.B. Minipakete von „Toblerone", „Ferrero Küsschen", „Ferrero Roché", „Mon Cherie" etc. Aber selbst in diesem Bereich ist wieder ein Trend zu verbuchen, die Verpackungen größer und damit teurer werden zu lassen. So werden z.B. „Mars" und „Twix" auch in extra großen Snackverpackungen angeboten, und wer „Ritter Sport Minis" konsumieren möchte, muß gleich ein 10er-Paket kaufen.

„Mars", „Milky Way" u.ä. Schokoriegel werden seit neuestem in Großpaketen „+ 1 Riegel meeehr! Inhalt" angeboten. Der dazugehörige Hinweis wird optisch durch die Schreibweise „meeehr!" mit drei „e" und Ausrufezeichen zum Blickfang gemach, was gleichzeitig als

Zeichen für eine intensive Betonung in der gesprochenen Sprache interpretiert werden soll.[143]

„Unox" bietet den Kunden ein sogenanntes „Schlemmer-Trio" bestehend aus drei verschiedenen Soßen in einem Set an. Neben der Interpretation, daß es sich bei diesem Set um ein günstiges Angebot handelt, soll zusätzlich als Vorteil interpretiert werden, daß man drei verschiedene Produkttypen zu einem vorteilhaften Preis erwerben kann, d.h. die Soßen für den Grillabend können mit dem Kauf eines einzigen Sets ohne weiteren Aufwand abgedeckt werden.

Eine sinnvolle Portionierung eines Produktes durch die Verpackung läßt sich an einer einfachen Grundregel festmachen: Ist es realistisch, daß die Zielgruppe das Produkt vor dem Verderb komplett verbrauchen kann? Wenn dies nicht der Fall ist, werden viele Konsumenten auf kleiner portionierte Alternativen umschwenken.

Desweiteren ist bei der Frage der Portionierung die Verwendungshäufigkeit zu beachten. Es gibt Produkte, die eher selten verwendet werden. Aus diesem Grund schrecken große Packungen und ein hoher Preis vom Kauf ab. Dies ist z.B. bei ungewöhnlichen Gewürzen der Fall oder bei Sekundenkleber.

Ein weiterer Aspekt ist der Transport. Produktverpackungen mit einer großen Portionsmenge werden oft groß und schwer. Dies ist z.B. bei 1,5l Getränkeverpackungen der Fall (Tetra-Pak oder Plastikflasche). So wird man bei den alltäglichen Getränken keine 1,5l

---

143     Die Betonung des Wortes „meeehr!" in der gesprochenen Sprache ergibt sich von selber, wenn das Wort gesprochen wird, wie es geschrieben steht. Hierbei handelt es sich um eine ikonische Unterstützung der Semantik von „mehr".

Glasflasche finden. Hier wurde zugunsten der Transportabilität auf Plastik umgeschwenkt.[144]

Der Faktor Transport nimmt z.B. auch auf die Portionierung von Cornflakes- und Waschmittelverpackungen großen Einfluß. Cornflakeskartons mit mehr als 375g Inhalt würden eine Einkaufstasche alleine zum Transport benötigen und damit nur einen sehr einseitigen Einkauf zulassen. Waschmittelkartons mit mehr als 10kg Gewicht könnten von einem Verbraucher durchschnittlicher Statur schlecht aus dem Regal gehoben, geschweige denn ohne Hilfsmittel zum Auto oder nach Hause transportiert werden.

**e)     Ist die Verpackung auf ihren spezifischen Einsatz ausgerichtet?**

Diese Frage steht in engem Zusammenhang mit der Möglichkeit, ein Produkt zu transportieren und zu lagern.

Die Ausrichtung auf einen spezifischen Einsatz ist z.B. bei flüssigen Produkten in Tetra Paks, Spülmitteln oder Klebern in Plastikflaschen relevant. In diesen Fällen ist es sinnvoll bis notwendig, die Verpackung mit einer Schütt- bzw. Tropfvorrichtung auszustatten. Besonders Spülmittel- und Kleberflaschen verärgern die Kundschaft, wenn beim Gebrauch unvermittelt eine riesige Produktmenge aus der Flasche strömt. Gerade bei Kleber kann dabei einiges Unheil angerichtet werden.

Zum spezifischen Nutzen einer Verpackung kann auch gehören, daß sie z.B. als Geschenk geeignet ist. Dementsprechend werden Parfums in edlen Flakons und Pralinen in noblen Schachteln angeboten. Geschenkverpackungen sind im übrigen die einzigen Verpackungen, bei

---

[144]     Bei Sekt- und Champagnerflaschen wird die 1,5-Liter-Magnum Ausführung als Zeichen für Exklusivität interpretiert. Bei einem derartigen Luxusartikel steht der Faktor "Praktikabilität" im Hintergrund.

denen es von Seiten der Käufer sogar erwünscht ist, daß die Hülle mehr Inhalt verspricht als tatsächlich darin ist.

Es gibt in der Tiefkühltruhe z.B. portioniertes Spaghetti-Eis. Der spezifische Nutzen der Verpackung des Eises wurde insofern berücksichtigt, als daß selbiges in Desserttöpfchen aus Plastik angeboten wird. Dabei läßt sich der Plastikdeckel abnehmen und als Fuß unter das Töpfchen klemmen - und schon hat man einen Eisbecher.

**f)    Ist die Verpackung praktisch?**

Eng mit den Aspekten der Transportierbarkeit, der Lagerung, der Portionierung und des spezifischen Nutzens verbunden steht die Frage, ob eine Verpackung auch praktisch ist.

So sind z.B. 6er Pakete Tiefkühlpizza **nicht** praktisch, weil sie nicht in das üblicherweise im Kühlschrank integrierte Tiefkühlfach passen. Für diese Kartons benötigt man eine extra Tiefkühltruhe. Es gibt eine ganze Reihe von Tiefkühlprodukten, die sich nur zum Kauf eignen, wenn man einen separaten Gefrierschrank besitzt.

Sehr praktisch dagegen sind wiederverschließbare Ausgießvorrichtungen bei Tetra Paks. Geöffnete Tetra-Paks passen oft nicht aufrecht in die Kühlschrankfächer. Insbesondere die 1,5l Paks lassen sich nur in der Kühlschranktür unterbringen und das nur längs mit viel Platzverbrauch. Seit es die wiederverschließbare Ausgießvorrichtung gibt, können Tetra Paks auch quer in die Kühlschranktür gestellt werden, ohne daß man Gefahr läuft, daß die Flüssigkeit beim Öffnen und Schließen der Kühlschranktür ausläuft.

Die Minipäckchen von Tempo sind ebenfalls praktisch, weil sie in jede Handtasche und in viele Hosentaschen passen. Unpraktisch dagegen ist Ketchup in Glasflaschen, weil man endlos braucht, bis er dort herausläuft und dann meist herausgeschossen kommt und das Essen ungenießbar macht.

Praktisch ist z.B. auch die "denk mit aktiv Reisetube" ein Waschmittel für unterwegs, daß sich ohne Probleme auch in kleinem Gepäck unterbringen läßt.

**FAZIT:**

Folgende Fragestellungen lassen sich für den ersten Punkt eines Analysemodells für Produktverpackungen festhalten:

Für das Analysemodell sind folgende technisch orientierte Fragen zu vermerken:

- **Schützt die Verpackung das Produkt und die Umwelt ausreichend?**
- **Läßt sich das Produkt in der Verpackung angenehm transportieren?**
- **Ist es möglich, das Produkt in der Verpackung entsprechend zulagern?**
- **Portioniert die Verpackung das Produkt sinnvoll?**
- **Ist die Verpackung auf ihren spezifischen Einsatz ausgerichtet?**
- **Ist die Verpackung praktisch?**

## 3.2 Die Verpackung als Zeichen

Das Resümee der zeichentheoretischen Auseinandersetzung mit dem Thema "Verpackungen" (Kap. 2.1) ergab, daß eine Verpackung im Idealfall selbst zum Zeichen wird - zum Zeichen für das Produkt. Bei einer ersten Konfrontation mit der Verpackung im Laden wird in der Regel entweder das symptomische oder das ikonische Interpretationsverfahren angewendet. Das symptomische Verfahren wird eingesetzt, wenn die Verpackung bis dato noch nicht bekannt ist und von ihrer Beschaffenheit kausal auf den Inhalt geschlossen wird (z.B. Tetra Pak - Flüssigkeit). Das ikonische Interpretationsverfahren wird angewendet, wenn die Verpackung bereits aus der Werbung bekannt ist. Die Verpackung im Regal wird assoziativ interpretiert aufgrund ihrer Ähnlichkeit zu der Verpackung aus der Werbung. In jedem Fall soll die Verpackung über hochfrequente Konfrontation mit den Kunden regelbasiert interpretiert und damit zum Symbol für das Produkt werden. Im Idealfall wird die Verpackung bei sehr häufigen Konfrontationen mit dem Konsumenten reflexartig bzw. ähnlich dem Interpretationsverfahren der Symptome interpretiert. Mit dieser schnellen Form der Interpretation ist die Verpackung als Zeichen für ein Produkt zur Selbstverständlichkeit geworden, so geschehen z.B. bei der „Coca-Cola" Flasche.

Darüber hinaus sollen auch die zentralen Zeichen auf der Verpakkung längerfristig zu Symbolen werden. So werden z.B. Firmenzeichen und -logos bei häufiger Konfrontation symbolisch interpretiert. Genauso werden aber auch die Bilder auf den Frontseiten auf Dauer nicht mehr ikonisch, sondern symbolisch bzw. reflexartig interpretiert. Ein Apfel auf der Frontseite eines Tetra-Paks wird dann auf einen Blick ebenso als Zeichen für Apfelsaft interpretiert wie die rote Schleife für „Persil" (Waschmittel). Aber auch die

Farbe einer Verpackung kann zum Symbol ihrer selbst werden. Würde man versuchen, „Milka" in roten Tafeln anzubieten, Apfelsaft in orangen Tetra-Paks oder Orangensaft in lilanen, würde niemand auf Anhieb das Produkt, das sich hinter der Verpackung verbirgt, erkennen. Es würde vermutlich sogar zu Verwechslungen kommen.

Für das Analysemodell sind folgende Fragen festzuhalten:

- Ist die Verpackung prototypisch?
- Hat die Verpackung Symbolcharakter?
- Sind auf der Verpackung Bilder, die Symbolcharakter haben?
- Sind auf der Verpackung Zeichen, die Symbolcharakter haben?
- Hat die Farbe der Verpackung Symbolcharakter?
- Wird die Verpackung reflexartig interpretiert?

## 3.3 Zeichen auf Verpackungen

### 3.3.1 Die Zeichen auf Verpackungen

Bevor die Analyse der einzelnen Zeichenarten beginnt, ist es sinnvoll, alle Zeichen in einer Übersicht zusammenzustellen, die auf der gewählten Verpackung vorhanden sind, um im Anschluß eine Zuordnung vorzunehmen.

Die meisten Zeichen auf den Produktverpackungen dienen der Kommunikation mit den Konsumenten. Dementsprechend lassen sie sich auch nach der nach Keller vorgestellten Klassifikation als Index, Ikon oder Symbol identifizieren. Dazu ist das jeweilige Interpretationsverfahren zu untersuchen, mit Hilfe dessen die Zeichen verstanden werden.

Darüber hinaus ist die Intention zu erforschen, mit der die Zeichen auf der Verpackung eingesetzt wurden, denn nur so läßt sich ihr Sinn entschlüsseln.

Über den spezifischen Sinn des zielgerichteten Einsatzes der Zeichen lassen diese sich jeweils wiederum Kategorien zuordnen. So kommt es, daß einem Zeichen durchaus mehrere Klassifikationsmerkmale zugesprochen werden können.

### 3.3.2 Die Bildzeichen auf der Verpackung und ihre Intention

Bildzeichen gehören nach Keller häufig zur Klasse der Ikone. Sie stehen in der Regel aufgrund ihrer Ähnlichkeit mit dem Produkt oder einer Zutat in Beziehung zu selbigem. Dementsprechend werden Bildzeichen auch assoziativ über die Ähnlichkeit der Abbildung mit ihrem Referenzobjekt interpretiert und verstanden.

Darüber hinaus befinden sich oft auch Abbildungen auf Verpackungen, die z.B. Verwendungserläuterungen visuell unterstützen sollen. Ebenso werden auf Verpackungen z.T. auch Abbildungen aufgedruckt, die ausschließlich der Produktwerbung dienen. Die meisten dieser Bilder und Graphiken lassen sich zunächst durch das ikonische Interpretationsverfahren verstehen. Da Verpackungen jedoch die Eigenschaft haben, dem Kunden in der Werbung und im Laden immer wieder zu begegnen, werden insbesondere die Graphiken auf den Frontseiten der Verpackungen bei hochfrequenten Begegnungen mit den Konsumenten mit der Zeit zu Symbolen. Dann wird das assoziative Schlußverfahren durch ein regelbasiertes Interpretationsverfahren abgelöst. Der Vorteil dabei ist, daß ein regelbasiertes Schlußverfahren automatisierter und damit schneller abläuft als das assoziative. Insbesondere bei Produkten, die von einem Verbraucher immer wieder gekauft werden, läuft das Interpretationsverfahren der Bilder irgendwann ähnlich der Interpretation von Symptomen ab. Die Interpretationsregel lautet dann z.B.: "Immer, wenn ich eine goldene Kaffeebohne auf einer Verpackung sehe, handelt es sich um „Tchibo"-Kaffee ". Es wird ein kausaler Zusammenhang zwischen einem graphischen Element auf der Produktverpackung und dem Produkt hergestellt. Das graphische Element der goldenen Kaffeebohne ist dann in Kombination mit der typischen Form des Kaffeepaketes ebenso ein prototypisches Erkennungszeichen wie der rote Punkt auf der Möwenschnabelattrappe. Das symptomische Interpretationsverfahren läuft sehr stark automatisiert und reflexartig ab und damit besonders schnell.

Darüber hinaus können Graphiken komplizierte Texte visuell unterstützen bzw. gänzlich übernehmen. So sind Pfeile beispielsweise bereits über regelhaften Gebrauch zum Symbol für eine Bewegungsrichtung geworden. Dementsprechend können in der Graphik zum Öffnen des Verschlusses von „Vitafit"-Apfelsaftverpackung die symbolischen Elemente der Pfeile in dem ungewohnten Kontext der ikonischen Elemente des Verschlusses und der Finger schnell und einfach interpretiert werden.


Es gibt auf Produktverpackungen auch Bilder, die mit reiner Blickfangfunktion ohne zusätzliche Zeichenqualität installiert wurden, bzw. bei denen man sich nicht die Mühe gemacht hat, einen Zusammenhang zum Produkt herauszuarbeiten. Zum Zwecke des Blickfangs werden gerne Bilder oder Formen verwendet, die auf eine sexuell ansprechende Wirkung bei den Kunden abzielen. Diese Werbepraxis ist insbesondere bei Autozubehörkatalogen und auf den Flaschen alkoholischer Getränke beliebt[145]. Man kann die erotischen Zeichen auf Flaschen alkoholischer Getränke dahingehend interpretieren, daß unterschwellig auf den enthemmenden Zustand hingewiesen werden soll, der durch den Konsum des Produktes ausgelöst werden kann, der wiederum dazu führen kann, daß man leichter Personen des anderen Geschlechtes kennenlernt oder man selber kennengelernt wird. Ein direkter Zusammenhang des Zeichens mit dem Produkt besteht jedoch oft nicht und wird von Seiten des Anbieters auch nicht vorgestellt.[146]

Nicht alle Bildzeichen auf Produktverpackungen lassen sich direkt interpretieren. Wenn einem z.B. auf einer Schokoladenschachtel das Gesicht eines Jungen entgegenstrahlt oder ein Waschmittelkarton durch eine knallrote Schleife auffällt, dann handelt es sich zunächst ebenfalls um Ikone, denn die Abbildungen zeigen eindeutige Ähnlichkeiten zu einem Referenzobjekt. Das jeweilige Referenzobjekt ist in diesen beiden Fällen allerdings nicht das Produkt. In solchen Fällen bedarf es bei der Interpretation noch eines Zwischenschrittes. Im Griceschen Sinne ist insbesondere bei der Betrachtung der kommunikativen Zeichen auf Produktverpackungen davon auszugehen, daß sie intendiert sind. Allerdings darf bei den Produktverpackungen von Standardkonsumartikeln nicht davon ausgegangen werden, daß die Betrachter mit intensiven Interpretationsbemühungen versuchen werden, den tieferen Sinn dieses Ikons zu ergründen. Dementsprechend einfach muß es sein, den Zusammenhang herzustellen, und dementsprechend unterstützend muß in der Werbung gearbeitet werden.

---

[145] „Bacio Chardonet frizzante" ist z.B. mit einer erotisch dargestellten Frau auf dem Etikett ausgestattet und Coca Cola-Flaschen sind von ihrer Form her dem Körper einer Frau nachempfunden und sollen beim Anfassen erotisierend wirken.

[146] Beispielsweise bei Parfum hingegen kann eine weibliche Flaconform durchaus im Zusammenhang mit dem Produkt interpretiert werden.

Darüber hinaus sollte der Kontext der anderen Zeichen der Interpretation dienlich sein.

Dann ist für die Verbraucher leicht zu erfassen, daß das strahlende Gesicht des Jungen auf der Schokoladenschachtel neben der Aufschrift "Kinderschokolade" die Zielgruppe demonstrieren soll. Das gesunde und fröhliche Aussehen des Jungen, das Lächeln, das den Blick auf strahlend weiße Zähne freigibt, sind Merkmale, die durch unsere gesellschaftliche Erfahrung mittlerweile regelbasiert und damit symbolisch interpretierbar sind. Nur zufriedene Kinder lachen, und strahlend weiße Zähne hat man nur, wenn man sich gesund ernährt. Diese Interpretationsregeln, die unbewußt beim Betrachten des gesamten Bildes abgerufen werden sollen, sollen anschließend auf das Produkt in der Verpackung übertragen werden: Das Produkt macht die Kinder zufrieden und ist gesund. Eine bewußte Reflexion dieser Merkmale würde allenfalls den Schluß zulassen, daß die Schokolade die Kinder zufrieden macht, nicht aber, daß sie gesund ist. Zu diesem Zweck befindet sich neben der Abbildung eines Milchglases der ergänzende Hinweis "- Kakao + Milch". Auch in der Werbung wird die Schokolade wegen ihres hohen Milchanteils als Beitrag zu einer gesunden Ernährung gelobt.

Das Gesicht auf der Kinderschokoladenschachtel ist bis heute nicht verändert worden, weil es mittlerweile zum Symbol und damit zum Erkennungszeichen für Kinderschokolade geworden ist

Ebensowenig ist auf den ersten Blick ersichtlich, was eigentlich eine rote Schleife auf einem Waschmittelkarton zu suchen hat, wo es sich dabei wahrlich nicht um ein Produkt handelt, das zum Verschenken geeignet ist. Mit der roten Schleife kann folgendes Schlußverfahren initiiert werden: Die rote Schleife auf dem Persilkarton ist das Ikon einer roten Schleife einer Geschenkverpackung. Ähnlich dem metaphorischen Verfahren ist die rote Schleife auf der Produktverpackung eingesetzt, um den Charakter eines Geschenkes zu demonstrieren - ein Geschenk des Herstellers (der Firma „Henkel") an die Verbraucher.

Geschenke werden in der Regel sorgfältig ausgewählt und sollten qualitativ anspruchsvoll sein. Diese Merkmale sollen nun zunächst assoziativ auf die mit der roten Schleife als Geschenk gekennzeichnete Persilverpackung übertragen werden. Bei ausreichend frequenter Begegnung mit dieser Verpackung wird die rote Schleife zum Symbol, weil das Interpretationsverfahren nicht mehr regelbasiert, sondern assoziativ abläuft. Im Idealfall ist die Gebrauchsregel der roten Schleife als Markenzeichen des Persilkartons so in Fleisch und Blut übergegangen, daß sie ähnlich einem Symptom einen Reflex auslöst, der das Produkt Persil mit allen Qualitäten erkennen und in den Einkaufswagen stellen läßt. Dann wirkt die vollständig verinnerlichte Regel des Gebrauchs wie ein Kausalzusammenhang.

Für die Analyse der Bildzeichen auf Produktverpackungen von Standardkonsumartikeln bleiben folgende Fragestellungen festzuhalten:

- Bildet das Bildzeichen ein reales Objekt ab und ist aufgrund der Ähnlichkeit zu interpretieren?
- Ist die Abbildung abstrakt und damit erläuterungsbedürftig?
- Wird das Bild nach dem ikonischen Interpretationsverfahren interpretiert?
- Wird das Bild nach dem symbolischen Interpretationsverfahren interpretiert?
- Ist ein direkter Schluß möglich oder bedarf es Zwischenschritte bzw. Erläuterungen?
- (Dies gilt auch bei objektgetreuen Abbildungen, die nicht in direktem

157

Zusammenhang mit dem Produkt stehen.)
- Kann das Bildzeichen ohne Probleme im intendierten Sinn interpretiert werden?
- Paßt das Bildzeichen in das Verpackungskonzept?
- Erzeugt das Bildzeichen bei der Zielgruppe positive Geneigtheit oder eine
  ablehnende Haltung?

### 3.3.4 Die sprachlichen Zeichen

Die sprachlichen Zeichen lassen sich aus verschiedenen Perspektiven betrachten. Sie lassen sich mit Hilfe der verschiedenen Disziplinen der Linguistik gewinnbringend untersuchen, z.B. über eine grammatikalische, semantische oder semiotische Analyse.

An diesem Punkt der Entwicklung eines Analysemodells erachte ich es für sinnvoll, zunächst die Untersuchungskriterien und deren möglichen Erkenntnisgewinn bezüglich der Form zusammenzustellen, um darauf aufbauend inhaltliche Aspekte und textuelle Referenzen zu bearbeiten. Bei der Anwendung des Analysemodells auf konkrete Fallbeispiele wird zu überprüfen sein, ob diese Vorgehensweise praktikabel ist.

Zusammenfassend sollen die sprachlichen Zeichen tabellarisch vorgeführt werden, die üblicherweise auf Verpackungen verwendet werden. Die Übersicht erhebt keinen Anspruch auf absolute Vollständigkeit. Sie soll nicht als Reglement verstanden werden, sondern als Orientierungshilfe zum Wiederfinden von sprachlichen Zeichen auf den verschiedensten Verpackungen in ihrem individuellen Zusammenhang.

## a) Auf der Frontseite

- der Name des Produktes und des Herstellers
- die Gattungsbezeichnung
- eine Überschrift
- ein Slogan
- diverse isolierte sprachliche Elemente
- kurze Hinweise, z.B. Warnhinweise
- Hinweise auf Sonderaktionen
- knappe Werbetexte

## b) Auf der Rückseite

- der Name der Firma und des Produktes
- die Gattungsbezeichnung
- Benutzerinformationen wie Zubereitungshinweise, Bedienungsanleitungen,    Funktionshinweise etc.
- Inhaltsstoffangaben oder Zutaten
- Nährwerttabellen bei Nahrungsmitteln
- ausführliche Werbetexte mit Informationen über Hersteller, Herstellungsverfahren, ausgewählte Inhaltsstoffe, Anwendungen u.v.m.
- Info-Hotlines und Kundenservicehinweise
- Entsorgungshinweise
- ein Slogan
- diverse isolierte sprachliche Elemente

- diverse Sonderaktionen wie Preisausschreiben, Bastelvorlagen, Sammelbilder oder Kampagnen
- zuweilen herstellerbezogene Zeichen wie Chargennummern, Strichcodes für Scanner etc.

## c) Auf den Seiten:

- der Name des Produktes und des Herstellers
- die Gattungsbezeichnung
- ein Slogan[147]

## d) Der Boden und der Deckel

- der Name des Produktes und des Herstellers
- die Gattungsbezeichnung
- ein Slogan
- das Verfalls- oder Herstellungsdatum
- diverse isolierte sprachliche Elemente[148]

## e) Die Innenseiten

- der Name des Produktes und des Herstellers
- Gattungsbezeichnung
- zusätzliche Informationen und Hinweise (z.B. Rezeptvariationen)
- Hinweise auf Sonderaktionen (Sammelspiele, Preisausschreiben)
- besonderes Zubehör (z.B. Bestellkarten für diverse Artikel)

---

[147] Im Prinzip finden hier alle sprachlichen Zeichen Platz, für die auf der Rückseite kein Raum war, jedoch werden die Seiten häufig nicht voll ausgenutzt.

[148] Meistens wird der Boden jedoch gar nicht bedruckt, weil diese Fläche von den Kunden nur selten betrachtet wird

## 3.4 Verschiedene Arten sprachlicher Zeichen auf Produkt-verpackungen

Die am meisten verwendete Klasse sprachlicher Zeichen auf Produktverpackungen sind die Wortzeichen. Aus diesem Grund bietet es sich an, die Wortzeichen ihrerseits in die gebräuchlichen Kategorien einzuteilen und jeweils einer separaten Betrachtung zu unterziehen.

Alle sprachlichen Zeichen, die nicht einer Kategorie der Wortzeichen zugeordnet werden können, sind für Verpackungen unüblich und werden dementsprechend der Kategorie "Sonstige" zugeordnet.

### 3.4.1 Die Substantive

Substantive werden sehr gerne zur textuellen Gestaltung von Produktverpackungen eingesetzt, insbesondere der Frontseiten. Ihre Eignung zur Benennung von Objekten und Objekteigenschaften macht ihren Einsatz unverzichtbar. Zur Klasse der Substantive gehören auch sämtliche Produktnamen, die allerdings in einer eigenen Subkategorie erfaßt und betrachtet werden.

Substantive werden auf den Frontseiten von Verpackungen mit Vorliebe dazu eingesetzt, einen Produktnamen zu ergänzen, etwa um eine Gattungsbezeichnung "Vollmilchschokolade" („Milka"), "Zahncreme" („elmex"), "Schmelzkäsezubereitung" („Bergfreund") u.v.m. Besonders bei abstrakten Produktnamen sind Ergänzungen um Gattungsbezeichnungen notwendig, um das Produkt allgemeinsprachlich zu kennzeichnen. Die Kunden haben dann die Möglichkeit, über die bekannten Regeln des Gebrauches des allgemeinsprachlichen Wortes, wie z.B. der Gattungsbezeichnung, auf die Gebrauchsregeln des Produktnamens bzw. auf den Inhalt der Verpackung zu schließen. Die Gattungsbezeichnung dient dabei quasi als allgemeinsprachlich übersetzte Vokabel.

Darüber hinaus werden Substantive eingesetzt, um Inhaltsstoffe zu kennzeichnen. Meist geschieht dies in Form einer knappen und kleingedruckten Aufzählung auf der Rückseite der Verpackung. Substantive eignen sich ebenfalls, um Charaktereigenschaften von Produkten zu kennzeichnen, z.B. "Delikatesse", "Diätprodukt", „Bio..." etc.

Beliebt ist es auch, durch Ergänzungen ganz „normale" Produktzutaten zu etwas Besonderem zu machen, um das Produkt stärker von anderen Alternativen zu differenzieren. So wird der Danone Fruchtjoghurt nicht einfach in den Sorten „Pfirsich" und „Vanille" angeboten, sondern die verschiedenen Typen heißen „Avellino Pfirsiche" und „Sambava Vanille". In diesem speziellen Fall ist es nicht unbedingt notwendig, die Gebrauchsregeln der Worte „Avellino" und „Sambava" zu kennen, um diese entsprechend der Intention der Anbieter interpretieren zu können. Hier kann es sogar einen Effekt bewirken, wenn man die Gebrauchsregeln nicht kennt – die Sorten werden zu etwas ganz Besonderem.

Die Eignung eines Substantives besteht in schlichten Sätzen darin, leicht als Subjekt identifizierbar zu sein. Da die Sätze auf Produktverpackungen zu Gunsten einer schnellen Erfaßbarkeit grundsätzlich kurz und parataktisch gehalten werden, findet man in den Verpackungstexten viele Substantive zur Kennzeichnung des Subjektes. Substantive machen das Objekt bzw. das Produkt in der Verpackung zum Subjekt des Verpackungskontextes.

Der ausschließliche Einsatz bekannter Substantive als sprachliche Symbole auf Produktverpackungen würde dem Bestreben nach Differenzierung der vielen Produktalternativen durch die Anbieter auf Dauer nicht genügen.

Mit Substantiven lassen sich schnell und einfach neue Wortkompositionen zusammenstellen wie „Fruchtzwerge" oder „Sonnenscheinfrühstück". Der Vorteil zusammengesetzter Substantive als neue Wortkreationen ist, daß man sie in der Regel ohne zusätzliche Erläuterungen erkennen und verstehen kann. Man erkennt in dem Neologismus sprachliche Symbole, deren Gebrauchsregeln bekannt und verinnerlicht sind. Es wird das symbolische Schlußverfahren zum Verstehen dieser Begriffe angewendet, mit dem Akzent auf der Kombination der Symbole. Sicherheitshalber erläutern die Anbieter zusätzlich ihre Neologismen in der Werbung und auf der Verpackung, so daß ein Verständnis garantiert ist.

Nicht zu empfehlen ist die Komposition von Wortungetümen wie *Multivitamidiätmehrfruchtnektar* („Punika"). Zwar sind die einzelnen Wortkomponenten durchaus verständlich, aber das Wort läßt sich insgesamt durch die Länge und die vielen Einzelkomponenten sehr schwer erfassen und noch schlechter behalten. Es ist davon auszugehen, daß die wenigsten Konsumenten die Wortkomponenten als einzelne Merkmale und Vorzüge des Saftes wahrnehmen - sie gehen in dem Gesamtkomplex unter und verschmelzen zu einer schlecht wahrnehmbaren Einheit. Es empfiehlt sich, einige Einzelaspekte des Wortes gesondert darzustellen, um den Rezipienten die Wahrnehmung zu erleichtern.

Schwieriger gestaltet sich das Verständnis von neuen Wortkombinationen, wenn man die Wortkomponenten nicht erkennt. Begriffe wie "Anti-Aging-System"(„Coral") lassen sich von Normalverbrauchern nicht auf Anhieb erschließen - sie müssen erläutert werden. Hier liegt eine Chance und eine Gefahr. Eine Chance, als wertsteigerndes und vorteilhaftes Merkmal interpretiert zu werden, hat solch ein Begriff nur, wenn er über ergänzende Werbung verständlich und attraktiv erläutert wird, so daß auch Kunden neugierig werden, die bislang andere Produkte gekauft haben. Gelingt dies nicht, läuft man Gefahr, daß die Verbraucher verunsichert werden, ob das Produkt zu ihren Bedürfnissen paßt.

Neologismen werden nicht nur im Bereich der Substantive eingesetzt. Daher wird dieses Stilmittel bei der Besprechung der anderen Wortklassen noch einmal aufgegriffen. Festzuhalten bleibt, daß auf Produktverpackungen bevorzugt Neologismen, bestehend aus substantivischen Wortkomponenten zu finden sind, da sich subjektivische Einheiten bilden lassen. Die Darstellung einzelner Komponenten wird verkürzt und der Kompaktbegriff läßt sich in der Regel leichter merken, es sei denn, es handelt sich um ein Wortungetüm.

Eine weitere bemerkenswerte Funktion von Substantiven ist ihre Eignung als Reiz- bzw. Schlüsselwort.
Bei Reiz- bzw. Schlüsselworten handelt es sich um Begriffe, deren Symbolwirkung durch einen aktuellen Medienbezug verstärkt wird, wie beispielsweise die Begriffe "Natur", "Umweltschutz", "Gesundheit" und Wortelemente mit Schlüsselreizeffekt wie „Öko" und „Bio" etc.
Ebenso haben solche Begriffe Reiz- und Schlüsselwortwirkung, die die Grundbedürfnisse und Grundmotivationen der Menschen ansprechen. Dazu zählen Begriffe aus den Themenkreisen "Leben", "gesellschaftliche Anerkennung", "Sexualität", "Sicherheit" u.ä. (vgl. Masolws Bedürfnispyramide Kap. 1.5.4).
Idealerweise wird die Reizwirkung eines Begriffes aus dem Themenkreis der Grundbedürfnisse aktuell in den Medien behandelt. Auf diesem Weg wird die Wirkung insofern gesteigert, als daß von einem derartigen Begriff für viele Kunden Signalwirkung ausgeht, wenn sie ihn auf einer Produktverpackung wiederfinden.

164

Alle Begriffe, die sich diesen Gruppen der Reiz- und Schlüsselworte zuordnen lassen, werden grundsätzlich nach dem symbolischen Verfahren interpretiert. Es werden für das Schlußverfahren die gelernten Regeln des Gebrauches des Begriffes herangezogen. In dem Moment, in dem ein Begriff verstärkt in den Medien auftritt, oder bei Begriffen aus dem Themenkreis der Grundbedürfnisse des Menschen, kann davon ausgegangen werden, daß den Rezipienten diese Substantive in einer wesentlich höheren Frequenz begegnen als die meisten anderen unserer Sprache. Aus diesem Grund wird der Einsatz der gelernten Regeln des Gebrauches zur Interpretation des Begriffes automatisiert bzw. zum Reflex. Das Wort wird dann zu einem Reiz, der eine reflexartige Interpretation auslöst, ähnlich der eines Index.

Worte aus dem Themengebiet "Natur", "Umweltschutz" und "Öko" erreichen eine so große Stimulanz und Akzeptanz, weil die Verwender über die Medien dahingehend konditioniert werden, daß sie ihr Gewissen beruhigen können, wenn sie etwas für die Umwelt tun, z.B. wenn sie umweltfreundliche Naturprodukte kaufen. In diesem Fall wird die gebräuchliche Regel des Einsatzes eines Begriffes aus diesem Themengebiet zur Interpretation um die Faktoren der sozialen Anerkennung und der Gewissensberuhigung ergänzt. Dementsprechend interpretieren die Verbraucher bei der Konfrontation mit einer Produktverpackung als Projektionsfläche für einen derartigen Begriff selbigen nach dem symbolischen Schlußverfahren mit den psychologischen Regelergänzungen, daß man mit dem Kauf des Produktes als Träger des Reizwortes soziale Anerkennung erwerben und darüber hinaus sein Gewissen beruhigen kann.

In diesem Zusammenhang wird z.B. die schmutzig-braune Farbe zum Kaufargument, weil es gelungen ist, den Kunden beizubringen, diese als Symbol für ein ökologisch wertvolles Recyclingprodukt zu interpretieren.

Es werden gerne auch substantivische Schlüssel- und Reizworte als Hinweis auf Qualität eingesetzt und manchmal sogar, um den Kunden eine Garantie an die Hand zu geben. Mit Hilfe von Gütesiegeln und Garantien wird versucht, für die Konsumenten neben einem reinen Qualitätsversprechen ein symbolisches Wiedererkennungszeichen bereit zu stellen, das aufgrund seiner institutionalisiert wirkenden Gestaltung eine stärkere Verbindlichkeit signalisieren soll.

Als Fragen bezüglich der Substantive für das Analysemodell lassen sich folgende festhalten:

- Werden Substantive als Reiz- und Schlüsselworte auf der Verpackung eingesetzt?
- Werden Stilmittel mit einer Wirkungsintention eingesetzt, und wirken diese tatsächlich im intendierten Sinn?
- Wird eine verkaufsfördernde Wirkung erzielt - sprechen die Substantive stilis-tisch (z.B. jugendlich, innovativ, originell, konservativ etc.) die Zielgruppe an?
- Sind die Substantive verständlich bzw. leicht zu interpretieren?
- Sind die Substantive im Sinne der Wirkungsintentionen gelungen umgesetzt? (z.B. Akzentuierung, Innovation, Leistungssteigerung, Attraktion, Qualität etc.)
- Sind die zentralen Substantive leicht erkennbar und merkbar?
- Werden Bedürfnisse/Motivationen mit diesen Begriffen gereizt?

### 3.4.2 Die Namen

Obwohl die Namen der Wortklasse der Substantive zuzuordnen sind, verdienen sie eine gesonderte Betrachtung.

Namen bilden in der Semantik eine besondere Kategorie von Worten. Sie werden vorgestellt als "Nägel", an denen identifizierende Beschreibungen aufgehängt werden, die sowohl der Sprecher als auch der Zuhörer mit dem Namen verbinden kann.[149] Dabei gilt es zu beachten, daß es sich bei dem hier präferierten zeichentheoretischen Ansatz bei den sogenannten "identifizierenden Beschreibungen" um die Zuordnungsregeln handeln muß, die sowohl dem Sender wie dem Empfänger der Namensbotschaft bekannt sein sollten.
Im Alltagsgebrauch können Namen ohne Kontext für sich alleine stehen und durch ihre Existenz eine Identifikation möglich machen, wenn dem Rezipienten die Zuordnungsregel des Namens zu einer Person, einem Produkt etc. bekannt ist. Sind Namen über einen frequenten Gebrauch ausreichend etabliert, wird beim Erscheinen des Namens - ähnlich dem Erscheinen eines Symbols - das Referenzobjekt nach dem regelbasierten Schlußverfahren abgerufen (vgl. Kap. 6.5.3). Namen sind Spezialfälle von Symbolen. Die regelbasierten Schlußprozesse, die sie auslösen, werden über einen hochfrequenten Gebrauch derart automatisiert abgerufen, daß reflexartig bei der Konfrontation mit dem Namen der Zusammenhang zum Referenzobjekt hergestellt wird.

Nach Peirce sind alle Eigennamen Indizes, da sie als Reaktionszeichen in einer wirklichen Verbindung mit ihrem Objekt stehen.[150] Die

---

[149]    vgl. Searle (1974), S. 258 (die Nagelmetapher) und S. 256

[150]    vgl. Peirce (1973), S. 93-95

Beziehung zwischen einem sprachlichen Zeichen und einer Firma bzw. einem Produkt kann arbiträr sein. Trägt das Produkt den Namen der Firma, so z.B. „Coca-Cola", und wird dieser Name hochfrequent verwendet, wird das indexikalische Namenszeichen, sobald es regelbasiert interpretiert wird, symbolisch für das Produkt eingesetzt.[151] Man stellt angesichts des „Coca-Cola"-Schriftzuges sofort die Referenz zu dem Getränk her.

Initialen sind Indizes für den ganzen Namen.[152] Jedoch weist Keller bei diesem Punkt darauf hin, daß nach einiger Zeit auch die Initialen dergestalt verinnerlicht werden, daß aus dem kausalen Schlußverfahren ein regelbasiertes wird, so daß sie auf lange Sicht ebenfalls zu Symbolen werden, wie z.B. bei CK für „Calvin Klein."[153]

Nach Römer sind Produktnamen "Appellativa der eigenen Art".[154] Diese Aussage betont stärker den kommunikativen Aspekt der Produktnamen: Sie sollen Konsumenten im wahrsten Sinne des Wortes ansprechen, denn seit dem Rückgang der „Tante-Emma-Läden" übernehmen die Produktverpackungen zusätzlich Verkäuferfunktion. Häufig stehen Produktnamen zwischen Gattungsbezeichnungen und Eigennamen. Man bestellt eine „Cola" und keine koffeinhaltige Limonade, man bittet um ein „Tesa" und nicht um durchsichtiges Klebeband, man braucht ein „Tempo" und verlangt kein Papiertaschentuch u.v.m.

---

[151] vgl. Nöth (1975), S. 32

[152] vgl. Nöth (1975), S. 32

[153] vgl. Keller (1995), S. 186 "Alles" bezieht sich hierbei auf sprachliche Ausdrücke, die symptomatisch, ikonisch, symbolisch oder metaphorisch interpretiert werden.

[154] vgl. Römer (1968), S. 54

Namen sind zur Produktvermarktung eine unersetzbare Wortklasse. Strategisch angewendet, lassen sich durch sie absatzträchtige Effekte erzielen.

Gotta bringt das Leistungsvermögen von Namen für das Produktmarketing auf den Punkt:

**"Namen dienen dazu, ein Produkt auf besondere Art und Weise hervorzuheben und es von Produkten oder Dienstleistungen anderer Hersteller zu unterscheiden."** [155]

Für Gotta haben Namen wie "Marlboro", „Persil", „Nivea", „Pampers" oder „Maggi" die besondere Eigenschaft, selbstverständlich mit der Annahme verwendet zu werden, daß jeder weiß, was gemeint ist. Obwohl sie wie andere Worte auch eine Buchstabenkombination sind, bewirken sie den Lerneffekt, daß eben diese Buchstabenkombination auf etwas Konkretes referiert. Der Lerneffekt funktioniert nach einem einfachen Prinzip:

**"Je konkreter ein Name dazu imstande ist, ein Produkt zu charakterisieren, desto größer ist die Chance, daß es tatsächlich identifiziert wird."** [156]

Hat sich ein Produktname längerfristig auf dem Markt etabliert, wird er Teil eines eigenen Wertesystems. Namen stellen nicht nur einen Bezug zu einem konkreten Referenzobjekt her, sondern sie vermitteln oft damit einhergehend eine ganze Produktphilosophie.
Produktphilosophien werden von Anbietern für viel Geld über die Werbung installiert. Es handelt sich dabei um ein ganzes Marketing-

---

[155]    Gotta (1988), S. 15
[156]    Gotta (1988), S. 15

konzept. Wer ein Päckchen „Marlboro"- Zigaretten kauft, kauft gleichzeitig eine Portion Freiheit und Abenteuer. Die gestandenen Cowboys aus der Werbung wecken die Träume vieler. Darüber hinaus wird der Markt über die Produktphilosophie dahingehend erweitert, daß das passende Outdoor-Equipment mit dem Zigarettenlogo angeboten wird. Die „Camelboots" und die allwetterfeste „Marlborojacke" machen das Angebot von Abenteuer und Freiheit glaubwürdiger, indem den Kunden die Ausrüstung für ein persönliches Abenteuer geliefert wird. Die Ausrüstung alleine reicht oft nicht aus, um die Kunden zu ihrem individuellen Abenteuer zu führen. Nachgeholfen wird dazu passend mit entsprechenden Events wie die "Marlboro-Tour" oder die "Camel-Trophy-Tour".[157]

Nebenbei lenken diese Attribute von den negativen Eigenschaften des Zigarettenkonsums ab.

Insbesondere Zigarettenanbieter nutzen die Möglichkeit, in weitere Märkte vorzudringen und ihr Angebot mit völlig anderen Produkten zu erweitern. Seit es in den USA verboten ist, direkt Werbung für Zigaretten zu schalten, ist dies die einzige Möglichkeit, das Produkt indirekt über andere Produkte aus dem Konzept zu bewerben.

Auch in diesem Fall sollen die Markennamen als Logo über hochfrequenten Einsatz zum Symbol werden. Bei der Konfrontation mit einer Zigarettenschachtel sollen die von den anderen Produkten her bekannten Gebrauchsregeln des Symbols auf diesen Kontext angewendet und mit denselben Werten in Verbindung gebracht werden.

---

[157] Man kann sich für diese Veranstaltungen bewerben. Ausgewählt werden und teilnehmen dürfen nur die Männer und Frauen, die genau in das Marketingkonzept der harten und sportlichen Abenteuertypen in der Freiheit passen. Indem diese Personen die Chance haben, an einem solchen gesponserten Abenteuer teilzunehmen, soll eine Identifikation mit der Produktphilosophie und mit den vermittelten Werten stattfinden. Darüber hinaus sollen die vermittelten Werte glaubwürdiger erscheinen, indem man den Konsumenten die Chance einräumt, sich selbst auf einer Outdoortour davon überzeugen zu können.

Den Kunden wird in diesem Fall nicht wie gewohnt erst ein Produkt vorgestellt und dann über die Werbung die Regeln des Einsatzes des Markennamens beigebracht, sondern es werden erst die Regeln vermittelt, die dann auf den Produktnamen angewendet werden sollen.

In der Werbung taucht deshalb der Name mindestens einmal im Originallogo auf, um in Verbindung mit dem Produkt gelernt und im Laden auf der Verpackung wiedererkannt zu werden.

Ideal ist es, wenn Fernseh-, Zeitungs-, Plakatwerbung und die Verpackung konzeptionell aufeinander abgestimmt werden. Ein gelungenes Beispiel ist das "Dany + Sahne"-Konzept. Über die Werbung im Fernsehen, in der Zeitung und auf Plakaten lernen die Konsumenten die exponiert dargestellte Verpackung kennen. In der Werbung der Printmedien wird der Becher schlicht mit dem Begriff "Lustobjekt" überschrieben. Der Produktname und das Verpackungsdesign sollen im Zusammenhang mit dieser zusätzlichen Gebrauchsregel, ein Lustobjekt zu sein, gelernt werden. Diese Maßnahmen soll garantieren, daß die Kunden im Laden den Becher wiedererkennen.

Dieses Beispiel zeigt jedoch gleichzeitig, daß es nicht einfach ist, den "Dany+Sahne"-Becher von den Me-Too Bechern mit gleich aussehendem zu differenzieren. Zwar werden die Kunden einerseits mit dem "Dany + Sahne"-Becher deutlich konfrontiert, gleichzeitig werden die No-Name-Becher aber auch mitbeworben, denn den Konsumenten prägt sich auch das Aussehen der Verpackung als separater Reiz ein. In den entsprechenden Geschäften kann dann der Anblick eines sehr ähnlich aussehenden No-Name-Bechers als Reiz genügen, um dieses Objekt als Lustobjekt in den Einkaufswagen zu stellen, ganz gleich, was darauf steht.

171

**"Namen sind mehr als nur die Aussprechbarkeit ihrer Buchstaben-reihenfolge".** [158]

Es wird in der Regel streng darauf geachtet, daß ein Produktname einzigartig auf dem Markt ist, zumindest in der jeweiligen Pro-duktsparte. [159]

Die Namen müssen auch internationalen Sprachtests standhalten. Insbesondere Autokonzerne haben bei der Namensfindung für Ihre Modelle schon folgenschwere Fehltritte begangen. So wird das "Uno" im Finnischen als "Trottel" interpretiert. So manches Kürzel hat ebenfalls seine Tücken: MR2 klingt im Französischen wie "mer-de". [160]

Der Aufwand für die Produktnamenfindung wird durch die Tatsache gerechtfertigt, daß es äußerst schwierig ist, einen einmal etablierten Produktnamen wieder zu ändern.

---

[158]
Gotta (1998), S. 17

[159]
Es gibt zur Namensfindung für Produkte und zur Überprüfung deren Ein-zigartigkeit auf dem Markt mittlerweile Agenturen. Diese Agenturen lassen eine Reihe von Mitarbeitern brainstormingartig Listen mit potentiellen Namen erstellen, nachdem sie ihnen charakteristische Eigen-schaften des Produktes an die Hand gegeben haben. Aus diesen Listen werden dann ein paar Namen ausgewählt, die in Frage kommen und rechtlich abgesichert. Das heißt, es wird gecheckt, ob der Name irgendwo auf der Welt schon als Produktname existiert. Desweiteren wird überprüft, ob der Name sich pro-blemlos in alle möglichen Sprachen implantieren läßt, ohne z.B. eine unangenehme Bedeutung zu erhalten. Diese Agenturen übernehmen die Haftung für eventuelle Fehlschläge. Schließlich werden über eine Mei-nungsforschung die Namen ausgewählt, die von den Konsumenten bevorzugt werden. Durch die Überprüfung des vorab ausgewählten Na-mens konnte als bekanntes Beispiel verhindert werden, daß die Firma „Rolls Royce" ein Modell namens "Silver Mist" (Silbernebel) auf den Markt brachte, denn wer möchte in Deutschland schon mit*Silbermist* her-umfahren.

[160]
vgl. Reichardt (1999)

172

Ein bekanntes Beispiel für eine Namensänderung ist der Schokoriegel "Twix". "Twix" hieß früher in Deutschland "Raider". Da der Schokoriegel in allen anderen Vertriebsländern "Twix" heißt, entschloß man sich, diesen Namen auch in Deutschland zu etablieren. Die Namensänderung war allerdings mit erheblichem Kosten- und Werbeaufwand verbunden. Die Verpackung blieb identisch, ebenso der Schriftzug. Die Konsumenten mußten lediglich lernen, was die Werbung explizit machte: "Raider heißt jetzt Twix". Das heißt, der Kunde muß lernen, die gelernte Gebrauchsregel für den Namen "Raider" jetzt auf den Namen "Twix" zu übertragen und anzuwenden.

Namensänderungen werden nur dann durchgeführt, wenn sie sich nicht vermeiden lassen, denn jeder Fehler dabei kann sich verheerend auswirken.[161] Es kann passieren, daß mit einer Namensänderung das mühsam aufgebaute Image verlorengeht und das Produkt nicht mehr erkannt und gekauft wird.

Gotta charakterisiert die wichtigsten Merkmale eines Namens:
- Er muß sich deutlich vom Namen des Wettbewerbs unterscheiden.
- Er muß schutzfähig sein.
- Er muß im Rahmen aller flankierenden Maßnahmen in der Lage sein, in den Augen der Verbraucher einen Wert zu verkörpern, der ihn deutlich vom Wert des Wettbewerbsproduktes unterscheidet und damit zum Kauf motiviert.
- Er muß aussprechbar, attraktiv und merkfähig sein.[162]

Eine Strukturanalyse von Markennamen durch Gotta und seine Mitarbeiter ergibt folgende Kategorisierung:[163]

---

[161]    vgl. Loewy (1953), S. 128
[162]    vgl. Gotta (1988). S. 18

### 3.4.3 Beschreibende Namen

Namen dieser Kategorie sagen konkret etwas über das Produkt und/oder die Produktleistung aus. Typische Vertreter dieser Kategorie sind Namen wie: "Mamorkuchen", "Salamipizza", "WC Frisch", "Müller Milch", "Dr. Oetker Vanille Pudding", "Zewa wisch und weg" u.v.m.

### 3.4.4 Assoziative Namen

Zu dieser Gruppe zählen Namen, die sich gleichzeitig als assoziative oder symbolträchtige Bezeichnungen charakterisieren lassen. Sie sollten nach Möglichkeit nicht nur das Produkt, sondern auch das dazugehörige Konzept vermitteln.

Namen wie "Tatü", "Spüli", "Yofresh" etc. referieren auf ein ganzes Sortiment verschiedener Produkttypen.

"Mr. Proper", "Ajax"[164], "Knack und Back" sind Namen, die einen Saubermann, einen Riesen und damit Kraft assoziieren lassen oder einfach das Geräusch, das beim Öffnen der Verpackung entsteht. Über regelmäßigen und damit auch regelhaften Gebrauch werden solche Namen zu Symbolen für das dazugehörige Produkt.

---

[163]    vgl. Gotta (1988), S. 21

[164]    Ajax ist ein Name aus der griechischen Sagenwelt, dem Belagerer von Troja; vgl. Lötscher (1987), S. 13

### 3.4.5 Artifizielle Namen

Namensvertreter dieser Kategorie sind in der Regel dem allgemeinen Wortschatz nicht bekannt bzw. es handelt sich dabei um Neologismen oder neue Wortkombinationen.

Namen wie "Sidolin", "Omo", "Lipton"[165], "4711", oder "le Tartare" müssen dem Konsumenten erläutert werden. Ist die Verbindung zwischen "Omo" zu Waschmittel, "Lipton" zu Eistee, "4711" zu Kölnisch Wasserparfum oder "le Tartare" zu einer Frischkäsezubereitung erst einmal her- und als Gebrauchsregel vorgestellt, ergibt sich der Sinn und die Bedeutung und kann gelernt werden.

Gotta nimmt eine Gegenüberstellung der Vor- und Nachteile der einzelnen Kategorien vor. Dabei kommt er zu folgendem Ergebnis:

"Beschreibende Namen besitzen den scheinbaren Vorteil, daß sie eine konkrete Produktbotschaft vermitteln, ohne auf zusätzliche Informationsmaßnahmen angewiesen zu sein. Was sie aber erst lebensfähig macht, ist der Absender. Was ist ein *Knusperzauber* ohne *Milka*, eine *klare Fleischbrühe* ohne *Maggi* wert? Solche Bezeichnungen laufen Gefahr, Sortenbezeichnungen zu werden, die kaum eine Chance besitzen, charakteristische Wesensmerkmale einer wirklichen Markenpersönlichkeit zu erreichen."[166]

Die meisten Unternehmen möchten ihre Produkte auch im Ausland anbieten. Dort sind viele deutsche Namen nicht aussprechbar oder

---

165    Sir Thomas Lipton ist der Name eines englischen Teefirmenbesitzers. Er hat oft um den Amerika-Pokal gesegelt, bzw. segeln lassen, konnte jedoch nie gewinnen. Jedoch gewann er auf diesem Weg an Bekanntheit. Auch in Deutschland gibt es noch immer jede Menge Lipton Tæsorten.

166    vgl. Gotta (1988), S. 21

wirken klanglich ungewöhnlich bis unangenehm. Beschreibende Namen werden im Ausland meistens nicht verstanden.

Darüber hinaus haben plakativ beschreibende Namen den großen Nachteil, nicht schutzfähig zu sein. Sie sind leicht nachzuahmen und demzufolge eine dankbare Quelle für die Anbieter von Me-Too-Produkten.

Demgegenüber steht der Vorteil der Schutzfähigkeit von assoziativen und artifiziellen Namen. Durch die Schutzfähigkeit ist es möglich, einen Namen in Besitz eines Unternehmens zu bringen und zu dessen hauseigenem Zeichen zu machen.[167]

Trotz der höheren Abstraktionsebene sind assoziative Namen in der Regel ohne "intensivere Kommunikationsunterstützung" einführbar.[168]

Es ist davon auszugehen, daß die Verbraucher im Laden bei dem Namen "Spüli" sofort und ohne größeren gedanklichen Aufwand den Rückschluß ziehen können, daß es sich um ein Spülmittel handelt, genau wie bei dem Namen "Schoko-Flokina-Kuchen" der Schluß nahe liegt, daß es sich um Kuchen mit Schokoflocken und bei „WC-Frisch" um einen Geruchsentferner für Toiletten handelt. Das

---

[167]    Allerdings gilt der Patentschutz nur für einen Produktsektor. So kann z.B. der Name "Tempo" sowohl für Taschentücher als auch für Spülmittel verwendet werden, ebenso der Name „Bounty" für einen Schokoriegel und eine Küchenrolle. Das engl. Wort "Bounty" läßt sich übersetzen mit "Großzügigkeit, Freigebigkeit, Belohnung". Nach dem Film "Meuterei auf der Bounty" erinnert der Name laut Lötscher (1987), S. 39 zusätzlich an ferne Südseeromantik.

[168]    vgl. Gotta (1988), S. 22

Schlußverfahren wird oft dadurch erleichtert, daß die Produkte in den entsprechenden Abteilungen angeboten werden.[169]

Idealerweise sind assoziative Namen sprachlich unabhängig, d.h. sie werden in verschiedenen Ländern vergleichbar verwendet, wie z.B. der Name des Waschmittels "Persil".[170]

Auch englische Namen eignen sich für den internationalen Einsatz.

Ein Nachteil der assoziativen Namen liegt in der Tatsache, daß sie oft einem Begriffsfeld entstammen, aus dem sich weitere Namen mit ähnlichen Assoziationen schöpfen lassen. Ein Beispiel ist das Me-Too-Produkt eines Billiganbieters zu "Nutella" - "Nutoca".[171]

Artifizielle Namen lassen sich wiederum in zwei Kategorien untergliedern. Dabei handelt es sich einmal um die Gruppe von Namen, für die es bereits eine Regel des Gebrauches gibt, die aber aus einem anderen Sprachraum stammt. "Wenn man weiß, daß Timotei der Name für eine schwedische Grassamenart ist, wurde uns plötzlich das Wissenskonzept verständlich. Und wenn man erfährt, daß Kaloderma aus den griechischen Begriffen „kalos" - „schön" und „derma" – „Haut" zusammengesetzt ist, dann ist das Produktversprechen eindeutig."[172] Ein artifizieller Name, der von einem anderssprachigen Terminus abgeleitet ist, definiert sich über die Tatsache als artifiziell,

---

169
     Es ist für eine Firma, die ein neues Produkt auf dem Markt etablieren möchte, ein erheblicher Kostenfaktor, den Platz für das Produkt im Ladenregal meterweise einzukaufen.

170
     „Persil" läßt sich als assoziativer Name klassifizieren, wenn man weiß, daß er aus den Anfangssilben seiner beiden Hauptinhaltsstoffe Perborat und Silikat zusammengesetzt wurde. Für diejenigen, die dies nicht wissen, läßt sich „Persil" auch den artifiziellen Namen zuordnen.

171
     Aus diesem Grund geben viele Firmen Geld dafür aus, die Namen, die dem Produktnamen ähnlich sind, ebenfalls zu schützen.

172
     Gotta (1988), S. 23

daß die allermeisten Konsumenten diese Herleitung nicht nachvollziehen können.

Die zweite Kategorie artifizieller Namen faßt diejenigen Produktnamen zusammen, die bis dato nicht im Sprachgebrauch verwendet werden, z.B. "Rei in der Tube", "Sidolin streifenfrei", "Pampers", "Chappi" u.s.w.
Der schwergewichtige Vorteil solcher artifizieller Namen ist, daß sie schutzfähig sind, und daß es meistens sehr schwierig ist, sie nachzuahmen.

Gotta insistiert mit Nachdruck auf der Tatsache, daß die Unternehmen viel zu oft beschreibenden oder assoziativen Namen den Vorzug geben. Das Hauptargument, mit dem diese Entscheidungen begründet werden, ist der hohe Kostenaufwand für die Bekanntmachung und Erläuterung eines sich nicht selbsterläuternden Namens. Für Gotta ist dieses Argument nicht akzeptabel, da große Investitionen notwendig sind, unabhängig davon, was für ein Name bekannt gemacht werden soll.[173]

Artifizielle Namen, die nicht über den allgemeinen Sprachgebrauch erschlossen werden können, werden mit beschreibenden Zusätzen wie "Sidolin streifenfrei", "Rei in der Tube" ausgewiesen.

Gotta erläutert, daß bei artifiziellen Namen die Verpackung die Funktion einer Visitenkarte übernimmt. So wie der Hausname eines Steuerberaters oder Rechtsanwaltes nichts über sein Berufsbild aussagt, sagt ein artifizieller Produktname noch nichts über die Art,

---

[173]    vgl. Gotta (1988), S. 24

178

Funktion und Leistung des Produktes aus. Es bedarf der entsprechenden Zusätze auf der Visitenkarte bzw. der Verpackung.[174]

Visitenkarten haben jedoch gegenüber Produktverpackungen den Vorteil, daß sie fast alle gleich aussehen und von der Struktur her ähnlich aufgebaut sind. Da es nur wenige Strukturelemente gibt und selten Graphiken verwendet werden, die von den eigentlichen Informationen ablenken, sind die Informationen einer Visitenkarte schnell erfaßt.

Gemeinsam haben Visitenkarten und Produktverpackungen, daß sich nach dem Erfassen des Namens und des Berufs- bzw. Produktzweiges relativ schnell entscheidet, ob der Kunde das Produkt oder die Unternehmensleistung benötigt.

Die Verpackungstexte haben dabei die schwierige Aufgabe zu leisten, die Kunden davon zu überzeugen, daß sie die Produktleistungen früher oder später bevorzugt vor Alternativen brauchen werden.

Zusammenfassend bieten artifizielle Namen folgende Vorteile:

- Eigenständigkeit und Unverwechselbarkeit
- Einsatzfähigkeit in unterschiedlichen Ländern
- Fähigkeit, ein Produktkonzept und das Positioning genauer zu repräsentieren.[175]

Ziel dieser Bemühungen ist es, die Namen der Produkte zu Markennamen zu machen und das Produkt damit zu einem Markenartikel.

---

[174]    vgl. Gotta (1988), S. 24
[175]    vgl. Gotta (1988), S. 28

179

### 3.4.6 Namensbildung als grammatikalische Formelbildung

Die Assoziationen zu einem Namen können über Suffixe und Präfixe in eine bestimmte Richtung katalysiert werden.
Für medizinische Produkte ist das Suffix "med" äußerst beliebt, z.B. „Hansamed", „Vivimed" etc. "Med" kann sogar als Circumflex eingebaut werden: "Wick MediNait". Für ökologische bzw. gesundheitsversprechende Produkte werden gerne Suffixe wie "vit" („Naturvit", „Vitafit", „Duravit", „Eivit", „Vitalis") und "fit" („Topfits", „Reisfit", „Onken Fitness") verwendet. Die Assoziationen sollen sein: med -Medizin, vit - Vitalität und fit - Fitness. Bei Fertigprodukten ist die Endung "fix" sehr beliebt, z.B. „Knorr Fix", „Maggi Fix" etc. „Fix" assoziiert fertig, flott und schnell - die Eigenschaften der Fertigküche von heute.

Handelt es sich um Produktnamen, bei denen Objektnamen noch rudimentär vorhanden sind, liegen verstümmelte Lexeme vor, deren Inhalt aber noch erkennbar ist.[176]

- „Butella" (Margarine, Lexem *Butter*)
- „Nutella" (Nuß-Nougat-Creme, Lexem *Nuß*)[177]
- „Milka" (Vollmilchschokolade, Lexem von engl. *milk*)[178]

Ergänzen läßt sich hier, daß das Produkt „Butella" sowohl von der Konsistenz als auch vom Namen her eine Kombination von Butter und „Sanella" (Margarine) ist.

---

[176] vgl. Römer (1968), S. 65
[177] vgl. Römer (1968), S. 65
[178] Die erste Milkaschokolade war Vollmilchschokolade. vgl. auch Lötscher (1987), S. 148

180

Endungen wie -al, -an, -in, -ol und -on werden bevorzugt für Heilmittel, Hygieneprodukte und Chemikalien verwendet, z.B. „Delial" (Sonnenmilch), „Sagrotan" (Desinfektionsmittel), „Sidolin" (Glasreiniger), „Odol" (Mundwasser ) und „Calgon" (Waschmaschinenentkalker).

Viele Produktnamen bestehen aus zwei Silben. Sie sind dann kurz, aber dennoch lang genug, um individuell und prägnant zu sein. Der Vorteil solch zweisilbiger Namen ist eine gute Merkfähigkeit, Eindeutigkeit und eine bequeme, da wenig aufwendige Handhabung.[179]
Produktnamen werden oft erweitert, indem ihnen Appellativa für die Warengattung, Zahlenkombinationen zur Differenzierung bzw. Artikelbezeichnungen oder sonstige Zusätze beigefügt werden. Daher entscheiden sich immer mehr Anbieter für mehrgliedrige Produktnamen.

Günstig sind viersilbige Wörter, aus zwei Wörtern bestehende Namen und Namen, die bereits eine semantische Nebenbedeutung haben.[180]
Vorteile bieten Namen, die Bestandteile des Firmennamens als Silben einfließen lassen (wie bei „Nesquick"/ Nestlé + Quick=schnell). Auf diesem Weg läßt sich nach Koppelmann eine Herkunftsklammer schaffen, die den Produktnamen an der bereits existierenden Bekanntheit und dem Firmenimage partizipieren läßt.[181]
Durch die Kombination eines Produktnamens mit dem Firmennamen entsteht im Sinne Gottas ein artifizieller Name. Eine derartige Kombination läßt sich meist aufgrund des angemeldeten Firmennamens

---

[179] Nach Lötscher (1987), S. 321 werden nach wie vor mit Vorliebe Autos, Seifen und Waschmittel mit zweisilbigen Produktnamen benannt.

[180] vgl. Koppelmann (1981), S. 49

[181] vgl. Koppelmann (1981), S. 49

ebenfalls ohne Probleme schützen. Ein gelunges Beispiel ist der Produktname "Jacobs Kaffee Zauber". Hierbei handelt es sich um eine Kombination aus Firmennamen, dem erkennungstypischen Hinweis auf das Produkt Kaffee und dem Schlüsselreizwort *Zauber*, das hier zweideutig eingesetzt wird. Einmal soll die Zubereitung des Schnellkaffees als Zauberei und damit als leicht und schnell vorgestellt werden. Gleichzeitig soll das Wort "Zauber" auch auf die Verzauberung des Konsumenten hinweisen, z.B. in eine wohltuenden Pause. Namenszusätze sind z.B. vorangestellte oder nachgestellte nominale Ergänzungen:[182]

so z.B. „Asbach Uralt", „Henkel trocken", „Kellogg's Cornflakes", „Eckes Edelkirsch", „Ritter Sport", etc.

Zweigliedrige Produktnamen bieten den Vorteil, daß die Hersteller den Objektnamen mit dem Firmennamen kombinieren können. Dadurch kann die Produktpersönlichkeit stärker betont werden. Es handelt sich dann nicht um irgendwelche Cornflakes, sondern um die von Kellogg's. Über häufig frequenten Gebrauch z.B. mit der Werbung lernen die Kunden einen solchen Namen als Einheit kennen. Begegnet ihnen im Laden eine Packung mit einer anderen Namenskombination, wird ihnen deutlich bewußt, daß es sich um ein anderes Produkt handelt.

Wird ein zweigliedriger Produktname häufig genug verwendet, dann kann nach dem Sprachwandelprinzip eine Verschmelzung stattfinden. Sprachbenutzer handeln grundsätzlich so rational wie möglich. Sie wollen unter dem kleinstmöglichen Aufwand den größtmöglichen Effekt erzielen. Um sicherzugehen, daß der Rezipient das Gesagte noch versteht, artikuliert man immer ein klein wenig mehr, als unbedingt notwendig ist. Dieses Phänomen wird Redundanzsteuerung

---

[182] vgl. Koppelmann (1981), S. 49

genannt.[183] Da es aufwendig ist, zwei einzelne Worte zu artikulieren, wird der Übergang fließend.

Wird der Firmenname als ein Namenselement angegeben, ist es leichter, weitere Produkte einzuführen, da sie sofort als Marke akzeptiert werden, z.b. „Jakobs Krönung", „Jacobs Cappuccino", „Jacobs Expresso" etc.

Drei- und mehrgliedrige Produktnamen bieten den Vorteil, daß sich das Angebot differenzierter beschreiben läßt, z.b.: "Jacobs Krönung light", "Kellogg's Knusper Flakes", "Nivea Haarpflege Pflegespülung".
Diese Namen werden oft nach einer Hierarchie strukturiert, z.b. Name des Anbieters, Produktsparte, spezielle Subkategorie.
Eine der aufwendigsten vielgliedrigen Namenkombinationen ist der Paradiesvogel aus der „Punicaoase": der 17 + 4 Mulitvitamindiätvielfruchtnektar, allerdings ist eine derartige Namenkombination zu unübersichtlich, wie im Zusammenhang mit den Neologismen schon erwähnt, um korrekt gelernt und behalten zu werden. (vgl. Kap. 2.15.1)

Dieser Name ist mit einer Metapher kombiniert: 17 + 4 wird normalerweise als Name für ein Glücksspiel verwendet. Die Metapher soll das Produkt insofern positiv charakterisieren, als daß 17+4 Früchte in dem Produkt enthalten sind und das Produkt damit als "Gewinn" interpretiert werden kann. Die Siegerregeln des Glücksspiels können auf das Produkt übertragen und in diesem neuen Wirkungszusammenhang nach den herkömmlich gelernten Gebrauchsregeln interpretiert werden.

---

[183] vgl. Keller (1994), S. 184f

Nach Römer ist der Lernerfolg wesentlich größer, wenn die Reihenfolge Apposition + Eigenname eingehalten wird, wie bei „Kaffee Hag" und „Creme Mousson"[184] oder „Schoko Leibniz".[185] Jedoch findet man diese Reihenfolge heute eher selten. Die Anbieter setzen darauf, daß der Firmen- bzw. Markenname leichter erlernt wird, wenn er zuerst genannt und dadurch in den Vordergrund gerückt wird. Desweiteren ist der Klang des Namens in dieser Reihenfolge oft angenehmer.

Bei neologistischen Wortkompositionen ist dringend darauf zu achten, welche Interpretationsmöglichkeiten in Betracht kommen und welche Assoziationen auf diesem Wege ausgelöst werden können. So ist beispielsweise der Name "Kindergesichtswurst" für eine Wurst, in der durch Fleischstückchen ein lustiges Kindergesicht dargestellt wird, ein Fehltritt. Der Name dieser Wurst war früher "Kinderwurst" und sollte eine spezielle Wurst für Kinder assoziieren. Aber auch bei dem Namen "Kindergesichtswurst" kann man unsicher sein: Wurst mit Kindergesicht, Wurst für das Kindergesicht oder Wurst aus Kindergesicht? Solche Mehrdeutigkeiten sollten vermieden werden.

## e)    Namen machen Marken

Namen sind auf Werbemaßnahmen angewiesen, die sie erläutern und über das strategische Einflechten in konkrete Lebenssituationen eine Verbindung zwischen dem Produktnamen und dem dazugehörigen Produkt herstellen.

---

[184]     vgl. Römer (1968), S. 74

[185]     Mittlerweile gehört die Firma Leibniz zum Anbieter Bahlsen.

So wurden beispielsweise über die Werbung die Assoziationen, die der Produktname "Lux" provoziert, kanalisiert und in die vom Hersteller gewünschte Richtung gelenkt.

Die Hersteller der Seife "Lux" erwiesen sich als hervorragende Marketing- und Kommunikationsstrategen, als sie in den von einer tiefen wirtschaftlichen Krise geprägten 30er Jahren erkannten, daß die Filmindustrie eines der wenigen profitablen Geschäfte der Zeit war. Neben den Schönheitsidealen der Zeit verkörperten Filmstars die Welt des Erfolges und des Luxus, von dem die Durchschnittsbürger nur träumen konnten und immer wieder gerne träumten. Die Strategie der "Lux"-Seifenhersteller knüpfte an diese heißbegehrte Wunschwelt an.

"Lux-Seife bemächtigte sich dieser Welt des Luxus und der Flucht aus der Wirklichkeit und sprach über die Filmsymbolik die Träume von Millionen junger Frauen an".[186]

Der Name "Lux" kommt von "Luxus" und soll eben diese Assoziation bewirken. Luxus, hohe Qualität und Pflege für die Haut, die sich eigentlich nur Stars leisten konnten, wurde für jeden erschwinglich angeboten. So avancierte "Lux-Seife" zu einer der bekanntesten und akzeptiertesten Seifen - der Luxus, sich ein bißchen "heile Haut" leisten zu können.

Nach wie vor boomt das Filmgeschäft. Die Stars sind jedoch universeller und individueller geworden. Konstant geblieben ist der Seifenkonsum im Haushalt und der Wunsch, ein bißchen vom Glamour und Jet Set der Berühmtheiten mitzubekommen.

Die Ansprüche der Zeit und das Angebot der Konkurrenz machen es immer wieder notwendig, ein Produkt zeitgemäß bzw. der Zeit ein

---

[186]    Black (1988), S. 82

bißchen voraus zu gestalten. So wurde die Konsistenz der "Lux-Seife" ein wenig verändert, ebenso die Form und die graphische Verpackungsgestaltung.

Die Stars in der Werbung haben sich geändert, doch der Name der Seife ist geblieben. Schönheit und Pflege sind nach wie vor Ansprüche, die besonders Frauen an sich stellen. Ein Produkt, das über so viele Jahre hinweg aus dem Munde der Berühmtheiten der Zeit diese Ansprüche zu erfüllen verspricht, schafft nach wie vor bei vielen Verbrauchern die Vertrauensbasis, die "Lux-Seife" auch heute noch regelmäßig in den Einkaufskorb wandern läßt.

Der Name des Basisproduktes "Lux-Seife" hat sich nicht geändert, dafür aber die Namen weiterer Produkte aus der Serie, z.B. heißt das „Lux" Duschgel jetzt "Lux Beauty Shower". Diese Benennung entspricht dem Trend der modernen Frau, nicht mehr mit einem Schminkkoffer auf Reisen zu gehen, sondern mit einem *Beauty Case*. Um auch die „Lux"-Seife der Beauty-Serie anzugleichen, wird auf der Verpackung der Zusatz "Beauty Soap" ergänzt. Der Name "Lux" gilt bei den Kunden als bekannter Markenname. Man versucht, über diesen Namen weitere Produkte leichter einführen zu können.

Nach Humboldt konstituieren Zeichen Sprache und damit Wirklichkeit. Er sucht immer wieder die Verknüpfung zwischen Zeichen und den Zeichen im Menschen.[187]

Saussure vertritt die Auffassung, daß Ausdruck und Inhalt der Zeichen immer mit einem Band von Assoziationen verbunden sind.[188]

Dementsprechend wird die Strategie, die hinter dem Namen "Lux" steckt auch aus einer anderen Perspektive deutlich. Der Name "Lux"

---

[187] vgl. Humboldt (1820) in Leitzmann (Hg.) (1905), S. 29

[188] vgl. EC 149, S. 28

wurde über ein assoziatives Verfahren entwickelt. Er steht am Ende einer Assoziationskette:

Lux - Luxus - Glamour - Schönheit - Pflege - Parfümerie - Seife - Lux

Diese Kette ist als gängiges Assoziationsschema konzipiert, so daß grundsätzlich bei jedem Verbraucher durch den Namen "Lux" als Reizwort aktiviert werden kann. Die Assoziationskette funktioniert prinzipiell bei jedem Verbraucher von der Struktur her nach demselben Schema. Dabei spielt es keine Rolle, daß die unterschliedlichen Verbraucher ganz verschiedene Schönheitsideale haben können.

Der Verbraucher wird mit dem Namen "Lux" in seiner typographischen Gestaltung auf der Verpackung oder in seiner lautlichen Ausprägungsform in der Werbung konfrontiert.

Lux ist kein gängiges Wort unserer Alltagssprache. Daher sind die Rezipienten genötigt, über das assoziative Interpretationsverfahren das präsentierte lautliche oder visuelle Erscheinungsbild mit einem Sinn zu verknüpfen. Der Name "Lux" hat unvollständig ikonischen Charakter aufgrund der Ähnlichkeit zu dem sprachlichen Symbol "Luxus".

"Lux" ist ein assoziativer Name, der mit dem Ziel eingesetzt wurde, den Konsumenten einen Impuls zu eigenen Assoziationen zu geben, die die Elemente der Assoziationskette des Namensfindungsprozesses wieder aufgreifen. Die Verbraucher werden dabei mit dem Anfang und dem Ende der Assoziationskette gleichzeitig konfrontiert. Damit soll die Interpretation automatisch auf das gelenkt werden, was dazwischen liegt. Auch hier ist daran zu erinnern, daß die Gebrauchsregeln des Namens "Lux" bei hochfrequenter Konfrontation gelernt werden und damit der Name zum Symbol wird.

Das Verfahren der gezielten Lenkung von Assoziationen sind Suggestionen, denn es handelt sich um eine Beeinflussung der Rezipienten zugunsten des Produktes.[189]

Bei dem genannten Beispiel wird versucht, über den regelmäßigen Gebrauch des Namens "Lux-Seife" im Zusammenhang mit dem Luxus berühmter Persönlichkeiten aus der Unterhaltungsbranche dem Namen eben diese Bedeutung zukommen zu lassen.

Dabei darf jedoch nicht außer Acht gelassen werden, daß es zwar ein relativ einheitliches Konzept über den Gebrauch des Wortes *Luxus* – „Lux" gibt, jedoch der Reiz und die spontanen Assoziationen für jeden ein bißchen anders sind, der jeweiligen Lebenssituation entsprechend. Aus diesem Grund ist es wichtig, daß der über die Werbung in Richtung des Luxus der Hollywoodstars kanalisierte Name "Lux" mit einem Artikel verbunden ist, der im Haushalt eines jeden für den ganz alltäglichen Luxus benötigt wird. Denn nur dann kann der individuelle Luxus der Verbraucher um einen Gebrauchsartikel angereichert werden, der vorgibt, trotz eines günstigen Preises die Anforderungen an einen Luxuskonsumartikel zu erfüllen.

---

[189] Suggestionen bilden eine Subkategorie der konversationellen Implikaturen (unausgesprochene Schlußfolgerungen) sowie eine Beeinflussung gegen den Willen einer Person (Fremdwörterduden 1990, S. 152). Assoziation kommt von lat. associare - sich verbinden. In der Psychologie ist dies ein Vorgang der Bewußtseinsverknüpfung von zwei oder mehreren Vorstdlungsaspekten (Bußmann 1990, S. 105).

## f)    Von einem Markennamen zu einer Produktfamilie

Die Firma Beiersdorf war seit den 20er Jahren führender Anbieter für eine Art "Volkshautcreme" auf dem Kosmetiksektor, die "Nivea Hautcreme". Doch in den 60er und 70er Jahren wurde der Umsatz rückläufig, da die Leute mit wachsendem Wohlstand speziellere Produkte für ihre ganz individuelle Pflege bevorzugten.

Um das Produkt vor dem Untergang zu bewahren, wurde in einer breit angelegten Studie ein Profil der „Nivea Creme" erstellt, deren charakteristische Eigenschaften die Verbraucher spontan ermittelten, ausgelöst durch die Konfrontation mit dem Markennamen.[190]

Es stellte sich dabei heraus, daß der Markenname "Nivea" nach wie vor bei den Verbrauchern für Ehrlichkeit und Qualität stand und deshalb deren größtes Vertrauen genoß sowie einen hohen Goodwill hatte. Man entschloß sich, den hohen Vertrauens-index nicht aufs Spiel zu setzen und beließ zunächst sowohl das Produkt als auch die Verpackung und den Produktnamen ohne Änderung.

Man vergrößerte den Distributionsbereich und schaltete eine sehr gewagte Werbekampagne. Der Spruch "Nivea - eine bessere gibt es nicht"[191] revitalisierte das grundsätzlich vorhandene Vertrauen der Kunden in die Qualität des Produktes.

Die Assoziationen der Verbraucher wurden bezüglich des Zeicheninhaltes des Namens „Nivea" dahingehend manipuliert, daß die schon gelernte Bedeutung "Nivea = Qualität" durch den Werbeslogan eine Steigerung erfuhr "Nivea = die beste Qualität".

---

[190]    vgl. Prick (1988), S. 91

[191]    Der „Nivea"-Werbespruch 1972 bereitete zunächst vielen Rechtsanwälten der Konkurrenz Kopfschmerzen. Schließlich wurde dieser Slogan aufgrund der Vorspielung möglicherweise falscher Tatsachen verboten. (vgl. Prick (1988), S. 91f)

Nach der Revitalisierung der „Nivea"-Creme werden ständig weitere Produkte entwickelt, die der Philosophie der Nivea-Creme entsprechen, z.B. „Nivea"-Sonnenschutzprodukte, „Nivea"-Shampoo, „Nivea"-Pflegespülung, „Nivea"-Babyprodukte, „Nivea"-Lotion, „Nivea"-Aftershave, „Nivea"-Lippenstifte, „Nivea"-Schminke u.v.m. Es wurde streng darauf geachtet, daß die Produkte einfach und unkompliziert sind. Sie sollten zwar Teilmärkte abdecken, jedoch universal nutzbar sein (keine Anti-Fett oder Anti-Schuppen-Shampoos), so daß die Verbraucher die bereits gelernten Attribute der „Nivea"-Creme problemlos bei dem Schlüsselreiz des Markennamens "Nivea" übertragen können.

Es ist der Firma Beiersdorf gelungen, aus einer Line-Extension auch eine Life-Extension zu entwickeln.

**g)    Es geht auch andersherum**

Normalerweise liegt zuerst das neu entwickelte Produkt vor, bevor ein Name dafür gefunden werden muß. Das es auch andersherum geht, bewies 1982 Maurice Roger, als er einen revolutionären Namen für einen neuen Duft fand, der noch entwickelt werden mußte: "Poison".

"Weil ein Duft 'nicht nur in der Nase ist, sondern auch im Kopf etwas bewegen muß' (Maurice Roger), wurde zuerst ein Name konzipiert".[192]

Der Begriff „Poison" (engl. Gift) findet als Name für ein Parfum metaphorische Verwendung. Diese Metapher sollte das faszinierende

---

[192]    ohne Autor, Spiegel Verlag (1988), S. 201

Wechselspiel zwischen Mann und Frau zum Ausdruck bringen und wie eine Waffe wirken.[193]

Ein Name wie „Poison" für einen Duft soll die Konsumenten dazu verleiten, ihn zu hinterfragen. Diese Strategie trägt zu einem größeren Bekanntheitsgrad des Parfums bei, denn über eine aktive Auseinandersetzung wird ein Produktname schneller verinnerlicht und gelernt. Diese Strategie konnte sehr erfolgreich umgesetzt werden.

**Fazit:**    **Der Name macht die Marke**

Der Markenname eines neu entwickelten Produktes kann immer nur Teil eines Ganzen sein. Eine Marke wird dem Konsumenten im Laden in der Verpackung präsentiert. Diese konstituiert sich aus dem Zusammenspiel zwischen Logo, Marken- bzw. Produktnamen, Farben, graphischer Gestaltung, Informationen und Hinweisen.

Im Zusammenhang mit den Produktnamen ergeben sich folgende Leitfragen für die Untersuchungsaspekte:

- Welcher Kategorie der Namen läßt sich der Produktname zuordnen?

**a)    beschreibender Name**

- Ist die Beschreibung durch den Namen produktadäquat ausgewählt?
- Ist es möglich, den Namen als Gattungsbezeichnung aufzufassen, so daß das Produkt nicht auf Anhieb als Markenartikel zu identifizieren ist?
- Ist der Name gut merkbar?

---

[193]    vgl. o.A. Spiegel Verlag (1988), S.201

**b)   assoziativer Name**

- Ist der Name produktadäquat ausgewählt?
- Ist das assoziative Interpretationsverfahren einfach und schnell durchzuführen?
- Oft sind bekannte Größen die Grundlage zur Bildung assoziativer Namen („Ajax", „Ariel", „der General" etc.). Assoziiert diese Größe eine geeignete bzw. produktadäquate Eigenschaft?
- Ist das Produkt bzw. eine Produkteigenschaft die Grundlage der Assoziation des Namens (z.B. „Spüli")?
- Gelingt es, den assoziativen Namen als Markennamen bekannt zu machen und damit selber zum Symbol werden zu lassen?
- Ist der assoziative Name leicht zu merken?
- Differenziert der assoziative Name das Produkt von anderen Alternativen?
- Ist der assoziative Name originell?
- Spricht der assoziative Name die Zielgruppe an?

**c)   artifizieller Name**

- Ist der Name produktadäquat ausgewählt?
- Ist das regelbasierte Interpretationsverfahren einfach und schnell durchzuführen?
- Oft sind bekannte Größen die Grundlage zur Bildung artifizieller Namenskompositionen („Kaloderma" etc.). Lassen diese Größen auf geeignete bzw. produktadäquate Eigenschaften schließen?
- Ist der Anbieter, das Produkt bzw. eine Produkteigenschaft die Grundlage der Namensneuschöpfung (z.B. ) und das Produkt aus diesem Grund leicht zu erschließen (Dextro Energen)?

192

### d) Wortneuschöpfung

- Ist der Name produktadäquat ausgewählt?
- Bei völlig unbekannten Wortneuschöpfungen kommt es darauf an, daß der Kunde über die Werbung schnell erfaßbare Erläuterungen bezüglich der Verwendungsregeln des Wortes lernt. Damit wird der artifizielle Name zum Symbol für das Produkt. Ist dies gelungen?

**Weitere Fragen:**

- Gelingt es, den artifiziellen Namen als Markennamen bekannt zu machen und damit selber zum Symbol werden zu lassen?
- Ist der artifizielle Name leicht zu merken?
- Differenziert der artifizielle Name das Produkt von anderen Alternativen?
- Ist der artifizielle Name originell?
- Spricht der artifizielle Name die Zielgruppe an?
- Ist es dem Anbieter mit seinen Marketingmaßnahmen gelungen, den Namen produktadäquat bekannt zumachen - gelingt es den Konsumenten dauerhaft über die Interpretation des Namens auf das Produkt zu schließen?
- Ist der Name gut merkbar (ist er leicht zu lesen und zu schreiben - z.B. "Freixenet" ist nicht leicht zu lesen)?
- Gibt es stilistische Besonderheiten, die die Merkbarkeit erleichtern sollen (z.B. Alliteration)?
- Ist der Klang des Namens angenehm?
- Mit welchem Aufwand muß der Name eingeführt werden?
- Vermittelt der Name einen Eindruck der Produktphilosophie?
- Läßt sich mit dem Namen eine Produktfamilie verbinden?
- Macht der Name eine Marke?
- Verkörpert der Name

a) ein positives Firmenimage?
b) ein positives Produktimage?
c) ein positives Konsumentenimage?
- Sind die Aspekte Anbieter, Produkt und Konsument referentiell miteinander        verknüpft?

Namen bzw. Substantive sind ein wirkungsintensives Gestaltungs-
element für Produktverpackungen. Ihre Wirkung läßt sich mit Hilfe
von Adjektiven noch verstärken.

### 3.4.7 Adjektive

Substantive lassen sich durch Adjektive flexibel beschreiben. Darüber hinaus können Aussagen polarisiert bzw. Akzente gesetzt werden.

Für Koppelmann sind für die Produktwerbung "vor allem die Adjektive bedeutungsvoll, heben sie doch die Qualitäten des Werbeobjektes besonders hervor".[194]

Häufig verwendete Adjektive in der Werbung sind Worte wie: *gut, mehr, schön, besser, frisch, neu, gesund, leicht*[195] und Variationen dazu.

Adjektive dienen der genaueren Definition der Substantive und können diesen einen individuellen Touch verleihen, z.B.:

"Jacobs Cappuccino. Die feine Kaffeespezialität mit dem unverwechselbaren Jacobs Aroma, cremigem Schaum und feinen Schokoflocken"[196].

In diesem Satz wird der Name des Anbieters „Jacobs" als Reizwort verwendet, als bereits bekannt vorausgesetzte Qualität. Jedes substantivische Merkmal wird durch ein Adjektiv angereichert, das die einzelnen Merkmale positiv aufwerten soll. Etwas unglücklich ist dabei aus stilistischer Sicht die zweimalige Wahl des gleichen Adjektives (*fein*). Dadurch erhalten die Schokoflocken keinen neuen eigenen Wert.

---

[194] Koppelmann (1981), S, 273

[195] vgl. Baumgart (1992), S. 138

[196] Jacobs Cappuccino

Das Besondere an „Jacobs Krönung" sind die Wortkompositionen (neben den Café Compositionen) und das "unverwechselbare Jacobs Aroma".

In dieser Wortkomposition wird der Begriff "Aroma" durch das beschreibend verwendete *unverwechselbar* in Kombination mit "Jacobs" definiert. Hinter dieser Strategie läßt sich die Absicht erkennen, die Kunden zu dem Schluß zu bewegen, daß das Aroma nicht mit Adjektiven der Alltagssprache ausreichend zu beschreiben ist, sondern in Kombination mit dem Markennamen zu einer eigenen Institution wird. Allerdings bleibt es den Kunden selbst überlassen, festzustellen, ob das Aroma stark, bitter, süß etc. ist.

Adjektiven kommt auf Verpackungen auch die Rolle zu, als Reiz- und Schlüsselwörter eingesetzt zu werden.

Viele Adjektive erhalten auf der Frontseite von Verpackungen einen exponierten Platz. Sie stehen entweder über, unter oder neben dem Produktnamen oder gänzlich alleine links oder rechts neben einer Graphik.

Es handelt sich dabei um vielversprechende Adjektive wie *neu, mega, ultra, supra, professionell, mehr* u.v.m.

Der Charakter dieser Adjektive ist in der Regel hypermodern. Sie haben eine "eye-catcher Funktion". Mit ihrer Hilfe läßt sich eine Verpackung "aufpeppen", ohne ein neues Design entwickeln zu müssen. Es geht dabei hauptsächlich darum, mit diesen Ausdrücken die Konkurrenzprodukte zu übertrumpfen.

Das Adjektiv *ultra* steht ganz oben auf der Hitliste adjektivischer Reizwörter. Das Wort "ultra" ist aus der Medizin und aus dem Welt-all bekannt, z.B. über den Begriff "Ultraschall".[197] Mit einer starken chemischen und biologischen Wirkung wird das sogenannte "ultra-violett" definiert.[198] "Ultra" verweist jedoch auch auf politische Zusammenhänge.[199] Die Assoziation mit einer extremen Größe ist in diesem Zusammenhang gewünscht.

"Ultra" ist mittlerweile auf einer ganzen Reihe von Verpackungen chemischer Substanzen wie Waschmittel und Reiniger an exponierter Stelle zu finden. Durch hochfrequenten Gebrauch verliert auch ein solches Wort den Reiz des Besonderen. Um ein Konkurrenzprodukt in seiner Wirkung gesteigert hervorzuheben, werden Ausdrücke wie "ultra plus" („Ultra plus und extra stark - 3 Wetter Taft") gewählt.

Jedoch sind die Steigerungsmöglichkeiten für einen Begriff wie "ul-tra" begrenzt. Daher wird auch wieder auf alt bewährtes zurückgegriffen, z.B. "ultra classic" (Ajax), oder "original ultra plus" (Palmolive).

Eine Kombination von "ultra" und "classic" ist jedoch nicht empfeh-lenswert. Es soll eine Leistungssteigerung des klassischen Produktes suggeriert werden. Jedoch referieren beide Adjektive auf gegensätzli-che Attribute, die bevorzugt in ihrem jeweiligen Wirkungsbereich (klassisch - futuristisch) verstärkt werden sollten (z.B. original clas-sic oder ultra plus) und nicht als Paradox gegenseitig ausgehebelt werden sollten. Die Reihe ließe sich fortsetzen, wenn die Konsu-menten bei weiteren Steigerungsversuchen bald mit "Gigaperls" konfrontiert würden, was der derzeitig aktuellen Computersprache

---

[197] vgl. Duden Fremdwörterlexikon (1990), S. 801 - Stichwort "Ultraschall". Es handelt sich dabei um Schallfrequenzen, die für das menschliche Ohr nicht mehr wahrnehmbar sind.

[198] vgl. ebd., Stichwort "ultraviolett"

[199] vgl. ebd., Stichwort "Ultra"= Extremist, *ultra*-rechts oder *ultra*-links, *Ultra*-Extremist etc.

angemessen wäre – ein „Gigaset" in Form einer Telefonanlage von Siemens gibt es ja schon.

Über das Adjektiv "professionell" wird ein Produkt wie "der General" personifiziert. Von der Konsistenz her handelt es sich bei diesem Produkt um eine chemische Substanz, die mit dem Status eines Profis ausgestattet wird. Es wird suggeriert, daß der Reiniger ebenso professionell arbeitet wie eine Putzkolonne. Leider putzt der Reiniger in der Realität noch nicht von selbst.

Die Anbieter des Waschmittels "Fairy ultra" haben sich etwas ganz Neues einfallen lassen, um die mittlerweile ausgereizten Adjektive wie "mega" und "ultra" zu ergänzen. Sie haben ihr Produkt "Fairy New Multi Active" genannt. Die englische Bezeichnung soll Internationalität suggerieren. Es handelt sich jedoch um Begriffe, die in Deutschland nicht befremdlich wirken. Neue *Multi-Aktivität* ist die Antwort auf *Ultra-Leistung*.

Ebenso haben sich die Anbieter vom "Tetesept Erkältungsbad" einen innovativen Namenszusatz einfallen lassen: "Tetesept, die Nr. 1". Damit wurde das Erkältungsbad vermessen an die Spitze sämtlicher Konkurrenzanbieter gestellt, denen als wirkungsvollstes Überzeugungsattribut ein Angebot zu einem besonders günstigen Preis bleibt.

Schwartau präsentiert die Marmeladensorte „Erdbeer/Orange" als „ unsere Marmelade des Jahres". Der Ausdruck „... des Jahres" ist ein feststehender Begriff und über die Regelhaftigkeit seines Einsatzes zum Symbol dafür geworden, daß jemand eine Ehrung bezüglich einer „besten Leistung" in einem Jahr erhalten hat. Lediglich der Zusatz „unsere" läßt darauf schließen, daß diese Marmelade nicht offiziell prämiert wurde, sondern lediglich von Schwartau Preisträger vorgestellt wird. Auf den ersten Blick fällt dieser Zusammenhang jedoch nicht unbedingt auf. Die Marmeladensorte wird durch diesen Hinweis deutlich von den anderen Sorten differenziert.

Auf den Verpackungen der verschiedensten Frühstückszerealien ist eine Flut von amerikanisierten adjektivischen Reiz- und Schlüssel-wörtern zu beobachten. Ebenso sind diverse Salzgebäck- und Süßwaren von dem Trend betroffen, daß Adjektive auf den Verpak-kungen verwendet werden, die den "American Way of Life" suggerieren. Häufig bilden derartige Adjektive Bestandteile des Na-mens. Besonders bevorzugt werden die Adjektive, die onomatopoetischen Charakter haben. Dazu gehören die "Kellogg's Crunchy Nuts" genauso wie die "Milky Way Crisp Rolls". "Crunchy" und "crispy" sind beides Adjektive, die Geräusche simulieren und suggerieren sollen, die beim Reinbeißen in das Produkt entstehen.

Von Adjektiven, die an einer exponierten Position auf Verpackungen installiert werden, wird ein hoher Index an Textcharakter abverlangt. Obwohl es sich nur um ein einziges Wort handelt, sollte es beim Kunden eine geschlossene Assoziationskette auslösen, die dem Ad-jektiv einen Kontext gibt.

Für das Analysemodell ergeben sich in bezug auf die Adjektive folgende Leitfragen für die Konzeption der Untersuchungsaspekte:

- Werden die Adjektive wirkungseffektiv als Reiz- bzw. Schlüsselwort auf der Produktverpackung eingesetzt?
  - alleine?
  - als Bilderänzung?
  - als Wortergänzung?
- Wie wirken die Adjektive?
  - ergänzend?
  - aufwertend?
  - vergleichend?
  - Sonstiges?
- Bieten sie einen sinnvollen Aspekt der Ergänzung?
- Wirken die Adjektive
  - glaubwürdig?
  - positiv?
  - aufbauschend?
  - Sonstiges?
- Sprechen die Adjektive die Zielgruppe an?
- Sind die Adjektive verständlich?
- Passen die Adjektive zum Stil der Verpackung?

### 3.4.8 Verben

Verben findet man selten auf Frontseiten von Verpackungen. Dort stehen in der Regel stichpunktartig angelegte Wortkonstruktionen, die als kurzer und prägnanter Blickfang durch Verben nur unnötig verlängert würden, zumal bei der prädikativen Verwendung von Verben die Satzstruktur entsprechend angeglichen werden müßte.

Nach Koppelmann dienen Verben dazu, das Dynamische, das Bewirkende herauszustellen.[200]

Auf Frontseiten begegnen uns Verbkonstruktionen wie "verbessert" („Poly Kur"), "angereichert" (Säfte), "wirkt" („Stodil" Bodenreiniger) und "macht" („Drano Rohrfrei")

Stark provokativ wirkt der Frontseitenaufdruck in einem separierten Kasten auf einer „Dr. Oetker" Tiefkühlpizza:
"Probieren und vergleichen Sie mit Ihrer Lieblingspizza beim Italiener!"[201]

Diese Aussage ist unverfänglich, da unverbindlich. Es wird suggeriert, daß die Tiefkühlpizza dem Vergleich standhält. Jedoch wird davon ausgegangen, daß die Konsumenten beim Lesen dieses Aufdruckes lediglich die eigene Alternative der Tiefkühlpizza in Anspruch nehmen. Sie sollen in ihrer Entscheidung bestätigt werden und das Produkt den Alternativen vorziehen.

Der Hauptverwendungsbereich für Verben sind umseitige Verpackungstexte. Handelt es sich um einen informativen Text, wird das Verb *sein* in der Form *ist* bevorzugt verwendet. Ebenso wie in aufgedruckten Bedienungs- und Zubereitungsanleitungen werden die

---

[200] vgl. Koppelmann (1981), S. 273

[201] „Dr. Oetker Küche Ristorante Pizza Calzone Speziale tiefgekühlt"

201

Verben gerne in einer Imperativkonstruktion vorgestellt, um die Rezipienten kurz und manchmal provokativ anzusprechen, z.Bmit "Kleb mich!"[202] Mit diesem Ausdruck werden die Rezipienten geduzt, was einen persönlich ansprechenden Ton erzeugen soll.

Ebenfalls beliebt sind imperativisch eingesetzte Konstruktionen in der dritten Person mit "Sie". Dabei wirkt der Befehlston abgemildert - und wird zu einem gut gemeinten Ratschlag. Ein schönes Beispiel bietet der Rückentext einer „Dr. Oetker Junge Küche Ristorante Pizza Salami tiefgefroren". Nebenbei bemerkt handelt es sich bei dem Produktnamen um eine siebengliedrige Wortkomposition, die vom Firmennamen über die Spartenbezeichnung immer spezieller wird. Der Text dazu lautet:

"Gönnen Sie sich doch öfter Genuß wie beim ‚Italiener'! Denn auf der Ristorante Speisekarte finden Sie jetzt auch die Pizza Calzone Speziale. Das ist eine typisch italienische Pizza-Tasche mit leckerer Füllung aus sonnengereiften Tomaten, Champignons, saftigem Schinken, herzhafter Salami und viel Käse in der gewohnten Ristorante Qualität. Genießen Sie die Calzone Speziale bei einem Glas Wein und Kerzenschein!"[203]

Die verwendeten Verben zielen auf Genuß und Lebensqualität.
Mit der Form "ist" wird wertneutral eine Palette von Zutaten vorgestellt, die durch dramaturgisch eingesetzte Adjektive schillernd belebt werden. Die verwendeten Adjektive kennzeichnen jedoch keine konkreten Merkmale, die Konsumenten als verbindliche Aussage einklagen könnten. "Typisch italienisch" ist genauso der

---

[202]  „Brand" Klebesiegel zum Wiederverschließen der Tüte

[203]  „Dr. Oetker Junge Küche Ristorante Pizza Salami tiefgekühlt"

subjektiven Einschätzung überlassen wie eine "leckere Füllung" und die "gewohnte Ristorante Qualität".

Zusammenfassend läßt sich festhalten, daß Verben auf Verpackungen meistens in einer Aufforderungskonstruktion mit "Sie" verwendet werden. Es werden über eine Form von "sein" nur dann Verbindlichkeiten eingegangen, wenn diese auch problemlos nachweisbar sind, wie z.B. bei Zutaten. Wenn es um die Beeinflussung subjektiver Wertigkeiten geht, werden meinungskatalysierende Verben vor meinungsvorgebenden bevorzugt. Man soll sich z.B. eine leckere Pizza gönnen und genießen (sie *schmeckt* gut, statt sie *ist* gut).

Es liegt in der Natur der Verben, Vorgänge und Tätigkeiten auszudrücken. Aus diesem Grund eignen sie sich hervorragend um Wirkungen, Wirkungsprozesse und Verbesserungen auszudrücken. Dementsprechend hoch ist die Frequenz von Verben wie "wirken" und "verbessern" auf Produktverpackungen.

Für das Analysemodell ergeben sich folgende Punkte:

- Sind die Verben verständlich?
- Welchen Charakter haben die Verben?
- Sind die Verben zielgruppenadäquat ausgewählt?
- Passen die Verben in den Kontext?
- Lassen sich die Verben sinngemäß interpretieren?

### 3.4.9 Sonstige Wortklassen

Alle weiteren Wortklassen, die Akzente setzen, lassen, sich in der Kategorie "Sonstige" gesammelt betrachten.

So ist z.B. als eines der beliebtesten attributiven Funktionswörter der Partikel "mit" auf den Frontseiten der Verpackungen zu finden. Die Anbieter halten "mit" den besonderen Wirk- und Inhaltsstoffen ihrer Produkte nicht hinter dem Berg. Sie versuchen, über eine deutliche Kennzeichnung der Besonderheiten auf den Frontseiten gegen die Konkurrenz aufzutrumpfen. "Mit" kennzeichnet nicht nur einen schlichten Inhaltsstoff, sondern exponiert ein besonderes Ingredient.

Ebenfalls häufig verwendet wird das Wörtchen "nach". Allerdings ist "nach" stärker dem Nahrungsmittelsektor vorbehalten. "Nach italienischer Art" („Jacobs Cappuccino") oder „nach „Hausfrauenart" (Schwartau) sind augenscheinlich nennenswerte Alternativen, wenn die Zutaten keine herausragenden Besonderheiten darstellen.

Darüber hinaus dienen derartige Zusätze, um darauf hinzuweisen, daß das Produkt in der Qualität dem eigentlichen Original (z.B. Hausfrauenart, Maggi Wirtshaus) standhält.

Auch mit Präpositionen wie "unter" und "über" lassen sich Wirkungseffekte erzielen. So werden sie z.B. auf der "Persil Megaperls Color"-Verpackung geschickt eingesetzt, indem eine faktischen Aussage gewertet wird, und selbige dadurch als Kaufargument zu präsentieren. "Unter 5%: Seife, Polycarboxylate" und "Über 30%: Zeolithe, (Sasil®) Persil Megaperls enthält Enzyme" sind als Aussagen gestaltet, die die Konsumenten schließen lassen, daß die faktischen Mengenangaben von negativen Inhaltsstoffen sehr gering und von positiven Inhaltsstoffen sehr reichlich eingehalten werden. Dabei ist davon auszugehen, daß der Durchschnittskunde die genannten Begriffe nicht konkret zu interpretiere weiß. Über derartige

Formulierungen soll er jedoch das Gefühl bekommen, die Zusammensetzung des Produktes einschätzen und bewerten zu können.

Auf Produktverpackungen werden gerne Fremd-, Fach- und Kunstworte eingesetzt.

## a) Fremdworte

Kennzeichnend für ein Fremdwort ist, daß es sich um einen sprachlichen Ausdruck handelt, der aus einer fremden Sprache in die Muttersprache übernommen wurde. Anders als ein Lehnwort ist ein Fremdwort bezüglich der Orthographie und Flexion noch nicht in das System der Muttersprache eingepaßt.

Wichtig ist hierbei, zu unterscheiden, welche Fremdwörter bereits eingedeutscht und damit als allgemein bekannt vorauszusetzen sind und welche nicht. Besonders für die Produktanbieter ist es empfehlenswert, streng darauf zu achten, ob ein Fremdwort erläuterungsbedürftig ist oder nicht, und inwieweit der ganze Text durch das Wort beeinflußt wird. Grundsätzlich sollte die Regel bei der Verpackungstextgestaltung gelten, daß ein (noch) nicht eingedeutschtes Fremdwort unbedingt erläutert werden sollte, um den Rezipienten das Verständnis zu erleichtern. Gut gemeinte Übersetzungsversuche scheitern dann, wenn es keine adäquate Übersetzungsmöglichkeit gibt und/oder die Übersetzung das Verständnis nur unnötig verkompliziert. Hier gilt die Regel, daß vor jeder Übersetzung zu überprüfen ist, ob der entsprechende Ausdruck den Sachverhalt wirklich angemessen wiedergibt und ob das Verständnis des Sachverhaltes durch die Übersetzung nicht beeinträchtigt wird.

Es gilt der Grundsatz, daß Fremdwörter, wenn sie seltener auftreten, wie alle wenig gebräuchlichen Wörter schwerer verständlich sind als muttersprachliche Wörter und daher so gut es geht vermieden werden sollten.[204]

So steht auf „Bonaqua"-Wasserflaschen, die häufig über Automaten zu erwerben sind, "sparkling" oder "non sparkling". Der Kunde wird mit einer derartigen Aufschrift genötigt, seine Fremdsprachenkenntnisse zu aktivieren. Leichter verständlich, aber weniger elegant ist in Deutschland der Aufdruck "mit Kohlensäure" oder "ohne Kohlensäure" gewesen.

Auf den verschiedensten Kosmetikartikelverpackungen findet man immer wieder den Hinweis: "dermatologisch getestet".[205] Die Aussage klingt wissenschaftlich und soll aus diesem Grund den Kunden imponieren. Das Wort "dermatologisch" ist für jemanden ohne Latein- oder Griechischkenntnisse ein unverständliches Fremdwort, das mit keinem Wort der deutschen Sprache Ähnlichkeit hat. Für die Kunden reduziert sich dann der Hinweis durch ein Nichtverstehen reduziert auf die Aussage, daß das Produkt getestet wurde. Wenn man auf ein Fremdwort nicht verzichten möchte, kann man den Kunden die Möglichkeit geben, den Begriff aus dem Kontext zu erschließen, etwa mit einem Satz wie: „Das Produkt wurde dermatologisch getestet und für hautfreundlich befunden."

Viele Anbieter hoffen, daß ihr Produkt mit einer Beschreibung gespickt mit Fremdworten an Wert gewinnt, weil es Internationalität und Exklusivität signalisiert. Jedoch ist abzuwägen, ob und in wie

---

[204]     vgl. Teigeler (1968), S. 39

[205]     z.B. auf einer „Timotei" Pflegespülungsflasche

weit eine verständlichere Verpackungsbeschriftung nicht einen Verkaufsvorteil bieten würde, insbesondere dann, wenn die Kunden auf eine verständliche Gebrauchs- oder Verbrauchsanleitung auf der Verpackung angewiesen sind.

**b)  Kunstworte**

Per Definition werden Kunstworte im Bereich der Werbesprache aus einzelnen Sprachelementen wie Silben, Wortteilen etc. neu zusammengestellt und kombiniert. Da diese neuen Worte oft aus einer Kombination bekannter Elemente bestehen, hoffen die Texter, daß die Rezipienten die Bedeutung der Worte aus den ihnen bekannten Elementen ableiten und erschließen können.[206]

Nicht immer wird ein Kunstwort aus der Not heraus gebildet, daß ein geeigneter Begriff im Wortschatz nicht vorhanden ist. Kunstwörter als eine Form von Wortneuschöpfungen bzw. Wortneukombination eignen sich z.B., um die Leser stärker affektiv-emotional anzusprechen, als dies mit einem entsprechenden allgemein gebräuchlichen Synonym möglich wäre („Rejuven Q 10 Night"-Creme (Juvena) statt Faltenbeseitigungscreme, oder „Sproodles" (Ariel) statt Brausetabletten).

Kunstworte sollen besondere Leistungen des Produktes kreativ hervorheben bzw. markieren.

Es sollen nicht nur die besonderen Leistungen auffällig gekennzeichnet werden, sondern diese sollen darüber hinaus markant von den Leistungen konkurrierender Produkte hervorgehoben werden.

Ein weiterer Aspekt für die Verwendung von Kunstwörtern ist die Möglichkeit, damit verschiedene Produkte firmenspezifisch zu kennzeichnen.

---

[206]  vgl. Krautmann (1981), S. 105

Die Firma Ferrero hat dies in ihrem Produktzweig "Schokolade für Kinder" sehr erfolgreich umgesetzt. Es wurden schlichte und sehr einfach verständliche Kunstworte gebildet, die als Namen eine ganze Produktpalette einheitlich kennzeichnen. Es handelt sich dabei um:

- „Kinderschokolade"
- „Kinderüberraschung"
- „Kinder-Country"
- „Kinder-Milchschnitte"

Jeder Name besteht aus einer Zusammensetzung zweier vollständiger Substantive. Durch die Verwendung kompletter Worteinheiten als Elemente für Wortneuschöpfungen ist ein gutes Verständnis garantiert. Die Rezipienten können von den Einzelwortbedeutungen auf die ganze Einheit schließen. In dem aufgezeigten Fall dient das Wortelement Kinder- prinzipiell dazu, den Rezipienten die Interpretation zu vereinfachen, daß es sich um ein Produkt handelt, das für Kinder besonders geeignet ist.

Viele Kunstwörter werden dergestalt gebildet, daß sie wie ein Fachwort aussehen, sozusagen mit "Profi-Look". Solche Kunstwörter mit 'Snob-Appeal' haben jedoch weniger die Aufgabe, verständlich und präzise zu informieren, sie sollen affektiv-emotional wirken.[207]

Als Fazit bleibt:

"Verwendet nie ein neues Wort, sofern es nicht drei Eigenschaften besitzt:

---

[207] vgl. Krautmann (1981), S. 105

208

Es muß notwendig,

es muß verständlich und

es muß wohlklingend sein."[208]

Dabei bleibt die Frage nach der Notwendigkeit von Fall zu Fall zu untersuchen. Ein seltenes Wort kann auch dann *notwendig* sein, wenn es z.B. besonders elegant oder stark differenzierend wirkt. Neben dem Wohlklang sollten aber auch Kriterien wie Originalität und Kreativität berücksichtigt werden.

## c)   Fachworte

Fachwörter entstammen in der Regel einer kompletten Fachsprache. Fachsprachen sind gekennzeichnet durch einen eigenen, von der Allgemeinsprache besonderen Wortschatz. Sie dienen der präzisen Kommunikation, meist über ganz spezifische Sachbereiche oder Tätigkeitsfelder. Durch eine exklusive Bedeutungsspezifizierung grenzen sich Fachwörter von Wörtern aus der Alltagssprache ab. Ihre Gebrauchsregel ergibt sich durch das Gebiet, für das sie gebildet wurden und die sprachliche Lücke, die sie dort zu füllen haben. Fachsprachen sind streng zu unterscheiden von Sondersprachen. Während Fachsprachen durch ein spezielles Sachgebiet bestimmt sind, sind Sondersprachen von einem definierbaren Personenkreis bestimmt.

Fachtermini sind in sämtlichen Texten, die für Personen über die Fachsprachensprecher hinaus veröffentlicht werden, Quelle von Verständnisproblemen. Die Schwierigkeit liegt für die Rezipienten meist

---

[208]    Schneider (1986), S. 53 in Gedenken an Voltaire (1937), Ratschläge an einen Journalisten

darin, daß sie sich die Spezialausdrücke aufgrund ihrer Fremdartigkeit nicht selbst herleiten können und ihnen auch eine Erschließung aus dem Zusammenhang versagt bleibt.

Ein weiteres Problem ist die Tatsache, daß, selbst wenn ein Kunde die verwendeten Fachwörter verstanden hat, nicht gleichzeitig auch sichergestellt ist, daß ihm klar wird, welchen Wert diese Angaben für ihn haben bzw., was er konkret mit den Angaben anfangen soll.

Es ist daher empfehlenswert, in Verpackungstexten von Produkten, wenn möglich, auf Fachworte zu verzichten, wenn sie für eine breitere Masse als Zielgruppe bestimmt sind. Statt dessen sollte versucht werden, den Sachverhalt mit bekannten Worten so kurz und doch so verständlich wie möglich darzustellen.

Es gibt Fälle, bei denen sich die Verwendung eines Fachwortes nur schwer vermeiden läßt. Meistens mangelt es an adäquaten Ausdrucksmöglichkeiten aus dem allgemein gebräuchlichen Wortschatz. Umschreibungen verkomplizieren einen Sachverhalt oft unnötig und schrecken die Konsumenten noch mehr ab.

Sehr hilfreich ist es, dem Kunden entsprechende Erläuterungen an die Hand zu geben sowie komplizierte Vorgänge mit Bildmaterial visuell zu unterstützen.

Der Informationsgehalt von Leistungsinformationen gewinnt dann an Relevanz für den Kunden, wenn er den Wert des Produktes bzw. seine Leistungen für sich persönlich abschätzen kann. Zu diesem Zweck ist es sinnvoll, Erklärungen beizufügen, mit deren Hilfe der Verbraucher Fachausdrücke und die spezifischen Leistungen in eine für ihn verständliche Sprache übersetzen kann.

Geschickt gelöst haben dieses Problem einige Hersteller von Lebensmitteln. Es ist mittlerweile für eine ganze Reihe von Lebensmitteln Pflicht, die Kilojouleangabe auf die Verpackung aufzudrucken. „Kilojoule" ist allerdings eine Einheit mit sehr großen Werten. Um die Verbraucher, die meist noch die alte Angabe „Kilokalorien" gewohnt sind, nicht zu verunsichern, lassen die meisten Anbieter die alte Angabeform in Kilokalorien mit den wesentlich niedrigeren Werten zusätzlich auf die Verpackung aufdrucken Sie werden häufig mit "Energie" überschrieben. Allerdings lassen diese Wertetabelle nur dann eine konkrete Einschätzung des Produktes zu, wenn man weiß, in welchem Verhältnis die Angaben desselben zu der Menge steht, die man täglich konsumieren darf/soll.

Eine gute Lösung bietet der Aufdruck auf „Bihun"-Suppen-Verpackungen. Es wird den Kunden der Vergleich an die Hand gegeben: "Diese Packung enthält weniger Kalorien als ein Apfel".[209]

Nicht nur kalorien- und ernährungsbewußte Menschen wissen, daß ein Apfel sehr wenig Kalorien enthält und daher ohne schlechtes Gewissen verzehrt werden darf. Der Trick dieser Angabe ist, das Gewissen der Kunden mit diesem Vergleich dergestalt zu beruhigen, daß sie sich wegen der Kalorien bzw. um ihre Figur keine Sorgen beim Verzehr der Suppe machen brauchen.

Die Firma „Coca-Cola" gibt an, der Kaloriengehalt ihres Produktes „Coca Cola light" betrage pro Glas nur eine Kalorie, und wirbt sogar damit.
Der Kaloriengehalt erscheint im Vergleich zu den Hunderterzahlen, die ansonsten auf den Produktverpackungen zu finden sind, unglaublich gering. Die Kunden haben das Gefühl, den genannten Wert einschätzen zu können, was sich insbesondere bei kalorienbewußten Menschen positiv auf die Kaufbereitschaft auswirkt.

---

[209]    Vgl. Bihunsuppenverpackung, Rückseite

Bei der Analyse der Wortneuschöpfungen ist oft sehr schwer zu rekonstruieren, ob nicht tatsächlich versucht wurde, ein neues Fachwort zu bilden, um ein semantisches Loch zu schließen.

Ebenfalls schwierig ist es, zu bestimmen, was überhaupt ein Fachwort ist und was nicht. Die meisten Worte, die auf Produktverpackungen verwendet werden, haben sich im allgemeinen Wortschatz zumindest so weit etabliert, daß sie ohne größere Erläuterungen verstanden werden.

Besonders schwierig ist es, zwischen echten Fachwörtern und den "Kunstwörtern im Profi-Look" zu unterscheiden. Dabei ist zu differenzieren, ob es sich um ein Produkt handelt, das von Spezialisten für einen kleinen Interessentenkreis entwickelt wurde, oder ob es sich um ein Produkt handelt, das als Standardkonsumartikel auf dem Markt etabliert werden soll.

Im ersten Fall ist es relativ unproblematisch, Fachworte in einem Verwenderkreis zu etablieren, da sowohl Anbieter als auch Käufer Mitglieder des spezifischen Sprachbenutzerkreises sind, z.B. im Bereich Computer, Motorradzubehör, Heimwerkerbedarf.

Ein gängiges Mittel in der Kosmetikindustrie ist es, mit Hilfe von Fachwortattrappen Wissenschaftlichkeit und Hochwertigkeit des Produktes zu suggerieren und gleichzeitig das Produkt von der (Über)Flut der Konkurrenzartikel zu differenzieren und damit zu separieren.

So steht z.B. auf einer umverpackenden Pappschachtel für eine Cremedose der Firma „L'Oréal" zu lesen: "L'Oréal Plénitude Hydra-Matité - Feuchtigkeitscreme mit absorbierenden Mikrospheren." Ein derartiger Satz wirft nicht die Frage auf, *ob* man studiert haben muß, um ihn zu verstehen, sondern *was*.

Drei Akzente in einer frontseitigen Aufschriftkonstruktion sollen vermeintlich französischen Charakter suggerieren. "Hydra" läßt sich von Wasser herleiten, was zu einer Doppelung des Merkmals in Kombination mit der Beschreibung "Feuchtigkeitscreme" führt. Optisch jedoch bleibt eine Merkmalsfülle durch die Vielzahl der Worte erhalten. Die "absorbierenden Mikrospheren" verleihen einer ganz prophanen Gesichtscreme ein mystisches Moment, denn durch die Charakterisierung dieser Mikrospheren mit einem Aktivität vorstellenden Partizip erhält die Creme ein lebendiges Moment und einen wissenschaftlichen Akzent.

Strategisch anspruchsvoll wird der Hinweis "Glanz-Regulierend" vorgestellt. Die Darstellung in zwei jeweils großgeschriebenen Worten exponiert die beiden Aspekte "Glanz" und "Regulation". Die vorteilhafte Präsentation einer Produkteigenschaft erfolgt hier über den Begriff "Regulierend". Es wird kein Ausschlußkriterium vorgestellt wie "schafft Glanz" oder "verhindert Glanz", sondern es wird ein aktives Produkt präsentiert, das sich flexibel dem individuellen Typ anpaßt und darüber suggeriert, immer den richtigen Teint zu treffen.


Etwas anders verhält es sich, wenn Experten Fachwörter für ihr Gebiet konzipieren, die aber einer breiteren Öffentlichkeit zugänglich und eingängig sein sollen. Zu denken ist dabei beispielsweise an die verschiedenen Waschmittelhersteller. Es wird dem Verbraucher suggeriert, daß das jeweilige Waschmittel nur von Experten entwickelt wurde. Dieser Aspekt wird bei der Produktvermarktung durch die Verwendung vermeintlicher Fachworte untermauert.

Hier gilt es ganz klar zu unterscheiden, ob es sich tatsächlich um Fachworte aus dem Benutzerkreis der Chemiker, Ingenieure, Technologen etc. handelt, oder ob es sich um die sogenannten „Kunstworte im Profi-Look" handelt, die dem Kunden Professionalität des Produktes suggerieren sollen und möglichst gleichzeitig in deren Wortschatz etabliert werden sollen.

Ein solcher Begriff aus der Waschmittelbranche ist auf der „Coral Intensiv-Packung" zu finden - "mit Anti-Aging-System". Bei diesem Begriff handelt es sich um ein Kunstwort, das zur Leistungsbeschreibung eines Standardkonsumartikels konzipiert wurde und Professionalität suggerieren soll. Da dieses Wort für eine große Zielgruppe entwickelt wurde und nicht dem Spezialwortschatz einer kleinen Gruppe Fachkundiger vorbehalten bleibt, kann es als künstliche Fachwortnachbildung bestimmt werden.

Dieser Begriff verdeutlicht, daß die Beschreibung Krautmanns, daß Kunstwörter, die wie Fachwörter konstruiert werden, weniger verständlich und präzise informieren, dafür affektiv emotional wirken sollten, nicht völlig zutreffend ist.[210]

Ein Wort wie "Anti-Aging-System" ist für die Kunden auf Anhieb nur schwer herzuleiten. Es bezieht sich auf eine Produktleistung und soll dem Kunden den Eindruck hochentwickelter Technologie bei der Produktentwicklung vermitteln. Von einer emotional-affektiven Wirkung kann nur insofern ausgegangen werden, als der Begriff den Kunden qualitativ hochwertige Leistungen suggeriert und darüber hinaus Werte wie Seriosität, Exklusivität und Vertrauen.

Demnach ist Krautmanns Aussage[211] dergestalt zu formulieren, daß zwischen folgenden Fachworten und Fachwortkonstruktionen zu unterscheiden ist:

*F*achworte, die von Angehörigen der Benutzergruppe der Fachsprache eingeführt werden. Derartige Fachworte beziehen sich in der Regel auf ganz spezifische Produkteigenschaften und/oder Leistungen und sollen die Kunden überzeugen. Sie bleiben aufgrund einer

---

[210]  vgl. Krautmann (1981), S. 105
[211]  vgl. Krautmann (1981), S. 103

kleineren und sehr speziellen Ziel- und Benutzergruppe nur einem kleinen Kreis von Fachkundigen vorbehalten.

Fachworte, die dem Wortschatz der Experten entstammen, die das zu vermarktende Produkt entwickelt haben. Derartige Fachworte sollen qualitativ hochwertige Technologien suggerieren und das Produkt von den Alternativen der Konkurrenz abheben. Auch hierbei steht die Überzeugungstaktik im Vordergrund.

Kunstworte im Profi-Look, um sich der Terminologie Krautmanns zu bedienen. Dabei handelt es sich um Wortneuschöpfungen oder neue Wortkombinationen, die wie Fachworte konstruiert werden, aber keiner speziellen Fachsprache vorbehalten sind, sondern in das allgemeine Sprachgut eingeführt und dort etabliert werden sollen.

Kunstworte, die wie Fachworte wirken können, aber nicht ausschließlich sachspezifisch ausgerichtet sind, sondern auch Bedürfnisse und Triebe der Konsumenten ansprechen sollen. Demzufolge kommt zu der rein sachlichen Überzeugungswirkung noch eine affektiv-emotionale Wirkungskomponente hinzu.

Kunstworte, Wortneuschöpfungen bzw. Neologismen, die einzig und allein zu dem Zweck gebildet werden, der Verpackungsaufschrift einen innovativen Touch zu verleihen mit der Möglichkeit, die Verbraucher spontan affektiv-emotional zu erreichen. Auf diesem Wege sollen die Kunden positiv zu dem Produkt gestimmt werden.

215

Für das Analysemodell festzuhalten bleibt:

---

- Werden mit Hilfe von Worten aus weiteren Klassen Akzente gesetzt?
- Ist die Wortwahl verständlich?
- Ist die Wortwahl sinnvoll oder wird der Text unnötig verkompliziert?
- Wie läßt sich die Wortwahl im Sinne einer Wirkungsintention charakterisieren?

---

### 3.4.10 Stilmittel

Die häufigsten Stilmittel, die auf Verpackungen zu finden sind, sind Steigerungen und Euphemismen.

**a)    Steigerungen**

Verschiedene Steigerungsformen sind ein beliebtes Mittel, sich von der Konkurrenz abzusetzen.

Die übliche Form ist ein gerichteter Vergleich, bei dem das vorliegende Produkt herausragend besser abschneidet. Es eignet sich in diesem Fall die Form des Komparativs, um das "bessere Abschneiden" zu verdeutlichen. Da es verboten ist, in Form von Konkurrenzwerbung auf andere Produkte Bezug zu nehmen, müssen sich die Anbieter mit Hilfe eines sogenannten "leeren Komparatives"[212] damit begnügen, die Vorteile des präsentierten Produktes als besser herauszustellen oder unverbindlich gegen eine allgemeine Variable abzugrenzen. Beliebt ist zu diesem Zweck ein Ausdruck wie "besser als herkömmliche Produkte" (Persil, Duracell).

---

[212]    vgl. Baumgart (1992), S. 57

Die höchste Steigerungsform ist der Superlativ. Der Superlativ bietet den Vorteil, daß er aufgrund von Überhöhung keinen Vergleich mehr verlangt. Er dient dazu, grammatikalisch den Gipfel positiver inhaltlicher Merkmale zu kennzeichnen („fit-fitter-taxofit", „Nivea Neu in Bestform"). Allerdings wird er trotz dieser Fähigkeit relativ sparsam verwendet, denn er wird gerne als aufschneiderisch und damit als unseriös interpretiert. Der Grund dafür ist die bereits erwähnte gesetzliche Regelung, daß Aussagen, die nicht 100%ig evident sind, nicht geäußert werden dürfen bzw. eingeschränkt werden müssen. Ein eingeschränkter Superlativ wirkt wie eine Karikatur seiner selbst. „Hakles" "wahrscheinlich das dickste und kostbarste Toilettenpapier weltweit" ist das vollmundige Versprechen, das beste Produkt ausgewählt zu haben, auch wenn es ein bißchen mehr kostet.

Es ist darüber hinaus möglich, ein Produkt aufzuwerten, indem man eine inhaltliche Steigerung z.B. über einen Slogan vorstellt, z.B.: „Salaggio – alles andere ist Wurst". „Salaggio" wird als Geflügelsalami vorgestellt, die eine neue Dimension von Wurst verkörpern soll.

## b)  Euphemismen

Euphemismen als Wortbeschönigungen sind auf Grund der vielen Wortneuschöpfungen auf Verpackungen kaum eindeutig nachzuweisen und unterliegen der jeweiligen Perspektive des Betrachters.
So kann z.B. die Bezeichnung "Fischstäbchen" als Euphemismus interpretiert werden, da dieses Produkt meist nichts anderes als Fischreste enthält. Ebenso fällt es empfindlichen Seelen schwer, die euphemistische Bezeichnung für das Insektenabwehrspray "Autan" als "Lotion im Pumpzerstäuber" zu akzeptieren.

Reine Euphemisem werden auf Verpackungen generell vermieden. Man würde mit einem direkten Euphemismus Gefahr laufen, daß die Aussage als Falschaussage gesetzlich angekreidet wird.[213]

Dennoch läßt es sich als Euphemismus interpretieren, wenn auf einem Tetra-Pak "Apfelsaft" als Produktbezeichnung aufgedruckt steht, und man bei genauerem Hinsehen feststellt, daß der Fruchtsaftgehalt lediglich 30% beträgt. Noch stärker verschönernd ist die Aussage "Fruchtsaftgetränk", in dem nicht einmal unbedingt Fruchtsaft enthalten sein muß – dieser kann durchaus chemisch substituiert werden.

### d) Personifizierungen

Personifizierungen sind ein beliebtes Mittel insbesondere auf Produktverpackungen für Kinder. Dabei lassen sich verschiedene Formen der Personifizierung unterscheiden:

- Das Produkt selber wird personifiziert (z.B. erhalten Schokocrossis plötzlich Augen und die Früchte auf dem Schwartau Multivitaminmarmelandenglas werden mit Gesichtern ausgestattet)[214]
- Das Produkt wird über eine Person sympathisch gemacht (z.B. „Putzi" auf Kinderzahncremetuben, der Hase auf „Nesquick"-Dosen etc.)
- Nicht das Produkt wird personifiziert, sondern ein Vertreter der Konsumenten. Hier werden mit Vorliebe Sympathieträger aus

---

[213] Nach dem UWG §3 ist es verboten, mit Falschaussagen über das Produkt zu werben.

[214] vgl. auch Abbildung S. 248

dem gesellschaftlichen Leben eingesetzt, wie Spitzensportler oder Filmstars, mit denen sich die meisten Verbraucher gerne identifizieren.

Personifizierungen werden eingesetzt, um die Anonymität des Produktes aufzuheben. Insbesondere der Einsatz von Personen mit hohen Bekanntheitsgrad soll Vertrauen in die Qualität des Produktes wecken. Personifizierte Produkte auf der Verpackung sollen helfen, Sympathien zu entwickeln, die kaufstimulierend wirken.

Auf Verpackungen lassen sich noch jede Menge andere Stilmittel wie Neologismen, Alliterationen („becker's bester", „Kellogg's Cornflakes", „Müller Milch" u.v.m.), Reime („Ehrmann - keiner macht mich mehr an...") finden. Dem Einfallsreichtum sind keine Grenzen gesetzt. Wichtig ist jedoch, daß die Stilmittel geeignete Akzente setzen und sich nicht negativ auf das Verständnis auswirken.

Analysefragen hierzu sind:

- Wird mit den Stilmitteln ein Akzent gesetzt?
- Ist die Wirkung der Stilmittel erfolgreich?
- Sind die Stilmittel zielgruppenadäquat?
- Welchen Charakter haben die Stilmittel?

### 3.4.11 Satzzeichen

Satzzeichen sind in der Regel nur in geschlossenen Texten auf Verpackungen zu finden oder wenn es gilt, einen Ausdruck ganz besonders hervorzuheben. Die Satzstrukturen stehen an Kürze und Prägnanz in Konkurrenz zu Pressetexten. Dementsprechend gestaltet sich auch die Verwendung von Satzzeichen:

**a) Der Punkt**

Punkte sind die am meisten verwendeten Satzzeichen innerhalb von Verpackungs-texten. Sie grenzen Aussagen und Informationen voneinander ab und schaffen dabei Satz- und Bedeutungseinheiten. Mit Punkten lassen sich gut strukturierte Texteinheiten konzipieren und Inhalte "auf den Punkt bringen". "So ein Pünktchen macht eine Sache wichtig".[215]

Allerdings eignen sich Punkte nur dann für die Gestaltung von Frontseiten, wenn dort konsequente Einheiten gebildet werden sollen. Auf Frontseiten wird jedoch eine elliptische Satzform ohne Satzzeichen bevorzugt, um die Kunden zu freien Assoziationen anzuregen und zu signalisieren, daß der Text nicht abgeschlossen ist.

**b) Ausrufezeichen**

Ausrufezeichen markieren in der Regel besonders beachtenswerte Sätze oder satzartige Elemente. Sie werden nicht nur zur Kennzeichnung von Warnhinweisen verwendet, sondern auch dann, wenn es Produktvertreibern darum geht, auf einen Produkthinweis besonders aufmerksam zu machen.

Bei einer derartigen Funktionsbeschreibung ist eine Flut von Ausrufungszeichen auf Verpackungen zu erwarten. Jedoch werden

---

[215]    Högn und Pomplitz (1990), S. 326

Ausrufungszeichen nicht nach dem Prinzip "viel nützt viel" verwendet, sondern nur dann, wenn es ganz explizit darum geht, einen Satzkern besonders hervorzuheben.

Ein Beispiel für die Markierung eines Satzkerns befindet sich auf sämtlichen Tetra Paks. Es handelt sich um den Slogan: "Tetra Pak. Irgendwie clever!"[216] Nach dem Gebot der Kürze und Prägnanz wird hier auch nur der für das Verständnis zentrale Satzteil schriftlich fixiert. Der unvollständige Satz soll als Ausruf des Staunens und des Bewunderns interpretiert werden.

**c)  Fragezeichen**

Fragezeichen dienen im alltäglichen Sprachgebrauch primär der Kennzeichnung eines für den Benutzer unklaren Sachverhaltes. Daraus leiten sich weitere Funktionen bzw. Stilmittel ab, wie rhetorische Fragen, Provokationen etc.

Aufgrund dieser Funktionsbeschreibung eignet sich das Fragezeichen als Satzzeichen für Verpackungstexte nicht, denn es geht dort darum, den Rezipienten Sicherheit bezüglich konkreter Informationen und Hinweise zu vermitteln.

Fragezeichen eignen sich in Verpackungstexten allenfalls zur Kennzeichnung eines Stilmittels wie der rhetorischen Frage: "Heute schon geschweppt?" („Schweppes") oder um z.B. eine Verbraucherhotline zu markieren: "Noch Fragen?", aber auch, um Fragen an das Gewissen der Konsumenten zu stellen.

Auf den „Balisto"- und „Bounty"-Schokoriegel Großpackungen wird mit einer witzigen Kampagne der Hinweis auf die neue Größe sprachlich mit dem Bedürfnis zu naschen kombiniert: „Lust 1 mehr aufzureißen?". Hierbei kennzeichnet das Fragezeichen eine indirekte

---

[216]    Slogan auf der Rückseite von Tetra Paks

Frage, die die Konsumenten dazu provozieren soll, auf den neuen Mengeninhalt aufmerksam zu werden.

**d)   Kommata**

Kommata verbinden Satzteile in mehrgliedrigen Sätzen miteinander. Mehrgliedrige Sätze widersprechen aber grundsätzlich dem Textkonzept für Verpackungen, wo eine einfache und kurze Aussagengestaltung im Vordergrund steht. Meistens haben Kommata in Verpackungstexten die Funktion, innerhalb einer Aufzählung die einzelnen Elemente zu gliedern.

**e)   Sonstige Satzzeichen**

Alle anderen Satzzeichen wie das Semikolon, der Doppelpunkt, der Gedanken- oder Bindestrich etc. besitzen auf Verpackungen Seltenheitswert und werden, wenn nötig, an konkreten Beispielen aufgegriffen und erläutert.

Im Rahmen des Analysemodells ist zu fragen:

- Sind die Satzzeichen sinn- und wirkungsvoll eingesetzt?

Nach der Betrachtung sprachlicher Einzelkomponenten geht es nun an die Untersuchung größerer Einheiten.

### 3.4.12 Phraseologismen

Viele Floskeln unserer Alltagssprache gehören in die Kategorie „Höflichkeit". Man spricht von sogenannten Phraseologismen der Höflichkeit (zu gut deutsch: *Höflichkeitsfloskeln*), wenn Standardsprüche geäußert werden, die zum guten Ton gehören. Deshalb dürfen Floskeln auch auf Verpackungen nicht fehlen.

So gibt es "Lindt Frohes Fest", "Ferrero Frohe Ostern" und eine ganze Reihe anderer Produktverpackungen mit den jahreszeitlich entsprechenden Festtagswünschen.

Diese Strategie soll gleich zweifach wirken: Einmal übermitteln die Anbieter auf diesem Weg dem höflichen Umgang entsprechend allen Konsumenten die passenden Festtagswünsche. Dadurch sollen die Sympathien der Kunden geweckt werden. Gleichzeitig sollen diese Produkte als Variationen aus dem Angebot herausstechen und einen weiteren Absatzmarkt bieten. Produktverpackungen mit Festtagswünschen stellen für die Käufer ein Kommunikationsmedium dar, das sich als Geschenk anbietet. Die Käufer können die Produktverpackung als Kommunikationsmedium verwenden, um ihre persönlichen Festtagswünsche zu übermitteln oder wenigstens zu ergänzen. Weitere Produktverpackungen mit einer solchen Mittlerfunktion sind "Merci", "Ferrero Küßchen", "Ein kleiner Dank"(Lindt), „Milka lila Herzen" (Suchard-Tobler) und "Herzlichst" (Lindt) u.a.

Diese Strategie wird hauptsächlich bei Artikeln der Süßwarenindustrie angewendet, da sie sich gut als Geschenk eignen. Empfehlenswert ist diese Strategie auch für diverse Artikel aus dem Kosmetikbereich, die sich gut verschenken lassen, oder aus dem Bereich Tiernahrung etc.

Vielleicht wird den Kunden eines Tages z.B. auf einer Zahnpastatube "guten Morgen" gewünscht oder auf diversen Nahrungsmitteln "guten Appetit".

Im Zusammenhang mit den Phraseologismen bleibt folgendes zu beachten:

---

- Setzen die Phraseologismen einen Akzent?
- Welchen Charakter haben die Phraseologismen?
- Paßt der Phraseologismus zum Kontext?
- Paßt er zum Produkt?
- Paßt er zur Zielgruppe?
- Wird er im intendierten Sinn interpretiert?

---

### 3.4.13 Der Verpackungstext

Die größte Schwierigkeit der geschlossenen Verpackungstexte ist, daß sie von den Käufern gerne ignoriert werden. Dementsprechend müssen sie stilistisch ansprechend gestaltet werden. Ein wichtiger Aspekt für eine zielgruppenadäquate Textgestaltung ist eine passende Wortwahl. Das alleine reicht aber nicht aus. Der Text muß flüssig und spannend zu lesen sein. Er muß verständlich und glaubwürdig sein. Er muß den Kunden Lust auf das Produkt machen und im Idealfall Lust auf weitere Produkte des Anbieters. Er sollte den Kunden das Gefühl vermitteln, mit dem Kauf des Produktes eine gute Wahl zu treffen, er muß überzeugen u.s.w.

Das sind viele Ansprüche an einen Verpackungstext. Wichtig ist, daß nicht einfach nur über die Produkteigenschaften erzählt wird, sondern daß die Vorzüge des Produktes, des Anbieters und die Vorteile für den Käufer argumentativ präsentiert werden. Die Rezipienten des Textes sollten nicht, wie das heute gerne praktiziert wird, zum Kauf überredet werden, sondern mit Argumenten überzeugt werden. Überzeugte Kunden sind gute Kunden, weil sie meist Stammkunden werden und Alternativen dann ignorieren.

Folgende Grundtypen von Argumentationsstrategien lassen sich unterscheiden:

Eine sehr beliebte Strategie ist die argumentative **Steigerung des Wertes**.
Dabei unterscheidet man:

a)      **Prime Value**: Ein Wert, der auf das Material bezogen wird („besonders kostbare Rohkaffees" – „Tschibo").

b)      **Labor Value**: Ein Wert, der auf das Bearbeitungsverfahren bezogen wird („Nestlé Forschungszentrum" – „Nestlé LC 1")

c)      **Symbolic Value**: Ein Wert, der innerhalb der Kultur als besonders wichtig betrachtet wird und als dessen Träger das Objekt erscheint (z.B. „Frosch, das umweltschonende Spülmittel").

Lassen sich bei einem Produkt keine besonderen Produkteigenschaften hervorheben, wird gerne mit **allgemeinen Überzeugungsformeln** gearbeitet:

- der Kommunikator signalisiert eigene Überzeugung und Begeisterung (Sympathieträger auf der Verpackung, z.B. Karen Mulder auf „Yogurette" oder Steffi Graf auf „Apollinaris"-Flaschenetiketten)

- der Kommunikator verpflichtet die Rezipienten, auf den Bezugsrahmen einzugehen ("Wünschen Sie weitere Informationen?" "Heute schon geschweppt?")

- Rezipienten glauben grundsätzlich lieber der Meinung eines Rezipienten, als der marktschreierischen Art eines unbekannten Texters. (Sie haben entschieden...)[217]

Nach Karmasin lassen sich folgende **Argumentationstypen** unterscheiden:[218]

**a)    Das semantische Argument**
Gerechtfertigt, kritisiert oder behauptet wird hier über einen bestimmten Sprachgebrauch. Ein Beispiel bietet der Slogan: "Nur wo Nutella draufsteht, ist auch Nutella drin!"

**b)    Das genetische Argument**
Der Anbieter rechtfertigt sich für ein Produktmerkmal oder stellt es sogar positiv heraus, indem er angibt, daß eine gesetzliche Norm erfüllt wird (z.B. "ohne Konservierungsstoffe" als Hinweis auf Brot oder die Aufschrift „mit Vitamin C", obwohl es sich dabei um Ascorbinsäure handelt, die dem Produkt als Antioxidationsmittel zugefügt werden mußte – z.B. auf diversen Limonadenflaschen).

**c)    Das historische Argument**
Bei dieser Argumentationsstrategie stützt der Anbieter seine Argumente auf Erfahrungen der Vergangenheit („Tchibo Feine Milde" wird "mit all unserer langjährigen Erfahrung geröstet").

**d)    Das komparative Argument**
Hierbei wird ganz diskret der Vergleich mit der Konkurrenz angestrebt, z.B. „besser als herkömmliche Waschmittel" (Persil).

---

[217]    vgl. Ogilvy (1964), S. 145

[218]    vgl. Karmasin (1993), S. 414

## e)  Das teleologische Argument

Es wird darauf hingewiesen, daß zum Erreichen eines bestimmten Ziels vernünftigerweise folgende Mittel einzusetzen sind, beispielsweise diverse Diätprodukte zur Erhaltung einer jugendlich sportlichen Figur („Du Darfst").

Meiner Ansicht nach ist hier unbedingt die Klasse der Pseudoargumente zu ergänzen.

## f)  Das Pseudoargument

Es werden Sachverhalte als kaufstimulierende Argumente eingesetzt, die sich bei genauerem Hinsehen als nicht stichhaltig enttarnen lassen.

Wenn z.B. auf der Verpackung für das Toilettenpapier "ecolution"[219] versucht wird, argumentativ zu werben mit dem Hinweis: „Die Verpackung löst sich in kürzester Zeit in Wasser auf und belastet nicht die Umwelt", handelt sich eindeutig um ein Pseudoargument. Bei genauerer Lektüre stellt man fest, daß sich die Verpackung zwar in Wasser auflöst, daß sie aber deshalb noch lange nicht eliminiert ist. Auch im aufgelösten Zustand verschmutzen die Verpackungsmoleküle das Wasser, sie sind nur nicht mehr auf Anhieb sichtbar. Beseitigt ist die Verpackung durch ihre Wasserlöslichkeit noch lange nicht.

Ebenso ist es ein Pseudoargument, wenn der Joghurt Nestlé LC 1 als "ein täglicher Beitrag für Ihre Gesundheit" präsentiert und mit dem

---

219    Der Name "ecolution" ist der Klasse der assoziativen Namen zuzuordnen. Assoziiert werden der in der Biologie beheimatete Begriff "Evolution" und der politische Begriff "Revolution". Versucht wird über diese Wortkombination dem Produkt einen progressiven Charakter zu vermitteln, der als Produkterlebnisqualität Beruhigung des ökologischen Gewissens und gleichzeitig das Gefühl innovativer Aktivität erwirken soll.

Hinweis beworben wird, daß der "lactobacillus adophilus" die Darmflora positiv stimuliert. Die meisten Konsumenten werden bei der
Lektüre dieses Hinweises vergessen, daß Millionen von „Lactobazil-
len" bereits ihre Darmflora bevölkern und stimulieren. Bei einem
Verhältnis ein paar zu ein paar Millionen erscheint die im Nestlé
Forschungszentrum getestete Wirkungskraft des Bakterium gleich
weniger beeindruckend.

Ebenso verbergen sich hinter dem vielversprechenden Zusatz „Mit
natürlichen Pflege-Lipiden" (Palmolive) nicht etwa besondere Pfle-
gesubstanzen.
Der Begriff „Lipide" wird in den Naturwissenschaften i. d. R. dazu
verwendet, diverse Fettmoleküle zu bezeichnen. Es wird darauf gebaut, daß das Fachwort Wissenschaftlichkeit suggeriert. Mit dem
Wissen um die gebräuchliche Verwendungsregel des Begriffes „Lipide" verliert das Argument an Überzeugungskraft. Der Pflegewert
von Fettmolekülen bleibt für den Einzelnen individuell zu bestimmen.

Für den Einsatz der Argumente werden folgende **Techniken** umgesetzt:

- das didaktische Lehrbeispiel (Zahncremes)
- der experimentelle Beweis (Toilettenpapier)
- die magische Wirkung („Mr. Proper")
- das persönliche Zeugnis („Saft")
- der Rat einer Autorität (von Medizinern empfohlen)
- die Referenz einer Norm („mehr als der Tagesbedarf an...")
- die Rechtfertigung („der Umwelt zuliebe")[220]

---

[220] vgl. Fritz (1974), S. 90

Um zu garantieren, daß eine Vielzahl von Argumenten, die über einen Text impliziert werden, ohne Probleme verstanden wird, müssen die Argumente so formuliert werden, daß sie mit Hilfe der verschiedenen Interpretationsverfahren, ausgehend von einer regelbasierten Bedeutung der Worte, leicht verstanden werden können.

**Verbotene Argumente** sind tunlichst zu vermeiden. Die Konkurrenz beobachtet streng und wartet nur, den anderen Anbietern ein Negativimage über die Veröffentlichung von Gesetzeswidrigkeiten zu bescheren und diese darüber hinaus über Klagen auch finanziell zu schädigen.

Gemäß § 3 UWG, der Generalklausel über irreführende Werbung, ist es grundsätzlich untersagt, zu Lasten der Konkurrenz zu argumentieren.[221]

a)  Dabei ist zu beachten, daß eine verbotene irreführende Werbung auch mittels objektiv zutreffender Werbeaussagen erfolgen kann, wenn sie geeignet sind, z.B. den Verkehr irrezuführen. (z.B. "einziger Handwerksbetrieb" am Ort, wenn gleichwertige Leistungen auch von Nichthandwerksbetrieben am selbigen Ort durchgeführt werden können).

b)  Ebenso stellt die Werbung mit Selbstverständlichkeiten einen Verstoß gegen § 3 UWG dar, wenn beispielsweise mit Standards geworben wird, die entweder gesetzlich vorgeschrieben oder sonst den Verkehrsgepflogenheiten entsprechen und damit von allen Wettbewerbern erfüllt werden müssen. Beispielsweise ist eine Aussage wie "hergestellt aus garantiert nicht chemisch be-

---

[221]  Schönefelder (1998), Kap 73, S. 1; Köhler (1995), vgl. auch Haidl (1996) und vgl. Högn und Pomplitz (1990), S. 30

handelten Mehlen" unzulässig, da klar ist, daß dies generell nicht erlaubt ist.

c) Eine Irreführung besteht auch dann, wenn bestimmte Tatsachen verschwiegen werden, für die gesetzliche Aufklärungspflichten bestehen. (z.B. müssen Zigarettenschachteln mit dem Aufdruck versehen werden: „Rauchen gefährdet Ihre Gesundheit")

d) Objektiv falsche Werbebehauptungen fallen gleichfalls unter die Verbotsnorm.

e) Ebenso können nicht ernst gemeinte Werbeangaben eine Irreführung beinhalten, wenn die     Gefahr besteht, daß sie ernst genommen werden könnten („z.B. Für'n Appel und 'n Ei"- als Preisangabe.[222])

f) Auch irreführende Blickfangwerbung ist verboten, wenn der hervorgehobene Blickfang durch den nachfolgenden Text relativiert wird.

Nach dem § 3 UWG ist die Nachahmung fremder Werbung grundsätzlich zulässig, solange kein Copyright verletzt wird. Dies wird jedoch verboten, wenn ein Erinnerungseffekt an vorausgegangene Werbekampagnen kreiert wird.

Entgegen der weit verbreiteten Annahme besteht kein ausdrückliches Verbot vergleichender Werbung. Sie wird jedoch unzulässig, wenn

---

[222]  Bei der Preisangabe "Für'n Appel und 'n Ei" wurde bei einem öfentlichen Verkehrsmittel-Unternehmen davon ausgegangen, daß die Kunden ein derart abwegiges Angebot als nicht ernstzunehmen akzeptierten. Die Kunden jedoch nutzten diese Chance, um dem Unternehmen eins auszuwischen und bekamen vom Gericht Recht. Generell besteht jedoch keine Haftungspflicht bei Angaben, die offensichtlich nicht wörtlich zu nehmen sind.

für den Verbraucher auch ohne Namensnennung erkennbar wird, zu welchem Produkt ein Bezug hergestellt wird. Desweiteren verstößt vergleichende Werbung gegen § 1 UWG, wenn die Produkte der Mitbewerber zugunsten der eigenen Alternative kritisiert und abgewertet werden.

Nach einer EU-Richtlinie, die bis April 2000 umgesetzt sein muß, ist vergleichende Werbung grundsätzlich zulässig, sofern bestimmte Voraussetzungen erfüllt sind. Hierzu zählt, daß der Vergleich nicht irreführend sein darf, daß nachprüfbare und typische Eigenschaften miteinander verglichen werden und der Mitbewerber nicht herabgesetzt oder verunglimpft wird.

Der Bundesgerichtshof hat in einem Urteil entschieden, daß eine vergleichende Werbung, die den Maßstäben der Richtlinie entspricht, schon heute umgesetzt werden darf.[223]

Neben den inhaltlichen Aspekten können auch die typographischen Eigenschaften eines Verpackungstextes ausschlaggebend wirken, ob ein Text gelesen wird oder nicht. So darf z.B. die Schrift nicht zu klein gewählt werden. Sie sollte möglichst ohne Lupe lesbar sein. Darüber hinaus sind viele Farbkombinationen schlecht lesbar. In jedem Fall sind Farben zu vermeiden, die von Farbenblinden nicht identifiziert werden können, wie rot und grün.

---

[223] Urteile vom 05.02.1998 – I ZR 211/95 – und vom 23.04.1998 – I ZR 2/96, Die Original-Presse-Mitteilung ist nachzulesen unter der URL: http://www.jura.uni-sb.de/Entscheidungen/Bundesgeriche/BGH /zivil/vergwerb.html

Für das Analysemodell ergeben sich in bezug auf die Verpackungstexte folgende Untersuchungskriterien:

- Wird der Fokus des Rezipienten auf den Text gelenkt?
- Ist der Text gut wahrnehmbar?
  a) Typographie
  b) Farben
- Wirkt der Text einladend?
- Ist der Text leicht und flüssig lesbar?
- Ist der Text verständlich?
- Wirkt der Text schlüssig?
- Ist der Text originell?
- Wirkt der Text glaubwürdig?
- Wirkt der Text überredend?
- Werden überzeugende Argumente eingesetzt?
- Handelt es sich um Pseudoargumente?
- Ist der Text sprachlich zielgruppenadäquat?
- Ist der Text stilistisch ansprechend?
- Wird der Fokus der Rezipienten
  a) auf den Text gelenkt?
  b) durch den Text gelenkt?
- Macht der Text "Lust" auf das Produkt?
- Werden neben dem Produkt noch ein oder mehrere ideelle Werte versprochen?
- Ist der Text passend in das gesamte Verpackungskonzept integriert?

### 3.4.14 Der Inhalt

Inhaltlich lassen sich die Verpackungstexte grob vier Aspekten zuordnen:

- produktbezogener Inhalt
- firmenbezogener Inhalt
- kundenbezogener Inhalt
- ergänzender Inhalt (z.B. Kampagnen, Gewinnspiele)

Prinzipiell sollten bei der inhaltlichen Gestaltung von Texten alle vier Aspekte berücksichtigt werden. Der Text sollte die drei Größen: Kunde-Produkt-Firma miteinander verbinden und ergänzen. Es sind nicht immer auf den Produktverpackungen alle Inhaltsaspekte zu finden, mindestens aber der produktbezogene Inhaltsaspekt sollte auf der Verpackung vorhanden sein. Dies läßt sich z.B. auf Schokoriegeln aus Platzgründen lediglich über den Produktnamen umsetzen. In solchen Fällen bedarf es unbedingt ergänzender und erläuternder Werbung. Es sollte darauf geachtet werden, daß der Inhalt stimmig ist und wenigstens indirekt eine Beziehung zu einem der vier Aspekte erkennen läßt.

Besonders beliebt ist es, auf Kaffeeverpackungen den Text zur Erläuterung der Rohstoffe über einen Mythos aus dem Herkunftsland zu entwickeln („Mild'or"-Kaffee) oder über sinnliche Text- und Bildsequenzen („Nestlé" Cappuccino). Die Gefahr besteht dabei, daß die Kunden bei solchen Texten nicht direkt den Sinn erschließen können, damit nicht erkennen, welchen Nutzen sie aus dem Lesen des Textes ziehen könnten, und deshalb werden solche Texte oft nicht oder nicht ganz gelesen. Lediglich wenn die Wort- und Bildsequenzen kurz, prägnant und ansprechend sind, kann man oft nicht umhin, die eigene

Neugier dahingehend zu befriedigen, daß man herausfindet, was sich hinter diesen Zeichen verbirgt.

Ein wichtiger Inhaltsaspekt ist die Produkt- und Firmenphilosophie und damit einhergehend das Image des Produktes. Insbesondere Firmen, die mehr als ein Produkt anbieten, versuchen ihre Produkte im Rahmen eines Konzeptes mit spezifischen Schwerpunkten zu vermarkten. So hält z.B. „Nivea" bei der Vielzahl der neu auf den Markt gebrachten Produkte nach wie vor an den Grundwerten "Qualität", "Basiskosmetik" und "Nicht-Spezialisierung" fest. Auch die Produkte, die unter dem Firmennamen "Frosch" auf den Markt gebracht werden, werden alle im Rahmen der corporate identity und dem daran orientierten Marketingkonzept als Ökoprodukte vorgestellt und als besonders schonend und umweltverträglich charakterisiert. Genauso gibt es Firmen, die versuchen, ihre Produktphilosophie und damit ihr Image an einer bestimmten Form des Lifestyles zu orientieren. Geeignete Beispiele hierfür sind Marlboro mit den harten freiheits- und abenteuerliebenden Cowboys und dem „Marlboro" Outdoor-Equipment, genauso wie „El'Vital" für die mode- und selbstbewußte Frau von heute wirbt.

Es wird versucht, über die Werbung unter Einsatz der verschiedensten kommunikativen Medien die Produktphilosophie zu einem Zeichen der Kategorie Symbole zu machen. Wenn dies gelingt, wird ein ganzer atmosphärischer Komplex zum Symbol für eine Firma bzw. für ein Produkt. Man erkennt dann z.B. die „Marlboro"-Werbung im Kino schon an den Bildern und der Musik, ohne daß der Name genannt wird.

Eine Produkt- bzw. Firmenphilosophie alleine reicht noch nicht aus. Es muß auch ein positives Image in den Reihen der Verbraucher aufgebaut werden. Das Image bestimmt die Mund-zu-Mund-Propaganda. Gelingt es einmal, eine positive Einstellung der Kunden dem Produkt und dem Anbieter gegenüber zu gewinnen, wird diese auch nicht so schnell wieder revidiert. Das Image konstituiert sich aus den Grundwerten der Produktphilosophie, die entsprechend vermarktet werden müssen. Darüber hinaus ist die Beliebtheit bzw. das Ansehen in der Konsumentenschaft entscheidend für das allgemeine Image eines Produktes. Oft entscheidet der Beliebtheitsgrad im sozialen Umfeld des Konsumenten über Kauf oder Nichtkauf und nicht die wahre Qualität eines Produktes. So wird z.B. "Tuffi"- oder „Landliebe"-Milch bevorzugt gekauft, wegen des positiven Images und dem hohen Bekanntheitsgrad, das über die Werbung bei den Konsumenten installiert wurde. Dabei ist gerade bei Milch in der Regel kaum ein Qualitätsunterschied festzustellen. Lediglich die Verpackungen sind unterschiedlich designed.

Mit der Firmenphilosophie müssen die spezifischen Werte der Zielgruppe angesprochen werden oder allgemeine Werte wie Umweltschutz glaubwürdig als Werte des Produktes vorgestellt werden. Über die Werbung mit entsprechenden Sympathieträgern kann unterstützend dazu beigetragen werden, daß die potentiellen Kunden die Werte als Produkteigenschaften kennen- und schätzen lernen, Sympathie für das Produkt entwickeln und sich daraus ein positives Image konstituiert. Die Eigenschaften des Produktes sollten dann jedoch nicht allzu enttäuschend sein.

Es gilt zu vermeiden, daß bezüglich des Images ein Phänomen ähnlich wie bei „McDonalds" eintritt: Die Mehrheit äußert sich negativ über „McDonalds" aber nach den Verkaufszahlen geht die Mehrheit hin. Mit einem positiven Image könnten die Verkaufszahlen noch gesteigert werden.

Ein wichtiger Aspekt bezüglich des Inhaltes sind die Themen. Neben dem Produkt, der Firma oder den Konsumenten können durchaus auch andere Themen behandelt werden. Häufig wird das eigentliche Thema - das Produkt - über Umwege eingeleitet, wie beispielsweise auf „Mild'Or" Kaffeeverpackungen das Produkt über einen Naturmythos vorgestellt wird. Eine beliebte Strategie ist, auf Produktverpackungen Kampagnen aufzudrucken, die indirekt das Produkt bewerben. Ziel ist es, über die Kampagnen ein positives Produkt-, Firmen- und Markenimage aufzubauen. Für die Kampagnen werden z.T. Sympathieträger beauftragt, das Produkt zu bewerben (z.B. „Karen Mulder" für „Yogurette", Steffi Graf auf „Apollinaris-Flaschenetiketten" oder das Radrennteam „Deutsche Telekom" für „Nestlé Sporties") und sich selbst als Konsument vorzustellen. Beliebte Themen von Kampagnen sind aber genauso Gewinnspiele, diverse Mottos (z.B. „Winter-Langnese") oder soziales Engagement u.v.m.

Eine bemerkenswerte Kampagne hat die Firma „Alfred Ritter GmbH & CoKG" auf ihren „Ritter Sport" Schokoladenverpackungen initiiert. In Zusammenarbeit mit dem „World Wide Found for Nature" (WWF) erhielten die Schokoladen den Titel "Choc for Life", der kombiniert mit der Abbildung eines vom Aussterben bedrohten Tieres auf den Frontseiten die Gemüter bewegen soll. Auf der Rückseite befindet sich eine kurze Information zu dem bedrohten Tier und das Angebot zu weiteren Informationen. Der Titel "Choc for Life" ist auf der Rückseite noch einmal zusammen mit dem „Ritter Sport-Logo" zu lesen, um den Konsumenten den Zusammenhang zwischen dem Schokoladenanbieter und dem Artenschutz zu verdeutlichen (s. Abbildung 5).

Umwelt- und Artenschutzengagement werden gesellschaftlich hoch bewertet. Über eine sozial positiv bewertete Aktivität versucht die Firma „Ritter Sport" zusätzlich Verbraucher zu aktivieren. Ihnen wird suggeriert, über den Kauf der Schokolade gleichzeitig eine gutes Werk zu tun und damit auch ihr Gewissen beruhigen zu können. Leider wird auf der Verpackung nur eine namentliche Beziehung zum WWF hergestellt. Es finden sich keinerlei Hinweise auf eine finanzielle Unterstützung durch die Einnahmen der verkauften „Choc for Life"-Schokoladen oder ähnliche Hinweise, die die Glaubwürdigkeit der Zusammenarbeit unterstützen würden.

Dadurch wird der positive Eindruck der Kampagne geschmälert. Der WWF wird lediglich über die Schokolade stärker publik gemacht, ebenso die Schokolade über den WWF. Der Effekt ließe sich über eine z.B. finanziell unterstützende Maßnahme wesentlich verstärken. Auf diese Weise würde der Kaufanreiz der Schokolade durch ein emotionales Attribut katalysiert, wie "wenn ich diese Schokolade bevorzugt kaufe, unterstütze ich den Artenschutz".

Nach dem gleichen Schema ist die Kampagne "111 Jahre Gerolsteiner 111 Brunnen für Äthiopien!" konzipiert (s. Abbildung 5). Auf jeder Gerolsteiner-Getränkeflasche befindet sich ein Bild von Karlheinz Böhm im Einsatz seiner Äthiopienhilfe und der Hinweis "Partner der Aktion SAT. 1 Menschen für Menschen". Jedoch entpuppt sich die Kampagne bei genauerem Hinsehen als "Fake", denn man unterstützt die Aktion nicht etwa durch den Kauf des Produktes, sondern durch eine zusätzlich auszufüllende Teilnahmekarte oder durch eine direkte Spende auf das angegebene Konto. Wer etwas Gutes (für sein Gewissen) tun möchte – muß auch bezahlen. Gerolsteiner unterstützt die Kampagne lediglich durch Werbung.

Bei wenig genauem Hinsehen im Laden entsteht der Eindruck, daß die Verpackung eine zusätzliche Produkterlebnisqualität verspricht – ein gutes Gewissen.

Auch mit weniger aufwendigen Kampagnen wird gerne an das Gewissen der Konsumenten appelliert. So werden z.B. „EiVit"-Eierkartons mit Hinweisen ausgestattet, die in Anlehnung an bereits bekannte Verkehrsschilder dergestalt konzipiert sind, daß es einer nicht besonders hohen Frequenz der Begegnung bedarf, um sie als Symbol für kontrollierte Freilandeier zu erlernen.

Der textuelle Appell an das Gewissen erfolgt hierbei gleich auf zwei Eben. Mit dem Aufdruck: „Kontrolliert vom Bund gegen den Mißbrauch der Tiere e.V." wird versucht, in den Kunden das Bedürfnis zu wecken, selber aktiv gegen Mißbrauch der Tiere zu werden, indem nur noch kontrollierte Eier gekauft werden. Damit einhergehend wird der höhere Preis dieser Eier gerechtfertigt. Daran angegliedert ist die Produktwerbung: „EiVit das andere Ei für eine moderne und bewußte Ernährung". Auch mit diesem Hinweis wird an das Gewissen appelliert, denn es wird versucht, den Kunden für seine Ernährung zu sensibilisieren. Der Begriff „Ernährung" ist mittlerweile in Deutschland zu einem Schlüsselreiz geworden. Der Begriff ist zum Symbol geworden, für die bewußte Auseinandersetzung mit dem eigenen Körper und der Umwelt, sowie für die Verantwortung und Sorge für beide Aspekte (s. Abbildung 4).

Beide Aspekte werden ganz gezielt als Kaufargumente eingesetzt.

Für das Analysemodell gilt es, folgende Aspekte bezüglich des Inhaltes der Verpackungstexte zu berücksichtigen:

- Ist der Inhalt des Textes produktadäquat?
- Ist der Inhalt des Textes kundenbezogen?
- Ist der Inhalt des Textes anbieterbezogen?
- Werden zu diesen drei Aspekten inhaltlich ergänzende Aspekte vorgestellt?
- Wird ein umfassendes Konzept zu einer Firmen- und damit auch zu einer Produktphilosophie präsentiert?
- Wird das Produkt sympathisch gemacht?
- Werden im Rahmen der Produktphilosophie positive Werte der Zielgruppe vorgestellt?
- Gelingt es, diese positiven Werte als Produkteigenschaften glaubhaft zu machen?
- Ist der Anbieter mit einem positiven Image behaftet?
- Ist das Produkt mit einem positiven Image behaftet?
- Wird die Zielgruppe über die Verpackung mit einem positiven Image behaftet?
- Wird die Verpackung mit Sympathieträgern ausgestattet?
- Trägt das Image zum Verkaufserfolg bei?
- Appelliert die Verpackung
  - an das Gewissen?
  - an den Mutter-/Vaterinstinkt?
- Verspricht die Verpackung
  - soziale Anerkennung?
  - Bedürfnis-/Triebbefriedigung?
  - einen Mehrwert?
  - Sonstiges?

Diese Aspekte sind in Kombination mit den Textmerkmalen zu betrachten. Darüber hinaus ist der Gesamteindruck zu überprüfen.

239

## 3.4.15    Der Gesamteindruck

Unter folgender Leitfrage sind sämtlich zu überprüfende Kriterien
noch einmal zusammengefaßt:

| |
|---|
| • Wie ist der Gesamteindruck der Verpackung? |

Alle Untersuchungsaspekte der einzelnen Kapitel ergeben zusammen
ein komplettes Analysemodell:

## IV a: Konzeption einer Checkliste:

### 4.1 Die Checkliste

Das folgende Analysemodell soll unparteiisch Hilfestellung geben für die Auseinandersetzung mit Produktverpackungen, sei es aus der Perspektive der Anbieter bezüglich der Konzeption, der Überprüfung, der Verbesserung, des Vergleiches u.v.m., sei es von Seiten der Konsumenten bezüglich des Vergleiches, der Leistung der Verpackung, des individuellen Nutzens etc.

Anhand des Analyserasters sollen Verpackungen schnell erfaßt, untersucht, verglichen und diskutiert werden können. Dabei erhebt das Modell keinen Anspruch an Vollständigkeit. Es erhebt jedoch den Anspruch, eine sinnvoll strukturierte, praktikabel einsetzbare und vielseitige Meßlatte vorzugeben. Das Fazit der Auseinandersetzung wird ein subjektives sein, wie auch die Beantwortung der einzelnen Analysekriterien. In diesem Wissen soll das Modell unterstützen, eine individuelle Diagnose einer Produktverpackung zu entwickeln.

Es läßt sich dann ein repräsentatives Analyseergebnis erzielen, wenn die Untersuchung in einer größeren geeigneten Personengruppe durchgeführt- und die Ergebnisse miteinander korreliert werden. Idealerweise wird eine Analyse mit dem Ziel durchgeführt, den Marktwert der Verpackung zu testen, in einer repräsentativen Auswahl von Probanden einer potentiellen Zielgruppe.

Letztendlich entscheidend für den Markterfolg sind das gesamte Marketingkonzept des Anbieters inklusive aller Werbemaßnahmen und natürlich das Produkt, seine faktisch feststellbare Qualität, sein individueller Nutzen, der persönliche Mehrwert für den Kunden sowie das Preis-Leistungsverhältnis u.ä. Faktoren.

Im folgenden wird zunächst das Analysemodell vorgestellt und im zweiten Teil die zeichentheoretischen Untersuchungsaspekte an ausgewählten Anwendungseinsätzen auf die Praktikabilität in der Praxis überprüft.

Das Modell eignet sich sowohl für die Analyse einer einzelnen Verpackung, um diese zu optimieren u.ä., als auch für den Vergleich mehrerer Verpackungskonzepte. Dabei ist jedoch unbedingt darauf zu achten, daß für eine Gegenüberstellung Verpackungen ausgewählt werden, die vergleichbar sind. Das heißt, es sollten beispielsweise keine Schokosnackverpackungen mit Pralinenschachteln verglichen werden, sondern entweder nur Schokosnackverpackungen oder nur Pralinenschachteln.

Jeder Punkt ist danach zu bewerten, ob

a)    das Item überhaupt auf der Verpackung vorhanden ist und wenn ja,

b)    wie es auf einer Skala von 1-10 Punkten zu bewerten ist.

Der Maßstab ist dabei nicht die maximale Punktzahl, sondern die Punktzahl, die maximal im Rahmen von einer Verpackung in einer Sparte erreicht wurde.

Die Items sollen als Anregung dienen,

a)    mit welchen Mitteln man eine Verpackung gestalten kann,

b)    welche Wirkungseffekte erzielt werden können.

Um Verpackungen vergleichen zu können, die naturgemäß nicht mit allen Items ausgestattet sind, sei es aus Platzgründen oder aus dem Verlangen nach einer schlichten Gestaltung, wird zu jeder Analysegruppe am Ende eine Durchschnittsnote ausgewertet. Aus allen

Durchschnittsnoten wird nach Abschluß der Analyse die Gesamtnote berechnet, indem die Einzelnoten summiert und durch die Anzahl der Einzelnoten geteilt werden.

Bei dieser Methode ist jedoch darauf hinzuweisen, daß die Einzelaspekte der Analyse betrachtet werden sollten, wenn man sich einen Eindruck über die spezifischen Eigenschaften der Verpackung beschaffen möchte, die in der Gesamtnote nicht ausgedrückt werden können.

Es ist durchaus möglich, ausgesuchte Kriterien besonders zu gewichten, indem man die Ergebnispunktzahl durchgängig mit dem Faktor zwei oder drei multipliziert. So könnte man z.B. das Kriterium der „Originalität" in einer Analyse besonders betonen.

Wenn von vornherein nur ausgewählte Kriterien interessieren, können diese auch losgelöst von dem kompletten Fragebogen alleine bearbeitet werden.

**Das Analysemodell zur Gestaltung von Verpackungskonzepten mit dem Schwerpunkt der textuellen Kompositionen:**

**1.) Technisch orientierte Fragen**

1.) Schützt die Verpackung das Produkt und die Umwelt ausreichend?

Bitte ankreuzen:

| ← | O | O | O | O | O | O | O | O | O | O | → |
|---|---|---|---|---|---|---|---|---|---|---|---|
| Nein | 1 | 2 | 3 | 4 | 5 | 6 | 7 | 8 | 9 | 10 | Ja |

Kommentar:

_____

2.) Läßt sich das Produkt in der Verpackung angenehm transportieren?

Bitte ankreuzen:

| ← | O | O | O | O | O | O | O | O | O | O | → |
|---|---|---|---|---|---|---|---|---|---|---|---|
| Nein | 1 | 2 | 3 | 4 | 5 | 6 | 7 | 8 | 9 | 10 | Ja |

Kommentar:

_____

3.) Ist es möglich, das Produkt in der Verpackung entsprechend zu lagern?

Bitte ankreuzen:

| ← | O | O | O | O | O | O | O | O | O | O | → |
|---|---|---|---|---|---|---|---|---|---|---|---|
| Nein | 1 | 2 | 3 | 4 | 5 | 6 | 7 | 8 | 9 | 10 | Ja |

Kommentar:

_____

4.)  Portioniert die Verpackung das Produkt sinnvoll?

Bitte ankreuzen:

← O O O O O O O O O O →

Nein 1  2  3  4  5  6  7  8  9  10  Ja

Kommentar:

_____

5.)  Ist die Verpackung auf ihren spezifischen Einsatz hin ausgerichtet?

Bitte ankreuzen:

← O O O O O O O O O O →

Nein 1  2  3  4  5  6  7  8  9  10  Ja

Kommentar:

_____

6.)  Ist die Verpackung praktisch?

Bitte ankreuzen:

← O O O O O O O O O O →

Nein 1  2  3  4  5  6  7  8  9  10  Ja

Kommentar:

_____

## 2.) Die Bildzeichen

1) Bildet das Bildzeichen eine reales Objekt ab? (Wenn Nein - weiter mit Frage 2)

Ist das Bildzeichen aufgrund der Ähnlichkeit zum realen Objekt einfach zu interpretieren?

Bitte ankreuzen:

| ← | O | O | O | O | O | O | O | O | O | O | → |
|---|---|---|---|---|---|---|---|---|---|---|---|
| Nein 1 | 2 | 3 | 4 | 5 | 6 | 7 | 8 | 9 | 10 | Ja |

2.) Ist die Abbildung abstrakt und damit erläuterungsbedürftig?

Bitte ankreuzen:

| ← | O | O | O | O | O | O | O | O | O | O | → |
|---|---|---|---|---|---|---|---|---|---|---|---|
| Nein 10 | 9 | 8 | 7 | 6 | 5 | 4 | 3 | 2 | 1 | Ja |

3.) Wird das Bild nach dem ikonischen Interpretationsverfahren interpretiert?

Bitte ankreuzen: O    O

         Ja    Nein (weiter mit Frage 4)

4.) Wird das Bild nach dem symbolischen Interpretationsverfahren interpretiert?

Bitte ankreuzen:

| ← | O | O | O | O | O | O | O | O | O | O | → |
|---|---|---|---|---|---|---|---|---|---|---|---|
| Nein 1 | 2 | 3 | 4 | 5 | 6 | 7 | 8 | 9 | 10 | Ja |

5.)     Ist ein direkter Schluß möglich oder bedarf es Zwischen-
        schritte bzw. Erläuterungen (Auch bei objektgetreuen
        Abbildungen, die nicht in direktem Zusammenhang mit dem
        Produkt stehen)?
Bitte ankreuzen:

← O   O   O   O   O   O   O   O   O   O   →
Nein 1   2   3   4   5   6   7   8   9   10   Ja
Kommentar:

_____

6.)   Kann das Bildzeichen ohne Probleme im intendierten Sinn
interpretiert werden?
Bitte ankreuzen:

← O   O   O   O   O   O   O   O   O   O   →
Nein 1   2   3   4   5   6   7   8   9   10   Ja

7.)   Paßt das Bildzeichen in das Verpackungskonzept?
Bitte ankreuzen:

← O   O   O   O   O   O   O   O   O   O   →
Nein 1   2   3   4   5   6   7   8   9   10   Ja
Kommentar:

_____

8.)   Wirken die Bildzeichen originell?
Bitte ankreuzen:

← O   O   O   O   O   O   O   O   O   O   →
Nein 1   2   3   4   5   6   7   8   9   10   Ja

9.)   Verleihen die Bildzeichen der Verpackung Pepp?

Bitte ankreuzen:

| ← | O | O | O | O | O | O | O | O | O | O | → |
|---|---|---|---|---|---|---|---|---|---|---|---|
| Nein | 1 | 2 | 3 | 4 | 5 | 6 | 7 | 8 | 9 | 10 | Ja |

10.)   Wirken sie innovativ?

Bitte ankreuzen:

| ← | O | O | O | O | O | O | O | O | O | O | → |
|---|---|---|---|---|---|---|---|---|---|---|---|
| Nein | 1 | 2 | 3 | 4 | 5 | 6 | 7 | 8 | 9 | 10 | Ja |

11.)   Wirken sie ausgefallen?

Bitte ankreuzen:

| ← | O | O | O | O | O | O | O | O | O | O | → |
|---|---|---|---|---|---|---|---|---|---|---|---|
| Nein | 1 | 2 | 3 | 4 | 5 | 6 | 7 | 8 | 9 | 10 | Ja |

12.)   Wirken sie exklusiv?

Bitte ankreuzen:

| ← | O | O | O | O | O | O | O | O | O | O | → |
|---|---|---|---|---|---|---|---|---|---|---|---|
| Nein | 1 | 2 | 3 | 4 | 5 | 6 | 7 | 8 | 9 | 10 | Ja |

13.)   Wirken sie langweilig?[224]

Bitte ankreuzen:

| ← | O | O | O | O | O | O | O | O | O | O | → |
|---|---|---|---|---|---|---|---|---|---|---|---|
| Nein | 10 | 9 | 8 | 7 | 6 | 5 | 4 | 3 | 2 | 1 | Ja |

---

[224]   Bei dieser Frage handelt es sich um ein gedrehtes Item. Dieses soll den Zweck erfüllen, daß die Fragen nicht stupide angekreuzt, sondern jeweils überlegt angekreuzt werden.

14.) Sonstiges? Hier kann ein selbstgewähltes Item zur Analyse der Bildzeichen eingesetzt und im Anschluß bewertet werden:

_____

Bitte ankreuzen:

← O O O O O O O O O O →
Nein 1 2 3 4 5 6 7 8 9 10 Ja

15.) Erzeugt das Bildzeichen bei der Zielgruppe positive Geneigtheit?
Bitte ankreuzen:

← O O O O O O O O O O →
Nein 1 2 3 4 5 6 7 8 9 10 Ja

16.) Hat die Farbe der Verpackung Zeichencharakter – wird die Farbe der Verpackung nach dem symbolischen Verfahren als Zeichen für das Produkt in der Verpackung interpretiert?
Bitte ankreuzen:

← O O O O O O O O O O →
Nein 1 2 3 4 5 6 7 8 9 10 Ja

## 3.) Die Substantive

1.) Werden Substantive als Reiz- und Schlüsselworte auf der Verpackung eingesetzt?
Bitte ankreuzen:

← O O O O O O O O O O →
Nein 1 2 3 4 5 6 7 8 9 10 Ja

2.) Welche substantivischen Stilmittel lassen sich feststellen?

_____

Wurden Neologismen eingesetzt?[225]

Bitte ankreuzen: O     O

          Ja     Nein (weiter mit Frage 5)

3.) Ist der Neologismus verständlich?

Bitte ankreuzen:

← O O O O O O O O O O →

Nein 1 2 3 4 5 6 7 8 9 10 Ja

4.) Bei zusammengesetzten Wortkomplexen: Ist das Zusammenfassen der Einzelkomponenten sinnvoll?

Bitte ankreuzen:

← O O O O O O O O O O →

Nein 1 2 3 4 5 6 7 8 9 10 Ja

5.) Wird eine verkaufsfördernde Wirkung erzielt - sprechen die Substantive stilistisch die Zielgruppe an?[226]

_____

[225] Meiner Ansicht nach sind Neologismen auf Produktverpackungen, sofern sie verständlich sind, positiv zu bewerten, da sie in der Konzeption aufwendig sind und in ihrer Wirkung sehr effektiv. Sie eignen sich hervorragen, um ein Produkt auf dem Markt zu differenzieren.

[226] Bei diesem Item besteht die Chance, Punkte zu sammeln. Zur Chancengleichheit können auch nur die tatsächlich erkennbaren Charakteristika bewertet werden. Dementsprechend muß ein innovatives Substantiv nicht unbedingt gleichzeitig auch seriös sein. Wenn eine Firma auf "Jugendlichkeit" setzt, bekommt sie deshalb keine schlechte Note bei den anderen Eigenschaften.

a) Wirkt die Verpackung dadurch jugendlich?

Bitte ankreuzen:

← O O O O O O O O O O →
Nein 1 2 3 4 5 6 7 8 9 10 Ja

b) innovativ?

Bitte ankreuzen:

← O O O O O O O O O O →
Nein 1 2 3 4 5 6 7 8 9 10 Ja

c) originell?

Bitte ankreuzen:

← O O O O O O O O O O →
Nein 1 2 3 4 5 6 7 8 9 10 Ja

d) seriös?

Bitte ankreuzen:

← O O O O O O O O O O →
Nein 1 2 3 4 5 6 7 8 9 10 Ja

e) Sonstiges? Hier kann ein selbstgewähltes Item eingesetzt und bewertet werden.

_____

Bitte ankreuzen:

← O O O O O O O O O O →
Nein 1 2 3 4 5 6 7 8 9 10 Ja

6.) Sind die Substantive verständlich bzw. leicht zu interpretieren?

Bitte ankreuzen:

← O O O O O O O O O O →

Nein 1 2 3 4 5 6 7 8 9 10 Ja

7.) Sind die Substantive im Sinne der Wirkungsintentionen gelungen umgesetzt? (z.B.Akzentuierung, Innovation, Leistungssteigerung, Attraktion, Qualität etc.)

Bitte ankreuzen:

← O O O O O O O O O O →

Nein 1 2 3 4 5 6 7 8 9 10 Ja

8.) Sind die zentralen Substantive leicht erkennbar und merkbar?

Bitte ankreuzen:

← O O O O O O O O O O →

Nein 1 2 3 4 5 6 7 8 9 10 Ja

9.) Werden Bedürfnisse/Motivationen mit diesen Begriffen gereizt?

Bitte ankreuzen:

← O O O O O O O O O O →

Nein 1 2 3 4 5 6 7 8 9 10 Ja

## 4. Die Namen

1.) Welcher Kategorie der Namen läßt sich der Produktname zuordnen?

**a)** **beschreibender Name**

        O   (Ja)           O    (Nein - weiter mit b)

2.) Ist die Beschreibung durch den Namen produktadäquat ausgewählt?

Bitte ankreuzen:

← O O O O O O O O O O →
Nein 1 2 3 4 5 6 7 8 9 10 Ja

3.) Ist es möglich, den Namen als Gattungsbezeichnung aufzufassen, so daß das Produkt nicht auf Anhieb als Markenartikel zu identifizieren ist?

Bitte ankreuzen:

← O O O O O O O O O O →
Ja 1 2 3 4 5 6 7 8 9 10 Nein

4.) Ist der Name gut merkbar?

Bitte ankreuzen:

← O O O O O O O O O O →
Nein 1 2 3 4 5 6 7 8 9 10 Ja

**b)    assoziative Namen**

      O    (Ja)           O    (Nein - weiter mit c)

1.)    Ist der Name produktadäquat ausgewählt?

Bitte ankreuzen:

←   O   O   O   O   O   O   O   O   O   O   →
Nein 1   2   3   4   5   6   7   8   9   10   Ja

2.)    Ist das assoziative Interpretationsverfahren einfach und schnell durchzuführen?

Bitte ankreuzen:

←   O   O   O   O   O   O   O   O   O   O   →
Nein 1   2   3   4   5   6   7   8   9   10   Ja

3.)    Oft sind bekannte Größen die Grundlage zur Bildung asso-
       ziativer Namen („Ajax", „Ariel", „der General" etc.).
       Assoziiert diese Größe eine geeignete bzw. produktadäquate
       Eigenschaft?

Bitte ankreuzen:

←   O   O   O   O   O   O   O   O   O   O   →
Nein 1   2   3   4   5   6   7   8   9   10   Ja

Kommentar:

_____

4.)    Wird das Produkt bzw. eine Produkteigenschaft in geeigneter
       Weise zur Grundlage der Assoziation des Namens gemacht
       (z.B. „Spüli")?

Bitte ankreuzen:

←   O   O   O   O   O   O   O   O   O   O   →
Nein 1   2   3   4   5   6   7   8   9   10   Ja

5.) Gelingt es, den assoziativen Namen als Markennamen bekannt zu machen und ihn damit selber zum Symbol werden
zu lassen?

Bitte ankreuzen:

← O   O   O   O   O   O   O   O   O   O   →
Nein 1   2   3   4   5   6   7   8   9   10   Ja

6.) Ist der assoziative Name leicht zu merken?

Bitte ankreuzen:

← O   O   O   O   O   O   O   O   O   O   →
Nein 1   2   3   4   5   6   7   8   9   10   Ja

7.) Differenziert der assoziative Name das Produkt von anderen
Alternativen?

Bitte ankreuzen:

← O   O   O   O   O   O   O   O   O   O   →
Nein   1   2   3   4   5   6   7   8   9   10
Ja

8.) Ist der assoziative Name originell?

Bitte ankreuzen:

← O   O   O   O   O   O   O   O   O   O   →
Nein 1   2   3   4   5   6   7   8   9   10   Ja

9.) Spricht der assoziative Name die Zielgruppe an?

Bitte ankreuzen:

← O   O   O   O   O   O   O   O   O   O   →
Nein 1   2   3   4   5   6   7   8   9   10   Ja

## c)   artifizielle Namen

O   (Ja - 10 Bonuspunkte)[227]                    O   (Nein)

1.)   Wie ist der Name gebildet?

a)   Wortkomposition aus bekannten Elementen?

O   (Ja)                    O   (Nein - weiter mit d)

2.)   Ist der Name produktadäquat ausgewählt?

Bitte ankreuzen:

←   O   O   O   O   O   O   O   O   O   O   →
Nein 1   2   3   4   5   6   7   8   9   10   Ja

2.)   Ist das regelbasierte Interpretationsverfahren einfach und schnell durchzuführen?

Bitte ankreuzen:

←   O   O   O   O   O   O   O   O   O   O   →
Nein 1   2   3   4   5   6   7   8   9   10   Ja

4.)   Oft sind bekannte Wortkomponenten die Grundlage zur Bildung artifizieller Namenskompositionen („Kaloderma" etc.). Lassen diese auf geeignete bzw. produktadäquate Eigenschaften schließen?

Bitte ankreuzen:

←   O   O   O   O   O   O   O   O   O   O   →
Nein 1   2   3   4   5   6   7   8   9   10   Ja

---

[227] Ich vergebe für artifizielle Namen Bonuspunkte, da dieser Typ Name mit sehr viel Aufwand eingeführt und den Kunden beigebracht werden muß. Ideal ist ein artifizieller Name kombiniert mit einer Produktbeschreibung, denn dann hat man sowohl den Aspekt der Verständlichkeit als auch die Aspekte Innovation, Originalität und Produktdifferenzierung berücksichtigt.

5.) Ist der Anbieter, das Produkt bzw. eine Produkteigenschaft die Grundlage der Namensneuschöpfung (z.B. ) und das Produkt aus diesem Grund leicht zu erschließen (Dextro Energen)?

Bitte ankreuzen:

← O O O O O O O O O O →
Nein 1   2   3   4   5   6   7   8   9   10   Ja

**d) Wortneuschöpfung**

1.) Ist der Name produktadäquat ausgewählt?

Bitte ankreuzen:

← O O O O O O O O O O →
Nein 1   2   3   4   5   6   7   8   9   10   Ja

2.) Bei völlig unbekannten Wortneuschöpfungen kommt es darauf an, daß der Kunde über die Werbung, schnell erfaßbare Erläuterungen etc. die Verwendungsregeln des Wortes lernt. Damit wird der artifizielle Name zum Symbol für das Produkt. Ist dies gelungen?

Bitte ankreuzen:

← O O O O O O O O O O →
Nein 1   2   3   4   5   6   7   8   9   10   Ja

3.) Gelingt es, den artifiziellen Namen als Markennamen bekannt zu machen und ihn damit selber zum Symbol werden zu lassen?

Bitte ankreuzen:

← O O O O O O O O O O →
Nein 1   2   3   4   5   6   7   8   9   10   Ja

4.)   Ist der artifizielle Name leicht zu merken?

Bitte ankreuzen:

←   O   O   O   O   O   O   O   O   O   O   →
Nein 1   2   3   4   5   6   7   8   9   10   Ja


5.)   Differenziert der artifizielle Name das Produkt von anderen Alternativen?

Bitte ankreuzen:

←   O   O   O   O   O   O   O   O   O   O   →
Nein 1   2   3   4   5   6   7   8   9   10   Ja


6.)   Ist der artifizielle Name originell?

Bitte ankreuzen:

←   O   O   O   O   O   O   O   O   O   O   →
Nein 1   2   3   4   5   6   7   8   9   10   Ja


7.)   Spricht der artifizielle Name die Zielgruppe an?

Bitte ankreuzen:

←   O   O   O   O   O   O   O   O   O   O   →
Nein 1   2   3   4   5   6   7   8   9   10   Ja


**e) Allgemeines zum Namen**

1.)   Welchen Charakter hat der Name:

a)   Wirkt er seriös?

Bitte ankreuzen:

←   O   O   O   O   O   O   O   O   O   O   →
Nein 1   2   3   4   5   6   7   8   9   10   Ja

b)     Verleiht er der Verpackung Pepp?

Bitte ankreuzen:

| ← | O | O | O | O | O | O | O | O | O | O | → |
|---|---|---|---|---|---|---|---|---|---|---|---|
| Nein 1 | 2 | 3 | 4 | 5 | 6 | 7 | 8 | 9 | 10 | Ja |

c)   Wirkt er innovativ?

Bitte ankreuzen:

| ← | O | O | O | O | O | O | O | O | O | O | → |
|---|---|---|---|---|---|---|---|---|---|---|---|
| Nein 1 | 2 | 3 | 4 | 5 | 6 | 7 | 8 | 9 | 10 | Ja |

d)   Wirkt er ausgefallen?

Bitte ankreuzen:

| ← | O | O | O | O | O | O | O | O | O | O | → |
|---|---|---|---|---|---|---|---|---|---|---|---|
| Nein 1 | 2 | 3 | 4 | 5 | 6 | 7 | 8 | 9 | 10 | Ja |

e)   Wirkt er exklusiv?

Bitte ankreuzen:

| ← | O | O | O | O | O | O | O | O | O | O | → |
|---|---|---|---|---|---|---|---|---|---|---|---|
| Nein | 1 | 2 | 3 | 4 | 5 | 6 | 7 | 8 | 9 | 10 |

Ja

f)   Wirkt er langweilig?

Bitte ankreuzen:

| ← | O | O | O | O | O | O | O | O | O | O | → |
|---|---|---|---|---|---|---|---|---|---|---|---|
| Nein 10 | 9 | 8 | 7 | 6 | 5 | 4 | 3 | 2 | 1 | Ja |

g)       Sonstiges? Hier kann ebenfalls ein selbstgewähltes Item ein-
         gesetzt und bewertet werden.

Bitte ankreuzen:

← O   O   O   O   O   O   O   O   O   O   →
Nein 1   2   3   4   5   6   7   8   9   10  Ja

2.)      Ist es dem Anbieter mit seinen Marketingmaßnahmen gelun-
         gen, den Namen produktadäquat bekannt zu machen - gelingt
         es den Konsumenten dauerhaft, über die Interpretation des
         Namens auf das Produkt zu schließen?

Bitte ankreuzen:

← O   O   O   O   O   O   O   O   O   O   →
Nein 1   2   3   4   5   6   7   8   9   10  Ja

3.)      Ist der Name gut merkbar?
Bitte ankreuzen:

← O   O   O   O   O   O   O   O   O   O   →
Nein 1   2   3   4   5   6   7   8   9   10  Ja

4.)      Ist der Name leicht zu lesen und zu schreiben - (z.B. *Freixe-
         net* ist nicht leicht zu lesen)?[228]

Bitte ankreuzen:

← O   O   O   O   O   O   O   O   O   O   →
Nein 1   2   3   4   5   6   7   8   9   10  Ja

---

[228]
         Die Firma "Marten" hat eines ihrer Produkte mit dem italienisch klingen-
         den Namen "Salaggio" (Geflügelsalami) ausgestattet. Um allzugroßen
         Verstehens-, Aussprache-, Schreib- und Merkproblemen entgegenzuwir-
         ken, wurde eine Werbung als reine Sprachübung gestaltet. Einer spricht vor
         und ein Chor antwortet – zuerst falsch. Durch die Korrektur sollen die
         Kunden bewußt auf eine mögliche Fehlerquelle bei der Aussprache hinge-
         wiesen werden daß der Name anders gesprochen als geschrieben wird. Sie
         erfahren dabei gleichzeitig, wie der Name geschrieben wird, was die Wie-
         dererkennung im Laden erleichtert.

5.) Gibt es stilistische Besonderheiten, die die Merkbarkeit erleichtern sollen (z.B. Alliteration)?

Bitte ankreuzen:

| ← | O | O | O | O | O | O | O | O | O | O | → |
|---|---|---|---|---|---|---|---|---|---|---|---|
| Nein 1 | 2 | 3 | 4 | 5 | 6 | 7 | 8 | 9 | 10 | Ja |

6.) Ist der Klang des Namens angenehm?

Bitte ankreuzen:

| ← | O | O | O | O | O | O | O | O | O | O | → |
|---|---|---|---|---|---|---|---|---|---|---|---|
| Nein | 1 | 2 | 3 | 4 | 5 | 6 | 7 | 8 | 9 | 10 |

Ja

7.) Mit wie viel Aufwand wird der Name eingeführt?

Bitte ankreuzen:

| ← | O | O | O | O | O | O | O | O | O | O | → |
|---|---|---|---|---|---|---|---|---|---|---|---|
| wenig 1 | 2 | 3 | 4 | 5 | 6 | 7 | 8 | 9 | 10 | viel |

8.) Vermittelt der Name einen Eindruck der Produktphilosophie?

Bitte ankreuzen:

| ← | O | O | O | O | O | O | O | O | O | O | → |
|---|---|---|---|---|---|---|---|---|---|---|---|
| Nein 1 | 2 | 3 | 4 | 5 | 6 | 7 | 8 | 9 | 10 | Ja |

9.) Läßt sich mit dem Namen eine Produktfamilie verbinden?

Bitte ankreuzen:

| ← | O | O | O | O | O | O | O | O | O | O | → |
|---|---|---|---|---|---|---|---|---|---|---|---|
| Nein 1 | 2 | 3 | 4 | 5 | 6 | 7 | 8 | 9 | 10 | Ja |

10.) Wird der Name als Begriff mit scharfen Rändern interpretiert?

Bitte ankreuzen:

| ← | O | O | O | O | O | O | O | O | O | O | → |
|---|---|---|---|---|---|---|---|---|---|---|---|
| Nein 1 | 2 | 3 | 4 | 5 | 6 | 7 | 8 | 9 | 10 | Ja |

261

11.) Wird der Name als Begriff mit unscharfen Rändern interpretiert?[229]
Bitte ankreuzen:

| ← | O | O | O | O | O | O | O | O | O | O | → | |
|---|---|---|---|---|---|---|---|---|---|---|---|---|
| Nein | 10 | 9 | 8 | 7 | 6 | 5 | 4 | 3 | 2 | 1 | Ja |

12.) Macht der Name eine Marke?
Bitte ankreuzen:

| ← | O | O | O | O | O | O | O | O | O | O | → | |
|---|---|---|---|---|---|---|---|---|---|---|---|---|
| Nein | 1 | 2 | 3 | 4 | 5 | 6 | 7 | 8 | 9 | 10 | Ja |

13.) Verkörpert der Name
a)    ein positives Firmenimage?
Bitte ankreuzen:

| ← | O | O | O | O | O | O | O | O | O | O | → | |
|---|---|---|---|---|---|---|---|---|---|---|---|---|
| Nein | 1 | 2 | 3 | 4 | 5 | 6 | 7 | 8 | 9 | 10 | Ja |

b)    ein positives Produktimage?
Bitte ankreuzen:

| ← | O | O | O | O | O | O | O | O | O | O | → | |
|---|---|---|---|---|---|---|---|---|---|---|---|---|
| Nein | 1 | 2 | 3 | 4 | 5 | 6 | 7 | 8 | 9 | 10 | Ja |

c)    ein positives Konsumentenimage?
Bitte ankreuzen:

| ← | O | O | O | O | O | O | O | O | O | O | → | |
|---|---|---|---|---|---|---|---|---|---|---|---|---|
| Nein | 1 | 2 | 3 | 4 | 5 | 6 | 7 | 8 | 9 | 10 | Ja |

---

[229] Die Interpretation eines Produktnamens als Name mit unscharfen Rändern ist nicht vorteilhaft für eine gezielte Produktdifferenzierung auf dem Markt, die allerdings einen gewissen Aufwand verlangt.

d)   Sind die Aspekte Anbieter, Produkt und Konsument referentiell miteinander verknüpft?

Bitte ankreuzen:

← O   O   O   O   O   O   O   O   O   O   →
Nein 1   2   3   4   5   6   7   8   9   10   Ja


## 5.)   Die Adjektive

1.)   Werden die Adjektive wirkungseffektiv als Reiz- bzw. Schlüsselwort auf der   Produktverpackung eingesetzt?

   a)   allein

Bitte ankreuzen:

← O   O   O   O   O   O   O   O   O   O   →
Nein 1   2   3   4   5   6   7   8   9   10   Ja

   b)   als Bilderänzung

Bitte ankreuzen:

← O   O   O   O   O   O   O   O   O   O   →
Nein 1   2   3   4   5   6   7   8   9   10   Ja


   c)   als Wortergänzung

Bitte ankreuzen:

← O   O   O   O   O   O   O   O   O   O   →
Nein 1   2   3   4   5   6   7   8   9   10   Ja

2.)   Wie wirken die Adjektive?

a)   ergänzend?

Bitte ankreuzen:

← O   O   O   O   O   O   O   O   O   O   →
Nein 1   2   3   4   5   6   7   8   9   10   Ja

b)   aufwertend?

Bitte ankreuzen:

| ← | O | O | O | O | O | O | O | O | O | O | → |
|---|---|---|---|---|---|---|---|---|---|---|---|
| Nein | 1 | 2 | 3 | 4 | 5 | 6 | 7 | 8 | 9 | 10 | Ja |

c)   vergleichend?

Bitte ankreuzen:

| ← | O | O | O | O | O | O | O | O | O | O | → |
|---|---|---|---|---|---|---|---|---|---|---|---|
| Nein | 1 | 2 | 3 | 4 | 5 | 6 | 7 | 8 | 9 | 10 | Ja |

d)   glaubwürdig?

Bitte ankreuzen:

| ← | O | O | O | O | O | O | O | O | O | O | → |
|---|---|---|---|---|---|---|---|---|---|---|---|
| Nein | 1 | 2 | 3 | 4 | 5 | 6 | 7 | 8 | 9 | 10 | Ja |

e)   positiv?

Bitte ankreuzen:

| ← | O | O | O | O | O | O | O | O | O | O | → |
|---|---|---|---|---|---|---|---|---|---|---|---|
| Nein | 1 | 2 | 3 | 4 | 5 | 6 | 7 | 8 | 9 | 10 | Ja |

f)   aufbauschend?

Bitte ankreuzen:

| ← | O | O | O | O | O | O | O | O | O | O | → |
|---|---|---|---|---|---|---|---|---|---|---|---|
| Nein | 10 | 9 | 8 | 7 | 6 | 5 | 4 | 3 | 2 | 1 | Ja |

g)   Sonstiges? Hier kann ein selbstgewähltes Item eingesetzt und bewertet werden:

_____

Bitte ankreuzen:

| ← | O | O | O | O | O | O | O | O | O | O | → |
|---|---|---|---|---|---|---|---|---|---|---|---|
| Nein | 1 | 2 | 3 | 4 | 5 | 6 | 7 | 8 | 9 | 10 | Ja |

3.)   Bieten sie einen sinnvollen Aspekt der Ergänzung?
Bitte ankreuzen:

← O  O  O  O  O  O  O  O  O  O  →
Nein 1  2  3  4  5  6  7  8  9  10  Ja

4.)   Sprechen die Adjektive die Zielgruppe an?
Bitte ankreuzen:

← O  O  O  O  O  O  O  O  O  O  →
Nein 1  2  3  4  5  6  7  8  9  10  Ja

5.)   Wirken die Adjektive verständlich?
Bitte ankreuzen:

← O  O  O  O  O  O  O  O  O  O  →
Nein 1  2  3  4  5  6  7  8  9  10  Ja

6.)   Passen die Adjektive zum Stil?
Bitte ankreuzen:

← O  O  O  O  O  O  O  O  O  O  →
Nein 1  2  3  4  5  6  7  8  9  10  Ja

7.)   Wirken die Adjektive originell?
Bitte ankreuzen:

← O  O  O  O  O  O  O  O  O  O  →
Nein 1  2  3  4  5  6  7  8  9  10  Ja

8.)   Wirken die Adjektive witzig?
Bitte ankreuzen:

← O  O  O  O  O  O  O  O  O  O  →
Nein 1  2  3  4  5  6  7  8  9  10  Ja

9.) Verleihen die Adjektive der Verpackung Pepp?

10.) Wirken die Adjektive innovativ?
Bitte ankreuzen:

← O O O O O O O O O O →
Nein 1 2 3 4 5 6 7 8 9 10 Ja

11.) Wirken die Adjektive ausgefallen?
Bitte ankreuzen:

← O O O O O O O O O O →
Nein 1 2 3 4 5 6 7 8 9 10 Ja

12.) Wirken die Adjektive langweilig?
Bitte ankreuzen

← O O O O O O O O O O →
Nein 10 9 8 7 6 5 4 3 2 1 Ja

13.) Sonstiges? Hier kann eine selbstgewähltes Item eingesetzt und bewertet werden:

_____

Bitte ankreuzen:

← O O O O O O O O O O →
Nein 1 2 3 4 5 6 7 8 9 10 Ja

**6.)  Die Verben**

1.)    Sind die Verben verständlich?

Bitte ankreuzen:

←   O   O   O   O   O   O   O   O   O   O   →

Nein 1   2   3   4   5   6   7   8   9   10   Ja

2.)    Wirken die Verben dynamisch?

Bitte ankreuzen:

←   O   O   O   O   O   O   O   O   O   O   →

Nein 1   2   3   4   5   6   7   8   9   10   Ja

3.)    Wirken die Verben aktivierend/motivierend?

Bitte ankreuzen:

←   O   O   O   O   O   O   O   O   O   O   →

Nein 1   2   3   4   5   6   7   8   9   10   Ja

4.)    Wirken die Verben originell?

Bitte ankreuzen:

←   O   O   O   O   O   O   O   O   O   O   →

Nein 1   2   3   4   5   6   7   8   9   10   Ja

5.)    Wirken die Verben innovativ?

Bitte ankreuzen:

←   O   O   O   O   O   O   O   O   O   O   →

Nein 1   2   3   4   5   6   7   8   9   10   Ja

6.)    Wirken die Verben ausgefallen?

Bitte ankreuzen:

←   O   O   O   O   O   O   O   O   O   O   →

Nein 1   2   3   4   5   6   7   8   9   10   Ja

267

7.)  Wirken die Verben exklusiv?

Bitte ankreuzen:

← O O O O O O O O O O →

Nein 1  2  3  4  5  6  7  8  9  10  Ja

8.)  Wirken die Verben langweilig?

Bitte ankreuzen

← O O O O O O O O O O →

Nein 10  9  8  7  6  5  4  3  2  1  Ja

9.)  Sonstiges? Auch hier besteht wieder die Möglichkeit, ein selbstgewähltes Item einzusetzen und zu bewerten.

_____

Bitte ankreuzen:

← O O O O O O O O O O →

Nein 1  2  3  4  5  6  7  8  9  10  Ja

10.)  Sind die Verben zielgruppenadäquat ausgewählt?

Bitte ankreuzen:

← O O O O O O O O O O →

Nein 1  2  3  4  5  6  7  8  9  10  Ja

11.)  Passen die Verben in den Kontext?

Bitte ankreuzen:

← O O O O O O O O O O →

Nein 1  2  3  4  5  6  7  8  9  10  Ja

12.)  Lassen sich die Verben sinngemäß interpretieren?

Bitte ankreuzen:

← O O O O O O O O O O →

Nein 1  2  3  4  5  6  7  8  9  10  Ja

## 7.) Sonstige Worte

1.) Werden mit Hilfe von Worten weiterer Klassen Akzente gesetzt?

O (Ja)                              O (Nein - weiter mit Frage 8)

Bitte ankreuzen:

← O O O O O O O O O O →

Nein 1 2 3 4 5 6 7 8 9 10 Ja

2.) Wirkt die Wortwahl verständlich?

Bitte ankreuzen:

← O O O O O O O O O O →

Nein 1 2 3 4 5 6 7 8 9 10 Ja

3.) Wirkt die Wortwahl sinnvoll (oder wird der Text unnötig verkompliziert)?

Bitte ankreuzen:

← O O O O O O O O O O →

Nein 1 2 3 4 5 6 7 8 9 10 Ja

4.) Wirkt diese Wortwahl originell?

Bitte ankreuzen:

← O O O O O O O O O O →

Nein 1 2 3 4 5 6 7 8 9 10 Ja

5.) Wirkt diese Wortwahl innovativ?

Bitte ankreuzen:

← O O O O O O O O O O →

Nein 1 2 3 4 5 6 7 8 9 10 Ja

6.)  Wirkt diese Wortwahl ausgefallen?

Bitte ankreuzen:

← O O O O O O O O O O →
Nein 1 2 3 4 5 6 7 8 9 10 Ja

7.)  Wirkt diese Wortwahl exklusiv?

Bitte ankreuzen:

← O O O O O O O O O O →
Nein 1 2 3 4 5 6 7 8 9 10 Ja

8.)  Wirkt die Wortwahl langweilig?

Bitte ankreuzen

← O O O O O O O O O O →
Nein 10 9 8 7 6 5 4 3 2 1 Ja

9.)  Sonstiges? Hier kann ein selbstgewähltes Item eingesetzt und
bewertet werden:

---

Bitte ankreuzen:

← O O O O O O O O O O →
Nein 1 2 3 4 5 6 7 8 9 10 Ja

**8.)    Die Stilmittel**

1.)    Wird mit Stilmitteln ein publikumswirksamer Akzent gesetzt?

←   O   O   O   O   O   O   O   O   O   O   →

Nein 1   2   3   4   5   6   7   8   9   10   Ja

2.)    Ist die Wirkung der Stilmittel erfolgreich?
Bitte ankreuzen:

←   O   O   O   O   O   O   O   O   O   O   →

Nein 1   2   3   4   5   6   7   8   9   10   Ja

3.)    Wirken die Stilmittel zielgruppenadäquat?
Bitte ankreuzen:

←   O   O   O   O   O   O   O   O   O   O   →

Nein 1   2   3   4   5   6   7   8   9   10   Ja

4.)    Wirken die Stilmittel originell?
Bitte ankreuzen:

←   O   O   O   O   O   O   O   O   O   O   →

Nein 1   2   3   4   5   6   7   8   9   10   Ja

5.)    Wirken die Stilmittel blickfangend?
Bitte ankreuzen:

←   O   O   O   O   O   O   O   O   O   O   →

Nein 1   2   3   4   5   6   7   8   9   10   Ja

6.)    Wirken die Stilmittel innovativ?
Bitte ankreuzen:

←   O   O   O   O   O   O   O   O   O   O   →

Nein 1   2   3   4   5   6   7   8   9   10   Ja

7.)   Wirken die Stilmittel ausgefallen?

Bitte ankreuzen:

← O O O O O O O O O O →
Nein 1 2 3 4 5 6 7 8 9 10 Ja

8.)   Wirken die Stilmittel exklusiv?

Bitte ankreuzen:

← O O O O O O O O O O →
Nein 1 2 3 4 5 6 7 8 9 10 Ja

9.)   Wirken die Stilmittel langweilig?

Bitte ankreuzen:

← O O O O O O O O O O →
Nein 10 9 8 7 6 5 4 3 2 1 Ja

10.)   Sonstiges? Hier kann ein selbstgewähltes Item eingesetzt und
      bewertet werden:

_____

Bitte ankreuzen:

← O O O O O O O O O O →
Nein 1 2 3 4 5 6 7 8 9 10 Ja

## 9.)   Die Satzzeichen

1.)   Sind die Satzzeichen sinn- und wirkungsvoll eingesetzt?

Bitte ankreuzen:

← O O O O O O O O O O →
Nein 1 2 3 4 5 6 7 8 9 10 Ja

## 10.  Phraseologismen

1.)     Setzen die Phraseologismen einen Akzent?
Bitte ankreuzen:

← O O O O O O O O O O →
Nein 1   2   3   4   5   6   7   8   9   10   Ja

2.)     Wirken sie verständlich?
Bitte ankreuzen:

← O O O O O O O O O O →
Nein 1   2   3   4   5   6   7   8   9   10   Ja

3.)     Wirken sie gut merkbar?
Bitte ankreuzen:

← O O O O O O O O O O →
Nein 1   2   3   4   5   6   7   8   9   10   Ja

4.)     Wirken sie originell?
Bitte ankreuzen:

← O O O O O O O O O O →
Nein 1   2   3   4   5   6   7   8   9   10   Ja

5.)     Wirken sie blickfangend?
Bitte ankreuzen:

← O O O O O O O O O O →
Nein 1   2   3   4   5   6   7   8   9   10   Ja

6.)     Verleihen sie der Verpackung Pepp?
Bitte ankreuzen:

← O O O O O O O O O O →
Nein 1   2   3   4   5   6   7   8   9   10   Ja

7.)   Wirken sie innovativ?

Bitte ankreuzen:

← O O O O O O O O O O →
Nein 1 2 3 4 5 6 7 8 9 10 Ja

8.)   Wirken sie ausgefallen?

Bitte ankreuzen:

← O O O O O O O O O O →
Nein 1 2 3 4 5 6 7 8 9 10 Ja

9.)   Wirken sie exklusiv?

Bitte ankreuzen:

← O O O O O O O O O O →
Nein 1 2 3 4 5 6 7 8 9 10 Ja

10.)   Wirken sie langweilig?

Bitte ankreuzen:

← O O O O O O O O O O →
Nein 10 9 8 7 6 5 4 3 2 1 Ja

11.)   Sonstiges? Hier kann ein selbstgewähltes Item eingesetzt und
bewertet werden:

_____

Bitte ankreuzen:

← O O O O O O O O O O →
Nein 1 2 3 4 5 6 7 8 9 10 Ja

12.)   Paßt der Phraseologismus zum Kontext?

Bitte ankreuzen:

← O O O O O O O O O O →
Nein 1 2 3 4 5 6 7 8 9 10 Ja

13.) Paßt er zum Produkt?

Bitte ankreuzen:

| ← | O | O | O | O | O | O | O | O | O | O | → |
|---|---|---|---|---|---|---|---|---|---|---|---|
| Nein 1 | 2 | 3 | 4 | 5 | 6 | 7 | 8 | 9 | 10 | Ja |

14.) Paßt er zur Zielgruppe?

Bitte ankreuzen:

| ← | O | O | O | O | O | O | O | O | O | O | → |
|---|---|---|---|---|---|---|---|---|---|---|---|
| Nein 1 | 2 | 3 | 4 | 5 | 6 | 7 | 8 | 9 | 10 | Ja |

15.) Wird er im intendierten Sinn interpretiert?

Bitte ankreuzen:

| ← | O | O | O | O | O | O | O | O | O | O | → |
|---|---|---|---|---|---|---|---|---|---|---|---|
| Nein 1 | 2 | 3 | 4 | 5 | 6 | 7 | 8 | 9 | 10 | Ja |

## 11. Der Text

1.) Ist der Text gut wahrnehmbar in bezug auf:

    a) Typographie?

Bitte ankreuzen:

| ← | O | O | O | O | O | O | O | O | O | O | → |
|---|---|---|---|---|---|---|---|---|---|---|---|
| Nein 1 | 2 | 3 | 4 | 5 | 6 | 7 | 8 | 9 | 10 | Ja |

    b) Farben?

Bitte ankreuzen:

| ← | O | O | O | O | O | O | O | O | O | O | → |
|---|---|---|---|---|---|---|---|---|---|---|---|
| Nein 1 | 2 | 3 | 4 | 5 | 6 | 7 | 8 | 9 | 10 | Ja |

2.) Wirkt der Text einladend?

Bitte ankreuzen:

← O O O O O O O O O O →
Nein 1 2 3 4 5 6 7 8 9 10 Ja

3.) Ist der Text leicht und flüssig lesbar?

Bitte ankreuzen:

← O O O O O O O O O O →
Nein 1 2 3 4 5 6 7 8 9 10 Ja

4.) Ist der Text verständlich?

Bitte ankreuzen:

← O O O O O O O O O O →
Nein 1 2 3 4 5 6 7 8 9 10 Ja

5.) Wirkt der Text schlüssig?

Bitte ankreuzen:

← O O O O O O O O O O →
Nein 1 2 3 4 5 6 7 8 9 10 Ja

6.) Ist der Text originell?

Bitte ankreuzen:

← O O O O O O O O O O →
Nein 1 2 3 4 5 6 7 8 9 10 Ja

7.) Wirkt der Text glaubwürdig?

Bitte ankreuzen:

← O O O O O O O O O O →
Nein 1 2 3 4 5 6 7 8 9 10 Ja

8.)   Wirkt der Text überredend?

Bitte ankreuzen:

| ← | O | O | O | O | O | O | O | O | O | O | → |
|---|---|---|---|---|---|---|---|---|---|---|---|
| Nein | 10 | 9 | 8 | 7 | 6 | 5 | 4 | 3 | 2 | 1 | Ja |

9.)   Werden überzeugende Argumente eingesetzt?

Bitte ankreuzen:

| ← | O | O | O | O | O | O | O | O | O | O | → |
|---|---|---|---|---|---|---|---|---|---|---|---|
| Nein | 1 | 2 | 3 | 4 | 5 | 6 | 7 | 8 | 9 | 10 | Ja |

10.)   Handelt es sich um Pseudoargumente?

Bitte ankreuzen:

| ← | O | O | O | O | O | O | O | O | O | O | → |
|---|---|---|---|---|---|---|---|---|---|---|---|
| Nein | 10 | 9 | 8 | 7 | 6 | 5 | 4 | 3 | 2 | 1 | Ja |

11.)   Ist der Text sprachlich zielgruppenadäquat?

Bitte ankreuzen:

| ← | O | O | O | O | O | O | O | O | O | O | → |
|---|---|---|---|---|---|---|---|---|---|---|---|
| Nein | 1 | 2 | 3 | 4 | 5 | 6 | 7 | 8 | 9 | 10 | Ja |

12.)   Ist der Text stilistisch ansprechend?

Bitte ankreuzen:

| ← | O | O | O | O | O | O | O | O | O | O | → |
|---|---|---|---|---|---|---|---|---|---|---|---|
| Nein | 1 | 2 | 3 | 4 | 5 | 6 | 7 | 8 | 9 | 10 | Ja |

13.)   Hier ist Platz für die jeweils individuelle Bewertung der sprachlichen Gestaltung des Textes. Um Vergleichbarkeit auch bei verschiedenen Anwendern zu gewährleisten, werden hier die Kategorien von vier Wortklassen bereitgestellt, die jeweils in Bezug auf zwei Eigenschaften mit Punkten von 1-10 bewertet werden können aber nicht müssen.[230]

Bereitgestellt sind folgende Wortklassen zur zweifachen Individualbewertung:

a)   Substantive

-   Eigenschaft

1:_____

Bitte ankreuzen:

← O   O   O   O   O   O   O   O   O   O   →

Nein 1   2   3   4   5   6   7   8   9   10   Ja

-   Eigenschaft

2:_____

Bitte ankreuzen:

← O   O   O   O   O   O   O   O   O   O   →

Nein 1   2   3   4   5   6   7   8   9   10   Ja

b)   Adjektive

-   Eigenschaft

1:_____

Bitte ankreuzen:

← O   O   O   O   O   O   O   O   O   O   →

Nein 1   2   3   4   5   6   7   8   9   10   Ja

---

[230] Die Textgestaltung ist dermaßen vielfältig, daß hier die Interessen des Anwenders die Bewertung bestimmen sollen.

- Eigenschaft

2:_____

Bitte ankreuzen:

← O O O O O O O O O O →

Nein 1 2 3 4 5 6 7 8 9 10 Ja

c) Verben

- Eigenschaft

1:_____

Bitte ankreuzen:

← O O O O O O O O O O →

Nein 1 2 3 4 5 6 7 8 9 10 Ja

- Eigenschaft

2:_____

Bitte ankreuzen:

← O O O O O O O O O O →

Nein 1 2 3 4 5 6 7 8 9 10 Ja

d) sonstige Wortklasse:

_____

- Eigenschaft

1:_____

Bitte ankreuzen:

← O O O O O O O O O O →

Nein 1 2 3 4 5 6 7 8 9 10 Ja

- Eigenschaft

2:_____

14.) Trägt der Text zu einer Wertsteigerung des Produktes bei?

Bitte ankreuzen:

← O O O O O O O O O O →

Nein 1 2 3 4 5 6 7 8 9 10 Ja

15.) Wirkt der Text innovativ?

Bitte ankreuzen:

← O O O O O O O O O O →

Nein 1 2 3 4 5 6 7 8 9 10 Ja

16.) Wird der Fokus der Rezipienten

     a)    auf den Text gelenkt?

Bitte ankreuzen:

← O O O O O O O O O O →

Nein 1 2 3 4 5 6 7 8 9 10 Ja

     b)    durch den Text gelenkt?

Bitte ankreuzen:

← O O O O O O O O O O →

Nein 1 2 3 4 5 6 7 8 9 10 Ja

17.) Macht der Text "Lust" auf das Produkt?

Bitte ankreuzen:

← O O O O O O O O O O →

Nein 1 2 3 4 5 6 7 8 9 10 Ja

18.) Werden neben dem Produkt noch ein oder mehrere ideelle Werte versprochen?

Bitte ankreuzen:

← O O O O O O O O O O →

Nein 1 2 3 4 5 6 7 8 9 10 Ja

19.) Ist der Text passend in das gesamte Verpackungskonzept integriert?

Bitte ankreuzen:

← O O O O O O O O O O →
Nein 1 2 3 4 5 6 7 8 9 10 Ja

## 12. Der Inhalt

1.) Ist der Inhalt produktadäquat?

Bitte ankreuzen:

← O O O O O O O O O O →
Nein 1 2 3 4 5 6 7 8 9 10 Ja

2.) Ist der Inhalt kundenbezogen?

Bitte ankreuzen:

← O O O O O O O O O O →
Nein 1 2 3 4 5 6 7 8 9 10 Ja

3.) Ist der Inhalt anbieterbezogen?

Bitte ankreuzen:

← O O O O O O O O O O →
Nein 1 2 3 4 5 6 7 8 9 10 Ja

4.) Werden zu diesen drei Aspekten inhaltlich ergänzende Aspekte
vorgestellt?

Bitte ankreuzen:

← O O O O O O O O O O →
Nein 1 2 3 4 5 6 7 8 9 10 Ja

5.) Wird ein umfassendes Konzept zu einer Firmen- und damit auch zu einer Produktphilosophie präsentiert?

Bitte ankreuzen:

← O O O O O O O O O O →
Nein 1 2 3 4 5 6 7 8 9 10 Ja

6.) Wird das Produkt sympathisch gemacht?

Bitte ankreuzen:

← O O O O O O O O O O →
Nein 1 2 3 4 5 6 7 8 9 10 Ja

7.) Werden im Rahmen der Produktphilosophie positive Werte der Zielgruppe vorgestellt?

Bitte ankreuzen:

← O O O O O O O O O O →
Nein 1 2 3 4 5 6 7 8 9 10 Ja

8.) Gelingt es, diese positiven Werte als Produkteigenschaften glaubhaft zu machen?

Bitte ankreuzen:

← O O O O O O O O O O →
Nein 1 2 3 4 5 6 7 8 9 10 Ja

9.) Ist der Anbieter mit einem positiven Image behaftet?

Bitte ankreuzen:

← O O O O O O O O O O →
Nein 1 2 3 4 5 6 7 8 9 10 Ja

10.) Ist das Produkt mit einem positiven Image behaftet?

Bitte ankreuzen:

← O O O O O O O O O O →

Nein 1 2 3 4 5 6 7 8 9 10 Ja

11.) Wird die Zielgruppe über die Verpackung mit einem positiven Image behaftet?

Bitte ankreuzen:

← O O O O O O O O O O →

Nein 1 2 3 4 5 6 7 8 9 10 Ja

12.) Wird die Verpackung mit Sympathieträgern ausgestattet?

Bitte ankreuzen:

← O O O O O O O O O O →

Nein 1 2 3 4 5 6 7 8 9 10 Ja

13.) Trägt das Image zum Verkaufserfolg bei?

Bitte ankreuzen:

← O O O O O O O O O O →

Nein 1 2 3 4 5 6 7 8 9 10 Ja

14.) Appelliert der Verpackungstext:

    a)    an das Gewissen?

Bitte ankreuzen:

← O O O O O O O O O O →

Nein 1 2 3 4 5 6 7 8 9 10 Ja

    b)    an den Mutter-/Vaterinstinkt?

Bitte ankreuzen:

← O O O O O O O O O O →

Nein 1 2 3 4 5 6 7 8 9 10 Ja

15.) Verspricht der Verpackungstext:

   a)    soziale Anerkennung?

Bitte ankreuzen:

← O O O O O O O O O O →
Nein 1 2 3 4 5 6 7 8 9 10 Ja


   b)    Bedürfnis-/Triebbefriedigung?

Bitte ankreuzen:

← O O O O O O O O O O →
Nein 1 2 3 4 5 6 7 8 9 10 Ja


   c)    einen Mehrwert?

Bitte ankreuzen:

← O O O O O O O O O O →
Nein 1 2 3 4 5 6 7 8 9 10 Ja


   d)    Sonstiges? Auch hier kann wieder ein selbstgewähltes Item eingesetzt und bewertet werden.

_____

Bitte ankreuzen:

← O O O O O O O O O O →
Nein 1 2 3 4 5 6 7 8 9 10 Ja


16.) Ist die Verpackung mit einer Kampagne ausgestattet, die zum Verkaufserfolg beiträgt?

Bitte ankreuzen:

← O O O O O O O O O O →
Nein 1 2 3 4 5 6 7 8 9 10 Ja

## 13.  Der Gesamteindruck

Wie wirkt der Gesamteindruck der Verpackung?
1.)    stimmig?
Bitte ankreuzen:

← O O O O O O O O O O →
Nein 1  2  3  4  5  6  7  8  9  10  Ja

2.)    verständlich?
Bitte ankreuzen:

← O O O O O O O O O O →
Nein 1  2  3  4  5  6  7  8  9  10  Ja

3.)    gut wahrnehmbar?
Bitte ankreuzen:

← O O O O O O O O O O →
Nein 1  2  3  4  5  6  7  8  9  10  Ja

4.)    praktisch?
Bitte ankreuzen:

← O O O O O O O O O O →
Nein 1  2  3  4  5  6  7  8  9  10  Ja

5.)    originell?
Bitte ankreuzen:

← O O O O O O O O O O →
Nein 1  2  3  4  5  6  7  8  9  10  Ja

6.) ausgefallen?

Bitte ankreuzen:

| ← | O | O | O | O | O | O | O | O | O | O | → |
|---|---|---|---|---|---|---|---|---|---|---|---|
| Nein | 1 | 2 | 3 | 4 | 5 | 6 | 7 | 8 | 9 | 10 | Ja |

7.) pfiffig?

Bitte ankreuzen:

| ← | O | O | O | O | O | O | O | O | O | O | → |
|---|---|---|---|---|---|---|---|---|---|---|---|
| Nein | 1 | 2 | 3 | 4 | 5 | 6 | 7 | 8 | 9 | 10 | Ja |

8.) langweilig?

Bitte ankreuzen:

| ← | O | O | O | O | O | O | O | O | O | O | → |
|---|---|---|---|---|---|---|---|---|---|---|---|
| Nein | 10 | 9 | 8 | 7 | 6 | 5 | 4 | 3 | 2 | 1 | Ja |

9.) innovativ?

Bitte ankreuzen:

| ← | O | O | O | O | O | O | O | O | O | O | → |
|---|---|---|---|---|---|---|---|---|---|---|---|
| Nein | 1 | 2 | 3 | 4 | 5 | 6 | 7 | 8 | 9 | 10 | Ja |

10.) seriös?

Bitte ankreuzen:

| ← | O | O | O | O | O | O | O | O | O | O | → |
|---|---|---|---|---|---|---|---|---|---|---|---|
| Nein | 1 | 2 | 3 | 4 | 5 | 6 | 7 | 8 | 9 | 10 | Ja |

11.) zielgruppenadäquat?

Bitte ankreuzen:

| ← | O | O | O | O | O | O | O | O | O | O | → |
|---|---|---|---|---|---|---|---|---|---|---|---|
| Nein | 1 | 2 | 3 | 4 | 5 | 6 | 7 | 8 | 9 | 10 | Ja |

12.) produktadäquat?

Bitte ankreuzen:

← O O O O O O O O O O →

Nein 1  2  3  4  5  6  7  8  9  10  Ja

13.) Verkörpert die Verpackung ein optimales Preis-
Leistungsverhältnis?

Bitte ankreuzen:

← O O O O O O O O O O →

Nein 1  2  3  4  5  6  7  8  9  10  Ja

Kommentar:

_____

14.) Wirkt die Verpackung qualitativ hochwertig?

Bitte ankreuzen:

← O O O O O O O O O O →

Nein 1  2  3  4  5  6  7  8  9  10  Ja

Gesamtpunktzahl: _____

Kommentar: _____

## VI b: Die Anwendung

## 4.2 Einführung

In diesem Teil soll die Anwendung des Analysemodells und damit die Praktikabilität der theoretischen Grundlagen des ersten Teils überprüft werden. Es werden drei Beispiele für eine Analyse vorgestellt. Einmal wird es sich um eine ganz schlichte Verpackung handeln. In einem zweiten Durchlauf wird die Anwendung des Analysemodells an einem etwas aufwendiger gestalteten Verpackungsobjekt demonstriert. In einer letzten Untersuchung wird eine sehr komplex ausgestattete Produktverpackung bearbeitet. Nach der kompletten Analyse werden jeweils die Unterschiede der alternativen Verpackungen präsentiert, um die Möglichkeiten, ein Ranking zu erstellen, zu demonstrieren.

Ich habe mich dazu entschlossen, drei verschiedene Produktverpackungen von 100%igem Apfelsaft exemplarisch mit dem Modell zu analysieren. 100%iger Apfelsaft ist ein durchschnittliches Konsumgut, das sowohl von Männern, Frauen und Kindern über alle Schichten hinweg konsumiert wird. Dementsprechend gibt es grundsätzlich keine produktspezifische Zielgruppe.

Zwei dieser Verpackungen sind relativ ähnlich. Sie wurden gewählt, um zu zeigen, daß das Modell sowohl den direkten Vergleich zweier wenig unterschiedlicher Verpackungen leisten kann, wie auch den Vergleich völlig unterschiedlicher Verpackungen. Analyse drei wird dementsprechend an einem völlig anderen Typ Apfelsaftverpackung demonstriert. Darüber hinaus ist es Ziel zu veranschaulichen, daß mit Hilfe des Modells jede Verpackung individuell auf Stärken und Schwächen hin untersucht werden kann.

Eine derartige Untersuchung von Produktverpackungen erachte ich insofern für sinnvoll, als daß sie dazu beiträgt, die Verpackung zu optimieren.

Die Frage, warum nicht auch eine ganz besonders schlichte Verpackung im Stil der No-Name-Produktverpackungen analysiert wird, hat ihre Berechtigung.
Dazu festzuhalten bleibt, daß die Analyse für eine derart wenig aufwendig gestaltete Verpackung aufgrund der wenigen gestalterischen Elemente sehr dürftig ausgefallen wäre. Der entscheidende Vorzug einer derartigen Verpackung ist der geringe Preis. Der Wert an Attraktivität und Kaufanreiz jedoch ist gleich Null.

## 4.3 Analyse I:    "vita*fit* Apfelsaft"

Bei „Vitafit Apfelsaft" handelt es sich um die Hausmarke der Markendiscounterkette „Lidl".

"Vitafit Apfelsaft"-Verpackungen sind im Verhältnis zum gesamten Verpackungsangebot relativ schlicht gestaltet. Der Tetra-Pak bietet ein repräsentatives Beispiel für eine Apfelsaftverpackung und eignet sich daher auch für den Vergleich.

Im folgenden wird die Verpackung Schritt für Schritt exemplarisch anhand des Analysemodells untersucht. Dabei werden die Einzelbewertungen mit einem kurzen Kommentar zur Entscheidungsfindung präsentiert (Abbildung 6).

### 1.)    Technisch orientierte Fragen

1.)    Schützt die Verpackung das Produkt und die Umwelt ausreichend?
Bitte ankreuzen:

← O O O O O O O ⊗ O O →
Nein 1  2  3  4  5  6  7  8  9  10  Ja

Kommentar:    Die Verpackung ist flexibel und damit wenig knautschanfällig und dicht. Tetra-Paks platzen jedoch zuweilen, wenn sie herunterfallen, und manchmal weisen die Schweißnähte undichte Stellen auf.

2.)    Läßt sich das Produkt in der Verpackung angenehm transportieren?
Bitte ankreuzen:

← O O O O O ⊗ O O O O →
Nein 1  2  3  4  5  6  7  8  9  10  Ja

Kommentar:    Der 1,5l -Pak ist für die Einkaufstasche etwas groß und schwer.

3.) Ist es möglich, das Produkt in der Verpackung entsprechend zu lagern?

Bitte ankreuzen:

← O O O O O ⊗ O O O O →
Nein　1　2　3　4　5　6　7　8　9　10
Ja

Kommentar:　Auch für die Lagerung im Kühlschrank ist die Verpackung etwas groß. Insbesondere wenn der Pak geöffnet ist, paßt er nicht optimal in die Kühlschranktür.

4.) Portioniert die Verpackung das Produkt sinnvoll?

Bitte ankreuzen:

← O O O O O O ⊗ O O O →
Nein 1　2　3　4　5　6　7　8　9　10　Ja

Kommentar:　Die Bewertung der Portionierung durch die Verpakkung ist von Verbrauchsgewohnheiten der Konsumenten abhängig. Der Apfelsaft sollte möglichst schnell aufgebraucht werden, wenn er einmal angebrochen wurde. Daher ist die Portionierung in 1,5l Paks nur sinnvoll, wenn man den Apfelsaft in größeren Mengen konsumiert. Dann allerdings ist diese Portionierung sehr praktisch.

5.) Ist die Verpackung auf ihren spezifischen Einsatz hin ausgerichtet?

Bitte ankreuzen:

← O O O O O O O O ⊗ O →
Nein 1　2　3　4　5　6　7　8　9　10　Ja

Kommentar:　Die Verpackung ist speziell für den Einsatz zur Aufbewahrung von Flüssigkeiten konzipiert. Sie wird der Lagerung des Produktes im Kühlschrank ebenfalls gerecht.

6.)   Ist die Verpackung praktisch?

Bitte ankreuzen:

← O O O O O O ⊗ O O O →
Nein 1 2 3 4 5 6 7 8 9 10 Ja

Kommentar: Mit der Ausgieß- und Wiederverschließvorrichtung ist die Verpackung im Gebrauch relativ praktisch, wenn auch etwas groß. Die Größe ist beim Transport und bei der Lagerung nicht optimal.

**Durchschnittsnote: 43:6 = 7,1**

## 2.   Die Bildzeichen

1.)     Bildet das Bildzeichen eine reales Objekt ab? (Wenn Nein - weiter mit Frage 2.)
        Ist das Bildzeichen aufgrund einer Ähnlichkeit einfach zu interpretieren?

Bitte ankreuzen:

← O O O O O O O O O ⊗ →
Nein 1 2 3 4 5 6 7 8 9 10 Ja

3.)     Ist die Abbildung abstrakt und damit erläuterungsbedürftig? (Wenn Nein - weiter mit der nächsten Frage)

Bitte ankreuzen:

← O O O O O O O O O O →
Nein 1 2 3 4 5 6 7 8 9 10 Ja

3.) Wird das Bild nach dem ikonischen Interpretationsverfahren interpretiert?

Bitte ankreuzen: ⊗    O

              Ja    Nein

4.) Wird das Bild nach dem symbolischen Interpretationsverfahren interpretiert?

Bitte ankreuzen: ⊗                        O

              Ja (10 Sonderpunkte)      Nein

Kommentar: Der Apfel wird auf Tetra-Paks mittlerweile regelbasiert als Hinweis auf Apfelsaft interpretiert. Damit ist er Symbol geworden.

5.) Ist ein direkter Schluß möglich?

(Auch bei objektgetreuen Abbildungen, die nicht in direktem Zusammenhang

      mit dem Produkt stehen.)

Bitte ankreuzen:

←   O   O   O   O   O   O   O   O   O   ⊗   →

Nein 1   2   3   4   5   6   7   8   9   10  Ja

Kommentar: Die Abbildung ist fotorealistisch und bildet originalgetreu einen Apfel ab. Aufgrund der großen Ähnlichkeit ist ein direkter Schluß ohne Zwischenschritte möglich. Eine Interpretation im intendierten Sinn ist ohne Probleme möglich.

6.) Kann das Bildzeichen ohne Probleme im intendierten Sinn interpretiert werden?

Bitte ankreuzen:

←   O   O   O   O   O   O   O   O   O   ⊗   →

Nein 1   2   3   4   5   6   7   8   9   10  Ja

Kommentar:    Eine Interpretation im intendierten Sinn ist ohne Probleme möglich.

7.)    Paßt das Bildzeichen in das Verpackungskonzept?
Bitte ankreuzen:

| ← | O | O | O | O | O | O | O | O | O | ⊗ | → |
|---|---|---|---|---|---|---|---|---|---|---|---|
| Nein 1 | 2 | 3 | 4 | 5 | 6 | 7 | 8 | 9 | 10 | Ja |

Kommentar:    Der Apfel paßt optimal in das Verpackungskonzept. Auf dem grünen Hintergrund wird das Bildzeichen als zentrales blickfangendes Element eingesetzt.

8.)    Wirken die Bildzeichen originell?
Bitte ankreuzen:

| ← | ⊗ | O | O | O | O | O | O | O | O | O | → |
|---|---|---|---|---|---|---|---|---|---|---|---|
| Nein 1 | 2 | 3 | 4 | 5 | 6 | 7 | 8 | 9 | 10 | Ja |

Kommentar:    Der Apfel ist alles andere als originell, sondern absoluter Standard.

9.)    Verleihen sie der Verpackung Pepp?
Bitte ankreuzen:

| ← | ⊗ | O | O | O | O | O | O | O | O | O | → |
|---|---|---|---|---|---|---|---|---|---|---|---|
| Nein 1 | 2 | 3 | 4 | 5 | 6 | 7 | 8 | 9 | 10 | Ja |

10.)    Wirken sie innovativ?
Bitte ankreuzen:

| ← | ⊗ | O | O | O | O | O | O | O | O | O | → |
|---|---|---|---|---|---|---|---|---|---|---|---|
| Nein 1 | 2 | 3 | 4 | 5 | 6 | 7 | 8 | 9 | 10 | Ja |

11.) Wirken sie ausgefallen?

Bitte ankreuzen:

| ← | ⊗ | O | O | O | O | O | O | O | O | O | → |
|---|---|---|---|---|---|---|---|---|---|---|---|
| Nein | 1 | 2 | 3 | 4 | 5 | 6 | 7 | 8 | 9 | 10 | Ja |

12.) Wirken sie exklusiv?

Bitte ankreuzen:

| ← | ⊗ | O | O | O | O | O | O | O | O | O | → |
|---|---|---|---|---|---|---|---|---|---|---|---|
| Nein | 1 | 2 | 3 | 4 | 5 | 6 | 7 | 8 | 9 | 10 | Ja |

13.) Wirken sie langweilig?

Bitte ankreuzen:

| ← | O | O | O | O | O | O | O | ⊗ | O | O | → |
|---|---|---|---|---|---|---|---|---|---|---|---|
| Nein | 10 | 9 | 8 | 7 | 6 | 5 | 4 | 3 | 2 | 1 | Ja |

14.) Sonstiges?

Nein._____

Bitte ankreuzen:

| ← | O | O | O | O | O | O | O | O | O | O | → |
|---|---|---|---|---|---|---|---|---|---|---|---|
| Nein | 1 | 2 | 3 | 4 | 5 | 6 | 7 | 8 | 9 | 10 | Ja |

15.) Erzeugt das Bildzeichen bei der Zielgruppe positive Geneigtheit?

Bitte ankreuzen:

| ← | O | O | O | O | O | O | O | ⊗ | O | O | → |
|---|---|---|---|---|---|---|---|---|---|---|---|
| Nein | 1 | 2 | 3 | 4 | 5 | 6 | 7 | 8 | 9 | 10 | Ja |

Kommentar:    Der Apfel entspricht mit der rot-gelben Farbe und dem grünen Blatt dem klassischen Stereotyp eines frischen Obstes, der das Wasser im Mund zusammenlaufen läßt und zum Reinbeißen einlädt.

16.) Hat die Farbe der Verpackung Zeichencharakter – wird die Farbe der Verpackung nach dem symbolischen Verfahren als Zeichen für das Produkt in der Verpackung interpretiert?

Bitte ankreuzen:

← O O O O O O O O O ⊗ →
Nein 1  2  3  4  5  6  7  8  9  10  Ja

**Durchschnittsnote: 76 : 13 = 5,8**

### 3.) Die Substantive

1.) Werden Substantive als Reiz- und Schlüsselworte auf der Verpackung eingesetzt?

Bitte ankreuzen:

← O O O O O O O ⊗ O O →
Nein 1  2  3  4  5  6  7  8  9  10  Ja

Kommentar: Das Substantiv "Apfelsaft" wird als zentrales Reiz- und Erkennungswort auf der Front- und Rückseite eingesetzt. Für meinen Geschmack müßte der Begriff origineller gestaltet sein als eine plakative Produktbezeichnung, um die vollen 10 Punkte zu erhalten.

2.) Welche Stilmittel lassen sich feststellen?

<u>keine</u>

Wurden z.B. Neologismen eingesetzt?

Bitte ankreuzen: O  ⊗
                 Ja  Nein

3.)  Ist der Neologismus verständlich?

Bitte ankreuzen:

← O O O O O O O O O O →

Nein 1 2 3 4 5 6 7 8 9 10 Ja

4.)  Bei zusammengesetzten Wortkomplexen: Ist das Zusammenfassen der  Einzelkomponenten sinnvoll?

Bitte ankreuzen:

← O O O O O O O O O O →

Nein 1 2 3 4 5 6 7 8 9 10 Ja

5.)  Wird eine verkaufsfördernde Wirkung erzielt - sprechen die
Substantive stilistisch  die Zielgruppe an?

a)  jugendlich?

Bitte ankreuzen:

← O O O O O O O O O O →

Nein 1 2 3 4 5 6 7 8 9 10 Ja

b)  innovativ?

Bitte ankreuzen:

← O O O O O O O O O O →

Nein 1 2 3 4 5 6 7 8 9 10 Ja

c)  originell?

Bitte ankreuzen:

← O O O O O O O O O O →

Nein 1 2 3 4 5 6 7 8 9 10 Ja

d)    seriös?

Bitte ankreuzen:

← O O O O O O O O O O →
Nein 1  2  3  4  5  6  7  8  9  10  Ja

Kommentar:    Das Wort "Apfelsaft" ist stilistisch gesehen neutral.
Es soll ebenso wie das Produkt alle Konsumenten ansprechen. Aus
diesem Grund habe ich hier keine Punkte für spezielle Eigenschaften
vergeben.

e)    Sonstiges?
      Nein

Bitte ankreuzen:

← O O O O O O O O O O →
Nein 1  2  3  4  5  6  7  8  9  10  Ja

6.)   Sind die Substantive verständlich bzw. leicht zu interpretieren?
Bitte ankreuzen:

← O O O O O O O O O ⊗ →
Nein 1  2  3  4  5  6  7  8  9  10  Ja

Kommentar:    Das Wort "Apfelsaft" ist ein gebräuchliches Wort
der deutschen Sprache. Es ist eindeutig verständlich und ohne Probleme nach dem regelbasierten Verfahren zu interpretieren. Durch
die hohe Frequenz des Wortes *Apfelsaft* ist davon auszugehen, daß
das Wort reflexartig interpretiert werden kann.

7.)   Sind die Substantive im Sinne der Wirkungsintentionen gelun-
      gen    umgesetzt?    (z.B.    Akzentuierung,    Innovation,
      Leistungssteigerung, Attraktion, Qualität etc.)
Bitte ankreuzen:

← ⊗ O O O O O O O O O →
Nein 1  2  3  4  5  6  7  8  9  10  Ja

Kommentar: Das Substantiv wirkt rein erläuternd. Es wird kein Akzent gesetzt bzw. es läßt sich keine weitere Wirkungsintention erkennen.

8.) Sind die zentralen Substantive leicht erkennbar und merkbar?
Bitte ankreuzen:

← O O O O ⊗ O O O O O →
Nein 1   2   3   4   5   6   7   8   9   10   Ja

Kommentar: Das Substantiv "Apfelsaft" ist zwar leicht erkennbar, aber aufgrund des neutralen bzw. allgemeinen Charakters nicht besonders gut merkbar.

9.) Werden Bedürfnisse/Motivationen mit diesen Begriffen gereizt?
Bitte ankreuzen:

← O O O O ⊗ O O O O O →
Nein 1   2   3   4   5   6   7   8   9   10   Ja

Kommentar: Das Zusammenspiel zwischen dem Substantiv "Apfelsaft" und dem Bild ist zwar ansprechend, aber nicht besonders motivierend bzw. triebreizend, da es dem Stereotyp einer Apfelsaftverpackung entspricht und dementsprechend vertraut ist.

Neben dem Substantiv *Apfelsaft* befinden sich noch die Substantive *Apfelsaftkonzentrat* und *Fruchtsaftgehalt* auf der Verpackung. Beide dienen der Erläuterung von Eigenschaften des Apfelsaftes. Aber auch mit diesen Substantiven sind schlichte beschreibende Vertreter dieser Kategorie gewählt, die nicht aufwendig präsentiert werden. Inhaltlich verwundert es, daß der Begriff "Apfelsaftkonzentrat" unterstrichen und damit als positiv hervorgehoben präsentiert wird. Die Regeln des Gebrauchseinsatzes sind für Durchschnittsverbraucher nicht eindeutig bekannt. Für den Verbraucher sind die Angaben *Apfelsaft* und

*100%* maßgeblich zur Produktinterpretation. Daher werden die beiden anderen Substantive hier nur kurz vorgestellt.

**Durchschnittsnote: 29 : 5 =     5,8**

**4.)   Die Namen**

1.)   Welcher Kategorie der Namen läßt sich der Produktname zuordnen?

**b)     assoziative Namen**

⊗   (Ja)                    O    (Nein - weiter mit c)

1.)   Ist der Name produktadäquat ausgewählt?

Bitte ankreuzen:

←   O   O   O   O   ⊗   O   O   O   O   O   →

Nein 1   2   3   4   5   6   7   8   9   10   Ja

Kommentar:     Der Name "vitafit" bezieht sich auf ein Produkterlebnis, das nicht zu den grundsätzlichen Charakteristika des Produktes gehört. Man könnte diesen Namen auch allen möglichen anderen Produkten zuordnen.

2.)   Ist das assoziative Interpretationsverfahren einfach und schnell durchzuführen?

Bitte ankreuzen:

←   O   O   O   O   ⊗   O   O   O   O   O   →

Nein 1   2   3   4   5   6   7   8   9   10   Ja

Kommentar:     Die Namenskomponente *fit* ist bekannt. *Vita* hingegen muß als die lateinische Version des Wortes *Leben* erkannt und interpretiert werden. Darüber hinaus assoziiert *vita* auch den ersten Teil des Wortes *Vitamine*, sowie des Wortes *Vitalität*. In allen Interpretationen macht die Namenskombination Sinn: fit leben, fit durch Vitamine, vital und fit.

3.) Oft sind bekannte Größen die Grundlage zur Bildung asso-
ziativer Namen („Ajax", „Ariel", „der General" etc.).
Assoziiert diese Größe eine geeignete bzw. produktadäquate
Eigenschaft?

Bitte ankreuzen:

| ← | O | O | O | O | O | O | O | ⊗ | O | O | → |
|---|---|---|---|---|---|---|---|---|---|---|---|
| Nein 1 | 2 | 3 | 4 | 5 | 6 | 7 | 8 | 9 | 10 | Ja |

Kommentar: Zu den bekannen Wortelementen bitte den Kommentar zu Frage 2 lesen. Apfelsaft ist gesund und erfrischend und
wird gerne als isotonisches Sportgetränk konsumiert, um dem Körper
verlorene Mineralien wieder zuzuführen. Der Name assoziiert eine
geeignete Produkteigenschaft.

4.) Wird das Produkt bzw. eine Produkteigenschaft in geeigneter Weise
zur Grundlage der Assoziation des Namens gemacht (z.B. Spüli)?
Bitte ankreuzen:

| ← | O | O | O | O | O | O | O | ⊗ | O | O | → |
|---|---|---|---|---|---|---|---|---|---|---|---|
| Nein 1 | 2 | 3 | 4 | 5 | 6 | 7 | 8 | 9 | 10 | Ja |

Kommentar: Vitalität und Fitness sind keinesfalls Produkteigenschaften von Apfelsaft, aber sie werden glaubwürdig als solche
verkauft.

5.) Gelingt es, den assoziativen Namen als Markennamen bekannt zu machen und damit zum Symbol werden zu lassen?
Bitte ankreuzen:

| ← | O | O | O | ⊗ | O | O | O | O | O | → |
|---|---|---|---|---|---|---|---|---|---|---|
| Nein 1 | 2 | 3 | 4 | 5 | 6 | 7 | 8 | 9 | 10 | Ja |

Kommentar:    Es werden kaum zusätzliche Marketingmaßnahmen betrieben wie TV-Werbung o.ä. Daher ist der Name bislang maximal bei den Stammkunden der Lidl-Kette Markensymbol geworden.

6.)    Ist der assoziative Name leicht zu merken?

Bitte ankreuzen:

← O     O   O   ⊗   O   O   O   O   O   →

Nein 1   2   3   4   5   6   7   8   9   10   Ja

Kommentar:    Prinzipiell ist es nicht schwierig, diesen Namen zu behalten. Das Hauptaugenmerk des Kunden ist jedoch auf die substantivische Produktbeschreibung "Apfelsaft" gerichtet, mittels derer er das Produkt erkennt und kauft. Der Name wird dadurch in den Hintergrund gedrängt.

7.)    Differenziert der assoziative Name das Produkt von anderen Alternativen?

Bitte ankreuzen:

← O   O   O   O   O   O   ⊗   O   O   O   →

Nein 1   2   3   4   5   6   7   8   9   10   Ja

Der Name "vitafit" präsentiert Standardreizworte, die auf vielen anderen Lebensmitteln zu finden sind. In Kombination mit dem Wort *Apfelsaft* differenziert der Name das Produkt kaum noch.

8.)    Ist der assoziative Name originell?

Bitte ankreuzen:

← O   O   O   O   ⊗   O   O   O   O   O   →

Nein 1   2   3   4   5   6   7   8   9   10   Ja

9.)   Spricht der assoziative Name die Zielgruppe an?
Bitte ankreuzen:

← O   O   O   O   O   O   ⊗   O   O   O   →
Nein 1   2   3   4   5   6   7   8   9   10   Ja

**Allgemein zum Namen**

1.)   Welchen Charakter hat der Name:
a)   Wirkt er seriös?
Bitte ankreuzen:

← O   O   O   O   ⊗   O   O   O   O   O   →
Nein 1   2   3   4   5   6   7   8   9   10   Ja

b)   Verleiht er der Verpackung Pepp?
Bitte ankreuzen:

← O   O   O   O   O   O   ⊗   O   O   O   →
Nein 1   2   3   4   5   6   7   8   9   10   Ja

c)   Ist er innovativ?
Bitte ankreuzen:

← O   O   O   O   O   ⊗   O   O   O   O   →
Nein 1   2   3   4   5   6   7   8   9   10   Ja

d)   Ist er ausgefallen?
Bitte ankreuzen:

← O   O   O   O   O   ⊗   O   O   O   O   →
Nein 1   2   3   4   5   6   7   8   9   10   Ja

e)    Ist er exklusiv?

Bitte ankreuzen:

←    O    O    O    O    ⊗    O    O    O    O    O    →

Nein 1    2    3    4    5    6    7    8    9    10    Ja


f)    Ist er langweilig?

Bitte ankreuzen:

←    O    O    O    O    ⊗    O    O    O    O    O    →

Nein 10    9    8    7    6    5    4    3    2    1    Ja


g)    Sonstiges?

Kommentar:Der Name paßt zum Trend Jugendlichkeit und Fitness.

Bitte ankreuzen:

←    O    O    O    O    O    O    O    ⊗    O    O    →

Nein 1    2    3    4    5    6    7    8    9    10    Ja


2.)    Ist es dem Anbieter mit seinen Marketingmaßnahmen gelungen, den Namen produktadäquat bekannt zumachen - gelingt
es den Konsumenten dauerhaft über die Interpretation des
Namens auf das Produkt zu schließen?

Bitte ankreuzen:

←    O    O    O    O    O    O    O    ⊗    O    O    →

Nein 1    2    3    4    5    6    7    8    9    10    Ja

Kommentar:    Der Name "vitafit" ist nicht mit besonderen Marketingmaßnahmen bekannt gemacht worden. Jedoch gelingt es den
Kunden dauerhaft vom Namen auf das Produkt zu schließen, weil die
Produktbeschreibung "Apfelsaft" ins Zentrum des Blickfeldes gerückt wurde.

3.) Ist der Name leicht zu lesen und zu schreiben - (z.B. *Freixenet* ist nicht l eicht zu lesen)?

Bitte ankreuzen:

← O O O O O O O ⊗ O O →
Nein 1    2    3    4    5    6    7    8    9    10    Ja

Kommentar:     Der Name ist ohne Probleme zu lesen. Ungewöhnlich ist jedoch die Kleinschreibung.

4.) Gibt es stilistische Besonderheiten, die die Merkbarkeit erleichtern sollen (z.B. Alliteration)?

Bitte ankreuzen:

← O O O O O ⊗ O O O O →
Nein 1    2    3    4    5    6    7    8    9    10    Ja

Kommentar:     Die Buchstaben "v, f, i, t" sollen eine Klangsymmetrie erzeugen.

5.) Ist der Klang des Namens angenehm?

Bitte ankreuzen:

← O O O O ⊗ O O O O O →
Nein 1    2    3    4    5    6    7    8    9    10    Ja

Kommentar:     Der Klang ist etwas hart, was Sportlichkeit charakterisieren kann.

6.) Mit welchem Aufwand muß der Name eingeführt werden?

Bitte ankreuzen:

← O O O O O ⊗ O O O O →
wenig 10    9    8    7    6    5    4    3    2    1    viel

Kommentar:     Durch die Beschreibung "Apfelsaft" ist lediglich ein durchschnittlicher Aufwand notwendig.

7.)  Vermittelt der Name einen Eindruck der Produktphilosophie?
Bitte ankreuzen:

← O O O O ⊗ O O O O O →
Nein 1  2  3  4  5  6  7  8  9  10  Ja


8.)  Läßt sich mit dem Namen eine Produktfamilie verbinden?
Bitte ankreuzen:

← O O O O O O O O ⊗ O →
Nein 1  2  3  4  5  6  7  8  9  10  Ja
Kommentar:    Der Name wird mit diversen Lidl-Produkten in
Verbindung gebracht.


9.)  Wird der Name als Begriff mit scharfen Rändern interpretiert?
Bitte ankreuzen:

← O O O O O O O O O O →
Nein 1  2  3  4  5  6  7  8  9  10  Ja


10.)  Wird der Name als Begriff mit unscharfen Rändern interpretiert?
Bitte ankreuzen:

← O O O O O O ⊗ O O O →
Nein 10  9  8  7  6  5  4  3  2  1  Ja
Kommentar:    Es wird nicht explizit auf die Besonderheiten des
Produktes hingewiesen, die es von anderen unterscheiden.


11.)  Macht der Name eine Marke?
Bitte ankreuzen:

← O O O O ⊗ O O O O O →
Nein 1  2  3  4  5  6  7  8  9  10  Ja
Kommentar:    Der Name wird zum Markennamen durch die Viel-
zahl der Produkte, die mit ihm gekennzeichnet werden.

12.) Verkörpert der Name

a)  ein positives Firmenimage?

Bitte ankreuzen:

← O O O O O ⊗ O O O O →

Nein 1  2  3  4  5  6  7  8  9  10  Ja

Kommentar:   Hier sind meiner Ansicht nach keine besonderen Bemühungen zu erkennen.

b)  ein positives Produktimage?

Bitte ankreuzen:

← O O O O O O ⊗ O O O →

Nein 1  2  3  4  5  6  7  8  9  10  Ja

Kommentar:   Auch hier fehlen meiner Ansicht nach entsprechende Anstrengungen.

c)  ein positives Konsumentenimage?

Bitte ankreuzen:

← O O O O O O ⊗ O O O →

Nein 1  2  3  4  5  6  7  8  9  10  Ja

Kommentar:   Hier müßten entsprechende Maßnahmen erarbeitet werden.

d)  sind die Aspekte Anbieter, Produkt und Konsument referentiell miteinander verknüpft?

Bitte ankreuzen:

← O O O O O O ⊗ O O O →

Nein 1  2  3  4  5  6  7  8  9  10  Ja

Kommentar:   Es läßt sich dahingehend ein referentieller Zusammenhang interpretieren, als daß die Kombination der assoziativen Namenselemente „vita" – als Hinweis auf Vitamine gedeutet werden kann und „fit" als Hinweis auf „Fitness". In der Kombination wäre die Interpretation „vitafit" – „Vitamine vom Produkt = Fitness für

307

den Konsumenten". Ein expliziter Hinweis wäre hier jedoch empfehlenswert.

**Durchschnittsnote:** 180 : 29 = 6,2

**Die Punkte 5 bis 12 entfallen, da keine weiteren Textelemente vorhanden sind.**

### 13.) Der Gesamteindruck

1.   Wie wirkt der Gesamteindruck der Verpackung?
1.)  stimmig?
Bitte ankreuzen:

← O O O O O O O O O ⊗ →
Nein 1  2  3  4  5  6  7  8  9  10  Ja

2.)  verständlich?
Bitte ankreuzen:

← O O O O O O O O O ⊗ →
Nein 1  2  3  4  5  6  7  8  9  10  Ja

3.)  gut wahrnehmbar?
Bitte ankreuzen:

← O O O O O O O O O ⊗ →
Nein 1  2  3  4  5  6  7  8  9  10  Ja

4.)   praktisch?

Bitte ankreuzen:

| ← | O | O | O | O | ⊗ | O | O | O | O | O | → |
|---|---|---|---|---|---|---|---|---|---|---|---|
| Nein | 1 | 2 | 3 | 4 | 5 | 6 | 7 | 8 | 9 | 10 | Ja |

5.)   originell?

Bitte ankreuzen:

| ← | O | ⊗ | O | O | O | O | O | O | O | O | → |
|---|---|---|---|---|---|---|---|---|---|---|---|
| Nein | 1 | 2 | 3 | 4 | 5 | 6 | 7 | 8 | 9 | 10 | Ja |

6.)   ausgefallen?

Bitte ankreuzen:

| ← | ⊗ | O | O | O | O | O | O | O | O | O | → |
|---|---|---|---|---|---|---|---|---|---|---|---|
| Nein | 1 | 2 | 3 | 4 | 5 | 6 | 7 | 8 | 9 | 10 | Ja |

7.)   pfiffig?

Bitte ankreuzen:

| ← | O | O | O | ⊗ | O | O | O | O | O | O | → |
|---|---|---|---|---|---|---|---|---|---|---|---|
| Nein | 1 | 2 | 3 | 4 | 5 | 6 | 7 | 8 | 9 | 10 | Ja |

8.)   langweilig?

Bitte ankreuzen:

| ← | O | O | O | O | O | O | O | O | O | ⊗ | → |
|---|---|---|---|---|---|---|---|---|---|---|---|
| Nein | 10 | 9 | 8 | 7 | 6 | 5 | 4 | 3 | 2 | 1 | Ja |

9.)   innovativ?

Bitte ankreuzen:

| ← | ⊗ | O | O | O | O | O | O | O | O | O | → |
|---|---|---|---|---|---|---|---|---|---|---|---|
| Nein | 1 | 2 | 3 | 4 | 5 | 6 | 7 | 8 | 9 | 10 | Ja |

10.) seriös

Bitte ankreuzen:

← O O O O O O O O O O →
Nein 1   2   3   4   5   6   7   8   9   10   Ja

11.) zielgruppenadäquat?

Bitte ankreuzen:

← O O O O O O ⊗ O O O →
Nein 1   2   3   4   5   6   7   8   9   10   Ja

12.) produktadäquat?

Bitte ankreuzen:

← O O O O O O ⊗ O O O →
Nein 1   2   3   4   5   6   7   8   9   10   Ja

13.) Verkörpert die Verpackung ein optimales Preis-Leistungsverhältnis?

Bitte ankreuzen:

← O O O O O O O O ⊗ O →
Nein 1   2   3   4   5   6   7   8   9   10   Ja

Kommentar: Der Preis von 1,29 DM für 1,5L Apfelsaft im Tetra-Pak ist sehr gut und liegt im Vergleich weit vorne. Der Satz "Apfelsaft aus Apfelsaftkonzentrat Fruchtgehalt: 100%"verspricht absolute Qualität aufgrund der Reinheit des Apfelsaftes. Tatsächlich jedoch ist bei dieser Angabe nicht abzuschätzen, ob es sich um Saft qualitativ hochwertiger Äpfel handelt, oder vielleicht sogar um Saft von Äpfeln, die chemisch behandelt wurden.

14.) Ist die Verpackung qualitativ hochwertig?

Bitte ankreuzen:

← O O O O ⊗ O O O O O →

Nein 1 2 3 4 5 6 7 8 9 10 Ja

Kommentar: Die Verpackung ist aus dem üblichen Tetra-Pak-Karton hergestellt. Sie wirkt daher weder besonders hoch- noch besonders minderwertig. Sie entspricht dem Durchschnitt.

**Durchschnittsnote: 71 : 13 = 5,5**

- Gruppe 1: 7,1
- Gruppe 2: 5,8
- Gruppe 4: 6,2
- Gruppe 13: 5,5
- **Insgesamt: 24,6 : 46 = 6,2**

**Kommentar:** Die Verpackung ist schlicht, aber technisch praktikabel gestaltet. Durch die einfache Struktur und die gut wahrnehmbaren Elemente ist sie für die Konsumenten leicht zu interpretieren und wiederzuerkennen. Verpackung, Bild, Farbe und Produktbezeichnung bilden eine Einheit, die mittlerweile Symbol für eine stereotype Apfelsaftverpackung geworden ist. Dadurch ist das Produkt "vitafit" nicht optimal von anderen Alternativen zu differenzieren. Es empfiehlt sich, mehr Wert auf eine stärker wirkungsintendierte und akzentuierende Gestaltung zu legen, da die Verpackung insgesamt einen eher gut durchschnittlichen Eindruck macht.[231]

---

[231] Diesem Produkt ist das "Lidl-Stammklientel" sicher, so daß auch ohne weitere Marketingmaßnahmen ein beständiger Markt garantiert ist.

## 4.4 Analyse II: "rio d'oro" Apfelsaft

"Rio d'oro Apfelsaft" ist von der frontseitigen Gestaltung dem "Vitafit"-Apfelsaft ganz ähnlich. Entsprechend der ähnlichen Gestaltung, sind auch die Noten für die ersten Kategorien fast identisch. Aus Platzgründen werden hier nur die Ergebnisse vorgestellt (s. Abbildung 7).

**1.) Technisch orientierte Fragen:**

Hier wurde als Durchschnittsnote eine 6,8 im Gegensatz zur 7,1 von "vitafit" ermittelt. Ausschlaggebend für diese Differenz war das Fehlen einer wiederverschließbaren Ausgießvorrichtung. Zudem fassen die "rio d'oro"-Apfelsaftpakete nur 0,75l, die halbe Menge von "vitafit". Damit sind die Paks zwar erheblich leichter zu transportieren und auch etwas platzsparender im Kühlschrank unterzubringen, aber auch viel zu schnell leer. Im Verhältnis gesehen ist der "rio d'oro" Apfelsaft teurer. [232]

**2.) Bildzeichen**

Zu den Bildzeichen ist zu bemerken, daß auch bei diesem Tetra-Pak als Motiv ein Apfel gewählt wurde, diesmal allerdings vor einem hellgrünen Hintergrund. Im Zentrum des Bildes befindet sich eine Apfelhälfte, die den Kunden den Blick auf das Innere des Apfels frei- und damit das Gefühl geben soll, man habe nichts zu verbergen. Die Apfelhälfte ist zwar auch auf dem "vitafit"-Pak vorhanden, aber nicht im Blickfeld des Betrachters, sondern auf der Seite.

---

210 Die Bewertung setzt sich aus folgenden Einzelnoten zusammen: 1.) 8, 2.) 8, 3.) 8, 4.) 5, 5.)
6, 6.) 6;     $41 : 6 = 6,8$

Insgesamt sind die beiden Bildzeichen auf den Frontseiten nicht besonders ausgefallen. Sie differenzieren die Marke nur durchschnittlich von anderen Alternativen.

Das Bild auf der Rückseite ist vorteilhaft umgesetzt. Die "rio d'oro"-Verpackung befindet sich vor einem im Landhausstil karierten Hintergrund inmitten von Äpfeln, von denen ein Exemplar und eine Apfelhälfte auf der Frontseite zu sehen ist. Das Bild soll den Betrachter zu dem Schluß inspirieren, daß gesunde Äpfel, wie sie neben der Verpackung zu sehen sind, den Rohstoff (Apfelsaft) für den Verpackungsinhalt bieten. Positiv ist der Wiedererkennungs- und damit der Lerneffekt der erneuten Präsentation der Verpackung in Frontansicht.

Aus diesem Grund wurde ein besseres Ergebnis für "rio d'oro" mit 6,0 im Vergleich zu 5,5 für "vitafit" erreicht. Eine ansprechende Gestaltung der Frontseite als Blickfang ist für die Bewertung ausschlaggebend.[233]

### 3.)  Substantive

In der Kategorie der Substantive hat "rio d'oro" ebenfalls besser abgeschnitten. Das Ergebnis wurde positiv beeinflußt durch den zusätzlichen Aufdruck "ohne Zuckerzusatz". Auch "vitafit Apfelsaft" ist ohne Zucker, dennoch wird diese Eigenschaft nicht direkt genannt, sondern nur über die Angabe "Fruchtsaftgehalt 100%" impliziert. Diese Angabe befindet sich ebenfalls auf der "rio d'oro"-Verpackung. Mit dem Hinweis "ohne Zuckerzusatz" wird ein weiterer Schlüsselreiz auf der Verpackung installiert, mit dem zusätzlich ein bestimmtes Klientel angesprochen wird: die Gruppe der ernährungs- und kalorienbewußten Konsumenten. Aus diesem Grund habe

---

[233]    Die Einzelnoten: 1.) 10, 2.) 10, 4.) 10, 5.) 10, 6.) 10, 7.) 8, 8.) 2, 9.) 2, 10.) 2, 11.) 2, 12.) 2, 13.) 3, 15.) 8, 16.) 10  89 : 14 = 6,4

ich die Durchschnittsnote 6,2 für "rio d'oro zu 5,8 für "vitafit" vergeben.[234]

### 4.)  Der Name

Ebenso wie bei dem "vitafit"-Produkt wird kein eigener Produktname
angegeben. Als Erkennungszeichen wird die Produktbezeichnung
"Apfelsaft" und als übergeordneter Markenname "rio d'oro" eingesetzt. "Rio d'oro" ist ein assoziativer Name, der aus dem Italienischen
mit "Fluß des Goldes" übersetzt werden kann. Als entsprechend
wertvoll soll das Getränk interpretiert werden.

Meiner Ansicht nach gelingt diese Assoziation dem Durchschnittskon-
sumenten jedoch nicht auf Anhieb, da es sich beim Spanischen um eine
weniger geläufige Sprache handelt. Aus diesem Grund wurde der Name
"rio d'oro" mit 5,2 deutlich geringer bewertet als "vitafit" mit 6,2.[235]

Die Kategorien 5 bis 10 entfallen, da keine entsprechenden Items auf
der Verpackung vorhanden sind.

### 11.)  Der Text

Auf dem Tetra-Pak sind zwei Texte aufgedruckt, ein rückseitiger
Haupttext und ein Hinweistext auf der Seite. Vornehmlich wird der
Werbetext auf der Rückseite besprochen. Bei Items, die auch auf den
Seitentext zutreffen, werden diese gesondert genannt. Sie werden
jedoch nicht in die Bewertung miteinbezogen, da es sich um einen

---

[234]
    Die Einzelnoten: 1.) 8, 6.) 10, 7.) 3, 8.) 5, 9.) 5;     31 : 5 = 6,2

[235]
    Die Einzelnoten:  1.) 5, 2.) 5, 3.) 8, 4.) 0, 5.) 7, 6.) 5, 7.) 5, 8.) 5, 9.) 5,
    Name allgemein 1a) 5, 1b) 6, 1c) 6, 1d) 6, 1e) 5, 1f) 5 2.) 8, 3.) 6, 4.) 3, 5.)
    6, 6.) 6, 7.) 5, 8.) 5, 9.) 9, 10.) 5, 11.) 5, 12.) 5, 13.a) 5, 13.b) 5, 13.c) 3,
    13.d) 1; 155 : 30 = 5,2

allgemeinen informativen Text zum grünen Punkt handelt, der nicht als direktes Item der Verpackung gewertet werden darf.

1.) Ist der Text gut wahrnehmbar

a) Typographie

Bitte ankreuzen:

← O O O O O O ⊗ O O O →

Nein 1  2  3  4  5  6  7  8  9  10  Ja

Kommentar : Die Schrift dürfte etwas größer sein.

b) Farben

Bitte ankreuzen:

← O O O O O O O O ⊗ O →

Nein 1  2  3  4  5  6  7  8  9  10  Ja

Kommentar: Die Farben sind ähnlich einem Früchtekorb im Landhausstil aufeinander abgestimmt.

2.) Wirkt der Text einladend?

Bitte ankreuzen:

← O O O O O O O O ⊗ O →

Nein 1  2  3  4  5  6  7  8  9  10  Ja

Kommentar: Die Überschrift "Die schönsten Äpfel sind vierek-kig" macht neugierig. Einerseits ist der Wortlaut aus der „Milka"-Reklame "Die schönsten Pausen sind lila" schon bekannt, andererseits wird ein spannender Einstieg durch eine unmögliche Aussage provoziert.

Die Überschrift "Recycling lebt vom Mitmachen" wirkt schon alleine als Aufruf und lädt daher nicht zum Lesen des nachfolgenden Textes ein.

3.)   Ist der Text leicht und flüssig lesbar?

Bitte ankreuzen:

← O O O O O O ⊗ O O O →

Nein 1   2   3   4   5   6   7   8   9   10   Ja

Kommentar:   Die langen Sätze und die Gedankenstriche dürften noch im Hinblick auf ein leichteres Verständnis bearbeitet werden.

4.)   Ist der Text verständlich?

Bitte ankreuzen:

← O O O O ⊗ O O O O O →

Nein 1   2   3   4   5   6   7   8   9   10   Ja

Kommentar :   Der Text ist zwar lustig aufgemacht, aber nicht unbedingt auf Anhieb bei einem ersten Überfliegen zu verstehen. Es stellt sich die Frage, wieso die Äpfel im Dreieck springen, weshalb ein Tetra-Pak verpackungstechnisch eine runde Sache ist, was den Tetra-Pak vitaminschonend macht u.ä.. Erst bei genauerem Hinsehen wird deutlich, daß der Text nicht der Produktbeschreibung dient, sondern eine Werbung für Tetra-Paks ist. Der zweite Text ist leicht verständlich.

5.)   Wirkt der Text schlüssig?

Bitte ankreuzen:

← O O O O ⊗ O O O O O →

Nein 1   2   3   4   5   6   7   8   9   10   Ja

Kommentar:   Bei genauer Betrachtung läßt sich der Text als schlüssig nachvollziehen.

6.)   Ist der Text originell?

Bitte ankreuzen:

← O O O O O O O O ⊗ O →

Nein 1   2   3   4   5   6   7   8   9   10   Ja

Kommentar:    Der Text erfüllt das Kriterium der Originalität sehr gut und differenziert dadurch das Produkt eindeutig von Alternativen. Der zweite Text ist rein informativer Natur, daher wird das Kriterium der Originalität hier bei der Gestaltung nicht berücksichtigt.

7.)    Wirkt der Text glaubwürdig?

Bitte ankreuzen:

← O O ⊗ O O O O O O O →
Nein 1    2    3    4    5    6    7    8    9    10    Ja

Kommentar:    Es ist nicht glaubwürdig, wenn Äpfel personifiziert werden und sie sich angeblich freuen, daß ihr Saft in den Tetra-Pak kommt.

Für Text zwei in Form eines Hinweises auf der Seite ist das Item "Glaubwürdigkeit" eine heikle Angelegenheit. Als Entsorgungshinweis sollte das Kriterium "Glaubwürdigkeit" selbstverständlich sein. Durch den gesellschaftlichen Streit über Sinn und Unsinn des grünen Punktes hat der grüne Punkt allgemein an Glaubwürdigkeit verloren.

8.)    Wirkt der Text überredend?

Bitte ankreuzen:

← O O O O O ⊗ O O O O →
Nein 10    9    8    7    6    5    4    3    2    1    Ja

Kommentar:    Es werden Eigenschaften und Kriterien genannt, die weiter erläuternd ausgeführt werden sollten, z.B. was macht den Tetra-Pak recyclebar oder wieso ist er vitaminschonend?

9.)    Werden überzeugende Argumente eingesetzt?

Bitte ankreuzen:

← O O O O O ⊗ O O O O →
Nein 1    2    3    4    5    6    7    8    9    10    Ja

317

Kommentar:     Es werden Argumente in Form von Reizworten wie "Vitaminschonend" und "recyclebar" eingesetzt. Auch der Mehrwert für die Kunden wird genannt. Dabei handelt es sich um eine teleologische Argumentationsform. Mit Hinter-grundinformationen könnte die Überzeugungskraft gesteigert werden.

10.)  Handelt es sich um Pseudoargumente?

Bitte ankreuzen:

← O O O O O ⊗ O O O O →

Nein 10  9  8  7  6  5  4  3  2  1  Ja

Kommentar:     Teilweise handelt es sich um Pseudoargumente, z.B. bei den scheinbar erfreuten Äpfeln und den kraftvoll zugreifenden Konsumenten.

11.)  Ist der Text sprachlich zielgruppenadäquat?

Bitte ankreuzen:

← O O O O O O O O ⊗ O →

Nein 1  2  3  4  5  6  7  8  9  10  Ja

Kommentar:     Die textuelle Gestaltung ist insofern relativ zielgruppenadäquat, als die blickfangende Frontseite absolut seriös und zielgruppenneutral gestaltet ist. Die Idee, mit dem rückseitigen ausgefallenen Text, insbesondere junge Leute als Zielgruppe anzusprechen, aber auch alle anderen potentiellen Kunden, muß mit einem sehr guten Ergebnis belohnt werden.

12.)  Ist der Text stilistisch ansprechend?

Bitte ankreuzen:

← O O O O O O O ⊗ O O →

Nein 1  2  3  4  5  6  7  8  9  10  Ja

Kommentar:     Stilistisch ist der Text insofern ansprechend, als er in einem lockeren Umgangston gestaltet wurde. Zu einer Wirkungssteigerung hätten jedoch weitere Stilelemente eingearbeitet werden können.

13.) Hier ist Platz für die jeweils individuelle Bewertung der sprachlichen Gestaltung der Worte im Text. Um Vergleichbarkeit auch bei verschiedenen Anwendern zu gewährleisten, werden hier die Kategorien von vier Wortklassen bereitgestellt, die jeweils in Bezug auf zwei Eigenschaften mit Punkten von 1-10 bewertet werden können, aber nicht müssen.[236]

Ich möchte für dieses Beispiel die Wortklasse der Adjektive unter Berücksichtigung der Adverbien an dieser Stelle bewerten, da diese Wortklasse im Gegensatz zu allen anderen Kategorien strategisch wirkungsintendiert eingearbeitet wurde.
Die Adjektive und Adverbien werden beschreibend, ergänzend und wertsteigernd eingesetzt. Dabei fehlt ihnen aber jegliche Innovation. Aus diesem Grund bewerte ich die Wortklasse wie folgt:

14.) Wertsteigerung:

← O   O   O   O   O   O   O   ⊗   O   O   →
Nein 1   2   3   4   5   6   7   8   9   10   Ja
Kommentar:   Besonders die Adjektive und Adverbien *vitaminschonend, recyclebar, prima, bruchsicher, gesund, kraftvoll, richtig, praktisch*, nützlich tragen zu einer Wertsteigerung bei. Jedoch könnte diese Wortklasse z.B. durch entsprechende Steigerungsformen noch wirkungsvoller in Szene gesetzt werden.

---

[236] Die Textgestaltung ist dermaßen vielfältig, daß hier die Interessen des Anwenders die Bewertung bestimmen soll.

15.) Innovation:

← O ⊗ O O O O O O O O →

Nein 1   2   3   4   5   6   7   8   9   10   Ja

Kommentar:     Etwas ungewöhnlich ist das umgangssprachliche Wort "prima" zur Beschreibung der Stapelbarkeit. Ansonsten ist mehr Innovation beim Einsatz der Worte insgesamt gefragt.

16.) Wird der Fokus der Rezipienten
      a)     auf den Text gelenkt?

Bitte ankreuzen:

← O O O O ⊗ O O O O O →

Nein 1   2   3   4   5   6   7   8   9   10   Ja

Kommentar:     Zwar macht die Überschrift neugierig, jedoch werden auf der Frontseite keine Maßnahmen installiert, die auf den rückseitigen Text verweisen.

      b)     durch den Text gelenkt?

Bitte ankreuzen:

← O O O O ⊗ O O O O O →

Nein 1   2   3   4   5   6   7   8   9   10   Ja

Kommentar:     Der Fokus der Kunden wird nicht besonders engagiert durch den Text gelenkt, denn Überschrift und Text sind durch ein Bildzeichen getrennt, so daß viele Leser schon nach der Betrachtung des Bildzeichens den Blick wieder abwenden, auch wenn die Überschrift neugierig macht und somit auf den Text verweist.

17.) Macht der Text "Lust" auf das Produkt?

Bitte ankreuzen:

← O O O O O O ⊗ O O O →

Nein 1 2 3 4 5 6 7 8 9 10 Ja

Kommentar: Durch die spritzigen Formulierungen wird Lust auf den Text gemacht.

18.) Werden neben dem Produkt noch ein oder mehrere ideelle Werte versprochen?

Bitte ankreuzen:

← O O O O O ⊗ O O O O →

Nein 1 2 3 4 5 6 7 8 9 10 Ja

Kommentar: Indirekt wird mit dem Adjektiv *recyclebar* der soziale Mehrwert "Umweltverträglichkeit" versprochen.

19.) Ist der Text passend in das gesamte Verpackungskonzept integriert?

Bitte ankreuzen:

← O O O O O ⊗ O O O O →

Nein 1 2 3 4 5 6 7 8 9 10 Ja

Kommentar: Der Text könnte fließender in das Gesamtkonzept eingearbeitet werden, dann würde auch der Fokus der Konsumenten stärker durch den Text gelenkt.

**Durchschnittsnote: 126 : 20 = 6,3**

**12.) Der Inhalt des Textes**

1.) Ist der Inhalt produktadäquat?

Bitte ankreuzen:

← O O O O O ⊗ O O O O →

Nein 1 2 3 4 5 6 7 8 9 10 Ja

Kommentar:    Es könnten noch mehr produktadäquate Eigenschaften explizit beschrieben werden.

2.)    Ist der Inhalt kundenbezogen?
       (Werden die Kunden z.B. direkt angesprochen u.ä.?)
Bitte ankreuzen:

← O   O   O   O   O   ⊗   O   O   O   O   →
Nein 1   2   3   4   5   6   7   8   9   10   Ja

Kommentar:    Der Kunde wird zwar direkt angesprochen, aber nur
in bezug auf das Zugreifen, nicht auf den expliziten individuellen
Mehrwert.

3.)    Ist der Inhalt anbieterbezogen?
Bitte ankreuzen:

← O   O   O   ⊗   O   O   O   O   O   O   →
Nein 1   2   3   4   5   6   7   8   9   10   Ja

Kommentar:    Der Text ist anbieterbezogen, allerdings hauptsächlich in bezug auf den Anbieter der Tetra Paks und weniger auf die
Produktanbieter.

4.)    Werden zu diesen drei Aspekten inhaltlich ergänzende Aspekte
vorgestellt?
Bitte ankreuzen:

← O   O   O   O   O   O   O   O   ⊗   O   →
Nein 1   2   3   4   5   6   7   8   9   10   Ja

Kommentar:    Die Verpackung und das System "Der Grüne Punkt"
werden deutlich in den Vordergrund gerückt.

5.) Wird ein umfassendes Konzept zu einer Firmen- und damit auch zu einer Produktphilosophie präsentiert?

Bitte ankreuzen:

← ⊗ O O O O O O O O O →

Nein 1 2 3 4 5 6 7 8 9 10 Ja

Kommentar: Es wird weder eine "rio d'oro"-Produkt- noch Firmenphilosophie vorgestellt, sondern die Tetra-Pak-Philosophie.


6.) Wird das Produkt sympathisch gemacht?

Bitte ankreuzen:

← O O O O O O O O ⊗ O →

Nein 1 2 3 4 5 6 7 8 9 10 Ja

Kommentar: Durch den witzigen und umgangsprachlichen Text auf der Rückseite wird zunächst die Verpackung sympathisch gemacht. Die Verpackung wird als zusätzliche Produktqualität vorgestellt, die ein qualitativ hochwertiges Produkt hochwertig umhüllt.


7.) Werden im Rahmen der Produktphilosophie positive Werte der Zielgruppe vorgestellt?

Bitte ankreuzen:

← O O ⊗ O O O O O O O →

Nein 1 2 3 4 5 6 7 8 9 10 Ja

Kommentar: Es werden nur indirekt Werte der Zielgruppe vorgestellt, wie z.B. "gesund", "praktisch", "vitaminschonend", "recyclebar", "natürlich bruchsicher" und "kraftvoll".

8.) Gelingt es, diese positiven Werte als Produkteigenschaften glaubhaft zu machen?

Bitte ankreuzen:

← O O O O ⊗ O O O O O →
Nein 1 2 3 4 5 6 7 8 9 10 Ja

Kommentar: Die Produkteigenschaften könnten über erläuternde Hintergrundinformationen stärker glaubhaft vorgestellt werden.


9.) Ist der Anbieter mit einem positiven Image behaftet?

Bitte ankreuzen:

← O O O O O O ⊗ O O O →
Nein 1 2 3 4 5 6 7 8 9 10 Ja

Kommentar: Der Text läßt insofern einen positiven Eindruck bezüglich des
Firmenimages zu, als daß die Anbieter sich bemüht geben, ein hochwertiges Produkt in einer umweltschonenden Verpackung anzubieten.


10.) Ist das Produkt mit einem positiven Image behaftet?

Bitte ankreuzen:

← O O O O ⊗ O O O O O →
Nein 1 2 3 4 5 6 7 8 9 10 Ja

Kommentar: Es werden keine expliziten Maßnahmen auf der Verpackung installiert, um das Produkt mit einem positiven Image auszustatten. Die Verpackung als Teil des Produktes wird jedoch mit einem überaus positiven Image ausgestattet. Hier sollte noch mehr Augenmerk auf das Produkt gelegt werden.

11.) Wird die Zielgruppe über die Verpackung mit einem positiven Image behaftet?

Bitte ankreuzen:

← O O O O O O ⊗ O O O →
Nein 1 2 3 4 5 6 7 8 9 10 Ja

Kommentar:     Dem Kunde wird durch das Wort "recyclebar" indirekt ein umweltschützendes Image zugesprochen.

12.) Wird die Verpackung mit Sympathieträgern ausgestattet?

Bitte ankreuzen:

← O O O O O O O O O O →
Nein 1 2 3 4 5 6 7 8 9 10 Ja

Kommentar:     Die Verpackung ist mit keinem Sympathieträger ausgestattet.

13.) Trägt das Firmenimage zum Verkaufserfolg bei?

Bitte ankreuzen:

← O O O ⊗ O O O O O O →
Nein 1 2 3 4 5 6 7 8 9 10 Ja

Kommentar:     Es wird kein explizites Image aufgebaut, das zum Verkaufserfolg beiträgt. Durch die intensive Tetra-Pak-Werbung wird jedoch die Verpackung mit einem positiven Image ausgestattet, das zum Verkaufserfolg beiträgt.

14.) Appelliert die Verpackung:

    a)     an das Gewissen?

Bitte ankreuzen:

← O O O O O ⊗ O O O O →
Nein 1 2 3 4 5 6 7 8 9 10 Ja

Kommentar:     Das Wort "recyclebar" sowie der seitwandige Hinweis appellieren an das Gewissen bezüglich des Umweltschutzes.

b)    an den Mutter-/Vaterinstinkt?

Bitte ankreuzen:

←⊗ O    O    O    O    O    O    O    O    O    O    →
Nein 1    2    3    4    5    6    7    8    9    10    Ja

15.)  Verspricht die Verpackung:

a)    soziale Anerkennung

Bitte ankreuzen:

←    O    O    O    O    O    ⊗    O    O    O    O    →
Nein 1    2    3    4    5    6    7    8    9    10    Ja

Kommentar:    Soziale Anerkennung wird durch den Faktor Umweltschutz unterschwellig suggeriert. Dieser Aspekt sollte deutlicher
herausgearbeitet werden.


b)    Bedürfnis-/Triebbefriedigung

Bitte ankreuzen:

←    ⊗    O    O    O    O    O    O    O    O    O    →
Nein 1    2    3    4    5    6    7    8    9    10    Ja

Kommentar:    Der Ausdruck "Damit Sie auch morgen noch kraftvoll zugreifen können" kann dahingehend interpretiert werden, daß
das Grundbedürfnis der körperlichen Erhaltung mit dem Produkt
befriedigt werden kann.

c)    einen Mehrwert?

Bitte ankreuzen:

←    O    ⊗    O    O    O    O    O    O    O    O    →
Nein 1    2    3    4    5    6    7    8    9    10    Ja

Kommentar:    Es wird lediglich der Faktor "Umweltschutz" auf
der Verpackung installiert.

d)    Sonstiges?

Nein_____

16.)    Wird die Verpackung mit einer Kampagne ausgestattet, die
        zum Verkaufserfolg beiträgt?

Bitte ankreuzen:

← O  O  O  O  ⊗  O  O  O  O  O  →

Nein 1    2    3    4    5    6    7    8    9    10    Ja

Die "Tetra-Pak"-Kampagne locktert die Verpackung etwas auf und
verleiht ihr etwas Witz und „Pepp". Sie trägt jedoch insofern nicht
besonders zum Verkaufserfolg bei, da die Kunden einerseits im Laden die Kampagne auf der Rückseite nicht sehen und somit bei der
Kaufentscheidung nicht berücksichtigen und andererseits die „Aldi"-
Marken von einem relativ festen Klientel konsumiert werden.

**Durchschnittsnote: 86 : 18 = 4,7**

Kommentar: Der witzige Text ist eine gute Werbekampagne für die
Tetra-Paks. Jedoch wäre es empfehlenswert, die spezifischen Vorzüge des Produktes ebenfalls den Kunden explizit vorzustellen und
somit das Produkt stärker auf dem Markt zu differenzieren.

**13.) Der Gesamteindruck**

Wie wirkt der Gesamteindruck der Verpackung?

1.) stimmig?

Bitte ankreuzen:

← O O O O O O O O O ⊗ →

Nein 1 2 3 4 5 6 7 8 9 10 Ja

Kommentar: Die Farben der Verpackung sind gut aufeinander abgestimmt. Zu einem stimmigen Verpackungskonzept trägt auch die Graphik auf der Rückseite bei, die die komplette Verpackung im Kontext einer Vielzahl von Äpfeln darstellt, von denen einer auf der Frontseite zu sehen ist.

2.) verständlich?

Bitte ankreuzen:

← O O O O O O O ⊗ O O →

Nein 1 2 3 4 5 6 7 8 9 10 Ja

Kommentar: Der Text könnte in bezug auf das Verständnis noch verbessert werden.

3.) gut wahrnehmbar?

Bitte ankreuzen:

← O O O O O O O O O ⊗ →

Nein 1 2 3 4 5 6 7 8 9 10 Ja

Kommentar: Die Verpackung ist gut wahrnehmbar und es ist leicht zu erkennen, was sich darin befindet.

4.) praktisch?

Bitte ankreuzen:

← O O ⊗ O O O O O O O →

Nein 1 2 3 4 5 6 7 8 9 10 Ja

Kommentar: Die Verpackung ist aufgrund der kleineren Portion und der fehlenden Ausgießvorrichtung weniger praktisch als "vitafit".

5.) originell?

Bitte ankreuzen:

← O O O ⊗ O O O O O O →

Nein 1 2 3 4 5 6 7 8 9 10 Ja

Kommentar: Der Text auf der Rückseite steigert den Faktor "Originalität", wenn auch der Text nur indirekt auf das Produkt eingegangen wird.

6.) ausgefallen?

Bitte ankreuzen:

← O O O O ⊗ O O O O O →

Nein 1 2 3 4 5 6 7 8 9 10 Ja

siehe Kommentar zu 5.))

7.) pfiffig?

Bitte ankreuzen:

← O O ⊗ O O O O O O O →

Nein 1 2 3 4 5 6 7 8 9 10 Ja

Kommentar: Die Verpackung ist unterdurchschnittlich pfiffig gestaltet, was auch der rückseitige Text nicht auffangen kann.

8.) langweilig?

Bitte ankreuzen:

← O O O O ⊗ O O O O O →

Nein 10 9 8 7 6 5 4 3 2 1 Ja

Kommentar: Die Verpackung an sich ist langweilig. Sie wird durch den rückseitigen Text aufgepeppt.

9.) innovativ?

Bitte ankreuzen:

← O O ⊗ O O O O O O O →

Nein 1   2   3   4   5   6   7   8   9   10   Ja

Kommentar:     Die Wahl eines umgangssprachlichen Stils ist innovativ. Empfehlenswert sind weitere innovative Elemente zur
stärkeren Differenzierung von den Konkurrenzprodukten.

10.) seriös?

Bitte ankreuzen:

← O O O O O ⊗ O O O O →

Nein 1   2   3   4   5   6   7   8   9   10   Ja

11.) zielgruppenadäquat?

Bitte ankreuzen:

← O ⊗ O O O O O O O O →

Nein 1   2   3   4   5   6   7   8   9   10   Ja

Kommentar:     Das Produkt wird nicht speziell für eine besondere
Zielgruppe vorgestellt. Dementsprechend wird nur indirekt auf die
Bedürfnisse der Zielgruppe eingegangen. Hier besteht noch Bedarf.

12.) produktadäquat?

Bitte ankreuzen:

← O O ⊗ O O O O O O O →

Nein 1   2   3   4   5   6   7   8   9   10   Ja

Kommentar:     Besondere Produktleistungen werden nicht explizit
hervorgehoben.

13.) optimal im Preis-Leistungsverhältnis?

Bitte ankreuzen:

← O O O O O O O ⊗ O O →
Nein 1    2    3    4    5    6    7    8    9   10   Ja

Kommentar:     Das Preis-Leistungsverhältnis ist im Vergleich attraktiv.[237]

14.) qualitativ hochwertig?

Bitte ankreuzen:

← O O O O ⊗ O O O O O →
Nein 1    2    3    4    5    6    7    8    9   10   Ja

Kommentar:     Die Qualitätsmerkmale wie „100%iger Fruchtgehalt" oder die Vorzüge der Verpackung sollten stärker in den Vordergrund gerückt werden.

**Durchschnittsnote: 76 : 14 = 5,4**

- Gruppe 1:     6,8          Gruppe12: 4,7
- Gruppe 2:     6,4          Gruppe 13:5,4
- Gruppe 3:     6,2          Insgesamt: 41 : 7 = 5,9
- Gruppe 4:     5,2
- Gruppe 11:  6,3

**Kommentar:**    Dieses Ergebnis zeigt, was auch der Blick auf die Frontseiten beweist: die Verpackungen sind sich auf dem ersten Blick sehr ähnlich. Ein schlechteres Abschneiden der Praktikabili-

---

[237]    Im Vergleich zu anderen Anbietern ist der Preis von 0,99.- Mark pro Pak attraktiv.

tät[238] der 0,75L-Verpackung wird durch das gute Ergebnis im Faktor „Originalität" des rückseitigen Textes der „rio d'oro"-Verpackung ausgeglichen. Der Text ist zwar originell und ausgefallen, aber nicht optimal wirkungseffektiv umgesetzt, und vor allem wird das Beziehungsdreieck "Produkt-Kunde-Anbieter" nicht berücksichtigt. Die spezifischen Produkteigenschaften werden nicht explizit herausgearbeitet und die Argumentation bleibt an der Oberfläche. Auch diese Verpackung bleibt bei der Bewertung guter Durchschnitt.[239] Hier zeigt sich: mehr (Verpackungsaufdruck) ist nicht unbedingt mehr (Attraktivität).

---

[238] Es stellt sich für mich bei dieser Analyse heraus, daß 1,5 Liter Tetra-Paks nicht praktisch sind, weil sie in der Einkaufstasche schwer sind und nicht in die Kühlschranktür passen. Für den größeren Konsum sind 0,75 Liter Paks allerdings ebenfalls ungeeignet, da sie zu schnell aufgebraucht sind. Ideal sind 1 Liter Paks.

[239] Ebenso wie bei der Lidl-Verpackung, ist diesem Produkt das "Aldi-Stammklientel" sicher, so daß auch ohne weitere Marketingmaßnahmen ein beständiger Markt garantiert ist.

332

## 4.5 Analyse III: "beckers bester" Apfelsaft

Als drittes Beispiel habe ich eine "beckers bester"-Apfelsaftflasche ausgewählt, weil diese überdurchschnittlich aufwendig gestaltet wurde, insbesondere was das textuelle Design betrifft (s. Abbildung 8).

**1.) Technisch orientierte Fragen**

Zu den technisch orientierten Fragen läßt sich festhalten, daß die Verpackung in einer Glasflasche eine Reihe Vorteile bietet, aber auch einen Nachteil.

Eine Flasche schützt das Produkt und auch die Umwelt grundsätzlich sehr gut. Die einzige Schwachstelle ist der Verschluß. Durch die Ausstattung des Verschlusses mit einem Plastikring als Plombe, ist dieser Schwachpunkt bis zum ersten Gebrauch ziemlich sicher. Glasflaschen mit einem Liter Fassungsvermögen sind relativ schlecht zu transportieren. Sie sind schwer, unflexibel und es besteht die Gefahr, daß sie bei stärkeren Stößen zerbrechen. Die Lagerung hingegen macht wenig Schwierigkeiten. Die Flasche paßt gut in die Standardkühlschranktür. Sie ist wiederverschließbar. Die Portionierung von einem Liter bietet sich für ein Kühlschrankgetränk an, das nicht Gefahr läuft, durch Kohlensäureverlust schnell schal zu werden. Die Verpackung ist auf nichts anderes als auf ihren spezifischen Nutzeneinsatz hin ausgerichtet. Plastikflaschen bieten den Vorteil, beim Transport leichter zu sein und nicht so leicht kaputtzugehen. Die Verpackung nimmt eine Menge Platz ein und ist aufgrund des etwas schwierigeren Transportes nicht optimal praktisch. Insgesamt habe ich als Note für diese Kategorie eine 7,8 vergeben.[240]

---

[240] Diese Bewertung setzt sich aus folgenden Einzelnoten zusammen: 1.) 9, 2.) 5, 3.) 8, 4.) 9, 5.) 9, 6.) 7; 47 : 6 = 7,8

## 2.) Bildzeichen

Auf den Etiketten sind mehrere Bildzeichen abgedruckt. Zentral ist das Bildzeichen auf dem frontseitigen Hauptetikett. Es handelt sich dabei um die Kombination eines Ikons, das assoziativ und symbolisch interpretiert wird. Der Apfel wird symbolisch und der Tropfen dem Apfel assoziativ interpretiert. Empfehlenswert ist, einen größeren Ausschnitt des Apfels zu zeigen, damit dieser leichter erkannt werden kann. Alle anderen Abbildungen bilden entweder stilisiert ein reales Objekt ab (Haus auf dem Flaschenhalsetikett, Baum auf der Rückseite) oder es handelt sich um ein bereits gelerntes Symbol (das Umweltzeichen). Bis auf das Tropfen-Apfelbildzeichen sind alle Bilder sehr gut in das Verpackungskonzept integriert. Erstgenanntes Bild dürfte noch ansprechender in die Gesamtgestaltung eingearbeitet werden.

Die Bildzeichen dürften insgesamt noch wirkungsvoller gestaltet werden.

Ein großer Vorzug ist die Tatsache, daß die beckers bester Glasflaschen durchsichtig sind und den Blick freigeben auf die Originalfarbe des Apfelsaftes. Die Farbe kann auf diesem Wege optimal als Symbol für das Produkt wirken.

Daher vergebe ich hier die Gesamtnote 6,7.[241]

---

[241] Diese Bewertung setzt sich aus folgenden Einzelnoten zusammen: 1.) 7, 2.) 7, 3.) 5, 5.) 8, 6.) 7, 7.) 8, 8.) 6, 9.) 6, 10) 6, 11.) 6, 12.) 6, 13.) 6, 15.) 6; 16.) 10; 94 : 14 = 6,7

### 3.) Die Substantive

Frontseitig sind folgende Substantive zu bewerten: *Qualität, Qualitätsgarantie, Stiftung Warentest, Extraqualität, ohne Zuckerzusatz, Fruchtgehalt, Apfelsaft, Apfelsaftkonzentrat, Mehrweg* und die Unterschrift *Becker*.

Alle diese Substantive sind entweder allein oder nur in einem ganz kurzen Textfragment eingesetzt. Sie alle haben Schlüsselreizfunktion. Dabei ist festzuhalten, daß die Schlüsselreize inhaltlich sehr vielschichtig angelegt sind. Mit "Stiftung Warentest" wird ein übergeordnetes Beurteilungsmedium angegeben, das gesellschaftlich anerkannt ist.

Ebenso verhält es sich mit dem Hinweis "Umweltzeichen weil Mehrwegflasche". Dieses Textfragment ist auf das Kürzestmögliche reduziert, um den Kausalzusammenhang auszudrücken. Dabei wird die Gewichtung der beiden Substantive verstärkt.

Zu den Substantiven, die das Produkt selbst betreffen, ist zu bemerken, daß die textuelle Basis dieselbe ist wie auf den beiden besprochenen Tetra-Paks: "Apfelsaft aus Apfelsaftkonzentrat", "Fruchtgehalt 100% ohne Zuckerzusatz". Diese Substantive sind auch typographisch mit roter Farbe in Szene gesetzt. Darüber hinaus wird ihre Wirkung durch den Einsatz weiterer Substantive mit Schlüsselreizfunktion ergänzt. Das Substantiv *Apfelsaft* wird überschrieben mit "Extraqualität", was der Kunde als Exklusivität der Ware interpretieren soll. Ergänzend wird das Produkt durch das Substantiv "Qualitäts-Garantie" aufgewertet. Durch die Schreibweise in zwei Worten, verbunden mit einem Bindestrich, werden die einzelnen Aspekte der Zusammensetzung in ihren Einzelwerten stärker betont.

Der Hinweis "Für Qualität bürgen wir mit unserem Namen" und die Unterschrift "Becker" soll Vertrauen schaffen, weil eine Bezugsperson angegeben wird, die die Verantwortung für das Produkt übernimmt.

Die textuelle Gestaltung wurde in bezug auf die Substantive sehr aufwendig konzipiert und umgesetzt. Insbesondere die Vielfalt der Aspekte und die Wirkungsintention des Einsatzes von Reizwörtern, die die Motivation und Bedürfnisse der Kunden ansprechen, gaben den Ausschlag für die sehr gute Note 9,0.[242] Mit "ausgezeichnet" (10 Punkte) wurden in diesem Block die leichte Erkennbarkeit, Verständlichkeit, Interpretierbarkeit und Merkbarkeit der Substantive bewertet. Noch verbessert werden könnte der Aspekt der Bedürfnismotivation.

**4.)  Der Name**

Der Name "beckers bester" scheint auf Anhieb nicht ganz einfach einzuordnen zu sein. Ich ordne den Namen der Kategorie der assoziativen Namen zu, denn es soll eine Produkteigenschaft assoziiert werden. Die Einarbeitung des Namens des Firmeninhabers "Becker" gibt einen guten Ansatzpunkt, eine persönliche Bezugsperson vorzustellen, die eine Qualitätsgarantie des Produktes verantwortet. Die Produkt-adäquanz wird sichergestellt, indem eine Produkteigenschaft bzw. eine Eigenschaft, die als Produkteigenschaft suggeriert wird, als Bestandteil des Namens eingearbeitet wird. Die Interpretation ist schnell und einfach durchzuführen. Durch aufwendige Werbemaßnahmen ist es gelungen, den Markennamen bekanntzumachen und damit zum Symbol werden zu lassen. Es gelingt sogar, den Namen auf eine ganze Produktfamilie auszuweiten - die "beckers beste"-Fruchtsäfte. Der Name differenziert das Produkt von anderen Alternativen. Jedoch ist er nicht besonders originell, innovativ oder

---

[242]
Die Einzelnoten:  1.) 9, 5d) 10, 5e) Exklusivität:9, 6.) 8, 7.) 9, 8.) 10, 9.) 8;
63: 7 = 9,0

pfiffig. Das wird jedoch durch einen höheren Wert für das Merkmal "Exklusivität" aufgefangen. Das Stilmittel der Alliteration erleichtert die Merkbarkeit. Die Referenzbeziehung zum Kunden dürfte auf der Frontseite stärker berücksichtigt werden.[243]
Insgesamt wird mit der Note 7,9 ein gutes Ergebnis für den Namen erreicht.

## 5.) Die Adjektive

Auf der Frontseite sind zwei Adjektive zentral, die Qualitätsangabe "köstlich" und die Note "sehr gut" von der übergeordneten Bewertungsinstitution "Stiftung Warentest". Das Adjektiv "klar" wird hier nicht extra bewertet, da es sich dabei lediglich um ein Unterscheidungsmerkmal zu "trüben" Apfelsaft handelt und nicht um ein speziell eingesetztes Reizwort. Empfehlenswert ist, die Phrase "für Qualität bürgen wir mit unserem Namen" um das Adjektiv *gut* zu ergänzen. Damit würde dem Kunden impliziert, daß der Name schon eine etablierte Institution ist.
Die Bewertung der "Stiftung Warentest" ist glaubwürdig. Bei der Produktbeschreibung "köstlich" handelt es sich um ein subjektives Bewertungskriterium, das nicht 100%ig glaubwürdig wirken kann.

---

[243]
    Die Einzelnoten:  b) 1.) 9, 2.) 8, 4.) 9, 5.) 9, 6.) 9, 7.) 8, 8.) 4, 9.) 8, allgemein 1a) 7, 1b) 7, 1c) 7, 1d) 8, 1e) 7, 2.) 8, 3.) 9, 4.) 9, 5.) 10, 6.) 8, 7.) 7, 8.) 8, 9.) 9, 10.) 9, 11.) 9, 12.) 8, 13.a) 8,13b) 8, 13c) 7, 13d) 5
    222 : 28 = 7,9

1.)   Werden die Adjektive wirkungseffektiv als Reiz- bzw. Schlüsselwort auf der   Produktverpackung eingesetzt?
        -   alleine?
Bitte ankreuzen:

← O   O   O   O   O   O   ⊗   O   O   O   →
Nein 1   2   3   4   5   6   7   8   9   10   Ja

        -   als Bildergänzung
Bitte ankreuzen:²⁴⁴

← O   O   O   O   O   O   O   O   O   O   →
Nein 1   2   3   4   5   6   7   8   9   10   Ja

        -   als Wortergänzung
Bitte ankreuzen:

← O   O   O   O   O   O   O   O   O   O   →
Nein 1   2   3   4   5   6   7   8   9   10   Ja

2.)   Wie wirken die Adjektive?
        a)        ergänzend?
Bitte ankreuzen:

← O   O   O   O   O   O   O   O   O   O   →
Nein 1   2   3   4   5   6   7   8   9   10   Ja

        b)        aufwertend?
Bitte ankreuzen:

← O   O   O   O   O   O   O   O   ⊗   O   →
Nein 1   2   3   4   5   6   7   8   9   10   Ja

---

²⁴⁴   Es werden keine Adjektive als Bildergänzung eingesetzt.

c) vergleichend?

Bitte ankreuzen:

| ← | O | O | O | O | O | O | O | O | ⊗ | O | → |
|---|---|---|---|---|---|---|---|---|---|---|---|
| Nein | 1 | 2 | 3 | 4 | 5 | 6 | 7 | 8 | 9 | 10 | Ja |

d) glaubwürdig?

Bitte ankreuzen:

| ← | O | O | O | O | O | ⊗ | O | O | O | O | → |
|---|---|---|---|---|---|---|---|---|---|---|---|
| Nein | 1 | 2 | 3 | 4 | 5 | 6 | 7 | 8 | 9 | 10 | Ja |

e) positiv?

Bitte ankreuzen:

| ← | O | O | O | O | O | O | O | O | ⊗ | O | → |
|---|---|---|---|---|---|---|---|---|---|---|---|
| Nein | 1 | 2 | 3 | 4 | 5 | 6 | 7 | 8 | 9 | 10 | Ja |

f) aufbauschend?

Bitte ankreuzen:

| ← | O | O | O | ⊗ | O | O | O | O | O | O | → |
|---|---|---|---|---|---|---|---|---|---|---|---|
| Nein | 10 | 9 | 8 | 7 | 6 | 5 | 4 | 3 | 2 | 1 | Ja |

g) Sonstiges

_____

Bitte ankreuzen:

| ← | O | O | O | O | O | O | O | O | O | O | → |
|---|---|---|---|---|---|---|---|---|---|---|---|
| Nein | 1 | 2 | 3 | 4 | 5 | 6 | 7 | 8 | 9 | 10 | Ja |

3.) Bieten sie einen sinnvollen Aspekt der Ergänzung?

Bitte ankreuzen:

| ← | O | O | O | O | O | O | O | O | O | O | → |
|---|---|---|---|---|---|---|---|---|---|---|---|
| Nein | 1 | 2 | 3 | 4 | 5 | 6 | 7 | 8 | 9 | 10 | Ja |

4.)   Sprechen die Adjektive die Zielgruppe an?

Bitte ankreuzen:

← O O O O O O O ⊗ O O →
Nein 1 2 3 4 5 6 7 8 9 10 Ja

5.)   Wirken die Adjektive verständlich?

Bitte ankreuzen:

← O O O O O O O O ⊗ O →
Nein 1 2 3 4 5 6 7 8 9 10 Ja

6.)   Passen die Adjektive zum Stil?

Bitte ankreuzen:

← O O O O O O O O ⊗ O →
Nein 1 2 3 4 5 6 7 8 9 10 Ja

7.)   Wirken die Adjektive originell?

Bitte ankreuzen:

← O O O O ⊗ O O O O O →
Nein 1 2 3 4 5 6 7 8 9 10 Ja

8.)   Wirken die Adjektive witzig?

Bitte ankreuzen:[245]

←⊗ O O O O O O O O O O →
Nein 1 2 3 4 5 6 7 8 9 10 Ja

---

[245]   Die Adjektive wirken überhaupt nicht witzig.

9.)   Verleihen die Adjektive der Verpackung Pepp?

Bitte ankreuzen:

| ← | O | O | O | ⊗ | O | O | O | O | O | O | → |
|---|---|---|---|---|---|---|---|---|---|---|---|
| Nein | 1 | 2 | 3 | 4 | 5 | 6 | 7 | 8 | 9 | 10 | Ja |

10.)  Wirken die Adjektive innovativ?

Bitte ankreuzen:

| ← | O | O | O | O | ⊗ | O | O | O | O | O | → |
|---|---|---|---|---|---|---|---|---|---|---|---|
| Nein | 1 | 2 | 3 | 4 | 5 | 6 | 7 | 8 | 9 | 10 | Ja |

11.)  Wirken die Adjektive ausgefallen?

Bitte ankreuzen:

| ← | O | O | O | O | ⊗ | O | O | O | O | O | → |
|---|---|---|---|---|---|---|---|---|---|---|---|
| Nein | 1 | 2 | 3 | 4 | 5 | 6 | 7 | 8 | 9 | 10 | Ja |

12.)  Wirken die Adjektive langweilig?

Bitte ankreuzen

| ← | O | O | O | O | ⊗ | O | O | O | O | O | → |
|---|---|---|---|---|---|---|---|---|---|---|---|
| Nein | 10 | 9 | 8 | 7 | 6 | 5 | 4 | 3 | 2 | 1 | Ja |

13.)  Sonstiges?

Sie sind exklusiv!

Bitte ankreuzen:

| ← | O | O | O | O | O | O | O | O | ⊗ | O | → |
|---|---|---|---|---|---|---|---|---|---|---|---|
| Nein | 1 | 2 | 3 | 4 | 5 | 6 | 7 | 8 | 9 | 10 | Ja |

Der Einsatz der wirkungsintendierten Adjektive ergibt die Note 107 :
16 = 6,7. Der Einsatz der Adjektive ist positiv zu bewerten. Das Ergebnis würde noch weit besser ausfallen, wenn die Adjektive etwas
origineller ausgewählt worden wären. Darüber hinaus sollten subjek-

tive Bewertungen vermieden werden, da unter ihnen der Faktor "Glaubwürdigkeit" leidet.

Eine Bewertung der Kategorien 6 - 9 entfällt, da keine entsprechenden Merkmale auf der Flasche vorhanden sind.


## 10.  Phraseologismen

1.)    Setzen die Phraseologismen einen Akzent?
Bitte ankreuzen:

←   O   O   O   O   O   O   O   ⊗   O   O   →
Nein 1   2   3   4   5   6   7   8   9   10   Ja

Kommentar:    Der Phraseologismus "Für die Qualität bürgen wir mit unserem Namen" setzt einen Akzent auf den Aspekt "Qualität".

2.)    Sind sie verständlich?
Bitte ankreuzen:

←   O   O   O   O   O   O   O   O   O   ⊗   →
Nein 1   2   3   4   5   6   7   8   9   10   Ja

3.)    Sind sie gut merkbar?
Bitte ankreuzen:

←   O   O   O   O   ⊗   O   O   O   O   O   →
Nein 1   2   3   4   5   6   7   8   9   10   Ja

Kommentar:    Die Merkbarkeit des Phraseologismus spielt in diesem Fall keine Rolle, da er nicht zu den Kernaussagen gehört.

4.)    Wirken sie originell?

Bitte ankreuzen:

← O    O    O    O    ⊗    O    O    O    O    O    →

Nein 1    2    3    4    5    6    7    8    9    10    Ja

Die Originalität ist lediglich durchschnittlich.


5.)    Wirken sie blickfangend?

Bitte ankreuzen:

← O    O    O    O    ⊗    O    O    O    O    O    →

Nein 1    2    3    4    5    6    7    8    9    10    Ja

Für einen Blickfang ist der Phraseologismus zu klein gedruckt.


6.)    Verleihen sie der Verpackung Pepp?

Bitte ankreuzen:

← O    O    O    O    ⊗    O    O    O    O    O    →

 Nein    1    2    3    4    5    6    7    8    9    10
 Ja


7.)    Wirken sie innovativ?

Bitte ankreuzen:

← O    O    ⊗    O    O    O    O    O    O    O    →

Nein 1    2    3    4    5    6    7    8    9    10    Ja


8.)    Wirken sie ausgefallen?

Bitte ankreuzen:

← O    O    O    O    ⊗    O    O    O    O    O    →

Nein 1    2    3    4    5    6    7    8    9    10    Ja

9.) Wirken sie exklusiv?

Bitte ankreuzen:

← O O O O O ⊗ O O O O →

Nein 1   2   3   4   5   6   7   8   9   10   Ja

Kommentar:     Der exklusive Charakter könnte durch Einsatz einer adjektivischen Ergänzung wie "bürgen wir mit unserem *guten* Namen" gesteigert werden.


10.) Wirken sie langweilig?

Bitte ankreuzen:

← O O O O O ⊗ O O O O →

Nein 10   9   8   7   6   5   4   3   2   1   Ja


11.) Sonstiges?

     Der Phraseologismus schafft ein persönliches Verhältnis und damit Vertrauen für die    Kunden.

Bitte ankreuzen:

← O O O O O O O O O ⊗ →

Nein 1   2   3   4   5   6   7   8   9   10   Ja

12.) Paßt der Phraseologismus zum Kontext?

Bitte ankreuzen:

← O O O O O O O O O ⊗ →

Nein 1   2   3   4   5   6   7   8   9   10   Ja


13.) Paßt er zum Produkt?

Bitte ankreuzen:

← O O O O O O O O O ⊗ →

Nein 1   2   3   4   5   6   7   8   9   10   Ja

14.) Paßt er zur Zielgruppe?

Bitte ankreuzen:

← O O O O O O O O O ⊗ →
Nein 1 2 3 4 5 6 7 8 9 10 Ja

15.) Wird er im intendierten Sinn interpretiert?

Bitte ankreuzen:

← O O O O O O O O O ⊗ →
Nein 1 2 3 4 5 6 7 8 9 10 Ja

**Die Gesamtnote für diesen Phraseologismus beträgt: 107 : 15 = 7,1**

## 11.) Der Text

Sämtliche Textelemente sind insgesamt nicht gut wahrnehmbar. Sie alle sind zu klein gedruckt und typographisch wenig hervorgehoben. Man könnte dieses Problem einfach lösen, indem man die großen weißen Flächen für die Ausgestaltung nutzt. Die Farben sind insbesondere beim Namen und den Textfragmenten auf der Frontseite nicht optimal gewählt. Die Namenskomponente "bester" sollte nicht schwarz geschrieben werden, da diese Farbe in Kontrast zum grünen "beckers" negative Assoziationen auslösen könnte. Die Farbe Rot wird allgemein als Symbol für "Gefahr" interpretiert. Eine Signalwirkung könnte auch gut mit einer freundlicheren Farbe erzielt werden.
Der rückseitige Text ist mit einem Bildzeichen unterlegt, das assoziativ als Apfelgarten interpretiert wird. Die Schrift auf diesem Hintergrund sollte deutlicher gestaltet werden, um die Lesbarkeit zu erleichtern.
Aufgrund der schlechten Lesbarkeit sind die Textelemente nicht optimal einladend. Geschickt ist jedoch die einleitende persönliche Ansprache "Verehrte Kundin, verehrter Kunde". Diese Einladung

zum Lesen interpretiere ich, ausgehend von der Wortwahl, als Zeichen für Exklusivität. Darüber hinaus läßt sich diese Ansprache als ausgesprochen höflich und fein charakterisieren.

Die Texte sind relativ leicht und flüssig lesbar und ohne Probleme verständlich. Die Schlüssigkeit der Texte wird durch den Einsatz einer Argumentationsstruktur erreicht. Im Gegensatz zum "rio d'oro"-Text wird das Kriterium der Originalität hier überhaupt nicht berücksichtigt. Das Produkt soll absolut seriös angeboten werden. Dafür ist der Text glaubwürdig und wirkt dementsprechend wenig überredend. Die Argumente referieren einen faktischen Tatsachenbestand und sollen aus diesem Grund überzeugen. Allerdings entlarvt sich das Argument "Frei von Konservierungsmitteln ohne Farbstoffe" durch den Zusatz "laut Lebensmittelgesetz" selbst als Pseudoargument.

Der Einfluß des Aspektes der Zielgruppenadäquanz ist sprachlich insofern festzustellen, als mit stilistisch sehr seriösen und konservativ anmutenden Formulierungen eine exklusivere Zielgruppe angesprochen wird. Jedoch ist der Text nicht zu speziell gestaltet, so daß keine Gruppe ausgegrenzt wird.

Stilistisch sind die Texte nur durchschnittlich ansprechend. Es fehlt an Witz und Pepp, sie wirken etwas steif.

Als Auswahlkategorie habe ich die Adjektive gewählt und in bezug auf Stilistik und Wertsteigerung mit *sehr gut* bewertet. Es handelt sich um das Adjektiv "bester", die auf den Namen referieren und damit doppeldeutig eingesetzt sind. Jedoch könnte dieses Adjektiv noch konsequenter eingearbeitet werden.

Der Fokus der Rezipienten könnte stärker auf und durch den Text gelenkt werden, um nicht nur über den Faktor Qualität "Lust auf das Produkt zu machen".

Neben dem Produkt wird zusätzlich die Leistung eines wichtigen Beitrages zu einer gesunden Ernährung als ideeller Wert versprochen.

Insgesamt könnte der Text fließender in das Gesamtverpackungskonzept eingearbeitet werden und in der Gestaltung ansprechender umgesetzt werden.

**Insgesamt wird in der Kategorie Text die Note erzielt:**
**$122 : 21 = 5,8$** [246]


## 12.) Der Inhalt

Der Inhalt der Texte ist sehr produktadäquat. Er ist anbieterbezogen durch Einsatz der Pronomen *Wir* und *unsere*. Dem Aspekt "Kundenbezogenheit" wird durch die Anrede "verehrte Kundin, verehrter Kunde" und den Allgemeinplatz "gesunde Ernährung" Folge geleistet. Jedoch ließe sich dieses Kriterium deutlicher herausarbeiten, indem man den direkten Mehrwert für den individuellen Kunden aufzeigt, z.B. über eine Formulierung wie "ein Beitrag zu Ihrer gesunden Ernährung", oder "Wir verwenden Früchte in bester Qualität für Sie".

Der Ausdruck "Fruchtsäfte und Nektare" vermittelt den Eindruck einer umfassenden Firmen- und Produktphilosophie. Hier ist anzuraten, die modale Verbform "können einen wichtigen Beitrag zur gesunden Ernährung leisten" durch die aktive Form "leisten einen wichtigen Beitrag zu einer gesunden Ernährung" zu ersetzen. Auf diese Weise erhielte die Formulierung einen zweifelsfreien Charakter und würde glaubhafter.

Mit diesem Ausdruck wird ein Appell an das Gewissen gerichtet, für die Gesundheit Sorge zu tragen. Dieser Appell ließe sich verstärken,

---

246
    Die Einzelnoten: 1a) 2, 1b) 5, 2.) 6, 3.) 8, 4.) 8, 5.) 8, 6.) 1, 7.) 7, 8.) 6, 9.) 7, 10.) 3, 11.) 7, 12.) 6, 13a) 5, 13b) 2, 14.) 8, 15.) 6, 16.) 7, 17.) 6, 18.) 10, 19.) 10    gesamt: 128 : 21 = 6,1

wenn die Adressaten explizit genannt würden. Damit einhergehend könnte z.B. auch an den Mutter-/Vaterinstinkt appelliert werden. Durch eine Ergänzung einer witzigen, innovativen oder originellen Formulierung könnte das Produkt noch sympathischer gemacht werden. Auch der Einsatz eines Sympathieträgers neben der Unterschrift des Unternehmensinhabers wäre ein geeignetes Mittel für diesen Zweck.

Durch die Installation des Urteils "sehr gut" der Stiftung Warentest wird der Faktor der Glaubhaftigkeit des Produktes erheblich gesteigert.

"beckers bester"-Fruchtsäfte konnten sich über die Werbung mit dem Image eines seriösen und renommierten Unternehmens etablieren.

Der Aspekt "Image der Zielgruppe" sollte jedoch stärker betont werden. Dieser Wert wird automatisch gesteigert, wenn explizit ein ideeller Mehrwert für die Konsumenten genannt wird.

Die Verpackung verspricht keine soziale Anerkennung. Der Aspekt der Bedürfnis-/Triebbefriedigung dürfte stärker herausgearbeitet werden. Es wird neben dem Genußwert des Produktes ("köstlich") der Beitrag zur gesunden Ernährung als Mehrwert angegeben.

Insgesamt könnten die Aspekte, die der Beurteilung als Grundlage dienen, mit dem vorhandenen guten Potential an Text noch stärker herausgearbeitet werden. Dieses Mal ergibt sich für die Gruppe "Inhalt" eine Note von: $109 : 18 = 6,0$ .[247]

---

[247]     Die Einzelnoten:  1.) 8, 2.) 4, 3.) 7, 4.) 6, 5.) 7, 6.) 4, 7.) 9, 8.) 8, 9.) 8, 10.) 8, 11.) 4, 12.) 5, 13.) 7, 14a) 7, 15a) 3, 15b) 0, 15c) 6, 15d) 8        109 : 18 = 6,0

## 13.) Der Gesamteindruck

Der Gesamteindruck der Verpackung ist stimmig und verständlich, aber insbesondere die Texte sind schlecht wahrnehmbar. Die Verpackung ist relativ praktisch, aber wenig originell. Die Etiketten sind zwar nicht auffallend pfiffig, aber dennoch aufwendig gestaltet, und sie werden durch die Vielzahl der eingearbeiteten Elemente nicht langweilig. Der Aspekt der Neuwertigkeit bzw. der Innovation könnte stärker berücksichtigt werden.
Die Verpackung ist produktadäquat gestaltet, sie suggeriert bzw. rechtfertigt das Preis-Leistungsverhältnis über das Bewertungskriterium der qualitativen Hochwertigkeit. Jedoch sollte noch stärker auf die Zielgruppe eingegangen werden und die Vorteile des Kaufes von "beckers bester"-Apfelsaft stärker argumentativ expliziert werden.[248]

Insgesamt ergab sich für diese Verpackung die Note:

- Gruppe 1:     7,8            Gruppe 10: 7,1
- Gruppe 2:     6,7            Gruppe 11: 6,1
- Gruppe 3:     9,0            Gruppe 12: 6,0
- Gruppe 4:     7,9            Gruppe 13: 7,0
- Gruppe 5:     6,7            Insgesamt: 64,3 : 9 = 7,1

Der gezielte Einsatz wirkungsintendierter sprachlicher Gestaltungselemente spiegelt sich in diesem guten Ergebnis wider. Das Verhältnis dieses positiven Ergebnisses zu dem durchschnittlichen Ergebnis der beiden einfacheren Verpackungen zeigt, daß sich die Mühe des gezielten Einsatzes sprachlicher Wirkungsmedien lohnt.

---

[248]    Die Einzelnoten für den Gesamteindruck: 1.) 8, 2.) 8, 3.) 3, 4.) 7, 5.) 6, 6.) 7, 7.) 6, 8.) 6, 9.) 7, 10.) 9, 11.) 8, 12.) 8, 13.) 7, 14.) 8; 98 : 14 = 7,0

Dennoch ließe sich das Ergebnis mit den genannten Empfehlungen noch steigern.

Diese drei Beispiele demonstrieren die Praktikabilität des Analysemodells, das sich sowohl für die Untersuchung und Bewertung einer einzelnen Verpackung eignet, als auch für den Vergleich.

# V.   Schlußteil

## 5.1   Wer liest eigentlich Verpackungsaufschriften?

Nach der Analyse und Interpretation von Verpackungsaufschriften stellt sich berechtigterweise die Frage, ob denn Verpackungsaufschriften überhaupt gelesen werden und eng damit einhergehend, ob der ganze Aufwand überhaupt lohnt.

Selbstverständlich werden Verpackungsaufschriften gelesen - jedoch nicht immer alle und nicht unbedingt auf einer Verpackung alle Aufschriften. Wenn die Konsumenten auf Ge-, Verbrauchs- oder Anwendungshinweise angewiesen sind, ist es einfacher, den Fokus dergestalt zu leiten, daß noch weitere Informationen aufgenommen werden. So informieren sich z.b. viele Kunden über die Zubereitung ihrer Iglo Fischstäbchen über die entsprechenden Hinweise auf der Rückseite dieser Verpackung. Dabei wird der Blick zusätzlich über ergänzende und werbende Produktinformationen geleitet. Dazu gehört die ausführliche Beschreibung des Alaska Seelachs, der als ausgewählte und qualitativ besonders hochwertige Zutat vorgestellt wird.

Produktverpackungen werden im Laden studiert, wenn man sich entweder generell über das Produkt und dessen Handhabung informieren möchte oder wenn man aus verschiedenen Alternativen die augenscheinlich beste auswählen möchte.

Zu Hause werden Produktverpackungen in der Regel dann besonders sorgfältig studiert, wenn die aufgedruckten Informationen für Ge- und Verbrauch und die Entsorgung notwendig erscheinen. Zuweilen werden Verpackungen auch dann studiert, wenn eine interessante Kampagne eine zusätzliche Leistung verspricht, z.B. Rezepte, Gewinnspiele, Kampagnen für einen guten Zweck u.v.m..

Dementsprechend ist es empfehlenswert, ergänzende Produktinformationen soweit möglich mit notwendigen zu kombinieren – dann sind die

Chancen besonders groß, daß sie rezipiert und eventuell auch behalten werden. Darüber hinaus sollten frontseitig interesseweckende Hinweise angebracht sein, die motivieren, umseitige Informationen zu lesen. Dabei sind Bilder und Farben immer ein geeignetes Mittel, die Blicke zu fangen.

Zuweilen werden Verpackungen an ganz ungewöhnlichen Orten studiert: Die Toilette kann zuweilen einer der wenigen Orte der Ruhe und Ungestörtheit sein. Allerdings tritt bei längeren Sitzungen zuweilen Langeweile auf, so daß zu allem Greifbaren gegriffen und dieses studiert wird. So geschehen auch bei einer solchen Sitzung von Luise F. Pusch, die beschreibt:
"Frau gerät immer mal wieder in Badezimmer, Örtchen oder wie ihr es nun nennen wollt, in denen sie nichts Vernünftiges zu lesen findet. Vielleicht gehört ihr auch zu jenen Unverdrossenen, die sich in derartigen Notfällen dann eben mit vergleichsweise dürftigem Lesefutter begnügen - was so in Reichweite ist, Zahnpastatuben, Cremedöschen, Deodorants. Ich jedenfalls hatte neulich Gelegenheit, eingehend eine o.b.-Schachtel zu studieren. [...] Ich las also mäßig unterhalten, bis ich auf folgende Information stieß: "Die Menstruation ist bei jedem ein bißchen anders."[249] Ein solcher Fehler[250] darf nicht passieren. Frau Pusch reklamierte diesen Fauxpas und erhielt als Dankeschön ein großzügiges Werbegeschenk.

---

[249] Pusch (1991), S. 149

[250] Der Fehler liegt für feministisch orientierte Frauen in der von ihnen als männlich interpretierten Form "jedem". Dabei ist die Aussage, daß die Menstruation bei jedem ein bißchen anders sei nach Pusch insofern falsch, als daß "jedem" auf einem ausschließlich von Frauen gekauften Artikel wie Tampons dennoch eindeutig auf einen Mann referiere.

## 5.2 Witzige Verpackungsaufdrucke

*Dafür stehen Sie sogar nachts auf!*

### Allgemeine Bemerkung

Niemand ist ein Genie, alles muss erlernt werden. Wenn Sie Ihr **KI-STOP** zum ersten Mal benutzen, so verstehen Sie vielleicht nicht auf Anhieb die richtige bzw. beste Anwendung. Regen Sie sich darüber nicht auf, bleiben Sie ruhig; Sie sind Motorradfahrer, also wissen Sie sich zu helfen. Sie werden auf jeden Fall Ihren Reifen ab- und remontieren, egal wie lange Sie dazu brauchen, was mit normalen Werkzeug nicht der Fall ist.
Wir danken Ihnen für Ihr Vertrauen in **KI-STOP**, und wünschen Ihnen Gute Fahrt!

## 5.3 Zusammenfassung der Ergebnisse und Resümee

In diesem abschließenden Kapitel sollen die wichtigsten Ergebnisse der vorliegenden Arbeit zusammengefaßt und ein Resümee gezogen werden.

Es war Ziel, eine Antwort auf die Frage zu finden, wie man es erreicht, ein Produkt aus dem breiten Angebot heraus zu exponieren und erfolgreich zu verkaufen.

Eine Antwort auf diese Frage ist, daß die Produktverpackung ein vielschichtiges Potential an Möglichkeiten bietet, ein Produkt optisch, haptisch und manchmal sogar akustisch (z.B. über das ansprechende Geräusch beim Öffnen einer Coca-Cola-Dose) zu bewerben. Für diese Arbeit standen die optischen Wirkungsvariablen im Vordergrund. Zu den optischen Wirkungsvariablen zählen die Zeichen auf einer Produktverpackung, angefangen von den Wort- bzw Schriftzeichen über die graphischen und Bildzeichen bis hin zu den Zahlzeichen. Dabei ist zu berücksichtigen, daß eine Produktverpackung mit ihrer Form und auch ihrem Gesamteindruck selber ebenfalls über Zeichenwirkung verfügen kann.

Als „silent salesman" übernimmt die Verpackung in den heute üblichen Selbstbedienungswarenhäusern zusätzlich eine Verkäuferfunktion. Sie kann clever eingesetzt als Kommunikationsmedium im Sinne des Produktanbieters nutzbar gemacht werden. Da Kommunikation vorzugsweise mittels Sprache und über Bilder geschieht, die auf Verpackungen in Form von Schriftzeichen und visuellen Zeichen eingesetzt werden, bot es sich an, die Produktverpackung aus einer linguistischen Perspektive heraus zu untersuchen. Dazu wurde ein praktikabler zeichentheoretischer Ansatz ausgewählt und auf seine Anwendbarkeit bezüglich der Analyse von Produktverpackungen überprüft (vgl. Kap. 6). Aus den vielen alternativen Theorien habe ich mich für den gebrauchstheoretischen Ansatz entschieden, wie er von Keller vorgestellt wird. Es zeigte sich, daß dieser Ansatz hervorragend geeignet ist, die Zeichen auf den Produktverpackungen und die Produktverpackungen als Zeichen zu klassifizieren und die dazugehörigen Interpretationsverfahren, die von seiten der Kunden notwendig werden zu untersuchen.

Bei der Bearbeitung der ausgesprochen umfangreichen textuellen Gestaltungselemente von Produktverpackungen konnte herausgestellt werden, daß diese als eigene Textsorte klassifiziert werden können. Diese Feststellung ist von Interesse, da Verpackungsaufschriften als kommunikative Handlungen konzipiert und eingesetzt werden, mit einer häufig situationsspezifischen Intention, die in manchen Fällen sogar auf eine Rezipientenerwartung trifft (z.B. Ge-, Verbrauchs- und Bedienungsanleitungen, aber auch bei Produktinformationen u.ä.). Es ist durchaus empfehlenswert, die Makrostruktur der Verpackungstexte dergestalt zu entwickeln, daß der Fokus der Konsumenten über die gesamte Verpackung gelenkt wird. Mit dem Einsatz von übergreifenden Strukturen kann erreicht werden, daß die Verbraucher mehr als die nur unbedingt für sie relevanten Informationen aufnehmen. Auf diesem Wege können den Rezipienten zusätzliche Argumente vorgestellt werden. Die Beratung der Kunden wird dann ausführlicher, was dazu führen kann, daß die Kunden stärker von dem vorliegenden Produkt überzeugt werden. Der Fokus der Rezipienten wird z.B. über die Lektüre der Zubereitungsinformationen zu weiteren Produktinformationen geleitet. Dabei sollte der Einsatz zusätzlich überzeugender Kaufargumente das Produkt stärker von anderen Alternativen differenzieren und deutlich auf dem Markt positionieren.

Unter Berücksichtigung vieler anderer wichtiger sprachwissenschaftlicher Aspekte, wie z.B. die Auseinandersetzung mit den Produkt-, Firmen- und Markennamen oder mit dem Einsatz von Stilmitteln wie Neologismen, Fremdworten und mit der Konzeption verschiedener Argumentationsstrategien und deren Wirkungspotential etc., erwies sich der gebrauchstheoretische Ansatz darüber hinaus insofern als praktikabel, als daraus ein Analysemodell zur Beurteilung von Produktverpackungen entwickelt werden konnte.

Ziel des Analysemodells war es, ein Raster zu entwickeln, daß einerseits die Möglichkeit bietet, die einzelne Verpackung insbesondere auf die Qualität ihrer textuellen Gestaltung hin zu untersuchen. Dabei sollten die praktischen Voraussetzungen einer Verpackung jedoch nicht unberücksichtigt bleiben. Zu diesem Zweck wurde ein Fragebogen entwickelt, der die vorhandenen Aspekte einer Verpackung bewerten läßt und auf Lücken aufmerksam macht.

Der Zeitpunkt des Einsatzes des Analysemodells kann sowohl vor der Einführung einer neuen Verpackung auf dem Markt gewählt werden, als auch zur Überprüfung einer bereits länger schon eingesetzten Verpackung.

Der Fragebogen wurde nicht nur zu dem Zweck konzipiert, Verpackungen zu analysieren. Idealerweise lassen sich aus der Untersuchung einer Verpackung Empfehlungen ableiten, wie selbige noch optimiert werden kann und welche Mängel behoben werden sollten, um das Produkt mit seiner Verpackung noch stärker zu differenzieren und damit deutlicher auf dem Markt zu positionieren.

Desweiteren wurde angestrebt, einen Kriterienkatalog zu entwickeln, der neben der Einzelfallanalyse auch den gerichteten Vergleich von Verpackungen untereinander möglich macht und es erlaubt, ein Ranking der überprüften Verpackungen aufzustellen.

Um eine repräsentative Untersuchung mittels des Fragebogens durchzuführen, ist dringend zu empfehlen, möglichst viele Personen mit der Verpackungsanalyse nach den Vorgaben des Kriterienkataloges zu beauftragen.

Es wurde Wert darauf gelegt, daß der Vergleich von Verpackungen auch dann möglich ist, wenn diese von der Menge ihrer gestalterischen Elemente vollkommen unterschiedlich konzipiert wurden oder wenn die Art dieser Elemente völlig unterschiedlich sind.

Zusätzlich sollte das Analysemodell Untersuchungen erlauben, die auf einen spezifischen Schwerpunkt fokussiert sind. Mit der Möglichkeit, Multiplikationsfaktoren einzusetzen, konnte auch diesem Anspruch genüge getan werden.

Wichtig ist, nicht nur die einzelnen Charakteristika einer Verpackung zu untersuchen, sondern immer auch das gesamte Erscheinungsbild und das Zusammenspiel der Merkmale zu berücksichtigen.

Da der Fragebogen flexibel ergänzt oder gekürzt und gewichtet werden kann, läßt er sich zur Analyse aller mir bekannten Verpackungen heranziehen und eignet sich als Basis für alle möglichen Untersuchungen mit den verschiedensten Schwerpunkten.

## 5.4  Fazit und Ausblick

Als Fazit bleibt festzuhalten, daß Verpackungen als ausgesprochen wirkungsintensives Kommunikationsmedium eingesetzt werden können.
Sie können die Kaufentscheidung der Kunden entscheidend beeinflussen.
Es ist sinnvoll, eine Verpackung bevor sie auf den Markt kommt und während sie auf dem Markt ist, immer wieder hinsichtlich ihrer Qualität zu überprüfen. Dabei sollten nicht nur die technischen Gesichtspunkte von Interesse sein – auch der kommunikative Aspekt einer Verpackung sollte regelmäßig aktualisiert und den Gegebenheiten des Marktes angepaßt werden. Dabei kann das vorgestellte Analysemodell sinnvoll Hilfestellung leisten.
Verpackungsaufschriften lassen sich als Textsorte klassifizieren, wenn man bereit ist, von der strengen Definition des Begriffes „Text" insofern abzusehen, als nicht immer ein geschlossener Textkorpus auf die Verpackungen aufgedruckt wird. Jedoch lassen sich die verschiedenen textkonstituierenden Maßnahmen in Kombination mit den graphischen Elementen in ihrer Gesamtheit als eigenes Textgenre begreifen. Mehr als in vielen anderen Texten werden die textuellen Elemente wirkungsintendiert eingesetzt. Sie leisten einen großen Beitrag zum Erfolg eines Produktes, von dem die Existenz des Anbieters abhängig ist. Idealerweise erfolgt die Kommunikation mittels der Verpackung zu den Konsumenten in Kombination mit den anderen Werbemedien wie Funk-, Fernseh-, Plakat- oder Direktwerbung.

Die Linguistik kann in diesem Feld einen wichtigen Anwendungseinsatz finden. Diese Wissenschaft bietet eine notwendige und nützliche Perspektive für die Auseinandersetzung des Kommunikationsmedium Sprache und Schrift.

Mein Anliegen war es, zu zeigen, daß linguistische Disziplinen nicht nur abstrakte theoretische Konstrukte bereitstellen, die jeglichen Realitätsbezugs entbehren. Ich hoffe, es ist gelungen zu zeigen, daß die Sprachwissenschaften weit mehr zu bieten haben – u.a. eine sinnvolle Grundlage der theoretischen und praktischen Auseinandersetzung mit dem Medium, das eines der spannensten, facettenreichsten, bewegensten und kommunikativsten ist, und die Gesellschaften stark bestimmt: die Sprache.

Es ist allen Anbietern von Produktverpackungen anzuraten, das kommunikative Potential selbiger zu nutzen. Den Konsumenten ist zu empfehlen, das ein oder andere Mal ein bißchen genauer hinzuschauen – dann kaufen sie vielleicht nicht „die Katze im Sack".

## Literaturverzeichnis:

- **Angehrn, Otto (1968):**
  „Marktsegmentierung als Absatzmethode."
  In: GFM Mitteilungen zur Markt- und Absatzforschung, Heft 2

- **Angehrn, Otto (1973):**
  „System des Marketing". Bern: Verlag Paul Haupt

- **Angermann, Hartmut; Vogel, Günter (1984b):**
  „dtv-Atlas zur Biologie".
  München: Deutscher Taschenbuchverlag GmbH & Co.KG

- **Arroyabe, Estanislao (1982):**
  „Peirce: eine Einführung in sein Denken".
  Hanstein: Verlagsgruppe Athenäum, Hain und Scriptor

- **Atkin, K. (1978):**
  „Observation of Parent-Children Interaction in Supermarket Decison-Making".
  Journal of Marketing 42, H. 4, S. 41-45,

- **Aristoteles:**
  „Aristoteles Perihermenias oder Lehre vom Satz (Des Organon zweiter Teil)". Herausgegeben von Rolfes,
  Eugen, Leipzig: Felix Meiner Verlag (1920)

- **Baumgart, Manuela (1992):**
  „Die Sprache der Anzeigenwerbung. Eine linguistische Analyse aktueller Werbeslogans". Konsum und Verhalten Bd. 37, Physica-Verlag, Heidelberg

- **Behaegel, Julien (1991)**
  „Brand Packaging - Die Verpackung als Medium".
  München: Artemis & Winkler Verlag

- **Bräuer, Helmut (1957)**
  „Die Verpackung als absatzwirtschaftliches Problem".
  Marktwirtschaft und Verbrauch. Schriftenreihe der Gesellschaft für Konsumforschung e.V.,
  Kallmünz/Opf: Verlag Michael Laßleben.

- **Braem, Harald (1985):**
  „Träume in Blech und Papier. Alte Zigarettenschachteln als Sammelobjekt".
  Bern, Stuttgart: Verlag Paul Haupt

- **Brand, Horst W. (1978):**
  „Die Legende von den geheimen Verführern: kritische Analysen zur unterschwelligen Wahrnehmung und Beeinflussung".
  Basel: Beltz Verlag

- **Buck, Alex; Vogt, Matthias (1996.):**
  „Designermonographien". Mappe.
  Berlin: Ernst-Verlag

- **Bund Deutscher Werbeberater und Werbeleiter e.V. (1964):**
„Werbung...freiheit und verantwortung".
Essen: Wirtschaft und Werbung Verlagsgesellschaft m.b.H.

- **Conen, Dieter (1985):**
„Wirkung von Werbesprache. Eine experimentelle Untersuchung
zur Interaktion von Bild und Text".
München: GBI-Verlag

- **Corell, Prof. Werner (1992):**
„Menschen durchschauen und richtig behandeln – Psychologie
für Beruf und Familie".
München: mvg- Moderne Verlagsgesellschaft mbH

- **Crowel, Wim; Weidemann, Kurt (1968):**
„Verpackung-international". Stuttgart: Gerd Hatje Verlag

- **Cruse, D. A. (1991⁴):**
„Lexical Semantics". Cambridge: The Bath Press

- **Debrunner, Peter (1977):**
„Die Verpackung als Marketinginstrument. Kosten und Nutzen
ihres Einsatzes".
Zürich: Diss. Juris Druck und Verlag

- **Dichter, Ernest (1964):**
„Handbuch der Kaufmotive". Düsseldorf: Econ Verlag

- **Dichter, Ernest (1981):**
„Das Grosse Buch der Kaufmotive". Düsseldorf: Econ Verlag

- **Franck, Dorothea (1980):**
  „Grammatik und Konversation". Königstein/Ts.: Scriptor

- **Frege, Gottlob:**
  "Nachgelassene Schriften und wissenschaftlicher Briefwechsel".
  Herausgegeben von: Hermes, Hans; Kambartel, Friedrich; Kailbach, Friedrich Band I,
  Hamburg: Felix Meiner Verlag (1969)

- **Frege, Gottlob:**
  „Schriften zur Logik und Sprachphilosophie".
  Aus dem Nachlass hgg. von Gottfried Gabriel.
  Hamburg: Felix Meiner Verlag (1971)

- **Frege, Gottlob:**
  „Funktion, Begriff, Bedeutung – Fünf logische Studien".
  Herausgegeben von: Patzig, Günther,
  Göttingen: Vandenhoeck & Ruprecht Verlag (1994[7])

- **Freud, Siegmund:**
  „Freud Biologie der Seele. Jenseits der psychoanalytischen Legende". Herausgegeben von Frank J. Suloway, Köln: Hohenheim Verlag (1979)

- **Frieling, Dr. Heinrich (1980):**
  „Farbe hilft verkaufen. Farbenlehre und Farbenpsychologie für Handel und Werbung".
  Frankfurt: Muster-Schmidt-Verlag

- **Fritz, Thomas (1994):**
  „Die Botschaft der Markenartikel. Vertextungsstrategien in der Werbung". Probleme der Semiotik Bd.15,
  Tübingen: Verlag Brigitte Narr GmbH

- **Fürst, Reimar (1973):**
  „Verpackung - gelobt, getadelt, unentbehrlich - 1 Jahrhundert Verpackungsindustrie".
  Wien: Econ Verlag

- **Gotta, Manfred (1988)**
  „Die Rolle des Markennamens im Marektingmix: Global Branding und die Zukunft von Markennamen".
  In: Spiegel-Verlag Rudolf Augstein GmbH & Co. KG Marketingabteilung Hamburg, S. 15ff

- **Grice, Paul H. (1975):**
  „Logik und Konversation". In: Meggle, Georg (Hg): „Handlung, Kommunikation, Bedeutung".
  Frankfurt am Main: Suhrkamp

- **Hacker, Karin (20.07.1997):**
  „Der Beitrag der Verpackung zur Profilierung eines Markenartikels beim Verbraucher. - Theoretische Grundlagen und empirisches Beispiel". Diplomarbeit Trier

- **Haidl, Heinz, K. (1996):**
  „Die anlehnende vergleichende Werbung in Deutschland und in der Europäischen Union".
  München: Verlag v. Florentz GmbH

- **Hardt-Mautner, Gerlinde (1992):**
  „The silent salesman oder: die Verpackung als Werbeträger.
  Eine linguistisch-semiotische Annäherung".
  In: Internationale Zeitschrift für Fachsprachenforschung- didaktik
  und Terminologie.
  „Fachsprache" - int. journal of LSP. 14. Jahrgang
  Heft 3-4, Wien: Braunmüller

- **Hayakawa, Samuel Ichiye (1972³):**
  „Language in Thought and Action".
  New York u.a.: Harcourt Brace Jovanovich, Inc.

- **Hermanns, Arnold (4/1972):**
  „Die Werbeaussage als determinierende Variable bei der Soziali-
  sation durch Werbung".
  In: „Jahrbuch der Absatz und Verbraucherforschung" S. 292f

- **Hermanns, Arnold (1972):**
  "Sozialisation durch Werbung. Sozialisierungswirkungen von
  Werbeaussagen in Massenmedien".
  Düsseldorf: Bertelsmann Univ. Verlag

- **Högn, Ernst; Pomplitz, Hans-Jürgen (1990):**
  „Der erfolgreiche Werbetexter".
  Landsberg am Lech: mi Verlag moderne Industrie

- **Humboldt, Wilhelm von:**
  „Über das vergleichende Sprachstudium in Beziehung auf die verschiedenen Epochen der Sprachentwicklung". In: Leitzmann, A. (Hg): "Wilhelm von Humboldts Werke." Bd. 4, B. Berlin: Behr's Verlag (1905)

- **Jacobi, Helmut (1963):**
  „Werbepsychologie- Ganzheits- und Gestaltpsychologische Grundlagen der Werbung".
  Wiesbaden: Betriebswirtschaftlicher Verlag

- **Kaltenbach, H. G.(1963):**
  „Die Rolle von Produkt und Verpackung in der Marktkommunikation".
  Essen: Verlag W. Girardet

- **Karmasin, Helene (1993):**
  „Produkte als Botschaften: was macht Produkte einzigartig und unverwechselbar?; Die Dynamik der Bedürfnisse und die Wünsche der Konsumenten; die Umsetzung in Produkt und Werbe-konzeption".
  Wien: Ueberreuter

- **Katona, George (1962):**
  „Die Macht des Verbrauchers". Düsseldorf: Econ-Verlag

- **Katz Elihu und Lazarsfeld, Paul F. (1964):**
  „Personal influence – The Part Played by People in the Flow of Mass Communication".
  New York: The Free Press

- **Keller, Rudi (1994$^2$):**
  „Sprachwandel Von der unsichtbaren Hand in der Sprache".
  Tübingen und Basel: Francke Verlag

- **Keller, Rudi (1995):**
  „Zeichentheorie Zu einer Theorie semiotischen Wissens".
  Tübingen und Basel: Francke Verlag

- **Kirchler, Dr. Erich (1989):**
  „Kaufentscheidungen im privaten Haushalt".
  Göttingen: Verlag für Psychologie

- **Kirsch-Postma, Martje Anje (1978):**
  „Studien zur Werbesprache - rhetorische und psychologische
  Aspekte". Hamburg: Diss.

- **Knappe, Hans-Joachim (1981):**
  „Informations- und Kaufverhalten unter Zeitdruck".
  Frankfurt: Verlag Peter D. Lang GmbH

- **Köhler, Helmut (1995):**
  „Gesetz gegen den unlauteren Wettbewerb, mit Rabattgesetz und
  Preisangaben    verordnung".
  München: C.H. Beck'sche Verlagsbuchhandlung

- **Koppelmann, Udo (1971):**
  „Grundlagen der Verpackungsgestaltung. Ein Beitrag zur marke-
  tingorientierten Produktforschung".
  Berlin/Herne: Verlag Neue Wirtschafts-Briefe

- **Koppelmann, Udo (2/1972):**
  „Grundlagen eines Mittelsystems der Produktgestaltung".
  In: „der Markt." Wien S.173

- **Koppelmann, Udo (1981):**
  „Produktwerbung". Köln u.a.: W. Kohlhammer GmbH

- **Krautmann, Dr. Axel (1981):**
  „Zur Analyse von Verständlichkeitsproblemen bei der Gestaltung
  von Gebrauchsanleitungen". Köln

- **Kroeber-Riel, Werner (1992):**
  „Konsumentenverhalten". Müchen: Vahlen Verlag

- **Kurz, Gerhard (1982):**
  „Metapher, Allegorie, Symbol".
  Göttingen: Vandenhoeck & Ruprecht

- **Lakoff, George (1987):**
  „Woman, Fire and Dangerous Things – What Categories Reveal
  about the mind".
  Chicago: University of Chicago Press

- **Leitherer, Eugen; Wichman, Hans (1987):**
  „Reiz und Hülle. Gestaltete Warenverpackungen des 19. und 20.
  Jahrhunderts".
  Basel: Birkehäuser Verlag

- **Loewy, Raymond (1953):**
  „Häßlichkeit verkauft sich schlecht. Die Erlebnisse des erfolgreichsten Formgestalters unserer Zeit".
  Düsseldorf: Econ-Verlag GmbH

- **Männicke, Dr. Adolf (1957):**
  „Die Warenverpackung als ein Faktor der betrieblichen Absatzpolitik".
  Berlin: Duncker & Humblot

- **Maslow, Abraham, H. (1977):**
  „Motivation und Persönlichkeit".
  Olten und Freiburg im Breisgau: Walter-Verlag

- **Medeyros, Monika (1990$^2$):**
  „Anmutungshafte Verpackungsgestaltung als Mittel der Produktpolitik". Köln: Fördergesellschaft Produkt-Marketing e.V.

- **Meggle, Georg (Hg) (1979):**
  „Handlung, Kommunikation, Bedeutung".
  Frankfurt am Main: Suhrkamp

- **Morris, Charles William (1981):**
  „Zeichen, Sprache und Verhalten". Wien: Ullstein

- **noAH (Directory of international package Design) (1992):**
  „Les pachagines Du Monde". Japan Creators Assoziation

- **Nöth, Winfried (1975):**
  „Semiotik. Eine Einführung mit Beispielen für Reklameanalysen". Tübingen: Max Niemeyer Verlag

369

- **Ogilvy, David (1975$^2$):**
  „Geständnisse eines Werbemannes".
  Wien Düsseldorf: Econ Verlag

- **Osgood, Charles E. (1959):**
  „The Representional Model and Research Methods". In: Sola
  Pool I. de (HG): Trends in Content Analysis. o.O.

- **Osgood, Charles E.; Suci, George .J.; Tannenbaum, Perci H.
  (1967):**
  „The Measurement of Meaning".
  Urbana: University of Illinois Press

- **Packard, Vance (1958):**
  „Die geheimen Verführer. Der Griff nach dem Unbewußten in
  Jedermann".
  Düsseldorf: Econ Verlag GmbH

- **Peirce, Charles Sanders:**
  „Lectures on Pragmatism". Hamburg: Felix Meiner Verlag
  (1973)

- **Peirce, Charles S.:**
  „Phänomen und Logik der Zeichen". Herausgegeben und über-
  setzt von Helmut Pape,
  Frankfurt am Main: Suhrkamp Verlag (1993)

- **Petersen, B. Martin. (Hg) (o.J.):**
  „Graphis Packaging 5. An international survey of Package Design".
  Zürich: Graphis Press Corp.

- **Platon:**
  „Sämtliche Werke". Band II, herausgegeben von: Otto, Walter
  F.; Grassi, Ernesto; Plamböck, Gert. In der Übersetzung von:
  Schleiermacher, Friedrich, mit der Stephanus-Numerierung,
  Hamburg: Rowohlt Taschenbuch Verlag GmbH (1957[15])

- **Reichhardt, Philip (1999):**
  „Uns fehlen die Worte". Die Zeit Nr. 21/20. Mai 1999, Kap. Leben,
  S.3

- **Römer, Ruth (1968):**
  „Die Sprache der Anzeigenwerbung". Bd. 4: Sprache der Ge-
  genwart. Schriften des Institutes für deutsche Sprache,
  Düsseldorf: Pädagogischer Verlag Schwann

- **Rosch, Eleanor; Boyes-Braem, Penny; Gray, Wayne; John-
  son, David; Mervis, Carolyn (1975):**
  „Basic Objects in Natural Categories". Working Paper Nr. 43,
  Berkeley: Language Behavior Research Laboratory

- **Roth, E. (1967):**
  „Einstellungen als Determination individuellen Verhaltens".
  Göttingen: o.V.

- **Sander, Horst (1972):**
  „Die Verpackung als Informationsmedium. Eine absatzwirt-
  schaftliche und werbepsychologische Untersuchung der
  Informationsleistung der Konsumgüterverpackung".
  Bochum: Diss.

- **Schilder-Bär, Lotte; Bignens, Christoph (Hg), Museum für Gestaltung Zürich:**
„Hüllen füllen. Verpackungsdesign zwischen Bedarf und Verführung". Anläßlich der Ausstellung vom 28.05 - 31.07.1994, Sulgen: Verlag Niggli AG

- **Schneider, Wolf (1986):**
„Wörter machen Leute. Magie und Macht der Sprache". München: R.Piper GmbH & Co.KG

- **Schönefelder, Dr. Heinrich (Hg) (1998[20]):**
„Deutsche Gesetze – Sammlung des Zivil-, Straf- und Verfahrensrechts". München: C.H. Beck'sche Verlagsbuchhandlung

- **Somogyi, Andreas (1972):**
„Die absatzwirtschaftlichen Bestimmungsfaktoren einer marktgerechten Packung". Aarau: Keller-Verlag

- **Spiegel-Verlag Augstein, R. GmbH & CoKG, Marketingabteilung (Hg) (1988):**
„Brand News", Hamburg: Spiegel-Verlag

- **Swankin, D. (1967):**
„Irreführende Verpackung - die amerikanische ‚Truth-in-Packaging-Bill'". In: „Verpackung und Konsument". Bd. 36 Schriftenreihe der Stiftung „Im Grüne", Bern und Stuttgart: Verlag Paul Haupt

- **Teigeler, Peter (1968):**
"Verständlichkeit und Wirksamkeit von Sprache und Text".
Stuttgart: Nadolski

- **Trömmel-Plötz, Senta (1982)**
"Frauensprache: Sprache der Veränderung".
Frankfurt am Main: Fischer-Verlag

- **Vater, Heinz (1992):**
"Einführung in die Textlinguistik. Struktur, Thema und Referenzen in Texten".
München: Wilhelm Fink Verlag

- **Wachtel, Joachim (1965):**
"Vom Ballenbinder zur Selbstbedienung". Berlin: Bertelsmann

- **Watzlawick, Paul; Beavin, Janet H.; Jackson, Don D. (1974[4]):**

"Menschliche Kommunikation – Formen, Störungen, Paradoxien".
Stuttgart: Hans Huber Verlag

- **Wawrzyniak. Zdzislaw (1980):**
"Einführung in die Textwissenschaft".
Warschau: Pa'nstwowe Wydawnictwo Naukowe-Verlag

- **Wilss, Wolfram (1989):**
"Anspielungen. Zur Manifestation von Kreativität und Routine in der Sprachverwendung"
Tübingen: Max Niemeyer Verlag

- **Wittgenstein, Ludwig:**
  „Philosophische Untersuchungen". In: Werkeausgabe Bd. 1, S. 225-
  560,
  FaM: Suhrkamp (1984)

- **Wittgenstein, Ludwig:**
  „Wittgensteins philosophische Untersuchungen". Herausgegeben
  von: Ludwig; Savigny, Eike von,
  Frankfurt am Main: Vittorio Klostermann Verlag (1994²)


**Darüber hinaus empfehlenswerte Literatur zu dem Thema:**

- **Berekoven, Ludwig; Eckert, Werner; Ellenrieder, Peter (1991):**
  „Marktforschung, methodische Grundlagen und praktische An-
  wendung".
  Wiesbaden: Dr. Th. Gabler GmbH

- **Blumenthal, Peter (1983):**
  „Semantische Dichte: Assoziativität in Poesie und Werbespra-
  che". Konzepte der Sprach- und Literaturwissenschaft,
  Tübingen: Niemeyer Verlag

- **Bodmer, W.; Darms, L.; David, M.; Devaud, L. u.a. (1967)**
  „Verpackung und Konsument". Bd. 36 Schriftenreihe der Stif-
  tung „Im Grüne",
  Bern und Stuttgart: Verlag Paul Haupt

- **Bost, Dr. Erhard (1987):**
  „Ladenatmosphäre und Konsumentenverhalten".
  Heidelberg: Physica-Verlag

- **Bräuer, Helmut (1957):**
  „Die Verpackung als absatzwirtschaftliches Problem".
  Marktwirtschaft und Verbrauch. Schriftenreihe der Gesellschaft
  für Konsumforschung e.V.,
  Kallmünz/Opf: Verlag Michael Laßleben

- **Christofolini, Peter M. (1972):**
  „Verkaufsförderung in der Praxis".
  Düsseldorf/Wien: Econ-Verlag

- **Bund Deutscher Werbeberater und Werbeleiter e.V. (1964):**
  „Werbung...freiheit und verantwortung".
  Essen: Wirtschaft und Werbung Verlagsgesellschaft m.b.H.

- **Davis, Kenneth R. (1961):**
  „Marketing Management". New York: Ronald Press

- **Eco, Umberto (1972):**
  „Einführung in die Semiotik".
  Autorisierte deutsche Ausgabe von J. Trabant,
  München: Willhelm Fink Verlag

- **Eisendle, Reinhard und Miklautz, E. (1992):**
  „Produktkulturen. Dynamik und Bedeutungswandel des Konsums".
  Frankfurt am Main: Campus Verlag

- **Ellinger, Theodor (1966):**
  "Die Informationsfunktion des Produktes".
  Köln/Opladen: Westdeutscher-Verlag

- **Festinger, Leon (1978):**
„Theorie der kognitiven Dissonanz". Bern: Huber-Verlag

- **Gäfgen, Gerard (1968):**
„Theorie der wirtschaftlichen Entscheidung". Tübingen: Mohr

- **Gass, Franz Ulrich (1958):**
„Besser werben mit Humor. Ein heiterer Verkaufshelfer".
Stuttgart: Verlag Dr. Heinrich Seewald

- **Geiger, S. und Heyn, W. (1970):**
„Informationstheoretische Probleme der Werbung".
In: Behrens, K. Chr. (Hg): „Handbuch der Werbung".
Wiesbaden: Gabler-Verlag

- **Gossage, Howard Luck (1967):**
„Ist die Werbung noch zu retten?" Düsseldorf: Econ Verlag

- **Gutjahr, Gert (1974):**
„Markt- und Werbepsychologie". Bände. 1 u. 2,
Heidelberg: Sauer Taschenbücher für die Wirtschaft

- **Haselhoff, O.W.; Flockenhaus, K.F.; Lauer, K.;
Hoffmann, H.J. (1965):**
„Eine faktorielle Technik der psychologischen, semantischen und
informationellen Anzeigenanalyse". Berlin u.a

- **Hausenblas, K. (1985):**
„Zu den Prinzipien des Textaufbaus oder: Text ohne Stil?"
In: Hlavsa Zdenek/Viehweger, Dieter (eds.), S. 25-27

- **Herstatt, Johann David. (1985):**
„Die Entwicklung von Markennamen im Rahmen der Neupro-
duktplanung". Europäische Hochschulschriften Reihe 5,
Volks- und Betriebswirtschaft; 597
Frankfurt, Bern, New York: Lang-Verlag

- **Kaas, K.-P. (1977):**
„Empirische Preis-Absatzfunktion bei Konsumgütern".
Berlin u.a.: Axel Springer-Verlag

- **Kainz, Friedrich (1956):**
„Psychologie der Sprache. Spezielle Sprachpsychologie". Bd. 4,
Stuttgart: Enke Verlag

- **Kalverkämper, Hartwig (1989):**
„Orientierung zur Textlinguistik".
Tübingen: Max Niemeyer Verlag

- **Kassarjian, Harold H. (1982):**
„Consumer Psychology". o.O.

- **Kotler, Philipp (1974):**
„Marketing-Management. Analyse, Planung und Kontrolle".
Stuttgart: Poeschel-Verlag

- **Kropff, Hanns Ferdinand Josef (1953):**
„Die Werbemittel und ihre psychologische, künstlerische und
technische Gestaltung".
Essen: Giradet

- **Kuhlmann, E. (01.09.1971):**
  „Organisation der Marketing-Kommunikation".
  In: Absatzwirtschaft. Heft 17, S. 15-33

- **Langer, Inghard.; Schulz von Thun, Friedmann; Tausch, Reinhard (1974):**
  „Verständlichkeit in Schule, Verwaltung, Politik und Wissenschaft".
  München, Basel: Reinhardt

- **Lapp, Edgar (1992):**
  „Linguistik der Ironie". Tübinger Beiträge zur Linguistik 368,
  Tübingen: Gunter Narr-Verlag.

- **Lersch, Philipp (1970[11]):**
  „Aufbau der Person". München: Barth Verlag

- **Lindner, Rolf (1977):**
  „Das Gefühl von Freiheit und Abenteuer: Ideologie und Praxis in der Werbung".
  Frankfurt: Campus Verlag GmbH

- **Lötscher**, Andreas (1992[2]):
  „Von Ajax bis Xerox: ein Lexikon der Produktnamen". Zürich: Artemis & Winkler

- **Maletzke, Gerhard (1963):**
  „Psychologie der Massenkommunikation".
  Hamburg: Hans Bredow Institut

- **Meyer, Paul Georg (1983):**
  „Sprachliches Handeln ohne Sprechsituation. Studien zur theoretischen und empirischen Konstitution von illokutiven Funktionen in >situationslosen< Texten".
  Tübingen: Max Niemeyer Verlag

- **Michlick, Paul (1967):**
  „Geheimnisse der Werbesprache". Essen: Verlag W. Girardet

- **Müller, H.P. (1992):**
  „De gestibus non est disputandum? Bemerkungen zur Diskussion um Geschmack, Distinktion und Lebensstil".
  In. Eisendle, R. und Miklautz, E. (Hg): „Produktkulturen. Dynamik und Bedeutungswandel des Konsums".
  Frankfurt: Campus Verlag

- **Paszkowiak, E. (1970):**
  „Display-Werbung". In: Behrens, K.Chr. (Hg):
  „Handbuch der Werbung".
  Wiesbaden: Gabler Verlag, S. 579-586

- **Pompl, M. (1974):**
  „Werbestil". In: Tietz, B. (Hg): „Handwörterbuch der Absatzwirtschaft".
  Stuttgart: Poeschel

- **Reeves, R. (1960):**
  „Werbung ohne Mythos". München

- **Reinmann, Horst (1968):**
„Kommunikations-Systeme, Umrisse einer Soziologie der Vermittlungs- und Mitteilungsprozesse".
Tübingen: Mohr

- **Reinmöller, Dr. Patrick (1955):**
„Produktsprache. Verständlichkeit des Umganges mit Produkten durch Produktgestaltung". Beiträge zum Produktmarketing Bd. 25, Köln: Fördergesellschaft Produkt-Marketing e.V.

- **Sahihi, Armann (1987):**
„Kauf mich!: Werbe-Wirkung durch Sprache und Schrift".
Weinheim und Basel: Beltz Verlag

- **Schaff, Adam (1973):**
„Einführung in die Semantik". Reinbeck bei Hamburg: Rowohlt

- **Scheuch, E.K.(2/1972):**
„Der Einfluß der Verbrauchereigenschaften auf die Warengestaltung". In: Der Markt Nr.42 Wien

- **Scitovski, Tibor (1977):**
„Psychologie des Wohlstandes".
Frankfurt am Main: Campus-Verlag

- **Silbermann, A.; Luthe, H. O. (1969):**
„Massenkommunikation". In: König, P. (Hg): „Handbuch der empirischen Sozialforschung".
Bd.II, Stuttgart, S.675-734

- **Spiegel, Bernd (1970):**
  „Werbepsychologische Untersuchungsmethoden".
  Berlin: Duncker & Humblot

- **Sprenzinger, Jürgen (1996):**
  „Sehr geehrter Herr Maggi". München: Knaur

- **Stern, H. (1962):**
  „The Significance of Impulse Buying Today".
  In: „Journal of Marketing" Heft 2, S. 59-62

- **Volckaert, J. (1972):**
  „Verpackung". In: „Management Enzyklopädie. Das Manage-
  mentwissen unserer Zeit in 6 Bänden". Band 6,
  München: mi-Verlag

- **Wallendorf, M. und Zaltmann, G. (1984$^2$):**
  „Readings in Consumer Behavior". Wiley-Verlag, New York u.a.

- **Werlich, Egon (1975):**
  „Typologie der Texte. Entwurf eines textlinguistischen Modells
  zur Grundlegung einer Textgrammatik".
  Quelle & Meyer Heidelberg: UTB – Uni-Taschenbuch

- **Zellweger, H. U. (3/1971):**
  „Marketing als System betrachtet".
  In: „La Publicité en Suisse". S.149-153

**Nachschlagewerke:**

- Duden Band 1
  „Rechtschreibung der deutschen Sprache". Hrsg. vom Wissenschaftl. Rat d. Dudenredaktion: Günther Drosdowski

- Duden Band 5
  „Fremdwörterduden". Hrsg. vom Wissenschaftl. Rat d.
  Dudenredaktion: Günther Drosdowski

- **Lange-Kowal, Ernst Erwin und Weymuth, (1982):**
  „Eduard Langenscheidts Taschenwörterbuch Französich".
  Berlin u.a.: Langenscheidt Verlag

- **Klatt, Edmund und Roy, Dietrich (1983):**
  „Langenscheidts Taschenwörterbuch Englisch".
  Berlin u.a.: Langenscheidt Verlag

- **Menge, Hermann (1984):**
  „Langenscheidts Taschenwörterbuch Lateinisch".
  Berlin u.a.: Langenscheidt Verlag

- **„Brockhaus – Die Enyklopädie in 24 Bänden" (1996)**
  20. überarbeitete und aktualisierte Auflage, Leipzig: Brockhaus

- **Kluge, Friedrich (1989[22]):**
  „Etymologisches Wörterbuch der deutschen Sprache". völlig neu
  bearbeitet von Elmar Seebold,
  Berlin u.a.: De Gruyter Verlag

## Fortsetzung von Seite 2

...Wie reizvoll ist allein schon die Vielfalt der Hinweise auf die Stelle, wo das Haltbarkeitsdatum steht:
Haltbar bis siehe Seitenlasche
Mindestens haltbar bis Ende: siehe Monats- und Jahresangabe Etikettenunterrand
Haltbar bis Ende: Tubenfalz
Haltbar bis zum 15: 1 2 3 4 5 6 7 8 9 10 11 12 94 95 96 97 (eine der ersten zwölf und eine der letzten vier Zahlen sind mit einer Kerbung versehen)
und der unvergängliche Klassiker
Haltbar bis siehe Beutelschweißnaht
Beutelschweißnaht! Mit einem solchen Wort als Aperitif schmekken die Aromastoffe doppelt naturidentisch. Oft ist auch die Nummer eines Verbrauchertelephons angegeben, bei dem man sich »wertvolle Anregungen« holen kann: »Ihr Riesenappetit-Schwabentopf schmeckt irgendwie gar nicht anregend. Was kann ich tun?« »Geben Sie doch vor dem Anrichten einen halben Liter Sherry hinzu.«

Gelegentlich wird auf Verpackungen Ernährungszubehör angepriesen, z.B. eine praktische Knusperdose für Knäckebrot. Wer würde nicht gerne wissen, was das für Menschen sind, die eine solche Knäckebrotbox tatsächlich bestellen? ...

Wer die Antwort auf die Frage wissen möchte, der kann die Kurzgeschichte lesen in:

Goldt, Max: „Schließ einfach die Augen und stell dir vor, ich wäre Heinz Klunker." Ausgesuchte Texte 1991-1994, Haffmans Verlag 1994, S. 69ff

# Abbildungen

Abbildung 1

Abbildung 2

Abbildung 3

Abbildung 4

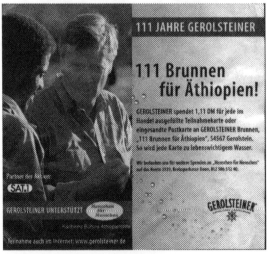

Abbildung 5

Abbildung 6

**Recycling lebt vom Mitmachen.**

Damit dieser Tetra Pak recycelt werden kann, sind wir auf Ihre Mithilfe angewiesen: Bitte entleeren Sie ihn vollständig. Ziehen Sie die Laschen nach außen, falten Sie ihn flach zusammen und geben Sie ihn in die gelbe Tonne oder entsprechenden Behälter. Dann können wir neue nützliche Dinge aus ihm herstellen. Für Sie und unsere Umwelt.

Abbildung 7

Abbildung 8

Herstellung: Libri Books on Demand
ISBN 3-8311-0256-2